**GAUTENG AND
SUN CITY**
Pages 306–325

**BLYDE RIVER
CANYON AND
KRUGER**
Pages 326–343

GAUTENG AND
MPUMALANGA

• Polokwane

Mbombela •
(Nelspruit)

PRETORIA/TSHWANE
Johannesburg •

MBABANE
SWAZILAND

THE EAST COAST
AND INTERIOR

• Kimberley

Bloemfontein •

MASERU

LESOTHO

• Durban

**DURBAN AND
ZULULAND**
Pages 278–297

Graaff-Reinet

Port
Elizabeth

**THE SOUTHERN
CAPE**
Pages 218–231

**THE GARDEN
ROUTE TO
GRAHAMSTOWN**
Pages 232–253

**WILD COAST,
DRAKENSBERG
AND MIDLANDS**
Pages 262–277

EYEWITNESS TRAVEL

SOUTH
AFRICA

EYEWITNESS TRAVEL

SOUTH
AFRICA

Main contributors:
Michael Brett, Philip Briggs,
Brian Johnson-Barker
and Mariëlle Renssen

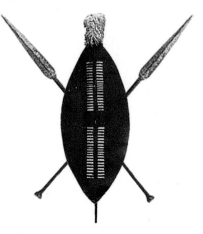

LONDON, NEW YORK,
MELBOURNE, MUNICH AND DELHI
www.dk.com

Produced by Struik New Holland Publishing (Pty) Ltd,
Cape Town, South Africa

MANAGING EDITOR Claudia Dos Santos
MANAGING ART EDITORS Peter Bosman, Trinity Loubser-Fry
EDITORS Gill Gordon, Gail Jennings
DESIGNERS Simon Lewis, Mark Seabrook
MAP CO-ORDINATOR John Loubser
PRODUCTION Myrna Collins
PICTURE RESEARCHER Carmen Watts
RESEARCHER Jocelyn Convery

Dorling Kindersley Limited
EDITORIAL DIRECTOR Vivien Crump
ART DIRECTOR Gillian Allan
MAP CO-ORDINATOR David Pugh

MAIN CONTRIBUTORS
Michael Brett, Philip Briggs, Brian Johnson-Barker, Mariëlle Renssen

PHOTOGRAPHERS
Shaen Adey, Roger de la Harpe, Walter Knirr

ILLUSTRATORS
Bruce Beyer, Annette Busse, Bruno de Robillard,
Steven Felmore, Noel McCully, Dave Snook

Printed and bound by South China Printing Co. Ltd., China

First American Edition, 1999

13 14 15 16 10 9 8 7 6 5 4 3 2 1

Published in the United States by DK Publishing,
375 Hudson Street, New York, New York 10014

Reprinted with revisions 2001, 2002, 2003, 2005, 2007, 2009, 2011, 2013

Copyright © 1999, 2013 Dorling Kindersley Limited, London

Published in the UK by Dorling Kindersley Limited.

A catalog record for this book is available from the Library of Congress.

ISSN 1542-1554
ISBN 978 0 75669 517 0

FLOORS ARE REFERRED TO THROUGHOUT IN
ACCORDANCE WITH EUROPEAN USAGE; IE THE "FIRST FLOOR"
IS THE FLOOR ABOVE GROUND LEVEL.

Front cover main image: Giraffes at the Itbala Game Reserve, KwaZulu-Natal

MIX
Paper from
responsible sources
FSC
www.fsc.org   FSC™ C018179

**The information in this
DK Eyewitness Travel Guide is checked regularly.**

Every effort has been made to ensure that this book is as up-to-date as
possible at the time of going to press. Some details, however, such as
telephone numbers, opening hours, prices, gallery hanging
arrangements and travel information are liable to change. The
publishers cannot accept responsibility for any consequences arising
from the use of this book, nor for any material on third party websites,
and cannot guarantee that any website address in this book will be a
suitable source of travel information. We value the views and
suggestions of our readers very highly. Please write to: Publisher,
DK Eyewitness Travel Guides, Dorling Kindersley, 80 Strand,
London WC2R 0RL, UK, or email: travelguides@dk.com.

CONTENTS

Vasco Da Gama

INTRODUCING SOUTH AFRICA

WILD SOUTH AFRICA

Camps Bay Beach, Cape Town

A male leopard patrols his territory at Londolozi Game Reserve

Red Disas on Table Mountain

Boschendal
Manor House
(see pp196–7)

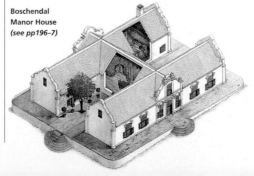

HOW TO USE THIS GUIDE

This guide helps you to get the most from a visit to South Africa, providing expert recommendations and detailed practical information. *Introducing South Africa* maps the country and sets it in its historical and cultural context. *Wild South Africa* is a detailed guide to wildlife viewing and safaris. The four regional sections, plus *Cape Town*, describe important sights, using photographs, maps and illustrations. Restaurant and hotel recommendations can be found in *Travellers' Needs*. The *Survival Guide* contains practical tips on everything from transport to personal safety.

CAPE TOWN

The "mother city" has been divided into three sight-seeing areas. Each has its own chapter opening with a list of the sights described. The *Further Afield* section covers many peripheral places of interest. All sights are numbered and plotted on an *Area Map*. Information on the sights is easy to locate as it follows the numerical order used on the map.

Sights at a Glance lists the chapter's sights by category: Museums and Galleries, Churches, Parks and Gardens, Historic Buildings, etc.

All pages relating to Cape Town have red thumb tabs.

A locator map shows clearly where the area is in relation to other areas of the city.

1 Area Map
For easy reference, sights are numbered and located on a map. City centre sights are also marked on the Cape Town Street Finder *maps (see pp169–77).*

2 Street-by-Street Map
This gives a bird's-eye view of the key areas in each sightseeing area.

Stars indicate the sights that no visitor should miss.

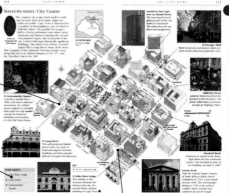

A suggested route for a walk covers the more interesting streets in the area.

3 Detailed Information
All the sights in Cape Town are described individually. Addresses, telephone numbers and other practical information are also provided for each entry. The key to the symbols used in the information block is shown on the back flap.

GAUTENG AND SUN CITY

1 Introduction

A general account of the landscape, history and character of each region is given here, explaining both how the area has developed over the centuries and what attractions it has to offer visitors today.

SOUTH AFRICA AREA BY AREA

Apart from Cape Town, the rest of the country has been divided into ten regions, each of which has a separate chapter. The most interesting towns and sights to visit are numbered on a *Regional Map* at the beginning of each chapter.

Each area of South Africa can be easily identified by its colour coding, shown on the inside front cover.

2 Regional Map

This shows the main road network and gives an illustrated overview of the whole region. All interesting places to visit are numbered and there are also useful tips on getting to, and around, the region.

Story boxes explore specific subjects further.

3 Detailed Information

All the important towns and other places to visit are described individually. They are listed in order, following the numbering on the Regional Map. Within each entry, there is further detailed information on major buildings and other sights.

For all the top sights, a Visitors' Checklist provides the practical information you will need to plan your visit.

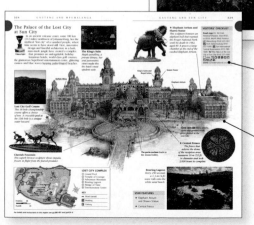

4 South Africa's Top Sights

The historic buildings are dissected to reveal their interiors; national parks have maps showing facilities and trails. The most interesting towns or city centres have maps, with sights picked out and described.

INTRODUCING SOUTH AFRICA

DISCOVERING SOUTH AFRICA

South Africa – the "Rainbow Nation" – has been described as offering the whole world in one country. The variety of scenery is outstanding: from beautiful forests to dramatic coastlines and vibrant cities. This is also a country with 11 official languages and a multifaceted culture as a result. Whether you want to experience exciting extreme

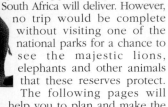

An African elephant

sports, superb wine tours or fantastic shopping opportunities, South Africa will deliver. However, no trip would be complete without visiting one of the national parks for a chance to see the majestic lions, elephants and other animals that these reserves protect. The following pages will help you to plan and make the most out of this incredible country.

Aerial view of Cape Town from Green Point

CAPE TOWN

- Shopping at the V&A Waterfront
- The legislative capital
- Dramatic Table Mountain
- Outstanding beaches

Set against the ocean and overlooked by the imposing Table Mountain, Cape Town is arguably the most scenic city in South Africa. It has always been a cosmopolitan place, and this is reflected in the shops at the **V&A Waterfront** *(see pp136–8)*, which will impress even the most discerning of visitors.

The grand public buildings and excellent museums, such as the **Castle of Good Hope** *(see pp126–7)*, are indicative of Cape Town's importance as South Africa's legislative capital, as are the imposing statues and monuments that punctuate the many parks and gardens. Cape Town also offers some of the best

national parks in the country. **Table Mountain** *(see pp132–3)* is easily reached by cable car, and it provides breathtaking panoramic views. Make sure to check the weather forecast first, however, since the summit can be shrouded in mist. Further along the coast lies the **Cape Riviera** *(see p147)*, which boasts excellent beaches that are very popular with both tourists and locals. Be aware that traffic can get congested along the coast, although the beaches are well worth the effort.

CAPE WINELANDS

- Fascinating wine tours
- Cape Dutch architecture
- Historic Stellenbosch

With a history in wine-making stretching back more than 350 years, it is not surprising that South Africa offers such excellent **wine tours** *(see p194 and p201).*

The visits provide a fascinating insight into the industry, not to mention the opportunity to sample the end product.

The Cape Winelands are blessed with a landscape of green rolling hills overlooked by jagged mountain peaks. The architectural heritage left by the Dutch and French adds to the region's charm. A particularly good example of the style is **Boschendal Manor House** *(see pp196–7).* The larger towns are just as picturesque as the white-washed farmhouses that dot the area. **Stellenbosch** *(see pp190–93)*, in particular, is worth visiting for the different styles of Cape Dutch architecture that line the peaceful streets. Other attractions include the **Worcester Museum** *(see pp204–5)*, the enticing wayside inns and some of the best restaurants in the country.

Terraced vineyards in the Cape Winelands region

◁ The Eastern Buttress, Devil's Tooth and Inner Tower formations of the Drakensberg mountain range

The vast underground complex of the Cango Caves

WESTERN COASTAL TERRACE

- **Floral Namaqualand**
- **Towering Cederberg Mountains**
- **Seafood fresh from the sea**

The best time to visit the Western Coastal Terrace is in the spring (September–November), after the winter rains – the heaviest rainfall of the year in this part of the country. This is when **Namaqualand** *(see pp216–17)* bursts into colourful bloom. The **Cederberg Mountains** *(see pp214–15)* are a spectacular, if surreal, sight. Formed from tectonic activity, the twisted landscape is perfect for hiking explorations.

The **West Coast National Park** *(see pp212–13)* is one of South Africa's most important wetlands. But this is not the only delight the ocean has to offer. The open-air *skerm* (restaurants) serve a range of delicious fresh seafood, and are the perfect place to stop for an informal meal.

SOUTHERN CAPE

- **The spectacular Four Passes**
- **Wild coastline**
- **Exploring Cango Caves**
- **Whale watching at Hermanus**

A rural wonderland, the Southern Cape is shadowed by the great ridge of the Overberg Mountains. The **Four Passes** *(see pp228–9)*, which traverse the peaks, are some of the world's most scenic mountain drives.

The coastline is equally dramatic, culminating in the wild **Cape Agulhas** *(see p225)*. Here the cold Atlantic Ocean crashes into the warmer waters of the Indian Ocean, producing treacherous conditions for even the most experienced of sailors and swimmers.

For the more intrepid visitor, the **Cango Caves** *(see p229)* are an excellent day out. The cathedral-like vastness of the Great Hall ends with a claustrophobic hole in the rock known as The Letterbox, through which visitors can "post" themselves.

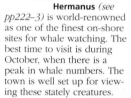

Colourful Namaqualand

Hermanus *(see pp222–3)* is world-renowned as one of the finest on-shore sites for whale watching. The best time to visit is during October, when there is a peak in whale numbers. The town is well set up for viewing these stately creatures.

GARDEN ROUTE TO GRAHAMSTOWN

- **Exotic flowers and forests**
- **Tsitsikamma**
- **Excellent hiking trails**
- **Port Elizabeth's golden beaches**

Never was an area more aptly named than the exotic and beautiful Garden Route. There are many cultivated blooms to see here, but the real draw are the forests of indigenous African hardwoods found in the **Tsitsikamma** section of the **Garden Route National Park** *(see pp244–5)*. Two of the most popular hiking trails in the country can be found here, but visitors should be aware that they must carry all their provisions with them.

The year-round balmy weather and well-planned trails through unspoilt woodlands have also contributed to making this one of the best regions for hiking. The seven-day, 108-km (67-mile) **Outeniqua Hiking Trail** *(see p241)* leads walkers through the forests that surround **Knysna** *(see pp240–41)*.

The ocean is never far away in the Garden Route, and there are many places to stop and enjoy the coastline. **Port Elizabeth** *(see pp246–9)* is one of the friendliest cities in South Africa. The golden beaches are understandably popular, but don't miss out on the city's beautiful architecture, or the exciting marine attractions at **Bayworld** *(see p249)*.

A scenic stretch of coastline in the Garden Route region

WILD COAST, DRAKENSBERG AND MIDLANDS

- Mighty uKhahlamba Peaks
- Historic battlefield tours
- Mountainous Lesotho
- Gandhi statue in Pietermaritzburg

Known to the Zulu as *uKhahlamba* – "a barrier of spears" – the mighty Drakensberg Mountains look down on the lush valleys that have long provided rich grazing. The hunter-gatherer San Bushmen made this region their home, and traces of their lives can be seen in the beautiful rock art in the **uKhahlamba-Drakensberg Park** *(see pp270–71)*. The area was later colonized by Xhosa, Zulu, Afrikaner and British people, leading to a succession of fierce conflicts. A **battlefields tour** *(see p274)* takes in such immortal sites as Blood River, Rorke's Drift and Ladysmith.

Though entirely surrounded by South Africa, **Lesotho** *(see pp268–9)* is an independent country, and the mountain refuge of the self-governing Basotho tribe. Abundant flora, fauna, rock art and fossil deposits make this the perfect destination for anyone who loves outdoor pursuits. **Pietermaritzburg**

The rugged landscape of the Drakensberg Mountains

High-rise buildings dominating the Johannesburg skyline

(see pp276–7) has many interesting monuments, including one of Gandhi, who began his fight against racial inequality here.

A group of Zulu warriors performing a tribal dance

DURBAN AND ZULULAND

- Bustling Durban
- Thrilling game parks
- Zulu heritage

The country's biggest port, and third-largest city, **Durban** *(see pp282–7)* is a popular destination in KwaZulu-Natal. The city's large Indian population adds another dimension to the nation's rich cultural mix, and the beautiful **Juma Masjid Mosque** *(see p284)* and **Temple of Understanding** *(see p285)* are well worth visiting. Durban has a fairly high crime rate, so it is best for visitors to stay within the main tourist areas.

The region is also home to some of South Africa's best game parks. Situated in the north are rich reserves of bush and grassland that are the perfect habitat for the

"Big Five": lions, leopards, rhinos, buffaloes and elephants. **Hluhluwe-Imfolozi Game Reserve** and **Ithala Game Reserve** *(see pp294–5)* offer excellent opportunities to view these wild creatures.

The legacy of the Zulu warriors is never far away, and **Shakaland** *(see p293)* is a fantastic reconstruction of a typical village.

GAUTENG AND SUN CITY

- Big business in Jo'burg
- Vibrant Soweto
- Pretoria/Tshwane – the administrative capital
- The Palace of the Lost City

Dynamic **Johannesburg** *(see pp310–13)* is a city of contrasts, with affluence and poverty found within a short distance of each other. **Sandton** *(see p317)* has become a wealthy suburb with great shopping and entertainment, but **Soweto** *(see p317)* has yet to feel the effects of the improved economy. The township can be visited as part of a guided tour, and it's worth joining one for the vibrant music and art. It is not advisable, however, to go on your own.

The administrative capital, **Pretoria/Tshwane** *(see pp320–21)*, has many elegant monuments and buildings. Less expected are the purple jacaranda trees, which burst into bloom each spring.

An alternative to cultural pursuits is the **Palace of the Lost City** casino *(see pp324–5)*, which is devoted to all forms of entertainment.

BLYDE RIVER CANYON AND KRUGER

- Scenic Panorama Route
- Incredible national parks and reserves
- The waterfalls tour
- Beautiful Swaziland

Some of the most incredible landscapes in South Africa are found where the land drops from the northern peaks of the imposing Drakensberg Mountains to the seemingly endless bush-lands of the veld far below. A spectacular scenic drive known as the **Panorama Route** *(see p333)* provides a good overview, with plenty of pull-in points to take in the view. **Kruger National Park** *(see pp338–41)*, the oldest game reserve in the world, offers the same beautiful scenery, but with the added attraction of the "Big Five". It can be easy to concentrate on just these wonderful animals, but be aware that the park is also home to many other species, including cheetahs, croco-diles and baboons.

Scoured by a fast-flowing river, the **Blyde River Canyon** *(see p333)* is vast in extent, and there are more waterfalls here than in any other area of South Africa. **Lisbon Falls** *(see p331)* is the highest, with an impressive 90-m (295-ft) drop. The beautiful kingdom of **Swaziland** *(see pp342–3)* provides excellent hiking opportunities through high-lands and nature reserves.

A flock of Karoo lambs at a farm in the town of Graaff-Reinet

SOUTH OF THE ORANGE

- Unique Karoo landscape
- Vast sheep ranches
- Graaff-Reinet's architecture
- Hardy mountain zebras

The Orange River is the largest and longest river in South Africa, but to the immediate south is a scrub-land area where water is always scarce. Named by the Khoina Tribe, the Karoo ("land of great thirst") may seem inhospitable, but it supports many plant and animal species. The **Karoo National Park** and **Camdeboo National Park** *(see p356)* were set up to conserve the region's unique heritage.

The area is also home to large sheep ranches that produce huge quantities of mutton and wool. **Cradock** *(see p360)* is the hub of the sheep-farming business and has a lovely church modelled on London's St-Martin-in-the-Fields. **Graaff-Reinet** *(see pp358–9)* grew up around the magistrate's court that

was established here in 1786. The town is known for its beautiful Cape Dutch architecture. The **Mountain Zebra National Park** *(see p360)* was created to save the Cape mountain zebra from extinction. The park has been successful in its efforts, and there is now a population of about 600 animals.

NORTH OF THE ORANGE

- Kimberley's diamond rush
- Bloemfontein – the judicial capital
- Wild Kalahari Desert

Formerly a quiet farming district, **Kimberley** *(see pp370–71)* was the scene of the world's greatest diamond rush. The famed Big Hole is a vast man-made crater that yielded an incredibly rich haul, including the Star of Africa diamond, the largest gem of this type ever found.

Bloemfontein *(see pp372–3)* is the judicial capital of South Africa and has an entirely different atmosphere. There are many grand build-ings here, including the Old Presidency and the Appeal Court. The cool and leafy King's Park provides a respite from the formal archi-tecture and is a pleasant place to stop for lunch.

The Kalahari Desert has been protected by the forma-tion of the **Kgalagadi Trans-frontier Park** *(see p369)*, Africa's largest national park. The desert is home to 19 species of carnivore, including lions, cheetahs, brown hyenas and tawny eagles.

Lions relaxing in the sands of the Kalahari Desert

Putting South Africa on the Map

The southernmost country on the African continent, South Africa is roughly five times the size of Britain. It covers an area of 1,223,201 sq km (472,156 sq miles) and has a population of around 50 million. The sovereign kingdom of Lesotho lies within its borders. The Atlantic, which washes its western shores, and the Indian Ocean, which laps the East Coast, meet at Cape Agulhas, Africa's most southerly tip. To the north of South Africa lie the neighbouring states of Namibia, Botswana, Zimbabwe, Swaziland and Mozambique.

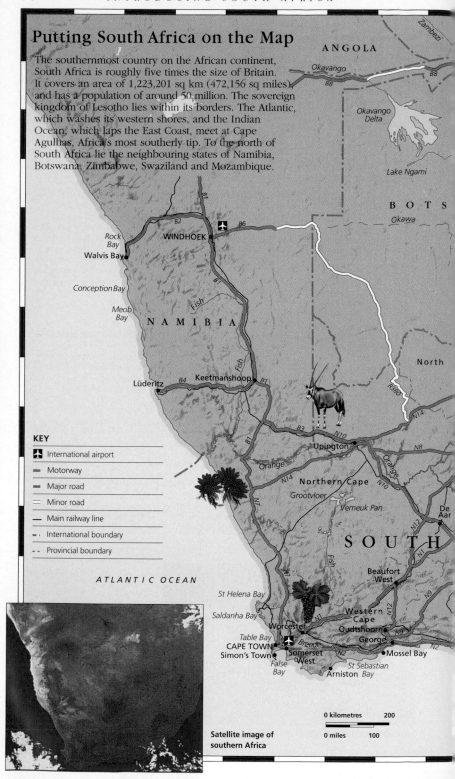

ANGOLA

Zambezi

Okavango

B8

B8

Okavango Delta

Lake Ngami

B O T S

Okawa

B1

B2

B6

WINDHOEK

Rock Bay

Walvis Bay

Conception Bay

B1

Meob Bay

Fish

N A M I B I A

North

Fish

Lüderitz

B4

Keetmanshoop

B1

B3

R380

N14

B1

N10

Upington

N8

Orange

Orange

N14

Northern Cape

Grootvloer

Verneuk Pan

De Aar

N12

S O U T H

N1

Fish

Beaufort West

N9

KEY

- ✈ International airport
- ▬ Motorway
- ▬ Major road
- ▬ Minor road
- — Main railway line
- ‑·‑ International boundary
- ‑‑‑ Provincial boundary

ATLANTIC OCEAN

St Helena Bay

Saldanha Bay

Table Bay

CAPE TOWN

Simon's Town

False Bay

Worcester

Breede

Somerset West

Western Cape

Oudtshoorn

George

N9

N2

Mossel Bay

St Sebastian Bay

Arniston

0 kilometres 200

0 miles 100

Satellite image of southern Africa

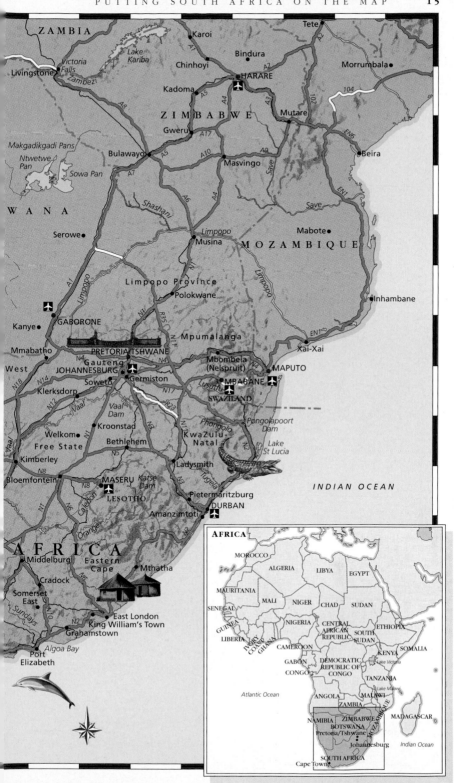

Road Map of South Africa

International airports at Johannesburg, Cape Town and Durban link South Africa with the rest of the world, while domestic airports serve many of the smaller centres. International ocean liners dock at the ports of Cape Town, Durban and Port Elizabeth. An efficient road network spans the vast interior, linking cities and towns. This book divides the country into ten regions, with a separate chapter for Cape Town. Officially South Africa has nine provinces.

KEY

- ✈ International airport
- Motorway
- Major road
- Minor road
- Main railway line
- International boundary
- Provincial boundary

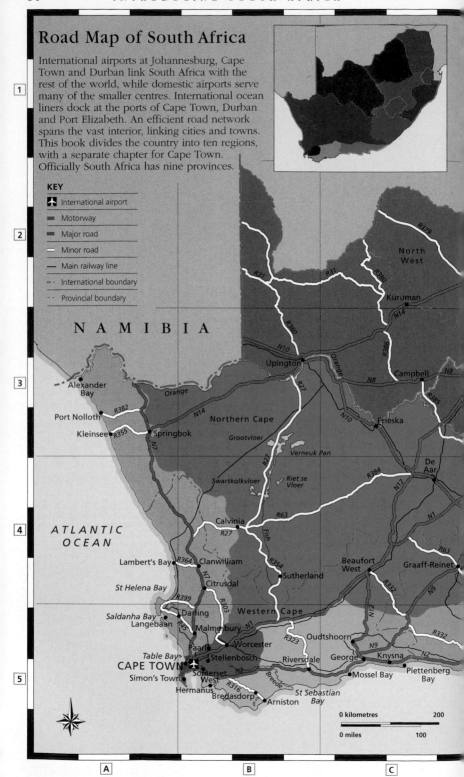

NAMIBIA

North West

Kuruman

Upington

Campbell

Alexander Bay

Orange

Port Nolloth

Kleinsee

Springbok

Northern Cape

Grootvloer

Prieska

Verneuk Pan

De Aar

ATLANTIC OCEAN

Swartkolkvloer

Riet se Vloer

Calvinia

Lambert's Bay

Clanwilliam

Sutherland

Beaufort West

Graaff-Reinet

Citrusdal

St Helena Bay

Western Cape

Saldanha Bay

Langebaan

Darling

Malmesbury

Worcester

Oudtshoorn

George

Knysna

Paarl

Stellenbosch

Riversdale

Mossel Bay

Plettenberg Bay

Table Bay

CAPE TOWN

Simon's Town

Somerset West

Hermanus

Bredasdorp

Arniston

St Sebastian Bay

0 kilometres   200

0 miles   100

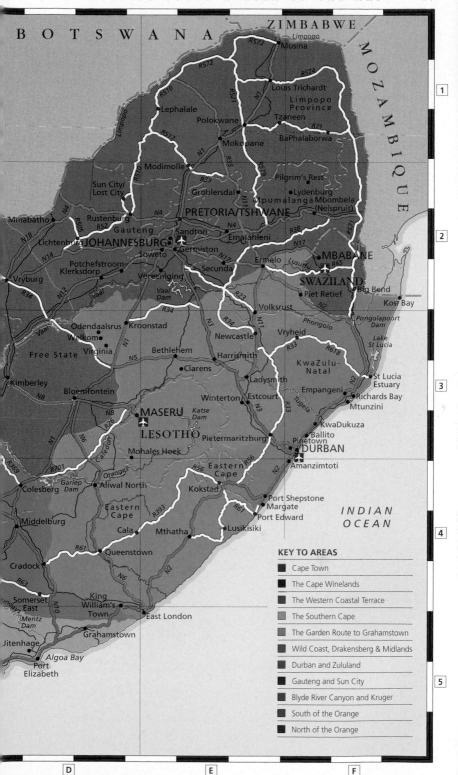

KEY TO AREAS

- Cape Town
- The Cape Winelands
- The Western Coastal Terrace
- The Southern Cape
- The Garden Route to Grahamstown
- Wild Coast, Drakensberg & Midlands
- Durban and Zululand
- Gauteng and Sun City
- Blyde River Canyon and Kruger
- South of the Orange
- North of the Orange

A PORTRAIT OF
SOUTH AFRICA

Blue skies, game parks, wilderness areas, and the promise of a sun-drenched holiday are what draws most visitors to South Africa. While the country continues to be troubled by deep-rooted racial divisions, the determination of its people to begin anew makes it an inspiring and beautiful place to explore.

South Africa, roughly the size of Spain and France combined, encompasses an astonishing diversity of environments: from the dramatic arid moonscapes of the northwest to the forest-fringed coastline of the Garden Route; from the flat, dry Karoo interior to the craggy Drakensberg in the east; the manicured vineyards of the Cape to the spring flower fields of Namaqualand. South Africa is the only country in the world that can lay claim to an entire floral kingdom within its borders. Centred on a small area in the Western Cape, *fynbos* (literally "fine-leaved bush") comprises a unique variety of proteas, ericas and grasses.

King protea

The many wildlife parks further north are home to the Big Five: buffaloes, elephants, leopards, lions and rhinos, while the wetlands and marine reserves along the east coast teem with sea creatures and colourful birds, great and small, that are often overlooked.

And then there are the beaches, favourite holiday destination of the locals, for boardsailing, swimming, surfing, angling, and suntanning.

The "rainbow people of God" is how former Anglican Archbishop Desmond Tutu described the South African nation – this conglomeration of beliefs, traditions, and heritages living within a country of breathtaking natural wonders.

Acacia trees survive along the parched fringes of the Kalahari desert

◁ A young Zulu dancer in traditional costume

Groote Schuur Hospital, where the world's first successful heart transplant was carried out in 1967

Yet, these stark contrasts do not exist in scenery alone. Many observers speak of two worlds within one country: a first and a third. Although 60 per cent of the continent's electricity is generated in South Africa, more than half of the nation's households still have to rely on paraffin, wood and gas for light, cooking, and heating their homes.

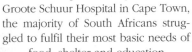

Pouring gold bars

The modern South African state began as a halfway station. Dutch traders of the 17th century, on long sea voyages to their colonies in the East, replenished their stores at the Cape. A fertile land, South Africa is still largely self-reliant today, compelled to become so as a result of the long period of international political isolation that resulted from its former policy of racial discrimination known as *apartheid* (apartness).

South Africa became a world producer of gold and petroleum. Impressive advances were made in communication, weapons technology and mining, but apartheid stood in the way of harmony and economic growth. In the late 1960s, while the world's first human heart transplant was performed at Groote Schuur Hospital in Cape Town, the majority of South Africans struggled to fulfil their most basic needs of food, shelter and education.

Farm labourers relaxing on a hay wagon, West Coast

PEOPLE AND SOCIETY

In a land of such differences, it is hardly surprising that South Africans lack a collective identity. In 1994, English, Afrikaans and nine Bantu tongues were recognized as official languages. Afrikaans, derived from Dutch and altered through contact with other tongues, is spoken by 13 per cent of the population.

South Africa's cultural mix has its roots in a colonial past. The original hunter-gatherer inhabitants of the Cape were joined, about 1,000 years ago, by migrating Bantu-speakers from the north. In the 17th century, European settlers appeared – first the Dutch, then the British and French – with their slaves from Indonesia, Madagascar, and India. Later followed indentured labourers from India. Settlers and slaves alike brought with them their culinary traditions, and if there is a national cuisine it is Cape Malay: mild lamb and fish curries sweetened with spiced fruit. Although seafood is relished, South Africans are really a meat-loving nation. The outdoor *braai* (barbecue) is popular all around the globe, but no one does it quite like South Africans, with fiercely guarded secret recipes, and competitions for the best *boerewors* (a kind of sausage) and *potjiekos* (a tasty stew prepared in a three-legged cast iron pot).

Religion crosses many of the cultural and social divides. The African independent churches have a large following, as their approach includes aspects of tribal mysticism, and a firm belief in

Feast day preparations in a Cape Town mosque

Penny whistler

the influence of ancestral spirits. The Dutch Reformed, Roman Catholic, Presbyterian, and Anglican churches draw worshippers from all population groups. Islam is strongly represented in the Western Cape, while Buddhists and Hindus are mainly found in Durban.

CULTURE AND SPORT

An awareness of African identity is increasingly apparent. Music, which has always played a central part in traditional ceremony and celebration, clearly leads the way. Regular church choir-festivals attest to the popularity of, especially, gospel and choral harmony. The distinctive sound of Zulu *mbube* (unaccompanied choral singing) has become one of South Africa's best-known exports.

African choir performing gospel and harmonies

Sindiwe Magona is the author of several books about her life as a black South African woman

In the cities, although the tunes are much influenced by popular North American music, jazz, soul, *kwela* (characterized by the piercing sound of the penny whistle), *kwaito* (transient pop), rock and reggae all have a strong local flavour.

The white Afrikaner's cultural heritage, accumulated over centuries of isolation from the European motherland, today embraces a powerful body of prose and poetry *(see pp28–9)*, and a distinctive musical tradition. Afrikaans songs tend to be nostalgic, often evoking gentler times. By contrast, the music of the coloured people is lively, distinguished by bouncy melodies and cheerful, racy lyrics that belie the sadness and indignities of the past.

During the dark years of apartheid, oppression and suffering offered ready-made source material for the arts, but contemporary writers are moving away from racial introspection towards more universal themes.

Most South Africans are passionate about sport – increasingly so since the end of the sports boycott. The Rugby World Cup, which was held in Cape Town and other cities in 1995 and won by a jubilant South Africa, probably did more than anything else to unite the nation. South Africa won the tournament again in 2007. Soccer, cricket, boxing, horse racing and athletics also draw expectant crowds. The country hosted the soccer World Cup in 2010.

SOUTH AFRICA TODAY

The best point from which to chart the end of apartheid is the then President FW de Klerk's unbanning of the African National Congress (ANC), along with the Communist Party and Pan-Africanist Congress (PAC).

On 11 February 1990, ANC leader Nelson Mandela was released from the Victor Verster Prison near Paarl. He had been imprisoned since 1963.

Amid escalating violence, negotiations began for a peaceful transition to democracy. Finally, on 27 April 1994, all South Africans voted. The ANC secured 63 per cent, and Nelson Mandela became the first black president of the "New South Africa".

Cape minstrel

The new constitution, approved in May 1996, has arguably the most enlightened Bill of Rights in the world, outlawing discrimination on the

South Africa's rugby team celebrates its World Cup victory in 2007

South Africans enjoy the outdoors, as here, on popular Clifton beach in Cape Town

grounds of ethnic or social origin, religion, gender, sexual orientation and language. Yet, many citizens still live very close to poverty and, despite the country's wealth of natural resources, advanced technology and sophisticated infrastructure, the gap between South Africa's privileged and its poor is ever wider. Tough times lie ahead, but the nation looks to the future applying Nelson Mandela's maxim: "It is not easy to remain bitter if one is busy with constructive things."

South Africa's children have a special place in "Madiba's" heart

NAME CHANGES

South Africa is in a state of transition, and nowhere is that more apparent than in the process, begun in 1994, of renaming places and streets. The main objective has been to purge the map of apartheid associations – Verwoedburg, for instance was renamed Centurion. Other changes have included cosmetic spelling corrections, like Umfolozi to Imfolozi, and the adoption of dual names, such as uKhahlamba-Drakensberg (for the country's largest mountain range). Some new names – for example OR

Tambo Airport (formerly Johannesburg International; before that, Jan Smuts) – are now officially accepted and in everyday use. Others are still awaiting ratification years after they were first tabled; Tshwane (Pretoria) is a notable example. The whole process has been poorly managed, resulting in a great deal of confusion.

In this edition of *Eyewitness South Africa,* new names are used only where they have been formally accepted. Where the change is recent or the new name is not yet in widespread use, the old name is given in parenthesis after the new one. Readers should be aware, however, that the process is ongoing, and further changes are inevitable.

A bold mural in Johannesburg portrays the multicultural nation

The Contrasting Coasts

Two ocean currents influence the coastal climate of South Africa: the tropical Agulhas Current, which flows south down the East Coast, and the cold, north-flowing Benguela Current along the western shores. The two merge somewhere off lonely Cape Agulhas, Africa's most southerly cape. Together with the winds and mountains, these ocean movements determine the region's coastal variance: the aridity of the west versus the luxuriant forest in the east. The coastal fauna and flora, both terrestrial and aquatic, display interesting variations. Here, too, the west differs substantially from the east, as plants and animals have adapted to their specific environments.

Blue whales, *at 33 m (108 ft), the largest mammals on earth, are one of the whale species that frequent South African coastal waters during the Arctic winter.*

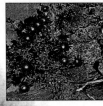

Drosanthemums *are low-growing plants, well adapted to arid West Coast conditions. They store precious water in their small, thick leaves and flower between August and October.*

Alexander Bay

0 kilometres 100
0 miles   50

ATLANTIC OCEAN

Cape Basin

St Helena Bay

Saldanha Bay

Table Bay

CAPE TOWN

False Bay

Cape Point

Cape Agulhas

A g u l h a s   B a n k

The black korhaan *inhabits dry coastal scrubland. The males are strikingly coloured and protect their territory with raucous calls. Females are an incon-spicuous mottled brown and avoid detection by standing perfectly still.*

At Cape Agulhas, the waters of the two currents converge.

West Coast rock lobster, *important to the region's economy, are harvested under special licence. They are not reared on a commercial basis.*

The Benguela Current flows north, carrying cold water from the Antarctic.

THE WEST COAST

Even in summer, water temperatures average only 14°C (57°F). This precludes the formation of rain-bearing clouds, and annual precipitation is below 250 mm (10 in). The lack of fresh water means that only tough succulents survive on dew from sea mists. The sea water, full of nutrients, sustains a rich and varied marine life.

Sea anemone

CAPE AGULHAS

Memorial plaque at Cape Agulhas

The southernmost point of the African continent is not Cape Point, but unassuming Cape Agulhas on the rocky east side of the windswept, shallow Danger Point headland. The Portuguese word *agulhas*, from which it gets its name, means "needles". It was here, early navigators discovered, that the compass needle was not affected by magnetic deviation, but pointed true north. A plaque is set into the rock and markers give the distances to international cities.

Various dolphin species *can be seen frolicking in the warm currents off towns like Durban and Margate. They usually occur in groups of 10 to 15 individuals.*

The genus *Crinum* *(amaryllis family) is commonly seen in swampy grass-land along the East Coast. It flowers in summer.*

The knysna lourie *(Tauraco corythaix) is found in the evergreen forests of southern and eastern South Africa. This elegant bird is most likely to be spotted flying between trees or hopping expertly along branches.*

INDIAN OCEAN

Natal Basin

Alwal Shoal

Umgeni River Estuary

St Lucia Marine Reserve

Kosi Bay

Algoa Bay

A g u l h a s   B a s i n

The warm Agulhas Current causes humid conditions along the East Coast.

Port Elizabeth crayfish *(or shoveller), one of many species of rock lobster found around the South African coast, has little commercial value.*

THE EAST COAST

The warm Agulhas Current that flows south through the Mozambique Channel creates hot, humid conditions along the East Coast. Vegetation is subtropical and mangrove forests flourish in the Umgeni River Estuary near Durban. The annual migration of big pilchard shoals is eagerly awaited by fish, bird and man. Coral reefs, rare in South African waters, are found in the St Lucia Marine Reserve.

Nudibranch

The Landscapes and Flora of South Africa

South Africa's flora has charmed visitors and intrigued botanists for years. Many species are widely distributed within the country, but each region has produced distinct characteristics, the result of varying geographic, climatic and soil conditions. In the more arid western reaches of the country, plants tend to be small and low-growing, flowering briefly after the winter rains, while further east open grassland and bushveld dominate. Along the East Coast grow lush subtropical coastal forests.

Aloe flower

THE CAPE FLORAL KINGDOM

Pelargonium

The Southwestern Cape, one of the world's six floral kingdoms, boasts around 8,500 different plants in an area less than four per cent of the southern African land surface. This so-called *fynbos* (fine-leaved bush) includes some 350 species of protea, as well as pelargoniums, ericas, reeds and irises. Most are endemic to the area, and are well represented in the Kirstenbosch National Botanical Garden *(see pp158–9)*.

SEMI-DESERT

Succulent

In southern Africa, true desert is confined to the Namib. The semi-desert Great Karoo region covers about one-third of South Africa. Its flora has evolved to withstand aridity and extreme temperatures. Many succulents, including the aloes, mesembryanthemums, euphorbias and stapelias, store water in their thick leaves or roots. The seeds of daisy-like ephemeral plants may lie dormant for years, only to germinate and flower briefly when the conditions are favourable *(see pp216–17)*. Trees tend to grow along seasonal river courses.

NAMAQUALAND *(see pp216–17)*

Many succulent plants in this region survive only through the condensation of nightly mists that roll in from the Atlantic Ocean. Adaptation has led to many bizarre species, such as the *kokerboom* (quiver tree), *halfmens* (half-human), and the insectivorous plants of the Stapelia family. Dwarf shrubs and scraggy bushes are widely spaced over dusty land that is bare for most of the year, until even modest winter rains raise dense, multi-hued crops of daisy-like *vygie* blossoms.

Vygies

TEMPERATE FOREST

Dense evergreen forests thrive in the high-rainfall area around Knysna *(see pp240–41)*. They produce lovely rare hardwoods such as stinkwood and yellowwood, two types that also occur along the subtropical coastal belt of KwaZulu-Natal. Knysna's temperate forests have a characteristic undergrowth of shrubs, ferns, fungi, and creepers, such as the wispy "old man's beard". Mature trees may reach a height of 60 m (195 ft), with a girth of seven metres (23 ft).

Forest fungus

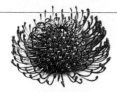

Erica patersonia is one of over 625 erica species that occur in the Southwestern Cape. It is mainly found along streams.

Protea grandiceps *is one of the most widely distributed of its species. It grows at the higher altitudes of coastal mountains.*

Pincushion proteas bloom from June to December in colours ranging from yellow to deep red. Flower heads last for up to three weeks and attract sunbirds and insects.

Ericas are found on Table Mountain, where Erica dichrus provides dense red splashes of colour.

Yellow pincushion proteas *grow on a tall shrub that is found near the coast.*

BUSHVELD

Large tracts of the interior are covered with tall grasses and low trees, most of them deciduous, fine-leaved and thorny. The Kruger National Park *(see pp338–41)* is an excellent example of several transitional types occurring between sparse shrub and savanna; here shrubs grow densely and larger tree types include marula, mopane and baobab. The large acacia family is characterized by pod-bearing trees and shrubs with clusters of small, golden-yellow flowers.

"Weeping boerbean" pod

HIGH MOUNTAIN

Mountain flora, zoned according to altitude and increasing severity of the environment, rises from dense heath to mixed scrub and grasses. A relatively small subalpine belt, 2,800 m (9,000 ft) above sea level, is confined to the Drakensberg region *(see pp270–71)*. Characteristic floral species are Helichrysum ("everlastings"), sedges and ericas. In many areas, annuals make brief, colourful spring appearances. Among the proteas growing in this region is the rare snow protea on the high peaks of

Watsonia   the Cederberg *(see pp214–15)*.

SUBTROPICAL COASTAL BELT

Brackish swamps, saline estuaries and lush plant growth are characteristic of the KwaZulu-Natal coast. Mangroves anchor themselves to their unstable habitat with stilt-like roots, while higher up on the banks grow palms and the broad-leaved wild banana of the Strelitzia family. A good example of typical East Coast vegetation can be seen at Kosi Bay *(see p297)*, where swamps surround lakes that are overgrown with water lilies and reeds. Dune forests and grasslands are dotted with wild palms.

Water lily

Literary South Africa

Afrikaans Bible

A rich literary tradition exists in all 11 national languages, which include nine Bantu tongues, mostly from the Nguni and Sotho branches. Most books were published in Afrikaans or English, while much of the African heritage was handed down orally. Books in African tongues are now beginning to enjoy a wider circulation, both locally and abroad, and are also appearing in foreign translation. Over the years, South Africa has inspired a number of outstanding authors and poets, among them Sir Percy FitzPatrick, Olive Schreiner, Sir Laurens van der Post, Nadine Gordimer and Mzwakhe Mbuli.

CJ Langenhoven wrote *Die Stem*, one of the two national anthems

Painting by Credo Mutwa, taken from the book *African Proverbs*

TRADITIONAL AFRICAN STORIES

Many African communities have an oral tradition of stories, genealogies, proverbs and riddles that have been passed down from generation to generation.

Izibongo, simplistically translated as praise songs, are very complex oral presentations delivered by a skilled performer known as *mbongi*. This rhythmic form of poetry uses exalted language, rich in metaphor and parallelisms. At Nelson Mandela's inauguration, two *izibongo* were performed in isiXhosa.

Among the best written works are Samuel Mqhayi's historic *Ityala Lamawele* (Lawsuit of the Twins) and A Jordan's *Ingqumbo Yeminyanya* (The Wrath of the Ancestors), both in isiXhosa, and Thomas

Mofolo's *Chaka* in Sesotho, BW Vilakazi's *Noma Nini* in isiZulu, and Sol Plaatjie's *Mhudi* in Setswana.

English publications of traditional African tales, novels and poetry include *Indaba My Children* and *African Proverbs* by Credo Mutwa.

Actor Patrick Mynhardt dramatizes Herman Charles Bosman's *A Cask of Jerepigo*

AFRIKAANS LITERATURE

The Dutch spoken by the colonial authorities formed the basis of a local tongue that became known as Afrikaans, or simply *die taal* (the language). Efforts to translate the Bible into Afrikaans led to a vigorous campaign to have the language formally recognized. A direct result of these tireless efforts was the publication of almost 100 books before 1900.

The descriptive prose and lyrical poetry of literary greats like Gustav Preller, CJ Langenhoven, DF Malherbe and Totius (Jacob Daniël du Toit), who delighted in the use of their new language, helped to establish Afrikaans as the lingua franca.

Later writers, like PG du Plessis and Etienne Le Roux, placed Afrikaans literature in a wider context, while Adam Small and Breyten Breytenbach used it as a form of political and social protest against the white Afrikaner establishment.

"Afrikanerisms", deliberate use of Afrikaans words and sentence construction when writing in English, is a literary device used in Pauline Smith's *The Beadle*, and in Herman Charles Bosman's humorous short story *A Cask of Jerepigo*. Both works describe the life, joys and hardships of a rural Afrikaner community.

Afrikaans became a hated symbol of oppression during the apartheid years yet, today, it is more widely spoken than any other local tongue.

Jock of the Bushveld statue in the Kruger National Park

ENGLISH POETRY AND PROSE

Olive Schreiner's *Story of an African Farm* (1883), first published under a male pseudonym, presented the rural Afrikaner to an international audience for the first time. The book was startling, also, for its advanced views on feminism – sentiments that the author expanded on in *Woman and Labour* (1911).

Percy FitzPatrick's *Jock of the Bushveld* (1907) became one of the best-known of all South African titles. A blend of romantic adventure and realism, it tells the story of a transport rider and his dog on the early gold fields.

Later popular authors who achieved international sales include Geoffrey Jenkins, and Wilbur Smith whose novels, such as *Where the Lion Feeds*, have made him one of the world's best-selling writers. A more thought-provoking genre is that of Stuart Cloete's *The Abductors*, once banned in South Africa, and Sir Laurens van der Post's touching description of a dying culture in *Testament to the Bushmen*.

The works of André P Brink and JM Coetzee dealt mainly with social and political matters that were often viewed by the apartheid regime as attacks on the establishment. Brink's critical *Looking on Darkness* (1963) became the first Afrikaans novel to be banned in South Africa.

The 1924 publication of *The Flaming Terrapin* established Roy Campbell as a leading poet. Although the hardships of black South Africans had been highlighted in Herbert Dhlomo's short stories and Peter Abrahams's *Mine Boy*, it was the subject matter of race relations in *Cry the Beloved Country* (1948) by Alan Paton that attracted the world's attention.

As one of several superb female writers, Nadine Gordimer (*A Sport of Nature* and *July's People*, among others) became the recipient of a Nobel Prize for Literature in 1991. The author contributed greatly to the standard of writing in South Africa, and her struggle against another of the apartheid era's crippling laws – censorship – paved the way for many others. Rose Zwi's

Local edition of *A Sport of Nature*

Another Year in Africa is an insight into the life of South Africa's Jewish immigrants, while the autobiographical *To My Children's Children* is Sindiwe Magona's account of a youth spent in the former homeland of Transkei, and of the daily struggle in Cape Town's townships.

CONTEMPORARY LITERATURE

Autobiographies and travelogues, popular genres for modern local writers, offer insights into the lives of South Africans. Nelson Mandela's *Long Walk to Freedom* was a national bestseller. *Country of My Skull* is Antjie Krog's narrative of her two years spent reporting on the Truth and Reconciliation Commission, while *Beckett's Trek* and *Madibaland* by Denis Beckett, and Sarah Penny's *The Whiteness of Bones* are entertaining jaunts through South Africa and its neighbours. Zakes Mda's award-winning *Ways of Dying* gives the reader a glimpse of the professional mourner, while Ashraf Jamal's *Love Themes for the Wilderness* takes a life-affirming trip into contemporary urbanity.

STRUGGLE POETRY

During the apartheid years, conflict and the repression of Africans provided recurring themes. Produced orally in various Bantu tongues and in written form in English, the new means of expression was termed "Struggle Poetry". Oswald Mtshali's *Sounds of a Cowhide Drum* (1971) signalled the shift in black poetry from lyrical themes to indirect political messages in free verse. Other creators of this form of

Mongane Wally Serote, poet and politician

protest were Mzwakhe Mbuli, known as "the people's poet", Mafika Gwala, James Matthews, Sipho Sepamla, Njabulo Ndebele and Mongane Wally Serote. Their verse expressed disapproval of the socio-political conditions in the country and was, at the same time, a conscious attempt to raise the level of awareness among their people.

South African Architecture

Diverse factors have influenced building styles in South Africa: climate, social structure, and the state of the economy have all shaped the country's homes. In earlier days, when suitable raw materials were often unavailable, ingenious adaptations resulted. Variations included the *hartbeeshuisie* (hard-reed house), a pitched-roof shelter built directly on the ground, and the beehive-shaped "corbelled" huts, built of stone in areas where structural timber was unobtainable, as in the Northern Cape. Modern South African building and engineering skills have kept abreast with international trends, and many different styles can be seen throughout the country.

Weaving the reed fence surrounding a traditional Swazi village

INDIGENOUS ARCHITECTURAL STYLES

Most traditional rural dwellings, often called "rondavels", are circular in shape. The conical roofs are traditionally constructed of a tightly woven reed or grass thatch, while the walls may be made of mud blocks mixed with cow dung, or consist of a framework of woven branches, covered with animal hide. Most of these homes, except the *matjieshuise* of the arid Namaqualand nomads for whom rain was no threat, are well insulated and waterproof. In recent times, materials like corrugated iron, plastic sheeting and cardboard have become popular, especially in informal settlements on the outskirts of cities.

Zulu "beehives" *are a community effort. The stick framework is erected by the men, and the women thatch it.*

The *matjieshuise* *(houses made of mats) of Khoina nomads consisted of portable hide- or reed-mats on a stick frame.*

Xhosa huts *are built of mud. The circular type shown here has largely been replaced by rectangular patterns.*

A capping of clay covers the ridge of the roof to keep the thatch in place.

The thatch is made of sheaves of grass or reed.

Windows and decorations are symmetrically placed around the door.

Wall designs are hand-painted.

Low outside wall

Ndebele homes *are, perhaps, the most eye-catching local style. The walls of the rectangular structures are traditionally painted by women, using bright primary colours. No stencils are used for the bold geometric motifs.*

Ndebele wall detail

Basotho huts, *originally circular, are built of blocks of turf, mud, or stone, and plastered with mud. In rural areas, walls are still decorated with pebbles, but the use of paint is spreading.*

CAPE DUTCH ARCHITECTURE

The vernacular of the Western Cape, recognized by its symmetrical design and prominent gables, evolved around the mid-18th century from a simple row of thatched rooms whose sizes depended on the length of the available beams. The forms of the gables were derived from the Baroque architecture of Holland. End gables prevented the roof from being torn off by high winds, while the centre gable let light into the attic.

Gable of Franschhoek Town Hall

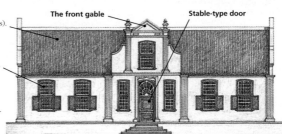

Thatching reed was widely available in the *vleis* (swamps).

The front gable

Stable-type door

Sash windows had many small panes, and only the lower half could be opened.

Rhone, *near Franschhoek, is a good example of an 18th-century homestead. The front gable dates back to 1795.*

GEORGIAN ARCHITECTURE

Modest examples of 18th-century Georgian-style architecture, with plain front pediments and flat roofs, survive along the narrow, cobbled streets of Cape Town's Bo-Kaap, or "Malay Quarter".

The neighbourhood of Artificers' Square in Grahamstown also has fine examples. Here, the houses display typical many-paned, sliding sash windows, plain parapets and a fanlight above the entrance.

Geometric brick detail

The chimney was designed to complement the house.

The roof is protected by slate tiles.

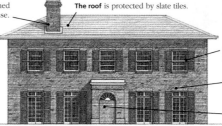

Louvre shutters reduce the harsh glare of the sun.

Bertram House, *completed in 1839, is Cape Town's only surviving brick Georgian house.*

Precise brick-laying adds attractive detail.

The wind lobby excludes draughts.

VICTORIAN ARCHITECTURE

The romantic Victorian style with its decorative cast-iron detail, brass fittings, and stained-glass windows became extremely popular, especially in Cape Town, around the turn of the century. Here, too, terrace housing, pioneered in 18th-century England by the Adam Brothers, provided affordable housing for a burgeoning middle-class. Fine examples may be seen in suburbs like Woodstock, Observatory, Mowbray and Wynberg.

***Broekie* lace detail, Prince Albert**

Cast-iron decorations were called *broekie* lace, because they resembled the lacy edging of ladies' drawers.

Ornamental gable

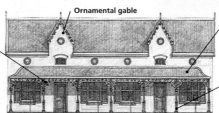

A corrugated iron awning covers the verandah.

Oom Samie se Winkel (see p190), *in Stellenbosch, displays a marked Cape Dutch influence. The porch encouraged patrons to linger.*

Cast-iron supports hold up the awning.

Multicultural South Africa

San Bushman rock painting

The South African nation is composed of a medley of different beliefs and cultures. Early influences, such as the languages and religions of slaves from India, Madagascar, Indonesia, West and East Africa and Malaysia, are preserved by their descendants. South Africa's mineral wealth drew settlers from other parts of Africa, as well as Asia, America and Europe – heritages still reflected in today's faces. Most coloured people live in the former slave-owning Western Cape area, while many Indians live around Durban, where their ancestors worked on sugar plantations.

Weaving is an important skill, and many Sotho, Xhosa and Tswana wear patterned or sombre ochre blankets as over-garments. In the northerly parts of Limpopo Province live the Venda, with a tradition, unusual in South Africa, of building in stone. The Venda are one of the few groups that traditionally used a drum as a musical instrument. Wood sculptures by leading Venda artists are treasured pieces.

The Wartburger Hof in KwaZulu-Natal looks like an alpine lodge

Very few San Bushmen still hunt and live in the traditional way

THE KHOI

Khoi rock paintings, often found in caves overlooking the plains below, offer tantalizing evidence of the practical skills and the spiritual nature of the people who were almost certainly South Africa's original human inhabitants. *(See Drakensberg pp270–71 and Kagga Kamma p214.)* Many were hunter-gatherers, living lightly on the natural bounty of the land.

Under pressure from more material cultures, some Khoi withdrew inland, where their descendants (the San Bushmen) are still today found in parts of Namaqualand and in the Northern Cape.

Other Khoi eventually threw in their lot with the Dutch settlers. Many of today's Cape Coloured people are descended from them.

THE BANTU-SPEAKERS

The Bantu languages are indigenous to Africa, although not related to those of the Khoi. Each group has its own complex system of cultures and relationships, although Westernized culture is replacing many of the older, traditional ways. Cattle and cattle pens *(kraals)* have an important place in Zulu, Xhosa and Ndebele cultures, and Zulu handicrafts include works in earthenware, iron and wood. Basket-making and weaving are other skills. The Xhosa, most of whom live in the Eastern Cape, are known for their beautifully designed and executed beadwork. The Ndebele of the Limpopo Province and Gauteng are renowned for their remarkably colourful and intricate beadwork, and their decorative painting applied to buildings is particularly eye-catching.

THE EUROPEAN COLONISTS

The first European settlers, in 1652, were Dutch and German. European politics further affected the composition of the Cape population, when French Huguenots were settled here from 1688, and French and German regiments were periodically brought in to boost the local defences against Britain. The British, however, took permanent possession of the Cape in 1806 and, during the

Many Xhosa women smoke long-stemmed pipes

depression that followed the Napoleonic Wars, dispatched several thousand settlers to farm in the Eastern Cape. More (pro-British) German settlers arrived after the Crimean War, and many British ex-soldiers elected to stay in South Africa, or returned to it, after the South African War of 1899–1902 and the World Wars. The British custom of hot Christmas dinner, for example, prevails in many quarters, despite its unsuitability in the local climate.

Franschhoek, near Cape Town, retains some of the atmosphere of a French wine-growing region, while Eastern Cape villages settled by Germans still carry the names of German cities, such as Berlin and Hamburg.

ASIAN ORIGINS

East Indian islanders who opposed Dutch colonization of their territory in the 17th and 18th centuries were banished to the Cape of Good Hope. Slaves imported from Indonesia and the Indian subcontinent swelled the size of the oppressed minority. Nearly all of them belonged to the Islamic faith, while many others converted.

During the 19th century, thousands of indentured Indians worked in the sugar cane fields of KwaZulu-Natal, and elected to stay on at the end of their contract. In KwaZulu-Natal, Cape Town and Gauteng, the striking Eastern mosques and temples are a noteworthy architectural feature. Religious festivals are regularly observed, and the bustling oriental markets yield a treasure trove of spices, jewellery and handicrafts.

AFRIKANERS

The term "Afrikaner" was first recorded in 1706, as referring to a South African-born, Afrikaans- (or Dutch-) speaking white person. In more recent times, however,

During Afrikaner festivals, traditional costumes are worn

just the first-language use of Afrikaans has become the identifying factor. Afrikaner men are often associated with a love for outdoor sport (especially rugby) and a passion for the *braai* (barbecue).

The tunes delivered by a *Boere-orkes* (literally "farmers' band") consist of concertina, banjo, piano accordion, and fiddles, and bear great similarity to North American "country" music.

THE COLOURED PEOPLE

The term "Cape Coloured" has now been in use for almost two centuries to define members of what is sometimes called "the only truly indigenous population".

Many of these people are descended from relationships between settlers, slaves and local tribes, and many slave names survive in the form of surnames such as Januarie,

Temple dancing is still being taught in Durban

November, Titus, Appollis, Cupido and Adonis.

The most skilled fishermen, livery men as well as artisans were traditionally found in the Asian and Coloured communities, and many of the Cape's beautiful historic buildings were their creations.

A young Muslim girl prepares flower decorations for a festival

FROM ALL QUARTERS

Compared with other countries such as the United States and Australia, South Africa offered little scope for unskilled or semi-skilled white labour from Europe. However, small but steady numbers of immigrants did arrive, especially from Eastern European countries like Yugoslavia, Poland and Bulgaria.

South Africa has many citizens from Italy, Greece, Portugal and the Netherlands, as well as Jewish communities. These and other groups have formed common-interest societies seen at their most picturesque during colourful community carnivals.

Sport in South Africa

Given the country's favourable climate, sport plays a major role in the lives of many South Africans. In recent years, generous government funding and corporate sponsorship have resulted in the development of sporting facilities in the previously disadvantaged communities, encouraging much as yet unexplored talent. Sports events that are held in the major centres take place in world-class stadiums with superb facilities. Seats for the important matches are best bought through Computicket *(see p431)*, while those for lesser events are obtainable directly at the respective venues.

Test matches are played by the national team, known as the Springboks, against the national sides of other rugby-playing nations.

In 1995 and 2007, South Africa won the Rugby World Cup (contested every four years). The local rugby season begins in early February, continuing through the winter months and ending in late October with the Currie Cup Finals *(see p36)*.

Soccer attracts spectators from all sectors of South African society

SOCCER

Soccer is played all over South Africa, in dusty township streets and in the elite professional clubs. The most popular clubs attract huge spectator and fan followings, and can easily fill 80,000-seat stadiums for top matches. The soccer leagues are contested by clubs, and, unlike other major sports such as rugby and cricket, there is little emphasis on representation at provincial level.

The national soccer team, known as Bafana Bafana, has had success in the biennial African Cup of Nations, winning the contest in 1995 (when South Africa hosted the tournament) and reaching the finals in 1998. The team, ranked among the world's top 40, qualified for the World Cup Finals for the first time in 1998. In 2010, South Africa hosted the FIFA World Cup. Except for the hottest summer months (Dec–Feb), soccer is played year round.

RUGBY UNION

Rugby is played at all levels – from school to regional club, and from provincial to national stage.

Teams from the 14 provincial unions contest the Currie Cup every season. These 14 unions supply players to the five regional teams that fight for victory in the Super 15, an international and regional tournament involving South Africa, as well as Australia and New Zealand.

CRICKET

South Africa has long been a major force in the world of cricket. Played during the summer months, cricket is a sport enjoyed by thousands of players and spectators at various levels, from club and provincial competitions to international test matches.

Development programmes have discovered great talent among the youth of once-disadvantaged communities.

Four-day provincial games and the more popular one-day matches are held, while five-day tests are contested between South Africa and visiting national teams. One-day and day/night limited-overs international and provincial matches are particularly popular, usually played to packed stands.

The demand for tickets to these games is high, and advance booking is available through Computicket outlets countrywide or the cricket union hosting the match.

Rugby games draw crowds of up to 50,000 to the provincial stadiums

Two Oceans Marathon runners pass the crowds at Constantia Nek

MARATHONS AND ULTRA-MARATHONS

Long-distance running is both a popular pastime and a serious national sport. South Africa boasts a number of the world's fastest marathon runners, such as Josiah Thugwane who won a gold medal in the 1996 Olympics.

The strenuous 56-km (35-mile) Two Oceans Marathon, which takes place around the Cape Peninsula on Easter Saturday, and the energy-sapping 85-km (53-mile) long Comrades Marathon, run between the KwaZulu-Natal cities of Durban and Pietermaritzburg in June, are two of the most difficult, yet popular, ultra-marathons in the country. Both events attract thousands of international and local entrants.

With its excellent training facilities and fine summer weather, South Africa is a popular place for European athletes to train during the winter months in Europe. During this season, the international Engen Grand Prix Athletics Series is held in various South African cities.

GOLF

South Africa boasts some of the finest golf courses in the world, and has also produced some of the world's finest golfers. The golfing prowess of Gary Player is legendary, while Ernie Els and Trevor Immelman rank among the top golfers in the world. Each December, Sun City hosts the Nedbank Golf Challenge (see p37), where 12 contestants compete for the largest prize in the world – 1.25 million dollars. The South African Golf Tour attracts professional golfers from around the globe.

Two popular local events are the South African Open, which is held in November, and the Alfred Dunhill PGA, in December.

CYCLING

Apart from various local professional events, the Cape Peninsula hosts the largest timed cycle race in the world, the annual Cape Argus Pick 'n Pay Cycle Tour. Over 35,000 sweaty cycling enthusiasts, some dressed in flamboyant costumes, race or trundle 105 km (65 miles) around the Peninsula on the second Sunday in March. About one-third of the contestants is from overseas.

EQUESTRIAN SPORTS

Horse racing, until recently the only legal form of gambling in the country, has been an enormous industry for many years. The "Met" (Metropolitan Stakes) held in Cape Town in January, and the Durban July are major social events, with fashion and high stakes the order of the day. Show jumping and horse trials attract crowds every spring to venues such as Inanda near Johannesburg.

The Cape to Rio race leaves Table Bay with huge fanfare

WATERSPORTS

South Africa's coastline offers superb opportunities for sports enthusiasts. The Mr Price Pro surfing event, held in Ballito each July, is a major attraction. Cape Town is a popular port of call for round-the-world yacht races, and is also the starting point for the Cape to Rio event that takes place early in January every three years.

Sun City's Golf Course hosts the Nedbank Golf Challenge

SOUTH AFRICA
THROUGH THE YEAR

Though organized festivals are a relatively new feature in South Africa, long, sunny days have given rise to a number of festivities, many of them outdoors. Cities, towns and villages host festivals to celebrate a variety of occasions: the start of the oyster and wildflower seasons; the citrus, apple or grape harvest; even the arrival of the southern right whale from its arctic breeding grounds – all are reason for celebration. The arts, music, religion, language and sport also take their places on the calendar of events. The diversity of festivals emphasizes the disparate origins of South Africa's many peoples and their gradual coming together as a single nation.

Dancers, FNB Dance Umbrella

SPRING

All across the country, but especially noticeable in the semi-arid Western and Northern Cape regions, the onset of warmer weather raises colourful fields of wildflowers. In wildlife reserves throughout South Africa, the newborn of various species will soon be seen.

SEPTEMBER

Arts Alive *(Sep)*, Johannesburg *(see pp310–11)*. An exciting urban arts festival, with performers ranging from world-class musicians to children eager to show off the skills they have acquired at the workshops.
Wildflower Show *(late Sep)*, Darling *(see p211)*. The show displays the unique West Coast flora and cultivated orchids.

Whale Festival *(last week in Sep)*, Hermanus *(see p222)*. From early spring onwards, the southern right whales and their calves can be seen close to shore in and around Walker Bay.
Prince Albert Agricultural Show *(Sep)*, Prince Albert *(see p227)*. Prince Albert proudly celebrates its agricultural heritage with this show featuring arts and crafts, horse displays, food stalls and entertainment.
Kalahari Kuierfees *(Sep)*, Upington *(see p368)*. Music, choir contests and fun on the Orange River.
Magoebaskloof Haenertsburg Spring Festival *(Sep–Oct)*, Magoebaskloof. A bustling arts, crafts and entertainment fair, held in a forest setting.

Orchids from Darling

OCTOBER

Currie Cup Finals *(late Oct)*. The location varies from year to year. Rugby match between the two best provincial teams.
Macufe (Mangaung Cultural African Festival) *(Oct)*, Bloemfontein *(see pp372–3)*. A festival with jazz, gospel, kwaito and classical music, plus drama, comedy and arts and crafts.
Bosman Weekend *(Oct)*, Groot Marico. A celebration of writer Herman Charles Bosman in the town where many of his stories are set.
Rocking the Daisies *(Oct)*, Darling *(see p211)*. A popular music festival showcasing top South African bands, as well as comedy, children's entertainment, wine tastings and a food and craft market.
Sabie Forest Fair *(Oct)*, Sabie. This fair offers arts and crafts stalls and local entertainment around a unique Forestry Museum.

NOVEMBER

Cherry Festival *(third week in Nov)*, Ficksburg. Celebrate South Africa's commercially grown cherries and asparagus.
National Choir Festival *(Nov–Dec)*, Ellis Park Arena, Johannesburg *(see pp310–11)*. The culmination of a national competition.

The Oude Libertas open-air amphitheatre

SUMMER

Most tourists visit South Africa during the long summer months. The local long school holidays extend from December well into January. With many South African families traditionally heading for the seaside and wildlife reserves, this is when the roads are at their busiest. Summer is a season spent outdoors. Christmas lunch is more likely to be celebrated around an informal *braai* (barbecue) than at a dining table. Over much of the country, summer rain arrives in the form of short, noisy thunder showers.

Shooting the Camps Drift rapids on the Dusi River

Carols by Candlelight

DECEMBER

Carols by Candlelight *(pre-Christmas).* These colourful Advent celebrations take place in all of the major towns and cities.
Strawberry Lights Festival *(Dec–Jan),* Somerset West *(see p188).* Main Street display of festive lights in rural Somerset West.
Miss South Africa, Sun City *(see p322).* A glittering, old-fashioned beauty pageant for the nine provincial beauty queens, one of whom will be crowned Miss South Africa.
Nedbank Golf Challenge, Sun City *(see p322).* An internationally renowned golfing event with 12 of the world's best golfers.

JANUARY

Summer Sunset Concerts *(every Sun, Jan–Mar),* Kirstenbosch National Botanical Garden, Cape Town *(see pp158–9).* Outdoor musical performances.
Maynardville Open-Air Theatre *(Jan–Feb),* Wynberg, Cape Town *(see p164).* Shakespearean plays in a city park.
Oude Libertas Arts Programme *(Jan–Mar),* Stellenbosch *(see pp192–3).* Performances in an elegant amphitheatre.
Minstrel Carnival *(2 Jan),* Cape Town *(see p22).* A colourful musical procession culminates in concerts at Cape Town Stadium.

FEBRUARY

FNB Dance Umbrella *(Feb–Mar),* Braamfontein, Johannesburg *(see pp310–11).* One of South Africa's most important dance events.

Cherries

Kavadi Festival *(Jan–Feb),* Durban *(see pp282–5).* A Hindu festival during which many penitents pierce their flesh with hooks and draw beautifully decorated carts through the streets.
Dusi Canoe Marathon *(second week in Feb),* Pietermaritzburg *(see pp276–7).* A three-day canoe marathon to the mouth of the Umgeni River.
Up the Creek *(Feb),* Breede River, near Swellendam *(see pp226–7).* A four-day music festival with three stages set up on the banks of the Breede River.
Prickly Pear Festival *(Feb–Mar),* Uitenhage, Port Elizabeth *(see pp246–9).* A celebration of traditional South African food, such as *braais, potjiekos* (stews made in three-legged cast-iron pots), ginger beer and bunnychow (curry served in a half loaf of bread).

Cape Town's minstrels are a colourful sight in early January

AUTUMN

When deciduous trees and grapevines begin to shed their leaves, a new round of country fairs is ushered in. The harvest festivals of many small towns celebrate crops like potatoes and olives; even sheep and gems are cause for cheerful get-togethers. A number of wine festivals are held from Paarl in the fertile Western Cape to Kuruman in the arid Northern Cape.

Over a million followers of the Zionist Church gather at Easter

MARCH

Rand Show *(Mar–Apr)*, Johannesburg *(see pp310–11)*. What began as an agricultural show has become a blend of entertainment and consumerism.
Lamberts Bay Kreeffees *(Mar)*, Lamberts Bay *(see pp210–11)*. *Kreef* is Afrikaans for crayfish, and *fees* means both festival and feast. Stalls sell West Coast seafood, and there are also live bands.

APRIL

Cape Town International Jazz Festival *(first weekend in Apr)*, Cape Town *(see pp132–5)*. A two-day affair featuring nearly 40 international and African acts performing on five stages. The musical extravaganza is accompanied by a series of photographic and art shows.

Zionist Church gathering *(Easter)*, near Polokwane (formerly Pietersburg, *see p328*) in the Northern Province. More than a million followers of this African Christian church gather at Moria (also known as Zion City) over the Easter weekend. The largest Christian gathering in South Africa.
Fire-walking *(Easter)*, Umbilo Hindu Temple, Durban *(see pp282–5)*. Devout Hindus, after careful spiritual preparation, walk uninjured across a bed of red-hot coals.
Two Oceans Marathon *(Easter)*, Cape Town.

Devotee at a Hindu temple

This 56-km (35-mile) marathon *(see p35)* around the Cape Peninsula is a qualifying race for the Comrades' Marathon.
Klein Karoo Arts Festival *(Apr)*, Oudtshoorn *(see p230)*. A mainly Afrikaans cultural festival.
Prince Albert Olive, Food & Wine Festival *(Apr)*, Prince Albert *(see p227)*. Live music, a cycle race, and an olive-stone spitting competition, plus food and wine tastings.
Ladysmith Show *(Apr)*, Ladysmith, KwaZulu-Natal. An agricultural show with many craft stalls and entertainment.
Splashy Fen Music Festival *(last weekend in Apr)*, Splashy Fen Farm, Underberg, KwaZulu-Natal. A popular festival with performances in mainstream, alternative, folk and traditional music styles.
Pink Loerie Mardi Gras *(Apr–May)*, Knysna *(see p240)*. A four-day gay festival, with charity-led events, exhibitions and food stalls.

MAY

Calitzdorp Port and Wine Festival *(May)*, Karoo *(see p228)*. A celebration of the region's famous port-style wine.

Amusement park at the Rand Show in Johannesburg

WINTER

Dry season for most of the country, only the winter-rainfall area along the South-western and Southern Cape coast is lush and green at this time. Inland, days are typically warm, although nightly frosts are common in high-lying areas. Snowfalls occur on the mountains of the Western and Eastern Cape and in the KwaZulu-Natal and Lesotho highlands. Late winter is particularly good for game-watching, as the thirsty wildlife gathers around waterholes.

JUNE

Comrades' Marathon *(mid-Jun)*, between Durban and Pieter-maritzburg. This ultra long-distance running event attracts top-class runners from all over the world *(see p35)*.

JULY

National Arts Festival *(early to mid-Jul)*, Grahamstown *(see pp252–3)*. An extremely popular two weeks of local and international drama, film, dance, visual arts and music.
July Handicap *(first Sat in Jul)*, Greyville Race Course, Durban *(see pp282–3)*. This is the glamour

Safari wildlife-viewing drive at Sabi Sabi, Mpumalanga

event of the South African horseracing fraternity.
Knysna Oyster Festival *(early Jul)*, Knysna *(see p240)*. The festival, centred on the commercial oyster beds in Knysna Lagoon, coincides with a forest marathon.

Knysna oyster

Berg River Canoe Marathon *(Jul)*, Paarl *(see pp200–1)*. A strenuous four-day canoe race that provides some high excitement and is staged annually when the river is in full flood.
Mr Price Pro *(see pp260–61) (mid-Jul)*, Ballito *(see p292)*. This popular week-long surfing championship attracts the world's best surfers and hordes of spectators.

High fashion, July Handicap

AUGUST

Standard Bank Joy of Jazz *(Aug)*, Johannesburg *(see pp310–11)*. Jazz festival with local and international acts.

Agricultural and Wildflower Show *(late Aug)*, Piketberg. The quality of this flower show, as well as the vivid-ness of the colours and the range of species on display, depends entirely on the rainfall during the preceding winter.
Hantam Vleisfees, *(last weekend in Aug)*, Calvinia. Located in the Northern Cape, Calvinia is sheep country. The festival is a celebration of meat in all its forms: stewed, curried or grilled. The three-day event also offers music concerts, a vintage-car rally, and the glittering Miss Vleisfees competition.
Cars-in-the-Park *(early Aug)*, Pretoria/Tshwane *(see pp320–21)*. Gleaming vintage vehicles are displayed by proud owners.
Oppikoppi Bushveld Festival *(Aug)*, Northam/Limpopo, north of Sun City. Alternative rock festival.

PUBLIC HOLIDAYS

New Year's Day (1 Jan)
Human Rights Day (21 Mar)
Good Friday (Apr)
Family Day (Apr)
Freedom Day (27 Apr)
Workers' Day (1 May)
Youth Day (16 Jun)
National Women's Day (9 Aug)
Heritage Day (24 Sep)
Day of Reconciliation (16 Dec)
Christmas Day (25 Dec)
Day of Goodwill (26 Dec)

National Arts Festival, Grahamstown

The Climate of South Africa

Situated halfway between the Equator and the Antarctic, South Africa has a temperate climate with short-term exceptions in certain locations. Day temperatures can soar to 50°C (122°F) over low-lying coastal plains in summer and drop to -16°C (3°F) during a winter's night over the higher plateau areas. Rainfall increases from west to east. The most popular time of year to visit South Africa is during the summer months, from December to February, but winter days are sunny and cool and best for game viewing.

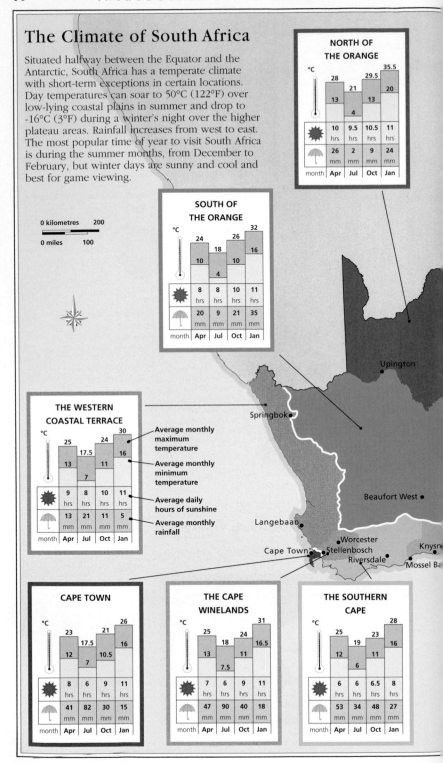

NORTH OF THE ORANGE

°C				35.5
	28	21	29.5	20
	13		13	
		4		
☀	10 hrs	9.5 hrs	10.5 hrs	11 hrs
☂	26 mm	2 mm	9 mm	24 mm
month	Apr	Jul	Oct	Jan

SOUTH OF THE ORANGE

°C			26	32
	24	18		16
	10		10	
		4		
☀	8 hrs	8 hrs	10 hrs	11 hrs
☂	20 mm	9 mm	21 mm	35 mm
month	Apr	Jul	Oct	Jan

THE WESTERN COASTAL TERRACE

°C			24	30
	25	17.5		16
	13		11	
		7		
☀	9 hrs	8 hrs	10 hrs	11 hrs
☂	13 mm	21 mm	11 mm	5 mm
month	Apr	Jul	Oct	Jan

Average monthly maximum temperature

Average monthly minimum temperature

Average daily hours of sunshine

Average monthly rainfall

Upington

Springbok

Beaufort West

Langebaan

Worcester

Cape Town Stellenbosch

Riversdale Knysn

Mossel Ba

0 kilometres   200

0 miles   100

CAPE TOWN

°C			21	26
	23	17.5		16
	12		10.5	
		7		
☀	8 hrs	6 hrs	9 hrs	11 hrs
☂	41 mm	82 mm	30 mm	15 mm
month	Apr	Jul	Oct	Jan

THE CAPE WINELANDS

°C			24	31
	25	18		16.5
	13		11	
		7.5		
☀	7 hrs	6 hrs	9 hrs	11 hrs
☂	47 mm	90 mm	40 mm	18 mm
month	Apr	Jul	Oct	Jan

THE SOUTHERN CAPE

°C			23	28
	25	19		16
	12		11	
		6		
☀	6 hrs	6 hrs	6.5 hrs	8 hrs
☂	53 mm	34 mm	48 mm	27 mm
month	Apr	Jul	Oct	Jan

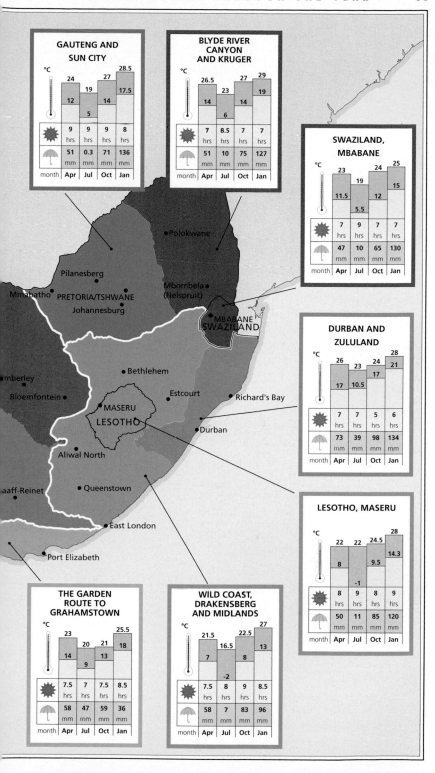

GAUTENG AND SUN CITY

°C	24	19	27	28.5
	12		14	17.5
		5		

☀	9 hrs	9 hrs	9 hrs	8 hrs
☂	51 mm	0.3 mm	71 mm	136 mm
month	Apr	Jul	Oct	Jan

BLYDE RIVER CANYON AND KRUGER

°C	26.5	23	27	29
	14		14	19
		6		

☀	7 hrs	8.5 hrs	7 hrs	7 hrs
☂	51 mm	10 mm	75 mm	127 mm
month	Apr	Jul	Oct	Jan

SWAZILAND, MBABANE

°C	23	19	24	25
	11.5		12	15
		5.5		

☀	7 hrs	9 hrs	7 hrs	7 hrs
☂	47 mm	10 mm	65 mm	130 mm
month	Apr	Jul	Oct	Jan

DURBAN AND ZULULAND

°C	26	23	24	28
	17		17	21
		10.5		

☀	7 hrs	7 hrs	5 hrs	6 hrs
☂	73 mm	39 mm	98 mm	134 mm
month	Apr	Jul	Oct	Jan

LESOTHO, MASERU

°C	22	22	24.5	28
	8		9.5	14.3
		-1		

☀	8 hrs	9 hrs	8 hrs	9 hrs
☂	50 mm	11 mm	85 mm	120 mm
month	Apr	Jul	Oct	Jan

THE GARDEN ROUTE TO GRAHAMSTOWN

°C	23	20	21	25.5
	14		13	18
		9		

☀	7.5 hrs	7 hrs	7.5 hrs	8.5 hrs
☂	58 mm	47 mm	59 mm	36 mm
month	Apr	Jul	Oct	Jan

WILD COAST, DRAKENSBERG AND MIDLANDS

°C	21.5	16.5	22.5	27
	7		8	13
		-2		

☀	7.5 hrs	8 hrs	9 hrs	8.5 hrs
☂	58 mm	7 mm	83 mm	96 mm
month	Apr	Jul	Oct	Jan

Polokwane

Pilanesberg

Mmabatho

PRETORIA/TSHWANE

Johannesburg

Mbombela (Nelspruit)

MBABANE
SWAZILAND

Kimberley

Bloemfontein

Bethlehem

Estcourt

Richard's Bay

MASERU
LESOTHO

Durban

Aliwal North

Graaff-Reinet

Queenstown

East London

Port Elizabeth

THE HISTORY
OF SOUTH AFRICA

The ancient footprints discovered at Langebaan, a cast of which is now in the South African Museum in Cape Town, were made 117,000 years ago. They are the world's oldest traces of anatomically modern man, *Homo sapiens sapiens*. Other early hominid remains found at the Sterkfontein caves in Gauteng and at Taung near Bloemfontein belong to the group known as *Australopithecus africanus*.

Jan van Riebeeck, the founder of Cape Town

The African and European civilization drifted towards a cultural collision when the Dutch East India Company set up a refreshment station in Table Bay. The year was 1652, and the colonizers had come not just to visit, but to stay. On the whole, the Dutch sought to establish amicable relationships with the local Khoi, but the inability to understand one another doomed many attempts, and the pattern of relations over the subsequent centuries was set. Rivalry over water and grazing soon turned into open hostility, first around the bay and then further inland as Dutch "burghers" sought new land. Isolated clashes with indigenous groups escalated into the bitter frontier wars of the 18th and 19th centuries, a situation further aggravated by the arrival of the 1820 British settlers. Although outnumbered, the settlers' muskets, cannons and horses were an advantage that led to a prevailing sense of white supremacy, with both colonial and republican governments denying people of colour their rights.

Ironically, it was the exploitation of black labour in the mines of Kimberley and Johannesburg that ignited the spark of African nationalism, while the segregation and, later, apartheid laws of the mid-1900s focused world attention and pressure on South Africa. The release of Nelson Mandela in 1990 was the beginning of a transformation that set the country on a new course: the road to democracy.

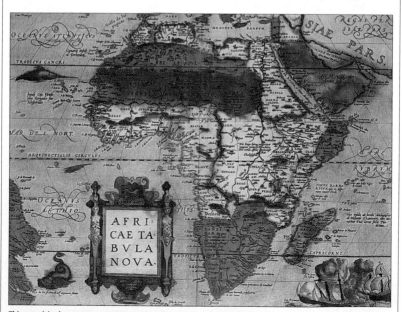

This surprisingly accurate map was produced in 1570 by Abraham Ortelius from Antwerp

◁ Ancient San Bushman paintings adorn many rock walls like this one in the Cedarberg, Western Cape

Prehistoric South Africa

Stone Age grinding tool

Some 2–3 million years ago, long after the dinosaurs, *Australopithecus africanus* inhabited South Africa's plains. *Australopithecines* were the ancestors of anatomically modern people whose remains in South Africa date at least as far back as 110,000 years. Rock art created by Bushman hunter-gatherers over the past 10,000 years is widely distributed. Some 2,000 years ago, pastoral Khoi migrated south-westward, while black farming communities settled the eastern side of the country. Their descendants were encountered by the 15th-century Portuguese explorers.

EARLY MAN

■ *Distribution in South Africa*

Australopithecus africanus
In 1925, Professor Raymond Dart, then dean of the University of the Witwatersrand's medical faculty, first identified man's ancestor based on the evidence of a skull found near Taung, North West Province.

Langebaan Footprints
Homo sapiens *tracks at Langebaan Lagoon are around 117,000 years old. They are the world's oldest fossilized trail of anatomically modern human beings.*

Karoo Fossils
Diictodon *skeletons found in the Karoo (see p356) belonged to mammal-like reptiles that tunnelled into the mud along river banks some 255 million years ago.*

CRADLE OF MANKIND
Based on the evidence of fossilized remains from the Sterkfontein caves *(see p318)* and other sites in South and East Africa, palae-ontologists believe that people evolved in Africa. Stone tools and bone fragments indicate that modern humans lived and hunted in South Africa some 110,000 years ago.

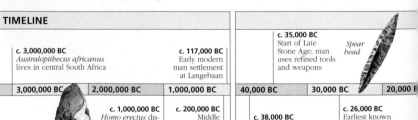

TIMELINE

c. 3,000,000 BC Australopithecus africanus lives in central South Africa		c. 117,000 BC Early modern man settlement at Langebaan	c. 35,000 BC Start of Late Stone Age; man uses refined tools and weapons	*Spear head*
3,000,000 BC	**2,000,000 BC**	**1,000,000 BC**	**40,000 BC**	**30,000 BC**	**20,000 B**
Hand axe	c. 1,000,000 BC Homo erectus displaces earlier ape-like hominid species	c. 200,000 BC Middle Stone Age	c. 38,000 BC Iron ore is mined for its pigment at Ngwenya in Swaziland	c. 26,000 BC Earliest known example of rock art (Namibia)

Early Goldsmiths
Gold ornaments, discovered in Mapungubwe grave sites in 1932, belonged to an Iron Age civilization that flourished until the end of the 12th century.

Sanga cattle were introduced into South Africa by Bantu-speaking tribes.

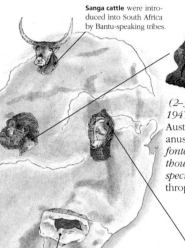

"Mrs Ples"
(2–3 million years). In 1947, the skull of an Australopithecus africanus *found at the Sterkfontein Caves was first thought to belong to a species called* Plesianthropus transvaalensis.

Lydenburg Heads
Seven clay heads found near Lydenburg (see p330) in Mpumalanga date back to AD700. The experts believe they were used in rituals.

Rock Paintings
South Africa is a rich storehouse of prehistoric art. Some paintings are thought to date back 10,000 years, while others were painted as little as 200 years ago.

WHERE TO SEE PREHISTORIC SOUTH AFRICA

The Natal Museum in Pietermaritzburg *(p277)*, McGregor Museum in Kimberley *(p370)* and National Museum of Natural History in Pretoria/Tshwane *(p321)* hold important collections of rock art, archaeological and palaeontological artifacts. Rock paintings can be seen in the Cederberg of the Western Cape *(p215)* and in the Drakensberg in Lesotho *(pp268–9)* and KwaZulu-Natal *(pp270–71)*. Cape Town's South African Museum *(p130)* has dioramas of early people. Bloemfontein's National Museum *(p372)* and the museum in Lydenburg *(p330)* exhibit fossil finds. The Sterkfontein Caves *(p318)*, where Mrs Ples was found, are near Krugersdorp. Many of these museums can assist visitors with information on outings to individual sites.

Bushman Cave Museum *is an open-air site in the Giant's Castle Reserve (see pp270–71).*

The Sudwala Caves *(see p330) feature an interesting timeline display on the evolution of man.*

c. 8,000 BC Microlithic ne toolkit of the Bushman culture		**c. AD 200** Black farmers and iron-workers settle south of the Limpopo River and plant sorghum crops			*San Bushman bow and arrows*	
10,000 BC	**AD 1**	**AD 350**	**AD 700**	**AD 1050**		**AD 1400**
	c. AD 1 Nomadic Khoi herders, originally from Botswana, move southwest into Cape coastal territory	*Sorghum*		**c. 1400** Stone settlements of Sotho people expand from the Highveld into present-day Free State		

Explorers and Colonizers

Bartolomeu Dias (1450–1500)

Portuguese navigators pioneered the sea route to India, but it was the Dutch who set up a fortified settlement at the Cape in 1652. The indigenous Khoi who initially welcomed the trade opportunities were quickly marginalized. Some took service with the settlers, while others fled from the Dutch *trekboers* (migrant graziers). In 1688, the arrival of French Huguenot families swelled the numbers of the white settlers, driving even more Khoi away from their ancestral land.

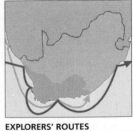

EXPLORERS' ROUTES
➤ Dias 1488 ➤ Da Gama 1498
▓ Cape colony 1795

The Caravels of Dias
In 1988, a replica of the ship commanded by Bartolomeu Dias 500 years before retraced his voyage from Lisbon to Mossel Bay. The ship is now housed in Mossel Bay's Bartolomeu Dias Museum complex (see pp236–7).

Unique Early Postal Systems
In the 15th and 16th centuries, Portuguese captains anchored in Mossel Bay and left messages for each other engraved on flat rocks. The stones soon became a type of post box, with letters stored beneath them.

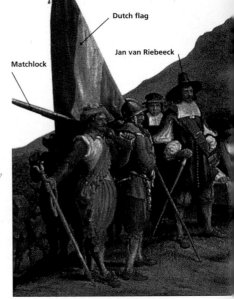

Dutch flag

Jan van Riebeeck

Matchlock

JAN VAN RIEBEECK'S ARRIVAL
On 6 April 1652, Jan van Riebeeck landed at the Cape to establish a permanent settlement for the Dutch East India Company. The first commander of the new outpost and his wife, Maria de la Quellerie, are commemorated by statues erected near the site of their historic landing.

TIMELINE

1486 Portuguese sail as far as today's Namibia

c. 1500 Shipwrecked Portuguese sailors encounter Iron Age farmers along South Africa's south coast

1400	1450	1500	1550

Vasco da Gama

1498 Vasco da Gama discovers the route to India around the Cape of Good Hope

1510 Dom Francisco d'Almeida, viceroy of Portuguese India, and 57 of his men are killed by Khoi in Table Bay

The Vereenigde Oost-Indische Compagnie (VOC)

Several small trading companies joined in 1602 to form the Dutch East India Company (VOC). It was granted a charter to trade, draw up treaties and maintain an army and a fleet. The VOC was dissolved in 1798.

Beads and trinkets were offered as gifts to the Khoi.

Autshumao, leader of the local *Strandlopers* (a people living near the sea who ate mainly fish and mussels) had been taken to Java by the British in 1631. He had a basic knowledge of English and was able to negotiate with the Dutch.

Animal skins were worn by the native peoples of the Cape.

Superior Weaponry

Matchlocks secured the settlers' advantage over the clubs and throwing spears of the Khoi, and the bows and poisoned arrows used by the San Bushmen.

Almond Hedge

A remnant of the hedge that was planted to discourage unauthorized trading with the Khoi can be seen at Kirstenbosch National Botanical Gardens (see pp158–9).

WHERE TO SEE EXPLORERS AND COLONIZERS

Mossel Bay's museum complex houses a replica of Dias's caravel (pp236–7), as well as the old milkwood tree in which passing sailors left messages for their fellow mariners. The Castle of Good Hope in Cape Town (pp126–7) is South Africa's oldest surviving structure. The Huguenot Memorial Museum in Franschhoek (p198) honours the French heritage of the town and contains antique furniture and paintings. Early colonial artifacts are on display at the Iziko Slave Lodge in Cape Town (p124).

The De Kat Balcony, at the Castle of Good Hope in Cape Town, was designed by sculptor Anton Anreith.

The French Huguenots

Fleeing from religious persecution in France, about 200 Huguenots arrived at the Cape of Good Hope in 1688. They were assigned farms around Franschhoek (see pp198–9), where they planted vineyards.

1594 Portuguese barter with Khoi in Table Bay

Maria de la Quellerie

1652 Jan van Riebeeck and his wife, Maria de la Quellerie, arrive in Table Bay

1693 Sheik Yusuf is exiled to the Cape after instigating a rebellion in Java. His *kramat* (shrine) near Faure (Western Cape) is revered by Muslims

1600	1650	1700	1750

1608 The Dutch barter with Khoi clans for food

1658 War against Khoi follows cattle raids and killing of settlers

1688 Huguenot refugees settle at the Cape

1713 Smallpox epidemic kills unknown hundreds of Khoi, as well as many white settlers

British Colonization

By 1778, settler expansion had reached the Eastern Cape and the Great Fish River was proclaimed the eastern boundary of the Cape Colony. As this was Xhosa territory, local herdsmen were deprived of their pastures and a century of bitter "frontier wars" ensued. In 1795, following the French Revolution, British forces were able to occupy the Cape. Having returned it to the Netherlands in 1802, they reclaimed it in 1806 and instituted a government-sponsored programme that assigned farms in the Zuurveld area to British settlers. To the east, Shaka Zulu was just beginning to build a powerful empire.

Hitching post, Graaff-Reinet

SETTLER EXPANSION

▢ 1814   — Cape today

Battle of Muizenberg (1795)
In this battle for possession of the Cape, British warships bombarded Dutch outposts at Muizenberg (see p153). Britain was victorious and thus acquired a halfway station en route to India.

Blockhouse ruins

FORT FREDERICK
In the 19th century, many private homes were fortified, and a succession of outposts and frontier forts were built in the Eastern Cape. Few were attacked; almost all are now in ruin. Fort Frederick in Port Elizabeth *(see pp246–7)* has been restored and is a superb example of what these frontier fortifications looked like.

Grave of Captain Francis Evatt, who oversaw the landing of the 1820 settlers.

Rustenburg House
After the battle of Muizenberg, the Dutch surrendered the Cape to Britain. The treaty was signed in this house in Rondebosch, Cape Town. Its present Neo-Classical façade probably dates from around 1803.

TIMELINE

1750 Worldwide, Dutch influence begins to wane	**1770** Gamtoos River made boundary of Cape Colony	**1778** Great Fish River made boundary of Cape Colony	**1789** Merino sheep are imported from Holland and thrive in South Africa
1750	1760	1770	1780
1751 Rijk Tulbagh appointed Dutch Governor of the Cape (1751–71)		**1779** A year after it is made boundary of the Cape Colony, settlers and Xhosa clash at the Fish River – the first of nine frontier wars	

Merino sheep

Battle of Blaauwberg (1806)
This battle between the Dutch and the British was fought at the foot of the Blouberg, out of range of British warships. Outnumbered and poorly disciplined, the Dutch defenders soon broke rank and fled.

The 1820 Settlers
About 4,000 Britons, mostly artisans with little or no farming experience, settled around Grahamstown (see pp252–3).

The **Powder Magazine** could hold some 900 kg (2,000 lb) of gunpowder.

Entrance

WHERE TO SEE BRITISH COLONIZATION

The museums in Mthatha (the capital of the former Transkei) and the University of Fort Hare in Alice (in the former Ciskei) have interesting collections of colonial artefacts. Old weapons and ammunition, uniforms, maps, and even letters and medical supplies are displayed in the Military Museum at the Castle of Good Hope in Cape Town *(pp126–7)*. The museums in King William's Town, Queenstown and Grahamstown *(pp252–3)* exhibit collections of frontier-war memorabilia. The excellent MuseuMAfricA in Johannesburg *(p310)* has a superb collection of old prints and paintings.

MuseuMAfricA has three permanent exhibitions and various temporary displays.

Shaka Zulu
This gifted military strategist became Zulu chief after the death of Dingiswayo in 1815. Shaka introduced the assegaai (short spear) and united lesser clans into a Zulu empire.

The Xhosa
The Xhosa had farmed in the Zuurveld (present Eastern Cape) for centuries. The arrival of the 1820 Settlers caused friction and dispute.

1795 Battle of Muizenberg and first British occupation	**1800** The *Cape Town Gazette* and *African Advertiser* are first published	**1806** Battle of Blaauwberg. Second British occupation of the Cape	**1818** Shaka's military conquests in Zululand begin	*Typical settler house* **1820** 4,000 British settlers arrive in Grahamstown		**1829** The Khoina are released from having to carry passes. The University of Cape Town is founded
	1800		**1810**	**1820**		**1830**
...93 Lombard ...nk, the first ...nk in the ...untry, opens Cape Town	**1802** Lady Anne Barnard, whose letters and diaries give an insight into colonial life, leaves the Cape	**1814** British occupation of the Cape is ratified by the Congress of Vienna	**1815** The Slagter's Nek rebellion, led by anti-British frontiersmen, ends with judicial executions near Cookhouse (Eastern Cape)		**1828** Shaka is murdered by his half-brother, Dingane	

Colonial Expansion

A Voortrekker woman's bonnet

The British colonial administration met with hostility from the Cape's Dutch-speaking community. Dissatisfied Voortrekkers (Boer pioneers) headed east and north in an exodus that became known as the Great Trek. In 1838, Zulu chief Dingane had one group of Voortrekkers killed, but in the subsequent Battle of Blood River his own warriors were beaten. A short-lived Boer republic, Natalia, was annexed by Britain in 1843. By 1857, two new Boer states, Transvaal and Orange Free State, landlocked and impoverished but independent, had been consolidated north of the Orange and Vaal rivers.

VOORTREKKER MOVEMENT

☐ *1836 Great Trek*

☐ *British territory by 1848*

Emancipated Slaves

The freeing of 39,000 Cape Colony slaves in 1834 angered Boer farmers who relied on slave labour. The British decision was not due entirely to philanthropism; it was simply cheaper to employ free labour.

THE GREAT TREK

Dissatisfied with the British administration, convoys of Boer ox wagons trekked inland to seek new territory. The pioneers, armed with cannons and muskets, were accompanied by their families, black and coloured retainers and livestock. Each wagon was "home" for the duration of the journey and contained all that the family owned. At night, or under attack, the convoy would form a laager – a circle of wagons lashed together with chains.

The Battle of Vegkop

In 1836 the Ndebele found themselves in the path of trekker expansion northwards. Traditional weapons were no match for blazing rifles. The 40 Voortrekkers beat off an attack by 6,000 Ndebele warriors at Vegkop, killing 430, but losing most of their own sheep, cattle and trek oxen.

Barrels were used to store food, water and gunpowder.

Wagon chest

The drive shaft was attached to the yoke which was placed around the neck of the oxen.

TIMELINE

1838 Battle of Blood River follows the murder of Voortrekker leader, Piet Retief, and his men

Dingane

1830	1835	1840

1834 Slaves freed subject to a four-year "apprenticeship". Sixth Frontier War erupts; Voortrekkers travel to present-day Free State, KwaZulu-Natal, Northern Province and Namibia

1836 The Great Trek begins

1839 Boer Republic of Natalia is proclaimed

The Battle of Blood River
On 16 December 1838, the river ran red with blood as a 468-strong burgher commando defeated 12,500 Zulu warriors in retribution for the killing of Piet Retief.

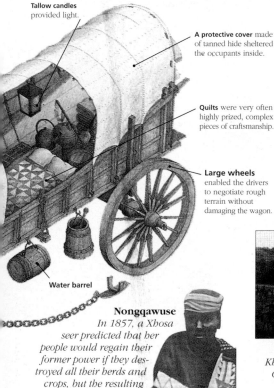

Tallow candles provided light.

A protective cover made of tanned hide sheltered the occupants inside.

Quilts were very often highly prized, complex pieces of craftsmanship.

Large wheels enabled the drivers to negotiate rough terrain without damaging the wagon.

Water barrel

Nongqawuse
In 1857, a Xhosa seer predicted that her people would regain their former power if they destroyed all their herds and crops, but the resulting famine further weakened their position.

WHERE TO SEE THE COLONIAL EXPANSION
British colonial history is well covered in cultural history and battle site museums nationwide. Museums at Grahamstown *(pp252–3)*, Port Elizabeth *(pp246–7)*, King William's Town and East London have displays of old weapons, maps and pioneer artifacts. MuseuMAfricA *(p310)* in Johannesburg exhibits historic documents, war memorabilia and maps. Kleinplasie Open-air Museum *(pp204–5)* is a living showcase of the lifestyles and farming processes of the Voortrekkers.

The Battle of Blood River Memorial, Dundee, shows a recreated, life-size laager.

The Kat River Rebellion
Khoina settlers on the Kat River in the Cape had fought for the government without compensation, but rebelled in the war of 1850. With their defeat, their land passed to white ownership.

1845	1850	1855	1860

1846 Seventh Frontier War (War of the Axe)

1850 Eighth Frontier War, in which the Kat River Khoina join the Xhosa

1854 Britain withdraws from the Orange River Sovereignty

1856 British and German settlers placed on Eastern Cape border; the Colony of Natal is granted a representative government

1852 The Cape is granted representative government by Britain. Zuid-Afrikaansche Republiek (Transvaal) is formed

1853 Stamps available in the Cape Colony for the first time

First postage stamp

1857 Thousands of Xhosa living between the Keiskamma and Great Kei rivers (Eastern Cape) perish in a famine resulting from an ill-advised prophecy

Clash for Gold and Diamonds

The crown of England

The discovery of diamonds in the Northern Cape laid the foundation for South Africa's economy and created a massive migrant labour system. Subsequent strikes of gold in the east of the country promised an untold source of wealth best exploited under a single British authority. African kingdoms and two Boer republics were coerced to join a British confederation. Resistance to the British masterplan led to a series of skirmishes that culminated in the South African (Boer) War of 1899–1902.

AREAS OF CONFLICT

☐ *Boer strongholds, war zones*

Gold Fever
Finds of alluvial gold at Pilgrim's Rest (see p331) and Barberton preceded the 1886 discovery of Johannesburg's Main Reef.

Leander Jameson (1853–1917)
After the discovery of the Transvaal gold reefs, Jameson masterminded a failed revolt intended to topple President Paul Kruger of the Transvaal Republic.

Cecil John Rhodes (1853–1902)
This ruthless financier became involved in organizing the Jameson Raid in 1896, while he was prime minister of the Cape. The interference in the affairs of another state effectively ended his political career.

TIMELINE

1867 A 21-carat diamond is found near Hopetown in the Northern Cape

1878 Walvis Bay (in today's Namibia) is proclaimed British territory

1860	1865	1870	1875

Cut diamond

1877 Britain annexes South African Republic

1871 Diamonds found at Colesberg Kopje (Kimberley). Gold found in Pilgrim's Rest

1879 Britain invades the Zulu kingdom of Cetshwayo, adjoining their colony of Natal

Jan Christiaan Smuts
General Smuts (1870–1950) played prominent roles in the South African War and in both World Wars. He also helped to draft the United Nations Charter, and was twice prime minister of South Africa (1919–24 and 1939–48).

WHERE TO SEE THE CLASH FOR GOLD AND DIAMONDS

Coach tours include the major sites on the Battlefields Route (*p274*) in KwaZulu-Natal. Audiotapes for self-guided tours are available at the Talana Museum (*p274*). Gold Reef City (*pp314–15*) is an evocative re-creation of Johannesburg in the 1890s. The Kimberley Mine Museum (*p371*) is one of several excellent historic sites in Kimberley.

Museum at Kimberley Mine Big Hole in Kimberley.

Isandhlwana Hill

Bayonets had to be used when the British ran out of ammunition.

Shields covered with cow hide were used to ward off the bayonets.

The *assegaai* (short stabbing spear) was useful in close combat.

British casualties were high; only a handful of men escaped alive.

BATTLE OF ISANDHLWANA

In an effort to subjugate the fiercely independent Zulu, British officials provoked several incidents. In 1879, a 1,200-strong British and colonial force was annihilated by 20,000 Zulu warriors at Isandhlwana Hill.

Modern Warfare

The South African War (1899–1902) was the first fought with high-velocity rifles and mechanical transport. Although the Boers were good shots and horsemen and could live off the land, limited manpower as well as the loose and informal structure of their armies counted against them.

1884 Lesotho becomes British protectorate	**1886** Discovery of the Main Reef on Witwatersrand (Gauteng)	**1894** Kingdom of Swaziland becomes British protectorate	**1896** Jameson Raid into Transvaal fails. Rinderpest kills countless head of cattle as well as wild animals	**1902** South African War ends
1880	**1885**	**1890**	**1895**	**1900**
1881 Boers defeat British army at Majuba	**1883** Olive Schreiner publishes *Story of an African Farm* **1885** Britain annexes part of Bechuanaland (Botswana)	**1893** Mohandas Karamchand Gandhi arrives in Durban to practise law	*Winston Churchill as war correspondent in South Africa*	**1899** Start of South African War. Sabie Game Reserve declared (forerunner of today's Kruger National Park)

Mahatma Gandhi

The Apartheid Years

"Free Mandela"

In 1910, the Union of South Africa became a self-governing colony within the British Commonwealth. The future of black South Africans was largely left undecided, leading to the founding of the South African Native National Congress (later known as the ANC) in 1912. The Great Trek centenary of 1938 renewed the white Afrikaner's hope for self-determination. In 1948, the Afrikaner-based National Party (NP) came to power and, by manipulating the composition of parliament, managed to enforce a series of harsh laws that stripped black South Africans of most of their basic human rights. In 1961 Prime Minister Verwoerd led the country out of the Commonwealth and into increasing political isolation.

APARTHEID SOUTH AFRICA

— *Provincial boundaries (1994)*

▓ *Homelands up to 1984*

Delville Wood
One of the most vicious battles of World War I was fought at Delville Wood, in France. For five days, 3,000 South African soldiers held out against the German line.

The Great Trek Centenary
The ox wagons rolled again in 1938, headed for a solemn celebration in Pretoria, where the first stone of the Voortrekker Monument (see p321) was laid. This re-enactment of the Great Trek was an impressive display of Afrikaner solidarity, patriotism and political strength.

BURNING PASS BOOKS
The 1952 Natives Act required all black men over 16 to carry a pass book (permit to work in a "white" area) at all times, and show it to the police on demand. In 1956 the law was extended to women. In 1960, thousands burned their pass books at township police stations countrywide. The law was repealed in 1986.

TIMELINE

1905 Cullinan Diamond found at Premier Diamond Mine	**1907** Sir James Percy FitzPatrick writes *Jock of the Bushveld*	**1912** South African Native National Congress founded (later becomes ANC)	**1928** Kirstenbosch Botanical Gardens and University of South Africa founded	**1936** First printing of the Bible in Afrikaans
1900		**1910**	**1920**	**1930**
1904 President Paul Kruger dies *President Paul Kruger*	**1910** Formation of the Union of South Africa	**1914** South Africa declares war on Germany. Boer rebellion put down by Union government. The first National Party formed in Bloemfontein	**1922** Miners' rebellion breaks out at coal mines in Witbank	**1927** Compulsory racial segregation declared in many urban areas

APARTHEID

Afrikaans for "separateness", this term was used as a slogan by the National Party, which brought it into force as a policy after winning the 1948 election. In keeping with racial classification laws, skin colour dictated where people were allowed to live, be educated, work and even be buried. Sex "across the colour bar" was punishable by imprisonment. Loss of land was among the system's most terrible inflictions.

Security police "house calls" enforced apartheid laws

WHERE TO SEE THE APARTHEID YEARS

District Six Museum *(p125)*, on the edge of this former Cape Town precinct, shows what life was like in this largely Muslim community before it was cleared under the Group Areas Act, starting in 1966. Exhibits at the Mayibuye Centre, University of the Western Cape, depict the struggle for democracy. The Iziko Slave Lodge *(p124)* in Cape Town, MuseuMAfricA *(p310)* in Johannesburg and the Red Location Museum *(p248)* in Port Elizabeth also have interesting displays. The Voortrekker Museum and Monument *(p321)* in Pretoria/Tshwane offer an insight into Afrikaner Nationalism.

MuseuMAfricA in Johannesburg shows the living conditions in a township like Sophiatown.

District Six, "the life and soul of Cape Town", was declared a white area in 1966.

African Nationalism

Drum, first published in the 1950s, was important for black journalists. Not afraid to criticize the white regime, they rekindled African Nationalism.

Apartheid's Architects

Dutch-born Hendrik Verwoerd (1901–66), prime minister from 1958 until his assassination, and Charles Robberts Swart (1894–1982), the minister of justice, implemented many apartheid measures.

First edition of Afrikaans Bible

1948 National Party elected as the country's government

1950 Communism is outlawed

1955 Petrol is made from coal for the first time in South Africa

1958 Hendrik Verwoerd becomes prime minister of South Africa

1940	1950	1960

1939 South Africa declares war on Germany

1949 Prohibition of Mixed Marriages Act, the first of many apartheid laws, is passed by Parliament

1960 Police shoot 69 demonstrators at Sharpeville. Whites-only referendum opts for a republic

Age of Democracy

Buttonhole,
1992 Referendum

The laws imposed by the white Nationalist government outraged black African societies, and the decree that Afrikaans be the language of instruction at black schools sparked off the revolt of 1976. States of emergency came and went, and violence increased. It became clear that the old system of administration was doomed. In 1990, State President Frederik Willem de Klerk undertook the first step towards reconciliation by unbanning the ANC, Communist Party and 34 other organizations, and announcing the release of Nelson Mandela.

THE NEW SOUTH AFRICA
— *Provincial boundaries*

A World First
Christiaan Barnard (right) made medical history in 1967 when he transplanted a human heart.

Desmond Tutu won a Nobel Peace Prize (1984) and Martin Luther King Peace Prize (1986) for his dedicated anti-apartheid campaign.

The Soweto Riots
On 16 June 1976, police fired on black students protesting against the use of Afrikaans in their schools. The picture of a fatally wounded boy became a world-famous symbol of this tragic struggle.

Arts Against Apartheid
The Black Christ (by Ronald Harrison) was inspired by the Sharpeville Massacre and banning of the then ANC president Chief Albert Luthuli (depicted as Christ). Banned for years, it now hangs in the Iziko South African National Gallery *(see p131).*

DEMOCRATIC ELECTION
On 27 April 1994, South Africans went to the polls – many for the first time. Five days later the result was announced: with 63 per cent of votes in its favour, the African National Congress (ANC) had achieved victory in all but two provinces and Nelson Mandela was the new State President.

TIMELINE

1961 South Africa becomes a republic outside the British Commonwealth

Old flag

1971 International Court and UN Security Council recognize Namibia and revoke South Africa's mandate on the country

1980 ANC bombs Sasolburg Oil Refinery in the Free State

1990 Namibia independence ANC unbanned Nelson Mandela release

1960	1965	1970	1975	1980	1985

1962 Nelson Mandela jailed. Start of UN-imposed sanctions

1963 Guerrilla war begins in South West Africa (Namibia)

1966 Prime Minister Verwoerd assassinated. Lesotho gains its independence

1968 Swaziland gains independence

1976 Soweto riots erupt. Flight of foreign capital from South Africa

1984 New constitution for tricameral parliament

The new flag

Kwaito – Sound of a New Generation
Boom Shaka was a pioneering kwaito group that emerged in the 1990s. A uniquely South African sound, kwaito *was born in the townships of Gauteng. The lyrics are influenced by toyi-toyi (protest) chants.*

Free At Last
On 11 February 1990, after almost three decades in custody, Nelson Mandela emerged from the Victor Verster prison near Paarl. The high-profile event was watched by millions around the world.

Independent Electoral Commission monitor

Cricket World Cup 1992
Political change in South Africa saw the national cricket team included in a world event for the first time in over 20 years.

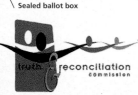

Ballot paper

Sealed ballot box

Freedom of Speech
The early 1980s saw flamboyant Evita Bezuiden-hout (see p211) on stage for the first time. Her outspoken, satirical views on internal politics made her famous in South Africa and abroad.

Sanctions Lifted
In 1993, trade sanctions (intro-duced in 1986) were lifted and brands became available again.

The Truth and Reconciliation Commission (TRC)
Established in 1994 under the chairmanship of former Archbishop of Cape Town Desmond Tutu, this commission aimed to determine the motives behind political crimes committed during the apartheid years.

1994 ANC wins first democratic election. Nelson Mandela becomes president	**1995** South Africa hosts and wins the Rugby World Cup	**1998** Truth and Reconciliation Commission hearings begin **1999** Second democratic election	**2004** The ruling party, ANC, wins a landslide election, taking 70 per cent of the votes	**2010** South Africa hosts the soccer World Cup	
	1995	2000	2005	2010	2015
1992 Referendum held regarding FW de Klerk's policy of change. South Africa participates in the Olympic Games, the first time since 1960		**2003** Walter Sisulu, a key member of the ANC and Nelson Mandela's mentor, dies at the age of 91	**2005** The Geographical Names Committee recommends that Pretoria change its name to Tshwane	**2009** The ANC wins the national elections; Jacob Zuma becomes president	

Leopard reclining on a tree branch ▷

WILD
SOUTH AFRICA

THE SAFARI EXPERIENCE

There is something hugely satisfying about South Africa's wild places. Partly it's the liberating sense of space in the greatest reserves, many of them the size of small countries; but mostly it's the thrill of sighting a fascinating assortment of wildlife, so familiar from television, here made living flesh. Be it lions roaring on a moonlit night or jackal cubs at play, the safari offers limitless natural wonder.

A Swahili word that means journey, the term "safari" came into popular usage in the early 20th century to describe the trophy-hunting expeditions popularized by the likes of Theodore Roosevelt, Ernest Hemingway and Karen Blixen. By the late 1960s, these gun-toting safaris had largely become a thing of the past, as a combination of factors – dwindling wildlife numbers, increased conservation awareness and the greater international mobility offered by jet travel – ushered in the era of the photographic safari. Today, tourists arrive in Africa not with guns but with cameras, and the modern safari industry is able to accommodate them in a variety of ways, from simple campsites and government rest camps to the exclusive, eco-friendly tented camps and lodges of the private reserves.

One surviving legacy of the colonial hunting era is the notion of the Big Five – lions, leopards, elephants, rhinos and buffaloes *(see pp72–3)*. Ticking them off the list is considered a rite of passage. Certainly there are few experiences more thrilling than the sight of a herd of elephants marching peacefully across the savannah or of a leopard lying in a tree, but safari should never become limited to an obsessive quest for a quintet of select beasts. With more than 300 protected areas to choose from, South Africa has plenty to keep wildlife-lovers occupied for months, if not years. Its many and diverse nature reserves range from the hippo- and crocodile-filled estuaries of iSimangaliso Wetland Park and the towering peaks of the uKhahlamba-Drakensberg to the red dunes and dry riverbeds of the remote Kgalagadi Transfrontier Park, home to gemsboks and springboks. Further south, Table Mountain National Park protects a host of endemic species, unique to South Africa, such as Cape mountain zebras and bonteboks.

Tourists on a game drive

Three springboks grazing, Kgalagadi Transfrontier Park

◁ Safari-goers watching a herd of Cape buffaloes, Sabi Sand Game Reserve

PRACTICAL INFORMATION

Arranging a safari is a fairly straightforward procedure. The biggest hurdles at the planning stage will be choosing between a self-drive adventure or an organized safari and deciding which reserves to visit – with the diversity of South Africa's national parks and wildlife reserves, visitors are spoiled for choice. If opting

Yellow-billed hornbill

for the DIY approach, it is easy to book everything online – the South African National Parks website *(see p67)* is extremely user-friendly. For the less adventurous, there are plenty of reputable tour operators in South Africa and elsewhere to offer specialist guidance and set transport and accommodation arrangements in place *(see p67)*.

Elephants gather at a watering hole in Addo Elephant National Park

BEST TIME TO GO

The best season for game viewing is winter (July to September), when the dry weather forces animals to gather around rivers and waterholes. The disadvantages are that animals aren't in optimal condition and the winter landscape is stark.

Summer (November to January) brings high rainfall, and the landscape becomes green and lush. This is the best time of year for viewing flora, though the wildlife will be more widespread and difficult to spot. The wide availability of water also leads to a higher threat of malaria in risk areas.

While many people come for the Big Five *(see pp72–3)* and get a thrill in the pursuit of spotting them, it is also possible to relish the opportunity to spend quiet time in remote bush, take unbelievable hikes and view striking landscapes and lesser-known animal life. Each of the parks and reserves offers something exceptional, and the following pages will help visitors decide where they want to go.

ORGANIZED AND INDEPENDENT TOURS

Most of the safari companies operate out of Cape Town, Durban and Johannesburg, arranging accommodation and game-viewing trips as part of an organized tour. The cost of trips varies from budget excursions to more expensive holidays. Many safari companies offer package deals, which are often great value for money. It can be an easier option to let an organization take care of all the planning, but if so, it is best to choose a company that is recognized by the

Southern Africa Tourism Services Association (SATSA). A few companies are listed on p67. Going on your own can be cheaper, and it allows for greater flexibility to explore. Hiring a car, booking self-catering accommodation and obtaining maps and information are all easy to arrange.

PLANNING YOUR TRIP

Most of the parks fall within three groups: **South African National Parks** (SANParks), **CapeNature** and **KZN Wildlife**. Contacting these organizations is a good first step, along with checking their websites and those of safari companies. Seasonal and promotional specials happen periodically and are often found in the travel sections of leading newspapers.

The Wild Card provides unrestricted access to SANParks for a year, and is a sensible investment if your itinerary includes visits to more than one reserve.

Most parks can be visited by car, since roads and gravel paths are generally well kept. However, just after the rainy season (January to April), a 4x4 vehicle is a more suitable

Bontebok National Park, part of the SANParks group

A typically South African *braai* in the bush

option. Also note that not all petrol stations accept credit cards. Air-conditioning may seem a necessity when the weather is warm, but try to keep the car windows open to experience fully the sounds and smells of the bush. The best speed for game viewing is 15 km/h (10 mph). To see which animals are in any particular area, check the sightings boards at the entrance of the camps. Wildlife identification books available in camp shops are also useful, and it may be a good investment to buy a pair of binoculars.

Essential items to pack include: comfortable clothes to cover exposed areas from insects (preferably in dull colours so as not to disturb the wildlife); a hat; sunblock; sunglasses; and a camera.

ACCOMMODATION

To avoid disappointment, it is best to book as far in advance as possible, especially over South African school and public holidays. Accommodation at national parks ranges from campsites, huts and safari tents to self-contained chalets and cottages. There is generally a choice of a private or shared bathroom and kitchen. In most national parks, bedding, towels, a fridge and cooking utensils are included. When booking self-catering accommodation, bear in mind that not all parks have well-stocked shops, and you may have to take some or all of your supplies with you. Once a reservation has been made, the company should send you

a leaflet detailing all of the facilities at the camp.

The ultimate wildlife accommodation is in luxurious lodges at private game reserves, mostly around the Kruger National Park. Prices are high, but they usually include accommodation, meals and game activities, and sometimes drinks. These lodges are a good option for visitors who have never experienced a safari before because there are well-informed rangers who lead game-viewing outings, so there is a much greater chance of sighting some wildlife.

CHOOSING AN ITINERARY

The best times to view game are early mornings and late afternoons. Be sure to return before the camp gates shut, just before dark.

Game drives, walks and night drives can be booked at the camp offices after arrival. They usually depart at dawn, last a few hours, and are often the best way to explore the area. Wilderness trails are longer and involve staying at a remote base camp and going on walks with an armed ranger. These can be booked months in advance.

The private reserves generally plan the itinerary for their guests, although there is room for flexibility. Typical activities include drinks at dawn, followed by guided game viewing, sundowners and night drives with dinner.

SAFETY TIPS AND HEALTH ISSUES

It is recommended that you approach a sighting quietly, turn off the car engine and allow space for the vehicle in front to reverse if necessary. Never feed animals, because once they are dependant on food from humans, they become aggressive and have to be shot. Stay in your car at

all times. If your car breaks down in the park, wait until a park ranger comes to help. Other visitors will be able to pass on a message to the authorities.

Water and drinks are essential to prevent dehydration. Anti-malaria prophylactics are recommended for those visiting risk areas, such as the Kruger. A doctor or travel clinic should be able to provide these. The highest-risk period is during the rainy season (December to April), when it is best to cover exposed skin with light clothing and insect repellents. A **24-hour Malaria Hotline** is available for further information.

Most camps in the parks provide ramped access for disabled visitors and, often, accessible toilets and specially adapted accommodation.

A close-up view of one of South Africa's Big Five

CHILDREN ON SAFARI

Parks and reserves in South Africa are well equipped for families. There are excellent game reserves outside of malaria areas where you can see the Big Five, and they are the best option for families with young children. It is also essential to find out the minimum age requirement of rest camps and lodges, and whether they are fenced in. Long drives can be dull, so it's worth considering hiring a guide to keep the children interested. It is also a good idea to bring a picnic and plan stops at waterholes.

Safaris, National Parks & Wildlife Reserves

South Africa has hundreds of parks and reserves, but most protect niche environments and cannot be considered true safari destinations. Even so, the first-time safari-goer faces a daunting array of possibilities, ranging from the vast Kruger National Park to the remote dunes of Kgalagadi and the lush subtropical landscapes of Hluhluwe-Imfolozi and iSimangaliso. Here, a brief region-by-region overview of the country's top reserves is provided to help narrow the options.

volcano, it has many attractions, including signs of early humankind in several Stone and Iron Age sites. The park's colourful bushveld and varied topography have made it particularly popular with artists and photographers.

Within an hour's drive of Johannesburg is the **Suikerbosrand Nature Reserve,** named after the protea (suikerbos) plant found throughout the area. This reserve is an excellent choice for outdoor enthusiasts as the Suikerbosrand mountain range provides first-rate hiking and mountain-biking opportunities. There are several day and overnight trails, plus the 700-m (765-yd) Toktokkie trail, which has been designed with disabled visitors in mind – it has wide paved paths and there are several benches to stop at.

GAUTENG AND MPUMALANGA

The flagship of South Africa's game reserves and ultimate destination for the wildlife fanatic is the **Kruger National Park**, with its 150 mammal and 500 bird species. There are also sites of historical and archaeological interest in the northern areas. Trails on offer include 4x4, wilderness and mountain biking, while golfers will love the unfenced nine-hole course at Skukuza.

The **Madikwe Game Reserve** is situated in the corner of the Northwest Province bordering on Botswana. A so-called "transition zone" on the edge of the Kalahari Desert, the region has a unique ecology with an enormous variety of flora and fauna, and several rare species occur here naturally. Madikwe is one of the few game reserves in the world that represents the most sustainable land use for the area. To visit it, you must stay at one of the lodges.

Pilanesberg Game Reserve is also based in the transition zone. Lying in an ancient

THE EAST COAST AND INTERIOR

The **Golden Gate Highlands National Park** takes its name from the beautiful sandstone rock formations that change from purple to gold at sunset. The park provides many activities including guided walks, hiking trails, abseiling, canoeing and horse riding. Accommodation ranges from luxury log cabins in the mountains to a rest camp that is reminiscent of an 18th-century Basotho village. Bird-watchers should look out for the rare bearded vulture and bald ibis.

iSimangaliso Wetland Park is South Africa's most significant wetland reserve and a World Heritage Site that incorporates bushveld, sand forest, grassland, wetland, coastal forest, swamp, beach, coral reef and sea. The best time to visit is during the turtle breeding season from October to April, or in the whale-watching season from June to December. Other animals to keep an eye out for are hippos, crocodiles, pelicans, Caspian terns and fish eagles.

Set in the heart of Zululand where tribal kings once hunted, **Hluhluwe-Imfolozi Game Reserve** is renowned for rhino conservation and is home to over 6,000 white rhinos and 300 black rhinos. The park also has several excellent wilderness trails and guided walks. Accommodation ranges from the sumptuous Hill-top Camp to individual lodges and more rustic bush camps.

Thirsty big cats at a watering hole in the Kruger National Park

Spectacular views of the Karoo National Park, Arid Interior region

Tembe Elephant Park was established in an isolated corner of KwaZulu-Natal to conserve the region's remaining elephants. Today, around 1,300 of the largest African elephants in the world are found here. Although the park is best known for the Big Five, it is also home to a large number of bird species. Additionally, the reserve offers a rich cultural experience with folklore stories told in song and dance around the fire in the *boma* (gathering place).

A World Heritage Site, **uKhahlamba-Drakensberg Park** encompasses the highest range south of Kilimanjaro. The park is blessed with spectacular waterfalls and streams, rocky paths and sandstone cliffs, making it a great option for hikers, rock climbers and walkers. The mountains were home to the indigenous San people for 4,000 years, and the rock art is the largest and most concentrated collection in Africa. Hikers can even stay in caves that were once inhabited by the San Bushmen.

THE ARID INTERIOR

Ai-Ais Richtersveld Transfrontier Park is truly extraordinary, but it is not for visitors who want to see large game. The park is a wild landscape that at first seems desolate, but on closer inspection reveals a treasury of the world's richest desert plants. Miniature rock gardens cling to cliff faces, and the strange stem succulents known as *halfmens* can appear almost human when viewed from a distance. The park is only accessible in 4x4 or high-clearance vehicles, and other cars are not allowed to enter.

The **Karoo National Park** is the largest ecosystem in South Africa, with an enormous diversity of plant and animal life. There are several species worth looking out for, such as the endemic black wildebeest, Cape mountain zebra, springbok, five species of tortoise and the rare black eagle. Activities include a scenic drive along the Klipspringer Pass, a guided night drive, and hiking along several trails. The Karoo Fossil Trail has been specifically designed for disabled visitors.

Called the "Place of the Great Noise" by the indigenous Khoi people, **Augrabies Falls National Park** is named after the magnificent 56-m- (184-ft-) high powerful waterfall formed by the Orange River.

PLANNING YOUR TRIP This chart is designed to help you choose your safari. The parks and reserves are listed alphabetically for each area on the map above.	Big Five	On-site restaurant	Swimming pool	On-site fuel	Malaria risk	Suitable for children	Suitable for disabled	Guided game drives	Picnic sites	Shops	Television	Electricity	Information Centre	Internet café	Laundry	Medical service	Cellphone reception	Public telephones	Hiking/walking trails	Whale-watching
GAUTENG AND MPUMALANGA																				
Kruger National Park	•	•	•	•	•		•	•	•	•	•	•	•	•	•	•	•	•	•	
Madikwe Game Reserve	•	•	•				•	•		•		•			•	•	•	•		
Pilanesberg Game Reserve	•	•	•				•	•	•	•		•					•	•	•	
Suikerbosrand Nature Reserve						•	•		•			•							•	
THE EAST COAST AND INTERIOR																				
Golden Gate Highlands National Park		•	•	•		•	•		•	•	•	•	•			•		•	•	
Hluhluwe-Imfolozi Game Reserve	•	•	•	•	•	•	•	•	•	•		•	•			•	•	•	•	
iSimangaliso Wetland Park			•		•	•	•	•	•	•		•	•				•	•	•	•
Tembe Elephant Park	•		•		•			•				•								
uKhahlamba-Drakensberg Park	•	•	•			•	•		•	•		•	•				•	•	•	
THE ARID INTERIOR																				
Ai-Ais Richtersveld Transfrontier Park			•				•		•			•	•						•	
Augrabies Falls National Park	•	•	•	•		•	•		•	•		•	•				•	•	•	
Goegap Nature Reserve						•	•		•			•	•					•	•	
Karoo National Park	•	•	•			•	•		•	•		•	•			•		•	•	
Kgalagadi Transfrontier Park	•	•	•	•		•	•		•	•		•	•			•		•	•	
Namaqua National Park						•	•		•			•							•	
THE WESTERN AND SOUTHERN CAPE																				
Addo Elephant National Park	•	•	•	•		•	•	•	•	•		•	•			•		•	•	
Bontebok National Park						•	•		•	•		•	•				•	•	•	
De Hoop Nature Reserve						•	•		•	•		•	•		•	•	•	•	•	•
Table Mountain National Park		•	•			•	•		•	•		•	•			•		•	•	•
Tsitsikamma		•	•			•	•		•	•		•	•		•		•	•	•	•
Wilderness			•			•	•		•	•		•	•				•	•	•	•

Visitors should be aware that the approach to the falls is very slippery and people have fallen in the past. The area is known for its traditional domed huts and excellent bird life. Sudden temperature changes are not unusual, so it is worth bringing extra layers of clothing.

Colourful flowers bloom in spring at **Goegap Nature Reserve**. The circular walks and challenging mountain-bike trails attract many visitors. Accommodation includes a self-catering guesthouse, bush huts and camping sites.

Kgalagadi Transfrontier Park is an "international peace park" comprising Kalahari Gemsbok National Park in South Africa and the much larger Gemsbok National Park in Botswana. This desert of glistening red sand dunes bisected by two dry rivers covers almost twice the area of the Kruger National Park *(see p64)*. Accommodation is either in traditional rest camps or in unfenced wilderness camps, guarded by armed guides. Guests can experience the bush at close hand during their stay, so these sites are popular. The park is also famous for its gemsbok and birds of prey.

World-renowned for its spectacular displays of spring flowers, with butterflies and birds darting among the blooms,

Namaqua National Park is best visited during August and September. More than 1,000 of its estimated 3,500 plant species are unique to the park, which, though arid, is designated a biodiversity hotspot. As this is a developing park, there are no overnight accommodation facilities and the only place to stop for snacks and light refreshments is a stall at a nearby farm.

THE WESTERN AND SOUTHERN CAPE

Addo Elephant National Park is home to approximately 450 elephants, as well as the unique flightless dung beetle. The trail has a 500-m (547-yd) boardwalk, to accommodate people with mobility and sensory impairments. Overnight visitors can choose from safari tents, forest cabins, *rondavels*, and luxury guest houses, as well as caravan and camping sites.

Named after the species of antelope it was established to conserve, **Bontebok National Park** is a World Heritage Site. The park has a wonderful view of the Langeberg mountains, and as part of the Cape Floral Kingdom it has particularly rich flora. This is an ideal spot in which to relax

Penguins at play in Table Mountain National Park, Cape Town

by the tranquil Breede River and take a tour of the Wine Routes and surrounding areas.

De Hoop Nature Reserve is a special reserve with an abundance of marine life such as dolphins, seals and whales. More than 260 species of resident and migratory birds are also found here. There are several hikes to choose from, including the Whale Trail, which has five overnight stops and provides an excellent opportunity to explore the area.

Table Mountain National Park is a unique mix of natural wonders and the bustling city life of Cape Town. Unusually, entrance to the park is free, except at three points: the Cape of Good Hope, Silvermine and Boulders Beach, which is worth visiting to see the delightful

Young baboon, De Hoop Reserve

A floral feast for the eyes at the Namaqua National Park, the Arid Interior region

African penguins. The park is part of the Cape Floral Kingdom and has some of the most diverse wildlife in the world.

Garden Route National Park comprises three sections: Tsitsikamma, Wilderness and Knysna Lakes. Keen hikers can enjoy the Otter Trail in the Tsitsikamma section, stretching some 5 km (3 miles) to the sea, where the underwater trails, scuba diving and snorkelling are also worth experiencing. Visitors can frequently catch sight of dolphins and porpoises frolicking near the shoreline. During the migration season, southern right whales might be seen. The Wilderness section of the park is popular with hikers and bird-lovers alike. Bird-watchers should keep a look-out for the Knysna lourie and pied kingfisher here. There are plenty of other activities on offer, including abseiling and paragliding. In the Knysna Lakes section, private enterprises offer sailing, angling, boardsailing and power boating.

The Otter Trail in Tsitsikamma, Garden Route National Park

DIRECTORY

ORGANIZED AND INDEPENDENT TOURS

African Sky (USA)
Tel (830) 560-6173.
www.africansky.com

Expert Africa (UK)
Tel (020) 8232-9777.
www.expertafrica.com

Intrepid Travel (Australia)
Tel (1300) 018-871.
www.intrepidtravel.com

Southern Africa Tourism Services Association (SATSA)
Tel (086) 127-2872.
www.satsa.co.za

PLANNING YOUR TRIP

CapeNature
Tel (021) 483-0190.
www.capenature.org.za

KZN Wildlife
Tel (033) 845-1000.
www.kznwildlife.com

South African National Parks
Tel (012) 428-9111.
www.sanparks.org

HEALTH ISSUES

24-Hour Malaria Hotline *(082) 234-1800.*

GAUTENG AND MPUMALANGA

Kruger National Park
N4, R538, R569, or R536.
Tel (012) 428-9111.
www.sanparks.org

Madikwe Game Reserve
70 km (43 miles) N of Zeerust on R49.
Tel (018) 350-9931.
www.madikwe-game-reserve.co.za

Pilanesberg Game Reserve
50 km (31 miles) N of Zeerust on R49.
Tel (014) 555-1600.
www.pilanesberg-game-reserve.co.za

Suikerbosrand Nature Reserve
Outside Heidelberg.
Tel (011) 439-6300.

THE EAST COAST AND INTERIOR

Golden Gate Highlands National Park
R711 or R712.
Tel (058) 255-0000.
www.sanparks.org

Hluhluwe-Imfolozi Game Reserve
N2 to signposted turn-off at Mtubatuba.
Tel (033) 845-1000.
www.kznwildlife.com

iSimangaliso Wetland Park
N2 from Mtubatuba.
Tel (033) 845-1000.
www.kznwildlife.com

Tembe Elephant Park
N2 past Mkuze, Jozini turn-off.
Tel (031) 267-0144.
www.tembe.co.za

uKhahlamba-Drakensberg Park
N3 via Mooi River or Harrismith and Estcourt.
Tel (033) 845-1000.
www.kznwildlife.com

THE ARID INTERIOR

Ai-Ais Richtersveld Transfrontier Park
From Springbok, N7 to Steinkopf, Port Nolloth & Alexander Bay; gravel road to Sendelingsdrift.
Tel (027) 831-1506.
www.sanparks.org

Augrabies Falls National Park
N14, 120 km (74 miles) W of Upington.
Tel (054) 452-9200.
www.sanparks.org

Goegap Nature Reserve
E off N7; S of R14; 15 km (10 miles) SE of Springbok.
Tel (027) 718-9906.
www.northerncape.org.za

Karoo National Park
N1 to Beaufort West.
Tel (023) 415-2828.
www.sanparks.org

Kgalagadi Transfrontier Park
R360 from Upington.
Tel (054) 561-2000.
www.sanparks.org

Namaqua National Park
Off N7 route to Namibia.
Tel (027) 672-1948.
www.sanparks.org

THE WESTERN AND SOUTHERN CAPE

Addo Elephant National Park
N2 from city, then R335.
Tel (042) 233-8600.
www.sanparks.org

Bontebok National Park
Off N2.
Tel (028) 514-2735.
www.sanparks.org

De Hoop Nature Reserve
56 km (35 miles) E of Bredasdorp on dirt road.
Tel (028) 542-1253.
www.capenature.org.za

Garden Route National Park (Tsitsikamma; Wilderness; Knysna Lakes)
Tsitsikamma:
N2 from Plettenberg Bay;
Tel (042) 281-1607.
Wilderness:
Close to N2, 15 km (10 miles) from George;
Tel (044) 877-1197.
Knysna Lakes:
N2 from Plettenberg Bay.
Tel (044) 382-2095.
www.sanparks.org

Table Mountain National Park
Tel (021) 712-2337.
www.sanparks.org

Habitats at a Glance

Habitat types are determined by a variety of factors including climate, vegetation and geology. In South Africa, the most important of these factors are rainfall, soil type, altitude and latitude. Broadly speaking, rainfall is significantly high in the east, while soil is sandiest in the west, altitude is highest in the central highveld area and temperatures tend to be highest at more northerly latitudes. Much of South Africa has rainfall in summer, with perhaps 90 per cent of precipitation occurring between November and April. By contrast, the Western Cape has a winter-rainfall climate, while much of the Eastern Cape falls between these extremes.

FIELD GUIDE ICONS

- Diurnal
- Nocturnal
- Savannah woodland
- Semiarid
- Forest
- Highveld grassland
- Wetland
- Intertidal
- Fynbos

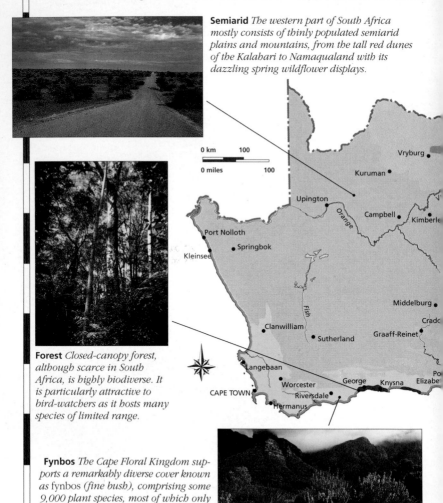

Semiarid *The western part of South Africa mostly consists of thinly populated semiarid plains and mountains, from the tall red dunes of the Kalahari to Namaqualand with its dazzling spring wildflower displays.*

Forest *Closed-canopy forest, although scarce in South Africa, is highly biodiverse. It is particularly attractive to bird-watchers as it hosts many species of limited range.*

Fynbos *The Cape Floral Kingdom supports a remarkably diverse cover known as* fynbos *(fine bush), comprising some 9,000 plant species, most of which only occur here – probably the world's greatest repository of floral endemics. Much of the wildlife is also unique to the region.*

0 km   100
0 miles   100

Vryburg
Kuruman
Upington
Campbell
Kimberle
Port Nolloth
Springbok
Kleinsee
Middelburg
Crado
Clanwilliam
Sutherland
Graaff-Reinet
Langebaan
Worcester
George
Knysna
Elizabe
CAPE TOWN
Riversdale
Hermanus
Orange
Fish

Highveld grassland

The largely high-lying central region of South Africa, rising to 3,480 m (11,420 ft) in the Drakensberg range, is dominated by open grassland. In the past century much of it has been lost to agriculture or urban development.

Termite hills provide an essential source of food for aardvarks

NICHE HABITATS

Within larger ecosystems exist many smaller micro-habitats. A termite hill not only supports its insect creators, but provides living space for small reptiles, food for aardvarks, and a handy vantage point for prowling cheetahs. Isolated *koppies,* or cliffs, support a unique set of creatures, from klip-springers to agama lizards, while puddles might provide a tempo-rary home to terrapins.

KEY

- ☐ Semiarid
- ☐ Savannah woodland
- ■ Forest
- ■ Wetland
- ■ Highveld grassland
- ☐ Intertidal
- ☐ Fynbos

Musina
Limpopo
Louis Trichardt
Mokopane Baphalaborwa
Rustenburg Mbombela (Nelspruit)
PRETORIA/ CITY OF TSHWANE
JOHANNESBURG
sdorp Vereeniging Ermelo MBABANE
Vaal Lusutfu
Phongolo
Newcastle Vryheid
Clarens Ladysmith
emfontein Tugela
MASERU KwaDukuza
Pietermaritzburg
DURBAN
Kokstad
Orange Port Edward
Lusikisiki
East London
Grahamstown

Savannah woodland *Much of the north and east is covered in savannah wood-land, mostly dominated by thorny acacia trees. In terms of viewing game, this is the most important habitat in South Africa.*

Wetland *There are several natural lakes in the iSimangaliso Wetland Park, but South Africa is generally a dry country, and most other fresh-water bodies are artificially dammed.*

Intertidal *The intertidal zone is the stretch of coast dividing the permanent tree line from the open sea. The northeast coastal belt features lush mangrove swamps and offshore coral reefs teeming with fish.*

FIELD GUIDE

*S*outh Africa's network of national parks and other protected areas are home to an astounding diversity of wildlife, from the Big Five (see pp72–3) to the trunk-necked giraffe, greyhound-like cheetah, elegant impala and diminutive dwarf mongoose. Bird enthusiasts can look forward to sighting an enormous variety of birds, and there are some 500 species of reptiles and amphibians.

The following pages are an introduction to some of the many wild creatures that inhabit South Africa. Some, such as the gregarious impala and comical warthog, will be seen several times daily on safari. Others, like lions and elephants, can usually be sighted at least once over the course of a few days. On the other hand, creatures such as the nocturnal aardvark and pangolin are so secretive that you could spend a year in the bush without catching so much as a fleeting glimpse. While the main focus of this field guide is mammals, a more generic overview of South Africa's varied cast of reptiles and amphibians is also provided, along with a few dozen of the more conspicuous and memorable bird species.

The vast Kruger National Park, in particular, is one of the world's top destinations for the Big Five and host to many other popular favourites, including the giraffe, wildebeest and

Chameleon climbing a branch

cheetah. These are just a fraction of what the country has to offer. But despite the relative profligacy of wildlife in South Africa, much biodiversity has been lost during the past three centuries of European settlement. The sable-like bluebuck and zebra-like quagga that once roamed the *fynbos*-strewn slopes of the Western Cape were hunted to extinction by the early settlers, while the protection of dwindling populations of fewer than 100 bonteboks, Cape Mountain zebras and white rhinoceros within national parks and game reserves saved these species from a similar fate. The conservation ethic that now prevails in South Africa is a relatively recent development, and it should never be taken for granted. For this reason, the descriptions that follow are accompanied by the International Union for Conservation of Nature (IUCN) Red List status of each species *(see p73)*.

A herd of zebras mixing with an impala herd for protection against predators

◁ Cheetah in a tree in the Kruger National Park

South Africa's Wildlife Heritage

Before the arrival of the white colonists, nomadic Khoina hunted wild animals for food, while to the east, Zulu and Venda traded in ivory and organized ceremonial hunts – but their spears and pitfall traps had little impact. When Europeans arrived on the scene in the 17th century, South Africa's wildlife seemed inexhaustible. By the mid-19th century, with their deadly weapons, the settlers had seen to it that the vast herds had disappeared – many species were in danger of extinction.

Conservation measures over the past century have brought about an amazing recovery, and South Africa's wildlife reserves are now among the finest in the world.

Giraffe

The klipspringer, *agile and sure-footed, occurs in mountainous areas throughout the country.*

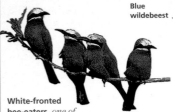

Blue wildebeest

White-fronted bee-eaters, *one of around 840 bird species recorded in the country, gather in flocks along rivers in the Kruger National Park. They catch and consume flying insects.*

Zebra

Nyala bulls can be distinguished from the similar-looking kudu by the orange colour of their lower legs.

Warthog

The hunt *is a brutal yet timeless African sequence. Cheetahs mainly prey on smaller antelopes, like springboks and impalas.*

AT THE WATERHOLE

In the dry winter months (May to September), an ever-changing wildlife pageant unfolds as animals gather at waterholes to drink. Wooden hides have been erected at waterholes in KwaZulu-Natal's Hluhluwe-Imfolozi (see p294) and Mkhuze game reserves, while the rivers in the Kruger National Park offer the best vantage points.

AFRICA'S BIG FIVE

This term originated from hunting jargon for the most dangerous and sought-after trophy animals. Today, they are still an attraction, with Kruger National Park (see pp338–41) the prime Big-Five viewing destination. Hluhluwe-Imfolozi, and the Pilanesberg and Madikwe reserves, too, are well-known sanctuaries.

Lions, *the largest of the African cats, live in prides of varying size controlled by one or more dominant males.*

The black rhinoceros *is in serious danger of extinction. It is distinguished from the white rhino by its longer upper lip.*

THE FIRST WILDLIFE RESERVES

By the mid-19th century, hunters had decimated the big game. Subspecies like the quagga (a type of zebra) and Cape lion had become extinct. As towns expanded, people began to view wildlife as an asset, and in 1889, the Natal *Volksraad* (people's council) agreed to establish a wildlife reserve. In 1894, a strip of land between KwaZulu-Natal and Swaziland became the Pongola Game Reserve, Africa's first conservation area. In 1898, President Paul Kruger signed a proclamation establishing the forerunner of a sanctuary that was later named Kruger National Park in his honour.

Quagga

Princeps demodocus demodocus, the attractive Christmas butterfly, is also known as the citrus swallowtail, and can be seen throughout South Africa from September to April. As its name suggests, the species often occurs in citrus groves.

IUCN RED LIST

Established in 1963, the International Union for Conservation of Nature (IUCN) Red List of Threatened Species uses a set of criteria to evaluate the extinction risk of more than 40,000 species and subspecies of plants and animals globally. Each taxon evaluated is assigned to one of the following categories:
• Extinct (EX) – No individuals known to survive, e.g. bluebuck.
• Extinct in the Wild (EW) – Survives only in captivity or as an introduced population outside its natural range.
• Critically Endangered (CE) – Extremely high risk of extinction in the immediate future, e.g. black rhino.
• Endangered (EN) – Very high risk of extinction within the foreseeable future, e.g. African wild dog.
• Vulnerable (VU) – Significant medium-term risk of extinction, e.g. lion.
• Least Concern (LC) – No significant risk of extinction at present, e.g. impala.
• Data Deficient (DD) – Insufficient information available for assessment.

Spotted hyenas *are one of the most interesting of African predators. Loose family groups are led by females who, due to high levels of male hormones, also have male genitalia.*

Female impala

Nyala cows, usually accompanied by dominant bulls, are often spotted in the woodlands of northern KwaZulu-Natal.

Vervet monkeys usually avoid arid habitats.

Waterholes dry out rapidly in the summer heat, and the animals suffer much hardship.

Oxpeckers and kudu *provide an example of the symbiosis that has evolved between different animals under the harsh African conditions. The birds free the antelopes of parasites, and also act as an alarm system at waterholes.*

Buffaloes *are the most abundant of the Big Five and occur in large herds. Old bulls become loners and may be extremely dangerous.*

Leopards *are shy cats that are largely nocturnal and often rest on tree branches.*

Elephants *live in tight-knit family groups led by a matriarch. The bulls remain solitary, or may band together to form bachelor herds.*

Cats

Secretive and solitary, cats belong to the family Felidae and are the most stealthy and efficient killers among carnivores. Also the most strictly carnivorous, they feed exclusively on other warm-blooded creatures, from sparrows and mice to buffaloes and giraffes. Although they differ greatly in colouration and size, all cats have a similar body plan to their familiar domestic counterpart, with an elongated body, long tail, small head, sensitive whiskers, prominent canines and keen bifocal vision. Much wild felid behaviour will be familiar to the average cat owner.

FAMILY

South Africa's seven felid species are traditionally split between three genera: Felis, with small- to medium-size cats; Panthera, with big cats distinguished by a larynx modification enabling them to roar; and Acinonyx, with the cheetah – the only felid with non-retractable claws.

CHEETAH
(SPECIES: ACINONYX JUBATUS)

BEST SEEN: Phinda, Kruger (central region), Sabi Sands

VU

This large spotted felid is the greyhound of the African bush, with a streamlined build, small head and unique non-retractable claws that cater to its specialist pursuit of sprinting. The world's fastest runner, it is capable of accelerating from standstill to a speed of 115 kmph (72 mph) in 4 seconds. Where most feline predators combine hunting with scavenging, the cheetah feeds exclusively on fresh meat. It is also unusual in that it hunts by day as well as at dusk, creeping to within 15–30 m (50–100 ft) of its prey before opening chase and, if successful, knocking down and suffocating its victim. Less solitary than most cats, the cheetah is often seen in pairs or small groups – either male coalitions of up to three brothers, or a female with cubs. In common with other cats, a cheetah will purr when content and growl, hiss and yelp when threatened or annoyed. Unlike the true big cats, it cannot roar. Instead, its most common vocalization, often made by a mother looking for her cubs, is a high-pitched, bird-like twitter known as "yipping". The cheetah has a restless temperament, and is often seen trotting determinedly through the grass, breaking step only to climb on a tree trunk or termite mound that presents itself as a lookout post. Once widespread in Asia, Arabia and Africa, it has suffered a massive range-retraction in recent times, and is now practically endemic to sub-Saharan Africa.

IUCN status VU: Vulnerable; LC: Least Concern

AFRICAN WILD CAT
(SPECIES: FELIS SILVESTRIS)

BEST SEEN: Sabi Sands, Kgalagadi, Kruger

LC

This small, elusive felid is closely related to its much rarer European counterpart. DNA evidence suggests that it is the sole wild ancestor of the domestic cat – and indeed it looks much like a domestic tabby, but with longer legs. A versatile hunter of rodents, birds and insects, it is the most widely distributed of all African predators, absent only from rainforest interiors and deserts. Its genetic integrity is under increasing threat as a result of interbreeding with feral domestic cats.

The African wild cat, a versatile hunter

BLACK-FOOTED CAT
(SPECIES: FELIS NIGRIPES)

BEST SEEN: Kgalagadi, Pilanesberg

VU

Endemic to southern Africa, this tiny cat is associated with sandy semiarid habitats, where it is very seldom seen. At a glance, it could be confused with the African wild cat, but it is much smaller, has shorter legs, and is heavily spotted as opposed to faintly striped. A nocturnal hunter, it preys mainly on small mammals such as gerbils, mice and elephant shrews.

The black-footed cat, nocturnal and seldom seen

CARACAL
(SPECIES: FELIS CARACAL)

BEST SEEN: Kgalagadi, Augrabies Falls

LC

The largest of Africa's "small cats", the caracal resembles the Eurasian lynx, although recent genetic studies suggest it has closer affinities to the serval. It has a fairly uniform tan coat, with light spotting sometimes distinguishable on the paler belly, and long tufted ears whose dark colouration is referred to in Turkish as *karakulak* (black ear), from which the cat gets its name. Because of this tufting, and some 20 muscles that control ear direction, it is exceptionally sharp of hearing, even by felid standards. An agile and versatile hunter, it is particularly skilled at taking birds in flight. Within South Africa, its range is confined to the extreme northwest.

Caracal, the cat most strongly associated with dry habitats

SERVAL
(SPECIES: FELIS SERVAL)

BEST SEEN: Kruger, uKhahlamba-Drakensberg, Ithala

LC

Superficially similar to the larger cheetah, the serval is a sleek spotted cat associated with rank grassland and other open non-forested habitats. It typically has streaky (as opposed to circular) black-on-gold spots, although speckled and melanistic morphs also occur. It has the longest legs in relation to body size of any felid, and very large ears – adaptations that help it locate prey in its preferred habitat of tall grassland. It feeds mainly on small mammals and birds, pouncing with a spectacular high spring, then delivering the fatal blow with one of its powerful claws. The serval is the most readily seen of the smaller felids, especially during the first 30 minutes after sunrise.

The serval, found in open habitats

Key to Field Guide icons *see p68*

Lion

The largest terrestrial predator in Africa, the lion is the most sociable and least secretive of the world's 36 cat species. Unusually among felids it seldom takes to the trees, and the adult male sports a regal blond or black mane. For most people, the charismatic "king of the jungle" is the ultimate African safari icon, so much so that it is often easy to forget that lions once ranged widely across Eurasia. Today, South Africa's lions are confined to a few protected areas. Elsewhere they have been hunted to extinction, and the continental population has plunged by an estimated 75 per cent since 1990.

Lions are remarkably indolent *creatures, spending up to 20 hours a day at rest. Though seldom active in the heat of the day, they often cover long distances at night.*

FAMILY AND BREEDING

The most sociable of cats, the lion generally lives in prides of five to ten animals, including an adult male, a few adult females and their offspring. Larger prides also occur, often involving male coalitions; one such grouping, active in Sabi Sands in 2010, had five adult males, four of them siblings. Prides defend their territories, which cover anything from 20 to 200 sq km (8–77 sq miles). Takeover battles are often fought to the death and result in the usurper killing all existing cubs, thereby encouraging the females back into oestrus sooner. Lions undergo an extraordinary mating ritual. A male and female pair off, mating briefly but violently at gradually increasing intervals of 12–25 minutes for up to 3 days, after which they return to their pride.

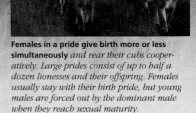

Females in a pride give birth more or less simultaneously *and rear their cubs cooperatively. Large prides consist of up to half a dozen lionesses and their offspring. Females usually stay with their birth pride, but young males are forced out by the dominant male when they reach sexual maturity.*

WHAT YOU MIGHT SEE

The first lion sighting often results in disappointment, as the animals loll indifferently in the shade. Observe them for a while, however, and one is bound to see exciting interactions. It is always worth staying with an isolated female and male pair, as they may well start mating; and if a lioness is lying low in the grass, looking intently into the distance, odds are she is part of a hunt.

Rivalry between adult males *can be intense and fights are often to the death.*

Grooming and social licking *are an important part of the daily ritual in any lion pride.*

IUCN status VU: Vulnerable

FEEDING

Hunting is normally a team effort undertaken by females, who rely on stealth more than speed. A common strategy is for one or two lionesses to herd their prey in the direction of other pride members lying hidden in tall grass. Males seldom take part in a hunt but are quick to exercise their feeding rights once a kill is made. Favoured prey includes antelope, and large prides can even bring down a giraffe or a buffalo.

A large male lion takes first pickings on a fresh giraffe kill

COMMUNICATION AND VOICE

Adult lions are most active around dusk and dawn, but cubs interact throughout the day, playing and mock fighting for hours on end. Subordinate individuals frequently stop to greet or groom dominant pride members, especially when they reunite after a period apart. The most common call, made by females as well as males, is a series of far-carrying moaning grunts that increase in volume, then fade away. As dominant males often move separately from the main pride (regrouping after a kill), this characteristic sound of the African night has the dual purpose of advertising the caller's presence to the pride and warning rivals off its territory.

A cub displays submissiveness to one of the adult males in the pride

Name: *Panthera leo*
Local names: *Mbube (Zulu), Shumba (Shangaan), Leeu (Afrikaans)*

Size Shoulder height: 100–130 cm (40–51 inches); Weight: up to 280 kg (617 lb).

Lifespan 12–15 years in the wild.
Population in South Africa 2,500–3,000.
Conservation status VU.
Gestation period 105–112 days.
Reproduction Females reach sexual maturity at three years and give birth to litters of two to six cubs every 18 months.

Habitat Most often in savannah, but range into all habitats except desert and rainforest.

Lion walking in front of tourist vehicle

Top places to see
Kruger, Sabi Sands, Kgalagadi, Madikwe, Pilanesberg.

Sighting tips
Look out for resting prides in the day. It is worth returning at dawn or dusk to catch them in action.

Friends and foes
In popular belief, lions are regal hunters and hyenas craven scavengers, but lions are as likely to steal a carcass from hyenas as to kill it themselves.

Facts and trivia
A Setswana expression used in tough times translates as "I've still got the lion by the balls" – the implication being that if you lose your grip, you're in trouble!

The main diet *of lions in South Africa comprises antelopes and other ungulates.*

Cubs *spend a large part of their day mock fighting and playing with each other, and sometimes with adults.*

A mating bout *often lasts for less than a minute and is accompanied by growling and hissing.*

Leopard

Paradoxically the most abundant yet most elusive of Africa's large predators, the leopard is distinguishable by its rosette-patterned coat, powerfully pugilistic physique and preference for dense cover. This determinedly nocturnal cat is the supreme solitary hunter, capable of creeping to within a metre of its prey before pouncing. Despite widespread persecution, the global leopard population stands at an estimated 500,000 individuals, ranging from Asia to South Africa. Sabi Sands *(see p341)* is the best place in the world for protracted sightings.

The melanistic leopard, *popularly known as a panther, is found mostly in Asia. However, there have been a few South African records of so-called pseudo-melanistic leopards, which have much denser black spots than normal.*

FAMILY AND BREEDING

The leopard is among the most solitary and territorial of cats. Adults live alone in well-marked territories that are never shared with individuals of the same sex, although males and females frequently have partial territorial overlap. Even so, a chance meeting between two individuals is usually accompanied by real or feigned aggression. Far smaller than males, female leopards come into oestrus every 6–7 weeks. At this time, males from bordering or overlapping territories will often fight to the death for coupling rights. Mating itself is an ill-tempered and abruptly executed affair, and the male has no involvement in rearing the cubs. Females give birth to litters of two to three cubs in a sheltered cave or thicket, and keep a close watch over them for the next 10–14 days, when the cubs' eyes open. Infant mortality is high; it is unusual for more than one cub to survive to adulthood. Cubs can fend for themselves at around one year, but usually stay close to their mother for another 6–12 months before becoming fully independent.

Leopard cubs *typically have greyer pelts than the adults. Leopards are famously solitary, and two individuals keeping peaceful company will almost certainly be a female and her cub.*

WHAT YOU MIGHT SEE

For most safari-goers, the leopard is the most ardently sought of the Big Five. It is most likely to be seen resting up in a tree, in which case it is often worth waiting to see whether there is a kill secured nearby, or if it decides to descend to the ground. Even more thrilling is to catch a leopard on the move, showing off its sleek yet pugilistic build to the full.

A creature of shadow, *cover and darkness, the leopard is most active after dark.*

Sharpened claws *are essential components in this cat's hunting and defensive arsenal.*

IUCN status LC: Least Concern

KEY FACTS

Leopard dragging prey, often three times its weight, into the canopy

FEEDING

The leopard is an adaptable and opportunistic hunter, feeding on anything from medium-sized antelopes to hares, birds, baboons, hyraxes and insects. It depends almost entirely on stealth, stalking silently through thick vegetation before emerging at the last possible moment to pounce and strangle its prey with its powerful jaws. In rainforests and other habitats where lions are absent, the leopard is typically the apex predator, and adults tend to be notably heavier than their savannah counterparts. A leopard will frequently carry a large kill high into the canopy, where it is safely out of the reach of less arboreal scavengers such as lions, hyenas and jackals.

COMMUNICATION AND VOICE

As might be expected of such a potentially fearsome creature known for its ability to survive in close, near-spectral proximity to humans, the leopard is not given to extensive vocalization. Males in particular advertise their presence with a repetitive rasping cough that sounds not unlike wood being sawed. Purring has also been recorded, probably indicating contentment during feeding. Territorial clashes between males are accompanied by snarling and hissing. However, the most remarkable feature of the leopard remains the capacity for furtiveness that ensures that the species still persists, although barely detected, in ranch-land and many other unprotected areas throughout Africa.

Display of affection between leopards, seldom observed in unrelated adults

Name: *Panthera pardus*
Local names: *Ingwe (Zulu), Nkwe (Sotho), Luiperd (Afrikaans)*

Size Shoulder height: 70–80 cm (28–32 inches); Weight: up to 90 kg (198 lb).

Lifespan 20 plus years.
Population in South Africa 8,000–10,000.
Conservation status LC.
Gestation period 3–4 months.
Reproduction Females reach sexual maturity at 2–4 years, when they come into oestrus.

Habitat Shows high habitat tolerance and might occur anywhere.

Leopard stalking a baboon

Top places to see
Sabi Sands, Kruger, Phinda.

Sighting tips
Leopards often take refuge in the lower branches of tall trees, where they may be detected by a tail flickering below the canopy.

Friends and foes
Leopards are the only large cats that regularly prey on baboons, which react hysterically to the cat, issuing a distinctive panicked alarm call that human trackers can recognize.

Facts and trivia
The leopard's name reflects an ancient belief that it is a hybrid between a lion (*leo*) and a panther (*pardos*).

The leopard is compulsively clean *and spends much of the day grooming itself.*

Although highly adaptable, *leopards favour habitats that offer them plenty of cover and camouflage.*

Leopards frequently spend their day *lying quietly in the branches of the upper canopy.*

Dogs and Hyenas

Cats aside, the two major families of large carnivore in South Africa, Canidae (dogs) and Hyaenidae (hyenas), are exciting to see in the wild. Indeed, spotted hyenas are probably the most socially complex of the region's carnivores, and it is riveting to watch clan members meet and greet at a den. Jackals, foxes and wild dogs are also at their boldest and most inquisitive while denning, offering plenty of opportunity to watch the pups at play.

FAMILY

Dogs and hyenas look similar, but their evolutionary lines split about 45 million years ago; the suborder Feliformia has cats, mongooses and hyenas; Caniformia has seals, bears, otters, pandas and dogs.

Young jackals often play in a puppy-like manner

BLACK-BACKED JACKAL
(SPECIES: CANIS MESOMELAS)

BEST SEEN: Kruger, Kgalagadi, Madikwe

LC

The more common of two closely related small dog species in South Africa, the black-backed jackal lives in pairs rather than packs. It is most active at dusk and dawn, and its shrill yelping is a characteristic sound of the African night. It has a shoulder height of 40 cm (16 inches), and an ochre coat offset by a prominent silver-flecked black saddle. An opportunistic feeder, it subsists on small mammals, birds and carrion, and is often seen lurking near lion kills.

SIDE-STRIPED JACKAL
(SPECIES: CANIS ADUSTUS)

BEST SEEN: Kruger

LC

Associated with brachystegia woodland, the side-striped jackal is more strictly nocturnal and less vocal than other jackals. It is similar in general colouration to the black-backed jackal, but with a pale stripe along the flanks. An adaptable omnivore seen singly or in pairs, it supplements a meat-based diet with fruit, grain and carrion. Its South African range is more or less restricted to the Kruger and adjacent private reserves.

The side-striped jackal also has a white-tipped tail

The small Cape fox, with its black-tipped tail

CAPE FOX
(SPECIES: VULPES CHAMA)

BEST SEEN: Kgalagadi, Pilanesberg

LC

The only true fox occurring in sub-Saharan Africa, the Cape fox is a secretive nocturnal species whose range runs from southern Angola to the Western Cape. With a grizzled grey back and browner underparts, its general colouration is jackal-like, but its long bushy tail precludes confusion with any other canid in the region. A versatile feeder, it has an exclamatory yap, and is heard more often than it is seen – unsurprisingly so, given that it was officially persecuted as vermin for over a century.

BAT-EARED FOX
(SPECIES: OTOCYON MEGALOTIS)

BEST SEEN: Kgalagadi, Augrabies Falls

LC

Easily distinguished from any jackal by its huge ears and black eye-mask, this small canid is not a true fox. A number of peculiarities – up to 50 sharp teeth, for instance – have led to it being placed in its own genus. Exclusively insectivorous, it tends to be nocturnal during the hot months and diurnal in the cooler ones. Pairs and small family groups can be seen throughout the year.

The large ears help detect subterranean insect activity

IUCN status EN: Endangered; VU: Vulnerable; LC: Least Concern

The blotchy brown coat of the spotted hyena

SPOTTED HYENA
(SPECIES: CROCUTA CROCUTA)

BEST SEEN: Kruger, Sabi Sands, Pilanesberg

LC

Africa's second-largest predator after the lion stands 1 m (3 ft) high at the shoulder, and weighs about 70 kg (154 lb), with females being larger than males. The most common and conspicuous large predator in many reserves, it is most often seen at dusk and dawn. Though highly vocal at night, its famous "laugh" is less commonly heard than a haunted whoooo-whoop that ranks as perhaps the definitive sound of the African night. The hyena has a complex social structure, living in wide-ranging clans of five to 25 animals that follow a strict matriarchal hierarchy and perform an elaborate ritual when two members meet. Powerfully built, it has a characteristic sloping back, bone-crushingly powerful jaws and a dog-like face and snout. Routinely portrayed as a giggling coward whose liveli-hood depends on scavenging from the noble big cats, it is actually an adept hunter, capable of killing an animal as large as a wildebeest.

The aardwolf is jackal-sized but hyena-shaped

AARDWOLF
(SPECIES: PROTELES CRISTATUS)

BEST SEEN: Pilanesberg, Madikwe, Kgalagadi

LC

A lightly built and strictly nocturnal Hyaenid, the aardwolf (literally, earth wolf) weighs 10 kg (22 lb) and is often mistaken for a jackal, from which, however, it differs in appearance by having a soft creamy striped coat and prominent dorsal mane. It is exclusively insectivorous, feeding almost entirely on two specific termite genera, and its distribution, generally in drier areas, is linked strongly to the presence of suitable nests, into which it burrows nose-first to feed.

AFRICAN WILD DOG
(SPECIES: LYCAON PICTUS)

BEST SEEN: Kruger, Hluhluwe-Imfolozi, Madikwe

EN

Africa's largest canid, also known as the hunting or painted dog, is small in comparison to a Eurasian wolf, and is distinguished from similar species in the region by its black, brown and cream coat. It typically lives in packs of five to 50 animals that hunt cooperatively, literally tearing apart prey on the run. Once so common that it was treated as vermin, it has suffered enormous losses in recent decades, partly through direct persecution and partly through the packs' susceptibility to infectious diseases spread by domestic and feral dogs. It is now Africa's second-most endangered large carnivore, with a total wild population of around 5,000. Of these, around 10 per cent are found in South Africa, mostly in the vicinity of the Kruger National Park, and a small number are resident within Hluhluwe-Imfolozi. It is legendarily nomadic, however, and might turn up in absolutely any bush habitat.

African wild dog packs may include up to 50 animals

BROWN HYENA
(SPECIES: HYAENA HYAENA)

BEST SEEN: Pilanesberg, Kgalagadi, Madikwe

VU

Endemic to the dry west of southern Africa, the brown hyena is a more solitary creature than its spotted counterpart, and a more dedicated scavenger, though it will hunt opportunistically. It is relatively lightly built, seldom weighing more than 50 kg (110 lb), and has a rather shaggy dark brown coat offset by creamy vertical stripes on its side and flanks, and a pale mane. It is the world's rarest hyena, and likely to be seen only on night drives.

Brown hyena, more solitary than its spotted namesake

Key to Field Guide icons *see p68*

Small Carnivores

South Africa supports a wide diversity of small carnivorous mammals, some very conspicuous and easily observed, others highly secretive and elusive. Falling firmly into the first category are the mongooses of the family Herpestidae, several species of which are likely to be seen in the course of any safari. The nocturnal viverrids and mustelids are generally less likely to be seen, although genets often become very tame in lodges where they are regularly fed.

FAMILY

Genets and civets belong to the most ancient of carnivore families, Viverridae, which is confined to Africa and Asia. Mustelidae, by contrast, is the most diverse carnivore family, represented by 55 species and 24 genera worldwide.

CAPE CLAWLESS OTTER
(SPECIES: AONYX CAPENSIS)

 LC

Arguably the largest of "small" carnivores, weighing as much as 35 kg (77 lb) in some cases, the Cape clawless otter is a dark brown piscivore with a bold white collar. While seen in any suitable wetland habitat, it is most common in waters where it can evade crocodiles.

HONEY-BADGER
(SPECIES: MELLIVORA CAPENSIS)

 LC

The honey-badger, or ratel, has a fearless temperament and pugilistic build, with a black body bisected by an off-white stripe down its back, a deceptively puppyish face and heavy bear-like claws. An opportunistic feeder, its diet includes snakes, scorpions and the soft parts of tortoises.

STRIPED WEASEL
(SPECIES: POECILOGALE ALBINCHA)

 LC

A widespread but uncommon resident of open grassland, the striped weasel is mostly black below and white on top, with an all-white tail. With its very short legs and almost cylindrical body shape, it could almost be mistaken for a snake at first glance. It preys almost exclusively on small rodents.

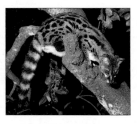

AFRICAN CIVET
(SPECIES: CIVETTICTIS CIVETTA)

 LC

Larger and heftier-looking than the related genets, the African civet is a long-haired omnivore with a black, white and gold coat. It feeds on small animals, including certain snakes, but will also eat fruits and roots. It is seen on night drives, pacing deliberately with its nose to the ground as if following a scent.

COMMON GENET
(SPECIES: GENETTA GENETTA)

 LC

Also known as the small-spotted genet, this is the most familiar member of a genus of cat-like predators represented by some eight species in sub-Saharan Africa. It regularly visits a few select lodges at night, and is quite often observed on night drives in Sabi Sands and other reserves.

BLOTCHED GENET
(SPECIES: GENETTA TIGRINA)

LC

Similar-looking to the common genet but with a black-tipped instead of a white-tipped tail, the blotched or large-spotted genet has a slender low-slung torso, spotted black-on-gold coat and a long striped tail. It is most likely to be seen on a night drive or scavenging around lodges after dark.

IUCN status LC: Least Concern

PREDATOR AND PREY

Small carnivores are often undiscerning feeders, snaffling up anything from insects to small rodents and birds, as well as fruit and carrion. The honey-badger is famed for its symbiotic relationship with the greater honeyguide, a bird which leads it to beehives and feeds on the scraps as the hive is torn apart. The Herpestidae mongooses are known to prey on snakes, but this behaviour is more common in Asia than in Africa, where they prey on small animals that are less well equipped to bite back.

Banded mongoose feasting on an egg

BANDED MONGOOSE
(SPECIES: MUNGOS MUNGO)

 LC

Among the most common and sociable of several mongoose species in South Africa, the banded mongoose is a slender cat-sized carnivore whose dark brown coat bears a dozen or so faint black stripes along the back. Diurnally active, it is typically seen in family bands of 10 to 20 members.

DWARF MONGOOSE
(SPECIES: HELOGALE PARVULA)

 LC

The diminutive and highly social dwarf mongoose has a shoulder height of 7 cm (2¾ inches). It is a light brown predator often seen in the vicinity of the termite mounds and hollowed dead branches that it uses as a home. Family members can sometimes be seen interacting near the den.

SLENDER MONGOOSE
(SPECIES: HERPESTES SANGUINEUS)

LC

A widespread species, the slender mongoose divides its time between foraging terrestrially and arboreally. Though quite variable in shade, it is almost always uniform grey or brown in colour with an elongated body and tail, the latter with a prominent black tip.

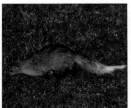

WHITE-TAILED MONGOOSE
(SPECIES: ICHNEUMIA ALBICAUDA)

 LC

About the size of a badger, this is the largest African mongoose. One of the most strictly nocturnal and solitary species, it is often observed by spotlight on night drives, when the combination of size and a bushy white tail render it unmistakable.

YELLOW MONGOOSE
(SPECIES: CYNICTIS PENCILLATA)

 LC

Endemic to the dry western region of southern Africa, this distinctive mongoose with a bushy orange-yellow coat has a habit of standing alertly on its hind legs. It favours sandy environments, where it lives in sprawling burrows with dozens of entrance holes. It is common in Kgalagadi Transfrontier Park.

MEERKAT
(SPECIES: SURICATA SURICATA)

LC

A highly distinctive diurnal mongoose, the meerkat lives underground in closely knit gangs of 20 or so individuals. It has monkey-like fingers with long claws, with which it digs, grooms and forages. Alert, intelligent and playful, it often stands on its hind legs, particularly when disturbed.

Key to Field Guide icons *see p68*

Primates

Intelligent, hyperactive and graceful, monkeys are among the most entertaining of creatures. They are well represented in equatorial Africa, where certain individual forests contain up to a dozen species, but rather less so in South Africa, where only three species are present. This lack of diversity is attributable to the paucity of suitably forested habitats. All South Africa's monkeys are Cercopithecids (cheek-pouch monkeys), an adaptable family of omnivores that fills many ecological niches from swamp forests to semiarid plains, and is named for its inner cheek pouch, which can hold as much food as a full stomach.

> **FAMILY**
>
> The three diurnal primate species that inhabit South Africa are all classified as Old World Monkeys (family Cercopithecidae) and placed in the sub-family Cercopithecinae (cheek-pouched monkeys).

BUSHBABIES
(FAMILY: GALAGONIDAE)

BEST SEEN: Kruger, Sabi Sands, Pilanesberg

Most species: Variable

More closely related to the lemurs of Madagascar than to the diurnal monkeys of the African mainland, bushbabies (or galagos) are endearing creatures, with wide round eyes and agile bodies that enable them to leap between trees. Formerly, only two species were recognized – greater and lesser bushbaby – but a pioneering study used calls and genital patterns to identify around a dozen species in East Africa alone. Pending a similar study in South Africa, the taxonomy of bushbabies in the region remains indeterminate. Seldom seen in daylight, bushbabies become very active after dark, and are often seen on night drives in reserves with suitable wooded savannah habitats.

The wide-eyed bushbaby, rarely seen in daylight

VERVET MONKEY
(SPECIES: CHLOROCEBUS [AETHIOPS] PYGERYTHRUS)

BEST SEEN: Kruger, Hluhluwe-Imfolozi, Durban

LC

Delightful or mischievous, depending on your point of view, the vervet monkey is one of the true characters of the African savannah. It lives in troops of 30–75 animals that are constantly engaged in interaction of one kind or another, whether fighting, grooming, carrying their young on their chest, clambering around branches in search of fruit, or raiding the nearest lodge's lunch buffet. Thought to be the world's most numerous primate species apart from humans, it is predominantly terrestrial, though it seldom strays too far from the trees in which it shelters when threatened. It is highly intelligent, boasting an array of different alarm calls that some scientists have likened to a rudimentary language. Smaller and lankier than any baboon, the vervet has a grizzled light olive or grey coat offset by a black face, white ruff and pale belly, though this rather dull colouration is offset in the male by a gaudy blue scrotum.

The highly intelligent vervet monkey

IUCN status LC: Least Concern

The chacma baboon, South Africa's largest primate

CHACMA BABOON
(SPECIES: PAPIO URSINUS)

BEST SEEN: uKhahlamba-Drakensberg, Kruger, Cape Peninsula

LC

Weighing up to 45 kg (99 lb), the chacma baboon is the largest primate in South Africa and probably the most widespread. Dark grey-brown in colouration, it is distinguishable from all other South African monkeys by its pugilistic build, inverted U-shaped tail, dog-like head and long fangs. Like the vervet monkey, the baboon is behaviourally fascinating, living in large, quarrelsome matriarchal troops whose social structure allows for regular inter-troop movement of males seeking dominance. An adaptable omnivore, the baboon is at home in almost any habitat from semi-desert to forest fringe, but is particularly fond of well-wooded savannah and mountains, where hikers are often alerted to its presence by a far-carrying barking call. Although mainly terrestrial, baboons feel safest when close to trees – their first path of retreat when predators (especially leopards) are in the vicinity. Baboons ordinarily steer clear of people, but they can become very aggressive in places where they have come to see them as a source of food, as in some parts of the Cape Peninsula. If encountered, they should be treated with extreme caution, as they can inflict a nasty bite.

BLUE MONKEY
(SPECIES: CERCOPITHECUS MITIS)

BEST SEEN: iSimangaliso, Hluhluwe-Imfolozi, Kruger (far north only)

LC

The most widespread of African forest monkeys and the only one whose distribution extends south of the Limpopo river, the blue monkey is also known by a number of other names – diademed, white-throated, Sykes, and samango – in different parts of its range, reflecting its high level of regional variability. Associated mainly with forest margins, it lives in troops of up to 10 animals that willingly travel riparian corridors through savannah habitats. It has a very limited distribution in South Africa, where it is confined to the northeast corner of the country – the KwaZulu-Natal coast, the Mpumalanga escarpment forests, and the riparian forest along the Limpopo and its tributaries bordering Zimbabwe. The blue monkey can be distinguished from other South African monkeys by its more arboreal behaviour and retiring nature, and its cryptic but rather beautiful coat – dark grey-blue with flecks of orange-brown on the back, and a white belly and throat.

The shy blue monkey spends most of its time in trees

Key to Field Guide icons *see p68*

African Bush Elephant

The world's largest land animal, the African elephant is one of the most enduringly exciting creatures encountered on safari, not only for its imposing bulk, but also for its complex social behaviour. Elephants are notable for two unique adaptations – a long trunk that combines immense strength with the sensitivity to isolate and tear out a single blade of grass, and outsized tusks that grow throughout its life, sometimes reaching lengths in excess of 3 m (10 ft).

Bloody combat *between male elephants is rare, since breeding rights are generally established within the community through mock fights which involve trunk-locking and tusk-clashing.*

FAMILY AND BREEDING

Elephants are intensely sociable creatures. Females and youngsters move around in close-knit matriarchal clans. Females typically come into oestrus between one and five years after giving birth. Once impregnated, they give birth about 22 months later. Unlike their female kin, males are generally booted out of their birth group in their early teens, after which they roam around singly or form bachelor herds, often tailing the larger breeding herds with which they share a territory. Males periodically come into musth, a sexually related condition characterized by a fifty-fold increase in testosterone levels; such elephants are unpredictable and best treated with caution by other elephants and humans alike.

Adult females maintain a vigilant watch *over their young until they are old enough to deter predators. A female gives birth to a 100-kg (220-lb) calf every 5 to 10 years. Each calf thus represents a major genetic investment for the matriarchal herd, and is raised communally. Matriarchal herds comprise up to four generations of sisters, daughters and grand-daughters, dominated by the oldest female.*

WHAT YOU MIGHT SEE

Elephants are interactive, and great entertainers. Their tusks are versatile tools, used to dig for salt or water, to tear bark, and even in self-defence. The trunk is employed to place food in the mouth and suck up water, and may be wielded threat-eningly in displays of dominance. When an elephant raises its trunk in your direction, trumpeting and stamping its feet, it is best to retreat.

Ears flap continuously *in hot weather to cool circulating blood below the thin skin.*

Faced with a potential threat, *a herd "periscopes" – moves its trunks around to investigate.*

IUCN status VU: Vulnerable

FEEDING

The trunk, used to reach high branches or dislodge ripe fruit

A versatile feeder, the African elephant is a mixed grazer-browser that spends up to 15 hours daily chomping some 200 kg (440 lb) of vegetable matter. It drinks up to 200 litres (44 gallons) daily, arriving at a waterhole a few hours after sunrise and often lingering on until late afternoon to play in the water or spray itself. Herds range widely in search of food, but concentrated populations in protected areas often cause serious environmental degradation by uprooting trees.

COMMUNICATION AND VOICE

It was long thought that aural communication between elephants was limited to bouts of trumpeting. In 1987 researchers discovered that the elephant's main means of communication are subsonic rumblings, below or at the edge of human perception, that can travel through the earth for several miles. These are picked up by the skin on the trunk and feet, allowing dispersed herds to coordinate their movements over a vast area. Elephants also have an exceptional sense of smell and good eyesight.

Elephants use their feet to sense the distant subsonic rumblings of a peer

---

Name: *Loxondonta africana*
Local names: *Ndlovu (Zulu), Tlou (Tswana), Olifant (Afrikaans)*

Size Shoulder height: 2.5–4 m (8–13 ft); Weight: up to 6,300 kg (13,890 lb).

Lifespan 65 years.
Population in South Africa 25,000.
Conservation status VU.
Gestation period 22 months.
Reproduction Typically, females first conceive in their early teens and give birth at 5-yearly intervals until their late 50s.

Habitat All habitats except desert.

Tourists watch an elephant cross the road

Top places to see
Addo Elephant, Tembe Elephant, Madikwe, Pilanesberg, Kruger.

Sighting tips
A trail of football-sized dung and mangled vegetation are sure signs that elephants have passed by.

Friends and foes
Elephant droppings are a treat for dung beetles, which feed almost exclusively on fecal matter.

Facts and trivia
The legend of elephant grave-yards has a factual basis. Old elephants whose last set of teeth has worn down gather in marshes to feed on waterlogged vegetation, until even that gets difficult and they starve to death.

Tusks and trunk *are both used to dig for subterranean water in riverbeds during the dry season.*

The trunk *is regularly used to tear juicy branches from the canopy and manoeuvre them into the mouth.*

Elephants spray themselves *with water or dust to help cool down under the hot tropical sun.*

Rhinoceros

With their armoured hide, massive bulk and fearsome horns, the world's five surviving rhino species represent one of the most ancient and impressive branches of the ungulate line. Sadly, all three Asian species are on the danger list, while their African counterparts are still in tentative recovery from the critical population declines that occurred during the 20th century. It is no exaggeration to say that South Africa stands at the forefront of rhino conservation; some 75 per cent of the world's surviving rhinos are protected within its borders.

The rhino and oxpecker *were long thought to have had a symbiotic relationship, with oxpeckers cleansing the rhino's skin of ticks and other pests. It is now known that oxpeckers also suck blood from cuts and wounds in their host's hide.*

The bond between mother and calf *is generally strong and lasts for 3–4 years. During the first 12 months, the calf is vulnerable to predation from lions and hyenas, and is protected aggressively by its mother. The female will eventually terminate the relationship once another calf is imminent.*

FAMILY AND BREEDING

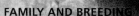

Adult rhinos are essentially solitary creatures, though not especially territorial. Both sexes are aggressive towards unfamiliar individuals but equable towards rhinos with neighbouring or overlapping territories, sometimes even pairing off temporarily. The bond between mother and calf, however, is more enduring. Courtship between rhinos is a protracted affair. In the case of the black rhino, the female scrapes her territorial dung piles vigorously, and the first male to pick up the scent trails behind her trying to cover it up with his own faeces. Prior to mating, the pair often indulge in noisy mock-sparring. Once the male is accepted, the two stay together for days or even weeks. A single calf weighing up to 50 kg (110 lb) is born 15–16 months later, and is fully mobile within days.

WHAT YOU MIGHT SEE

Black rhinos are reclusive animals that feed in thick bush. Most safari-goers consider themselves lucky to see one in the wild. White rhinos are more numerous, and easier to spot in the grasslands where they feed. Visitors may occasionally locate a mother and calf, or a few adults assembled at a wallow. Black rhinos tend to charge when disturbed; white rhinos are more passive.

IUCN status CE: Critically Endangered; VU: Vulnerable

An adult male defecates *at a communal dung post, signalling his passing to other rhinos.*

Rhinos enjoy wallowing in mud, *the colour of which often alters their own appearance.*

FEEDING

The black rhino is a dedicated browser, utilizing leaves, branches and fruits of at least 200 plant species, while the white rhino subsists mainly as a grazer. This dietary distinction is also accountable for the misleading names of black and white rhinos, both of which are a similar shade of grey in colour. The original Dutch name *weit* (wide) was an allusion to the square grass-cropping mouth of the white rhino, but was later mistranslated to "white", leaving the black rhino to be named by default. Rhinos feed mostly in the early morning and late afternoon, ideally retiring to a wallow or waterhole at midday, though the black rhino can go almost a week without drinking water if need be.

Black rhino plucking twigs with its prehensile upper lip

COMMUNICATION AND VOICE

Vocalizations, though complex and varied, are seldom observed during a casual rhino encounter. When two individuals meet, they may growl or trumpet to signal aggression, but will more likely snort in amicable greeting. Rhinos give a high-pitched alarm call when moderately threatened, and emit a loud pig-like squeal when seriously alarmed. Indirect communication between neighbours includes the sharing of common dung heaps at waterholes and feeding places, which allows every individual to know which other rhinos have passed by recently. In contrast to its acute sense of smell, it has poor sight; black rhinos have a focal range of less than 10 m (33 ft).

The awesome sight of two adult males locking horns in combat

KEY FACTS

Name: *Diceros bicornis (black); Caratotherium Simum (white)*
Local names: *Tshukudu (Sotho), Ubhejane (Zulu), Renoster (Afrikaans)*

 Size Shoulder height: 1.4–1.8 m (4½–6 ft) (black), 1.7–1.85 m (5½–6 ft) (white); Weight: up to 1,400 kg (3,086 lb) (black); up to 3,600 kg (7,937 lb) (white).

Lifespan 40–45 years.
Population in South Africa 2,000 (black), 16,500 (white).
Conservation status CE (black), VU (vulnerable).
Gestation period 16 months.
Reproduction Females mature sexually at 5 years and give birth to a calf every 3–4 years.

 Habitat Dense woodland and thicket (black); open woodland and grassland (white).

White rhinoceros in open woodland

 Top places to see Hluhluwe-Imfolozi, Kruger, Pilanesberg, Ndumo Ithala.

Sighting tips Mud wallows are good places to spot these elusive animals.

Friends and foes A full-grown rhino has little to fear from predators, but can be chased away by elephants.

Facts and trivia The main cause of the decline in Africa's rhino population is the mistaken belief that its horn has aphrodisiacal qualities.

Rhinos are solitary creatures *and seldom interact with each other or with different species.*

A black rhino might charge *at the slightest provocation, and can quickly reach an alarming 55 kmph (34 mph).*

Individual rhinos return daily *to favoured rubbing posts, gradually polishing the top smooth.*

African Buffalo

Africa's only wild ox, the African buffalo is similar in appearance to the Indian water buffalo and closely related to domestic cattle. Powerfully built, with a bulk of up to 800 kg (1,764 lb) and heavy, splayed horns, it is famed for its unpredictable temperament. Indeed, the "great white hunters" who coined the term Big Five regarded this ox as the most dangerous of foes. Buffaloes are the most numerous of the Big Five, with a continent-wide population estimated at almost a million, and are highly conspicuous in several South African reserves.

Affectionately known as Daga Boys *after an African word meaning mud, elderly male buffaloes tend to live singly or in small bachelor herds, and have a reputation for grumpiness, as well as for being quicker to charge than individuals in breeding herds.*

FAMILY AND BREEDING

The African buffalo is highly gregarious and non-territorial, generally moving in mixed-sex herds of 10 to 50 animals, with one dominant male and a hierarchical structure binding the adult females and non-dominant males. Females come into oestrus at the start of the rainy season and give birth to a single calf, or more infrequently twins, almost exactly a year later. Tensions between males run high during the mating season, with dominant bulls trying to pull rank and subordinate males fighting to challenge their breeding rights. The imposing bulk of an adult buffalo ensures that it has few natural enemies, and a strongly bonded herd will cooperate to chase away predators. Nevertheless, buffaloes are sometimes preyed upon by lions, with the predator occasionally coming off second best in the confrontation.

Seasonal aggregations of more than 1,000 buffaloes *can still be seen in some parts of South Africa, most notably in the central and northern Kruger National Park (see pp338–41).*

WHAT YOU MIGHT SEE

Buffaloes are less visibly interactive than certain other sociable animals. When a vehicle approaches a buffalo herd, the mass response will often be to stare down the vehicle or even to close in on it. While this can be quite intimidating, it signals curiosity – and chronic myopia – more than anything sinister. Buffaloes often support hitchhiking birds – cattle egrets, oxpeckers and starlings.

IUCN status LC: Least Concern

Rival males *often lock horns during the mating season, but serious injuries are rare.*

Buffaloes take to a wallow *during the day, more so than even rhinos and elephants.*

FEEDING

Buffalo herd gathering at a waterhole to drink and wallow

Primarily a grazer, the African buffalo requires a significant proportion of grass in its diet, although it can supplement this by browsing on low trees and shrubs. Large herds are common in most grassland habitats, while forests support smaller herds. The buffalo feeds throughout the day, but will readily adopt a nocturnal feeding pattern in areas where it is repeatedly disturbed. It must drink at least once every 24 hours, and also enjoys wallowing. Herds rarely stray more than 10–15 km (6–9 miles) away from a reliable water source.

COMMUNICATION AND VOICE

The African buffalo is generally far quieter than its mooing domestic counterpart when it comes to day-to-day communication. However, upon sighting a predator it makes an explosive snorting alarm call that swiftly mobilizes the rest of the herd into defensive mode. A threatened animal may also grunt aggressively. The buffalo has an acute sense of smell and exceptional hearing, but poor eyesight, for which reason a herd may often stand and stare myopically at a perceived intruder.

Buffalo herds tend to walk in single file when covering long distances

KEY FACTS

Name: *Syncerus caffer*
Local names: *Inyathi (Zulu), Nare (Tswana), Buffel (Afrikaans)*

Size Shoulder height: 1.2–1.7 m (4–6 ft); Weight: 500–800 kg (1,102–1,764 lb).

Lifespan 20–25 years.
Population in South Africa 30–60,000.
Conservation status LC.
Gestation period 11–12 months.
Reproduction Females mature at the age of 4–5 years and give birth to a single calf at the start of the rainy season.

Habitat Mostly non-arid environments.

Buffaloes on a private game reserve

Top places to see
Kruger, Hluhluwe-Imfolozi, Pilanesberg.

Sighting tips
The buffalo is still present in some places where unguided walking is permitted, such as the iSimangaliso Wetland Park.

Friends and foes
Cattle egrets flock around herds of buffalo to feed on insects that are disturbed as the mammals move through the grass.

Facts and trivia
The Zulu military formation "Impondo Zekomo" – Buffalo Horn – consisted of a strong body of troops with two flanking "horns" to cut off escape routes.

A courting male buffalo *will rest his head on the female's rump as a prelude to mating.*

Female calves *stay with their birth herd, but males may be forced out upon reaching sexual maturity.*

Large prides of lions *sometimes attempt to prey on buffaloes, with mixed success.*

Giraffes, the world's tallest land mammal

SOUTHERN GIRAFFE
(SPECIES: GIRAFFA CAMELOPARDALIS)

BEST SEEN: Kruger, Hluhluwe-Imfolozi, Pilanesberg

                                    LC

The world's heaviest ruminant and the tallest land mammal, the giraffe is a specialized canopy-feeder, browsing on high-grade leaf foliage at heights of up to 6 m (20 ft), though it will occasionally eat grass too. Giraffes typically move in impermanent groups of up to 15 animals, with individuals often leaving or joining at will; a herd may be all-male, all-female or mixed in composition. Males are significantly larger in size than females, and often engage in a form of behaviour called necking – intertwining their necks and heads and occasionally dealing out heavy blows. This has various functions, ranging from combat to a prelude to homosexual mounting, which is more frequent among giraffes than heterosexual coupling. Females normally have one calf, and give birth standing, with the newborn dropping up to 2 m (7 ft) to the ground, then standing up and suckling within 30 minutes.

COMMON HIPPOPOTAMUS
(SPECIES: HIPPOPOTAMUS AMPHIBIUS)

BEST SEEN: iSimangaliso, Kruger, Pilanesberg

                                                       VU

The most characteristic resident of Africa's rivers and freshwater lakes is the common hippo, whose purple-grey hairless hide, pink undersides and cheeks, barrel-like torso and stumpy legs render it unmistakable. Ears, eyes and nostrils are placed high on the skull, allowing it to spend most of its time submerged in the shallows. It feeds terrestrially, however, emerging between dusk and dawn to crop grass with its wide mouth, often ranging far from water in the process. The hippo is highly gregarious, living in pods of up to 30 members, and very territorial, with fights for dominance between males often resulting in serious injury or death. Contrary to appearance, the hippo is highly mobile on land and can easily attain a speed of above 32 kmph (20 mph). It can be very dangerous to humans, as it typically heads straight to the safety of the water when disturbed, mowing down anything in its path. The communal grunting of the hippo, a characteristic sound of waterside lodges, can be heard by day as well as after dark.

Hippos are poor swimmers, tending to stick to shallow water

IUCN status EN: Endangered; VU: Vulnerable; LC: Least Concern

The Cape mountain zebra has no shadow stripes

MOUNTAIN ZEBRA
(SPECIES: EQUUS ZEBRA)

BEST SEEN: Mountain Zebra, Goegap, Table Mountain

 EN

The mountain zebra is a vulnerable southern African endemic associated with dryish mountainous habitats up to 2,000 m (6,562 ft) above sea level. Two races are recognized, and regarded by some authorities as distinct species. The Cape mountain zebra is a *fynbos* endemic which was hunted close to extinction in the early 20th century, when the population bottlenecked at below 100 individuals, but has since bred up to an estimated population of 2,700. Hartmann's mountain zebra is near-endemic to Namibia, though a small South African population is protected within the Goegap Nature Reserve outside Springbok. In most respects, the mountain zebra is very similar to the South African race of plains zebra, from which it can be distinguished by the absence of shadow stripes, but it lives in smaller core herds which never form larger temporary aggregations.

The striping on a plains zebra reaches right under the belly

PLAINS ZEBRA
(SPECIES: EQUUS QUAGGA)

BEST SEEN: Kruger, Hluhluwe-Imfolozi, Sabi Sands

LC

More common than the mountain zebra, the plains zebra, or Burchell's zebra, is a grazer whose natural distribution ranges from Ethiopia to the Cape. The plains zebra is often seen in large ephemeral herds, but its core social unit is an aggressively defended non-territorial herd comprising one stallion, up to five mares and their respective foals. The purpose of the zebra's stripes is often cited as camouflage, breaking up the animal's outline in long grass, but this fails to explain their benefit in arid habitats. It is more likely that the striping is visually confusing to predators when the herd scatters. The quagga, a partially striped Western Cape endemic that was hunted to extinction in the early years of colonialism, is thought to have been a race of plain zebra (hence the Latin name *Equus quagga*).

Key to Field Guide icons see p68

Small Mammals

South Africa is best known for its rich megafauna, but the country also supports a fascinating variety of smaller and more obscure mammals. These range from diverse and highly conspicuous orders such as the rodents and bats, which keen observers are likely to encounter on a daily basis, to the more quirky and elusive aardvark and pangolin, all of which come close to topping the wish list of seasoned safari-goers.

FAMILY

Many of these animals are evolutionary one-offs. For instance, the aardvark is the only living member of the order Tubulidentata. By contrast, pigs belong to the same order as giraffes, camels and antelopes.

A pangolin, with its thick armour-plated scaling

GROUND PANGOLIN
(FAMILY: MANIDAE)

BEST SEEN: Kgalagadi

Most species: LC

Also known as scaly anteaters, pangolins are unobtrusive nocturnal insectivores whose name derives from the Malay *penguling*, a reference to their habit of curling into a tight ball when disturbed. The savannah-dwelling ground pangolin is the only species found in South Africa, where it is more or less confined to the northern border regions. Weighing up to 18 kg (40 lb), it is exceptionally unlikely to be seen in the wild.

Aardvarks use clawed feet to dig into termite mounds

AARDVARK
(SPECIES: ORYCTEROPUS AFER)

BEST SEEN: Sabi Sands, Kruger, Pilanesberg

LC

One of the most peculiar of African mammals, the aardvark – a Dutch name meaning earth pig – weighs up to 80 kg (176 lb). It is a shy, strictly nocturnal insectivore with a stout body, an arched back, pinkish skin, a heavy tail not unlike a kangaroo's and long upright ears. It uses an elongated snout and long, retractable sticky tongue to snaffle up as many as 50,000 termites in one night.

IUCN status LC: Least Concern

HYRAX
(ORDER: HYRACOIDEA)

BEST SEEN: Table Mountain, Mapungubwe, uKhahlamba-Drakensberg

                            All species: LC

Endemic to Africa, hyraxes are dwarfish relics of a once-prolific near-ungulate order more closely related to elephants than to any other living creature. The Cape rock hyrax (or dassie) *Procavia capensis* is a conspicuous resident of rocky slopes, where it lives in territorial family groups of up to 20 individuals. Confined to the forests of the eastern coastal belt, the seldom-seen southern tree hyrax *Dendrohyrax arboreus* is best known for its terrifying banshee-like call.

Hyraxes spend long periods basking in the sun

CAPE PORCUPINE
(SPECIES: HYSTRIX AFRICAEAUSTRALIS)

BEST SEEN: Widespread but seldom seen

LC

Porcupines are the largest of African rodents, though the species found in South Africa is not quite so bulky as its 27-kg (60-lb) East African counterpart. It is coated in long black-and-white quills, which occasionally betray its presence by rattling as it walks.

The long quills of the porcupine are modified hair

Fruitbats generally roost in colonies in trees

BATS
(ORDER: CHIROPTERA)

BEST SEEN: Common in most non-urban environments

Most species: Variable

Chiroptera (bats) is the second-most successful mammalian order, with 1,000-plus species globally. Although widely feared, no African bat sucks blood, and they play a vital ecological role in controlling flying insect populations. Small insect-eating bats are often seen hawking at dusk throughout South Africa, most commonly in game reserves and other relatively unspoilt habitats. The larger fruitbats tend to prefer forest and other wooded habitats, and are seldom seen in South Africa.

Th bushpig lives in dense forest and along rivers

BUSHPIG
(SPECIES: POTAMOCHOERUS LARVATUS)

BEST SEEN: Sabi Sands, Kruger, Hluhluwe-Imfolozi

LC

Larger, more hirsute and shorter-legged than the warthog, the bushpig is also fairly widespread in South Africa. It is less conspicuous as a result of its strictly nocturnal habits, its secretive nature and a preference for dense riverine and forested vegetation. The bushpig can be recognized by its small eyes, blunt snout, pointed, tufted ears and buckled toes. It has small tusks, and can be quite aggressive when cornered. It displays a high degree of colour variation, ranging from grey-brown to chestnut. Bushpigs are quite often seen after dark at the rest camp in Hluhluwe-Imfolozi Game Reserve, and you might well see traces of their foraging for roots on forest trails elsewhere in the country.

SPRINGHARE
(SPECIES: PEDETES CAPENSIS)

BEST SEEN: Kgalagadi, Augrabies Falls, Mapungubwe

LC

This peculiar and unmistakable rodent most resembles a miniature kangaroo, with powerful hind legs that enable it to cover up to 2 m (6 ft) in one bound. Sandy brown with a long black-tipped tail, it weighs up to 4 kg (9 lb) and is most likely to be seen after dark – initially as a pair of eyes bouncing around in the spotlight. By day, the springhare rests up in deep burrows in sandy soils, and is particularly common in the semiarid savannah of the Kalahari region.

The springhare, with its long black-tipped tail

COMMON WARTHOG
(SPECIES: PHACOCHOERUS AFRICANUS)

BEST SEEN: Kruger, Hluhluwe-Imfolozi, Pilanesberg

 LC

The most common and conspicuous of Africa's wild pigs, the warthog is a long-legged, slender-bodied swine that stands 80 cm (32 inches) high at the shoulder and weighs up to 150 kg (331 lb) in exceptional cases. It has an almost hairless grey coat, a long dorsal mane, upward-curving tusks and a trio of callus-like "warts" on its face. Family groups, a regular sight in many savannah reserves, are often seen trotting briskly away with long, thin tails stiffly erect. The warthog is an unfussy omnivore whose favoured food consists of roots and bulbs. It defends itself against predators by reversing into a burrow with tusks facing out aggressively. The common warthog's South African range is now confined to the north and east, but a similar-looking race of desert warthog *Phacochoerus aethiopicus*, also known from the Horn of Africa, inhabited the Cape until it was hunted out in the 1860s.

The tusks of the warthog are the largest of any swine

Key to Field Guide icons see p68

Antelopes

A constant of South Africa's wild places, antelopes thrive in every habitat from rainforest to desert. They range from the tiny blue duiker, which weighs about the same as a domestic cat, to the cattle-sized eland. Otherwise similar in appearance to deer, antelopes sport permanent horns rather than seasonal antlers. The family has its very own photogenic "Big Five", in the form of elands, kudu, gemsboks, sable antelopes and roan antelopes.

FAMILY

Antelopes split into two groups. The eland, greater kudu, nyala and bushbuck belong to the tribe Tragelaphini, more closely related to buffaloes than to other antelopes, which are split across six bovid subfamilies.

COMMON ELAND
(SPECIES: TAUROTRAGUS ORYX)

BEST SEEN: uKhahlamba-Drakensberg, Pilanesberg, Kgalagadi

LC

Also known as the Cape eland, Africa's largest antelope has a maximum shoulder height of 1.8 m (6 ft) and can weigh almost 950 kg (2,094 lb). The most overtly cow-like of the spiral-horned antelope, it is light tan in colour, with faint white vertical stripes, small unisex horns and a hefty dewlap. It moves in groups of about 10 animals, but larger parties are also seen. The eland was revered by the so-called Bushmen – hunter-gatherers who once inhabited South Africa – and is the animal most commonly depicted in their rock paintings.

The common eland, often depicted in rock paintings

The male greater kudu is unique in having horns that go into a full double spiral.

An adult male kudu sporting well-developed horns

GREATER KUDU
(SPECIES: TRAGELAPHUS STREPSICEROS)

BEST SEEN: Kruger, Pilanesberg, Mapungubwe

LC

The most magnificent of African antelopes, the greater kudu is second in stature only to the eland. It stands up to 1.5 m (5 ft) high and has a greyish coat with up to 10 vertical white stripes on each side. Males have massive double-spiralled horns. Small family parties are seen in dense woodland along dry-country watercourses. An accomplished jumper, it can clear fences twice its shoulder height. The greater kudu is the most common large antelope in unprotected parts of South Africa.

IUCN status VU: Vulnerable; LC: Least Concern

GEMSBOK (COMMON ORYX)
(SPECIES: ORYX GAZELLA)

BEST SEEN: Kgalagadi, Augrabies Falls, Pilanesberg

LC

This handsome dry-country antelope has a shoulder height of 1.2 m (4 ft), a cleanly marked grey, black and white coat, a long black tail and long straight horns that sweep back from the skull at the same angle as the forehead and muzzle. Seen in nomadic herds of up to 10 animals, it can survive without water for almost as long as a camel, obtaining all its needs from the plants it eats. It is naturally restricted to the more arid northwest of South Africa, but has also been introduced to the Pilanesberg National Park and other reserves outside that range.

The gemsbok, with its long straight horns

A lone sable antelope in woodland

SABLE ANTELOPE
(SPECIES: HIPPOTRAGUS NIGER)

BEST SEEN: Pilanesberg, Sabi Sands, Kruger (around Pretoriuskop and Letaba)

 LC

Among the largest and most handsome of antelopes, the male sable stands up to 1.4 m (4 ft 7 inches) at the shoulder and weighs up to 270 kg (595 lb). It has a jet-black coat offset by a white face, underbelly and rump, and its splendid decurved horns reach up to 1.4 m (4 ft 7 inches) in length. The female is less striking, with a chestnut-brown coat and shorter horns. Common elsewhere on the African continent, the sable is confined to the far northeast of South Africa, where it is very localized. Sightings are uncommon in Kruger National Park, but quite frequent in Pilanesberg.

ROAN ANTELOPE
(SPECIES: HIPPOTRAGUS EQUINUS)

BEST SEEN: Kruger (Letaba area), Pilanesberg

 LC

Similar in proportions to the sable antelope, the roan has short, decurved horns and a fawn-grey coat with a pale belly and light mane. Its South African distribution is comparable to that of the sable, but it is probably less common, with the Pilanesberg National Park offering perhaps the best opportunity of a sighting in the wild. Captive populations of roan are also held on some private ranches in the north of the country. Roan form groups of five to 15 animals, with a dominant male. Fighting among males for control of the herd is not uncommon. The closely related bluebuck is a *fynbos* endemic that was hunted to extinction in the 19th century and now survives only in the form of a few mounted specimens in museums.

The roan antelope, less common than the sable

COMMON WATERBUCK
(SPECIES: KOBUS ELLIPSIPRYMNUS)

BEST SEEN: Kruger, iSimangaliso, Hluhluwe-Imfolozi

VU

The largest and most distinctive member of the kob family, the common waterbuck stands up to 1.3 m (4 ft 3 inches) at the shoulder and weighs up to 240 kg (529 lb). It is recognized by its shaggy grey-brown to chestnut coat (which darkens with age), the male's large lyre-shaped horns, and the bold white inverted U-mark on its rump. Waterbuck are usually found in open grassland or woodland – almost always, as the name suggests, in the vicinity of standing water, although they spend relatively little time actually in the water. Herds consist of up to 10 individuals lorded over by a dominant male, who will defend his territory and mating rights with vigorous aggression. In his prime, a male will control a territory of around 120 hectares (297 acres).

A pair of common waterbucks

Key to Field Guide icons *see p68*

The impala, a fast runner and prodigious jumper

IMPALA
(SPECIES: AEPYCEROS MELAMPUS)

BEST SEEN: Kruger, Hluhluwe-Imfolozi, Madikwe

☐ ⋀⋀ ⚘   LC

A relative of the wildebeest, this elegantly proportioned medium-sized antelope has a chestnut coat with black-and-white stripes on the rump and tail. Males have magnificent black ringed horns. Impalas are usually seen in herds of over 100, dominated numerically by females and young. They are agile jumpers, and herds often jump in all directions to confuse predators. They are by far the commonest antelope in the Kruger National Park, whose impala population exceeds 100,000, and are also prolific in bush habitats elsewhere in the northeast, but don't occur naturally in the rest of the country. The much rarer black impala owes its colouration to a recessive gene.

RED HARTEBEEST
(SPECIES: ALCELAPHUS BUSELAPHUS)

BEST SEEN: Kgalagadi, Madikwe, Pilanesberg

☐ ⋀⋀ ⚘   LC

One of the more conspicuous large antelopes in the tropical grasslands of Africa, the hartebeest is similar in height to the related wildebeests, with large shoulders, a backward-sloping back, slender torso, pale yellow-brown coat, and smallish unisex horns whose somewhat heart-shaped appearance may be alluded to in its name (which is Dutch in origin). Males frequently climb on termite hills to scan, as a display of territorial dominance. Half a dozen races are recognized, the one present in South Africa being the red hartebeest. It only occurs naturally in the north, on the border with Botswana, but is farmed in many other parts of the country.

Red hartebeest, with its distinctive narrow face

Tsessebe, mainly found in open grassland

TSESSEBE
(SPECIES: DAMALISCUS LUNATUS)

BEST SEEN: Kruger (north only)

☐ ⋀⋀   LC

Known as the topi or tiang elsewhere in its range, the tsessebe comes across as a darker and glossier variation of the red hartebeest, with which it shares similar habits and a habitat preference for open grassland. It is dark brown in general colouration, with some black on the flanks and snout, and striking yellow lower legs. It is very rare in South Africa, with a natural range more or less confined to the Kruger National Park, where it is most likely to be seen on the eastern basaltic plains north of the Olifants River.

BLESBOK/BONTEBOK
(SPECIES: DAMALISCUS PYGARGUS)

BEST SEEN: Bontebok, Table Mountain, Golden Gate

☐ ⋀⋀ ⚘   LC

Endemic to South Africa, the blesbok and bontebok are smaller and more boldly marked relatives of the tsessebe that freely interbreed where their ranges overlap and are thus regarded as races of the same species. The bontebok is a *fynbos* endemic that was hunted to within 100 individuals of extinction prior to the creation of the eponymous national park in the 1930s, but since then the population has recovered to the thousands. The blesbok is a more numerous resident of highveld grassland in the centre of the country. Both are dark brown with white faces and legs.

Bontebok, found only in South Africa

Blue wildebeest running

BLUE WILDEBEEST
(SPECIES: CONNOCHAETES TAURINUS)

BEST SEEN: Kruger, Hluhluwe-Imfolozi, Sabi Sands

 LC

Although common in southern-hemisphere grassland habitats from the Serengeti-Mara to KwaZulu-Natal, the blue wildebeest is totally absent north of the equator. It is a highly gregarious creature, particularly in areas where it follows an annual migration, often assembling in groups of several hundred. Its dark grey-brown coat precludes confusion with other antelope, but at a distance it could be mistaken for a buffalo, although its slighter build and shaggy beard are distinguishing features.

A lone bushbuck grazing in a forest clearing

BUSHBUCK
(SPECIES: TRAGELAPHUS SCRIPTUS)

BEST SEEN: Kruger, Hluhluwe-Imfolozi, uKhahlamba-Drakensberg

 LC

The closest thing in Africa to a Bambi lookalike, the bushbuck is a widespread medium-sized antelope of forest and riparian woodland. The male is usually dark brown or chestnut in colour, while the more petite female is generally pale red-brown. Both sexes have white throat patches, and a variable combination of white spots and sometimes stripes on the coat. The bushbuck usually moves singly or in pairs and, although common, tends to be rather furtive.

BLACK WILDEBEEST
(SPECIES: CONNOCHAETES GNOU)

BEST SEEN: Golden Gate

LC

Another South African endemic hunted close to extinction by early European settlers, the black wildebeest or white-tailed gnu is rather more handsome than the more widespread blue wildebeest, from which it is most easily distinguished by its off-white mane and tail. Some authorities regard it as extinct in the wild, since the only surviving herds are farmed or semi-captive, but the population of several thousand is high enough for it to be IUCN-listed in the "Least Concern" category. It might be seen from the roadside on farmland anywhere in the central highveld northwest of Lesotho.

Black wildebeest bull

NYALA
(SPECIES: TRAGELAPHUS ANGASII)

BEST SEEN: Hluhluwe-Imfolozi, Kruger, iSimangaliso

LC

Intermediate in size between the related greater kudu *(see p96)* and bushbuck, the nyala typically occurs in small family groups in thicketed habitats close to water. The male is truly spectacular – dark chestnut-grey in general colouration, but with a grey-black leonine mane, light white stripes along the sides, yellow leg stockings and handsome lyre-shaped horns that can grow to a length of 80 cm (2 ft 8 inches). Hunted to near-extinction in most of its former range, the nyala would probably be listed as endangered were it not for the population of 25,000 animals (70 per cent of the global total) in northern KwaZulu-Natal.

The spectacular-looking male nyala

Key to Field Guide icons *see p68*

SPRINGBOK
(SPECIES: ANTIDORCAS MARSUPIALIS)

BEST SEEN: Kgalagadi, Augrabies Falls, Goegap

 LC

South Africa's national animal, the springbok is the only gazelle (that is, antelope of the genus *Gazella*, or related genera) found south of the Zambezi. It strongly resembles the East African "Tommy" (Thomson's gazelle), with fawn upperparts and creamy belly separated by a black side-stripe. Despite its iconic status, it is far rarer than it was in the 18th century; today it is largely confined to the extreme northwest of the country.

SUNI
(SPECIES: NEOTRAGUS MOSCHATUS)

BEST SEEN: Phinda, iSimangaliso, Ndumo

 LC

The suni is a small antelope of coastal forests and thickets whose posture, colouration and habits make it easy to confuse with a duiker. It has a more freckled coat than any duiker, however, and on close inspection it can also be distinguished by its backward-sweeping horns, large and almost rabbit-like ears, pronounced facial glands, and habit of flicking its black-and-white tail from side to side, rather than up and down.

COMMON DUIKER
(SPECIES: SYLVICAPRA GRIMMIA)

BEST SEEN: Kruger, Pilanesberg, uKhahlamba-Drakensberg

 LC

The least typical but most widespread and conspicuous of Africa's 18 duiker species, the common or grey duiker is a variably coloured resident of wooded savannah habitats that may be seen almost any-where in South Africa apart from forest interiors. Most often seen in pairs, it could be confused with steenbok, but it is generally greyer. The duiker has a unique identifier in the form of a black tuft of hair that divides its horns.

BLUE DUIKER
(SPECIES: PHILANTOMBA MONTICOLA)

BEST SEEN: Eshowe, Phinda, iSimangaliso

 LC

A widespread but shy resident of coastal forests, the blue duiker is the smallest South African antelope, with a height of about 35 cm (14 inches) and a weight of 5 kg (11 lb). It is one of a group of hunch-backed forest-dwellers that rank as perhaps the most elusive and least well under-stood of East African antelope. Seldom seen, it can be distin-guished by its white under-tail, which it flicks regularly.

NATAL RED DUIKER
(SPECIES: CEPHALOPHUS NATALENSIS)

BEST SEEN: Hluhluwe-Imfolozi, Phinda, iSimangaliso

 VU

The 46-cm- (18-inch-) tall Natal red duiker is among the South African representatives of a cluster of red duiker species, most of which are deep chestnut in colour with a white tail and black snout patch. A specialized forest-dweller confined to the eastern coastal littoral, it is liable to be confused only with the blue duiker or the suni, but it is more widespread than either and, when seen clearly, its rich colouration distinguishes it.

KLIPSPRINGER
(SPECIES: OREOTRAGUS OREOTRAGUS)

BEST SEEN: Mapungubwe, uKhahlamba-Drakensberg, Augrabies Falls

 LC

A relict of an ancient antelope lineage, the klipspringer (rock jumper) boasts several unusual adaptations to its mountain-ous habitat. Binocular vision enables it to gauge jumping distances accurately, it has a unique ability to walk on hoof tips, and its hollow fur insulates at high altitude. Pairs bond for life, and both sexes have a grizzled grey-brown coat, short forward-curving horns and an arched back.

IUCN status VU: Vulnerable; LC: Least Concern

REEDBUCK
(SPECIES: REDUNCA)

BEST SEEN: iSimangaliso, Kruger, uKhahlamba-Drakensberg

 LC

Two species of reedbuck occur in South Africa – the common and the mountain. Both are pale, skittish and lightly built grassland-dwellers with white underbellies and small horns. The common reedbuck, a lowland and mid-altitude species with short, forward-curving horns, is exceptionally common in iSimangaliso along the road to Cape Vidal. The chunkier and greyer mountain reedbuck is commonest in uKhahlamba-Drakensberg.

ORIBI
(SPECIES: OUREBIA OUREBI)

BEST SEEN: uKhahlamba-Drakensberg, KwaZulu-Natal (Midlands)

 LC

A patchily distributed small-to medium-sized antelope, the oribi has a shoulder height of around 50 cm (20 inches) and small straight unisex horns. It has a sandy coat with a white belly and can be recognized by the round black glandular patch below its ears. Typically seen in pairs or small herds in tall open grass, it tends to draw attention to itself with a trademark sneezing alarm call before rapidly fleeing.

STEENBOK
(SPECIES: RAPHICERUS CAMPESTRIS)

BEST SEEN: Kruger, Pilanesberg, Hluhluwe-Imfolozi

 LC

Somewhat resembling a scaled-down version of the oribi, the steenbok is a small antelope with tan upperparts, white underbelly and short straight horns. However, it tends to prefer thicker vegetation than the oribi, and its smaller size means it is more likely to be mistaken for a duiker. The name steenbok is Afrikaans for stone buck, and refers not to the animal's habitat, but to its habit of "freezing" when disturbed.

CAPE GRYSBOK
(SPECIES: RAPHICERUS MELANOTUS)

BEST SEEN: Table Mountain, De Hoop, Cedarberg Mountains

 LC

Endemic to *fynbos* and other thicket habitats in the Western and Eastern Cape, the Cape grysbok can be distinguished from other small antelope in its geographic range by its larger size, chunky build, tailless appearance and the combination of a flecked russet coat and white circles around the eyes. Despite being somewhat localized, it remains reasonably common in suitable habitats in the Western and Eastern Cape.

SHARPE'S GRYSBOK
(SPECIES: RAPHICERUS SHARPEI)

BEST SEEN: Kruger (central and northern regions), Mapungubwe

 LC

The core range of Sharpe's grysbok, the tropical counter-part to the Cape grysbok, lies north of the Limpopo, but it is sparsely distributed in suitable habitats – thickets and rocky slopes – in parts of Kruger National Park. The reddish, white-flecked coat and unusual grazing posture, with white rump tilted skywards, preclude confusion with other antelope in its range. Very timid, it sometimes retreats into aardvark burrows when threatened.

GREY RHEBOK
(SPECIES: PELEA CAPREOLUS)

BEST SEEN: uKhahlamba-Drakensberg, Mountain Zebra, Bontebok

 LC

This South African endemic is superficially similar to the mountain reedbuck, but has a woollier grey coat, a longer neck and snout, and distinctive elongated hare-like ears. Because it has several goat-like adaptations, it is something of a taxonomic enigma. Around 20 per cent of the global population lives in the uKhahlamba-Drakensberg, and it is commonly depicted in that park's ancient rock art.

Key to Field Guide icons *see p68*

Amphibians and Reptiles

Amphibians and reptiles tend to get a lot of bad press, and not entirely without reason, considering the Nile crocodile kills dozens of villagers annually and several snake species can inflict lethal bites. However, most reptiles are harmless to people and of great ecological value. These cold-blooded creatures maintain their body heat using external sources, for instance by basking in the sun. They are therefore prolific in warm climates and tend to be poorly represented at high altitudes.

AFRICAN BULLFROG
(SPECIES: PYXICEPHALUS ADSPERSUS)

LC

South Africa's largest frog species is an aggressive carnivore that weighs up to 2 kg (4 lb) and takes prey as large as rats. During the rains, it emits a memorable medley of lusty bellows and grunts. In the dry season it estivates, burying itself in a subterranean cocoon for months on end.

TREE FROGS
(FAMILY: HYPEROLIIDAE)

Variable

Africa's most diverse frog family, found in moist woodland habitats, tree frogs are small and brightly coloured, with long broad-tipped toes used to climb trees and reeds. A common species is the bubbling kassina, whose popping chorus is among the most wondrous of African sounds.

SKINKS
(FAMILY: SCINCIDAE)

Variable

Represented in South Africa by over a dozen species, skinks are small fleet-footed lizards with slender bodies, long tails and dark scaling. Among the more visible species are the variable, striped and rainbow skinks of the genus *Mabuya*, most of which are associated with rocks.

GECKOES
(FAMILY: GEKKONIDAE)

NE

The most diverse African lizard family, geckoes have lidless bug-eyes for nocturnal hunting and adhesive toes that allow them to run upside-down on smooth surfaces. Most familiar is the common house gecko, a translucent white lizard that can be seen in safari lodges in the Kruger area.

CHAMELEONS
(FAMILY: CHAMAELEONIDAE)

NE

These charismatic lizards are known for their colour changes (caused by mood rather than background), independently swivelling eyes and long sticky tongues that uncoil to lunge at insects. Most common is the flap-necked chameleon, but there are also several endemic dwarf chameleons.

AGAMAS
(FAMILY: AGAMIDAE)

NE

Agamas are medium to large lizards with bright plastic-looking scales – blue, purple, red or orange, depending on the species. The flattened head is generally differently coloured from the torso. Often observed basking on rocks, the male red-headed agama is particularly spectacular.

IUCN status LC: Least Concern; NE: Not Evaluated

HARMLESS SNAKES

Of the 120 snake species recorded in South Africa, only eight are classed as highly venomous. Most of the others are entirely harmless. Among the more common of these benign slitherers, snakes of the genus *Philothamnus* are generally bright green with large dark eyes, and are often seen near water. The widespread rhombic egg-eater, sometimes mistaken for a puff adder, can dislocate its jaws to swallow an egg whole, regurgitating the crushed shell in a neat package.

Rhombic egg-eater, a non-venomous snake

AFRICAN ROCK PYTHON
(SPECIES: PYTHON SEBAE)

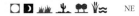 NE

Africa's largest snake, this python can reach lengths of 6 m (20 ft), and is very likely to be seen on safari. It is non-venomous, wrapping its body around its prey, swallowing it whole and slumbering for weeks or months while the digestive juices do their work.

MAMBAS
(GENUS: DENDROASPIS SPP)

 NE

Mambas are fast-moving and widely feared snakes that generally attack only when cornered. The 4-m (12-ft) black mamba, Africa's largest venomous snake, has a distinctive coffin-shaped head. The green mamba is smaller and shyer. Bites are rare but the venom is fatal.

COBRAS
(GENUS: NAJA SPP)

 NE

Cobras are long snakes – up to 3 m (10 ft) – whose trademark hoods open in warning when they raise their head to strike or spit venom into the target's eye. Bites are fatal, but spitting, though it can result in temporary blindness, causes little long-term damage if the venom is diluted with water.

BOOMSLANG
(SPECIES: DISPHOLIDUS TYPUS)

 NE

As its Afrikaans name suggests, the boomslang (tree snake) is almost exclusively arboreal. It is generally green in colour, but may also be brown or olive. Theoretically the most toxic of African snakes, it is back-fanged and passive, and, except on snake handlers, it has never inflicted a fatal bite.

ADDERS AND VIPERS
(FAMILY: VIPERIDAE)

 Variable

The puff adder's notoriously sluggish disposition means that it is more frequently disturbed than any other venomous snake – and is thus responsible for more bites than other species. Thickset and cryptically marked, it is most common in rocky areas, but also occurs in most bush habitats.

MONITORS
(FAMILY: VARANIDAE)

 NE

Africa's largest lizard, the Nile monitor can grow to be 3 m (10 ft) long, and is often seen along river margins. The closely related savannah monitor is a little smaller in size. Both species feed on meat and carrion and, though not normally dangerous, can inflict a nasty bite if cornered.

Key to Field Guide icons *see p68*

NILE CROCODILE
(SPECIES: CROCODYLUS NILOTICUS)

BEST SEEN: Kruger, iSimangaliso, Ndumo

    LC

Crocodiles have lurked in the lakes and rivers of Africa for at least 150 million years, and are the nearest thing alive to a relict of the Jurassic Era, as they are more closely related to dinosaurs than to any living creature. South Africa is home to the Nile crocodile, Africa's bulkiest and longest-lived predator, that grows to a maximum recorded length of 8 m (26 ft), weighs up to 1,000 kg (2,205 lb) and boasts a lifespan similar to that of humans. It occurs naturally in freshwater habitats, basking open-mouthed on the sandbanks before it slips, silent and sinister, into the water on the approach of a boat. The St Lucia Estuary in iSimangaliso Wetland Park harbours the country's densest population of Nile crocodiles, but they are also common in the rivers of the Kruger National Park.

A female lays up to 100 hard-shelled eggs in a small hole, covers them to protect them from predators, then returns three months later to carry the hatchlings to the water, where she leaves them to fend for themselves. The Nile crocodile feeds mainly on fish, but occasionally drags a mammal as large as a lion into the water. Several crocodile farms in South Africa breed these reptiles for their valuable hide, the best-known being located on the outskirts of St Lucia town.

The hide of dark, heavy scales is valued by commercial poachers to make handbags, shoes and other leather goods.

A crocodile can stay submerged in water without drawing breath for 45–60 minutes.

A Nile crocodile has about 80 teeth which are shed and replaced twice annually.

Crocodiles make for a primeval sight as they bask on a bank

TORTOISES
(FAMILY: TESTUDINIDAE)

BEST SEEN: Kruger, Addo Elephant, Pilanesberg

    Most species: Variable

The term tortoise is used to describe any terrestrial chelonian, an order of shelled reptiles that also includes freshwater terrapins and marine turtles. The most visible species on safari is the leopard tortoise, which is South Africa's largest terrestrial chelonian, occasionally weighing as much as 40 kg (88 lb). It can be recognized by the tall, domed, gold-and-black-mottled shell after which it is named. Often seen inching along game-reserve roads, the leopard tortoise has a lifespan of 50 years and few natural enemies, but its lack of mobility makes it susceptible to fast-spreading bush fires. It is also frequently hunted by local people. Another dozen species are recognized in South Africa, all but one of them endemic to the country. At up to 9 cm (3½ inches) long, the speckled padloper (literally, "roadwalker"), a Karoo endemic, is the world's smallest chelonian.

Like other reptiles, the leopard tortoise has scaled skin

IUCN status CE: Critically Endangered; EN: Endangered; LC: Least Concern

The long muscular tail is used to propel and steer through the water.

TERRAPINS
(FAMILY: PELOMEDUSIDAE)

BEST SEEN: iSimangaliso, Kruger, Ndumo

 Most species: LC

South Africa is home to four freshwater terrapin species, most of which are flatter and a plainer brown than any of the region's tortoises. They are usually seen in or close to water, sunning on partially submerged rocks or dead logs, or peering out from roadside puddles. Far and away the most common and widespread species is the marsh terrapin, which inhabits waterholes, puddles and other stagnant waterbodies in savannah habitats, but often wanders considerable distances on land in rainy weather. It estivates during the dry season, burying itself deep in mud only to re-emerge after the first rains – hence the local legend that terrapins drop from the sky during storms.

Marsh terrapin basking in the sun

Hawksbill turtle swimming gracefully through the reefs

MARINE TURTLES
(FAMILY: CHELONIOIDEA)

BEST SEEN: iSimangaliso

Most species: CE or EN

Five of the world's seven turtle species occur along the South African coast, and all are much larger than any indigenous tortoises or terrapins. Two species, the leatherback and loggerhead, breed on the beaches of northern KwaZulu-Natal, while the other three (olive ridley, hawksbill and green turtle, the latter named for the colour of its fat) are visitors that breed further to the north. An individual turtle lays several hundred eggs in the sand every season. After two months of incubation, the hatchlings make their way towards the sea, whose temperature will affect their sex – the cooler it is, the higher the proportion of males. In the late 19th century, marine turtles were common to abundant throughout their natural habitat, with some populations numbering well into the millions. Today, as a result of poaching and pollution, all but one species is classed as either endangered or critically endangered.

Key to Field Guide icons *see p68*

Birds

With a national checklist of 858 species, South Africa supports an exceptionally varied avifauna. The most prolific areas for birding are in the northeast (especially Kruger National Park, Ndumo Game Reserve and iSimangaliso Wetland Park), where enthusiasts may easily see up to 100 species in a day. Avian diversity is greatest from September to April, when migrants arrive and residents shed their drab plumage to emerge in brilliant breeding colours.

FAMILY

A growing body of genetic and fossil evidence suggests birds are most properly placed with crocodiles as the only living members of the Archosauria, a group that also includes the extinct dinosaurs.

The marabou, with a unique fleshy neck pouch

MARABOU STORK
(SPECIES: LEPTOPTILOS CRUMENIFERUS)

RELATIVES: saddle-billed stork, yellow-billed stork, open-billed stork

LC

A fabulously ungainly omnivore that stands 1.5 m (5 ft) tall, the marabou is identified by its scabrous bald head and inflatable flesh-coloured neck pouch. The most habitat-tolerant of South Africa's eight stork species, it may be seen near water, alongside vultures at a kill, or in urban environments. Its South African range is largely confined to the Kruger Park and surrounds.

HADEDA IBIS
(SPECIES: BOSTRYCHIA HAGEDASH)

RELATIVES: sacred ibis, glossy ibis, Southern bald ibis

LC

A characteristic bird of suburban lawns, hotel gardens and grassy wetlands, the hadeda is best known for its harsh onomatopoeic cackle, most often emitted on takeoff or in flight. Like other ibises, it is a robustly built bird that uses its long decurved bill to probe for snails and other invertebrates. Also common is the sacred ibis, which was revered and frequently mummified in ancient Egypt. The endemic Southern bald ibis is scarcer.

Hadeda ibis, known for its raucous "ha-ha-hadeda" call

Egyptian goose, seen in large lakes and open water

EGYPTIAN GOOSE
(SPECIES: ALOPOCHEN AEGYPTIACUS)

RELATIVES: spur-winged goose, yellow-billed duck, white-faced whistling duck

LC

South Africa supports 19 species of resident and migrant waterfowl, of which the largest is the spur-winged goose, but the most conspicuous is the ubiquitous Egyptian goose – a large rufous-brown bird that is very assertive and perpetually honking. Waterfowl populations tend to be densest during the European winter, when the Palaearctic migrants arrive.

AFRICAN DARTER
(SPECIES: ANHINGA RUFA)

RELATIVES: white-breasted cormorant, long-tailed cormorant, African finfoot

LC

Frequently seen perching on bare branches overhanging rivers and lakes, the African darter or snakebird looks like a distended cormorant, with a kinked serpentine neck almost as long as its torso and striking russet patches that glow off-gold in the right light. The gregarious, boldly marked white-breasted cormorant and the more solitary long-tailed cormorant are also common.

The African darter has a distinctive snake-like neck

IUCN status VU: Vulnerable; LC: Least Concern

Pelicans often roost communally on lakeshores

GREAT WHITE PELICAN
(SPECIES: PELECANUS ONOCROTALUS)

RELATIVES: pink-backed pelican

 LC

Easily recognized by their bulk, enormous wingspan and larder-like bills, South Africa's two pelican species are its largest water-associated birds. Most common is the great white pelican, an almost all-white bird with a large yellow pouch hanging from its long bill and black underwings that are clearly visible in flight. The smaller and more sparsely distributed pink-backed pelican has a pink-grey back and dark grey flight feathers. Both species are rather localized in South Africa, but might be seen on any large lake in synchronized flotillas of around six to 12 individuals.

Goliaths have the largest wingspan of any African heron

GOLIATH HERON
(SPECIES: ARDEA GOLIATH)

RELATIVES: grey heron, black-headed heron, great white egret, cattle egret

 LC

The herons and egrets of the Ardeidae family are among South Africa's most distinctive waterbirds. Most are tall and long-necked, and use their sharp, elongated bills to spear fish, frogs and other prey. The star of the group is the goliath heron, which stands up to 1.5 m (5 ft) tall and is commonest in the north and east. More prevalent, however, are the familiar Eurasian grey heron, black-headed heron and cattle egret.

GREATER FLAMINGO
(SPECIES: PHOENICOPTERUS ROSEUS)

RELATIVES: lesser flamingo

 LC

Represented by two species in South Africa, both of which are associated with flat, shallow pans, flamingos are pink-tinged birds that feed on algae and microscopic fauna, which are sifted through filters in their unique down-turned bills. They are very sensitive to water levels and chemical composition, and will easily relocate. The greater flamingo is the larger of the two species found in South Africa, but it is outnumbered by the lesser flamingo, which is much pinker, especially on the bill.

Flamingos, the most gregarious of waterbirds

BLUE CRANE
(SPECIES: ANTHROPOIDES PARADISEA)

RELATIVES: grey crowned crane, wattled crane

VU

South Africa's national bird stands up to 1.2 m (4 ft) tall and has a uniform silvery-blue plumage broken only by its white bulbous forehead and long black tail plumes. This handsome near-endemic has a declining population currently estimated at around 20,000. The blue crane is most often seen in grasslands and swampy habitats in the uKhahlamba-Drakensberg foothills, alongside the grey crowned and wattled cranes.

The blue crane, once revered by Zulu and Xhosa royalty

Key to Field Guide icons *see p68*

The lappet-faced vulture is usually seen singly or in pairs

LAPPET-FACED VULTURE
(SPECIES: TORGOS TRACHELIOTOS)

RELATIVES: white-backed vulture, hooded vulture, Cape vulture

   VU

Africa's largest raptor is a truly impressive bird, with a bald pink head, a massive blue-and-ivory bill and heavy black wings that spread open like a cape, reinforcing its menacing demeanour. It often shares kills with the region's five other carrion-eating vulture species, squabbling and squawking over the spoils. Capable of soaring on thermals for hours on end, this vulture ranks among the world's most powerful fliers, and its vision is practically unmatched in the animal kingdom. It is also unexpectedly fastidious, and will spend hours preening itself after feeding.

The broad-winged jackal buzzard in flight

JACKAL BUZZARD
(SPECIES: BUTEO RUFOFUSCUS)

RELATIVES: yellow-billed kite, chanting goshawk, harrier hawk

   LC

Named for its jackal-like call, this handsome, medium-large raptor has a black back and head, a striking chestnut breast (though some individuals are blotched black and white), a white throat band and a distinctive bright orange-red tail. Like other buzzards, it has long, broad wings, a relatively short tail and a stocky build. Probably the commonest large resident raptor in and around the uKhahlamba-Drakensberg, it is outnumbered by the duller migrant steppe buzzard in the northern winter.

IUCN status VU: Vulnerable; LC: Least Concern

AFRICAN FISH EAGLE
(SPECIES: HAKLIAEETUS VOCIFER)

RELATIVES: martial eagle, bateleur, Verreaux's eagle

     LC

Among the most evocative sounds of the bush is the far-carrying call of the African fish eagle, a high, piercing banshee wail delivered in duet, with both birds throwing back their heads dramatically. This strongly monogamous eagle is visually striking and distinctive, with black-and-white feathering against a rich chestnut belly and hooked yellow bill. It is a conspicuous resident of rivers and lakes, perching high in the branches of tall fringing trees, or soaring above the water for long periods, sweeping down occasionally to scoop a fish into its talons. It might be confused with another water-associated raptor, the osprey.

African fish eagles perch openly in the vicinity of water

VERREAUX'S EAGLE-OWL
(SPECIES: BUBO LACTEUS)

RELATIVES: barn owl, spotted eagle-owl, scops owl

   LC

Also known as the giant eagle-owl, Africa's largest nocturnal bird is most often seen near the large acacia trees in which it likes to breed. It is identified by its black eyes with pinkish eyelids that it closes during diurnal rest, and distinguish-ed from the similarly proportioned Pel's fishing owl by its grey-brown feathering, crested ears and bold black facial disk marks. Usually unob-trusive, it is sometimes heard hooting at night. As with other owls, it is feared as a harbinger of death in many South African cultures.

Verreaux's eagle-owls stand more than 60 cm (2 ft) tall

The secretary bird, the world's most atypical raptor

SECRETARY BIRD
(SPECIES: SAGITTARIUS SERPENTARIUS)

RELATIVES: no close relatives, affinities uncertain

 LC

A bizarre grassland bird with long skinny legs, a slender grey torso, long black tail and bare red face-mask, the 1.5-m- (5-ft-) tall secretary bird may have been named for its flaccid black crest, which recalls the quills used by Victorian secretaries. It is also claimed that "secretary" is a corruption of the Arabic *saqr-et-tair* (hunting bird). The family to which it belongs is thought to be ancestral to all modern eagles, buzzards and vultures. A terrestrial hunter, it feeds on snakes and lizards, which it stamps to death in a flailing dance ritual. It roosts in trees, but otherwise flies only when disturbed.

The flightless ostrich is associated with open landscapes

COMMON OSTRICH
(SPECIES: STRUTHIO CAMELUS)

RELATIVES: no close relatives in South Africa

LC

At a height of 2 m (7 ft 6 inches) and weighing more than 100 kg (220 lb), ostriches are the world's largest birds. Two very similar species are recognized, but the common ostrich (which has pink legs, as opposed to the Somali ostrich's blue legs) is the only one to occur in South Africa. A familiar resident of protected grassland areas, the larger male has a handsome black-and-white plumage, while the female is smaller and duller. Ostriches are farmed in the Oudtshoorn area (and elsewhere) for their feathers, eggs and low-cholesterol meat.

SOUTHERN GROUND HORNBILL
(SPECIES: BUCORVUS CAFER)

RELATIVES: trumpeter hornbill, silvery-cheeked hornbill, crowned hornbill

 LC

Ground hornbills are rather fantastic turkey lookalikes, with black feathers, white underwings, large casqued bills, conspicuous red throat and eye wattles, and long fluttering eyelashes. They are typically seen marching along in small family parties in open habitats, probing the ground for insects. Despite their terrestrial habits, they are strong fliers. Their low, booming call is most often heard shortly after dusk. The southern ground hornbill is confined to the eastern part of the country, where it is most common in protected savannah and woodland habitats, in particular the Kruger National Park and Sabi Sands.

The southern ground hornbill, with large red wattles

KORI BUSTARD
(SPECIES: ARDEOTIS KORI)

RELATIVES: Stanley's bustard, black-bellied korhaan, black korhaan

LC

Loosely related to cranes but more sturdily built, bustards and korhaans are medium to large ground birds associated with open habitats. The most conspicuous species is the kori bustard, the world's heaviest flying bird, weighing up to 12.5 kg (28 lb) and standing about 1.3 m (4 ft 3 inches) tall. Usually rather measured and stately in demeanour, it performs a manic courtship dance, raising and fanning its tail and flapping its wings up and down in apparent agitation.

The large size of the kori bustard renders it unique

Key to Field Guide icons *see p68*

HELMETED GUINEAFOWL
(SPECIES: NUMIDA MELEAGRIS)

RELATIVES: crested guineafowl, Swainson's francolin, coqui francolin

 LC

Guineafowl are large, gregarious ground birds with spotted white-on-grey feathers and blue heads. The distinctive helmeted guineafowl is common everywhere from Kirstenbosch Botanical Garden to the Kruger National Park. The striking crested guineafowl, with its "bad hair day" head-plumes, is restricted to forest and riparian woodland in the northeast of the country.

HAMERKOP
(SPECIES: SCOPUS UMBRETTA)

RELATIVES: no close relatives, affinities uncertain

 LC

The sole member of its family, the hamerkop is a rusty brown, rook-sized bird whose long, flattened bill and angular crest combine to create its hammer-headed appearance. This bird's proverbial massive and amorphous nest is normally constructed untidily over several months in a tree fork close to the water, and is made of litter, branches, mud and other natural and artificial objects.

AFRICAN JACANA
(SPECIES: ACTOPHILORNIS AFRICANUS)

RELATIVES: blacksmith plover, pied avocet, crowned plover

 LC

Also known as the lily-trotter, the African jacana is one of South Africa's most characteristic waterbirds, usually associated with lily pads and other floating vegetation, on which it is able to walk thanks to its exceptionally far-spreading toes. An unmistakable and very attractive bird, it has a rich chestnut torso and wings, white neck, black cap and blue bill and frontal shield.

YELLOW-BILLED HORNBILL
(SPECIES: TOCKUS FLAVIROSTRIS)

RELATIVES: African grey hornbill, red-billed hornbill

 LC

Often seen in rest camps and picnic sites in Kruger National Park, typical savannah hornbills of the genus *Tockus* are clownish birds with heavy decurved bills. One of the more common species is the yellow-billed hornbill. Most nest in holes in tree trunks. During the incubation period, the female plasters the entrance to seal herself in; the male feeds her through a slit until the eggs hatch.

CAPE SUGARBIRD
(SPECIES: PROMEROPS CAFER)

RELATIVES: Gurney's sugarbird

 LC

The larger of two species in the family Promeropidae, the Cape sugarbird is a striking nectar-eater (especially partial to flowering proteas) with a sunbird-like bill, orange chest, yellow vent and graduated tail that can be almost three times longer than the torso in the male. The similar but shorter-tailed Gurney's sugarbird inhabits the uKhahlamba-Drakensberg and escarpment region, with a range that extends into Zimbabwe.

AFRICAN HOOPOE
(SPECIES: UPAPA AFRICANA)

RELATIVES: green woodhoopoe, common scimitar-bill

LC

The African hoopoe is a handsome bird with orange, black and white colouration and a crest that is very striking when held erect. Seen singly or in pairs, it is most common in park-like habitats and hotel gardens, where it feeds on the lawn, poking around for insects with its long, curved bill. Its closest relatives are woodhoopoes – glossy-black birds with long tails and decurved bills.

GREY GO-AWAY BIRD
(SPECIES: CORYTHAIXOIDES CONCOLOR)

RELATIVES: Knysna loerie, purple-crested loerie

 LC

Endemic to Africa, go-away birds and loeries are vocal frugivores with elongated bodies, long tails and prominent crests. The grey go-away bird is named for its explosive onomatopoeic call. Far more beautiful are the green-and-red Knysna and purple-crested loeries. The former inhabits eastern coastal and montane forests; the latter is associated more with riparian woodland.

LILAC-BREASTED ROLLER
(SPECIES: CORACIUS CAUDATA)

RELATIVES: broad-billed roller, Eurasian roller, racket-tailed roller

 LC

One of the most popular and recognizable safari birds, the lilac-breasted roller is a robust, jay-like bird with a lilac chest, sky-blue underparts and gold back. It is often seen perching on an acacia branch, then swooping down to hawk on its prey. Four similar-looking roller species occur in bush habitats in South Africa, all indulging in the agile aerial displays to which their name refers.

LONG-TAILED WIDOW
(SPECIES: EUPLECTES PROGNE)

RELATIVES: white-winged widow, red bishop, golden bishop

 LC

Related to the smaller weavers, this black bird with red-and-white shoulder markings has an extraordinary long, droopy tail that gives it a total length of up to 80 cm (31½ inches) during the breeding season. It is often seen from the roadside, flying low over reedy marshes and highveld grassland, where it occurs alongside several other attractive but less dramatic widows and bishops.

WHITE-FRONTED BEE-EATER
(SPECIES: MEROPS BULLOCKOIDES)

RELATIVES: little bee-eater, southern carmine bee-eater, Eurasian bee-eater

 LC

A common resident of Kruger National Park and other bushveld reserves, this stunning bird has a bright green back, red neck and chest, cobalt vent and white head with black eye-stripe. Like other bee-eaters, it is a dashing insectivore whose sleek profile is determined by an upright stance, long wings and tail, and long decurved bill.

FORK-TAILED DRONGO
(SPECIES: DISCRURUS ADSIMILIS)

RELATIVES: square-tailed drongo

 LC

A characteristic savannah and woodland passerine, the fork-tailed drongo is an all-black insectivore that tends to hawk its prey from an open perch below the canopy. It is a bold and assertive character, and emits a wide array of indignant nasal calls. It is sometimes confused with black cuckoos, male black cuckoo-shrikes and black flycatchers, but none of the above have a comparably deep fork in their tail.

WHITE-BROWED COUCAL
(SPECIES: CENTROPUS SUPERCILIOSUS)

RELATIVES: red-chested cuckoo, yellowbill, Diederick's cuckoo

 LC

The white-browed coucal is a large, clumsy bird seen in rank grassland, marsh and lake margins. It has a white eye-strip and streaked underparts. It is most visible before rainstorms, which it tends to predict with a dove-like bubbling that gives it the name of rainbird. The coucal is related to cuckoos, which are common but secretive in African habitats.

Key to Field Guide icons *see p68*

AFRICAN FIREFINCH
(SPECIES: LAGONOSTICTA RUBRICATA)

RELATIVES: common waxbill, pin-tailed wydah, blue waxbill

 LC

Bright red with light spotting on the flanks, this ubiquitous but unobtrusive gem frequents gardens and lodge grounds. It is one of several small, colourful seedeaters in the family Estrildidae, most of which have conical bills whose waxen sheen gives them the common name of waxbill. They are parasitized by the related colourful wydahs.

BLACK-EYED BULBUL
(SPECIES: PYCNONOTUS BARBATUS)

RELATIVES: Cape bulbul, red-eyed bulbul, spotted nicator

LC

The black-eyed bulbul is one of the commonest birds in the northeast. Its counterparts in the southwest and northwest respectively are the very similar Cape and red-eyed bulbuls. All three are cheerful, habitat-tolerant garden birds with a bright tuneful song, slight crest and yellow vent. The main difference between them is eye colour (the Cape bulbul's eyes are white).

MALACHITE SUNBIRD
(SPECIES: NECTARINIA FAMOSA)

RELATIVES: collared sunbird, scarlet-chested sunbird, orange-breasted sunbird

LC

Sunbirds are small, restless nectar-eaters with long, decurved bills. In most species, the rather dowdy females are smaller and less conspicuous than the iridescent males. The widespread malachite sunbird, long-tailed and dazzling metallic green in colour, is arguably the most beautiful of these, and is associated with aloes and other flowering shrubs.

MASKED WEAVER
(SPECIES: PLOCEUS INTERMEDIUS)

RELATIVES: red-billed quelea, spotted-backed weaver, white-browed sparrow-weaver

LC

The *Ploceus* weavers are surely the most characteristic of African bird genera, and the masked weaver is probably the commonest species in South Africa. The dexterous male builds intricate, ball-shaped nests at the end of a thin hanging branch, which is stripped of leaves as protection against snakes. Once completed, the nest is inspected by the female, who deconstructs it ruthlessly if she deems it unsatisfactory.

CAPE WAGTAIL
(SPECIES: MOTACILLA CAPENSIS)

RELATIVES: African pied wagtail, long-tailed wagtail, orange-throated longclaw

LC

Frequently seen walking along the edge of rivers, lakes and swimming pools, the boldly marked grey-and-white Cape wagtail is easily identified by its incessantly bobbing tail. The most common and widespread wagtail in South Africa, it is outnumbered in the northeast by the African pied wagtail, and seasonally in some areas by the migrant yellow wagtail. The colourful longclaws and duller pipits are closely related.

SPECKLED MOUSEBIRD
(SPECIES: COLIUS STRIATUS)

RELATIVES: white-backed mousebird, red-faced mousebird

LC

This scruffy frugivore is the most widespread member of the order Coliidae, which is endemic to Africa and consists of half-a-dozen long-tailed and prominently crested species. It is generally seen in flocks of around five to eight birds. The name mousebird refers to its habit of shuffling nimbly along branches, though it might equally apply to its grey-brown colouration. Three species occur in South Africa.

IUCN status LC: Least Concern

OLIVE THRUSH
(SPECIES: TURDUS OLIVACEOUS)

RELATIVES: Cape robin-chat, common rock thrush, stonechat

 LC

The Turdidae is a diverse family of medium to small insectivores, represented by about 40 species and 15 genera in South Africa. Among the most recognizable is the olive thrush, which is often seen hopping around hotel lawns. The family also includes robin-chats, a group of orange, blue, black and white birds that are also common in gardens, but tend to prefer thicker cover.

AFRICAN PARADISE FLYCATCHER
(SPECIES: TERPSIPHONE VIRIDIS)

RELATIVES: Vanga flycatcher, chin spot batis, common wattle-eye

 LC

This hyperactive leaf-gleaning flycatcher tolerates most habitats apart from true desert. It might be seen anywhere, although local abundance is affected by complex seasonal intra-African movements. Usually bluish with an orange tail, it also has black-and-white and intermediate morphs. The male's tail can be up to three times the body length.

PIED KINGFISHER
(SPECIES: CERYLE RUDIS)

RELATIVES: Malachite kingfisher, giant kingfisher

 LC

Probably the most numerous and visible of South Africa's water-associated kingfishers, this black-and-white bird has a unique hunting method that involves hovering above open water then diving down sharply to spear a fish with its dagger-like bill. Other water-associated species range from the gem-like, finch-sized malachite kingfisher to the crow-sized giant kingfisher.

CRESTED BARBET
(SPECIES: TRACHYPHONUS VAILLANTII)

RELATIVES: black-collared barbet, red-fronted tinker-barbet, cardinal woodpecker

 LC

The repetitive trilling of the crested barbet – rather like a muted alarm clock – is one of the most distinctive sounds of the Kruger National Park. The bird is mainly yellow, but with a black-and-white back and bib, and red streaking on the face and belly. An equally conspicuous garden bird is the black-collared barbet, which has a red head and performs a haunting whirring duet.

CAPE GLOSSY STARLING
(SPECIES: LAMPROTORNIS NITENS)

RELATIVES: red-winged starling, plum-coloured starling, red-billed oxpecker

LC

Common and colourful, with cryptic but glossy green-blue feathering, red eyes and a faint black eye-stripe, this is the most widespread and visible of several beautiful South African starlings. Even more stunning is the plum-coloured starling, which occurs in riverine woodland and acacia bush, while the bulkier cliff-dwelling red-winged starling is often seen on Table Mountain.

FISCAL SHRIKE
(SPECIES: LANIUS COLLARIS)

RELATIVES: long-tailed shrike, crimson-breasted shrike, southern boubou

LC

This handsome resident of the South African highveld, usually seen perching openly on acacia trees or fences, is sometimes referred to as the butcher-bird, for its habit of impaling and storing its prey on thorns or barbs to eat later. The related southern boubou and spectacular crimson-breasted shrike are more furtive bush-shrikes that tend to betray their presence with antiphonal duets between male and female.

Key to Field Guide icons see p68

CAPE TOWN

Cape Town at a Glance

Cape Town lies on a small peninsula at the southern tip of Africa which juts into the Atlantic Ocean. It is South Africa's premier tourist destination and its fourth largest urban centre. Enriched by Dutch, British and Cape Malay influences, the cosmopolitan atmosphere is a unique blend of cultures. Lying at the foot of its most famous landmark, Table Mountain, Cape Town has a host of well-preserved historical buildings. Many, such as the Old Town House on Greenmarket Square, now house museums. Outside the city, attractions include Chapman's Peak Drive along a winding coastline, where sheer cliffs drop to the swirling sea below, and a tour of the vineyards around Franschhoek and Stellenbosch.

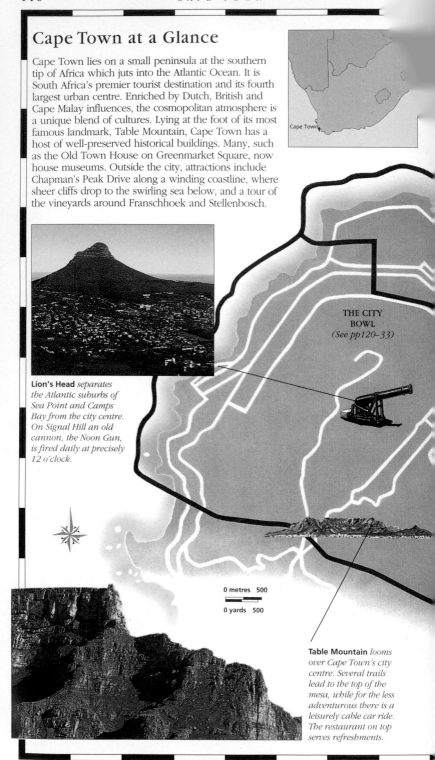

THE CITY BOWL
(See pp120–33)

Lion's Head *separates the Atlantic suburbs of Sea Point and Camps Bay from the city centre. On Signal Hill an old cannon, the Noon Gun, is fired daily at precisely 12 o'clock.*

0 metres   500

0 yards   500

Table Mountain *looms over Cape Town's city centre. Several trails lead to the top of the mesa, while for the less adventurous there is a leisurely cable car ride. The restaurant on top serves refreshments.*

◁ **Camps Bay beach, on the Atlantic seaboard, is a popular spot for sunbathing and people-watching**

Victoria Wharf Shopping Centre, *an upmarket complex at the Waterfront (see pp136–7), is a veritable shopper's delight. The modern structures have been designed to fit in with renovated older buildings.*

ROBBEN ISLAND
(See pp142–3)

0 metres 1,000

0 yards 1,000

The lighthouse *on Robben Island is 18 m (59 ft) high and was built in 1863. It stands near the "village", whose showpiece, the Governor's House, now offers accommodation for visiting dignitaries.*

V&A WATERFRONT
(See pp134–41)

The Grand Parade *is a lively market venue on Wednesdays and Saturday mornings. Wares range from fabrics, flowers and spices to cheap watches and toys. Beware of pickpockets, and don't carry expensive jewellery and cameras.*

GREATER CAPE TOWN AREA

Robben Island

Table Bay

Hout Bay

False Bay

0 kilometres 20

0 miles 10

Cape Point

The Castle of Good Hope *recreates the days of Jan van Riebeeck and the early settlers.*

The Cape Peninsula

209 m (686 ft) Cape of Good Hope

For four centuries, the Cape Peninsula's most prominent feature, Table Mountain, has been a welcome
landmark for travellers. A rugged mountain chain that
stretches from Table Bay to Cape Point soars out of
the sea to a height of 1,087 m (3,566 ft) above sea
level, dwarfing the high-rise buildings of the city and
its surrounding suburbs. The impressive front wall of
Table Mountain as well as the surrounding buttresses
and ravines are a spectacular natural wonder. The rock
formations and twisted strata indicate turbulent geological processes that span a 1,000-million-year history.

Smitswinkel Bay

PLATEAU

SWARTKOP
△ 678 m
(2,224 ft)
Simon's Town

GLENC

Fish

△ 507 m
(1,663 ft)
Muizenberg

TOKAI

Constantia
Winelands

Cape Point *juts into the southern Atlantic Ocean and forms the tip of the
peninsula's mountain chain. A scenic drive leads to the Cape of Good Hope*
(see p151) *that offers hiking and mountain biking trails. The less energetic
can ride the funicular to a lighthouse and superb views.*

The Constantia Winelands (see pp154–5) *nestle on the southeast
slopes of the peninsula's mountain range, within easy reach of
the city. The fertile slopes, combined with a mild Mediterranean
climate, create perfect conditions for choice grape cultivars.*

TABLE MOUNTAIN'S TABLECLOTH

The tablecloth

An old local legend tells of the
Dutchman, Jan van Hunks, who
engaged in a smoking contest
with a stranger on the slopes
of Devil's Peak. After several days,
the disgruntled stranger had to
admit defeat and revealed himself as the Devil. Vanishing in
a puff of smoke, he carried van
Hunks off with him, leaving behind wreaths of smoke curling
around Devil's Peak (which is where the cloud begins pouring over the mountain, forming the famous "tablecloth").

Funicular railway
Viewpoint
Walking/hiking
Mountain biking
Shipwreck
Whale watching

At Noordhoek, *the little rocky coves of the Atlantic seaboard give way to wide, unspoilt beaches. Noordhoek village is surrounded by smallholdings and horse farms, and outrides on the wide stretch of sand are popular.*

Llandudno *displays good examples of Cape granite, formed by rock melting under the earth's crust some 550 million years ago.*

The Sentinel *is an impressive rock outcrop that towers at the mouth of Hout Bay. It forms part of what is known as the Graafwater Formation, which lies above a base of Cape granite.*

Sea Point, *below Signal Hill, is built on metamorphic rock. This is the oldest of the peninsula's rock formations and weathers easily. Several road cuttings and old quarries in the area exhibit the red clayey soils that typify these strata.*

Kommetjie Lighthouse

Sun Valley
Kommetjie Beach
Noordhoek
CHAPMAN'S PEAK
593 m
(1,945 ft)
NSTANTIABERG
928 m
(3,044 ft)
THE SENTINEL ▲ 653 m
(2,142 ft)
FOREST TRACK
Hout Bay
Llandudno
NSTANTIA NEK
HOUT BAY MAIN
TWELVE APOSTLES
VICTORIA
BLE MOUNTAIN
▲ 1087 m
(3,566 ft)
S PEAK
TAFELBERG
Camps Bay
Clifton
LION'S HEAD
669 m
(2,195 ft)
KLOOF NEK
SIGNAL HILL
BEACH
E TOWN
SOMERSET
Sea Point

0 kilometres   5
0 miles   3

ND
borough
KOMMETJIE MAIN
CHAPMAN'S PEAK

THE CITY BOWL

Cape Town's Central Business District is cradled at the foot of Table Mountain. The city is bounded by Devil's Peak to the east and Lion's Head to the west. Table Bay harbour and the V&A Waterfront separate the city centre from the Atlantic Ocean. Visitors are often surprised by Cape Town's sophistication: it offers a plethora of culturally varied, exciting restaurants, and vibrant nightlife in the clubs and bars around Loop and Long streets. The many open-air markets and informal stalls with an ethnic African flavour are attractions in their own right, and nature lovers are enthralled by the city's scenic beauty. Early Cape Dutch and 19th-century Victorian architecture may be admired on a stroll through town. Particularly interesting buildings are Heritage Square on the corner of Shortmarket and Buitengracht streets, as well as the Blue Lodge on Long Street.

Jan Christiaan Smuts often hiked up Table Mountain

SIGHTS AT A GLANCE

Museums and Galleries

District Six Museum ❹
Iziko Bo-Kaap Museum ❽
Iziko Slave Lodge ❷
Iziko South African
  Museum and
  Planetarium ⓬
Iziko South African
  National Gallery ❿
South African
  Jewish Museum ⓫

Churches

Lutheran Church and
  Martin Melck House ❻

Parks and Gardens

Table Mountain pp132–3 ❾

Historic Buildings

Grand Parade and City Hall ❸
*Iziko Castle of Good Hope
  pp126–7* ❺
Iziko Koopmans-De Wet House ❼
Iziko Michaelis Collection ❶

0 metres 500
0 yards 500

KEY

▢ City Centre street-by-street map
   See pp122–3

▢ Gardens street-by-street map
   See pp130–31

🚂 Cape Town railway station

🚓 Police station

✝ Church

⊠ Post office

GETTING THERE

A network of highways leads into central Cape Town from all directions. The bus stop for coaches from upcountry is located at the railway station in Adderley Street.

◁ Cape Town's flower sellers are known for their jovial nature and sharp wit

Street-by-Street: City Centre

The compact city centre lends itself to walking, because most of its major sights are easily accessible. Cape Town is dissected by a number of thoroughfares, one of which is Adderley Street. The parallel St George's Mall is a lively pedestrian zone where street musicians and dancers entertain the crowds.

Frieze in the Koopmans-De Wet House Greenmarket Square, the focal point of the city, is lined with many historically significant buildings. One block west of here, towards Signal Hill, is Long Street. Some of the beautiful examples of the elaborate Victorian façades seen along this street are Bristol Antiques at No. 177 and the Blue Lodge at No. 206.

LOCATOR MAP
See Street Finder, map 5

★ Greenmarket Square
A produce market since 1806, and now a national monument, the cobbled square supports a colourful, daily open-air craft market. Among the historical buildings surrounding it is the Old Town House.

Malay Quarter

★ Long Street
This well-preserved historic street in the city centre is lined with elegant Victorian buildings and their graceful, delicate wrought-iron balconies.

Governme Avenue

KEY

– – – Suggested route

STAR SIGHTS
★ Iziko Slave Lodge
★ Long Street
★ Greenmarket Square

★ Iziko Slave Lodge
The exhibits at this museum illustrate the history of the site, the second-oldest colonial building in Cape Town ❷

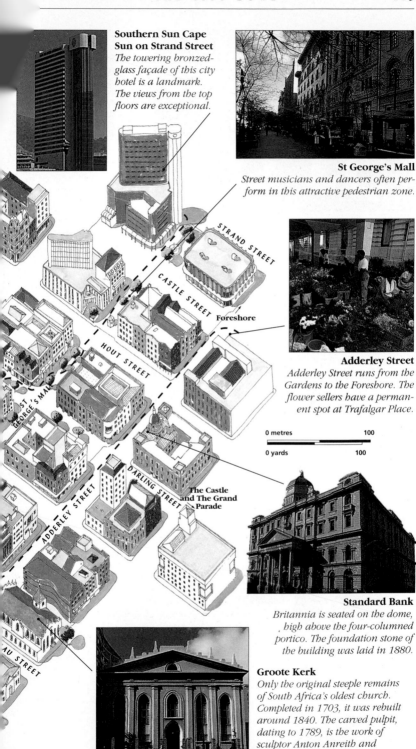

Southern Sun Cape Sun on Strand Street
The towering bronzed-glass façade of this city hotel is a landmark. The views from the top floors are exceptional.

St George's Mall
Street musicians and dancers often perform in this attractive pedestrian zone.

STRAND STREET

CASTLE STREET

Foreshore

HOUT STREET

ST GEORGE'S MALL

Adderley Street
Adderley Street runs from the Gardens to the Foreshore. The flower sellers have a permanent spot at Trafalgar Place.

| 0 metres | 100 |
| 0 yards | 100 |

DARLING STREET

ADDERLEY STREET

The Castle and The Grand Parade

AU STREET

Standard Bank
Britannia is seated on the dome, high above the four-columned portico. The foundation stone of the building was laid in 1880.

Groote Kerk
Only the original steeple remains of South Africa's oldest church. Completed in 1703, it was rebuilt around 1840. The carved pulpit, dating to 1789, is the work of sculptor Anton Anreith and carpenter Jan Jacob Graaff.

The Old Town House, where the Iziko Michaelis Collection is kept

Iziko Michaelis Collection ❶

Greenmarket Square. **Map** 5 B1.
Tel *(021) 481-3933.* ◯ *10am–5pm
Mon–Sat.* ● *1 May, 25 Dec.* **www**.
iziko.org.za

Located in the Old Town House, this national monument was built in 1755 in the Cape Rococo style. It initially served as the *"Burgherwacht Huys"* (house of the night patrol) and the magistrate's court; in 1839, it was claimed as a town hall by the newly formed municipality. After renovations in 1915, the building was handed over to the Union Government for use as an art gallery.

The original collection was donated to the city by the wealthy financier Sir Max Michaelis in 1914. It was added to by Lady Michaelis after the death of her husband in 1932. The collection consists of a world-renowned selection of Dutch and Flemish art from the 17th-century Golden Age.

The portraits are particularly interesting, offering an insight into Dutch society at the time.

In addition to the permanent collection, the gallery has a series of temporary exhibitions that have been designed to appeal to both locals and visitors alike.

After hours, the gallery becomes a cultural centre, hosting chamber-music concerts and lectures.

Iziko Slave Lodge ❷

Plaque on the Iziko Slave Lodge

Cnr Wale & Adderley sts. **Map** 5 B2.
Tel *(021) 467-7229.* ◯ *10am–5pm
Mon–Sat.* ● *Good Fri, 1 May, 25
Dec.* 📷 ✖ **www**.iziko.org.za

The first building on this site was a lodge that housed the slaves who worked in the Company's Garden *(see pp130–31)*. It was built around 1679 on land that originally formed part of the garden.

By 1807, new premises from which to administer the Cape colony were needed, and the Slave Lodge suited most requirements. Many slave inhabitants of the lodge were sold, while others were moved to the west wing of the building. The vacated area was turned into offices. In 1811, the west wing was also converted.

The people responsible for the conversion were the builder Herman Schutte, the sculptor Anton Anreith and the architect Louis Michel Thibault. As well as government offices, the lodge also housed the Supreme Court, the post office and the public library. The present building once extended into Adderley Street, but this portion had to be demolished when the road was widened. However, the original façade, designed by Thibault, has been restored to its former splendour.

Iziko Museums of Cape Town is working on transforming the Slave Lodge into a major site that increases public awareness of slavery, cultural diversity and the struggle for human rights in South Africa. The history of slavery at the Cape is illustrated with three-dimensional and audiovisual displays along with text, images and maps. A section that focuses on life at the lodge is currently being developed, based on archaeological and archival sources, as well as the memories of people who trace their roots to the time of slavery in the Cape.

THE MICHAELIS COLLECTION

This important art collection was established in 1914, when Sir Max Michaelis donated 68 paintings collected by Lady Phillips and Sir Hugh Lane. The gallery formally opened three years later, and today houses some 104 paintings and 312 etchings. It includes works by Frans Hals, Rembrandt, van Dyck, David Teniers the Younger, Jan Steen and Willem van Aelst. Although the collection is rather small in comparison to international galleries, it presents a valuable source of reference of the evolution of Dutch and Flemish art over two centuries. One of the most famous paintings in the collection is the *Portrait of a Lady* by Frans Hals.

Portrait of a Lady, **Frans Hals** (1640)

For hotels and restaurants in this region see pp380–85 and pp412–16

Many Cape Muslims have green-grocer stalls on the Grand Parade

Across the road from the Old Slave Lodge is the **Groote Kerk** (big church). Soon after their arrival at the Cape, the Dutch held religious services on board Jan van Riebeeck's ship, *Drommedaris*. Later, they used a small room at Castle Good Hope. However, they soon saw the need for a permanent site. A first, temporary structure at the northeast end of the Company's Gardens was replaced by a thatched church on the same site in 1700, at the order of Governor Willem Adriaan van der Stel.

The church was completely rebuilt in the 19th century, and the new building dedicated in 1841. All that remains of the original church today is the Baroque belfry, which, unfortunately, is now almost obscured by tall modern buildings.

Of interest in the church is the splendid original pulpit supported by carved lions. The story goes that sculptor Anton Anreith's original concept including the symbolic images of Hope, Faith and Charity was rejected as being too papist.

The façade of the church has high Gothic windows divided by bold pilasters. In front of the building is a statue of Andrew Murray,

**Andrew Murray
(1828–1917)**

minister of the Dutch Reformed Church in Cape Town from 1864–71.

> 🔒 **Groote Kerk**
> 43 Adderley St. **Map** 5 B2. **Tel** (021) 422-0569. ◯ 10am–2pm Mon–Fri. Ring ahead for a free guided tour.

Grand Parade and City Hall ❸

Darling St. **Map** 5 C2. **Tel** City Hall: (021) 400-2230. ◯ 8am–5pm Mon–Fri. ♿

The Grand Parade was the site van Riebeeck selected for his first fort in 1652. The structure was levelled in 1674 when the Castle of Good Hope *(see pp126–7)* was completed; until 1821 the area was used as parade and exercise ground for the troops. As buildings went up around the perimeter, greengrocers established fruit stalls, precursors of today's fleamarket, which operates from Monday to Friday. The site is now used both as a car park and as a venue for popular events.

Overlooking the Grand Parade is Cape Town's imposing City Hall. Built in 1905 in the elaborate Italian Renaissance style, it presents its elegant façades on four different streets.

A 39-bell carillon tower was added in 1923. The walls of the City Hall regularly resound to the soaring orchestral strains of the Cape Town Philharmonic,

formerly known as the Cape Town Symphony Orchestra. It is well worth getting tickets for the popular lunchtime and evening concerts, which can be booked through any branch of Computicket *(see p164)*.

District Six Museum ❹

25a Buitenkant St. **Map** B2. **Tel** (021) 466-7200. ◯ 9am–2pm Mon, 9am–4pm Tue–Sat. 📷 🖥️ www.districtsix.co.za

Up until the 1970s, the Sixth Municipal District of Cape Town was home to almost a tenth of the city's population. In 1965, the apartheid government declared the area "white", under the Group Areas Act of 1950. Removals began in 1968, and by 1982, more than 60,000 people had been forcibly uprooted from their homes and relocated 25 km (16 miles) away onto the barren plains of the Cape Flats.

The District Six Museum was launched in 1994 to commemorate the events of the apartheid era and preserve the memory of District Six as it was before the removals. It does this through a fascinating collection that includes historical documents, photographs, audio-visual recordings and physical remains of the area such as street signs.

Iziko Castle of Good Hope ❺

See pp126–7.

Cape Town's City Hall opposite the Grand Parade

Iziko Castle of Good Hope ⑤

Dutch East India (VOC) monogram, 17th century

Cape Town's Iziko Castle of Good Hope is South Africa's oldest structure. Built between 1666–79, it replaced an earlier clay-and-timber fort erected by Commander Jan van Riebeeck *(see p46)* in 1652. The castle overlooks the Grand Parade and is now a museum that also houses traditional Cape regiments and units of the National Defence Force.

Dolphin Pool
Descriptions and sketches made by Lady Anne Barnard (see p156) in the 1790s enabled the reconstruction of the dolphin pool over two hundred years later.

The Castle Moat
The restoration of the moat, which is a relatively recent addition to the castle, was completed in 1999.

Het Bakhuys

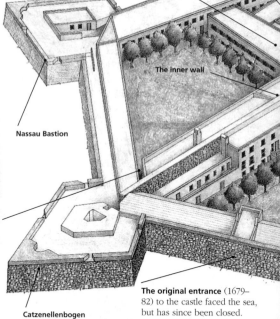

The inner wall

Nassau Bastion

The Archway
Slate, taken from a quarry on Robben Island (see pp142–3) in the 17th century, was used for the paving stones inside the castle.

Catzenellenbogen Bastion

The original entrance (1679–82) to the castle faced the sea, but has since been closed.

STAR FEATURES

- ★ The Castle Military Museum
- ★ William Fehr Collection
- ★ De Kat Balcony

★ The Castle Military Museum
On display is an array of military artifacts, as well as weapons and uniforms from the VOC and British periods of occupation of the Cape.

★ William Fehr Collection

Exhibits include paintings by old masters such as Thomas Baines, as well as period furniture, glass, ceramics and metalware.

VISITORS' CHECKLIST

Cnr Darling & Buitenkant sts.
Map 5 C2. **Tel** (021) 467-7223.
Cape Town station.
9:30am–4pm daily.
Key Ceremony 10am, noon.
1 Jan, 25 Dec. 11am,
noon, 2pm Mon–Sat.
www.iziko.org.za

Oranje Bastion

Entrance Gable
A teak copy of the original VOC gable reflects martial symbols: a banner, flags, drums and cannon balls.

Leerdam Bastion
Leerdam, Oranje, Nassau, Catzenellenbogen and Buuren were titles held by Prince William of Orange.

Colonnaded verandah

Moat

The Castle Entrance
The original bell, cast in Amsterdam in 1697, still hangs in the belfry. The coat of arms of the United Netherlands can be seen on the pediment above the gate.

Buuren Bastion

★ De Kat Balcony
The original staircase, built in 1695 as part of a defensive crosswall, divided the square into an inner and outer court, and was remodelled between 1786 and 1790.

Lutheran Church and Martin Melck House ❻

96 Strand St. **Map** *5 B1.* **Tel** *(021) 421-5854.* ☐ *10am–2pm Mon–Fri and for Sun services.*

Since the ruling authority was intolerant of any religion other than that of the Dutch Reformed Church, the Lutheran Church began as a "storeroom". Wealthy Lutheran businessman Martin Melck built it with the intention of modifying it into a place of worship once the religious laws were relaxed, and the first service was held in 1776. A few years later, the sexton's house was added.

From 1787–92, the German-born sculptor Anton Anreith embellished the church and added a tower. Today, both the church and the sexton's house are national monuments. The Martin Melck House, next door, was built in 1781 and declared a national monument in 1936. The building, a rare example of an 18th-century Cape townhouse that features an attic, plays host to the Gold of Africa Museum (Tel: (021) 405-1540; open Mon–Sat), featuring a collection of over 350 19th- and 20th-century gold objects from Mali, Senegal, Ghana and the Ivory Coast. The museum also houses temporary international exhibitions, a workshop, a gift shop and a restaurant.

The dining room in Iziko Koopmans-De Wet House

Iziko Koopmans-De Wet House ❼

35 Strand St. **Map** *5 B1.* **Tel** *(021) 481-3935.* ☐ *10am–5pm Mon–Fri.* 📷 *www.iziko.org.za*

This neo-classical home was built in 1701 when Strand Street, then close to the shore, was the most fashionable part of Cape Town. The building was enlarged in subsequent centuries; a second storey was added, and renowned French architect Louis Michel Thibault remodelled the façade around 1795 in Louis XVI-style. The De Wet family was the last to own the house. After the death of her husband, Johan Koopmans, Maria De Wet lived here with her sister, from 1880 until her death in 1906. Over the years, the De Wet sisters assembled the many fine antiques that can still be seen in the museum

today. Maria De Wet, apart from being a renowned society hostess who entertained guests like President Paul Kruger *(see p305)* and mining magnate Cecil John Rhodes *(see p52)*, was also responsible for taking the first steps to protect Cape Town's many historic buildings. It was thanks to her intervention that the destruction of part of the castle was prevented when the new railway lines were being planned.

Iziko Bo-Kaap Museum ❽

71 Wale St. **Map** *5 A1.* **Tel** *(021) 481-3938.* ☐ *10am–5pm Mon–Sat.* ● *Eid-ul-Fitr, Eid-ul-Adha, Good Fri, 25 Dec.* 📷 *www.iziko.org.za*

The Iziko Bo-Kaap Museum, which dates back to the 1760s, is the oldest house in the area still in its original form. The characteristic features are a *voorstoep* (front terrace) and a courtyard at the back, both emphasizing the social aspect of Cape Muslim culture. The museum focuses on the history of Islam in the Cape of Good Hope, highlighting its local cultural expressions.

The Bo-Kaap area has traditionally been associated with the Muslim community of South Africa, and the oldest mosque in the country is located on Dorp Street, just behind the museum.

Table Mountain ❾

See pp132–3.

The Lutheran Church on Strand Street

Malay Culture in Cape Town

The original Malays were brought to the Cape from 1658 onwards by the Dutch East India Company. Most of them were Muslims from Sri Lanka, Indonesian islands and India. A large proportion of them were slaves, while others were political exiles of considerable stature. After the abolition of slavery in the early 1830s, the Cape Malays (or Cape Muslims as they now prefer to be called) settled on the slope of Signal Hill in an area called Bo-Kaap ("above Cape Town") to be near the mosques that had been built there (Auwal Mosque dates from 1794). The Malays had a significant influence on the Afrikaans tongue, and many of their culinary traditions *(see pp408–9)* were absorbed by other cultures. Today, the Muslim community is very much a part of Cape Town: the muezzins' haunting calls, ringing out from minarets to summon the faithful, are an integral part of the city.

Mango atchar

STREETS OF THE BO-KAAP

Just above modern Cape Town, within easy walking distance of the city centre, lies the traditional home of the Cape Muslims. Here, narrow-fronted houses in pastel colours open onto cobbled streets.

Ornate parapets and plasterwork adorn the houses, most of which date from around 1810.

Cobbled streets still exist, but many of them have now been tarred.

Muslim tradition *dictates that formal attire be worn on festive occasions. This includes the traditional fez for men, while women don the characteristic chador (full-length veil or shawl).*

The fez, *of Turkish origin, is still worn occasionally, but knitted or cloth caps are more common nowadays.*

Signal Hill *is the traditional home of the Cape Muslim community. Many of the quaint, Bo-Kaap cottages have been replaced by modern apartment blocks higher up.*

The Mosque in Longmarket Street, *like many of the Bo-Kaap's mosques, stands wedged in-between the homes of residents. Religion is a fundamental part of every devout Muslim's life.*

Street-by-Street: Gardens

Jan van Riebeeck's famous vegetable garden, established
in 1652 to provide ships rounding the Cape of Good
Hope with fresh supplies, is still today known as the
"Company's Garden". It is a leafy, tranquil area that
contains an array of exotic shrubs and trees, an aviary
(records show that a "menagerie" existed here during
the time of governor Simon van der Stel), a conservatory and a sun dial dating back to 1787. There is also
an open-air restaurant. Nearby stands a Saffren pear
tree, planted soon after the arrival of Jan van Riebeeck,
which makes it the oldest cultivated tree in South
Africa. Look out for the disused old well, and the
tap that protrudes from the gnarled tree nearby.

LOCATOR MAP
*See Street Finder,
map 5*

KEY

– – – Suggested route

The garden is a
tranquil haven in
the city with water
features, lawns and
benches under tall,
old trees.

★ **Iziko South African Museum and
Planetarium**
*The museum concentrates on natural history,
archaeology, entomology and palaeontology.
The sophisticated equipment in the planetarium
reconstructs the southern night skies* ⓬

**South African Jewish
Museum**
*The entrance to this museum is
situated in the Old Synagogue,
the first synagogue built in
South Africa, in 1863* ⓫

Tabl
Mounta
Cablewa

STAR SIGHTS

★ Iziko South African
National Gallery

★ Iziko South African
Museum & Planetarium

★ Government Avenue

★ **Iziko South African
National Gallery**
*Temporary exhibitions
of contemporary local
artists augment the
permanent collection
of 6,500 paintings* ⓾

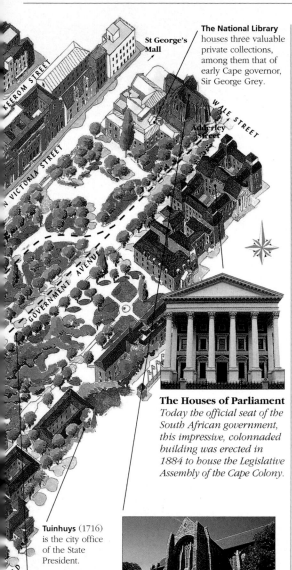

The National Library houses three valuable private collections, among them that of early Cape governor, Sir George Grey.

St George's Mall

The Houses of Parliament
Today the official seat of the South African government, this impressive, colonnaded building was erected in 1884 to house the Legislative Assembly of the Cape Colony.

Tuinhuys (1716) is the city office of the State President.

St George's Cathedral
This Anglican cathedral (1901) features stained glass by Gabriel Loire of Chartres and a Rose Window by F Spear.

★ Government Avenue
The original lemon tree lane has been replaced by tall, shady oak trees.

0 metres	100
0 yards	100

Iziko South African National Gallery ⑩

Government Ave, Company's Garden. **Map** 5 B2. **Tel** (021) 481-3970. ☐ 10am–5pm daily. ⬤ 1 May, 25 Dec. 🎫 📷 ⬛ ♿ 🏠 www.iziko.org.za

South Africa's premier gallery houses outstanding collections of British, French, Dutch, Flemish and South African paintings. Selections from the permanent collection change regularly to allow for a full programme of temporary exhibitions of contemporary photography, sculpture, bead-work, and textiles. They provide a great insight into the range of artworks produced in this country, the African continent and further afield.

South African Jewish Museum ⑪

88 Hatfield St. **Map** 5 A2. **Tel** (021) 465-1546. ☐ 10am–5pm Mon–Thu, Sun; 10am–2pm Fri. ⬤ Jewish hols. 📷 ♿ 🎫 🍴 www. sajewishmuseum.co.za

This museum, housed in a building opened in 2000 by Nelson Mandela, narrates the story of South African Jewry from its beginnings, setting it against the backdrop of the country's history. The interactive exhibits celebrate the pioneering spirit of the early Jewish immigrants and their descendants.

Iziko South African Museum and Planetarium ⑫

25 Queen Victoria St. **Map** 5 A2. **Tel** (021) 481-3800. ☐ 10am–5pm daily. ⬤ 1 May, 25 Dec. 📷 ♿ 🏠 www.iziko.org.za

Of special interest here are the coelacanth, reptile fossils from the Karoo, and the Shark World exhibition. There are also exceptional examples of rock art, including whole sections from caves.

The planetarium presents a diverse programme on the wonders of the universe.

Table Mountain

Cable car

The Cape Peninsula mountain chain is a mass of sedimentary sandstone lying above ancient shales deposited some 700 million years ago and large areas of granite dating back some 540 million years. The sandstone sediment which forms the main block of the mountain was deposited about 450 million years ago when the peninsula, then a part of Gondwana, lay below sea level. After the subsidence of the primeval ocean, the effects of wind, rain, ice and extreme temperatures caused erosion of the softer layers, leaving behind the characteristic mesa of Table Mountain.

Royal Visitors
In 1947, King George VI and the future Queen Mother accompanied Prime Minister Smuts on a hike.

Kirstenbosch National Botanical Garden
The garden (see pp158–9) nestles at the foot of the peninsula range. Three major trails and numerous paths lead up the mountain slopes.

HOL
BA

Kirstenbosch
National
Botanical
Garden

Ske

Window

SOUTHERN
SUBURBS

Contour Path

Forest
Station
P

Maclear's Bea
1,087 m (3,56(

Newlands

Newlands
Reservoir

T A B

Devil's Peak
1,000 m (3,280 ft)

University of
Cape Town

Rhodes
Memorial

King's
Blockhouse

Woodstock
Cave

P

Plumpudding Hill
291 m (955 ft)

Queen's
Blockhouse

Prince of Wales
Blockhouse

CITY CEN

CITY CENTRE AND FORESHORE

King's Blockhouse
This is the best preserved of the three 18th-century stone forts that were built during the first British occupation of the Cape (see pp48–9).

TABLE MOUNTAIN FAUNA AND FLORA

Disa orchid

Over 1,500 plant species of the 2,285 that make up the Cape Floral Kingdom of the peninsula can be found in the protected natural habitat of Table Mountain. They include *Disa uniflora* (also called Pride of Table Mountain), which mostly grows near streams and waterfalls, and several members of the regal protea family. Wildlife, consisting mostly of small mammals, reptiles and birds, includes the rare and secretive ghost frog that is found in a few perennial streams on the plateau.

Ghost frog

KEY

▬	Major road
▬	Road
--	Hiking trail
⁂	Viewpoint
🏃	Hiking trail starting point
🚲	Mountain bike access
❀	Wildflowers
P	Parking

The Plateau
The high plateau affords superb views of the Hely-Hutchinson reservoir and the Back Table, and southwards to False Bay and Cape Point.

VISITORS' CHECKLIST

Map 4 D5, E5, F5. 🛈 The Table Mountain Aerial Cableway Co, *(021) 424-8181. Cable cars every 10–15 mins.* ⬜ *daily.* ⬛ *in bad weather and for annual maintenance (2 wks Jul).* 🚌 *Adderley St or taxi from city centre.* 🅿 ♿ 📷 📷 www.tablemountain.net

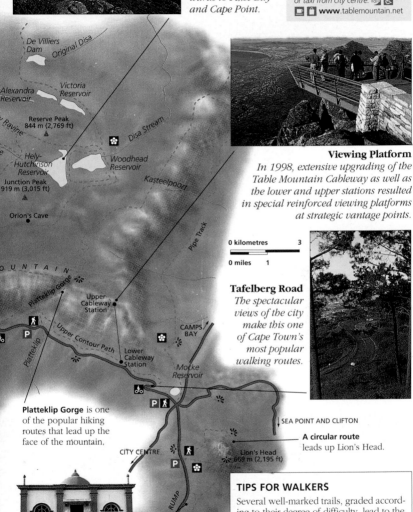

Viewing Platform
In 1998, extensive upgrading of the Table Mountain Cableway as well as the lower and upper stations resulted in special reinforced viewing platforms at strategic vantage points.

De Villiers Dam

Original Disa

Alexandra Reservoir

Victoria Reservoir

Reserve Peak 844 m (2,769 ft)

Disa Stream

Hely-Hutchinson Reservoir

Woodhead Reservoir

Junction Peak 919 m (3,015 ft)

Kasteelpoort

Orion's Cave

Pipe Track

| 0 kilometres | 3 |
| 0 miles | 1 |

M O U N T A I N

Platteklip Gorge

Upper Cableway Station

Upper Contour Path

Platteklip

Tafelberg Road
The spectacular views of the city make this one of Cape Town's most popular walking routes.

CAMPS BAY

Lower Cableway Station

Mocke Reservoir

Platteklip Gorge is one of the popular hiking routes that lead up the face of the mountain.

SEA POINT AND CLIFTON

A circular route
leads up Lion's Head.

CITY CENTRE

Lion's Head 669 m (2,195 ft)

LION'S RUMP

Kramat
This burial place of Goolam Muhamed Soofi is one of six Muslim shrines that form a holy circle around the Cape Peninsula.

Signal Hill 350 m (1,148 ft)

TIPS FOR WALKERS

Several well-marked trails, graded according to their degree of difficulty, lead to the summit. Hikers are advised to check with the Lower Cableway Station before setting out, since weather conditions may deteriorate without warning. Hiking on windy or misty days is not recommended. For safety reasons, do not hike alone.

Hikers on the plateau

V&A WATERFRONT

Logo of the V&A Waterfront

Cape Town's successful Waterfront project was named after the son of Queen Victoria. In 1860, a young Prince Alfred initiated the construction of the first breakwater in stormy Table Bay, by toppling a load of rocks that had been excavated from the sea floor into the water. The Alfred Basin, which was subsequently created, successfully protected visiting ships from the powerful gales howling around the Cape in winter that had previously caused an alarming number of vessels to founder.

Increased shipping volumes led to the building of the Victoria Basin to ease the pressure on Alfred. From the 1960s, the basins and surrounding harbour buildings gradually fell into disrepair. Then, in November 1988, the Waterfront Company set out to modernize, upgrade and develop the site. Today, visitors can stroll through the shopping areas and enjoy a meal in one of the many eateries, while watching the daily workings of the harbour.

In Table Bay, some 11 km (7 miles) north of the Waterfront lies Robben Island, the political enclave that gained international fame for the high-profile exiles incarcerated there. For most of its recorded history, the island has served as a place of confinement – for early slaves, convicts, lepers and the mentally unstable. In 1961, however, it became a maximum-security prison for leading political activists, among them Nelson Mandela. Today, the island is a protected area, and the former prison a museum.

SIGHTS AT A GLANCE

V&A Waterfront pp136–7 **1**   Robben Island pp142–3 **2**

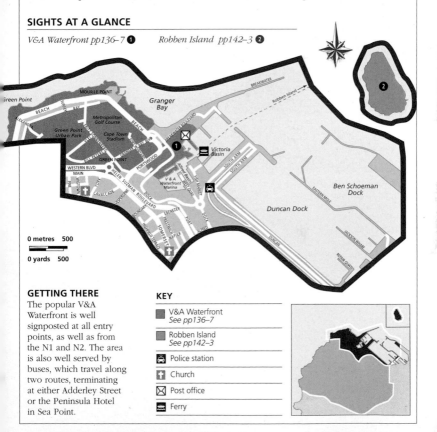

0 metres 500

0 yards 500

GETTING THERE

The popular V&A Waterfront is well signposted at all entry points, as well as from the N1 and N2. The area is also well served by buses, which travel along two routes, terminating at either Adderley Street or the Peninsula Hotel in Sea Point.

KEY

■	V&A Waterfront *See pp136–7*
■	Robben Island *See pp142–3*
🚓	Police station
✝	Church
⊠	Post office
⛴	Ferry

◁ **The clock tower at the V&A Waterfront, a shopping and entertainment complex that is part of a working harbour**

The V&A Waterfront ❶

The V&A Waterfront is a shopper's haven, offering
designer boutiques and others selling quirky hand-
painted clothing, health and beauty shops, homeware
and gift speciality stores, and more than 80 ethnically
diverse food outlets. Most eating places have harbour
views, and alfresco dining on the wharfs and waterside
platforms is extremely popular. Many bars and bistros
offer live music, while regular outdoor concerts are
staged at the Waterfront Amphitheatre. Excursions of all
kinds start at the Waterfront, from boat tours around
the harbour and to Robben Island, helicopter flips over
the peninsula to sunset champagne cruises off Clifton
Beach. The Waterfront is the port of call for visiting
cruise ships and boasts luxurious hotel accommodation.

LOCATOR MAP

Illustrated area

Extent of V&A Waterfront

Granger
Bay and Sea
Point

The Scratch Patch
*affords visitors the
opportunity to their
own selection of
polished semi-
precious stones,
such as amethyst
and tiger's-eye.*

Sea
Point

BEACH

Cape
Town

★ **Two Oceans Aquarium**
*Shatterproof glass tanks
and tunnels are filled
with shoaling fish such
as yellowtail, steenbras,
and musselcracker, as
well as penguins and even
a short-tailed stingray.*

STAR FEATURES

★ Two Oceans
Aquarium

★ Victoria Wharf
Shopping Centre

Foreshore

0 metres 50

0 yards 50

For hotels and restaurants in this region see pp380–85 and pp412–16

Table Bay Hotel
One of the best-appointed establishments at the V&A Waterfront, the glamorous Table Bay Hotel offers the ultimate in comfort and luxury. Each room has wonderful views of Table Mountain and the busy harbour.

BOULEVARD

QUAY 6

QUAY 5

Gateway to
Robben Island

Quay Four

ROAD

PIER HEAD

NORTH QUAY

To Clock
Tower Centre and
Diamond Museum

**★ Victoria Wharf
Shopping Centre**
Exclusive shops, cosy eateries and informal "barrow" stalls give this shopping centre a festive, market-day feel.

The V&A Waterfront Amphitheatre
This venue offers a vast array of musical and other events. Jazz, rock, classical concerts and the rhythms of traditional drumming take place here.

The Cape Grace Hotel
Another of the V&A Waterfront's fine accommodation offerings, The Cape Grace on West Quay has wonderful views.

VISITORS' CHECKLIST

Cape Town harbour. **Map** 2 D3–4, E3–4. ▮ *Visitors' Centre (021) 408-7600.* ▭ *Minibus taxi service operates daily from city centre.* ▭ *to Robben Island; N Mandela Gateway (see p143).* ◯ *9am–midnight.* ▧ *Dragon Boat Races (all year); Cape Town Boat Show (Oct); Volvo Ocean Race (Dec, every three years).* ▮ ▮ ▧ www.waterfront.co.za

Exploring the Waterfront

The V&A Waterfront is one of Cape Town's most visited attractions. The multibillion-rand redevelopment scheme incorporates ideas from other ventures, like San Francisco's harbour project. Easily accessible, it has its own bus services running to and from the city centre, and provides ample covered and open-air parking for vehicles. Major stores are open from 9am to 9pm, and most restaurants close well after midnight. Some of the city's most luxurious hotels are here.

Whitbread Round-the-World racers moor at the Waterfront

🐠 Two Oceans Aquarium

Dock Rd. **Map** 2 D4. **Tel** (021) 418-3823. ◯ 9:30am–6pm daily. 🎫 ♿ 🍴 🎁 www.aquarium.co.za

One of the top attractions in Cape Town, this complex aims to introduce visitors to the incredible diversity of sealife that occurs in the ocean around the Cape coast. A world first is the interesting exhibit of a complete river eco-system that traces the course of a stream from its mountain source down to the open sea.

One of the most fascinating features is the kelp forest, one of only three in the world. It is housed in a ceiling-high glass tank that holds various shoals of line fish swimming among the waving fronds. Apart from waterbirds like oystercatchers, there is a resident colony of African penguins and a touch pool, which has children exploring delicate underwater creatures such as crabs, starfish and sea urchins.

Alfred Basin (West Quay)

Off Dock Rd. **Map** 2 E4. ♿

Alfred Basin forms a crucial part of the working harbour, as fishing boats chug to the Robinson Graving Dock for repair and maintenance.

Alongside the dry dock is the Waterfront Craft Market, one of South Africa's largest indoor markets, which sells handcrafted gifts, toys, furniture and art. The **Iziko Maritime Centre** holds a model ship collection and includes the John H Marsh Maritime Research Centre, an important archive of photos of ships from the 1920s to the 1960s. The SAS *Somerset*, a former naval defence vessel, is also part of the centre.

Victorian clocktower

🏛 Iziko Maritime Centre

Union Castle Building, Dock Rd. **Tel** (021) 405-2880. ◯ 10am–5pm daily. ⬤ Good Fri, 25 Dec. 🎫

Victoria Basin

Map 2 E3.

Located in Quay 4, at the edge of the basin, the Quay Four Tavern offers superb views of the harbour and its constant boat traffic. Nearby, the Amphitheatre regularly stages free recitals and concerts, from the Cape Town Philharmonic Orchestra to African musicians and their energetic dance routines. Also in this area is the **Wheel of Excellence**, a 40-m (131-ft) high Ferris wheel with 30 air-conditioned cabins. There are great views across the Waterfront and Table Mountain from the top. In the **Red Shed Craft Workshop**, visitors can observe glass-blowers at work, buy hand-made pottery and ceramics, leathercraft, hand-painted fabrics, jewellery and gifts.

🎡 Wheel of Excellence

Quay 4. **Tel** (076) 276-6962. ◯ noon–6pm Wed, Thu & Sun; noon–8pm Fri & Sat. 🎫 www.capewheel.co.za

🎁 Red Shed Craft Workshop

Victoria Wharf. **Tel** (021) 408-7691. ◯ 9am–9pm Mon–Sat, 10am–9pm Sun & public hols. ♿

The Cape Town Diamond Museum

Cape Town Diamond Museum

1st Floor, Clock Tower Centre. **Map** 2 E4. **Tel** (021) 421-2488. ◯ 9am–9pm daily. 🎫 📷 www. capetowndiamondmuseum.org

Run by Shimansky, one of South Africa's leading diamond jewellers, this museum traces the history of diamonds from their underground formation to a sparkling gem. Exhibits document the Orange River diamond rush that started in 1867, and there are replicas of famous South African diamonds, such as the Cullinan and the Taylor-Burton. Visitors can also watch stones being cut and polished in the workshop.

Exhibits at the Two Oceans Aquarium

An innovative approach to education has assured the popularity and success of this venture. The complex is constantly upgraded to accommodate new exhibits, such as a fun gallery dedicated to frogs. All the exhibits introduce the public to unfamiliar aspects of the fragile marine environment and the need for its preservation. Young visitors, in particular, enjoy the hands-on experience. The wholesome Children's Play Centre offers an interesting programme, including daily puppet shows and supervised arts and crafts. Novel "sleep-overs" in front of the Predator Tank are a hit with children between the ages of six and 12. Adventurous visitors in possession of a valid scuba licence may book dives during the day, although not during feeding sessions in the Predator and Kelp tanks.

Starfish

THE DISPLAYS

The aquarium's displays are well planned and create an interesting, stimulating environment. Quite a few of them are interactive, offering visitors the opportunity to experience sealife at first hand. The latest technology is used to reveal the secrets of even the tiniest of sea creatures.

The interior *of the aquarium has been carefully designed to recreate various ocean and riverine habitats.*

The I & J Predator Tank *is a two-million-litre exhibit protected by shatterproof glass. The semi-tunnel surrounding the tank allows close encounters with turtles, yellowtails and ragged-tooth sharks.*

The Touch Pool *invites children to handle and examine sea dwellers like anemones and kelp.*

African penguins *have a small colony in the complex. There are also rockhopper penguins.*

The Intertidal Pool *contains mussels, barnacles, starfish, sea anemones and various sponges.*

A short-tailed stingray, *like this one, can be seen in the Predator Tank.*

Robben Island

World War II battery

Named "Robben Eiland" – seal island – by the Dutch in the mid-17th century, Robben Island has seen much human suffering. As early as 1636 it served as a penal settlement, and it was taken over by the South African Prisons Service in 1960. Its most famous inmate was Nelson Mandela, who spent 18 years here. When the last political prisoners were released in 1991, the South African Natural Heritage Programme nominated the island for its significance as a seabird breeding colony – it hosts more than 130 bird species. In 1997 the island was designated a museum, and in 1999 it was declared a UNESCO World Heritage Site.

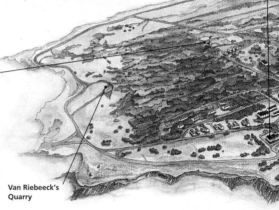

★ **Governor's House**
This splendid Victorian building dates from 1895 and was originally the home of the Island Commissioner. Today it serves as a conference centre and provides upmarket accommodation for visiting dignitaries and VIPs.

| 0 metres | 150 |
| 0 yards | 150 |

Van Riebeeck's Quarry

The Lighthouse
This lighthouse was built in 1863 to replace the fire beacons in use until then. It is 18 m (59 ft) high, and its beam can be seen from a distance of 25 km (15 miles).

STAR FEATURES

★ Governor's House

★ The Prison

★ Lime Quarry

POLITICAL PRISONERS

In the 18th century, high-ranking princes and sheikhs from India, Malaysia and Indonesia were sent to Robben Island by the Dutch East India Company for inciting resistance against their European overlords. The British banished rebellious Xhosa rulers to the island in the early 1800s. In 1963, Nelson Mandela and seven other political activists were charged with conspiracy against the state for their political beliefs and condemned to life imprisonment here.

Former inmate Nelson Mandela

VISITORS' CHECKLIST

Road map B5. **Tel** (021) 413-4220/1. 🚢 9 & 11am, 1 & 3pm daily (N Mandela Gateway, V&A Waterfront). 🌊 rough seas. 🎫 obligatory; book 2 days ahead (2 wks in high season). ♿ give ticket office advance notice. 📷 🏠 **www**.robben-island.org.za

Offshore Island

This flat, rocky island lies 11 km (7 miles) north of Cape Town in the icy Atlantic Ocean. Composed mainly of blue slate, it is only 30 m (98 ft) above sea level at its highest point. None of the trees on the island are indigenous.

Caspian Tern

This endangered migrant bird species breeds on the northern part of the island.

★ The Prison

Robben Island served as a place of banishment from 1658, when Jan van Riebeeck sent his interpreter here. The maximum security prison was completed in 1964.

Murray's Bay Harbour

The kramat was constructed in 1969 over the grave of an Indonesian prince. It is a place of pilgrimage for devout Muslims.

The Church of the Good Shepherd

Designed by Sir Herbert Baker, this stone church was built by lepers in 1895, for use by men only. Worshippers had to stand or lie because there were no pews.

Faure Jetty

★ Lime Quarry

Political prisoners, required to work in this quarry for at least six hours a day, suffered damage to their eyesight due to the constant dust and the glare of the sunlight on the stark white lime cliffs.

FURTHER AFIELD

Chacma baboons, Cape Point

In summer, the compact City Bowl bakes at the foot of Table Mountain's northern slopes, initiating a migration to the superb beaches of the Cape Riviera: Clifton, Camps Bay and Llandudno. Parking space is at a premium as sunseekers move on to the coastal villages of Hout Bay, Kommetjie and Scarborough, as well as Cape Point, with its dramatic ocean views. The wooded southern slopes of Table Mountain are cooler – it is known to rain in Newlands while the beaches of the Cape Riviera bask under clear skies. Also on the cool southern incline is Kirstenbosch National Botanical Garden, with its 7,000 plant species, and the world-famous wine estate Groot Constantia. On the popular False Bay coast, the water at Fish Hoek and Muizenberg is up to 5°C (10°F) warmer than along the western side of the Cape Peninsula.

SIGHTS AT A GLANCE

Historic Buildings
Groot Constantia pp154–5 **10**
Mostert's Mill **13**
Rhodes Memorial **14**
South African Astronomical Observatory **15**

Parks and Gardens
Kirstenbosch National Botanical Garden pp158–9 **11**
Ratanga Junction **16**

Suburbs
Cape Riviera **2**
Fish Hoek **8**
Green Point and Sea Point **1**
Hout Bay **3**
Muizenberg **9**
Newlands **12**
Noordhoek **5**
Simon's Town **7**

Nature Reserves
Cape of Good Hope, Table Mountain National Park **6**

Driving Tours
The Cape Peninsula **4**

20 km = 12 miles

KEY

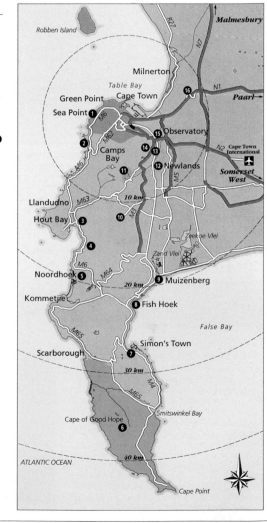

▮	Main sightseeing area
▮	Built-up area
▮	Reserve boundary
✈	International airport
▬	Motorway
▬	Major road
=	Minor road

◁ **Around 28 different indigenous cycad species can be seen at Kirstenbosch National Botanical Garden**

An aerial view of Sea Point on Cape Town's Atlantic seaboard

Green Point and Sea Point ❶

Main or Beach rds. **Map** 1 B4, 3 C1.

Since the development of the V&A Waterfront began in 1995, the real estate value in neighbouring seaside suburbs like Green Point and Mouille Point has soared. Beach Road, only a stone's throw from the sea, is today lined with expensive high-rise apartments, as well as trendy restaurants and up-market office blocks.

Green Point Common backs the residential strip. It started in 1657 as a farm granted to Jan van Riebeeck, but the soil proved unfit for cultivation. The sports complex on the common has hockey, soccer, rugby and cricket fields, bowling greens, and tennis and squash courts. Cape Town Stadium, built for the 2010 soccer World Cup, borders the Metropolitan Golf Course and the Green Point Urban Park. Green Point's red and white candy-striped lighthouse, built in 1824, is still functional. Its resonant fog-horn is notorious for keeping Mouille

Point's residents awake when mist rolls in from the sea.

Further along Beach Road lies the suburb of Sea Point. It, too, has undergone intensive development over the years and sports towering apartment blocks, hotels and offices. Sea Point used to be Cape Town's most popular entertainment strip. However, the opening of the V&A Waterfront provided a more convenient attraction, so Sea Point's glamour has faded somewhat, although the suburb still teems with restaurants, bars and night spots.

In the afternoon, the 3-km (2-mile) Sea Point promenade is abuzz with joggers, roller-bladers, children, tanned people-watchers and older residents strolling along with their lap dogs.

The promenade ends with a large parking area and the open-air **Sea Point Swimming Pool**, which is filled with filtered seawater and has an impressive diving pool.

Small sandy coves (packed with sunbathers in summer) dot the rocky shoreline. The tidal pools among the rocks are always a source of amaze-ment, particularly for children, who enjoy scrambling around looking for sea anemones, tiny starfish, shells and the occasional octopus. Other amenities along the promenade include a mini-golf course, a small maze, outdoor gyms and children's playgrounds.

Sea Point Swimming Pool
Beach Rd. **Tel** *(021) 434-3341.*
⬛ *Oct–Apr: 7am–7pm daily;*
May–Sep: 8:30am–5pm daily.
⬛ *only in bad weather.* 🈳

Mouille Point lighthouse has a foghorn to warn ships at sea

LION'S HEAD AND SIGNAL HILL

A fairly easy climb to the top of Lion's Head, 670 m (2,198 ft) high, affords views of the City Bowl and Atlantic coastline. Climbers can leave their cars at a parking area along Signal Hill Road (take the right-hand fork at the top of Kloof Nek Road), which opens to the contour path that encircles Lion's Head. At the end of Signal Hill Road is a viewpoint and another parking area. This spot is popular for its night views of the city, but be aware of safety issues and climb only when there is a full moon. Signal Hill is the site of Cape Town's noon gun, a battery originally built by the British in 1890 to defend the harbour. The cannon is fired daily at precisely noon.

The view from Lion's Head is spectacular

pe Riviera ❷

oria Rd. **Map** 3 B2–5.

nortly after the Sea Point
wimming Pool, Beach
Road runs via Queens into
Victoria Road. Bantry Bay,
Clifton and Llandudno are the
desirable addresses along this
steep stretch of coast, which
is known as the "Riviera" of
Cape Town because of the
million-dollar homes that
flank it. With incomparable
views and beautiful beaches
right on their doorsteps, this
is the haunt of the wealthy.

The coastal route extends
all the way to idyllic Hout
Bay, which lies over the saddle that separates the Twelve
Apostles mountain range
from the peak of Little Lion's
Head. The 12 impressive
sandstone buttresses, named
after the biblical apostles by
Sir Rufane Donkin, one-time
governor of the British Cape
Colony, flank the Riviera's
suburbs. First is **Bantry Bay**,
whose luxury apartments,
many supported on concrete
stilts, are built into the steep
mountain slope.

Trendy **Clifton** follows,
with its four famous small
beaches separated by granite
boulders. Fourth Beach is
especially popular among
families, as it has a car park
nearby, while the other three
are only accessible from the

A good meal and sweeping sea views at Blues in Camps Bay *(see p414)*

road via steep flights of stairs.
The Atlantic's waters are icy,
but the beaches are sheltered
from the strong southeasterly
gales by Lion's Head,
so during the summer
months all of the four
beaches are tremen-
dously popular with
sunseekers and the
resulting traffic con-
gestion is enormous.

Victoria Road con-
tinues along the
shore past **Maiden's
Cove**, which has a tidal pool
and good public facilities, and
Glen Beach, which has no
amenities but is frequented
nonetheless by surfers and
sunbathers. At **Camps Bay**,
the broad sweep of beach
lined with tall, stately palms
is another very popular spot,
although the southeaster tends
to bluster through here quite
strongly, especially during the
summer months. Backed by

**Strolling along
Camps Bay Beach**

Lion's Head and the mountain
chain known as the Twelve
Apostles, Camps Bay's
lovely setting has been
the inspiration for the
establishment of a
superb hotel, The Bay
(see p382), and a string
of good restaurants,
most of which offer
unrivalled sea views.

Arguably the city's
most beautiful little
beach, **Llandudno**,
lies about 10 km (6
miles) east of Camps Bay. The
small elite residential area,
settled on a rocky promontory
at the foot of the mountain
known as Little Lion's Head,
is first spotted from the cliff
top. Its curve of pristine white
beach and distilled turquoise
sea is a favourite spot to toast
the sunset. A 20-minute walk
to the west over the rocky
shore leads to secluded and
sheltered **Sandy Bay**, Cape
Town's nudist beach.

Camps Bay Beach with the Twelve Apostles in the background

Hout Bay ❸

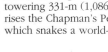

Scarlet ibis

Since the 1940s, Hout Bay has been an important fishing centre. It is also a pretty, residential area and a popular weekend resort. Its name derives from a diary entry made by Jan van Riebeeck in July 1653, in which he refers to "t'houtbaaijen", the wooded bays in the area. Hout Bay's fisheries centre on snoek and rock lobster, and include canning factories, a fishmeal plant and a fresh fish market. The 1 km-long (half-mile) beach is backed by low, scrub-covered dunes and flanked by tall mountains. To the west, the Karbonkelberg mountain range culminates in the towering 331-m (1,086-ft) Sentinel Peak. To the east rises the Chapman's Peak range, along the slopes of which snakes a world-famous scenic drive.

A colourful fishing trawler in the Hout Bay harbour

Exploring Hout Bay

Road map B5. 20 km (12 miles) S of Cape Town on M6 or M63. 🚌 from Cape Town station, Adderley St. 🛈 Main Rd. **Tel** (021) 790-1194. ⭘ daily. **www**.houtbaytourism.com

The green valleys of Hout Bay are threaded with oak-lined roads. Horse paddocks and stables are prolific; many local riding centres offer instruction and recreational horse riding. Residents walk their dogs on Hout Bay beach in the early mornings. The beach is also frequented by swimmers, paddlesurfers and, at its westernmost end, by windsurfers and Hobie Cat sailors. At the eastern edge of the bay, a 1.4-m (4.5-ft) high bronze statue of a leopard is perched on a rock pinnacle. It was cast in 1963 by the late Ivan Mitford-Barberton, a local artist. The village of Hout Bay itself offers a great variety of small coffee shops, restaurants, clothing and curio shops. Closer to the harbour there are a number of pubs, such as the popular Dunes Beach Bar, which has an open verandah that overlooks the beach and harbour.

At the start of the scenic coastal drive, Chapman's Peak Hotel is very well-positioned, with beautiful views across the bay; its terrace is popular in summer for seafood lunches and relaxed sundowners.

A work sculpted in memory of the mountain leopards

Mariner's Wharf

Harbour Road. **Tel** (021) 790-1100. ⭘ daily. ♿ 🍴 🖥 🎁 **www**.marinerswharf.com

Mariner's Wharf was built by a local family, the Dormans, whose predecessors farmed in the Hout Bay valley during the 1900s. It lies sandwiched between Hout Bay's beach and the busy little fishing harbour, and offers an open-air bistro, an upstairs seafood restaurant and a shop that sells marine-related curios. Visitors can also enjoy a stroll along the pier flanked by moored fishing boats. At weekends, the Bay Harbour Market is held in one of the old fishing factories. It features over 100 craft and food stalls and is popular for brunch and lunch, which are enjoyed at communal tables and accompanied by live music.

From the harbour, a number of tour operators launch regular cruises that take visitors out to watch sea birds and to photograph the Cape fur seal colony on Duiker Island. The ever-popular sunset cruises are also on offer and various local game-fishing companies organize expeditions off Hout Bay's shores to catch a variety of gamefish such as yellowfin and longfin tuna, broadbill swordfish and marlin.

A hiker's view of Hout Bay, seen from Chapman's Peak

Mariner's Wharf has an excellent fresh fish market

special breeding projects are the blue crane, the citron-crested cockatoo and the Egyptian vulture, which is extinct in South Africa.

Rare primates can also be seen at the sanctuary, such as the endangered pygmy marmoset and Geoffrey's tufted-ear marmoset. There are also terrapins, skinks and iguanas.

Hout Bay Museum

4 Andrews Rd. **Tel** (021) 790-3270.
◯ 8am–4:30pm Mon–Thu, 8am–4pm Fri. ● public hols. 🖼
This museum has interesting displays on the history of the Hout Bay valley and its people, focusing on forestry, mining and the fishing industry. The museum also organizes weekly guided nature walks into the surrounding mountains.

Environs: Just north of Hout Bay, the remarkable **World of Birds and Monkey Park** is presently the largest bird sanctuary in Africa and the second largest in the world. The high, landscaped, walk-through aviaries feature 400 bird species. Around 3,000 individual birds are kept in the sanctuary for rehabilitation purposes, many of them brought in injured. Others are endangered species introduced for captive breeding. Wherever possible, birds are released into their natural habitat as soon as they are fit to survive.

Visitors can watch them feed, build nests and incubate their eggs. The World of Birds also plays an important secondary role in educating the public on conservation and other environmental matters. Among the endangered bird species that have benefited from

🦅 World of Birds and Monkey Park
Valley Rd. **Tel** (021) 790-2730.
◯ 9am–5pm daily. 🖼 🚻 🔲 🛈
www.worldofbirds.org.za

Black-shouldered kite

LINEFISH OF THE WESTERN CAPE

The cold, nutrient-bearing water along the West Coast results in a greater number of fish than off the East Coast, but not as great a variety. The biggest catches are of red roman, kabeljou and white stumpnose. The uniquely South African national fish, the galjoen, has now become very rare. The deep gulleys along the rocky shores of the Western Cape, with their characteristic kelp beds, are perfect fishing spots for anglers.

Red Roman *Particularly tasty when stuffed and baked, this fish is found in great numbers off the Cape reefs.*

Snoek *Winter and early spring see the "snoek run", when this predatory fish migrates south in search of its prey – pilchards. Its rich, rather oily flesh is either canned, smoked or dried.*

Kabeljou (kob) *One of the most common food fishes, this is invariably served as the "linefish catch of the day".*

White stumpnose *A delicious sport fish, it is eagerly sought by ski-boat anglers.*

Yellowtail *This is one of the finest seasonal gamefish available in South African waters. The flesh is very firm and tasty, but can be coarse, especially in older and larger fish.*

Cape salmon *Its flesh is similar to that of its cousin, the kob, but more flavourful.*

Touring the Cape Peninsula ❹

Tours of the Cape Peninsula should start on the Atlantic coast and include Chapman's Peak Drive, a scenic route that took seven years to build. The drive, cut into the cliff face, has splendid lookout points with picnic sites. A highlight of the tour is the panorama at Cape Point, where the peninsula juts into the sea. The views encompass False Bay, the Hottentots Holland mountains and Cape Hangklip, 80 km (50 miles) away. The return journey passes the penguin colony at Boulders and goes through charming Simon's Town.

Chapman's Peak ①
The highest point rises to 592 m (1,942 ft). An observation platform is set on sheer cliffs which drop 160 m (525 ft) to the swirling seas below.

0 kilometres   5

0 miles   2

Kommetjie ②
Flashes from the powerful beams of Slangkop Lighthouse can be seen from Hout Bay at night.

KEY

▬	Tour route
=	Other roads
---	Park or reserve boundary
⸎	Viewpoint
➤	Shore-based whale watching

TIPS FOR DRIVERS

Length: 160 km (99 miles). From De Waal Drive via Camps Bay and Chapman's Peak Drive to Cape Point, returning through Simon's Town and Muizenberg, then back to the city via the M3. Chapman's Peak Drive is a toll road that may close in bad weather. Call (021) 790-9163 for more information.
Duration: It is advisable to do the route in two stages.

Map labels: PAARL, Cape Town, TABLE MOUNTAIN, N1, N2, AIRPORT, Disa, Constantia, Hout Bay, Tidal Lagoon, Kommetjie, Simon's Town, Fish Hoek, False Bay, Kom, CAPE OF GOOD HOPE, TABLE MOUNTAIN NATIONAL PARK, Cape of Good Hope, Cape Point, M6, M62, M63, M3, M64, M65, M4

Muizenberg ⑥
Muizenberg beach has flat, warm water and is safe for swimming.

Boulders ⑤
This accessible African penguin colony attracts many visitors each year.

Funicular ④
The Flying Dutchman funicular rail provides easy access to the lookout atop Cape Point.

Cape of Good Hope ③
There is a variety of wildlife here, including ostriches, boneboks, elands and zebras.

Horse riding on Noordhoek Beach is a popular pastime

Noordhoek ❺

Road map B5. Via Chapman's Peak Drive or Ou Kaapse Weg.

The best feature of this little coastal settlement is its 6-km (4-mile) stretch of pristine white beach. Strong currents make the water unsafe for swimming but it is popular with surfers and paddleskiers. The shore is good for horse riding and long walks (tourists are advised to walk in groups), while along its length lies the wreck of the *Kakapo*, a steamer that was beached here during a storm in 1900. Part of the Hollywood movie *Ryan's Daughter* was filmed here.

Environs: Another coastal hamlet, **Kommetjie**, adjoins a tidal lagoon situated inland from Noordhoek Beach. Long Beach, which stretches north as far as Klein Slangkop Point, is a venue for surfing championships and is very popular among boardsailors.

Scarborough, at the mouth of the Schuster's River, is a sought-after residential area. In summer, the seasonal lagoon is very popular.

Cape of Good Hope, Table Mountain National Park ❻

Road map B5. M4 via Simon's Town. **Tel** (021) 701-8692. ☐ Main gate: Oct–Mar: 6am–6pm (spring/summer) daily; Apr–Sep: 7am–5pm (autumn/ winter) daily; funicular: 9am–5pm daily. 🎫 ❌ 🍴 🎁 🐾 ♿ **www.** sanparks.org; **www.**capepoint.co.za

Strictly speaking, the Cape of Good Hope is the rocky headland that marks the most southwesterly point of the Cape Peninsula. Originally named Cape of Storms by Bartolomeu Dias in 1488, it was given its more optimistic title by King John of Portugal, who saw it as a positive omen for a new route to India.

Cape of Good Hope is also the name given to the southernmost sector (formerly referred to as the Cape of Good Hope Nature Reserve) of Table Mountain National Park, which encompasses the whole of the Table Mountain Chain from the southernmost point of the peninsula to Signal

Hill in the north. Most of the park is open access, with only three points at which conservation fees are payable: Boulders *(see p152)*, Silvermine and Cape of Good Hope.

Not surprisingly, this part of the park is exposed to gale-force winds, so the vegetation is limited to hardy milkwood trees and *fynbos*. Small antelopes live here, as do Cape mountain zebras. Visitors may also encounter troops of chacma baboons, which can sometimes be aggressive.

For stunning views from Cape Point, take the Flying Dutchman funicular up to the old lighthouse, 238 m (781 ft) above the crashing ocean waves. From here, a path leads down to the new lighthouse at Dias Point.

Along the park's east coast, the tidal pools at Venus Pool, Bordjiesrif and Buffels Bay attract hordes of tourists. A number of scenic walking trails along the west coast include the Thomas T Tucker shipwreck trail and the path to Sirkelsvlei; maps are available at the park's entrance gate.

Bonteboks, Cape of Good Hope

THE FLYING DUTCHMAN

The Flying Dutchman

This legend originated in 1641, when the Dutch captain Hendrick van der Decken was battling wild seas off Cape Point while sailing home. No match against the storm, his battered ship started sinking, but van der Decken swore that he would round the Cape, whether it took him until Judgement Day. Since then, many sightings of a phantom ship, its masts smashed and sails in shreds, have been reported in bad weather. The most significant was recorded in July 1881 in the diary of a certain midshipman sailing on HMS *Bacchante*. He was crowned King George V of England in 1910.

Classic architecture along the main road in Simon's Town

Simon's Town ❼

Road map B5. 🏃 58,000. 🚉 from
Cape Town station, Adderley St.
ℹ️ *Simon's Town Museum,
Court Rd, (021) 786-3046.*
🕐 *10am–4pm Mon–Fri,
10am–1pm Sat.* **www.**
simonstown.com

Picturesque Simon's
Town in False Bay
has been the base
of the South African
navy since 1957.
It was named after
Simon van der Stel
(see p154), who
visited this sheltered
little spot around 1687.

Since the Cape's winter
storms caused extensive
damage to the ships that
were anchored in Table
Bay, the Dutch East India
Company decided, in 1743,
to make Simon's Bay their
anchorage point during
the winter months.

From 1814, until handover
to South Africa, it served
as the British Royal Navy's
base in the South Atlantic.
The town's characterful hotels
and bars have been frequented
by generations of seamen.

Simon's Town's naval
history is best absorbed by
walking the "historical mile"
that begins near the railway
station and ends at the
Martello Tower on the East
Dockyard, taking in the
Simon's Town Museum, the
South African Naval Museum,
and the Warrior Toy Museum

African penguin

along the way. The Simon's
Town Museum is housed in
The Residency, believed to be
the town's oldest building. It
was built in 1777 as a weekend retreat for Governor
Joachim van Plettenberg.
Later, it also served as a
naval hospital. Among
the exhibits is a replica
of a World War II royal
naval pub and the
cramped quarters of
the original slave
lodge. Martello
Tower, the walk's
endpoint, was built
in 1796 as a defence
against the French.
Guided walks can be arranged
at the museum on request.

🏛 **Simon's Town Museum**
Court Rd. **Tel** *(021) 786-3046.*
🕐 *10am–4pm Mon–Fri,
10am–1pm Sat.* ● *1 Jan, Good
Fri, 25 Dec. Donations.* 📷 🎥

Environs: Between Simon's
Town and the Cape of Good
Hope sector of Table Mountain
National Park, the M4 passes
through charming settlements
that offer safe swimming and
snorkelling in a number of
protected bays such as Froggy
Pond, Boulders and Seaforth.
The big granite rocks after
which Boulders is named
provide excellent shelter when
the southeaster blows. A walk
along the beach between
Boulders and Seaforth leads to
secluded little coves. A major
attraction at Boulders is the
protected, land-based colony
of over 2,300 African penguins.

Further south, Miller's Point
has grassed picnic areas, a
slipway, and tidal rock pools.
The Black Marlin Restaurant
here is loved for its views and
fresh seafood. At Smitswinkel
Bay, a lovely cove lies at the
foot of a very steep path.

ABLE SEAMAN JUST NUISANCE

In Jubilee Square, overlooking Simon's Bay's
naval harbour, stands the statue of a Great
Dane. During World War II this dog was
the much-loved mascot of British sailors
based in Simon's Town. Just Nuisance,
formally enrolled in the Royal Navy,
was given the title Able Seaman.
When he died in a Simon's Town
naval hospital, he was honoured
with a full military funeral, which
was attended by 200 members of
the British Royal Navy. One room
at the Simon's Town Museum is
filled with memorabilia of the
unusual cadet.

Just Nuisance and friend

Fish Hoek ⑧

Road map B5. M4, False Bay.
⚐ *11,000.* ⚑ from Cape Town station, Adderley St.

Only recently was liquor allowed to be sold in Fish Hoek; until then it was a "dry" municipality. This condition had been written into a property grant made by Governor Lord Charles Somerset in 1818, and was only repealed in the 1990s.

The broad stretch of Fish Hoek beach is lined with changing rooms, cafés and a yacht club, and is popular with families and the sailing fraternity. Regattas are held regularly, and catamarans and Hobie Cats often line the beach. Jager's Walk, a pleasant pathway overlooking sea and beach, runs along the edge of the bay.

Environs: The M4 continues northwards, staying close to the shore. It passes through the seaside suburb of St James which has a small, safe family beach and is characterized by a row of wooden bathing huts that have all been painted in bright primary colours.

At the picturesque little fishing harbour of Kalk Bay, the daily catches of fresh fish, particularly snoek, are sold directly from the boats. The height of the snoek season varies, but usually extends from June to July. The Brass Bell restaurant, sandwiched between the railway station and the rocky shore, has a popular pub, good seafood

Muizenberg's beachfront seen from Boyes Drive

and, at high tide, waves crash against the breakwater between the restaurant and the sea. Kalk Bay is also popular for its many antique and art shops that line Main Road.

Muizenberg ⑨

Road map B5. M4, False Bay.
⚐ *5,800.* ⚑ from Cape Town station, Adderley St.

The name Muizenberg comes from the Dutch phrase *Muijs zijn berg*, meaning "Muijs's mountain". Wynand Willem Muijs was a sergeant who, from 1743, commanded a military post on the mountain overlooking the beach.

Muizenberg's white sands, which curve for 40 km (25 miles) around False Bay as far as the town of Strand, rightly earned the town its status as the country's premier holiday retreat in the 19th century. Traces of this early popularity are still visible in the now-shabby façades of once-grand beach mansions. Today a fast-food pavilion,

seawater pool and wide lawns attract young and old alike.

The railway station perches on a rocky section of shoreline, where the curve of the bay is known as Surfer's Corner, due to its popularity among surfers. There are several surf shops here that offer lessons for beginners.

Rhodes Cottage

Environs: Cecil John Rhodes, prime minister of the Cape Colony from 1890–95, started a trend when he bought Barkly Cottage in Muizenberg in 1899. Soon, holiday mansions began to mushroom at the seaside resort, although most were in stark contrast to his simple, stone-walled, thatch cottage. The cottage is today a museum in Main Road and has been renamed **Rhodes Cottage**.

It contains photographs and personal memorabilia of the powerful empire builder and statesman, including his diamond-weighing scale and the chest in which he carried his personal belongings.

🏛 **Rhodes Cottage**
246 Main Rd. **Tel** *(021) 788-9140.*
⚐ *10am–4pm daily.* ⚫ *25 Dec.*
🎟 *by donation.*

Fish Hoek beach offers safe bathing

Groot Constantia ⑩

The oldest wine estate in South Africa, Groot Constantia was built on land granted in 1685 to Simon van der Stel, newly appointed Commander of the Cape. On his death in 1712, the farm was subdivided into three parts and sold. After several changes of ownership, the portion with the manor house was bought in 1778 by Hendrik Cloete, whose family owned it for three generations thereafter and was responsible for the present appearance of the buildings. Today, as well as being a fully operational farm, Groot Constantia is also a popular tourist attraction, incorporating a museum belonging to the Iziko Museums group; its exhibits include furniture, paintings, textiles and ceramics.

Display of Carriages
A collection of carts and other implements tells the story of transport in the Cape's early colonial days.

★ **Cloete Wine Cellar**
This façade, commissioned by Hendrik Cloete and built in 1791, is attributed to Louis Thibault. The Rococo pediment was sculpted by Anton Anreith.

Cape Gable
The very tall gable of the manor house was added between 1799 and 1803. The sculpted figure of Abundance that decorates its lofty niche is the work of respected sculptor Anton Anreith.

★ **Manor House**
This museum contains an authentic representation of a wealthy, 19th-century farming household. Most of the antiques were donated by Alfred A de Pass, member of a Dutch family.

STAR FEATURES
★ Manor House
★ Cloete Wine Cellar
★ Jonkershuis

Groot Constantia
The Mediterranean climate of temperate summers and cool, rainy winters has ensured the success of the vines planted on this estate.

VISITORS' CHECKLIST

Road map B5. Groot Constantia off-ramp from M3 (Van der Stel Freeway) onto Ladies Mile. *Tel* (021) 794-5128. ⏲ 10am–6pm daily (to 5pm May–Sep). 🍷 cellar: 10am–4pm daily. **Iziko Museum** *Tel* (021) 795-5140. ⏲ 10am–5pm daily. 📷 ♿ 🍴 🛍 🚻

Vin de Constance
This naturally sweet Muscat de Frontignan by Klein Constantia (until 1712 part of the Groot Constantia estate) is made in the style of the early 18th-century wines.

★ Jonkershuis
Once the abode of the estate owner's bachelor sons, the quaint Jonkershuis is now a restaurant that serves traditional Cape dishes.

Trees in the front garden
included oak, chestnut, olive and banana. By 1695, some 8,401 had been planted.

THE DEVELOPMENT OF GABLE DESIGN

Government House (1756) is an example of the concave, or lobed, gable style.

Libertas (1771) has a convex-concave gable style, also called the Cape Baroque.

Klein Constantia (1799) has a classical gable, inspired by the Italian Renaissance.

Nederburg (1800) has a convex-concave outline, broken pediment and low pilasters.

Newlands Forest, a popular destination for weekend excursions

Kirstenbosch National Botanical Garden ⓫

See pp158–9.

Newlands ⓬

Road map B5. 🚆 *from Cape Town station, Adderley St.* 🚌 *Terminus in Strand St to Mowbray station.*

An exclusive suburb nestled at the foot of Table Mountain's southern slopes, Newlands is the headquarters for the Western Province rugby and cricket unions. The big Newlands sports grounds, which were renamed Newlands-Norwich in 1996, have served as the venue for many international matches. The rugby stadium can hold up to 50,000 spectators, and hosted the opening game of the 1995 Rugby World Cup *(see p34).*

Newlands Forest runs along the edge of the M3, a major route that links Muizenberg with the southern suburbs and the city centre. Local residents love to take long walks and exercise their dogs through the forest's tall blue gums, pines and silver trees, which are watered by the Newlands stream.

A little further on stands a beautifully restored national monument, **Josephine Mill**. This mill with its cast-iron wheel, was built in 1840 by the Swede, Jacob Letterstedt, on the bank of the Liesbeeck River, to grind wheat. It was named after the Swedish Crown Princess, Josephine.

Today, the mill is managed by Cape Town's Historical Society, and is Cape Town's only surviving operational mill. Demonstrations take place from Monday to Friday (at 11am and 3pm), and fresh biscuits and flour are for sale.

A pleasant restaurant in the grounds of the mill has outside tables next to the river.

🏛 **Josephine Mill**
13 Boundary Rd. **Tel** *(021) 686-4939.* ⏰ *10am–4pm Mon–Fri, 10am–2pm Sat.* 🎫 🎥 🍴
www.josephinemill.co.za

Josephine Mill

Mostert's Mill ⓭

Road map B5. Rhodes Drive.
🚌 *Golden Acre terminus in Strand St to Mowbray station.* **Tel** *(021) 761-9680.* ⏰ *phone to book.* 🎫
www.mostertsmill.co.za

This old-fashioned windmill dates to 1796 and stands on part of the Groote Schuur estate bequeathed to the country's people by financier Cecil John Rhodes *(see p52)*. Rhodes bought the estate in 1891, donating a portion to the University of Cape Town, which today sprawls across the lower slopes of the mountain, its red-tiled roofs and ivy-covered walls an unmistakable landmark above Rhodes Drive (M3). The mill was restored in 1936 with aid from the Netherlands.

Environs: Directly east of Mostert's Mill, in the suburb of Rosebank, is the **Irma Stern Museum**, dedicated to one of South Africa's most talented and prolific modern painters, who died in 1966. Her magnificent home, The Firs, features 200 paintings and her collection of antiques.

Travelling northwest from Mostert's Mill along the busy M3, the road curves around Devil's Peak to become De Waal Drive, which heads into the city centre. On the right is the famous Groote Schuur Hospital, where, in 1967, the world's first heart transplant was performed by Professor Christiaan Barnard. The story is told in the **Heart of Cape Town Museum**, inside the hospital, by way of life-size models in a re-created operating theatre. Tribute is paid to both the

LADY ANNE BARNARD (1750–1825)

A gracious Cape Georgian homestead in Newlands, now the Vineyard Hotel *(see p385)*, was once the country home of 19th-century hostess Lady Anne Barnard, who lived here from 1797 to 1802 with her husband Andrew, the colonial secretary. A gifted writer, she is remembered for her witty accounts of life in the new colony. She was also a talented artist: dainty sketches often accompanied her letters and the entries in her journal.

Lady Anne Barnard

Mostert's Mill dates back to 1796

heart donor, Denise Darvall, who had lost her life in a car accident, and the recipient, Louis Washkansky.

🏛 **Irma Stern Museum**
Cecil Rd, Rosebank. *Tel (021) 685-5686.* ⬜ *10am–5pm Tue–Sat.* ⬤ public hols. 🎫
www.irmastern.co.za

🏛 **Heart of Cape Town Museum**
Groote Schuur Hospital, Main Rd, Observatory. *Tel (021) 404-1967.* 📷 *9am, 11am, 1pm & 3pm daily; book in advance.* ⬤ *Good Fri, 25 Dec.* 🎫 www.heartof capetown.co.za

Rhodes Memorial ⓮

Road map B5. Groote Schuur Estate. Exit off M3.
ℹ *(021) 687-0000.* 🎫

Directly opposite Groote Schuur homestead – the state president's official Cape Town residence – the Rhodes Memorial overlooks the busy M3, and affords sweeping views of the southern suburbs.

The white granite, Doric-style temple on the slopes of Devil's Peak was designed by Sir Herbert Baker as a tribute to Cecil John Rhodes, and unveiled in 1912. It contains a bust of Rhodes by JM Swan, who also sculpted the eight bronze lions which guard the stairs. Beneath the bust is an inscription from "The Burial", written by one of Rhodes' good friends, Rudyard

Kipling. The focus of the memorial, however, is the bronze equestrian statue, titled "Physical Energy", which was executed by George Frederic Watts.

The sweeping views from the monument across the southern suburbs and out to the distant Hottentots Holland mountains are superb. Mixed oak and pine woodlands cover the mountain slopes around the memorial. They still harbour a small, free-living population of fallow deer, as well as a few Himalayan tahrs, first introduced on Groote Schuur estate in the 1890s by Cecil John Rhodes.

South African Astronomical Observatory ⓯

Road map B5. Off Liesbeeck Pkway, Observatory Rd. *Tel (021) 447-0025.* ⬜ *8pm on 2nd and 4th Sat of every month.* 📷 *groups of 10 or more must book.* www.saao.ac.za

The site for the Royal Observatory was selected in 1821 by the first Astronomer Royal stationed at the Cape, Reverend Fearon Fellows. Today, as the national headquarters for astronomy in South Africa, it controls the Sutherland laboratory in the Great Karoo and is

responsible for transmitting the electronic impulse that triggers the daily Noon Day Gun on Signal Hill *(see p133)*, thus setting standard time for the entire country.

Ratanga Junction ⓰

Road map B5. Off N1, 10 km (6 miles) N of Cape Town. *Tel (021) 550-8504.* ⬜ *phone for information.* ⬤ *25 Dec.* 🎫 www.ratanga.co.za

Ratanga Junction theme park logo

Ratanga Junction is the country's first full-scale theme park. This imaginative venue is situated north of the city centre on the N1, at the Century City shopping, hotel and office complex.

Ratanga Junction provides entertainment for the entire family. Chief among its many attractions are the thrilling tube ride through Crocodile Gorge, the spine-chilling Cobra roller coaster, and a breathtaking 18.5-m (60-ft) log-flume drop on Monkey Falls.

Also on offer are various shows, "jungle cruises", fun rides specifically designed for younger children and a nine-hole crazy-golf course. There are also family-friendly games that allow players to test their strength or their aim in a fun way. The Food Court, situated in The Walled City on Ratanga Island, offers a variety of food outlets.

The Rhodes Memorial, designed by Sir Herbert Baker

Kirstenbosch National Botanical Garden ⓫

In July 1913, the South African government handed over the running of Kirstenbosch estate (which had been bequeathed to the state by Cecil John Rhodes in 1902) to a board of trustees. The board established a botanical garden that preserves and propagates rare indigenous plant species. Today, the world-renowned garden covers an area of 5.3 sq km (2 sq miles), of which 7 per cent is cultivated and 90 per cent is covered by natural *fynbos* and forest. Kirstenbosch is spectacular from August to October when the garden is ablaze with spring daisies and gazanias.

Daisy

Proteas

★ Colonel Bird's Bath
Tree ferns and Cape Holly trees surround this pool, named after Colonel Bird, deputy colonial secretary in the early 1800s.

Van Riebeeck's Wild Almond Hedge
In the 1660s a hedge was planted to keep the Khoi out of the settlement and discourage illegal trading.

Birds
Proteas attract the endemic Cape sugarbirds.

Harold Pearson, first director of the garden, is buried above Colonel Bird's Bath.

Main entrance

★ Conservatory
This glasshouse, with a baobab at its centre, displays the flora from the country's arid areas, coastal fynbos, bulbs, ferns and alpines.

STAR FEATURES

★ Conservatory

★ Colonel Bird's Bath

★ Camphor Avenue

Braille Trail
A guide rope leads visually impaired visitors along this interesting 470-m (1,542-ft) long walk through a wooded area. Signs in large print and braille describe the plant species that grow along the trail.

VISITORS' CHECKLIST

Road map B5. Rhodes Ave turnoff on M3. 🚉 *Mowbray Station.* 🚌 *From Golden Acre in Adderley St and Mowbray Station; City Sightseeing Hop-On Hop-Off Mini Peninsular Tour bus.* **Tel** (021) 799-8782. ⏰ *8am–7pm daily (Apr–Aug: to 6pm).* 🎫 *10am Tue–Sat.* 🖼 🍴 🖥 📷 ♿ www.sanbi.org

0 metres 100

0 yards 100

Floral Splendour
After the winter rains, carpets of indigenous Namaqualand daisies and gazanias echo the flower display found along the West Coast (see p216).

Two Shops
The shop located at the upper entrance to the garden sells indigenous plants and seeds, while the lower shop offers a variety of natural history books, gifts and novelty items.

Parking

★ Camphor Avenue
This avenue of camphor trees was planted by Cecil John Rhodes in 1898 along his favourite ride – from his home at Groote Schuur to Constantia Nek.

SHOPPING IN CAPE TOWN

Cape Town is known as the international gateway to Africa, and the vast array of appealing shopping options supports its reputation. The bustling V&A Waterfront *(see pp136–8)*, in convenient proximity to the city centre, is just one of several large, sophisticated shopping complexes that offer everything under one roof – from fresh produce to high fashion and gourmet dining. Old and new contend for centre stage in the city

centre; antique jewellery and modern art are both worth searching for. The lively Long and Kloof streets, pedestrianized St George's Mall and the informal Greenmarket Square houses shops with a strong local flavour. The streetside art displays, buskers and stalls offering African masks, beadwork and carvings add to the vibrant atmosphere. Surrounding suburbs like Hout Bay regularly host outdoor craft stalls and noisy fish markets.

Bracelet made from beads and safety pins

OPENING HOURS

Most shops in the city centre and in the suburbs are open from 9am–5pm on weekdays, and from 9am–1pm on Saturdays. Major malls open at 9am and close between 7pm–9pm throughout the week and on most public holidays. Fridays are usually the busiest time of the week and many shops stay open until 9pm, although Muslim-owned businesses are closed between noon and 2pm. Supermarkets and many delis are open on Sundays.

SHOPPING MALLS

Cape Town's malls offer one-stop dining, entertainment, banking and shopping, with convenient parking facilities. **Canal Walk**, the largest, has more than 400 upmarket shops open till 9pm every day, and is a 10-minute drive from the city centre. With its children's

One of Cape Town's many malls

A relaxing corner of the busy Cape Quarter shopping mall

entertainment options and massive food court, it's an excellent choice for families.

The 185 shops in elegant **Cavendish Square** stock a range of high fashion, homewares and gourmet fare. The **V&A Waterfront**, a unique centre in the heart of the old harbour, is an attractive modern shopping venue offering outstanding jewellery, curios, make-up stores, restaurants and supermarkets.

Fashionable Capetonians prefer to browse at **Lifestyles on Kloof** and **Cape Quarter** in Green Point, which house home decor, art, fashion, beauty, health and lifestyle-related shops in a unique Cape Malay style building.

MARKETS

The cobblestoned **Greenmarket Square**, in the centre of Cape Town, is a vibrant craft market held Monday to Saturday, weather permitting.

Here one can buy African carvings, masks, drums, beadwork, jewellery, leatherwork, ceramics and handmade clothing.

The **Red Shed Craft Workshop** and the **Waterfront Craft Market**, both at the V&A Waterfront, are indoor venues open all week. Clothing, jewellery, mosaics and an array of textiles and artwork are available here.

On Sundays the best place to head to is the **Green Point Market**, in the parking area of the Green Point Urban Park, where everything from arts and crafts to plants and car parts is up for sale. **Milnerton Flea Market**, also held at weekends, is great for true bargain hunters, who can rummage through the junk to look for precious finds.

For African baskets, ceramics and shell art, visit the **Lion's Club of Hout Bay Arts and Craft Market** (open Sundays). The **Constantia Country**

Cobbled Greenmarket Square is one of the city's most popular markets

Living Market, held the third Saturday of the month, sells quality handwork.

Open-air markets also take place in Rondebosch and Kirstenbosch. The latter is a favourite with families, as children can play on the grass within sight of their parents. Remember to take cash with you: many markets don't accept credit cards.

The entrance to African Image

AFRICAN CRAFTS

African Image and the **Pan African Market** stock choice fabrics, ethnic furniture, beads, utensils and sculptures. **Africa Nova** specializes in locally produced handmade art, beautiful textiles from all over Africa and a range of unusual ceramic designs. **Heartworks** offers colourful beads, bags and glass, as well as innovative wood, wire and ceramic items.

In Newlands, the **Montebello Design Centre** is home to several artisan studios producing jewellery, textiles and pottery. The items made on-site are sold in the shop.

There is also a pleasant restaurant situated in the shade of several oak trees.

Another working artists' studio is **Streetwires**, which boasts more than 80 wire and bead artists under one roof, all creating enchanting items. The studio is open to visitors, and the artists chat to their clients while they work. **Monkeybiz**, with its distinctive yellow building painted with red monkeys, sells one-off beaded products made by township women in their homes rather than in factories. Profits from the beadwork support the Monkeybiz Wellness Clinic for HIV/AIDS-affected women.

Township tour itineraries often include a visit to the Khayelitsha Craft Market and the Sivuyile Craft Centre in Gugulethu (see p436).

BOOKS AND MUSIC

The most comprehensive bookstore chain in South Africa, **Exclusive Books** stocks newspapers, maps, guides, novels, CDs and a wide range of magazines. Some branches also have an in-store coffee shop.

Long Street is renowned for its bookstores. **Select Books** and **Clarke's Bookshop** both sell a variety of new, second-hand and collector's editions of southern African books; Clarke's also specializes in books on southern African art.

Wordsworth Books offers a wide range of fiction, biographies, coffee table volumes and other books. It has a particularly strong selection of South African interest and cookery titles. The book store at the **Kirstenbosch National Botanical Garden** sells travel, plant and wildlife guides specific to South Africa, as well as a range of titles for children. Fans of comic books, graphic novels and action figures will adore **Reader's Den** in Claremont.

There are a number of music megastores offering a range of commercial and more alternative CDs. **Musica**, open till late, is the largest in Cape Town. At the small, centrally located **African Music Store**, visitors are introduced to the exciting sounds of Africa.

FOOD AND WINE

New York Bagel in Sea Point has delicious bagels and a superb deli area. Head to **Mariner's Wharf Fish Market** for supplies of tasty fresh fish, and to **Melissa's The Food Shop** for an extensive range of attractively packaged handmade products.

Many supermarkets stock wine, but specialist shops can offer advice and freight facilities, and they are able to suggest Wine Route itineraries. **Vaughn Johnson's Wine & Cigar Shop** stocks a number of unusual Cape wines, such as Meerlust, Cordoba and Welgemeend. **Caroline's Fine Wine Cellar** stocks more than a thousand bottles, including classic imported wines from France, Italy, Spain and Australia. The shop also holds regular wine-tasting evenings.

Vaughn Johnson's Wine & Cigar Shop

Entrance to Naartjie, a popular children's clothes shop

HOMEWARE AND GIFTS

Imaginative homeware is readily available in Cape Town and shoppers will be spoiled for choice. In recent years, the city has witnessed a steady rise in lifestyle stores selling everything from kitsch china to stylish teapots.

The **Carrol Boyes Shop**, a perfect stop for gift shopping, sells designer cutlery, tableware and household items in silver, pewter, aluminium and steel.

Cape to Cairo, in Kalk Bay, offers a range of decorative objects from around the world, from Cuban antiques to Russian art. **Clementina Ceramics** stocks a selection of contemporary South African ceramics, which are sure to cheer up any kitchen.

Two household names in South Africa are the chains **@ Home**, ideal for trendy homeware and creative

pieces for the bathroom, bedroom and kitchen; and **Mr Price Home**, which is equally popular. Its wide range of fashionable household goods are sold at very reasonable prices.

ANTIQUES AND JEWELLERY

Quality antiques do not come cheap in Cape Town, but there is no shortage of wonderful items to buy.

In the city centre, both casual shoppers and serious collectors will enjoy browsing **Church Street Antique Market**, as well as the **Long Street Antique Arcade**, with its 12 antique shops. Both stock brassware, jewellery, old coins, china, vintage clothing and other interesting bric-a-brac. **Kay's Antiques** specializes in period jewellery from the Victorian to the Art Deco era.

Private Collections, in Green Point, has a fascinating stock of colonial Indian artifacts. Nearby, **Trade Roots** has a fine collection of antique Chinese country furniture and artifacts. Both are worth visiting just to browse through their interesting pieces.

The Shipwreck Shop in Hout Bay is a very unusual shop, specializing in maritime memorabilia, nautical antiques and fascinating shipwreck finds.

An unusual teapot from Carrol Boyes

Cape Town is renowned for its gold and jewellery, and the V&A Waterfront is a particularly good place to browse; **Olga Jewellery Design Studio** and **Uwe Koetter** are popular choices.

Both **The Diamond Works** and **Prins & Prins**, among others, offer tourists the chance to learn the art of diamond cutting, from the design stage to the finished product. At the end of the tour visitors can view a special collection of diamonds, with no obligation to buy.

CLOTHES AND ACCESSORIES

Cape Town has an eclectic collection of clothing shops. The **Young Designers Emporium (YDE)** showcases South Africa's younger design talent and offers the latest fashions at reasonable prices. **Hip Hop** has everything from custom-made suits to unique evening dresses described as "classic with a twist". **Klûk** is known for its exquisite couture and bridal wear; designer Malcolm Klûk apprenticed under John Galliano. Classic, well-cut garments can be found at **Hilton Weiner** and **Jenni Button**, and a selection of quality menswear stores can also be found in the major shopping malls.

Families may want to take some time to explore the children's clothes shops, which are excellent in Cape Town. **Naartjie** is one of the most popular, the 100 per cent cotton items come in bright colours and cute designs.

Before venturing into the great outdoors, head to **Cape Union Mart** for good-quality hiking and climbing gear, as well as camping equipment.

Shoppers who wish to pick up bags, hats and scarves, but are on a limited budget, should copy the locals and buy their accessories at factory shops. These outlets sell end-of-season stock often at huge discounts. Contact Cape Town Tourism for a list of stores.

The streamlined interior of Carrol Boyes Shop at the V&A Waterfront

DIRECTORY

SHOPPING MALLS

Canal Walk
Century City.
Tel (021) 529-9799/8.

Cape Quarter
Waterkant St. **Map** 2 D5.
Tel (021) 421-1111.

Cavendish Square
Dreyer St, Claremont.
Tel (021) 657-5620.

Lifestyles on Kloof
50 Kloof St. **Map** 5 A2.

V&A Waterfront
Map 2 D3.
Tel (021) 408-7600.

MARKETS

**Constantia Country
Living Market**
Cape Academy, Firgrove
Way. *Tel (021) 712-2124.*

Greenmarket Square
Cnr Shortmarket &
Burg sts. **Map** 5 B1.

Green Point Market
Green Point Urban Park.
Map 1 B4.
Tel (021) 439-4805.

**Lion's Club of
Hout Bay Arts
and Craft Market**
Village Green, Main Rd.
Tel (021) 790-1951.

**Milnerton
Flea Market**
Marine Drive, Milnerton.
Tel (021) 551-7879.

**Red Shed
Craft Workshop**
V&A Waterfront.
Map 2 D3.
Tel (021) 408-7846.

**Waterfront
Craft Market**
V&A Waterfront.
Map 2 D3.
Tel (021) 408-7600.

AFRICAN CRAFTS

African Image
Cnr Church & Burg sts.
Map 5 B1.
Tel (021) 423-8385.

Africa Nova
Cape Quarter, Green Point.
Map 2 D5.
Tel (021) 425-5123.

Heartworks
98 Kloof St, Gardens.
Map 4 F3.
Tel (021) 424-8419.

Monkeybiz
43 Rose St, Bo-Kaap.
Map 5 B1.
Tel (021) 426-0145.

**Montebello
Design Centre**
Newlands Ave, Newlands.
Tel (021) 685-6445.

Pan African Market
Long St. **Map** 5 A2.
Tel (021) 426-4478.

Streetwires
77 Shortmarket St,
Bo-Kaap. **Map** 5 B1.
Tel (021) 426-2475.

BOOKS AND
MUSIC

African Music Store
134 Long St. **Map** 5 B1.
Tel (021) 426-0857.

Clarke's Bookshop
211 Long St. **Map** 5 B1.
Tel (021) 423-5739.

Exclusive Books
Cavendish Sq, Claremont.
Tel (021) 674-3030.

**Kirstenbosch
National Botanical
Garden**
Rhodes Drive, Newlands.
Tel (021) 799-8782.

Musica
Cavendish Sq, Claremont.
Tel (021) 683-0665.

Reader's Den
Main Rd, Claremont.
Tel (021) 671-9551.

Select Books
232 Long St. **Map** 5 B1.
Tel (021) 424-6955.

Wordsworth Books
Gardens Centre, Gardens.
Map 5 B3.
Tel (021) 461-8464.

FOOD AND WINE

**Caroline's Fine
Wine Cellar**
Victoria Wharf,
V&A Waterfront.
Map 1 B1.
Tel (021) 425-5701.

**Mariner's Wharf
Fish Market**
Harbour Rd, Hout Bay.
Tel (021) 790-1100.

**Melissa's
The Food Shop**
Kloof St, Gardens. **Map** 5
A2. *Tel (021) 418-0255.*

New York Bagel
51 Regent Rd, Sea Point.
Map 3 C1.
Tel (021) 439-7523.

**Vaughn Johnson's
Wine & Cigar Shop**
Pierhead, Dock Rd, V&A
Waterfront. **Map** 2 E3.
Tel (021) 419-2121.

HOMEWARE AND
GIFTS

@ Home
Canal Walk, Century City.
Tel (021) 525-1940.

Cape to Cairo
Main Rd, Kalk Bay.
Tel (021) 788-4571.

Carrol Boyes Shop
Victoria Wharf, V&A
Waterfront. **Map** 2 E3.
Tel (021) 418-0595.

**Clementina
Ceramics**
The Old Biscuit Mill, 375
Albert Rd, Woodstock.
Tel (021) 447-1398.

Mr Price Home
Dreyer St, Claremont.
Tel (021) 671-0810.

ANTIQUES AND
JEWELLERY

**Church Street
Antique Market**
Church St Mall. **Map**
5 B1. *Tel (021) 438-8566.*

The Diamond Works
7 Coen Steytler Ave.
Map 2 E5.
Tel (021) 425-1970.

Kay's Antiques
Cavendish Sq, Claremont.
Tel (021) 671-8998.

**Long Street
Antique Arcade**
Long St. **Map** 5 A2.
Tel (021) 423-2504.

**Olga Jewellery
Design Studio**
Victoria Wharf, V&A
Waterfront. **Map** 2 E3.
Tel (021) 419-8016.

Prins & Prins
66 Loop St.
Map 5 B1.
Tel (021) 422-1090.

Private Collections
66 Waterkant St,
Green Point.
Tel (021) 421-0298.

**The Shipwreck
Shop**
Mariner's Wharf,
Hout Bay Harbour.
Tel (021) 790-1100.

Trade Roots
13 Hudson St,
Green Point.
Tel (021) 421-0401.

Uwe Koetter
Alfred Mall,
V&A Waterfront.
Map 2 E4.
Tel (021) 421-1039.

CLOTHES AND
ACCESSORIES

Cape Union Mart
Quay 4, V&A Waterfront.
Map 2 E3.
Tel (021) 425-4559.

Hilton Weiner
Burg St. **Map** 5 B1.
Tel (021) 424-1023.

Hip Hop
Cavendish St, Claremont.
Tel (021) 674-4605.

Jenni Button
Cavendish St, Claremont.
Tel (021) 683-9504.

Klûk
47 Bree St. **Map** 5 A1.
Tel (083) 377-7780.

Naartjie
Canal Walk, Century City.
Tel (021) 551-6317.

**Young Designers
Emporium (YDE)**
Cavendish Sq, Claremont.
Tel (021) 683-6177.

ENTERTAINMENT IN CAPE TOWN

Much of Cape Town's leisure activity centres on the beaches and mountains, but the city is developing a fine reputation for its nightlife and vibrant cultural events. Some of the best entertainment is found alfresco, with buskers and local beat poets fighting it out on the streets of the city. The grand flagship venue is the Artscape Theatre Centre, which draws audiences to local and international music performances,

The Artscape Theatre Centre

dance, cabaret, theatre and comedy. Cape Town has its own original form of jazz, which can be found in many of the restaurants, bars and clubs in and around Long Street. Capetonians are known to be laid-back and enjoy dinner followed by a visit to the cinema, but the city also caters for serious clubbers. Much of the action is concentrated on the trendy clubs and bars in the city centre and at the V&A Waterfront.

INFORMATION

For details of entertainment in the city, check the daily and weekend newspapers. They review and list events in the cinema, arts and theatre. Good choices include the *Cape Times*, *Cape Argus* on Tuesdays, *Mail & Guardian* on Fridays and *Weekend Argus*. Reviews and listings also appear in the magazine *Cape Etc*. The Cape radio station Good Hope FM mentions events from time to time, and the websites www.capetowntoday.co.za and www.mg.co.za may be helpful. For details of nightlife events, flyers are the best bet and are found all over the city. Try www.thunda.com and www.capetownlive.com for more information. Many venues have leaflets about forthcoming attractions, and the major venues have information telephone lines and

Computicket booking office, V&A Waterfront

websites. For information on all live performances, check **Computicket**, and for any other specific questions, **Cape Town Tourism** is also very helpful.

BOOKING TICKETS

Theatre seats can be reserved by calling Computicket or logging onto Computicket online. They have branches in

all the major centres country wide, which are open all day and some into the night. To book a theatre and dance performance at the Artscape theatre, contact **Dial-A-Seat**.

Telephone bookings for Ster-Kinekor cinemas can be made by calling **Ticketline**. There is also a dedicated **Cinema Call Centre** for bookings and information on Nu Metro films. Most theatres and cinemas don't accept telephone bookings without a payment by credit card.

DISABLED VISITORS

In general, most public buildings, museums and top visitor attractions cater for wheelchairs. **Kirstenbosch National Botanical Garden** provides good access for the disabled, and even has a special "touch and smell" area for visually impaired visitors. The **V&A Waterfront** also has specially designed parking bays, ramps and broad walkways. Most theatres are

The Baxter Theatre in Rondebosch

suitable for those in wheel-chairs. The Baxter Theatre has wheelchair positions located in certain areas; however, it's important to tell Computicket at the time of booking if a space is required. There are also adapted toilets and a lift to the restaurant.

At the back of specific Ster-Kinekor cinemas there is an area where people can comfortably sit in their wheel-chairs – check out the film section in newspapers to see which theatres are wheelchair-friendly. **Flamingo Tours** organizes holidays and tours for people with disabilities, and will be able to outline suitable venues.

BUDGET ENTERTAINMENT

Film-lovers on a budget will be happy to know that going to the cinema is a far cheaper activity in South Africa than in most other countries, and a bonus is that Tuesday is cut-price day at most cinemas.

On the music front, St George's Cathedral Choir gives performances free of charge – watch the press for details or telephone Computicket. From time to time, there are also free lunchtime concerts at the Baxter Theatre, showcasing the work of students from Cape Town University's **South African College of Music**.

The Amphitheatre at the V&A Waterfront often hosts free performances. On Heritage Day (24 September) look out for many free music festivals that are advertised by local press and radio.

Several word-class galleries offer free entrance, including

Summer concert, Kirstenbosch National Botanical Garden

Joao Ferreira Gallery (viewing of the gallery collection is by appointment only) and **Everard Read**.

It is also well worth considering buying the reasonably priced **Cape Town Pass** that allows free entry to over 50 of Cape Town's best attractions, as well as some 20 special offers and discounts.

OPEN-AIR ENTERTAINMENT

From December to March Kirstenbosch National Botanical Garden hosts the Summer Sunset Concert series where a wide variety of music is presented, from opera to rock and the local Philharmonic Orchestra. This is a great event for families, and spectators will enjoy the fresh air and attractive surroundings. Warm clothing is an essential as the weather can change suddenly.

Performances hosted by the University of Cape Town's **Little Theatre** and **Maynardville Open-air**

Theatre take place in January and February, when Shake-spearean plays are performed under the stars. These open-air events are very special and many theatre-goers take along a pre-performance picnic to enjoy in the park.

Other outdoor entertain-ments on offer include breathtaking acrobatic performances by the **South African National Circus School**; these take place in Observatory every weekend.

CINEMA

Mainstream Hollywood productions are extremely popular and provide the main fare in Cape Town's **Ster-Kinekor** and **Nu Metro** cinema complexes, as well as at **Cinema Prive**, which is more expensive but has big, comfortable seats and oak side-tables for drinks.

Art-house cinemas in Cape Town specialize in thought-provoking, independent films along with international art releases. **Cinema Nouveau** at the V&A Waterfront and **Cavendish Square** (the biggest non-mainstream cinema in the city) offer refreshing alter-natives to the usual Holly-wood fare. The charming **Labia Theatre**, originally an Italian embassy ballroom, has operated as an art-house cinema since the 1970s and caters for the more discerning viewer.

For an exclusive experi-ence, consider a private viewing at **Cine 12**, which is ideal for small groups.

Open-air concert at the Amphitheatre, the V&A Waterfront

Cape Town Philharmonic Orchestra and choir, centenary performance

CLASSICAL MUSIC AND OPERA

Cape Town City Hall offers classical music and opera performances in majestic surroundings. The **Artscape Theatre Centre** is the home of the **Cape Town Philharmonic Orchestra**, which usually gives performances on Thursday evenings. Occasionally, rather different concert venues are chosen, such as the Two Oceans Aquarium or the South African Museum. The Artscape stages opera and musicals, as well as popular lunchtime and Sunday afternoon concerts. There are 1,200 seats in the Opera House and the view is exceptional from every angle.

The Baxter Theatre Complex is where the South African College of Music performs its repertoire of chamber music, string ensembles, organ recitals and orchestral productions. It is also the venue for recitals by visiting soloists and chamber ensembles and it hosts occasional lunchtime concerts. **Cape Town Opera**, with its black soloists and chorus members, creates an inspiring listening experience. They perform at the Artscape and Baxter and give additional performances at the V&A Waterfront in February.

THEATRE AND DANCE

The **Artscape Theatre Centre** also hosts world-class performances of drama, ballet and satire, as well as experimental theatre and community and children's productions. It is one of the few venues in southern Africa with the facili-

ties to stage internationally known musicals such as *Les Misérables*, *Cats* and *Phantom of the Opera*, as well as big touring shows including *Spirit of Dance*, *Tap Dogs* and the St Petersburg State Academic Ballet. A calendar of events is available from the box office.

Another theatre and dance venue is the **Baxter Theatre Complex** in Rondebosch. The Main Theatre and Concert Hall show mainstream productions, whereas the intimate Studio Theatre hosts more challenging works.

In addition to the impressive **Cape Town City Ballet**'s contemporary and classical performances, Cape Town has a great variety of jazz, contemporary dance and hip hop companies performing styles such as African dancing, gumboots and Pantsula.

COMEDY

At the **Theatre on the Bay** in Camps Bay, farce is the standard fare, while at **Evita se Perron** in the town of Darling

(see p211), a short drive from Cape Town, the cutting wit of Pieter-Dirk Uys launches amusing attacks on current political issues. Both venues also have excellent cabaret and drag troupes.

Black comedians with one-man shows include Marc Lottering and Kurt Schoonraad. They are part of a post-apartheid comedy trend that reflects a new spirit in South Africa.

For fun interactive comedy, **Theatresports** takes place every Tuesday at **Kalk Bay Theatre**. It is all improvised by a team of professional actors, and each unique show is based entirely on the audience's suggestions.

Theatre on the Bay, Camps Bay

JAZZ, AFRICAN AND ROCK MUSIC

Cape Town's unique, indigenous style of jazz is heavily influenced by traditional African sounds. The legendary jazz musician Abdullah Ibrahim and other greats can be found playing at many of the venues around town. A fashionable spot is the **Winchester Mansions**

Cape Town City Ballet production of Giselle

Live sax playing at a Cape Town jazz festival

Hotel, which has Sunday brunch with live jazz. During the summer, St George's Mall buzzes with street music. **The Dubliner** on Long Street offers jazz on Sunday nights.

Two of the main jazz festivals are the Jazzathon at the V&A Waterfront in January and the Cape Town International Jazz Festival (previously known as the North Sea Jazz Festival) at the International Convention Centre at the end of March, which is the greatest jazz event on the continent.

The **Marimba Restaurant and Cigar Bar** is not to be missed on Thursday, Friday and Saturday nights, with its sounds of the African marimba fusing with jazz. It is a good idea to book early as it can be sold out weeks in advance. **Mama Africa** is popular with visitors, who come for its traditional percussion groups, hearty African menu, jungle-inspired decor and relaxed, fun atmosphere.

International live acts often perform at the **Cape Town Stadium**, while local rock bands favour the **Mercury Live and Lounge**, which is the leading live rock venue.

Other popular live music venues include **Dizzy's Pub, Cigar Bar and Lounge**, in Camps Bay, which features local cover bands and karaoke, and **Zulu Sound Bar**, which has live music most nights, ranging from rap bands to relaxed acoustic guitar jams.

CHILDREN'S ENTERTAINMENT

There is no need to worry that children will be bored in Cape Town. In addition to the endless outdoor activities that the city has to offer, there are plenty of family-friendly attractions too. For many kids, the thrilling amusement park Ratanga Junction *(see p157)* is top of the list, but the Two Oceans Aquarium *(see pp138–9)* is also a big hit with children. The **ice-skating rink** at the Grandwest Casino keeps kids occupied while the adults gamble.

In Observatory, the **Cape Town Science Centre** is a great complex with about 300 interactive displays. Another educational option is the **Planetarium**, where shows are held daily, including at weekends.

The V&A Waterfront often stages concerts and events during the holidays and the Zip Zap Circus at Easter is very popular.

Scratch Patch at the Waterfront and **Mineral World** in Simon's Town offer a fantastic activity. It involves digging for semi-precious gems – and kids get to keep what they have found.

CLUBS, BARS AND CAFES

It is not always easy to distinguish between the clubs and bars of Cape Town, as drinking and dancing usually take place in the same venue.

Trendy bars along the Camps Bay strip offer cocktails and sundowners – try **Café Caprice** if you're up for a showy summer scene and people-watching, or **Sand Bar**, a casual pavement café. Long Street in the City Centre provides an eclectic mix of places. Try **Fiction**, a DJ bar and lounge with electro, drum and bass and indie music, or the **Fireman's Arms** – a fun 1906 vintage-style bar that is also a popular place for watching sports on TV.

For sophisticated cocktails, champagne, caviar and oysters in an upmarket ambience, head straight to **Planet Champagne & Cocktail Bar** at Mount Nelson Hotel, or **Asoka** in arty Kloof Street.

There are dozens of clubs in Cape Town, varying from your standard disco-playing dance fare to profoundly alternative clubs, and the scene continues to grow. With a cigar bar, whisky lounge and regular events and DJs, one of the most fashionable is **The Bang Bang Club**.

The gay and lesbian scene in Cape Town is big and there's a wealth of clubs to choose from on the outskirts of the city centre, on the "Green Mile" strip in Green Point. A fun place to start an evening is **Beefcakes**, a gay-oriented restaurant with an amusing 1950s diner theme that is famous for its cheekily named burgers, late cocktail bar and regular drag shows.

Long Street has some of the best bars and clubs in Cape Town

DIRECTORY

INFORMATION

Cape Town Tourism
www.tourismcapetown.
co.za

Computicket
Tel (083) 915-8000.
www.computicket.com

BOOKING TICKETS

**Cinema Call Centre
(Nu Metro)**
Tel (0861) 246-362.

Dial-A-Seat
Tel (021) 421-7695.

**Ticketline
(Ster-Kinekor)**
Tel (082) 16789.

DISABLED VISITORS

Flamingo Tours
Tel (021) 557-4496.
www.flamingotours.co.za

**Kirstenbosch
National
Botanical Garden**
Rhodes Dr, Newlands.
Tel (021) 799-8899.

V&A Waterfront
Map 2 D3.
Tel (021) 408-7600.

BUDGET ENTERTAINMENT

Cape Town Pass
www.thecapetown
pass.co.za

Everard Read
3 Portswood Rd, V&A
Waterfront. **Map** 2 D3.
Tel (021) 418-4527.

**Joao Ferreira
Gallery**
80 Hout St. **Map** 5 B1.
Tel (021) 423-5403.

**South African
College of Music**
Tel (021) 650-2626.

OPEN-AIR ENTERTAINMENT

Little Theatre
Orange St. **Map** 5 A3.
Tel (021) 480-7129.

**Maynardville
Open-air Theatre**
Church St, Wynberg.
Tel (021) 421-7695.

South African National Circus School

2 Willow Rd, Observatory.
Tel (021) 692-4287.
www.sacircus.com

CINEMA

Cavendish Square
Dreyer St, Claremont.
Tel (082) 16789.

Cine 12
12 Apostles Hotel, Victoria
Rd, Camps Bay. **Map** 3
B5. *Tel (021) 437-9000.*

Cinema Nouveau
V&A Waterfront. **Map** 2
E3. *Tel (082) 16789.*

Cinema Prive
Canal Walk, Century City.
Tel (021) 555-2516.

Labia Theatre
Orange St and Kloof St.
Map 5 A2. *Tel (021) 424-
5927.* www.labia.co.za

Nu Metro
www.numetro.co.za

Ster-Kinekor
www.sterkinekor.com

CLASSICAL MUSIC & OPERA

**Artscape
Theatre Centre**
DF Malan St, Foreshore.
Map 5 C1.
Tel (021) 410-9800.
www.artscape.co.za

Cape Town Opera
Tel (021) 410-9807.
www.capetownopera.
co.za

**Cape Town
Philharmonic
Orchestra**
Tel (021) 410-9809.
www.cpo.org.za

THEATRE & DANCE

**Artscape
Theatre Centre**
*See Classical Music &
Opera.*

**Baxter Theatre
Complex**
Main Rd, Rondebosch.
Tel (021) 685-7880.
www.baxter.co.za

Cape Town City Ballet

Lovers Walk, Rosebank.
Tel (021) 650-2400.
www.capetowncityballet.
org.za

COMEDY

Evita se Perron
Darling Station, Darling.
Tel (022) 492-3930.
www.evita.co.za

Kalk Bay Theatre
Main Rd, Kalk Bay.
Tel (073) 220-5430.
www.kbt.co.za

Theatre on the Bay
Link St, Camps Bay.
Tel (021) 438-3301.
www.theatreonthebay.
co.za

Theatresports
Tel (072) 939-3351.
www.theatresports.co.za

JAZZ, AFRICAN & ROCK MUSIC

Cape Town Stadium
Green Point. **Map** 1 C3.

**Dizzy's Pub, Cigar
Bar and Lounge**
41 The Drive, Camps Bay.
Tel (021) 438-2686.

**The Dubliner
at Kennedy's**
251 Long St. **Map** 5 B2.
Tel (021) 424-1212.

**Mama Africa
Restaurant & Bar**
178 Long St. **Map** 5 B2.
Tel (021) 426-1017.

**Marimba Restaurant
and Cigar Bar**
Cape Town International
Convention Centre,
Lower Long St. **Map** 5
A2. *Tel (021) 418-3366.*

**Mercury Live
and Lounge**
De Villiers St,
Zonnebloem. **Map** 5 C3.
Tel (021) 465-2106.

**Winchester
Mansions Hotel**
221 Beach Rd. **Map** 1 B3.
Tel (021) 434-2351.

Zulu Sound Bar
98 Long St. **Map** 5 B2.
Tel (021) 424-2442.

CHILDREN'S ENTERTAINME

**Cape Town Scien
Centre**
370b Main Road,
Observatory. *Tel (021)
300-3200.* www.mtn
sciencecentre.org.za

Ice-skating rink
Grandwest Casino.
Tel (021) 535-2260.

Mineral World
Dido Valley Rd, Simon's
Town. *Tel (021) 786-2020.*

Planetarium
Queen Victoria St. **Map** 5
B2. *Tel (021) 481-3900.*
www.iziko.org.za

Scratch Patch
V&A Waterfront.
Tel (021) 419-9429.
www.scratchpatch.co.za

CLUBS, BARS & CAFES

Asoka
68 Kloof St. **Map** 4 F3.
Tel (021) 422-0909.

The Bang Bang Club
70 Loop St. **Map** 5 B1.
Tel (021) 418-0638.
www.thebangbang
club.co.za

Beefcakes
40 Somerset Road. **Map**
2 D5. *Tel (021) 425-9019.*
www.beefcakes.co.za

Café Caprice
Victoria Rd. **Map** 3 B5.
Tel (021) 438-8315.

Fiction
226 Long St. **Map** 5 B2.
Tel (021) 424-5709.

Fireman's Arms
Mechau St. **Map** 5 A1.
Tel (021) 419-1513.
www.firemansarms.co.za

**Planet Champagne
& Cocktail Bar**
78 Orange St. **Map** 5 A2.
Tel (021) 483-1948.
www.mountnelson.co.za

Sand Bar
31 Victoria Rd. **Map** 3 B5.
Tel (021) 438-8336.

APE TOWN STREET FINDER

The map references appearing with the sights, shops and entertainment venues that are mentioned in the Cape Town chapter refer to the maps in this section. The key map below shows the areas covered, including: the City Bowl, the Central Business District, the historical Gardens area and the V&A Waterfront. All the principal sights mentioned in the text are marked, as well as useful information like tourist information offices, police stations, post offices and public parking areas, always at a premium in the inner city. A full list of symbols appears in the key. Map references for Cape Town's hotels *(see pp380–85)* and restaurants *(see pp412–16)* have been included in the Travellers' Needs section.

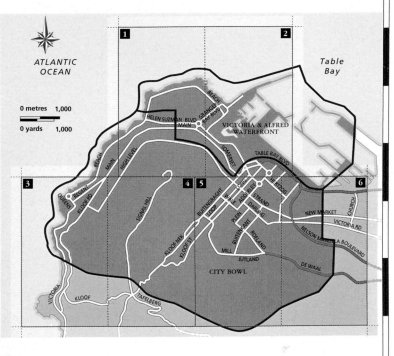

KEY

▣	Major sight
▣	Place of interest
▢	Other building
🚊	Railway station
🚌	Bus terminus
🚐	Minibus terminus
⛴	Ferry boarding point
🚕	Taxi rank
P	Parking

ℹ	Tourist information
✚	Hospital with casualty unit
👮	Police station
🚵	Mountain biking access
🏊	Bathing beach
✝	Church
C	Mosque
✡	Synagogue
⊠	Post office

☀	Viewpoint
═	Railway line
▬	Pedestrianized street
▬	Road (no public access)

SCALE FOR STREET FINDER PAGES

0 metres	400
0 yards	400

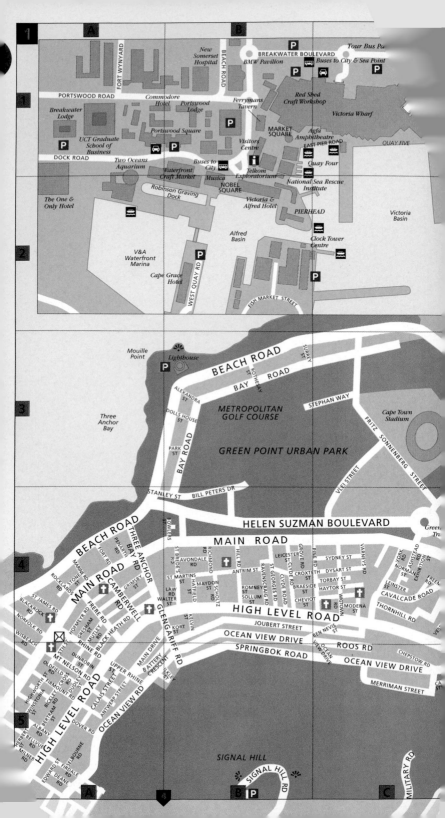

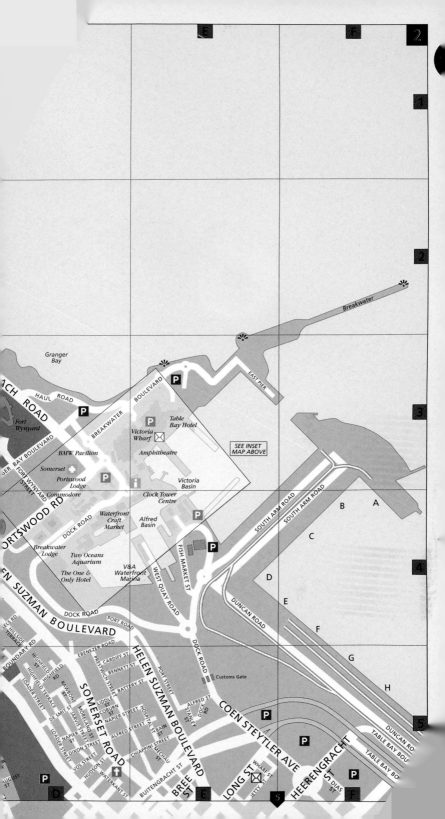

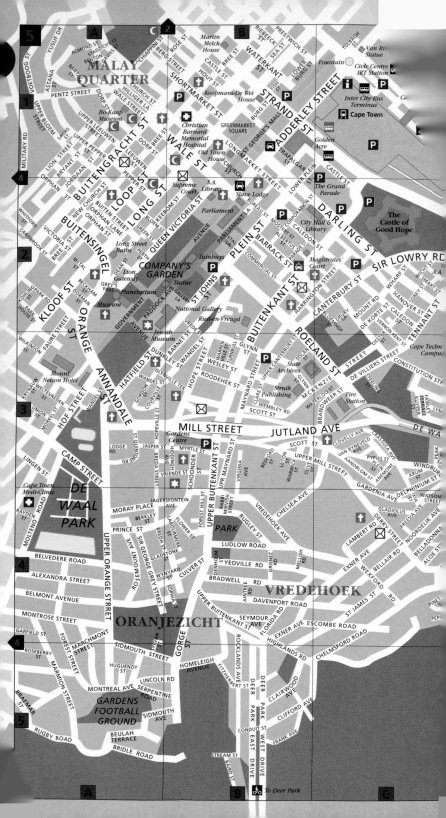

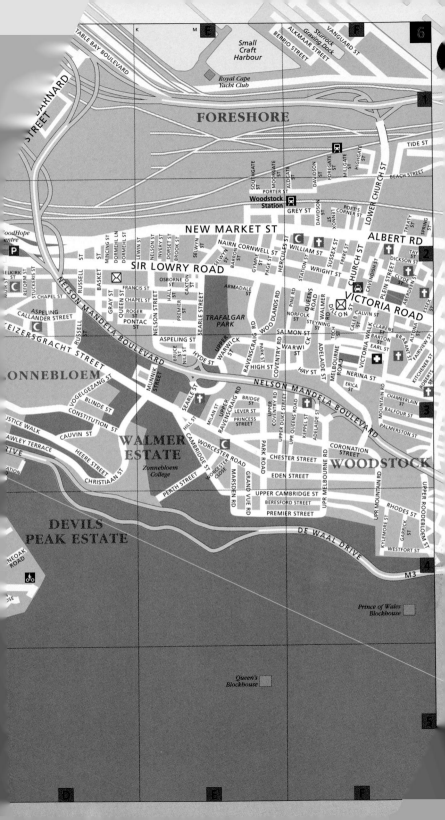

Cape Town Street Finder Index

THE WESTERN & SOUTHERN CAPE

Introducing the Western and Southern Cape

This region is dominated by a rugged mountain chain, comprising what is geologically known as the Cape folded mountains. The landscapes found in this territory are diverse. The arid and rather barren West Coast gives way to fertile winelands, cradled by jagged mountains. Beyond the terraced valleys, dramatic passes that traverse the massive mountain ranges of the Southern Cape are a testament to the efforts of early road builders. The spectacular Cango Caves lie here and, on the other side of the mountains, the magnificent Garden Route. All along the rocky coastline, which is one of the most dangerous in the world and where swells can reach up to 30 m (98 ft) in height, fishermen reap the harvest of the sea.

0 kilometres 50

0 miles   25

Namaqualand

A myriad wildflowers *occur in this region after good spring rains, when the dry West Coast comes alive with colour.*

THE WESTERN COASTAL TERRACE *(See pp206–17)*

The Manor House at Boschendal *near Fransch-hoek forms a stately backdrop for the vineyards of the estate. Wine tasting here is one of the highlights of the wine route.*

Cape Columbine

Boschendal Estate

Cape Columbine light-house *on the West Coast warns ships of the danger-ous rocks along the shore. It is the last manned light-house in South Africa.*

THE CAPE WINELANDS *(See pp186–205)*

THE SOUTHERN CAPE *(See pp218–31)*

Hermanus *is best known for the southern right whales that come here to give birth to their calves. The best time of year for whale watching is around September.*

◁ **In spring, double Namaqualand daisies provide carpets of colour**

Knysna Forest *is known for its tall stinkwood trees and ancient yellowwoods, some of which are 650 years old. The dense canopy is alive with birds, such as the elusive, emerald-green lourie.*

Port Elizabeth's *attractions include Bayworld, on the beachfront, where the highlight is the breeding colony of African penguins. In the city, a number of historic buildings date back to British colonial times.*

Addo Elephant National Park *in the Eastern Cape is a major tourist attraction. It is home to more than 450 elephants.*

THE GARDEN ROUTE
TO GRAHAMSTOWN
(See pp232–53)

Cango Caves

Knysna

Port Elizabeth

The Cango Caves *near Oudtshoorn contain many fascinating dripstone formations, caused by the constant percolation of water through limestone.*

Pinotage Wine-Making

Pinotage is a unique South African cultivar developed in 1925 by Stellenbosch University professor Abraham Perold, from a cross of pinot noir and cinsaut (then called hermitage). The world's first commercially bottled pinotage was released in 1961 under the Lanzerac label. The fruity, purple-red wine has since then achieved international acclaim. Pinotage comprises only a small percentage of South African total grape plantings, with most of the crop grown around Stellenbosch. There are small pinotage plantings outside of South Africa, notably in California and New Zealand.

Old grape press in the Stellenryck Museum, Stellenbosch

Pinot noir

Cinsaut

Pinotage

THE PINOTAGE CULTIVARS

Pinot noir, the noble cultivar from France's famous Burgundy district, contributed complexity, flavour, and colour, while cinsaut improved the yield. Today, pinotage is an early-ripening cultivar that results in a light- to medium-bodied wine with unique flavour characteristics.

*The large **oak barrels** used for maturation and storage of red wines are often decorated with hand-carved designs, like this beautiful example from the Delheim cellar in Stellenbosch.*

Stellenbosch *(see pp190–94)* is surrounded by gentle hills that are ideal for growing pinotage.

PINOTAGE INTERNATIONAL AWARDS

1987: Kanonkop (1985) – Beyers Truter voted Diners' Club "Winemaker of the Year"
1991: Kanonkop (1989 Reserve) – Robert Mondavi Trophy (USA)
1996: Kanonkop (1992) – Perold Trophy (International Wine and Spirit Competition)
1997: L'Avenir (1994) – Perold Trophy
1997: Jacobsdal (1994) – gold medal at Vin Expo Competition (France)

Two of South Africa's well-known pinotage labels

Lanzerac, in Stellenbosch, combines a luxury country hotel *(see p388)* with a working winery. Pinotage is one of a range of wines made by the estate.

WINE-MAKING PROCESS

natural product and winemakers
at care during harvesting, production
aturation to ensure that their wines are
gh quality and meet the requirements of
onsumer. Modern trends call for minimal
rference in the vineyard and cellar in order
allow the wines to "speak" for themselves.

Harvesting *is carefully timed to
achieve the best flavours and
characters from the grape.
Red grapes are traditionally
harvested later than white grapes,
to allow the development of riper
and more concentrated fruit.*

**Grapes are cut off the vine with sharp shears to
minimize damage to the mature berries**

Destalking *removes the stems, whose
high tannin content influences the
wine's flavour. The grapes are then
lightly crushed before being put into
a vat for fermentation to begin.*

**Destalker
and crusher**

**Fermentation
tank**

Fermentation *occurs over three to five
days. The juice is periodically pumped
over the "cap" formed by the skins to
extract the desired amount of colour
and tannin. After fermentation, the
juice is separated from the skins, and
matured before blending and bottling.*

**Storage tanks
and barrels**

Racking *is the transfer of fermented
wine from one tank or cask to another
to remove the "lees", sediments that
would cause the end product to appear
cloudy. Filtration and fining, often
using egg whites, removes impurities.*

Maturation *of pinotage
takes 12–15 months.
Traditionally, big vats
were used, but the
modern trend is to
use small barrels
made of French
or American
oak. The size of
the barrel, type
of wood and maturation
time combine to shape the character
of the wine. Once matured, the red
wines are ready for bottling.*

**Wooden
maturation
barrels**

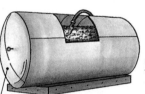

**The South African
Pinotage Producers,
Association**, *formed
in November 1995,
strives to maintain
a consistently high
standard for South
African pinotage. It
holds an annual com-
petition to judge the
year's ten best wines.*

Over 130 pinotages are made in South Africa

Whale-Watching

Shop sign in Hermanus

Some 37 whale and dolphin species and around 100 different types of shark occur in southern African waters. Only a small number come in close to the coast, however. Of the dolphins, bottlenose, common and Heaviside's are the most prolific, while common predatory sharks include the great white, tiger, ragged-tooth, oceanic white tip, bull (Zambezi), and mako. A large portion of the world's 4,000–6,000 southern right whales migrates north annually, with numbers increasing by seven per cent every year. They leave their subantarctic feeding grounds from June onwards to mate and calve in the warmer waters of the protected rocky bays and inlets that occur along the South African coastline.

WHALE-WATCHING

☐ Best vantage points

An albino calf was born in Hermanus in 1997.

Callosities *are tough, wart-like growths on the whale's skin, not barnacles as is often thought. Scientists use these unique markings to distinguish between individuals.*

THE SOUTHERN RIGHT WHALE

Early whalers named this species "southern right" *(Eubalaena australis)* because it occurred south of the Equator and was the perfect quarry. Its blubber was rich in oil, the baleen plates supplied whalebone for corsets, shoe horns and brushes, and when dead it floated, unlike other whales which sank. A protected species, it can migrate up to 2,600 km (1,615 miles) annually.

A characteristic V-shaped "blow" *can be seen when the southern right exhales. The vapour is produced by condensation, as warm breath comes into contact with cooler air.*

The "Whale Crier" *patrols the streets of Hermanus, blowing a kelp horn to inform passers-by of the best sightings of the day.*

WHALE ANTICS

The reasons for some types of whale behaviour are, as yet, unclear. Breaching, for example, may either indicate aggression or joyfulness; it may also simply help the animal get rid of lice.

Breaching: *the whale lifts its upper body out of the water and falls back into the sea with a massive splash.*

Southern right whales nurse their calves for at least six months.

Blowhole   Callosities

Lobtailing: *the flukes slap on the surface to produce a loud clap.*

Spyhopping: *the whale lifts its head vertically from the sea to observe what is happening on the surface.*

Shore-based whale watching is superb at Hermanus.

Humpback whales *are well known for their spectacular breaching behaviour, lifting their bodies well above the water. A striking feature of this species is its extremely long flippers.*

WHALE EXPLOITATION

In the years from 1785 to around 1805, some 12,000 southern right whales were killed off the southern African coast, but the northern right whale was the most ruthlessly hunted and is virtually extinct today. After the introduction of cannon-fired harpoons, humpbacks were the first large whale to be exploited. Some 25,000 were killed between 1908 and 1925. By 1935, when the League of Nations' Convention for the Regulation of Whaling came into effect, fewer than 200 southern right whales remained in southern African waters. Although numbers are increasing steadily, today's total population is only a fraction of what it once was.

Early whalers in False Bay

THE CAPE WINELANDS

T*he Cape's Winelands are a scenically enchanting region of lofty mountains and fertile valleys and slopes planted with orchards and vines. Nestled in the valleys are graceful Cape Dutch manor houses, of which stately Nederburg in Paarl (which hosts a famous wine auction), elegant Boschendal near Franschhoek and the charming Lanzerac Hotel in Stellenbosch are the best known.*

Stellenbosch was the first of the wineland towns to be established by Simon van der Stel, who had succeeded Jan van Riebeeck as governor in 1679. After van der Stel visited the area in November of that year and proclaimed it to be well watered and fertile, the first free burghers (early Dutch settlers who were granted tracts of land together with implements and oxen to help them establish farms) were sent to this valley to start a new life. Settlement in the Franschhoek valley followed with the arrival of the French Huguenots (Protestant refugees from Europe), and later Dutch as well as French pioneers established themselves in the Paarl area. The temperate Mediterranean climate of the Cape has ensured the survival of the early wine-making traditions.

The cool mountain and sea breezes create diverse conditions, and variable soil types – from the acidic and sandy alluvial soils of Stellenbosch to the lime-rich soils of Robertson – ensure a wide range of superb wines, both red and white, making South Africa the world's eighth-largest producer. Well over 100 estates, 66 co-operatives and more than 100 private cellars in the Western Cape support about 300,000 farm workers and their dependants.

Most of the estates and co-ops offer tastings, and the architectural legacy of the settlers is evident on a drive through any of the Wineland towns.

Klein Constantia in Cape Town is a particularly picturesque wine estate

◁ The Gazebo at Boschendal estate on the Franschhoek wine route

Exploring the Cape Winelands

After Table Mountain, the V&A Waterfront and Cape Point, the Winelands are the Western Cape's most popular attraction. The towns of Stellenbosch and Paarl are special for their elegant, gabled architecture, while Franschhoek enjoys an exquisite valley setting. Viewed from majestic mountain passes, the vineyards of Worcester and Robertson fit together like puzzle pieces, and the drawcard of Tulbagh *(see p211)* is its row of quaint, historical houses, meticulously restored after a devastating earthquake in 1969.

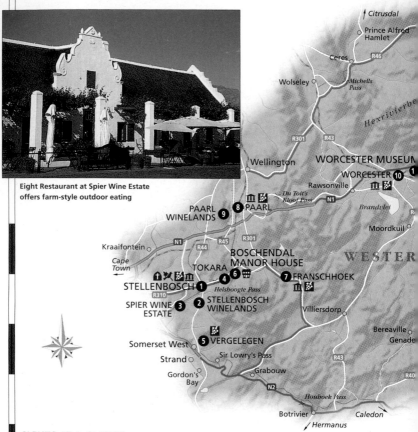

Eight Restaurant at Spier Wine Estate offers farm-style outdoor eating

SIGHTS AT A GLANCE

SEE ALSO

Delheim's vineyards, Stellenbosch

GETTING AROUND

The Winelands are served by two major national routes, the N1 and N2. All of the connecting principal roads are clearly signposted. Franschhoek, Paarl and Worcester are accessed from the N1, Stellenbosch from either the N1 or N2 national route. Robertson is reached from Worcester via the R60. The scenic mountain passes are well worth an excursion and own transport is essential if you wish to tour these areas. Alternatively, visitors can join one of the coach tours organized by major tour operators in Cape Town. Cape Town International is the closest airport.

Montagu is renowned for its hot springs

```
0 kilometres        50
0 miles        25
```

KEY

▬▬	Motorway
▬▬	Major road
═══	Minor road
▫▫▫	Untarred road
▬▬	Scenic route
▬▬	Main railway
──	Minor railway
✕	Pass

Rhebokskloof has converted a cellar into a cosy wine-tasting venue

Street-by-Street: Stellenbosch ●

Stained glass, Moederkerk

A centre of viticulture and learning, the historical university town of Stellenbosch is shaded by avenues of ancient oaks. The streets are lined with homes in the Cape Dutch, Cape Georgian, Regency and Victorian styles. Through the centuries, Stellenbosch has been ravaged by three fires, and several homes have had to be restored. The town is best explored on foot. Pamphlets of a walk are available from the tourist information bureau on Market Street; walking tours leave from the tourist office at 11am and 3pm daily.

The Burgher House was built in 1797. Its gable is an early example of the Neo-Classical style. The house is the headquarters of the Historical Homes of South Africa foundation.

VOC Kruithuis
The powder magazine of the VOC (Dutch East India Company) was built in 1777 to defend the early settlement. It now houses a small military museum.

Tourist information

Slave Houses, built around 1834 for the settlers' servants, are no longer thatched but still retain their original character.

★ Oom Samie se Winkel
In this "olde-worlde" village store (see p192) shoppers can step back in time and buy antiques, collectables, sticky toffee and biltong (see p408).

Libertas Parva and N2

KEY

– – – Suggested route

| 0 metres | | 250 |
| 0 yards | | 250 |

STAR SIGHTS

★ Oom Samie se Winkel

★ Dorp Street

For hotels and restaurants in this region see pp386–8 and pp417–18

St Mary's Anglican Church
*This church adjoins the town
square, Die Braak (fallow
land). Laid out in 1703, it
was used as a parade ground.*

Sasol Art Museum

Church Street is
the site of various
art galleries, as
well as D'Ouwe
Werf, one of South
Africa's oldest inns.

Village Museum and Moederkerk

Coetzenberg Sports Ground

Strand and Somerset West

La Gratitude's gable
is famous for the plaster
relief of the Lord's "all-
seeing" eye.

The Village Museum
*The historic houses that comprise
the Village Museum on Ryneveld
Street (see pp192–3) are decorated in different period styles
and are regarded as one of South
Africa's best restoration projects.*

The Rhenish Church
*The church was built in 1823
as a school for slaves' children
and "coloured" people.*

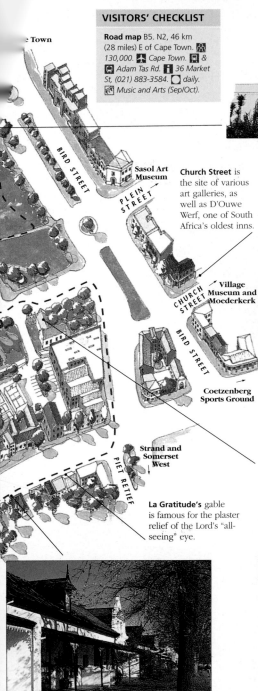

★ Dorp Street
*Some of the best-preserved historical façades in
Stellenbosch are found on this oak-lined street.*

Exploring Stellenbosch

The heart of the Winelands, this beautiful university town was founded in 1679 and is the historical cradle of Afrikaans culture. Its proud educational heritage began in 1863 with the establishment of the Dutch Reformed Theological Seminary. The Stellenbosch College was completed in 1886, the forerunner of the university, which was established in 1918. Today, the university buildings are beautifully integrated with the surrounding historical monuments, reinforcing the town's dignified atmosphere of culture and learning.

⊞ Rhenish Complex

Herte St. *Opening times of buildings vary and are subject to change.* **Tel** *(021) 883-3584 for information.*
This lovely group of old buildings, which is flanked by two modern educational centres – the Rhenish Primary School and the Rhenish Institute – is representative of most of all the architectural styles that have appeared in Stellenbosch over the centuries.

Parts of the Cape Dutch-style Rhenish parsonage are much older than the date of 1815 noted on the building's gable. The parsonage houses a museum of miniature rooms fitted with period furniture and a 50-sq-m (538-sq-ft) model railway set in a diminutive reconstruction of the landscape around Stellenbosch.

Leipoldt House, which was built around 1832, is an interesting combination of Cape Dutch and English Georgian architectural styles, while the Rhenish Church, facing Bloem Street, was erected in 1823 by the Missionary Society of Stellenbosch as a training centre and school for slaves and "coloured" people.

Oom Samie se Winkel

⊞ Oom Samie se Winkel

84 Dorp St. **Tel** *(021) 887-0797.*
◯ *8:30am–5:30pm (6pm summer) Mon–Fri, 9am–5pm (5:30pm summer) Sat, Sun.* ◉ *1 Jan, Good Fri, 25 Dec.*
This charming, restored Victorian shop, whose name means "Uncle Samie's Store", has been operating as a general store since 1904. Its original proprietor, bachelor Samie Volsteedt, used to live in the house next door. The store, a Stellenbosch institution

and a national monument, has bric-a-brac ranging from bottled preserves, basketry, candles and curios to 19th-century butter churns, plates and kitchen utensils. Visitors may also browse in Samie's Victorian Wine Shop for a special vintage or take tea under the leafy pergolas of the Koffiehuis restaurant.

🏛 Toy and Miniature Museum

Market St (next to tourist information office). **Tel** *(021) 887-2948.* ◯ *9:30am–5pm Mon–Sat, 2–5pm Sun.* ◉ *Sun (May–Aug).*
🅿 🛈 **www**.stelmus.co.za
The Toy and Miniature Museum offers a world of enchantment for both young and old and is well worth a visit. Housed in the old Rhenish Parsonage of 1815, the museum is the first of its kind in Africa. On display is an amazing collection of historical toys, including antique dolls and Dinky Toy motor cars, as well as a model railway-layout and miniature houses. The museum also boasts a number of finely detailed and exquisite 1:12 scale miniature rooms, each with delicate filigree work.

On sale in the small museum shop are furniture and accessories for dolls' houses, as well as mementos of the museum's unique treasures.

🏛 The Stellenbosch Village Museum

18 Ryneveld St. **Tel** *(021) 887-2948.* ◯ *9am–4:30pm Mon–Sat, 10am–4pm Sun.* ◉ *Good Fri, 25 Dec.*
🅿 ♿ 🛈 **www**.stelmus.co.za
This complex features houses from Stellenbosch's early settlement years to the 1920s, although the Edwardian and other early 20th-century houses are not open to the public. The museum includes four buildings. Schreuder House was built in 1709 by Sebastian Schreuder. It is the oldest of the houses and shows the spartan, simple lifestyle of the early settlers. Bletterman House, erected in 1789, belonged to Hendrik Bletterman, a wealthy *land-drost* (magistrate). Parts of

The Rhenish Complex, a splendid example of Cape Dutch architecture

ARTS AND CRAFTS IN STELLENBOSCH

Nurtured by Stellenbosch's environment of culture and learning, a community of artists, graphic designers, ceramicists and screen-printers has settled in the town. Multiple galleries and studios such as the Dorp Street Gallery at 176 Dorp Street and the Stellenbosch Art Gallery at 34 Ryneveld Street show the works of respected contemporary South African and local artists. Outside Stellenbosch, off Devon Valley Road, the Jean Craig Pottery Studio showcases all stages of its pottery production, and on Annandale Road, off the R310, visitors can watch spinners and weavers at work at Dombeya Farm. A detailed arts and crafts brochure is available from the Stellenbosch tourist information centre.

Work by Hannetjie de Clerq

The 18th-century middle-class Schreuder House at the Village Museum

Grosvenor House, the most elegant of the four, date back to 1782, but later additions to the house represent the Classicism of the 1800s. The house has period furnishings of the 1800s.

Constructed in 19th-century Victorian style, the interiors of Bergh House, occupied by Olof Marthinus Bergh from 1837 to 1866, accurately reflect the comfortable lifestyle of a wealthy burgher of the 1850s.

🏛 Sasol Art Museum

Eben Donges Centre, 52 Ryneveld St. **Tel** (021) 808-3691.
◯ 9am–4:30pm Mon–Sat.
● Good Fri, 25 Dec. 🖼 ♿ 📷
The interesting exhibition at the Sasol Art Museum focuses on anthropology, cultural history and art. Of particular interest to many visitors are the prehistoric artifacts, reproductions of San rock art and crafted utensils and ritual objects from South, West and Central Africa.

🏰 Van Ryn's Brandy Cellar

R310 from Stellenbosch, exit 33.
Tel (021) 881-3875. ◯ 9am–4:30pm
Mon–Sat (2:30pm Sat). ● public hols.
🖼 ♿ 📷 🏠 www.vanryns.co.za
At this cellar just southwest of Stellenbosch, where the well-known local brands Van Ryn and Viceroy are made, guided tours introduce the visitor to the intricate art of brandy production. Brandy courses are offered and include a lecture, an audiovisual presentation, as well as a brandy tasting and dinner.

Environs: The **Jonkershoek Nature Reserve** lies in a valley 10 km (6 miles) southeast of Stellenbosch that is flanked by the scenic Jonkershoek and Stellenbosch mountain ranges. The scenery is characterized by wooded ravines, pine plantations and montane *fynbos*, which in spring and summer includes tiny pink and white ericas, blushing bride *(Serruria florida)* and the king protea. The waterfalls and streams of the Eerste River provide abundant water for hikers, mountain bikers and horse riders. For the less energetic, there is a 12-km (7.5-mile) scenic drive into the mountains. Baboons and dassies may be sighted, and sometimes the elusive klipspringer. Of the many bird species in the reserve, the Cape sugarbird and malachite and orange-breasted sunbirds are most likely to be seen.

🏞 Jonkershoek Nature Reserve

Jonkershoek Rd. **Tel** (021) 866–1560. ◯ 8am–6pm daily.
● heavy rains (Jun–Aug). 🖼 📷
www.capenature.org.za

The sandstone mountains of the Jonkershoek Nature Reserve

Stellenbosch Winelands ❷

The Stellenbosch wine route was launched in
April 1971 by the vintners of three prominent
estates: Spier, Simonsig and Delheim. Today, the
route comprises a great number of estates and
co-operatives. Tasting, generally for a small fee,
and cellar tours are offered throughout the week
at most of the vineyards. A few of them can be
visited by appointment only and many are closed
on Sundays, so phoning ahead is advisable.

Saxenburg ①
Established as a farm in
1693, Saxenburg was turned
into a wine estate some 20
years ago. It has since become
a beacon of quality, winning
many accolades for its wines.
Tel *(021) 903-6113.*

Morgenhof ⑥
Established in 1692, this
historic farm is owned
by the Huchon-Cointreau
family of Cognac, in France.
Tel *(021) 889-5510.*

Delheim ⑦
Particularly atmospheric is Delheim's
wine cellar, with its brick arches,
wooden benches and mellow light.
Tel *(021) 888-4600.*

Thelema ⑤
A family-run estate,
Thelema is renowned for
producing quality wines.
Tel *(021) 885-1924.*

Neethlingshof ②
The Lord Neethling
restaurant in the old
manor house serves
Thai, Indonesian and
Vietnamese cuisine.
Tel *(021) 883-8988.*

KEY

▬	Motorway
▬	Tour route
=	Other roads
☀	Viewpoint

0 kilometres   5

0 miles   3

Ernie Els Wines ④
Established by
golfer Ernie Els, the
estate has wines that
are rated 93 points in
Wine Spectator.
Tel *(021) 881-3588.*

Spier Estate ③
This complex consists
of the manor house,
a riverside pub, farm
stall, two restaurants,
wine centre, a dam
and an open-air
amphitheatre.

TIPS FOR DRIVERS

Tour length: *Due to the great
number of wine estates, most
visitors tour three or four cellars,
stopping for lunch at one of the
superb estate restaurants.*
Getting there: *Visitors need a
car, unless they join an organized
tour from Cape Town.*

ـpier Wine Estate ❸

oad map B5. Stellenbosch. N2,
hen R310. **Tel** (021) 809-1100.
◯ tastings: 10am–4pm daily. 📷
♿ 🍴 📷 🎫 ◯ www.spier.co.za

Bounded by the Eerste River,
the Spier Wine Estate is one
of the oldest in the country. It
produced its first wine in 1712
and has buildings dating back
to 1767. The estate has undergone major renovations since
the early 1990s, when businessman Dick Enthoven purchased
it from the Joubert family.

Spier grows all the major
South African red grape varie-
tals – merlot, cabernet, shiraz
and pinotage – and produces
a good range of everyday reds
and whites, along with some
award-winning winemaker's
specials aimed at connoisseurs.

The world-class Moyo
restaurant *(see p418)* has
an excellent African fusion
menu, but there is also a
cheaper deli for those who
want to picnic on the rolling
lawns beside the lake.

There's plenty to do at this
family-friendly estate besides
eat and drink – you can visit
the cheetah outreach programme or bird of prey rehabilitation centre, follow a walking trail into the surrounding
protea-clad slopes, explore the
farm on horseback, browse
the well-stocked shop or visit
a craft centre promoting the
work of 90 local enterprises.

The estate is also home to
a luxury hotel with swimming
pool and conference facilities.

The vineyards surrounding the Tokara estate

Tokara ❹

Road map B5. Stellenbosch.
Off R310, on Helshoogte Pass.
Tel (021) 808-5900. ◯ 9am–5pm
Mon–Fri, 10am–3pm Sat & Sun.
📷 🍴 www.tokara.co.za

Merchant banker GT Ferreira
swapped his Sandton office
for the fresh Simonsberg air in
the early 1990s. Investment
and development at this
estate have been on a scale
seldom seen in South Africa.

Located up on the
Helshoogte Pass, Tokara
offers great views, art
exhibitions, fine food
and, above all, excellent
wines. The first bottling,
in 2000, was under
the Zondernaam
("without name") label:
it was an immediate
success, winning a
string of medals.

The estate also produces
brandy and olive oil. The

Choice white
wine of the area

restaurant is housed in a
striking elevated glass-and-
steel cube with wonderful
mountain views.

Vergelegen ❺

Road map B5. Somerset West.
Lourensford Rd from R44.
Tel (021) 847-1334. ◯ 9:30am–
4:30pm daily. ● Good Fri,
1 May, 25 Dec. 🎫 Summer:
10:30am, 11:30am & 3pm; winter:
11:30am & 3pm. 📷 🍴 📷
www.vergelegen.co.za

The vines and the five
old camphor trees in
front of the manor
house were planted in
1700, when the farm
belonged to Willem
Adriaan van der Stel.

Today, Vergelegen
is the property of
the Anglo-American
Group. The estate boasts a
unique cellar, built into the
slopes of Helderberg
Mountain. The ripe grapes
are fed into underground
destalking, crushing and steel
maturation tanks from above
the ground, thus maximizing
the effect of gravity and
minimizing bruising. This
results in a special brand
of velvet-smooth wines.

The estate also has a wine
museum and serves light
lunches in the charming Lady
Phillips Tea Garden (Lady
Florence Phillips lived here
from 1917 to 1940). The
extensive renovations undertaken by the Phillips revealed
the foundations of an octagonal
garden, built by Willem van
der Stel and now restored.

Visitors enjoying an outdoor meal at the Spier estate

For hotels and restaurants in this region see pp386–8 and pp417–18

Boschendal Manor House ⑥

Boschendal picnic basket

In 1685, Simon van der Stel granted the land on which the manor house stands to the French Huguenot Jean le Long. Originally named "Bossendaal" (which literally means "forest and valley"), the property was transferred in 1715, together with adjacent fertile farmland, to another Huguenot settler, Abraham de Villiers. It remained in the wine-farming de Villiers family for 100 years. Jan de Villiers built the wine cellar and coach house in 1796. His youngest son, Paul, was responsible for Boschendal Manor House in its present H-shaped form, which he built in 1812. Today, this historic estate is open to the public and offers a museum, a wine-tasting facility and restaurants.

The Back Entrance
Visitors to Boschendal enter the elegant Manor House via the gabled back door.

Crafted Room Dividers
Screens divided the front and back rooms in elegant Cape Dutch homes. Boschendal's original teak-and-yellowwood screen is decorated with geometric designs in dark ebony.

Rounded pilasters
supported the end gables. The front and back pilasters have a more classic design.

STAR FEATURES

★ Master Bedroom

★ Kitchen

★ Sitting Room

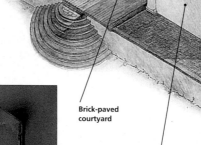

Brick-paved courtyard

★ Master Bedroom
This antique stinkwood four-poster bed was crafted in 1810 by local artisans. It is decorated with a hand-crocheted lace hanging and a light, embroidered cotton bedspread, both of which date from around 1820.

VISITORS' CHECKLIST

Road map B5. On R45
from Stellenbosch. **Tel** (021)
870–4200. ◯ 9:30am–5pm
daily. 🖼 ♿ 🍴 🛍 🏠
www.boschendal.com

★ Kitchen
*The original clay floor was washed
with a mixture of water and cow
dung to keep it cool and vermin-
free. Walls were painted dark
brown or red to hide the dirt.*

Long-Case Clock
*This Dutch long-case clock was
made by Carol Willem Bakker of
Groningen, in the Netherlands,
in the late 18th century.*

The sash windows are all
mounted by similarly curved
mouldings that reflect the
shape of the gables.

★ Sitting Room
*A gabled beefwood and stinkwood
cabinet-on-stand is the focal point of the
sitting room, which is resplendent with
Cape, Dutch and East Indian furniture.*

**The reception
room** has an
original section of
the 1812 wall frieze.

The drop-fanlight had to be
raised to allow visitors to enter.

FRIEZES
Painted wall decoration using oil-based
pigments is a craft believed to derive from
Europe. Pilasters and swags would feature
in reception and dining rooms, entwined
roses in drawing rooms and, in less
important rooms, a dado of a single colour
on a plain background would suffice. The
original 1812 wall frieze (in the reception
rooms) of black acorns and green leaves
was discovered during restoration in 1975.

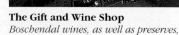

The Gift and Wine Shop
*Boschendal wines, as well as preserves,
souvenirs and gifts are sold at this shop.*

Franschhoek ❼

Farms in this beautiful valley encircled by the Franschhoek and Groot Drakenstein mountains were granted to several French Huguenot families *(see p47)* by the Dutch East India Company (VOC) in 1694. The new settlers brought with them considerable skill as farmers, crafters and viticulturists, leaving a marked influence on the area, which the Dutch

Victory statue named *De Fransche Hoek* (French Corner).

A collection of period furniture in the Franschhoek Huguenot Museum

Exploring Franschhoek

Upon arrival, the town's French heritage is immediately evident in lilting names like L'Ormarins and Haute Cabrière. The main attraction, besides an exquisite setting, is its gourmet cuisine, accompanied by the area's excellent wines. Around 30 restaurants *(see p417)* offer superb Malay, country and Provençale dishes.

Franschhoek's wine route was established in 1980 by Michael Trull, a former advertising executive. He formed the Vignerons de Franschhoek, with five founder cellars; today there are 20 estates.

A unique experience is a visit to **Cabrière Estate**. After an interesting cellar tour, host Achim von Arnim cleanly shears the neck off a bottle of his Pierre Jourdan sparkling wine with a sabre, an old technique known as *sabrage*, before serving the wine.

Visible at the top end of the main street is the **Huguenot Monument**, unveiled in 1948 to commemorate the arrival of the French settlers. A wide,

VISITORS' CHECKLIST

Road map B5. N1, exit 47, R45.
👥 *15,000.* 🚂 *Cape Town 79 km (49 miles) E.* ℹ️ *62 Huguenot St, (021) 876-2861.* ⭕ *daily.*
🎭 *Bastille Day (14 Jul).*

semi-circular colonnade frames three tall arches representing the Holy Trinity. Before them is the figure of a woman standing on a globe, with her feet on France. On a tall spire that surmounts the central arch is the "Sun of Righteousness".

🍷 Cabrière Estate

Tel *(021) 876-8500.* ⭕ *9am–5pm Mon–Fri, 10:30am–4pm Sat, 11am–4pm Sun.* ⭕ *public hols.* 🎫 *for groups (advance booking only).* ♿

🏛 Franschhoek Motor Museum

L'Ormarins Wine Estate, on the R45 outside Franschhoek. ***Tel*** *(021) 874-9000.* ⭕ *10am–5pm daily (to 4pm Sat–Sun).* 🖥 **www**.fmm.co.za
The museum charts the evolution of the automobile with a collection of some 220 vehicles, more than 80 of which will be on show at any one time.

🏛 Huguenot Memorial Museum

Lambrecht St. ***Tel*** *(021) 876-2532.* ⭕ *9am–5pm Mon–Sat, 2–5pm Sun.* ⭕ *Good Fri, 25 Dec.* 🖥 ♿ 🖥 📷
This museum functions mainly as a research facility covering the history and genealogy of the Cape's Huguenot families and their descendants. Of special note is a copy of the Edict of Nantes (1598), which permitted freedom of worship to Protestants in France, and a fine collection of old bibles, including one printed in 1636.

The Huguenot Monument in Franschhoek was built in 1943

For hotels and restaurants in this region see pp386–8 and pp417–18

Franschhoek's French Heritage

Franschhoek is a charming little country town with a distinctly French character. Wine-making traditions introduced by the early French Huguenot settlers are still pursued by viticulturists with surnames like Malherbe, Joubert and du Toit. Restaurants called Le Quartier Français and La Petite Ferme offer Provençale cuisine in light-filled, airy interiors, while Chez

The emblem of Cabrière Estate

Michel flies the French flag and serves delicacies like escargots, and Camembert marinated in Calvados brandy. Architecturally, the influence of French Classicism is evident in the graceful lines of the historic buildings. A good example is the Huguenot Memorial Museum, which was based on a design by the 18th-century French architect Louis Michel Thibault.

Freedom of religion *is symbolized by the dramatic central figure at the Huguenot Monument, which depicts a woman holding a bible in her right hand and a broken chain in the left.*

Refined classic gables *like that of the Huguenot Memorial Museum replaced the Baroque exuberance of earlier gables.*

The tricorn was worn by gentlemen.

Powdered wig

Mother-of-pearl buttons on garments were very fashionable.

THE FRENCH HUGUENOTS

After King Louis XIV of France revoked the Edict of Nantes in 1685, countless French Huguenots were forced to flee to Protestant countries. The Dutch East India Company's offer of a new life at the Cape of Good Hope was eagerly accepted by some 270 individuals.

Many Khoi were employed as slaves.

Hoop skirts were reinforced by stiff petticoats made from whalebone.

Grape presses *like this one, which stands outside the Huguenot Memorial Museum, were used by the French settlers to produce the first wines of the region.*

Restaurants *in Franschhoek exude typical French* joie de vivre *and ambience.*

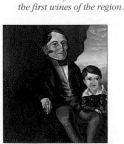

Rocco Catoggio *(1790–1858), depicted here with his grandson Rocco Cartozia de Villiers, married into a prominent Huguenot family.*

Paarl 🅸

In 1687 farms were allocated to early Dutch colonists in the pretty Berg River Valley, which is flanked to the north by Paarl Mountain. The name Paarl comes from the Dutch *peerlbergh* (pearl mountain), given to the outcrops by early Dutch explorer Abraham Gabbema when he spotted the three smooth domes after a rain shower. Mica chips embedded in the granite glistened in the sun, giving it the appearance of a shiny pearl. The town of Paarl was established in 1690.

The three granite domes on the outskirts of Paarl

Exploring Paarl

Large agricultural, financial and manufacturing companies are based in Paarl, making it a major player in the industry of the Western Cape. Its many tree-lined streets and graceful gabled homes, however, lend it a certain country charm. Paarl's 11-km (7-mile) Main Street, which runs along the Berg River, is shaded by oak trees and makes a very good starting point for exploring the town. A number of well-preserved 18th- and 19th-century Cape Dutch and Georgian houses are found along both sides of Main Street, some of the later ones displaying marked Victorian architectural influences.

Antique cupboard, Paarl Museum

La Concorde, a stately old structure in the Neo-Classical style built in 1956, is the head-quarters of the *Kooperatiewe Wijnbouwers Vereeniging* (KWV), the Cooperative Wine Farmers Association. The KWV was a controlling body which aimed to administer wine production, check the quality and develop export markets. It has since been privatized. Further

along Main Street, the **Paarl Museum** presents historical aspects of the town. Exhibits include a collection of stink-wood chairs, a Dutch linen press and yellowwood armoires. An excellent porce-lain collection features Imari, Kang Hsi, VOC and Canton pieces, and the kitchen is crammed with authentic utensils and furniture. Temporary displays on a wide field of related themes, such as the Khoina (*see pp46–7*), are arranged regularly.

Just off Paarl's Main Road lies **Laborie Estate**, first granted to a Huguenot settler in 1688. In 1774 it was acquired by Hendrick Louw, who subsequent-ly built the Cape Dutch homestead on it. It was care-fully restored after the KWV purchased the estate in 1972.

🏛 **Paarl Museum**
303 Main St. *Tel* (021) 872-2651. ☐ 9am–5pm Mon–Fri, 9am–1pm Sat. ◐ Good Fri, 25 Dec. 🖻 🖻 🖻

🍷 **Laborie Estate**
Taillefer St, off Main Rd. *Tel* (021) 807-3390. ☐ wine tastings: 9am–5pm daily (from 11am Sun). ◐ 1 Jan, 25 Dec. 🖾 book in advance. 🖾 🛦 🍴 www.laboriewines.co.za

---

VISITORS' CHECKLIST

Road map B5. On the N1. 🚗 150,000. ✈ Cape Town 56 km (35 miles) SW. 🚉 Paarl Station, Lady Grey St. 🚌 International Hotel, Lady Grey St. 🛈 216 Main Rd, (021) 872-4842. ☐ 8am–5pm Mon–Fri, 10am–1pm Sat, Sun & public hols. 🍷 Nederburg Wine Auction (Apr).

Environs: Just off Main Street, opposite La Concorde, is Jan Phillips Drive, an 11-km (7-mile) route to Paarl Mountain. The 500 million-year-old massif is the world's second-largest granite outcrop, after Uluru in Australia, and can be climbed with the aid of handholds.

The entrance to the Paarl Mountain Nature Reserve also lies on Jan Phillips Drive. From here, visitors can gain access to the **Language Monument** (*Taalmonument*). Designed by the architect Jan van Wyk, it was constructed around 1975, and is a tribute to the official recognition of the Afrikaans language 100 years earlier. The imposing monument is composed of three domes and three small pillars, all of vary-ing height and size, as well as a tall obelisk and a soaring column. Each of the elements acknowledges the linguistic influence and contribution of a different culture.

Language Monument
Signposted from Main St. *Tel* (021) 863-2800. ☐ 8am–5pm daily. 🛦 www.taalmuseum.co.za

The Language Monument, Paarl

Paarl Winelands Tour ❾

Picturesque wine farms spread out to either side of the imposing Paarl Mountain, with its three rounded domes. Estates dotted along its eastern slopes face the Klein Drakenstein and the Du Toitskloof mountains, while those on the west face look towards Table Mountain and False Bay.

Wine barrel

The vineyards around Paarl produce about one-fifth of South Africa's total wine crop. All of the estates on this route, which include well-known names like Nederburg and Laborie, offer wine tasting and sales on most days. Certain farms arrange cellar tours by appointment only.

Nederburg ⑤
Nederburg is famous for its annual Wine Auction, which showcases the spectrum of Cape wines.
***Tel** (021) 862-3104.*

Rhebokskloof Estate ①
This estate is named after the rhebok antelope that once lived in its valleys. ***Tel** (021) 863-8386.*

0 kilometres   3

0 miles   2

Fairview ②
The estate's Saanen goats can climb and enter this tower via a spiralling wooden ramp. Delicious goat's milk cheeses are sold.
***Tel** (021) 863-2450.*

Avondale ④
A top-quality organic producer, Avondale allows its wines to develop as naturally as possible.
***Tel** (021) 863-1976.*

WORCESTER

DU TOITSKLOOF PASS

KLEIN DRAKENSTEIN MTNS.

PAARL MOUNTAIN

Paarl Rock

Language Monument

LABORIE

Paarl

N1

SIMONSVLEI

N1

CAPE TOWN

R44

FRANSCHHOEK

R45

R44

R45

Berg

TIPS FOR DRIVERS

Getting there: *From Cape Town take exit 55 off the N1. This joins the R45, which then becomes Paarl's Main Street.*
Stopping-off points: *Simonsvlei and Laborie have formal restaurants.*
Tour length: *Depends on how many of the estates are visited (best limited to three or four).*

KEY

■ Motorway

■ Tour route

═ Other roads

Rupert & Rothschild Vignerons ③
Forged by two powerful families, R&R combines French and local winemaking on the historic Huguenot farm of Fredericksburg.
***Tel** (021) 874-1648.*

The road to Worcester leads through the scenic Dutoitskloof Pass

Worcester ⑩

Road map B5. N1 from Cape Town via Dutoitskloof Pass. 🚶 127,000. 🚉 Worcester Station. 🛈 25 Baring St, (023) 348-6244. ☐ Mon–Sat.

The city of Worcester, named after the Marquis of Worcester, the brother of one-time Cape governor Lord Charles Somerset, lies some 110 km (68 miles) east of Cape Town. It is the biggest centre in the Breede River Valley and the largest producer of table grapes in South Africa. Its wineries produce about one-quarter of the country's wine. Several of the estates, such as Nuy and Graham Beck, are open to the public for tastings and sales.

The attraction of a trip to Worcester is the drive through the Dutoitskloof Pass, which climbs to a height of 823 m (2,700 ft). Construction of the Huguenot Tunnel in 1988 shortened the pass by 11 km (7 miles), but

the route still affords scenic views of Paarl and the Berg River Valley.

At Church Square in the town, there is a Garden of Remembrance designed by Hugo Naude. The World War I Memorial is also here, along with a stone cairn erected at the time of the symbolic *Ossewa* (ox wagon) Trek of 1938 (*see p54*) that was undertaken to commemorate the historic Great Trek (*see pp50–51*).

Worcester's Dutch Reformed Church was built in 1832. However, the imposing Gothic-style steeple was added in 1927 after the original was blown away in gales.

The **KWV House of Brandy** offers the opportunity to learn more about the art

of brandy distillation through cellar tours with audio-visual presentations and tastings.

🏛 **KWV House of Brandy**
Cnr of Smith and Church sts.
Tel (023) 342-0255. ☐ tastings:
10am–3pm Mon–Fri; cellar tours:
10am (Afrikaans) and 2pm (English)
Mon–Fri. ● public hols. 🎟 ♿

Environs: The **Karoo Desert National Botanical Garden**, a short drive north of Worcester, contains plants that thrive in a semi-desert environment.

Jewel-bright mesembryanthemums are lovely in spring, while the unusual year-round species include the prehistoric welwitschias, and the *halfmens* (half-humans) and quiver trees. One area features plants grouped by regional and climatic zones. The succulent plant collection, the largest in Africa, is ranked by the International Succulent Organization as one of the most authentic of its kind in the world. There is also a trail with Braille text signs.

Old water pump in Worcester

🌿 **Karoo Desert National Botanical Garden**
Roux Rd, Worcester. **Tel** (023)
347-0785. ☐ 9am–7pm daily.
🎟 📷 (Aug–Oct only.) ♿ 🍴 🛍

Worcester Museum ⑪

See pp204–5.

The Dutch Reformed Church in Worcester

Robertson's Dutch Reformed Church

Robertson ⑫

Road map B5. R60 from Worcester or Swellendam. 🏘 *21,000.* ℹ *Cnr Reitz and Voortrekker sts, (023) 626-4437.* ◯ *daily.* 🎭 *Robertson Slow (Aug).* www.robertson62.com

Robertson lies in the Breede River Valley where sunny slopes create perfect conditions for vineyards and orchards. In addition to wine and table grapes, dried fruit is a major industry. The Robertson Wine Route comprises 48

Swan, Montagu Inn

cellars, many of which, like Van Loveren, are acclaimed for their choice Chardonnays.

Montagu ⑬

Road map B5. N15 fm Robertson. 🏘 *11,000.* ℹ *Bath St, (023) 614-2471.* ◯ *daily.*

The charm of Montagu lies in its many houses dating back to the early 1850s. In Long Street alone are 14 national monuments. The best-known feature is the

thermal springs (at a constant 43°C/109°F), situated 2 km (1 mile) from town.

The scenery of the northern edge of the Langeberg range has led to the establishment of trails for hikers, mountain bikers and 4WD enthusiasts.

The route to Montagu from Robertson passes through a 16-m (52-ft) long tunnel, above which stands the ruined Sidney Fort built by the British during the South African War.

Avalon hot springs in Montagu

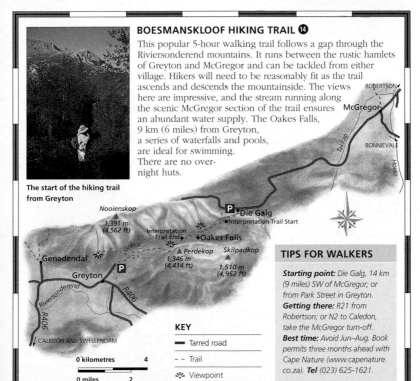

BOESMANSKLOOF HIKING TRAIL ⑭

This popular 5-hour walking trail follows a gap through the Riviersonderend mountains. It runs between the rustic hamlets of Greyton and McGregor and can be tackled from either village. Hikers will need to be reasonably fit as the trail ascends and descends the mountainside. The views here are impressive, and the stream running along the scenic McGregor section of the trail ensures an abundant water supply. The Oakes Falls, 9 km (6 miles) from Greyton, a series of waterfalls and pools, are ideal for swimming. There are no overnight huts.

The start of the hiking trail from Greyton

Nooienskop
1,391 m (4,562 ft)
Interpretation Trail End
Interpretation Trail Start
Die Galg
P
Oakes Falls
Perdekop
1,346 m (4,414 ft)
Skilpadkop
1,510 m (4,952 ft)
Genadendal
Gobos
Greyton
P
R406
Riviersonderend
R406
CALEDON AND SWELLENDAM
ROBERTSON
McGregor
Takkap
BONNIEVALE
Hoeks

KEY

━━ Tarred road

- - - Trail

🔆 Viewpoint

0 kilometres   4

0 miles   2

TIPS FOR WALKERS

Starting point: *Die Galg, 14 km (9 miles) SW of McGregor; or from Park Street in Greyton.*
Getting there: *R21 from Robertson; or N2 to Caledon, take the McGregor turn-off.*
Best time: *Avoid Jun–Aug. Book permits three months ahead with Cape Nature (www.capenature. co.za).* **Tel** *(023) 625-1621.*

Worcester Museum ⓫

The recreated buildings of this living "little farm" museum (previously known as Kleinplasie Open-Air Museum), which opened in 1981, portray the lifestyle of the early Cape pioneer farmer. Each one houses a particular home industry activity that was practised between 1690 and 1900. Here, visitors can watch brown bread being baked in an outdoor oven and the making of tallow candles and soap. At times the museum hosts seasonal activities such as wheat threshing and winnowing, grape treading and the distilling of *witblits* (a potent home-made brandy).

Candle holder

Tobacco Shed
Dried tobacco leaves are twisted together in this 19th-century, windowless farm shed.

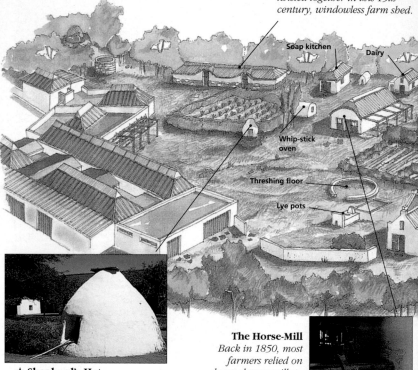

Soap kitchen

Dairy

Whip-stick oven

Threshing floor

Lye pots

★ **Shepherd's Hut**
Shepherds who tended distant flocks lived in temporary shelters like this one. In the treeless Karoo, domed stone roofs were used instead of wooden beams and trusses.

The Horse-Mill
Back in 1850, most farmers relied on horse-drawn mills to grind flour, a slow, laborious process.

STAR FEATURES

★ Shepherd's Hut

★ The Blacksmith

★ Labourer's Cottage

Canisters
This collection of 19th-century storage tins is displayed in the museum restaurant. Occasionally, these tins are found in "junk" stores today.

★ **The Blacksmith**
The smithy door, as well as the bellows used by the black-smith, date from 1820. The rest of the building has walls cast in clay and gables built from raw brick. The blacksmith can be seen daily, forging nails, hinges, forks and tripods.

★ **Labourer's Cottage**
Simply furnished and thatched with rye straw, one-roomed dwellings like this one date from the mid-19th century. They housed farm labourers and their families.

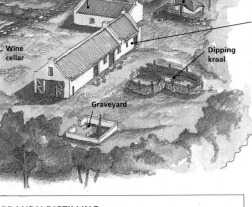

Farmhouse

Water mill

Wine cellar

Dipping kraal

Graveyard

Harness Room
This is a replica of an 1816 coach house, stable and harness room. The tanning of skins took place here, too.

BRANDY DISTILLING
Home-made brandies, first distilled in 1672 from peaches and apricots, became known as *witblits* (white lightning). To create this potent liquor, crushed fruit is fermented in large vats for ten days. The pulp is then poured into a brandy still and heated so that the alcohol evaporates. The resulting vapour is conducted from the dome of the still into a water-cooled condensation coil, which causes the alcohol to become liquid again. The first extraction, called the "heads", is discarded. Only the second, "the heart", is bottled; the rest is used as liniment.

Furnace Still

Coil

Brandy

Donkey Power
To draw water, a donkey rotated the bucket pump. Small buckets on a looped chain scooped water from the well and emptied it into irrigation furrows.

THE WESTERN COASTAL TERRACE

T*he dry, sunbaked landscape of South Africa's western coastal terrace is bounded to the east by the rugged Cederberg mountain range and to the west by the rocky, wind-blown Atlantic coastline. An unexpected surprise in this forbidding terrain is the appearance every spring of colourful fields of exquisite wildflowers in Namaqualand, the West Coast's most famous tourist attraction.*

The West Coast extends north of Cape Town to the Namibian border, where the fringes of the Namib desert epitomize the extremes of this vast, rain-deprived area. The arid, bleak and infertile vegetation zones support only hardy, drought-resistant succulents and geophytes (plants whose bulbs, corms or tubers store water and nutrients). The *fynbos* area south of Nieuwoudtville possesses a stark beauty, embodied in the weird forms of the Cederberg's outcrops that were eroded over millennia by wind and rain.

Further inland the country's wheat-belt centres on Malmesbury, and is an area of undulating golden corn whose texture changes constantly with the play of light on the rippling fields.

The upwelling of the Atlantic Ocean's cold Benguela Current along the coast brings rich phytoplanktonic nutrients to the surface, attracting vast shoals of pelagic fish (especially anchovies). This harvest from the sea supports an important fishing industry in the Western Cape. Saldanha Bay, a rather unappealing industrial town, is the fishing and seafood processing hub. It is also a major centre for the export of iron ore, which is mined at Sishen, further inland in the Northern Cape Province. Sishen is the site of the largest iron ore deposits in the world.

The Namaqualand is an arid belt stretching north of the Cederberg almost to the Namibian border, which is marked by the mighty Orange River. This belt only receives about 140 mm (6 inches) of rainfall during March and April, but the brief downpours provide sufficient moisture to clothe the landscape with colourful blooms from August to October every year.

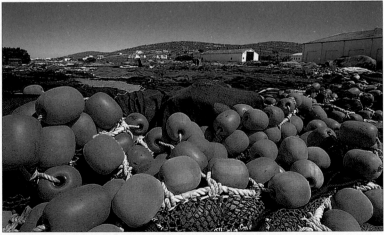

Fishing nets with bright yellow floats on the beach at St Helena Bay

◁ A carpet of yellow *Pentzia suffruticosa* frames this fisherman's cottage at Paternoster

Exploring the Western Coastal Terrace

Although first appearances seem to indicate that
the West Coast is a hot, barren wilderness, it
is a magnet to visitors during the spring months
when flowering daisies and gazanias paint the
landscape with bold colour splashes. The region
is also known for its spectacular walking and
hiking trails in the Cederberg mountains, which
are famous for their contorted rock formations
and breathtaking views. Along the coastline, the
cold waters of the Atlantic yield a vast array of
delicious seafood, from rock lobster and black
mussels to fresh linefish, which can be sampled
at a number of *skerms* (open-air restaurants)
that have been established on the beaches.

Fishing trawlers at anchor in Lamberts Bay harbour

The Wolfberg Arch in the Cederberg

SIGHTS AT A GLANCE

Cederberg **9**
Citrusdal **7**
Clanwilliam **8**
Darling **4**
Lamberts Bay **3**
Malmesbury **5**
Tulbagh **6**

West Coast **1**
West Coast National
Park pp212–13 **2**

Driving Tour
Namaqualand Tour **10**

GETTING AROUND

A car is essential for touring this region as no
regular public transport service exists. Private
coach companies do operate along this section
of coast, however. During the flower season,
a large number of organized coach tours are
available from operators based in Cape Town.
The N7, a major national route, runs straight up
the West Coast from Cape Town to the Namibian
border, with main roads leading off to the coast
and interior. Between Cape Town and St Helena
Bay, the R27 offers a more scenic route with
intermittent views of the coastline. The closest
international airport is in Cape Town.

0 kilometres 50

0 miles 25

olsdrif

7

einkopf

Bulletrap

ep *Upington* →

N14

Springbok

Burke's Pass

Kamieskroon

10

Garies

Groen

riep

Bitterfontein

Landplaas

Lutzville

Doring Bay

Kliprand

1024 m

Loeriesfontein

Nuwerus

Brandkop

Nieuwoudtville

Grootdrif Calvinia

Vanrhynsdorp R27

Vredendal

Klawer *Botterkloof Pass*

R364

WESTERN Doringbos

CAPE Uitspankraal

AMBERTS BAY 3

10 8 CLANWILLIAM

Leipoldtville Wuppertal

Elands bay Sandberg

Paleisheuwel 9

Noordkuil 7 CITRUSDAL

R27 Eendekuil

t. Helena Bay Velddrif

denburg Sauer De Hoek

aldanha *Groot Berg* Porterville

Hopefield R44

Langebaan Moorreesburg *Gydopas*

WEST COAST Riebeek

ATIONAL PARK Wes 6 TULBAGH

Yzerfontein 4 DARLING

1 5 MALMESBURY

WEST

COAST R27

Blouubergstrand Philadelphia

N7

Milnerton

Cape Town ↓

White Namaqualand daisies *(Dimorphotheia pluvialis)*, tall yellow bulbinellas *(Bulbinella floribunda)* and magenta *Senecio* open their petals to the sun

SEE ALSO

- *Where to Stay* pp389–90
- *Where to Eat* pp418–19

KEY

—	Major road
===	Minor road
·=·	Untarred road
—	Scenic route
----	Main railway
——	Minor railway
▬	International border
▬	Provincial border
▲	Summit
✕	Pass

Lookout, West Coast National Park

Fishermen drag their boat to the water at Paternoster

The West Coast ❶

Road map A4, A5.

From Cape Town, the R27 leads up the West Coast to the Olifants River, linking the coastal towns. Between Milnerton, Bloubergstrand and Melkbosstrand, Marine Drive (M14), which becomes Otto Du Plessis Drive, is a scenic road with wonderful views of the dunes and sea. Travelling north, the suburb of Bloubergstrand, today a sought-after residential area, is famous for its unsurpassed views of Table Mountain seen across the 16-km (10-mile) wide expanse of Table Bay, and lies at the foot of the Blouberg (blue mountain). The broad beaches and bays of Bloubergstrand are popular with watersports enthusiasts and families, although south-easterly summer gales can create windy conditions.

Heading north along the R27, silver domes come into view. They belong to Koeberg Nuclear Power Station, the only nuclear facility in Africa.

A left turn from the R27 onto the R315 leads to Yzerfontein, whose claim to fame is its prolific crayfish (rock lobster) reserves. The sweet-tasting flesh of this shellfish is a sought-after local delicacy and during the crayfishing season (Dec–Apr), the local campsite attracts countless divers and their families. Permits, allowing daily catches of four crayfish per person, are obtainable at any post office.

Continuing north on the R27, past the industrial fishing hub and harbour of Saldanha, is Vredenburg. From here, a 16-km (10-mile) drive leads to Paternoster, a typical little wind-blown fishing village with white-washed cottages. Legend recounts that the Portuguese sailors shipwrecked here recited the Paternoster (Our Father) to give thanks for their survival. The village

is a popular weekend retreat for Capetonians. Local regulations stipulate that new holiday cottages must be built in the traditional West Coast style.

Around a rocky headland, the village of **St Helena** perches at the edge of a sheltered bay. Just before the village a signposted turnoff leads to the monument commemorating Portuguese navigator Vasco da Gama's landing on these shores on St Helena's Day, 7 November, in 1497.

The fishing industry here benefits from the cold, north-flowing Benguela Current. It ensures a ready supply of rich nutrients that sustain the vast populations of anchovies and other shoals of pelagic fish.

West Coast National Park ❷

See pp212–13.

A seal pup relaxes on the rocks of Bird Island, Lamberts Bay

Lamberts Bay ❸

Road map A4. 🚶 *7,000.* 🚻 *Hoof St, (027) 432-1000.* 🕐 *Mon–Sat; also Sun during flower season.* **www**.lambertsbay.co.za

This little fishing town, an hour's drive west of Clanwilliam on the R364, was named after Rear-Admiral Sir Robert Lambert, a senior Royal Navy officer who monitored the marine survey of this section of coastline.

For visitors, the main attraction is **Bird Island**, which lies about 100 m (328 ft) offshore

---

OPEN-AIR SEAFOOD FEASTS

Along the West Coast, restaurateurs have established open-air eating places known as *skerms* (Afrikaans for "shelters") with names like Die Strandloper *(see p419)*, in Langebaan,

and Die Muisbosskerm *(see p418)*, in Lambert's Bay. Reed roofs provide shade and mussel shells are used as utensils, but the major appeal is the fresh seafood on offer: smoked angelfish, *snoek* (a large gamefish that tastes best when barbecued), spicy mussel stews, thin slices of *perlemoen* (abalone), and calamari.

Lunch at Die Strandloper

and is accessible via a break-water-cum-harbour wall. The island is a breeding ground for thousands of African penguins, Cape cormorants and the striking Cape gannet with its painted face. There is a small museum, and a viewing tower allows visitors to remain unobtrusive while observing the birds' behaviour.

Lamberts Bay Boat Charter offers trips of varying duration depending on interest. From August to October, groups of visitors are taken out to spot dusky dolphins and southern right whales, while penguins, Cape fur seals and Heaviside's dolphins, endemic to the West Coast, can be seen throughout the year.

✗ Bird Island
Tel (022) 931-2900. ⬤ *7am–5pm daily.* 🖳 *www.capenature.co.za*

➤ Lamberts Bay Boat Charter
Tel (073) 249-8977.
www.sadolphins.co.za

Darling ❹

Road map B5. R307. 🏠 *6,000.*
🛈 *Cnr Pastorie & Hill sts, (022) 492-3361.* 🎪 *Wildflower Show (Sep), Rocking the Daisies (Oct).*

Darling is surrounded by a farming region of wheat-fields, vineyards, sheep and dairy cattle, but the small town is best known for its annual springflower show *(see p36).*

Darling also lays claim to satirist Pieter-Dirk Uys *(see p166),* who gained fame for

A National Monument on historical Church Street in Tulbagh

the portrayal of his female alter ego, Evita Bezuidenhout, fictitious ambassadress of the equally fictitious homeland called Baphetikosweti. **Evita se Perron** (Evita's platform) is situated on a defunct railway platform and draws crowds to hear the hilarious, razor-sharp analyses of local politics.

🖼 Evita se Perron
Tel (022) 492-2831. 🖼 🍴 ♿ 🍷

Malmesbury ❺

Road map B5. 🏠 *21,000.*
🚉 *Bokomo Rd.* 🛈 *1 Church St, (022) 487-1133.* ⬤ *Mon–Fri.*

Malmesbury, the heart of South Africa's wheatland, lies in the *Swartland* (black country), a term that has, at times, been attributed to the

region's soil, at others to its renosterbush, a local shrub that turns a dark hue in winter. This town is South Africa's major wheat distributor and site of one of its largest flour mills. The surrounding wheat-fields undergo constant meta-morphosis, and the velvety shoots rippling in the breeze or cropped furrows with bales piled high are a lovely sight.

Tulbagh ❻

Road map B5. R44. 🏠 *18,000.*
🚉 *Station Rd.* 🚌 *along Church St.*
🛈 *4 Church St, (023) 230-1345.* ⬤
daily. **www**.*tulbaghtourism.co.za*

In 1700, Governor Willem Adriaan van der Stel initi-ated a new settlement in the Breede River Valley, naming it Tulbagh after his predecessor.

Encircled by the Witzenberg and Winterhoek mountains, in 1969 the town was hit by an earthquake measuring 6.3 on the Richter scale. Eight people died and many historic build-ings were badly damaged. The disaster resulted in a five-year restoration project undertaken along Church Street, lined with no less than 32 18th- and 19th-century Victorian and Cape Dutch homes. The oldest building, Oude Kerk (old church) Volksmuseum, dates back to 1743 and contains the original pulpit, pews and Bible. De Oude Herberg, Tulbagh's first boarding house (1885), is now a guest house and art gallery *(see p388).*

Cape gannets populate Bird Island in their thousands

West Coast National Park ❷

Watch out – tortoises on the road

The West Coast National Park encompasses Langebaan Lagoon, the islands Schaapen, Jutten, Marcus and Malgas, and the Postberg Nature Reserve, which is opened to the public each spring (Aug–Sep) when it is carpeted with colourful wildflowers like daisies and gazanias. The park is one of South Africa's most important wetlands, harbouring some 250,000 waterbirds including plovers, herons, ibis, and black oystercatchers. Antelope species such as elands, kudus and zebras can also be seen. Accommodation in the park consists of chalets and houseboats on the lagoon.

Cape Cormorants
Abundant on the coast, they feed on pelagic shoaling fish, but have been affected by overfishing.

SEABIRDS

Langebaan Lagoon, 15 km (9 miles) long, at an average depth of 1 m (3 ft), offers a sheltered haven for a great number of seabirds, including waders, gulls, flamingos, and pelicans. Resident and migrant species take advantage of the Atlantic's nutrient-rich water to rear their chicks.

The curlew sandpiper's curved bill enables it to probe for small crustaceans.

Hartlaub's gulls are endemic to the West Coast and forage for food along the shore in the morning hours.

Lesser flamingos, distinguished from greater flamingos by their smaller size and red bill, often congregate in large flocks.

White Pelicans
Langebaan Lagoon is home to one of only a handful of white pelican breeding colonies in southern Africa. The species feeds on fish, which it scoops up in the large pouch under its beak. Pelicans fly and feed information.

★ Geelbek Homestead
This educational centre in the park is a mine of fascinating information on the fauna, flora and ecology of the region. Bird-watchers can observe many different species from the nearby hide, and there is also a restaurant.

Plank
Stoney Head
Kreeftebaai
Vondeling Island
Kra
Sixteen Mile Beach
Churchhaven
Bird hide
Strandveld Educational Trail
Entrance
Yzerfontein

0 kilometres   5
0 miles   2.5

STAR FEATURE

★ Geelbek Homestead

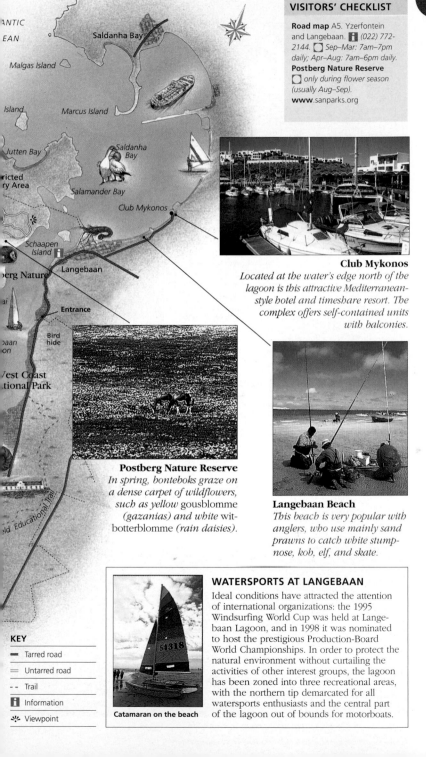

VISITORS' CHECKLIST

Road map A5. Yzerfontein
and Langebaan. ▮ *(022) 772-
2144*. ◯ *Sep–Mar: 7am–7pm
daily; Apr–Aug: 7am–6pm daily.*
Postberg Nature Reserve
◯ *only during flower season
(usually Aug–Sep).*
www.sanparks.org

Club Mykonos
*Located at the water's edge north of the
lagoon is this attractive Mediterranean-
style hotel and timeshare resort. The
complex offers self-contained units
with balconies.*

Postberg Nature Reserve
*In spring, bonteboks graze on
a dense carpet of wildflowers,
such as yellow* gousblomme
(gazanias) and white wit-
botterblomme *(rain daisies).*

Langebaan Beach
*This beach is very popular with
anglers, who use mainly sand
prawns to catch white stumpnose, kob, elf, and skate.*

WATERSPORTS AT LANGEBAAN

Ideal conditions have attracted the attention
of international organizations: the 1995
Windsurfing World Cup was held at Langebaan Lagoon, and in 1998 it was nominated
to host the prestigious Production-Board
World Championships. In order to protect the
natural environment without curtailing the
activities of other interest groups, the lagoon
has been zoned into three recreational areas,
with the northern tip demarcated for all
watersports enthusiasts and the central part
of the lagoon out of bounds for motorboats.

Catamaran on the beach

KEY

— Tarred road
= Untarred road
-- Trail
▮ Information
☆ Viewpoint

Zinc-roofed houses along Church Street in Clanwilliam

Citrusdal **7**

Road map B4. 🏔 *2,900.* ℹ️ *39 Voortrekker St, (022) 921-3210.* ⭕ *Mon–Fri.* **www**.*citrusdal.info*

Frost-free winters and the Olifants River Irrigation Scheme have made Citrusdal South Africa's third-largest citrus district. The first orchard was planted with seedlings from Van Riebeeck's garden at the foot of Table Mountain *(see pp132–3).* One tree, after bearing fruit for some 250 years, is now a national monument.

The Goede Hoop Citrus Cooperative has initiated scenic mountain bike trails around Citrusdal, like the old Ceres and Piekenierskloof passes.

Clanwilliam **8**

Road map B4. 🏔 *4,000.* 🚉 *from Cape Town station.* ℹ️ *Main Rd, (027) 482-2024.* ⭕ *Mon–Sat.*

Clanwilliam is the headquarters of the *rooibos* (red bush) tea industry. The shoots of the wild shrub are used to make a caffeine-free tea that is low in tannins and also considered to have medicinal properties *(see p408).*

Clanwilliam Dam, encircled by the Cederberg Mountains, stretches for 18 km (11 miles) and is popular with waterskiers. Wooden holiday cabins line the banks, and an attractive campsite has been established right at the water's edge.

Cederberg **9**

Road map B4. *Ceres. Algeria Cape Nature Conservation turnoff from N7.* ℹ️ *(027) 482-2403. Anyone wishing to hike or stay in the Cederberg area will require a permit.* 🅰 🚶 🎣 🔭

From the north, the Cederberg is reached via Pakhuis Pass and the Biedouw Valley, 50 km (31 miles) from Clanwilliam. Coming from the south, take the N7 from Citrusdal. The Cederberg range is a surreal

wilderness of sandstone peaks that have been eroded into jagged formations. It is part of the Cederberg Wilderness Area which was proclaimed in 1973 and covers 710 sq km (274 sq miles). The attraction of the range is its recreational appeal – walks, hikes, camping and wonderful views. The southern part, in particular, is popular for its dramatic rock formations: the Maltese Cross, a 20-m (66-ft) high pillar, and the Wolfberg Arch with its sweeping views of the area. At the Wolfberg Cracks, the main fissure measures over 30 m (98 ft). The snow protea *(Protea cryophila),* endemic to the upper reaches of the range, occurs on the Sneeuberg which, at 2,028 m (6,654 ft), is the highest peak. The Clanwilliam cedar, after which the area was named, is a species that is protected in the Cederberg Wilderness Area. At the southern end of the Cederberg is the **Kagga Kamma Private Game Reserve**, where visitors can go on game drives at sunrise and sunset, view Bushman and other examples of rock art, admire ancient Bushman living sites and take part in such activities as bird-watching, stargazing or hiking. Cottages and huts offer accommodation.

Road marker at Kagga Kamma

📷 **Kagga Kamma Private Game Reserve**
Southern Cederberg. **Tel** Tour reservations: (021) 872-4343 (prebook). ⭕ daily. 📷 🍴 (meals included). 🌐 **www**.kaggakamma.co.za

Scenic view over Clanwilliam Dam to the Cederberg mountains

Rock Formations of the Cederberg

During the Palaeozoic pre-Karoo era several hundred million years ago, the formations that over time became the Cape Folded Mountains were under water. Of the sandstones, shales and quartzites of these Cape formations, Table Mountain sandstone was the most resilient. In the Karoo Period, tectonic forces produced the crumpled folds of the Cape mountains. Subsequent erosion wore away the soft rock, leaving the harder layer. The resulting formations can be seen today in the Cederberg's twisted landscape. The original grey-coloured sandstone of the bizarre terrain has frequently been stained a rich red by iron oxides.

THE MALTESE CROSS

This unusual 20-m (66-ft) high rock formation, a day hike from Dwarsrivier Farm (Sanddrif), consists partly of Table Mountain sandstone. More resistant to erosion, it forms the upper portion of the cross.

Hiking
Paths made by woodcutters some 100 years ago now provide access for hikers.

Softer layers erode faster, causing a thinner base.

Cederberg Cedar
Some 8,000 trees are planted annually to ensure the survival of this endemic species. The cedars were once popularly used as telephone poles.

The scree slope, composed of fallen debris from above.

Wolfberg Cracks
Lovely views greet hikers at the Wolfberg Cracks, a 75-minute walk from the Wolfberg Arch.

Wolfberg Arch
The majestic Wolfberg Arch is the Cederberg's most unique formation. A favourite with photographers, it provides a natural frame for memorable images.

The arch, 30 m (98 ft) high, overlooks a region known as the Tankwa Karoo.

Bizarre rock sculptures supported on brittle pillars.

Cracks are caused by the expansion and contraction of the rock.

Erosion
Over aeons, wind and water have carved the Cederberg into a fairytale landscape. Pinnacles, arches and fissures resemble the strange castles of another world, while the rock outcrops seem alive with gargoyles and goblins.

Namaqualand Tour ❿

Gazania krebsiana

Namaqualand, an area of about 48,000 sq km (18,500 sq miles), from the Orange River in the north to the mouth of the Olifants River in the south, is a region of sharp contrasts. In spring, this scrub-covered, arid land blazes with colour – from fuchsia pinks to neon yellows and oranges – as a myriad daisies and flowering succulents open their petals to the sun. The seeds of the drought-resistant plants lie dormant in the soil during the dry months, but if the first rains (usually around March and April) are good, they burst into bloom from August to October.

0 kilometres 50
0 miles 25

Skilpad Wild Flower Reserve ⑥
Lying 17 km (11 miles) west of Kamieskroon, the reserve was bought by WWF-SA (World Wide Fund for Nature in South Africa) in 1993 to protect the area's plant life, and taken over by SANParks in 1998. The higher rainfall resulting from the reserve's proximity to the West Coast guarantees excellent displays. Bright orange daisies *(Ursinia* sp*)* and gazanias are at their most spectacular here.

Tienie Versfeld Wildflower Reserve ①
After attending the Darling wildflower and orchid shows, visitors can drive to this nearby reserve and view expanses of wildflowers in their natural habitat. Namaqualand's best displays vary from season to season, depending on the rainfall patterns.

Postberg Nature Reserve ②
This is the most popular flower-viewing spot among locals, as it is an easy day-trip from Cape Town, and visitors are not often disappointed at its multicoloured bands of annuals stretching as far as the eye can see.

KEY

◼ Tour route
═ Other roads
--- Park boundary
✵ Viewpoint
▣ Wildflower viewing

Goegap Nature Reserve ⑦
Situated 15 km (9 miles) east of Springbok, the "capital" of Namaqualand, the Goegap Nature Reserve's flat plains and granite koppies support hundreds of succulents. Over the years, the reserve has recorded 580 plant species within its boundaries.

Nieuwoudtville Wildflower Reserve ⑤
This reserve contains the world's largest concentration of geophytes (plants with bulbs, corms or tubers). Of the 300 plant species, the more prominent ones are the irises and lily family.

Vanrhynsdorp ④
This town is situated in the stony *Kners-vlakte* (a name that literally translates as "gnashing plains"). Spring ushers in dramatic displays of succulents such as *vygies*, and annuals like *botterblom* and *gousblom* (*Ursinia* sp).

Biedouw Valley ③
This valley is famous for its mesembryanthemums, a succulent species more commonly known by its Afrikaans name, *vygie*. Daisies and mesembryanthemums form the major group of Namaqualand's 4,000 floral species.

TIPS FOR DRIVERS

Tour length: Due to the extent of the area, trips can vary from one to three days. Contact **www**.capetown.travel for details of tour operators.
When to go: Flowers bloom Aug–Oct – call Namaqualand Information Bureau for the best viewing areas. Flowers only open on sunny days, and are best between 11am and 4pm; drive with the sun behind you and flowers facing you.
Where to stay and eat: Each town has its own hotel, as well as guesthouses and a campsite. Private homes may also offer accommodation.
🛈 Namaqualand Information Bureau, (027) 712-2820.
www.namaqualand.com

THE SOUTHERN CAPE

T*he Southern Cape's interior is characterized by its towering mountains, whose high-walled passes offer visitors a number of awe-inspiring scenic drives. The region's largest town, Oudtshoorn, upholds its reputation as the ostrich-farming capital, while on the coast, tourists are drawn to Hermanus every year to watch southern right whales from excellent vantage points along the coast.*

The quaint seaside towns of the Southern Cape lie in a region known as the Overberg, which extends east of the Hottentots Holland mountains and is defined to the north by the Riviersonderend mountains and the Langeberg and Outeniqua ranges. Along the coast, the Overberg stretches to the mouth of the Breede River, just north of the De Hoop Nature Reserve. Sir Lowry's Pass, a circuitous road that winds high above Gordon's Bay and offers splendid views across the False Bay coastline, is the gateway to the Overberg.

Early European settlers were prevented from crossing this formidable mountain barrier until Sir Lowry's Pass was constructed by Major Charles Michell in 1828. Before this, the Overberg was populated by the nomadic Khoina *(see pp46–7)*, attracted by abundant mountain water and grazing for

their herds. Elephant and other wildlife also roamed the area; in fact, the pass follows an ancient migratory trail, named *gantouw* (eland's path) by the indigenous peoples. As the settlers penetrated further into unexplored territory they faced another mountain barrier: north over the Langeberg and Outeniqua lay the Little Karoo, protected by the Swartberg mountains. It was in this territory that two of South Africa's greatest road builders, Andrew Geddes Bain and his son, Thomas Bain, made their fame. The spectacular Four Passes Tour *(see pp228–9)* is a worthwhile excursion; visitors can detour to the exquisite dripstone formations of the nearby Cango Caves or ride a giant bird at Oudtshoorn's ostrich farms.

At the coast, windswept Cape Agulhas marks the meeting point of the cold Atlantic and warm Indian oceans.

Thatched fishermen's cottages at Arniston (Waenhuiskrans)

◁ **An ancient stalagmite is bathed in eerie light at the Cango Caves, near Oudtshoorn**

Exploring the Southern Cape

An alternative route to the N2 over Sir Lowry's Pass, which drops down into wheatfields and farmland dotted with cattle and woolly merino sheep, is the R44, a scenic road that hugs the coastline from Gordon's Bay to Hermanus. Coastal hamlets like Cape Agulhas – official meeting point of two oceans – offer a calm contrast to the majestic passes that lead through the mountains. Oudtshoorn is where the mansions of former "ostrich barons" can be seen, and nearby lies the underground splendour of the Cango Caves.

Wind-blown sand dunes at De Hoop Nature Reserve

Rocky beach near Arniston's cave

GETTING AROUND

The N2 over Sir Lowry's Pass cuts right across the Southern Cape to Riversdale, where the R323 heads north to Oudtshoorn, the Cango Caves and the country's most dramatic passes, which are linked by the R328. All of the coastal towns are accessed via main routes feeding off the N2. The De Hoop Nature Reserve can be reached via an untarred road from both Bredasdorp and the N2. Coach tours offer day trips, otherwise public transport services are severely limited, so a car is essential for touring this region. The closest international airport is in Cape Town

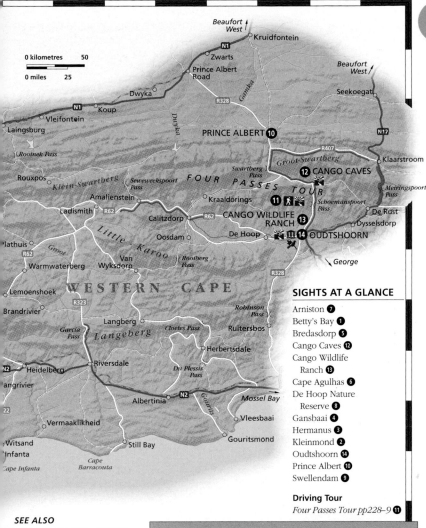

Beaufort
West
Kruidfontein

N1
Zwarts
Prince Albert
Road
Dwyka

Beaufort
West

Seekoegat

N1
Koup

Vleifontein

Laingsburg

Rooinek Pass

Rouxpos

Klaarstroom

N12

Klein-Swartberg

Seweweekspoort Pass

Amalienstein

Ladismith   R62

PRINCE ALBERT 🔟

Groot-Swartberg

Swartberg Pass

12 CANGO CAVES

FOUR PASSES TOUR

Kraaldorings   11   🚶

Schoemanspoort Pass

Meiringspoort Pass

De Rust

Calitzdorp   R62

CANGO WILDLIFE RANCH   13

Oosdam

Little Karoo

Groot

Van
Wyksdorp

Rooiberg Pass

De Hoop

14 OUDTSHOORN

Dysselsdorp

R328

George

Vlathuis   R62

Warmwaterberg

Lemoenshoek

Brandrivier   R323

WESTERN   CAPE

Langberg

Garcia Pass

Riversdale

Langeberg

Cloetes Pass

Robinson Pass

Ruitersbos

Herbertsdale

Du Plessis Pass

N2   Heidelberg

angrivier

22

Vermaaklikheid

Albertinia   N2

Gouritz

Mossel Bay

Vleesbaai

Witsand   Still Bay

Infanta

Cape Infanta   *Cape Barracouta*

Gouritsmond

SEE ALSO

- **Where to Stay** pp390–91
- **Where to Eat** p419

KEY

— Major road

===== Minor road

= = = Untarred road

— Scenic route

▬▬▬ Main railway

— Minor railway

▲ Summit

✕ Pass

A group of residents at High Gate Ostrich Farm, near Oudtshoorn

Betty's Bay ❶

Road map B5. R44 SE of Gordon's Bay.
👥 500. ✈ Cape Town International.
ℹ 14 Harbour Rd, Kleinmond, (028)
271-5657. www.ecoscape.org.za

This seaside village, named after Betty Youlden, the daughter of a property developer who lived here in the 1900s, is a popular weekend retreat. It is such a remote spot that electrification of some local homes occurred only in 1993.

Of significance is the **Harold Porter National Botanical Garden** on the slopes of the Kogelberg which rises behind Betty's Bay. Harold Porter, a partner in a property agents' business in the town, bought this tract of land in 1938 to preserve the rich mountain and coastal *fynbos* vegetation. Over 1,600 species of ericas, proteas and watsonias – one of the densest concentrations in the Southern Cape – attract sugarbirds and sunbirds. A permit is required for the Leopard Kloof Trail that runs through dense riverine forest to a picturesque waterfall. The penguin reserve at Stoney Point (open daily) protects a small breeding colony of African penguins.

Erica, Harold Porter Garden

🌿 Harold Porter National Botanical Garden

Tel (028) 272-9311. ⬜ 8am–4:30pm daily (to 5pm Sat, Sun, pub hols; 7pm summer). 📷 🖼
🚶 ℹ www.sanbi.org

Wide lagoon mouth and beach at Kleinmond

Kleinmond ❷

Road map B5. R44 E of Betty's Bay.
👥 2,900. ℹ 14 Harbour Rd, (028)
271-5657. www.ecoscape.org.za

Surrounding Kleinmond, the stony hills with their thin green veneer of *fynbos* scrub once harboured small bands of Khoi and runaway slaves. In the 1920s Kleinmond, at the foot of the Palmietberg, was a fishing settlement; today it is a holiday spot where rock angling for *kabeljou* (kob), and fishing for yellowtail and tunny are popular pastimes. Kleinmond Lagoon, where the Palmiet River reaches the sea, offers safe swimming and canoeing. Visitors can enjoy beautiful sea and mountain views from a well-planned network of hiking trails in the **Kogelberg Nature Reserve** and maybe even glimpse some of the dainty, shy gazelle species like klipspringers, as well as grysboks and steenboks that occur in the coastal fynbos and on the lower slopes of the mountain.

🌿 Kogelberg Nature Reserve

Off R44, 8 km (5 miles) W of
Kleinmond. **Tel** (028) 271-5138.
⬜ 7:30am–4pm daily. 🚶

Hermanus ❸

Road map B5. 👥 55,000.
🚃 Bot River 30 km (18 miles)
N on N2. ℹ Hermanus Stn,
Mitchell Street, (028) 312-2629.
www.hermanus.co.za

Originally established as a farming community by Hermanus Pieters, the town became a fashionable holiday and retirement destination due to the sunny climate and attractive location. Fisherman and sailors also found a relatively easy life, while visitors frequented the Windsor, Astoria and other august hotels. Today the town's grandeur is a little faded, but it still has plenty to offer most tourists.

The focal point of the town is the **Old Harbour Museum**, which traces the history of the town's whaling days, and contains a whale skull and old weapons. Fishermen's boats dating from 1850 to the mid-1900s lie restored and hull-up on the old ramp. On the higher rocks are *bokkom* stands, racks on which fish are hung to dry in the sun.

The tranquil Harold Porter Botanical Garden at Betty's Bay

For hotels and restaurants in this region see pp390–91 and p419

...manus is famous ...erb whale-watching ...ery year, southern right *(see pp184–5)* migrate ...he sub-Antarctic to calve ...e shelter of Walker Bay. ...y arrive in June and leave ...ain by December, but the ...eak whale-watching season is from September to October, when visitors are more than likely to sight the large mammals frolicking offshore. The town's official whale crier blows his kelp horn as he walks along Main Street, bearing a signboard that shows the best daily sighting places.

Hermanus has a beautiful coastline. Unspoilt beaches such as Die Plaat, a 12-km (7-mile) stretch from Klein River Lagoon to De Kelders, are perfect for walks and horseriding. A clifftop route extends from New Harbour to Grotto Beach; the regularly placed benches allow walkers to rest and enjoy the superb views. Swimming is generally safe, and there is a tidal pool below the Marine Hotel, to the east of the old harbour.

Activities nearby include the Rotay Way, a 10-km (6-mile) scenic drive, and the Hermanus Wine Route, which features four vineyards in the pretty Hemel en Arde Valley.

The popular Marine Hotel in Hermanus

Approximately 20 km (12.5 miles) east of Hermanus lies **Stanford**, a rustic crafts centre. The heart of this little village contains many historical homes built in the late 1800s and early 1900s, and has been proclaimed a national conservation area. The early school building and Anglican Church both date back to 1880, while the reputedly haunted Spookhuis (ghost house) is dated about 1885.

Fernkloof Nature Reserve boasts 40 km (25 miles) of waymarked footpaths, a 4.5-km (3-mile) circular nature trail and more than a thousand species of *fynbos*.

🏛 **Old Harbour Museum**
Market Square. *Tel (028) 312-1475.*
⊟ 9am–4:30pm Mon–Sat, noon–4pm Sun. ⬤ public hols. 🖼 ▣
www.old-harbour-museum.co.za

WHALE WATCHING IN HERMANUS

The World Wide Fund for Nature (WWF) has recognized Hermanus as one of the best land-based whale-watching spots on earth. October sees a peak in whale numbers (from 40 to 70 have been recorded). The mammals can be seen as close as 10 m (11 yd) away. Particularly special is the Old Harbour Museum's sonar link-up. A hydrophone buried in the seabed transmits the whale calls to an audio room on shore.

Cape Whale Coast logo

The rocky coastline around Hermanus offers good vantage points for whale watchers

Coming face to face with a great white on a shark-diving expedition

Gansbaai ❹

Road map B5. R43 SE of Hermanus. 🏠 22,000. 🚹 Gateway Centre, Kapokblom St, (028) 384-1439. ◯ daily. 🖳 **www**.gansbaaiinfo.com

The name Gansbaai (Bay of Geese) originates from the flocks of Egyptian geese that used to breed here.

Gansbaai is renowned for the tragedy of HMS *Birkenhead*. In February 1852, this ship hit a rock off Danger Point, 9 km (6 miles) away, and sank with 445 men – all the women and children were saved. To this day, the phrase "Birkenhead Drill" describes the custom of favouring women and children in crisis situations.

From Gansbaai there are several boat trips to Dyer Island, where you can watch great white sharks feed on the seals that breed on nearby Geyser Island. This area is also home to large numbers of African penguins, another food source for the great whites that congregate here. Nicknamed "Shark Alley", the channel between the islands and the mainland is a popular destination for water safaris and shark-diving expeditions.

Bredasdorp ❺

Road map B5. 🏠 9,800.

Bredasdorp lies in a region of undulating barley fields and sheep pasture. The town is a centre for the wool industry, but serves mainly as an access route to Cape Agulhas (via the R319) and Arniston (via the R316).

The town's most interesting feature is the **Shipwreck Museum**, which pays tribute to the southern coast's tragic history. This treacherous length of coastline has been labelled the "graveyard of ships" as its rocky reefs, gale-force winds and powerful currents make it one of the most dangerous in the world. Since 1552, more than 130 ships have foundered here, an average of one wreck per kilometre of coast.

The best time to visit the Bredasdorp Mountain Reserve is from mid-September to mid-October, when the countryside becomes bathed in colour from hundreds of blooms bursting into flower. An attractive, small garden has been created especially to showcase the indigenous wildflowers that are found here.

Figurehead, Shipwreck Museum

🏛 **Shipwreck Museum**
Independent St. **Tel** (028) 1240. ◯ 9am–4:30pm Mon, 11am–3:45pm Sat & Sun. 🌐
This museum was officially opened in April 1975 and is housed in an old rectory and church hall, both of which have been declared national monuments.

The rectory, built in 1845, is furnished like a 19th-century townhouse typical of South Africa's southern coast. The interiors and furnishings were influenced by the many shipwrecks that occurred along this capricious stretch of coastline. The salvaged wood, as well as ships' decor, frequently reappeared in door and window frames and in the ceiling rafters.

Many of the maritime artifacts that were donated have been incorporated into the refurbished home. The beautiful marble-topped washstand in the bedroom was salvaged from the *Queen of the Thames*, which sank in 1871, while the medicine chest came from the *Clan MacGregor*, which was shipwrecked in 1902.

The church hall, dating back to 1864, is now called the Shipwreck Hall. Its rather gloomy interior is a suitable environment for the interesting and diverse relics displayed in glass-cases, all of which were recovered from major shipwrecks in the area.

A 19th-century kitchen in the Shipwreck Museum at Bredasdorp

Arniston's fishermen live in Kassiesbaai

Cape Agulhas ❻

Road map B5. R319, 45 km
(28 miles) S of Bredasdorp. **Agulhas
National Park** *Tel* (028) 435-6222.
⬭ *daily.* 🖼 www.sanparks.org

Cape Agulhas was named by
early Portuguese navigators, the
first to round Africa in the
15th century. At the southernmost point of their journey,
the sailors noticed that their
compass needles were
unaffected by magnetic
deviation, pointing true north
instead. They called this point
the "Cape of Needles".

At this promontory,
where the tip of the African
continental shelf disappears
undramatically into the sea to
form what is known as the
Agulhas Bank *(see p24)*, the
Atlantic and Indian oceans
merge. The only physical
evidence of this convergence
is a simple stone cairn.

This is one of the
world's most treacherous
stretches of coast. The
often-turbulent waters
are shallow, rock-
strewn and subject to
heavy swells and strong

currents. This is the graveyard
for more than 250 once-proud
vessels, including the Japanese
trawler *Meisho Maru 38*,
whose rusting wreck can be
seen 2 km (1 mile) west of
the Agulhas Lighthouse.

The area around
the southernmost
tip of Africa
is now part of
the Agulhas
National Park.

🏛 **Lighthouse
and Museum**
Tel (028) 435-
6078. ⬭ *9am–*
5pm daily. 🖼 🍴
Agulhas Lighthouse,
whose design is
based on the
Pharos lighthouse
of Alexandria in
Egypt, was built in 1848.
After the Green Point lighthouse, it is the oldest working
lighthouse in southern
Africa. It fell into disuse,
but was restored and
reopened in 1988. Today,
its lamp is visible for
30 nautical miles.
There are 71 steps to
the top of the tower,
which affords superb
views of the coast
and seascape.

**A plaque at
Cape Agulhas**

Arniston ❼

Road map B5. 🚶 *1,500.*

Arniston's name originates
from the British vessel,
Arniston, which was wrecked
east of the settlement in
May 1815. Tragically,
of the 378
soldiers,
homebound
from Ceylon
(Sri Lanka),
only six
survived.

The little
fishing
settlement is
located some 24 km
(15 miles) southeast
of Bredasdorp off
the R316 and is
characterized by its
turquoise waters. The locals
call the village Waenhuiskrans
(wagonhouse cliff), after a
cave that is large enough to
accommodate several fully
spanned ox-wagons and is
situated 2 km (1 mile) south
of the modern Arniston Hotel.
The cave is accessible only
at low tide, however, and
visitors should beware
of freak waves washing
over the slippery rocks.

Kassiesbaai is a cluster
of rough-plastered and
thatched fishermen's
cottages with traditional
tiny windows to keep out
the midday heat. This little
village lies to the north of
Arniston, very close to
undulating white sand
dunes. Further to the south
lies Roman Beach, which
is especially good for
youngsters, with its gently
sloping seabed, rock pools
and caves. Continuing further
from here is a windy, wild
rocky point that attracts
many hopeful anglers.

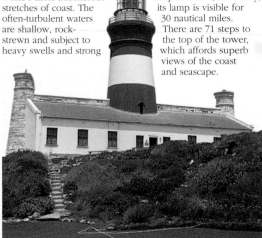

Agulhas Lighthouse is at the southernmost point of Africa

Mountain-biking in the De Hoop Nature Reserve

De Hoop Nature Reserve ❽

Road map B5. R319, 56 km (35 miles) W of Bredasdorp. **Tel** *(028) 542-1253.* ◯ *7am–6pm daily. Permits required.* www.capenature.co.za

This reserve, located some 15 km (9 miles) north of Arniston, encompasses a 50-km (30-mile) stretch of coastline, weathered limestone cliffs and spectacular sand dunes, some of which tower as high as 90 m (295 ft). De Hoop's main attraction is a 14-km (8-mile) wetland that is home to 12 of South Africa's 16 waterfowl species.

Thousands of red-knobbed coot, yellow-billed duck and Cape shoveller, as well as Egyptian geese, can be seen here, although populations do fluctuate with the water level of the marshland. The bird-watching is best between the months of September and April, when migrant flocks of Palaearctic waders arrive. Of the 13 species that have been recorded, visitors may expect to see ringed plover, wood and curlew sandpiper, greenshank, and little stint.

The rich variety of *fynbos* species includes the endemic Bredasdorp sugarbush *(Protea obtusfolia)*, stinkleaf sugar-bush *(Protea susannae)* and pincushion protea *(Leucospermum oliefolium)*.

Wildlife can also be seen in the reserve, and there is a short circular drive from the rest camp to Tierhoek. Species to look out for are the rare Cape mountain zebra and small gazelle, such as bontebok, grey rhebok and the rather shy and elusive mountain reedbuck.

For visitors who enjoy cycling, a mountain-bike trail traverses the Potberg section of the reserve, which contains a breeding colony of the rare Cape vultures. However, to avoid disturbing the birds the sites are not accessible.

Comfortable campsites and self-catering cottages are available for visitors who wish to stay overnight and experience the spectacular southern night sky almost free of light pollution.

Eland at the De Hoop Nature Reserve

Swellendam ❾

Road map B5. 🚶 *31,000.* ℹ️ *Oefeningshuis, Voortrek Street, (028) 514-2770.* ◯ *Mon–Sat.* www.swellendamtourism.co.za

Nestling in the shadow of the Langeberg Mountains, Swellendam is one of South Africa's most picturesque small towns. The country's third-oldest town, after Cape Town and Stellenbosch, Swellendam was founded by the Dutch in 1742 and named after the governor and his wife.

The thatched-roofed and whitewashed **Drostdy** was built by the Dutch East India Company in 1747 as the seat of the *landdrost*, or magistrate. It now serves as a museum of Dutch colonial life. Built shortly afterwards, the Old Gaol is situated at the rear of the Drostdy. Originally it was a simple, single-storey building with lean-to cells, but it was subsequently enlarged to include an enclosed courtyard created by linking the two cell blocks with high walls.

Near the museum is the *Ambagswerf* (trade yard), which features a smithy and wagonmaker's shop, a mill and bakery, a tannery, a cooperage and a coppersmith. Crafts demonstrations are held here regularly. Also on site is the pretty Mayville Cottage. Built between 1853 and 1855, it represents a transition of architectural styles, using both Cape Dutch and Cape Georgian influences. Outside the cottage is a well-designed rose garden featuring several heritage species.

Swellendam is renowned for its many fine old buildings, including the imposing Dutch Reformed church, with a whitewashed façade and an elegant clock tower. The **Oefeningshuis**, built in 1838 as a school for freed slaves, now serves as a tourist information centre. An interesting feature of the building is the clock designed for the illiterate: when the time painted on the sculpted clock face matches that on the real clock below, then it is time for worship.

The whitewashed Dutch Reformed church in Swellendam

Scenic view of the Swartberg Pass from the village of Prince Albert

Also of note are the splendid wrought-iron balconies and fittings of the Bulrski & Co shop, which opened for trade in 1880 opposite the Oefeningshuis, and the elegant Auld House on the same street.

🏛 Drostdy
18 Swellengrebel Street. *Tel* (028) 514-1138. ⬭ 9am–4:45pm Mon–Fri (also 9am–3:45pm Sat & Sun in summer). ⬤ 1 Jan, Easter, 25 Dec.
🖥 www.drostdymuseum.com

Environs: Bontebok National Park is 6 km (4 miles) outside Swellendam. This scenic wilderness was set up to protect the endangered species of antelope after which it was named. The bontebok has since recovered enough to share the habitat with several other introduced animals. Most of the park is accessible by car, and there are also several excellent self-guided walking trails.

The more challenging 74-km (46-mile) Swellendam Trail takes in the Marloth Nature Reserve, which is situated along the southern slopes of the Langenberg Mountains.

🏞 Bontebok National Park
Tel (028) 514-2735. ⬭ 7am–6pm daily. 🖥 www.sanparks.org

Prince Albert ⑩

Road map C5. 🏘 5,700.
🛈 Fransie Pienaar Museum, Church Street, (023) 541-1366.
⬭ daily. www.patourism.co.za

This pretty village, which is part of the Four Passes Tour *(see pp228–9)*, has several attractions. The **Fransie Pienaar Museum**, which hosts one of the world's largest fossil collections, also houses the tourist information centre, where guided walking tours of Prince Albert can be booked.

The **Prince Albert Gallery**, opposite the museum, was set up by local artists who wanted to find a venue to show their work. There are regular exhibitions of paintings, sculpture and photographs.

On Saturday mornings, in the square opposite the museum, there is a food and crafts market, and each April Prince Albert holds a popular olive, food and wine festival *(see p38)*, with stalls selling local produce, workshops, children's activities and guided walks.

Environs: The spectacular Swartberg Pass, key to the Karoo Desert, starts just 2 km (1 mile) from Prince Albert. The slopes of the pass provide the irrigation that makes the village an oasis in this arid area. The pass was built by the road engineer Thomas Bain after heavy floods in 1875 swept away the previous road, depriving local farmers of their link with the nearest seaports.

Nearby Sutherland houses the **South African Astronomical Observatory**, which boasts the largest telescope in the southern hemisphere. There are two guided tours daily; booking is essential.

🏛 Fransie Pienaar Museum
42 Church St. *Tel* (023) 541-1172. ⬭ 9:30am–4:30pm Mon–Fri, 9:30am–noon Sat, 10:30am–noon Sun. ⬤ public hols. 🖥

🏛 Prince Albert Gallery
Seven Arches, Church St. *Tel* (023) 541-1057. ⬭ 9am–4pm Mon–Fri, 9:30am–2pm Sat. Sun: call the number on the door. 🍴 pm only.

🏛 South African Astronomical Observatory
Tel (023) 571–2436.

Beautiful proteas blooming on the Swartberg Pass

Four Passes Tour ⓫

Northeast of De Hoop Nature Reserve, the N2 leads northwards over high mountains to the Little Karoo. This region, sandwiched between the Swartberg to the north and the Langeberg and Outeniqua mountains to the south, is surrounded by spectacular peaks which severely tested the genius of South Africa's famous road engineer, Thomas Bain. Most majestic of the four passes is the one that winds its way through the Swartberg.

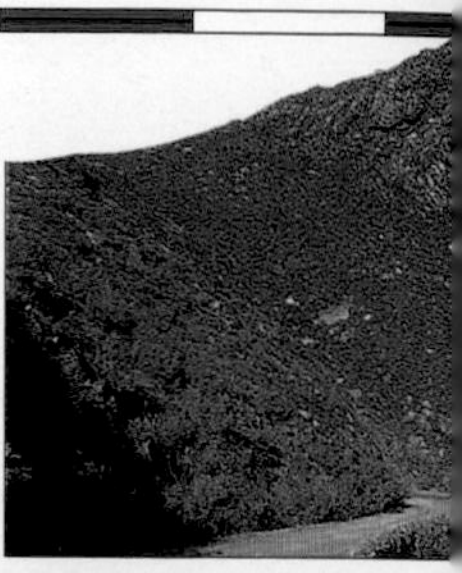

Seweweekspoort ①

A 15-km (9-mile) gravel route through sheer walls of rough-hewn rock criss-crosses a rivercourse that meanders through the Klein Swartberg mountains. Towering over the northern extent of the pass is the 2,325-m (7,628-ft) Seweweekspoort ("seven weeks pass") Peak. Local legend claims that this name refers to the time it used to take brandy smugglers to cross this route.

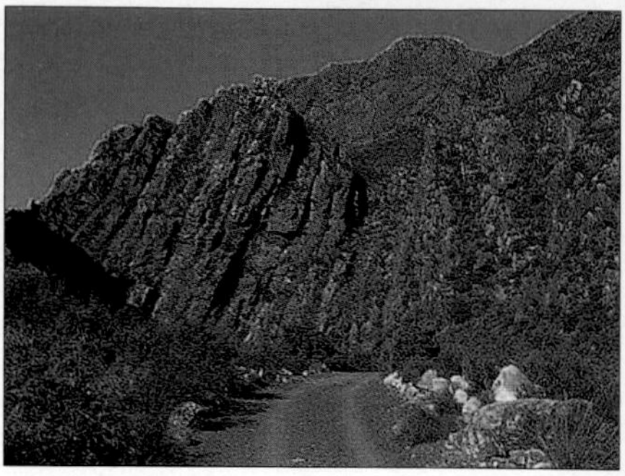

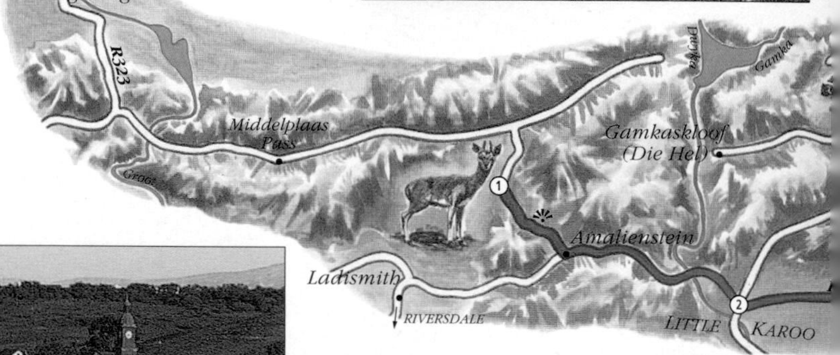

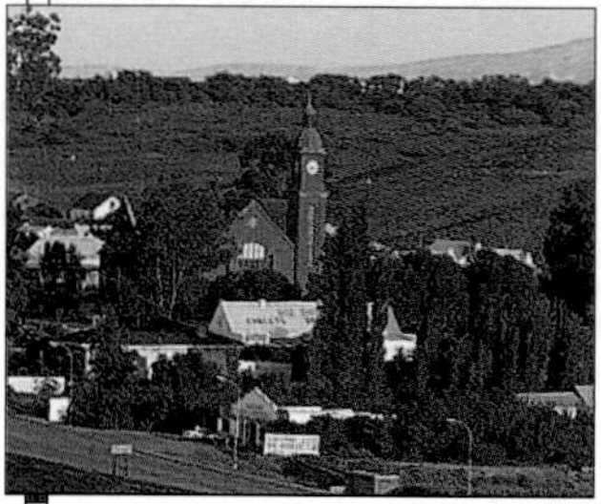

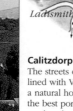

Calitzdorp ②

The streets of this Karoo village are lined with Victorian houses. Nearby is a natural hot-spring spa, and some of the best port wines in the country are produced at Boplaas, Die Krans Estate and the Calitzdorp Wine Cellar.

KEY

- Tour route
- Other roads
- Park boundary
- Viewpoint

0 kilometres 50

0 miles 25

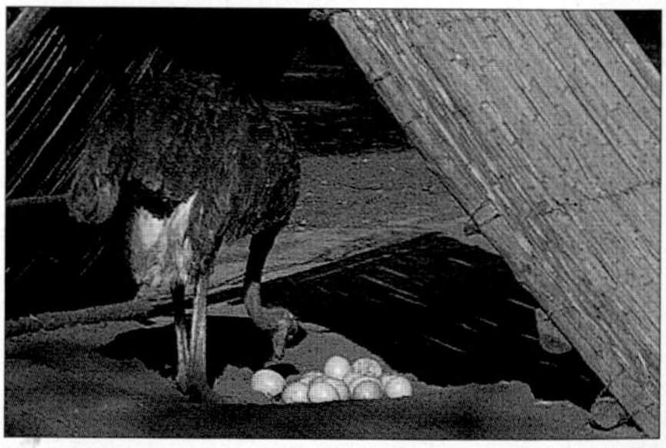

Oudtshoorn ③

The grand Victorian and Edwardian sandstone mansions in Oudtshoorn were built on the riches reaped during the ostrich-feather boom of the 1880s. Lucerne, the favourite food of ostriches, flourished in the Karoo climate, enabling farmers to raise these flightless birds commercially.

For hotels and restaurants in this region see pp390–91 and p419

Swartberg Pass ⑤
This spectacular 24-km (15-mile) gravel route took Bain's convict labour gang seven years to complete (1888).

TIPS FOR DRIVERS

Tour length: From Laingsburg: 337 km (209 miles); from Oudtshoorn: 175 km (109 miles).
Getting there: On the R323 turn left after 19 km (12 miles). After 50 km (31 miles) turn right for Seweweekspoort. Take the R62 at Amalienstein, then head north on the R328. Before Prince Albert turn onto the R407 via Meiringspoort. To return to Oudtshoorn take the N12.
When to go: In spring–autumn. Passes may close during Jun–Aug due to snowfalls.

Prince Albert ⑥
Traditional architecture (see p31) and a perennial spring watering fruit and olive trees make this isolated village an old-fashioned delight.

Schoemanspoort ④
This pass leads 10 km (6 miles) through a narrow chasm. It was built by Thomas Bain in 1862 along an existing bridle path near a mountain stream. Washed away in 1869, it took 11 years to rebuild the route above the flood level.

Meiringspoort ⑦
A 23-km-long (14-mile) tarred route runs along the valley of the majestic Groot River gorge. The sandstone cliffs, coloured deep red and burnt orange, loom above the pass in contorted folds, evidence of geological upheaval within the earth aeons ago.

Cango Caves ⑫

Road map C5. R328 from Oudtshoorn. **Tel** (044) 272-7410. ◯ 9am–5pm daily. ◯ 25 Dec. 🦽 🎥 every hour. 🍴 🛍 www.cangocaves.co.za

Deep in the foothills of the Swartberg Mountains lies an underground network of chambers and passages, where dissolved minerals have crystallized to form stalactites, stalagmites, and dripstone formations that resemble fluted columns and delicate, ruffled drapes.

The complex was first explored by Jacobus van Zyl after his herdsman stumbled upon the cave opening in 1780, but rock paintings and stone implements discovered near the entrance indicate that the site was occupied as early as 80,000 years ago.

Only Cango 1 is open to the public; access to Cango 2 and 3, discovered in 1972 and 1975 respectively, is prohibited to preserve the crystals. Some of the dramatic dripstone formations in Cango 1, which is 762 m (2,500 ft) in length, are the 9-m- (30-ft-) high Cleopatra's Needle which is believed to be some 150,000 years old, a dainty Ballerina and a Frozen Waterfall. The largest chamber is Van Zyl's Hall, 107 m (350 ft) long and 16 m (52 ft) high.

An hour-long standard tour takes in the first six chambers, while the full tour is a 1.5-hour hike with 416 stairs, which is best attempted only by the fit. The temperature inside is a constant 18°C (64°F), but humidity can reach an uncomfortable 99.9 per cent.

Stalagmite and stalactite dripstone formations in the Cango Caves

Visitors to Cango Wildlife Ranch can stroke tame cheetahs

Cango Wildlife Ranch ⑬

Road map C5. R328 to Cango Caves. **Tel** (044) 272-5593. ☐ 8am–5pm daily. 🎦 🚻 **www**.cango.co.za

The ranch lies 3 km (2 miles) north of Oudtshoorn. Since the establishment of the Cheetah Conservation Foundation in 1993, the ranch has ranked among the leading cheetah breeders in Africa and is one of the world's top five protection institutions. The breeding enclosure is not accessible, but visitors may enter a fenced area to interact with tame cheetahs. Other thrills include crocodile cage diving and the opportunity (depending on availability) to play with tiger or lion cubs. The centre also has a Bengal tiger breeding programme: there are several tigers at the ranch, and to date six rare white Bengal tigers have been born there.

Walkways elevated over a natural bushveld environment allow the visitor close-up views of other powerful hunters, including lions and jaguars. Crocodiles and alligators, of which there are about 30 for visitors to spot, are also bred at the ranch, and exotic snakes on show include a black mamba, a king cobra, a 4-m (13-ft) boa constrictor and a copperhead viper. There is a further breeding programme under way for the endangered blue duiker.

Nile crocodile at the Cango Wildlife Ranch

The ranch has a well-regarded programme of tours and special events, a fast-food outlet and a restaurant that serves, among other things, crocodile and ostrich meat.

Oudtshoorn ⑭

Road map C5. N12 from George. 🏠 123,500. 🛈 Baron van Reede St, (044) 279-2532. ☐ Mon–Sat. **www**.oudtshoorn.co.za

The town of Oudtshoorn was established in 1847 at the foot of the Swartberg Mountains, to cater to the needs of the Little Karoo's growing farming population. It gained prosperity when the demand for ostrich feathers – to support Victorian, and later Edwardian fashion trends – created a sharp rise in the industry in 1870–80.

The Karoo's hot, dry climate proved suitable for big-scale ostrich farming – the loamy soils yielded extensive crops of lucerne, which forms a major part of the birds' diet, and the ground was strewn with the small pebbles that are a vital aid to their somewhat unusual digestive processes.

Oudtshoorn's importance as an ostrich-farming centre continued for more than 40 years, and the town became renowned for its sandstone mansions, built by wealthy ostrich barons. But World War I and changes in fashion resulted in the industry's decline and unfortunately many farmers went bankrupt. Ostrich farming eventually recovered in the 1940s with the establishment of the tanning industry. Today, ostrich products include eggs and leather, meat and bonemeal. The town also produces crops of tobacco, wheat and grapes.

A sandstone "feather palace" on the outskirts of Oudtshoorn

For hotels and restaurants in this region see pp390–91 and p419

The early 20th-century sandstone façade of the CP Nel Museum

🏛 CP Nel Museum

3 Baron van Reede St. **Tel** (044) 272-7306. ⏱ 8am–5pm Mon–Fri, 9am–5pm Sat. ⬤ public hols. 🖼

This building, formerly the Boys' High School of Oudtshoorn, was designed in 1906 by the local architect Charles Bullock. Its green-domed sandstone façade is considered to be one of the best examples of stone masonry found anywhere in South Africa. The school hall was designed in 1913 by JE Vixseboxse.

The museum was named in honour of its founder, Colonel CP Nel. A series of dioramas traces the history of ostriches and the impact of ostrich farming on the town and its community. Displays also depict the cultural history and lifestyle of the people of the Klein Karoo region, and the museum prides itself on its excellent replica of an early 20th-century pharmacy. There is a section devoted to the vital role played by the Jewish community in the development of Oudtshoorn's feather industry.

A carved ostrich egg lamp

🏛 Le Roux Townhouse

146 High St. **Tel** (044) 272-3676. ⏱ 9am–1pm and 2–5pm Mon–Fri, Sat & Sun by app. ⬤ public hols. 🖼

Built around 1895, this is an outstanding example of the feather palaces of the time. As an annexe of the CP Nel Museum, it has exhibits of authentic European furniture from the period 1900–20 and a collection of porcelain, glassware and pieces made from Cape silver.

THE OSTRICH'S UNUSUAL EATING HABITS

Ostriches have neither teeth nor a crop, so have developed the habit of eating stones, which help to grind and digest their food. Perhaps by extension of this habit, or perhaps because they are naturally curious, there is little that an ostrich won't eat. A few years ago, an Oudtshoorn farmer was mystified by the theft of his washing – shirts, socks and trousers vanished every washday, until the death of one of his ostriches revealed the culprit. The birds have also been seen to eat babies' shoes, combs, sunglasses, buttons and earrings (ripped from the shirts and ears of tourists).

Spark plugs and bullet cases – ostriches eat almost anything

🐦 Highgate Ostrich Show Farm

Off R328 to Mossel Bay. **Tel** (044) 272-7115. ⏱ 8am–5pm daily. 🖼 🗣 multilingual. 📷 🎥

Located 10 km (6 miles) south of Oudtshoorn, this large farm offers a tour of its ostrich-breeding facilities where visitors can learn more about the various stages of the bird's development, and have an opportunity to cuddle the chicks, handle the eggs and visit an ostrich pen. The adventurous may even ride an ostrich. Those who don't have the nerve can watch jockeys take part in an ostrich derby. The tour length is 1.5 to 2 hours and the fee includes refreshments.

The curio shop offers ostrich-feather products, handbags, wallets, belts and shoes.

Coloured ostrich plumes are available in stores in Oudtshoorn

🐦 Safari Ostrich Show Farm

Off R328 to Mossel Bay. **Tel** (044) 272-7311/2. ⏱ 8am–5pm daily. 🖼 🗣 📷 🎥 www.safariostrich.co.za

Situated 5 km (3 miles) from Oudtshoorn, this show farm has over 2,500 ostriches. The conducted tours leave every half-hour and include an ostrich race and visits to the breeding camp and museum.

Place your bet on the race winner at one of the ostrich farms

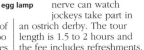

THE GARDEN ROUTE TO GRAHAMSTOWN

his magnificent stretch of coastline encompasses mountains, rivers, lagoons, lakes, beaches and the indigenous forests and wetlands of the Garden Route National Park, which comprises the Tsitsikamma, Wilderness and Knysna regions.

The Garden Route, backed by the Outeniqua, Tsitsikamma and Langkloof mountain ranges, extends all the way from Mossel Bay in the west to the Storms River Mouth in the east.

In 1780, French naturalist Francois Le Vaillant wrote: "Nature has made an enchanted abode of this beautiful place". In the 1800s, however, furniture makers began to value the indigenous hardwoods, and large tracts of Outeniqua yellowwood *(Podocarpus falcatus)*, ironwood *(Olea capensis)*, and the smaller stinkwood *(Ocotea bullata)* were felled by the European settlers. Of the original forest, only 650 sq km (251 sq miles) has survived, of which 430 sq km (166 sq miles) is on state land. Nowadays, plantations of exotic pines and bluegum supply the paper mills, as well as the furniture-making and building industries.

Tourists are drawn to the Garden Route for its scenic drives, forested walks and trails and pristine coastline, as well as the tranquil inland lakes and lagoons. The birdlife is spectacular. Knysna alone has recorded more than 230 different species, among them the African spoonbill, osprey and avocet. Of special interest among forest birds are the Knysna lourie and Narina's trogon.

Plettenberg Bay is an upmarket coastal retreat. Balmy weather attracts visitors even in the winter months.

Beyond the Garden Route, Port Elizabeth, the centre of South Africa's car-manufacturing industry, has lovely golden beaches and is famous for its Bayworld Complex.

The Wilderness is one of the most picturesque spots along the Garden Route

◁ A hanging bridge leads across Storms River Mouth in Tsitsikamma

Exploring the Garden Route to Grahamstown

The Garden Route, from Wilderness to the end of Tsitsikamma, where the N2 heads inland for the last stretch to Port Elizabeth, is a scenic treat. On leaving the town of Wilderness, vehicles can park at Dolphin's Point for an uninterrupted view of the coastline with its long white rollers. After Wilderness, the N2 hugs the coast almost all the way to Knysna. From here it passes through indigenous forest as far as Storms River. Between Nature's Valley and Storms River, detours can be made off the N2 to cross the spectacular old pass routes of Grootrivier and Bloukrans. Lush vegetation, mountains, lagoons, rivers and the sea combine to make this route a visual feast.

The beach at Nature's Valley

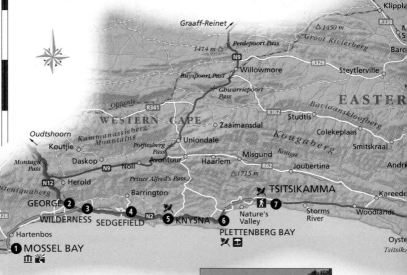

KEY

▬	Motorway
▬	Major road
═══	Minor road
▪═▪	Untarred road
▬	Scenic route
▬▬	Main railway
──	Minor railway
▬	Provincial border
▲	Summit
✕	Pass

People on a Nature Walk, at the picturesque Knsyna Lagoon

TTING AROUND

: N2 traverses the entire length of
Garden Route, from Mossel Bay
Port Elizabeth and beyond, on its
 up the east coast. Although
ch tours to the area are available,
el by car is ideal as it allows the
tor to explore the pretty coastal
ns along the way at leisure. The
en- and five-day hiking trails of
sikamma, as well as shorter forest
ks, may also entice visitors to
ger. There are domestic airports at
t Elizabeth and George.

At a waterhole in the Addo Elephant National Park

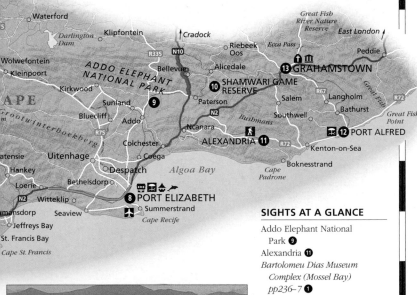

A view of Knysna Lagoon as seen from the Heads

Bartolomeu Dias Museum Complex (Mossel Bay) ❶

The Bartolomeu Dias Museum Complex, established in 1988, celebrates the 500th anniversary of Dias's historic landfall. A full-sized replica of his ship was built in Portugal in 1987 and set sail for Mossel Bay, arriving on 3 February 1988. Here, the 130-ton vessel was lifted from the water and lowered into the specially altered museum with its high, angled roof, clerestory windows and sunken floor for the keel.

★ The Caravel
The intrepid Spanish and Portuguese seafarers of the 15th and 16th centuries sailed into the unknown in small two- or three-masted ships like this.

Portuguese flag

Lateen sails are characteristic of Mediterranean ships.

Letter Box
Mail posted in this unusual post box in the museum complex is marked with a special postmark.

Post Office Tree
The 16th-century seafarers left messages for each other in a shoe suspended from a milkwood tree like this one, next to the museum building.

Rudder

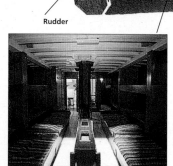

Barrels filled with fresh water were stored in the hold.

Crew Cabin
Cramped confines in the crew's quarters left little room for privacy on sea voyages that often lasted many months.

STAR FEATURES

★ The Caravel

★ Stained-Glass Windows

The **pennant** flown at the top of the main mast bore the Portuguese royal coat of arms (the House of Braganza).

The **red cross** of the Order of Christ was emblazoned on the sails of Portuguese sailing vessels.

★ **Stained-Glass Windows**
Three beautiful windows by Ria Kriek commemorate the early voyages of discovery. Shown here are the sails of the Dias caravel.

THE EPIC VOYAGE OF DIAS

A small fleet left Portugal around August 1487 under the command of Bartolomeu Dias *(see p46)*. The explorer made several landfalls on the West African coast, erecting *padrões* (stone crosses) along the way. In February 1488, he dropped anchor off the South African coast. The inlet he named after São Bras (St Blaize) is today called Mossel Bay.

Pulleys and ropes enabled sailors to furl and unfurl the sails at great speed.

Anchor

Rope ladder

Exploring Mossel Bay and the Bartolomeu Dias Museum Complex

One of the main attractions in the seaside town of Mossel Bay, situated 397 km (246 miles) east of Cape Town, is the interesting museum complex and the historic centre, both overlooking the harbour.

Seafaring history is the subject at the Bartolomeu Dias Museum Complex. Apart from the outstanding reconstruction of Dias's caravel, there are old maps, photographs and documents detailing the first explorations around the tip of Africa. The complex also includes the Protea Hotel Mossel Bay, which dates back to 1846 and is thought to be the oldest building in town.

The town is probably best known for its controversial and costly Mossgas development, initiated by the discovery of natural offshore gas fields.

But the real charm of the settlement lies in its natural beauty – fine beaches and walks. The 15-km (9-mile) St Blaize Hiking Trail winds along an unspoilt stretch of coastline from Bat's Cave to Dana Bay. Santos Beach, the only north-facing beach in South Africa, guarantees sunny afternoons and safe swimming.

Regular cruises take visitors out to **Seal Island**, while **White Shark Africa** offers shark cage dives or snorkelling and certification diving courses.

🚌 **Romonza–Seal Island Trips**
Mossel Bay Harbour.
Tel (044) 690-3101.

White Shark Africa
Cnr Kerk & Bland sts. **Tel** (044) 691-3796, (082) 455 2438.
www.whitesharkafrica.com

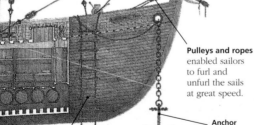

BARTOLOMEU DIAS MUSEUM COMPLEX

Protea Hotel Mossel Bay

Maritime Museum

MARKET ST

CHURCH ST

Tourist Information

P

SANTOS RD

Post Office Tree

GRAVE ST

Malay Graves

Munrohoek Cottages

Fountain

FOOTPATH

Ethno-Botanical Garden

Shell Museum

FOOTPATH

0 metres   100
0 yards   100

Protea Hotel Mossel Bay

George ❷

Road map C5. 🏠 183,000. ✈ 10 km (6 miles) NW of town. 🚉 George Station, Market St. 🚌 St Mark's Sq. ℹ 124 York St, (044) 801-9103. ⭘ Mon–Sat. www.visitgeorge.co.za

The wide streets of George were laid out in 1811 during the British occupation of the Cape. Named after King George III, the town was officially known as George's Drostdy. Today the Garden Route's largest centre, it primarily serves the farming community, with a focus on wheat, hops, vegetables, sheep and dairy cattle.

The **Outeniqua Transport Museum** provides an interesting insight into the history of steam-train travel in South Africa.

The **Outeniqua Nature Reserve** is the starting point for 12 day walks in the indigenous forest of the Outeniqua Mountains. At least 125 tree species grow here, and over 30 forest birds have been recorded. The Tierkop Trail is a circular overnight route that covers 30 km (18 miles) in two days. The difficult Outeniqua Trail covers 108 km (67 miles) in seven days.

🏛 **Outeniqua Transport Museum**
2 Mission St. **Tel** (044) 801-8288. ⭘ 8am–5pm Mon–Sat. 📷

🦋 **Outeniqua Nature Reserve**
Witfontein. On R28 NW of George. **Tel** (044) 870-8323. ⭘ 7:30am–4pm Mon–Fri. 📷 Permits at office.

Beach houses at Victoria Bay

Wilderness ❸

Road map C5. N2 12 km (7 miles) SE of George. 🏠 3,000. 🚉 Fairy Knowe. ℹ Milkwood Village, Beacon Road, (044) 877-0045. ⭘ Mon–Sat. www.tourism wilderness.co.za

Ten kilometres (6 miles) east of the city of George is South Africa's lake district. This chain of salt- and freshwater lakes at the foot of forested mountain slopes forms part of the Wilderness sector of the **Garden Route National Park**. Protecting some 30 km (19 miles) of unspoilt coastline, the park features two long white beaches – Wilderness and Leentjiesklip; however, note that swimming is not safe here due to the strong undercurrents.

Of the five lakes in this region, the three western-most ones – Island Lake, Langvlei and Rondevlei – are all linked and fed by the Touws River via a natural water channel called the Serpentine. Swartvlei is the largest and deepest lake, and it is connected to the sea by an estuary, although its mouth silts up for six months of the year. Groenvlei, which is the only lake not located within the Wilderness National Park, is not fed by any river and has no link to the sea. Instead, it receives its water through springs and rainfall; as a result, it is the least brackish.

Birdlife in the park is excellent, with as many as 79 of the country's waterbird species having been recorded. Five species of kingfisher can be spotted here – pied, giant, half-collared, brown-hooded and malachite. The area is also popular for angling and a variety of watersports, but these activities are restricted in order to protect the sensitive ecology of the area. Horse riding is permitted along Swartvlei's shores. A scenic drive starting at Wilderness runs along Lakes Road, which skirts the lake chain and meets up with the N2 at Swartvlei.

A malachite kingfisher

There are many hiking trails in and around Wilderness. With the magnificent Outeniqua range stretched along the northern perimeter of the area, you can ramble through natural forests on such trails as the Brown-Hooded Kingfisher Trail, the Pied Kingfisher Trail, the five-day Biking & Hiking Trail or the three-day Canoe & Hiking Trail. Those who prefer a less strenuous form of exercise can take the Wilderness Country Walk. Horse trails can be found or more extreme activities such as paragliding and abseiling can be enjoyed.

Steam locomotive at the Outeniqua Transport Museum

For hotels and restaurants in this region see pp391–4 and pp419–21

Paragliding over the beautiful coastline near Sedgefield

At Wilderness Heights the Map of Africa can be found, a forested area shaped like the African continent. Splendid views of the river valley can be admired from here.

Off the N2, between Wilderness and Sedgefield, is **Timberlake Farm Village**, a collection of charming wooden cabins with a café, a country deli and a wine shop. Activities here include a quad-bike course, a mountain bike trail, a delightful fairy-themed garden, an adventure playground for kids and a zipline cable ride between aerial platforms in the trees.

The **Goukamma Nature Reserve** borders on the Garden Route National Park and offers similar activities. The reserve supports grysboks and blue duikers.

Resident Cape clawless otters are also present, though they are seldom seen. Buffels Bay, a seaside resort located at the easternmost extent of the reserve, has a magnificent beach for walking, swimming and sunbathing.

🍴 **Garden Route National Park (Wilderness)**
ℹ️ (044) 877-1197.
◯ 7am–8pm daily. 🏞 🚶
www.sanparks.org

📷 **Timberlake Farm Village**
N2 between Wilderness and Sedgefield. **Tel** (044) 882-1211.
◯ 8am–5pm daily.
www.timberlakeorganic.co.za

🍴 **Goukamma Nature Reserve**
Wilderness. **Tel** (044) 802-5310.
◯ 8am–6pm daily.
🏞 🚶 ⚓ 🏊
www.capenature.co.za

Sedgefield ❹

Road map C5. N2 21 km (13 miles) E of Wilderness. 🏘 8,500.
🚗 Shell Garage, Main Street.
ℹ️ 30 Main Street, (044) 343-2010.
◯ Mon–Sat.

Twenty-one kilometres (13 miles) east of Wilderness is the small coastal town of Sedgefield, which can be a useful base for visitors to the Goukamma Nature Reserve (see left). Sedgefield also boasts a variety of its own attractions and this has resulted in some resort-type developments being built along the previously unspoilt beach front.

Sedgefield is well worth exploring, particularly if you are into water or adventure sports. For the most daring visitors, one-day paragliding courses with a full-time instructor are available at **Cloud Base Paragliding**.

Sedgefield Beach offers safe swimming, perfect for families, or you may fish for bass at Cola Beach, Myoli Beach, Swartvlei Beach or Gerike's Point. In addition to the several lakes and beaches, there are pretty forest and lakeside walking trails.

🪂 **Cloud Base Paragliding**
PO Box 446, Wilderness.
Tel (044) 877-1414 or
(082) 777-8474. **www**.cloudbase-paragliding.co.za

Fairy Knowe, a popular hotel near Wilderness

Paddle cruiser on the Knysna Lagoon

Knysna ❺

Road map C5. 👥 *77,000.* 🚌 *Main St.* 🚩 *40 Main St, (044) 382-5510.* ⭕ *Mon–Sat.* 🎭 *Oyster Festival (Jul).* **www**.visitknysna.co.za

A significant figure in Knysna's history was George Rex, who, according to local legend, was the son of King George III and his first wife Hannah Lightfoot, a Quaker (she never gained royal approval and was exiled after the birth of her son). The claim, made as a result of Rex's opulent lifestyle, was never proved. He played a leading role in developing the lagoon harbour, and his ship, the *Knysna*, regularly traded along the coast. At the time of his death, in 1839, he was the most prominent land-owner in the area.

Furniture, boat building and oysters cultivated in the lagoon are Knysna's major industries.

Environs: One of Knysna's most attractive features is the 17-km-long (11-mile) Knysna Lagoon, protected from the sea by two sandstone cliffs, the Knysna Heads.

George Rex Drive provides access to Leisure Island on the Eastern Head, from where there are superb views.

On the Western Head, which is accessible only via a ferry run by the **Featherbed Co.**, is the private Featherbed Nature Reserve. The four-hour excursion includes the boat trip, a 2.5-km (2-mile) guided nature walk known as the Bushbuck Trail, a short four-wheel-drive ride up to the top of the Western Knysna Head, and a buffet lunch; in fine weather this is served outside, under a grove of milkwood trees.

The Featherbed Co. also operates a fleet of other boats for sightseeing trips on the lagoon. The most popular is

Knysna lourie

the *John Benn*, a dou[ble-] storey pontoon and flo[ating] restaurant that departs daily on 90-minute cruis[es].

Angling, too, is a popu[lar] pastime. Fish are abundan[t] the area and catches inclu[de] white steenbras, stumpnose and blacktail. From Decemb[er] to April, fishermen can charte[r] deep-sea skiboats to try and net tuna, bonito and marlin.

South Africa's largest commercial oyster-farming centre is based at Knysna Lagoon. The delicious Pacific oysters (*Crassostrea gigas*) can be sampled on daily tasting tours organized by **Knysna Charters**, or at Jetty Tapas.

Another spot favoured by the locals is the mock-Tudor-style Crab's Creek, which has wooden benches under tall shade trees. Crab's Creek lies at the edge of the lagoon as one enters Knysna from the west.

About 6 km (4 miles) east of Knysna, a turnoff to Noetzie ends at a clifftop parking area. From here visitors can descend a path to a secluded bay that is guarded by five castles, all of which are private homes.

📧 **Featherbed Co.**
Knysna Waterfront Quays, Water-front Drive. **Tel** (044) 382-1693.
📧 for Featherbed Nature Reserve: 10am (with lunch) & 2:30pm (without lunch), more departures in high season; John Benn: 12:30pm (lunchtime cruise) & 5pm (6pm in summer) (sunset cruise). 🖥
www.knysnafeatherbed.com

Knysna Charters
Thesen Island. **Tel** (082) 892-0469.
www.knysnacharters.com

The Knysna Heads promontories guard the lagoon entrance

🌿 Knysna Forest

The magnificent indigenous forest that surrounds Knysna offers walking trails, scenic drives, cycling routes and picnic sites. Most notable of the hikes is the seven-day **Outeniqua Hiking Trail**, which traverses 105 km (65 miles).

Goldfields Drive leads to a picnic site at Jubilee Creek, which is lined with gold-panning relics, and then goes on to the old mineshafts and machinery of Millwood, a former gold-mining settlement.

From the **Diepwalle Forest Station** a 13-km (8-mile) scenic drive, a cycling route and the Elephant Walk lead through tall Outeniqua yellowwood, ironwood and stinkwood trees. The yellowwoods, which are often draped with lichen, the lush ferns and the twisted lianas create a fairy-tale atmosphere, where the lucky may spot a brilliant green Knysna lourie. In the Diepwalle State Forest is the King Edward Tree, a gigantic old Outeniqua yellowwood. It is 39 m (128 ft) tall with a circumference of 7 m (23 ft), and is believed to be 600 years old.

Kranshoek scenic drive, some 10 km (6 miles) east of Knysna, ends at a rocky coastline that falls sheer to the sea below. Back on the N2, the route crosses the "Garden of Eden", where many trees are labelled.

🥾 Outeniqua Hiking Trail
Knysna. *Tel* (044) 302-5606.

🌲 Diepwalle Forest Station
R339, 23 km (14 miles) N of Knysna. *Tel* (044) 382-9762. ⭕ 7:30am–4pm daily. 🥾 🎪 ⚙️ www.sanparks.org

One of the five private castles along Noetzie Beach

Plettenberg Bay ⑥

Road map C5. 🏘️ *75,000.* 🚌 Shell Ultra City, Marine Way. ℹ️ Main St. *Tel* (044) 533-4065. ⭕ Mon–Sat. **www**.plettenbergbay.co.za

Up-market Plettenberg Bay, 30 km (19 miles) east of Knysna, is the holiday playground of the wealthy. A coast of rivers, lagoons and white beaches, "Plett", as it is called by the locals, earned the name *Bahia Formosa* ("beautiful bay") from early Portuguese sailors.

The village is perched on red sandstone cliffs that rise above the coastline and the lagoon formed by the Keurbooms and Bietou rivers. Plett's most recognized feature is a large luxury hotel complex on Beacon Island.

South of the town, the **Robberg Nature and Marine Reserve** juts out into the sea, its cliffs rising to 148 m (486 ft) in places. A series of walking trails affords views of the dramatically churning seas and pristine secluded bays where anglers try their hand at catching elf, musselcracker, galjoen and

red roman in the deep, natural gulleys. Seals and dolphins are often seen, while whales occur in spring (Sep onwards).

Further along the coast, east of Plettenberg Bay, a winding scenic route off the N2 leads to Nature's Valley, a coastal resort that forms part of the Garden Route National Park *(see pp244–5),* and is studded with holiday homes.

🐾 Robberg Nature and Marine Reserve
Robberg Rd. *Tel* (044) 533-2125. ⭕ 7am–5pm (to 8pm Dec–Jan). *Permits required (avail. at the gate).* 📷 ⬇️ 🥾 www.capenature.co.za

The pansy shell is Plettenberg Bay's emblem

Beacon Island Lifestyle Resort seen from Signal Hill, Plettenberg Bay

THE KNYSNA FOREST ELEPHANTS

The last true forest elephant

During the 19th century, 400–500 elephants lived around Knysna and were perfectly adapted to the forest habitat. Ruthless hunting reduced their numbers drastically, and by the early 1900s only 50 of the gentle giants remained. Today, only a single one exists from the original herd. Two young elephants were introduced from the Kruger National Park, but the relocation venture failed. The last elephant is elusive and very shy, and is seldom seen. It belongs to the African elephant species *Loxodonta africana*, and is the only completely free-ranging elephant that remains in South Africa.

Tsitsikamma ⑦

Tsitsikamma is a San word meaning "place of abundant waters". This is part of the Garden Route National Park and extends for 68 km (42 miles) from Nature's Valley to Oubosstrand and stretches seawards for some 5.5 km (3 miles), offering licensed snorkellers and divers a unique "underwater trail". Within the park's boundaries lie two of South Africa's most popular hikes, the Tsitsikamma and Otter trails. Primeval forest, rugged mountain scenery and panoramic views contribute to their popularity with hikers.

Cape clawless otter

★ Yellowwood trees
Once considered inferior and used for building, today yellowwood is highly valued.

Bloukrans River gorge is the site of an overnight trail hut.

Fynbos
The typical vegetation of this area is coastal fynbos, which consists of low-growing species of ericas and proteas.

Tsitsikamma Trail   Keurbos △

Bloukrans River

△ Bloukrans

Cold Stream

N2
R102
Groot River
Bloukrans River
Bloukrans Forest Station
Vark River
R102
Coldstr
N2

Covie   Tsitsikamma

Nature's Valley   △ Kalander   André △   △ Otter Trail
Groot River Lagoon   Oak

Tsitsikamma Marine Reserve

Common dolphins
Hikers on the Otter Trail are sure to see dolphins frolicking in the waves.

STAR FEATURES

* ★ Otter Trail
* ★ Yellowwood trees
* ★ Tsitsikamma Trail

★ Otter Trail
This five-day coastal hike was the country's first official trail and stretches from the mouth of the Storms River to the superb beach at Nature's Valley. Hikers may spot whales, dolphins, seals and Cape clawless otters along the way.

★ **Tsitsikamma Trail**
*The relatively easy inland walking route leads 60 km
(37 miles) through fynbos and indigenous forest in the
Tsitsikamma mountains and takes five days to complete.*

VISITORS' CHECKLIST

Road map C5.
68 km (42 miles) E of
Plettenberg Bay on N2.
🏢 *Garden Route National Park:*
(042) 281-1607;
(012) 428-9111 (reservations
and permits for hiking trails).
🕐 *6:30am–7pm.*
Otter Trail: 41 km (25 miles).
Tsitsikamma Trail:
60 km (37 miles).
🌊 🍴 🏊 🚶 🍴 🏠 🏠
www.sanparks.org

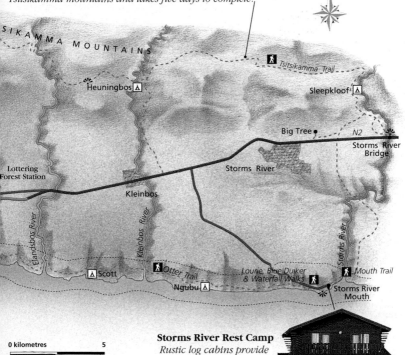

Storms River Rest Camp
*Rustic log cabins provide
cosy accommodation at
the start of the Otter Trail.*

| 0 kilometres | 5 |
| 0 miles | 5 |

KEY

═══ Motorway
━━━ Major road
▬▬▬ Tarred road
--- Trail
☀ Viewpoint
🚶 Hiking
Ⓐ Overnight trail huts

TIPS FOR WALKERS

*En route to Storms
River Mouth*

Visitors should be fit, and sturdy walking
shoes are essential. For the longer
hikes, all provisions as well as cooking
gear and sleeping bags must be carried,
as the overnight huts are only equipped
with mattresses. The Bloukrans River
along the Otter Trail can only be forded
by swimming or wading, so waterproof
backpacks are advised.

Street-by-Street: Port Elizabeth ❽

Statue of Queen Victoria

The third-largest port and fifth-largest city in the country, Port Elizabeth, part of the Nelson Mandela Bay Municipality, faces east across the 60-km (38-mile) wide sweep of Algoa Bay. Modern Port Elizabeth has spread inland and northward along the coast from the original settlement. It is often referred to as the "Friendly City" and its wide open beaches are popular with visitors. Among the many attractions in this sedate industrial city are a host of well-preserved historic buildings, splendid architecture, Bayworld, Donkin Reserve and the SA Marine Rehabilitation and Education Centre.

Donkin Lighthouse
Built in 1861, the lighthouse is in the Donkin Reserve.

★ Donkin Street
The row of quaint, double-storey Victorian houses lining this street was built between 1860–80. The entire street was declared a national monument in 1967.

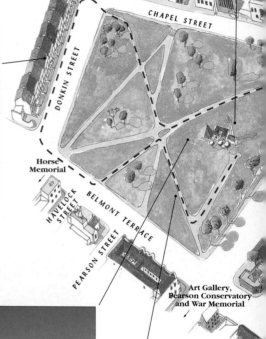

CHAPEL STREET

DONKIN STREET

Horse Memorial

HAVELOCK STREET

BELMONT TERRACE

PEARSON STREET

Art Gallery, Pearson Conservatory and War Memorial

Donkin Reserve is situated on a hillside overlooking the city.

Donkin Reserve
Overlooking the city and harbour, Donkin Reserve features the Opera House, a lighthouse, a flagpole and the touching memorial to Sir Rufane Donkin's wife Elizabeth, after which the city was named.

STAR SIGHTS

★ Donkin Street

★ City Hall

★ Fort Frederick

For hotels and restaurants in this region see pp391–4 and pp419–21

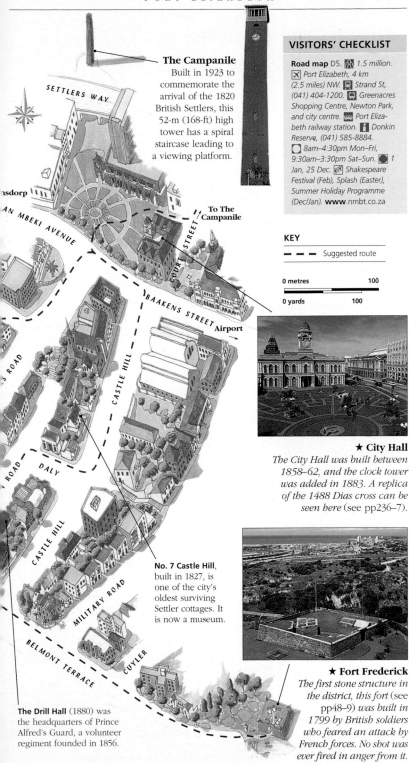

The Campanile
Built in 1923 to commemorate the arrival of the 1820 British Settlers, this 52-m (168-ft) high tower has a spiral staircase leading to a viewing platform.

SETTLERS WAY

ısdorp

AN MBEKI AVENUE

COURT STREET

To The Campanile

BAAKENS STREET

Airport

S ROAD

CASTLE HILL

ROAD

DALY

CASTLE HILL

MILITARY ROAD

BELMONT TERRACE

CUYLER

No. 7 Castle Hill, built in 1827, is one of the city's oldest surviving Settler cottages. It is now a museum.

The Drill Hall (1880) was the headquarters of Prince Alfred's Guard, a volunteer regiment founded in 1856.

VISITORS' CHECKLIST

Road map D5. 🏠 1.5 million. ✈ Port Elizabeth, 4 km (2.5 miles) NW. 🚌 Strand St, (041) 404-1200. 🚍 Greenacres Shopping Centre, Newton Park, and city centre. 🚃 Port Elizabeth railway station. 🛈 Donkin Reserve, (041) 585-8884. ◯ 8am–4:30pm Mon–Fri, 9:30am–3:30pm Sat–Sun. ◯ 1 Jan, 25 Dec. 🎭 Shakespeare Festival (Feb), Splash (Easter), Summer Holiday Programme (Dec/Jan). www.nmbt.co.za

KEY

– – – Suggested route

| 0 metres | 100 |
| 0 yards | 100 |

★ **City Hall**
The City Hall was built between 1858–62, and the clock tower was added in 1883. A replica of the 1488 Dias cross can be seen here (see pp236–7).

★ **Fort Frederick**
The first stone structure in the district, this fort (see pp48–9) was built in 1799 by British soldiers who feared an attack by French forces. No shot was ever fired in anger from it.

Exploring Port Elizabeth

Signpost

Port Elizabeth sprawls inland and northward on the windy shores of Algoa Bay. Many of the city's most popular attractions are situated along Humewood Beach. The city is proud of its settler heritage, and a wealth of historic buildings and museums, as well as memorials and statues, await exploration further inland. Since 2001, Port Elizabeth has been part of the Nelson Mandela Bay Municipality.

🏛 Donkin Reserve

Belmont Terrace. **1** *(041) 585-8884.* ☐ *8am–4:30pm Mon–Fri; 9:30am–3:30pm Sat–Sun.* ☀ *1 Jan, 25 Dec.* ☐

This park-like reserve, a national monument since 1938, contains the pyramid-shaped memorial that then acting governor of the Cape, Sir Rufane Donkin, dedicated to his late wife in 1820. The settlement was named Port Elizabeth in her honour.

Also here is the tallest flagpole in the continent, with a South African flag about the size of a tennis court.

The Horse Memorial

🏛 Horse Memorial

Cape Road.

During the South African War, Port Elizabeth was the port of entry for the horses of British soldiers. After the war, local resident Harriet Meyer raised money to honour the estimated 347,000 horses that had died. The statue by sculptor Joseph Whitehead, unveiled in 1905, was relocated to its present site in 1957. The inscription reads: "The greatness of a nation consists not so much in the number of its

Donkin Memorial

people or the extent of its territory as in the extent and justice of its compassion."

🌿 St George's Park

Park Drive.

The setting of the well-known play, *Master Harold and the Boys,* by Athol Fugard, this lovely park is home to the oldest cricket ground and bowling green in South Africa. It also contains tennis courts, a swimming pool, a botanic garden and several historic monuments, like the War Memorial in the north-east corner of the park.

The Pearson Conservatory, named after Henry Pearson who served as mayor of the city for 16 terms, was completed in 1882 and houses a collection of exotic plants. Always hire a tour guide to visit St George's Park, since it is not safe to walk alone.

🏛 Red Location Museum

New Brighton Township. **Tel** *(041) 408-8400.* ☐ *9am–4pm Mon–Fri, 9am–3pm Sat.*

This award-winning museum traces the struggle against apartheid through various exhibitions and interactive displays.

🛍 The Boardwalk

Marine Drive. **Tel** *(041) 507-7777.* Situated right on the seafront, this up-market shopping, dining and

entertainment complex also houses a casino with American roulette, blackjack and poker, plus the usual slots. Open to over-18s only.

⚓ Fort Frederick

Belmont Terrace. **Tel** *(041) 585-9711.* ☐ *sunrise–sunset daily.*

In 1799, a British garrison was sent to Algoa Bay to prevent an invasion by French troops supporting the rebel republic of Graaff-Reinet *(see pp358–9).* Small, square Fort Frederick *(see pp48–9)* was built on a low hill overlooking the mouth of the Baakens River, and named after the Duke of York, who was commander-in-chief of the British army at the time. Although it was defended by eight cannons, no salvoes were ever fired from them in an act of war. The arrival of the English settlers in 1820 was supervised by the commander of the garrison, Captain Francis Evatt, whose grave can be seen at the fort.

🏖 Humewood Beach

2 km (1 mile) S of the city centre.

The recreation hub of Port Elizabeth, Humewood Beach is bordered by Marine Drive, which provides quick access to all the attractions that line the shore. An attractive covered promenade provides welcome shelter from the wind and hosts a fleamarket at weekends. There is also an inviting freshwater and tidal pool complex nearby.

The gateway to The Boardwalk, an entertainment complex on Port Elizabeth's seafront

The all-important "19th hole" at Humewood Golf Club

Lifeguards are stationed at all the main beaches. Sailing and scuba diving are particularly popular here, and the windy expanse of Algoa Bay is often punctuated by the white sails of yachts.

Many hotels and holiday apartments line Marine Drive, and there are also numerous little restaurants and eateries.

On view at the snake park are snakes from around the world, including South African species like the puffadder and the green mamba.

Bayworld
Marine Drive. **Tel** (041) 584-0650.
9am–4:30pm daily.
25 Dec. **www**.bayworld.co.za

The jetty at Humewood Beach

Bayworld is an unusual combination of a natural and cultural history museum with an oceanarium and a snake park. At a different location, in the city centre, the Bayworld complex also includes No 7 Castle Hill, a Victorian house museum depicting the early Settler way of life.

The entrance to the main museum is lined with several open enclosures containing water birds. The fascinating exhibits inside include a marine gallery containing salvaged items and fully rigged models of early sailing ships.

An exhibition entitled "The First People of the Bay" features original artifacts of the Khoisan people. The Khoi arrived in Algoa Bay more than two millennia ago – long before any other population group. Items on display include medicinal herbs, musical instruments, rock art and clothing.

Environs: The championship **Humewood Golf Club**, some 3 km (2 miles) south along the coast from Humewood, is considered to be one of the best in South Africa. At the clubhouse, golfers can enjoy a well-earned drink and marvel at the splendid views across the bay.

About 3 km (2 miles) south of Humewood lies the cape that marks the entrance to Algoa Bay. **Cape Recife** and its surrounding nature reserve are an ideal destination for bird spotting and exploring the unspoilt rocky shore.

A 9-km-long (6-mile) hiking trail explores the reserve and traverses several different coastal habitats that include redbuds and dune vegetation. The route passes the Cape Recife lighthouse, a spot that is a favourite with divers. Near the lighthouse is the **SA Marine Rehabilitation & Education Centre (SAMREC)**, which rescues and rehabilitates marine birds – in particular, African penguins. Visitors can tour the premises and watch the penguins being fed (2:30pm daily). The Flying Penguin coffee shop is a good place to take a break.

Of the number of ships that have been wrecked at Cape Recife, the Greek vessel *Kapodistrias* was the most recent casualty. The bulk carrier struck Thunderbolt Reef in July 1985.

Humewood Golf Club
Marine Drive. **Tel** (041) 583-2137.
www.humewoodgolf.co.za

Cape Recife
Tel (041) 583-4004. sunrise–sunset daily. **www**.caperecife.co.za

SA Marine Rehabilitation & Education Centre (SAMREC)
Tel (041) 583-1830. 9:30am–5pm daily. 1 Jan, 25 Dec.
www.samrec.org.za

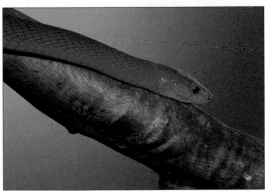

The green mamba, a venomous resident of Bayworld

Addo Elephant National Park ⑨

Road map D5. 72 km (45 miles) NE of Port Elizabeth. *Tel (042) 233-8600. Reservations: (012) 428-9111,* ⏰ *7am–7pm daily.* 🅿️ ✂️ 🍴 🚻 www.sanparks.org

In the past, elephants lived throughout the Cape Colony, but as the land was settled they were hunted to extinction. In 1919 Major Philip Pretorius was appointed to exterminate the last survivors and shot 120 over 11 months. Only 15 terrified elephants survived in the densest thickets.

When public opinion turned in their favour, a 68 sq km (26 sq mile) tract of surplus land was declared national park territory in 1931. However, the animals raided nearby farms at night and a suitable fence was needed to prevent escapes.

After numerous experiments, warden Graham Armstrong constructed a guard from railway tracks and elevator cables. By 1954, some 23 sq km (9 sq miles) had been fenced in this way, and the elephants were safely contained.

For many years, Addo resembled a large zoo. Oranges were placed below the rest camps at night to lure the shy beasts, while the stout fences separated visitors and animals. The herd responded well to protection – increasing to 265 by 1998 – making it necessary to enlarge their territory. Today, there are more

Dung beetles are protected in the park

than 450 elephants. The park, which includes the Zuurberg mountains to the north and a belt of coastal dunes to the south, covers 2,920 sq km (1,127 sq miles) and is the third-largest in the country.

Addo's rest camp has a shop, restaurant, swimming pool, caravan park and 61 chalets. A network of game-viewing roads allows visitors to explore the southern region of the park, which is the only park in the world to house the Big Seven: elephants, leopards, black rhinos, Cape buffaloes, lions and, in the marine section, great white sharks and southern right whales.

Other animals inhabiting the dense thicket include kudu, elands, hartebeests and bushbucks. But visitors tend to overlook one of the park's smallest and most fascinating creatures: the flightless dung beetle. Signs warn motorists not to drive over them.

Addo's dense *spekboom (Portulacaria afra)* bushland sustains the highest concentration of large mammals in the country. To monitor the effects that the elephant, black rhino and buffalo populations have on the vegetation, a botanical reserve has been established. A 6-km (4-mile) trail explores this reserve.

A herd of elephants at a waterhole in the Addo Elephant National Park

Shamwari Game Reserve ⑩

Road map D5. 72 km (44 miles) N of Port Elizabeth. *Tel (041) 407-1000.* 🅿️ ✂️ *11am–6pm daily (booking essential; lunch included).* 🎿 www.shamwari.com

At 200 sq km (77 sq miles), Shamwari is the largest private reserve in the Eastern Cape. It consists of undulating bushveld country in the catchment area of the Bushmans River. The recipient of several international awards, Shamwari is the brainchild of entrepreneur Adrian Gardiner, who originally bought the ranch in the hills near Paterson as a retreat for his family. Over the years, several neighbouring farms were incorporated and wildlife re-introduced. The reserve is now home to the Big Five *(see pp72–3)*, as well as zebras, giraffes and antelope species including elands, kudu, impalas, gemsboks, hartebeests, springboks and black wildebeests.

The reserve offers luxury accommodation *(see p394)* and an African wildlife experience that has attracted

A rustic chalet in the Addo Elephant National Park

For hotels and restaurants in this region see pp391–4 and pp419–21

many famous visitors, including the late Princess Diana. Rangers conduct game-viewing drives in open vehicles twice daily.

Shamwari was the first private reserve in the Eastern Cape to reintroduce large mammals to an area where they had become extinct, but there are now several more reserves in the vicinity of Addo Elephant National Park. They include Schotia Safaris (Tel (042) 235-1436; www. schotia.com), Amakhala Game Reserve (Tel (046) 636-2750; www.amakhala.co.za) and Pumba Private Game Reserve (Tel (046) 603-2000; www. pumbagamereserve.co.za).

Alexandria ⓫

Road map D5. R72, E of Port Elizabeth.

Alexandria was founded in 1856 around the Dutch Reformed Church. A dirt road, just west of town, crosses chicory fields before entering the enchanted Alexandria forest, which is home to 170 tree species including superb, towering specimens of yellowwood. The forest and the largest active dune system in South Africa lie within the **Woody Cape Nature Reserve**, which is part of the Addo Elephant National Park. The two-day, 35-km (22-mile) Alexandria Hiking Trail, one of the finest coastal walks in South

White rhino, Shamwari Game Reserve

Africa, passes through dense indigenous forest to reach sand dunes rising to 150 m (488 ft) above the sea, before returning via a circular route. Overnight huts are located at the start and at Woody Cape.

✖ Woody Cape Nature Reserve
8 km (5 miles) off R72. **Tel** (046) 653-0601. ◯ 7am–7pm daily. 🅿️ 🚶 bookings on (041) 468 0916. www.sanparks.org

Port Alfred ⓬

Road map D5. R72, 150 km (93 miles) E of Port Elizabeth. 🚶 18,000. ⌂ Halyards Hotel 🛈 Causeway Rd, (046) 624-1235. www.portalfred.co.za

Port Alfred, a charming seaside resort in the Eastern Cape, is well known for its

superb beaches. Those west of the river mouth are more developed, while those to the east are unspoilt and excellent for long walks. Kelly's Beach offers safe bathing. The entire stretch of coast is perfect for surfing and also popular with rock and surf fishermen.

Environs: The **Kowie Nature Reserve** has an 8-km (5-mile) hiking trail with various exit and entry points for those wanting shorter walks. It passes through a thickly forested canyon, and there are picnic sites next to the river. A variety of birds and small animals can be seen.

✖ Kowie Nature Reserve
R67, 5 km (3 miles) N of Port Alfred. **Tel** (046) 624-1235. ◯ 7am–7pm daily. 🅿️ (hiking permits available at the gate).

Many luxury yachts, catamarans and fishing vessels are moored at Port Alfred's marina

Grahamstown ⑬

Arts Festival logo

After the Fourth Frontier War of 1812, Colonel John Graham established a military post on an abandoned farm near the southeast coast. In an attempt to stabilize the region, the Cape government enticed 4,500 British families to the farmlands. Many of these "1820 Settlers" preferred an urban life, and Grahamstown became a thriving trading centre, home to the largest concentration of artisans outside Cape Town.

Exploring Grahamstown
Grahamstown is known for its 50 plus churches, university and superb schools. Its major attractions lie within a 500-m (1,625-ft) walk from the **City Hall** in High Street. Some 60 buildings have been declared national monuments, and a host of beautifully restored Georgian and Victorian residences line the streets.

🏛 Albany Museum Complex
Tel (046) 622-2312.
The complex incorporates five separate venues. Two of them, the **History and Natural Sciences museums**, display fossils, settler artifacts and Xhosa dress. Another, the **Old Provost**, opposite Rhodes University, was built in 1838 as a military prison. **Drostdy Gateway**, which frames the university entrance, is all that remains of the 1842 magistrate's offices. **Fort Selwyn** *(see pp48–9)*, adjacent to the 1820 Settlers Monument, was built in 1836 and was formally used as an artillery barracks. It offers scenic views of the town.

🏛 History and Natural Sciences museums
Somerset Street. *Tel (046) 622-2312.* ⬤ 9am–1pm, 2–4:30pm Mon–Fri; 9am–1pm Sat. ⬤ Good Fri, 25 Dec. 📷 ♿

🏢 Old Provost
Lucas Avenue. *Tel (046) 622-2312.* ⬤ by appointment only. 📷 ♿

🏢 Fort Selwyn
Fort Selwyn Drive. *Tel (046) 622-2312.* ⬤ by appointment only. 📷

⛪ Cathedral of St Michael and St George
High St. *Tel (046) 622-3976.* ⬤ 8am–4:30pm daily. ♿
The cathedral is the town's most prominent landmark – its spire towers 51 m (166 ft) above the town centre. The original St George's Church, built in 1824, is the oldest Anglican Church in South Africa, and the organ is one of the country's finest.

⛪ Methodist Church
Bathurst St. *Tel (046) 622-7210.* ⬤ daily. ♿
The Commemoration Church is noted for its Gothic Revival façade and lovely stained-glass windows. It was completed in 1850.

Drostdy Gateway, the entrance to Rhodes University

🏛 Observatory Museum
Bathurst Street. *Tel (046) 622-2312.* ⬤ 9am–1pm, 2–4:30pm Mon–Fri; 9am–1pm Sat. ⬤ Good Fri, 25 Dec. 📷 ♿ (except turret).
The attraction at this historic home and workshop of a mid-19th-century Grahamstown jeweller is the Victorian camera obscura in the turret, which projects images of the town on to a wall.

🏢 Rhodes University
Artillery Road. *Tel (046) 603-8111.* 📷 multi-entry ticket. **www.ru.ac.za**
This beautiful old university complex also houses the world-famous **South African Institute for Aquatic Biodiversity**, where the most interesting displays are two rare embalmed coelacanth specimens. This prehistoric species of deep-water fish was presumed extinct until its "discovery" in East London in 1939. There is also a collection of other marine and freshwater fish. Visitors interested in traditional African music should visit the **International Library of African Music**, which is also on the campus.

🏛 South African Institute for Aquatic Biodiversity
Rhodes University. *Tel (046) 603-5800.* ⬤ 8am–4pm Mon–Fri. ⬤ Good Fri, 25 Dec. **www.saiab.ac.za**

🏛 International Library of African Music
Rhodes University. *Tel (046) 603-8557.* ⬤ by appointment. ♿

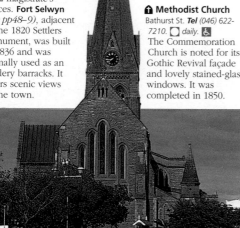

The Cathedral of St Michael and St George on High Street

For hotels and restaurants in this region see pp391–4 and pp419–21

🏛 National English Literary Museum

87 Beaufort St. **Tel** (046) 622-7042.
🕐 9am–1pm, 2–4:30pm Mon–Fri.
🌓 Good Fri, 25 Dec. ♿ **www**.
ru.ac.za/nelm

Preserved here are documents, early manuscripts and personal letters relating to South Africa's most important writers.

🏛 1820 Settlers Monument

Gunfire Hill. **Tel** (046) 603-1100.
🕐 8am–4:30pm Mon–Fri. ♿ 🛗 💻

Reminiscent of an old fort, this monument on Gunfire Hill was built in 1974 in the shape of a ship and commemorates the British families who arrived in the area in 1820. The modern Monument Theatre complex nearby is the main venue for the annual 11-day National Arts Festival *(see p39)*. Many paintings decorate the impressive foyer.

The Old Provost was once a military prison

Camera obscura in the Observatory Museum

Environs: 34 km (21 miles) north of Grahamstown lies the 445-sq-km (172-sq-mile) **Great Fish River Nature Reserve**. After the Fifth Frontier War of 1819, the land between the Keiskamma and Great Fish rivers was declared neutral territory, and British settlers were brought in to act as a buffer against the Xhosa incursions. Today, the area is the largest wildlife reserve in the Eastern Cape province, home to kudu, elands, hartebeests, hippos, black rhinos, buffaloes and leopards.

A two-day guided trail follows the river; hikers stay overnight in a tented camp.

🦌 Great Fish River Nature Reserve

R67 towards Fort Beaufort.
Tel (040) 653-8010. 🕐 daily.
www.ecparks.co.za

VISITORS' CHECKLIST

Road map D5. 🏘 *200,000*.
✈ *Port Elizabeth, 127 km (79 miles) to NE.* 🚉 *High Street.* 🚌 *Frontier Country Hotel, Bathurst St.* ℹ *63 High Street, (046) 622-3241.* 🕐 *8:30am–5pm Mon–Fri, 8:30am–noon Sat.* 🌓 *Good Fri, 25 Dec, pub hols.* 🎭 *National Arts Festival (Jul).* **www**.grahamstown.co.za

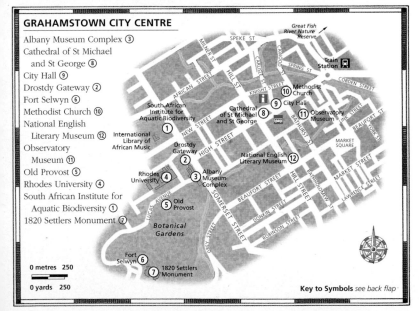

GRAHAMSTOWN CITY CENTRE

Albany Museum Complex ③
Cathedral of St Michael
    and St George ⑧
City Hall ⑨
Drostdy Gateway ②
Fort Selwyn ⑥
Methodist Church ⑩
National English
    Literary Museum ⑫
Observatory
    Museum ⑪
Old Provost ⑤
Rhodes University ④
South African Institute for
    Aquatic Biodiversity ①
1820 Settlers Monument ⑦

0 metres   250
0 yards   250

Key to Symbols *see back flap*

THE EAST COAST
AND INTERIOR

Introducing the East Coast and Interior

Crowned by southern Africa's highest mountains, a serrated spine that runs the length of this region, the Eastern Cape, Lesotho and KwaZulu-Natal offer rugged mountain scenery, undulating hills, and superb beaches. The powerful currents of the warm Indian Ocean carve the wave-battered cliffs of the Wild Coast. Although an almost continuous chain of coastal resorts extends 160 km (100 miles) south of Durban, Africa's largest port, much of the coastline remains unspoilt and accessible only along winding dirt roads. In the far north, subtropical forests and savannah provide a haven for an abundance of big game and birds, while coastal lakes and the ocean lure fishermen and holiday-makers.

Golden Gate National Park

Golden Gate Highlands National Park *in the northeastern Free State lies in the foothills of the Maluti mountains. Magnificent scenery, impressive sandstone formations like Sentinel Rock, abundant wildlife and pleasant walks are the attractions in this park* (see p271).

| 0 kilometres | 100 |
| 0 miles | 100 |

WILD COAST, DRAKENSBERG AND MIDLANDS *(See pp262–77)*

The Hole in the Wall *is situated just off the coast at the mouth of the Mpako River. It is one of the best-known sites on the romantic Wild Coast* (see p267).

Wild Coast

◁ **Loggerhead turtle hatchlings on Sodwana Bay beach, along the Maputaland coast**

Cape Vidal *separates the Indian Ocean and Lake St Lucia. It forms part of the iSimangaliso Wetland Park (see p296), which borders on the unspoilt Maputaland coast, the breeding ground of leatherback and loggerhead turtles.*

Sodwana Bay

DURBAN AND ZULULAND
(see pp278–97)

Pietermaritzburg

Church Street Mall *in Pietermaritzburg is surrounded by a number of historic buildings like the beautiful City Hall, which was built in 1893 (see p276).*

Durban's Beachfront, *a 6-km (4-mile) long stretch of hotels, restaurants and entertainment venues along the Indian Ocean shoreline, is also known as the Golden Mile (see p282).*

Zulu Culture

Clay pot

The reputation of being a fierce warrior nation, fuelled by written accounts of the 1879 Anglo-Zulu War, has been enhanced by dramatic films like *Zulu* and the internationally acclaimed television series *Shaka Zulu*. Many ites associated with Zulu history can be visited in the Ulundi, Eshowe and Melmoth districts of KwaZulu-Natal. It is true that the Zulu fought determinedly to defend their land, but their culture also reflects other, gentler, aspects in beadwork, pottery, basketry and dancing. In the remote Tugela River Valley and the northern parts of the province, rural people uphold many old customs.

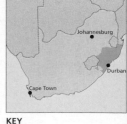

KEY

■ KwaZulu-Natal

Oxhide is stretched on the ground and cured to make clothing and shields.

Fence made of poles and woven reeds.

Zulu Beehive Hut
A framework of saplings is covered with plaited grass or rushes. A hide screen affords additional privacy.

ZULU CRAFTS

The Zulu people are renowned as weavers and for their colourful beadwork. Baskets and mats made from *ilala* palm fronds and *imizi* grass are very decorative and especially popular. Most baskets display the traditional triangle or diamond shape, a symbol representing the male and female elements. Shiny glass beads introduced by the early 19th-century traders created a new custom. Today, artistic beadwork forms an important part of Zulu culture. Every pattern and colour has symbolic significance, as in the *incwadi*, or love-letters, that are made by young women and presented to eligible men.

Zulu beadwork and spoon

Maize, the staple diet, is ground and boiled to form a stiff, lumpy porridge.

Basket weaver

Utshwala *(beer) is prepared by the women, using sorghum. The fermented liquid is then strained through long grass sieves to separate the husks.*

TRADITIONAL DANCING

In Zulu society, social gatherings almost always involve dancing. Most Zulu dances require a high level of fitness – and a lack of inhibition. While ceremonial dances can involve large crowds of gyrating, clapping and stamping performers, small groups of performers need only the encouragement of an accompanying drum and singing, whistling or ululating onlookers. Lore and clan traditions may be related through the dance; alternatively, the movements may serve as a means of social commentary.

Zulu dances require stamina and agility

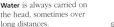

Water is always carried on the head, sometimes over long distances.

Grain Storage
To protect their grain from birds and rodents, the Zulu stored maize and sorghum in a hut on long stilts.

Clay pots, for water, grain or sorghum beer, are smoothed and decorated before firing.

THE ZULU KRAAL

Historically, the *umuzi* (Zulu kraal) was a circular settlement that enclosed several *uhlongwa* (beehive-shaped grass huts) grouped around an enclosure in which the cattle were corralled at night. Although the principle of the kraal continues, traditional architectural styles are seldom seen nowadays. Cement, bricks, concrete blocks and corrugated iron sheeting are the modern choices.

Cattle *are a symbol of wealth and play an important part in Zulu society. They are kept in a kraal (securely fenced enclosure) at night.*

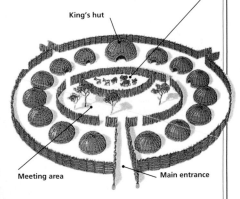

King's hut

Meeting area

Main entrance

Traditional weapons *are still an integral part of Zulu culture, even today, and men often carry wooden staffs and clubs. At political meetings and rallies, tempers tend to flare, and as a result the carrying of traditional weapons has been outlawed.*

Durban's Surfing Scene

In the 1960s, fibreglass surfboards replaced the canvas-covered wooden versions, causing a surge in devotees to the sport. Durban, with its warm currents, consistent waves and wide beaches, quickly became the surfing capital of the country. Some of the international greats the city has produced were Max Wetland, Shaun Thomson and Martin Potter, while current champions include Grant "Twiggy" Baker, Travis Logie and Jordy Smith. Although surfing venues can vary, favourite Durban hotspots are North Beach, New Pier, the Bay of Plenty and Snake Park. For the more experienced surfer, there is Cave Rock Bluff, south of the harbour.

Glen D'Arcy surfing logo

Jordy Smith, *one of a new breed of young surfers to come out of Durban, was crowned champion at the ISA World Surfing Games in California in October 2006.*

"Bottom turn" *is the term used to describe the manoeuvre at the base of a wave; it is often followed by a "floater", which is when the surfer floats across the top of the wave to generate speed.*

The perfect wave provides an exhilarating ride. Durban is famous for its superb waves.

Modern boards *are smaller, lighter and more manoeuvrable than the clumsy early models.*

Competition long boards must exceed 2.8 m (9 ft) in length and weigh between 5.2–7 kg (11–15 lbs).

Short boards are lighter, more manoeuvrable, and are not allowed to exceed 3.2 kg (7 lbs) to qualify for contests.

Wax is rubbed on the top of the board to improve the surfer's grip.

CAVE ROCK

Cave Rock is Durban's premier big-wave surf spot. The presence of a deep ocean channel (*see p25*) and a reef near the shore produces powerful big waves that compare with those that have made Hawai'i world-famous.

Shaun Thomson (*middle*) *became a local hero and surfing icon when he won the World Championship title in 1977.*

SURFING CULTURE

g has produced a unique
ientation and philosophy
ved by dedicated devotees
d the globe. Laid-back and
going, it strives for simplicity
centres on the enjoyment of
one of nature's most powerful
orces: water. Graffiti and murals
Durban integrate the thrills and
pills of surfing with the cityscape,
transforming the bland walls into
roaring tubes of salt and spray.

The lip forms as the base of
the wave encounters the reef.

Surf-wear fashion *is
a lucrative spin-off
industry. Imaginative
creations that reflect
surfing's way of life are
produced by brands
such as Quiksilver
and Billabong
and command
designer-wear prices.*

The tube of the wave
curls up and around
behind the surfer.

Surfing heroes,
*such as Kelly
Slater, enjoy cult
status wherever
they go. Each year,
big surf contests
draw devoted surf
"groupies" and
autograph hunters
to Durban's
beachfront.*

The Mr Price Pro *(formerly the Gunston 500) is South Africa's
premier surfing event and takes place over six days every July.
First staged in 1969 with prize money of R500, it was the first
professional surfing event to be held outside Hawai'i.*

SURFING LINGO

Tube – ride through the
concave curve formed by
the body of the wave.
Lip – the tip of the wave
(its most powerful part).
Barrel – ride through the
curve of a wave that ends
in the wave breaking on
the surfer.
Bomb – enormous wave.
Filthy – excellent surf.
Grommet – a beginner.
Shundies – thank you.
Tassie – a young woman.
Cactus – any person that
surfers do not like.

WILD COAST, DRAKENSBERG AND MIDLANDS

The Zulus call the jagged peaks of southern Africa's highest mountains ukhahlamba, *"a barrier of spears". Where the lofty summits of the Drakensberg slope down toward the coastline, the unspoiled Wild Coast promises excellent fishing and hiking.*

Some 1,000 years ago the lush, well-watered valleys of the Drakensberg were home to hunter-gatherer San Bushmen who stalked antelope with their bows and arrows. The colonizing vanguards of Zulu, Xhosa, Afrikaner and British soon drove them from the region, but, apart from the delicate paintings that survive under overhangs and in caves, the diminutive hunters left no evidence of their presence.

At the beginning of the 19th century, the Xhosa's heartland was part of the expanding Cape colony, while the centre of the Zulu kingdom stretched north of the Tugela River. Facing attacks on several fronts, the Basotho tribe sought refuge in the high mountains that would eventually become the kingdom of Lesotho. By 1848 the Kei River had become the frontier line between the British and Xhosa, while to the north, the territory between the Mzimkhulu and Tugela rivers was declared the Colony of Natal.

Over the centuries, countless territorial wars raged in this fertile region now known as the Midlands, and many of the old battle sites can still be visited today.

In 1976 the Xhosa territory of Transkei was officially declared "independent", but reincorporated into South Africa in 1994. This is an area of immense natural beauty and splendour. The enchanted coastline, too remote for modern development, has remained virtually unspoilt and offers secluded bays and beaches, rocky headlands and some of the best fishing to be found anywhere along the coast.

The sandstone buildings at the Rorke's Drift battle site

◁ Bushman's River and Giant's Castle in the Drakensberg range, seen from the Giant's Castle Game Reserve

Exploring the Wild Coast, Drakensberg and Midlands

The remote Lesotho highlands and the Drakensberg, southern Africa's highest mountain range, form the backbone of this region. Breathtaking views, and streams flowing through secluded valleys attract nature lovers, hikers, bird-watchers and trout fishermen. A plateau dotted with traditional Xhosa huts lies between the mountains and the Wild Coast's sheltered coves and forested cliffs. North of here, in the Natal Midlands, a pastoral landscape of green hills and forest patches serves as the perfect backdrop for charming country hotels, myriad arts and crafts enterprises and dairy farms.

The distant Champagne Castle, Monk's Cowl and Cathkin Peak in the Drakensberg mountains

KEY

▬	Motorway
▬	Major road
═══	Minor road
▪▪▪	Untarred road
▬	Scenic route
⌒	Main railway
—	Minor railway
▬	International border
—	Provincial border
✕	Pass

The memorial *laager* (encampment) on the site of the Battle of Blood River (1838), near Dundee

Johannesburg

Kroonstad

Ed

FRE

Odendaalsrus

Welkom

Virginia

Theunissen

Bloemfontein

Vals

Lind

Steyns

Ventersburg

Alemanskraal Dam

Sene

Rosenc

Winburg

Marquar

Ficksbur

Clocolan

Teyateyaneng

Westminster

Mase

Motimo N

Wepener

Ramabanta

Mafeteng

Bloemfontein

Breipaal

Dupleston

Smithfield

Zastron

Mohal-Hoek

Outhin

Rouxville

Orange

Goedemoed

Aliwal North

Sterkspruit

Vineyard

New Er

Burgersdorp

Clanville

Bar Eas

Swempoort

Steynsburg

Dordrecht

Ellio

Molteno

Hofmeyr

Lady Frere

Bailey

EASTE

Queenstown

Coetzeesberg

Tarkastad

Bolotwa

Cradock

Swart-Kei

Elandsdrift

Cathcart

Nqama

Winterberg

Daggaboersnek

Stutterheim

Kom

Bedford

Fort Beaufort

Bhisho

Port Elizabeth

Mdantsane

East Lon

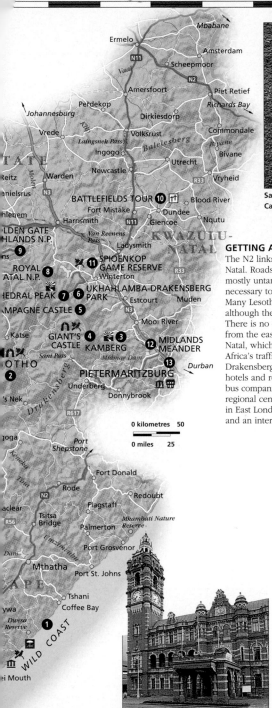

San Bushman rock art in the Giant's Castle Game Reserve, Drakensberg

GETTING AROUND

The N2 links East London with KwaZulu-Natal. Roads leading to the Wild Coast are mostly untarred and private transport is necessary to reach the remote beaches. Many Lesotho roads require a 4WD vehicle, although the network is being extended. There is no easy road access to Lesotho from the east. The N3 highway in KwaZulu-Natal, which carries one-tenth of South Africa's traffic, provides access to the Drakensberg resorts. Roads leading to the hotels and resorts are mostly tarred. Large bus companies offer regular services between regional centres. There are domestic airports in East London, Umtata and Pietermaritzburg and an international airport at Maseru.

SIGHTS AT A GLANCE

Cathedral Peak **7**
Champagne Castle **5**
Giant's Castle **4**
Golden Gate Highlands
  National Park **9**
Kamberg **3**
Lesotho pp268–9 **2**
Midlands Meander **12**
Pietermaritzburg **13**
Royal Natal National Park **8**
Spioenkop Game Reserve **11**
uKhahlamba-Drakensberg
  Park **6**
Wild Coast **1**

Tour
Battlefields Tour p274 **10**

SEE ALSO

- *Where to Stay* pp394–6
- *Where to Eat* pp421–2

The City Hall of Pietermaritzburg

The Wild Coast **❶**

The second-largest city in the Eastern Cape and the country's only river port, East London is a good starting point for exploring the shores of the former Transkei *(see p263)*. Appropriately named "Wild Coast", this area is one of South Africa's most under-developed, where rural communities adhere to age-old traditions, and spectacular beaches front a section of the Indian Ocean that is notorious for its shipwrecks. Much of the land here is communally owned by the Xhosa inhabitants.

East London's Orient Beach is popular with bathers and surfers

Exploring the Wild Coast

The Wild Coast is an outdoor paradise with rugged cliffs, an unspoilt coastline, sheltered bays and dense coastal forests. Most resorts, reserves and villages are accessible from the N2, but many roads are untarred and in poor condition. There is no public transport to speak of; the best option is the Baz Bus *(see p455)*, which covers the N2.

East London

Road map E5. 🏘 *808,000.*
✈ *R347, 12 km (7 miles) W of East London.* 🚉 *Station Rd.* 🚌 *Oxford St.* 🛈 *91 Western Ave, Vincent, (043) 721-1346.* ⭕ *daily.*

East London is a pleasant seaside town on the Buffalo River. Numerous good swimming beaches are washed by the warm waters of the Indian Ocean.

Among several interesting sites is the statue in front of the City Hall of Black Consciousness leader Steve Biko. Born in the Eastern Cape, he died under dubious circumstances while in police custody. The statue was unveiled by Nelson Mandela in 1997 to mark the 20th anniversary of Biko's death.

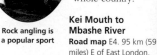

Rock angling is a popular sport

The **East London Museum**, established in 1921, has an interesting collection of natural and cultural exhibits, including fossils found in the region. There are also displays on maritime history and on the Xhosa people. .

🏛 **East London Museum**
319 Oxford St. **Tel** *(043) 743-0686.*
⭕ *9am–4:30pm Mon–Fri (to 4pm Fri), 10am–1pm Sat, 10am–3pm Sun.*
⭕ *Good Fri, 25 Dec.* 🖼 📷 ⓰
🖥 **www**.elmuseum.za.org

Morgan's Bay and Kei Mouth

Road map E4. Off the N2, 85 km (53 miles) E of East London. 🛈 *Morgan's Bay Hotel, (043) 841-1062.* **www**.morgan-bay-hotel.co.za
These coastal villages lie on a stretch of coast renowned for its scenery. At Kei Mouth, a pont transports vehicles across the Great Kei River to the former Xhosa "homeland" known as Transkei. The Morgan's Bay Hotel adjoins the beach, and the Ntshala Lagoon offers safe swimming. Walks along the cliffs afford superb views of the sea.

Further south, at Double Mouth, a spur overlooking the ocean and estuary provides one of the finest views in the whole country.

Kei Mouth to Mbashe River

Road map E4. 95 km (59 miles) E of East London.
The Kei River marks the start of the Wild Coast. Twenty rivers enter this 80-km (50-mile) long stretch, along which is strung a succession of old-fashioned family hotels. Kei Mouth is only an hour's drive from East London, making it a popular weekend destination.

Further north, Dwesa Nature Reserve extends along the coast from the Nqabara River. The reserve is home to rare tree dassies and samango monkeys. The grassland, coastline and forest are all pristine. On the eastern banks of the Mbashe River is the

---

COELACANTH

In 1938 a boat fishing off the Chalumna River mouth near East London netted an unusual fish. The captain sent it to the East London Museum, whose curator, Marjorie Courtenay-Latimer, contacted Professor JLB Smith, ichthyologist at Rhodes University. The fish belonged to a species believed to have become extinct with the dinosaurs. The reward offered for another *Latimeria chalumnae* was claimed only in 1952, when one was netted off the Comoros Islands. The coelacanth is steel-blue and covered in heavy scales; it is distinguished by its six primitive, limb-like fins.

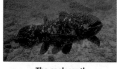

The coelacanth

For hotels and restaurants in this region see pp394–6 and pp421–2

Traditional Xhosa huts dot the hillsides of the former Transkei

Cwebe Nature Reserve. The adjoining reserves conserve 60 sq km (23 sq miles) of dense forest, home to bushbucks and blue duikers, as well as coastal grasslands inhabited by elands, hartebeests, wildebeests and zebras. A hiking trail follows the entire Wild Coast, but the section from Mbashe to Coffee Bay is the most spectacular.

Coffee Bay
Road map E4. Off the N2.
🏠 *Ocean View Hotel, (047) 575-2005/6.* **www**.oceanview.co.za
Allegedly named after a ship carrying coffee which was wrecked at the site in 1863, Coffee Bay is popular for fishing, swimming and beach walks. There are a number of superbly sited hotels set above the sandy beaches. A prominent detached cliff, separated from the mainland by erosion, has been named Hole in the Wall; it is a conspicuous landmark located 6 km (4 miles) south along the coast. Many centuries of swirling wave action have carved an arch through the centre of the cliff.

Umngazi Mouth
Road map E4. 25 km (16 miles) S of Port St Johns. 🏠 *Umngazi River Bungalows, (047) 564-1115.* **www**.umngazi.co.za
An idyllic estuary framed by forested hills, the Umngazi offers superb snorkelling, canoeing and board-sailing. Umngazi River Bungalows (*see p396*), on the northern bank is one of the leading resorts on the Wild Coast, and is renowned for its food and service. There is a lovely, sandy beach and the rugged coastline extends south to the cliffs that are known in Xhosa as *Ndluzulu*, after the crashing sound of the surf.

Mkambati Nature Reserve
Road map E4. Off R61 N of Port St Johns. 🏠 *Eastern Cape Parks, (043) 735-4400.* **www**.ecparks.co.za
Wedged between the Mzikaba and Mtentu rivers, Mkambati is the Wild Coast's largest nature reserve. Apart from conserving a 13-km (8-mile) long strip of grassland and unspoilt, rocky coastline, the reserve is known for its endemic plants such as the Mkambati palm, which is found only on the north banks of the rivers. Cape vultures breed in the Mzikaba Gorge. The Mkambati River flows through the reserve in a series of waterfalls of which Horseshoe Falls, near the sea, is the most striking.

Accommodation ranges from a stone lodge to cottages. Outdoor activities include swimming, fishing and horse riding. Animals include elands, springboks, blesboks, impalas, blue wildebeests and zebras. An added attraction is that the reserve is near the Wild Coast Sun Hotel and Casino (*see p288*).

The Xhosa word for Hole in the Wall, *esiKhaleni*, means "the place of sound"

Lesotho

Surrounded by South Africa, this mountain kingdom, or "Kingdom in the Sky" as it is sometimes referred to, achieved independence from Britain on 4 October 1966. The rugged highlands of Lesotho, which encompass the Drakensberg, Maluti and Thaba-Putsoa mountains, are a popular destination for visitors who enjoy camping, hiking and climbing. Lesotho also boasts fertile river valleys, a rich variety of flora and fauna, and a strong cultural heritage that is very much kept alive by the Basotho people.

Basotho hat

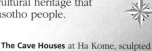
The Cave Houses at Ha Kome, sculpted from mud, are good examples of indigenous architecture.

★ **Teyateyaneng**
This town, easily accessible from Maseru, is the "craft capital" of Lesotho. The colourful woven jerseys, carpets and wall hangings are a local speciality.

Maseru
Founded by the British in 1869, Maseru lies on the Caledon River. The main attraction is Makoanyane Square, a monument to the Basotho who died in the two World Wars.

STAR FEATURES

★ Teyateyaneng

★ Katse Dam

★ Sani Pass

Snowfalls
In May and June the high country becomes a winter wonderland, attracting skiers and snowboarders.

For hotels and restaurants in this region see pp394–6 and pp421–2

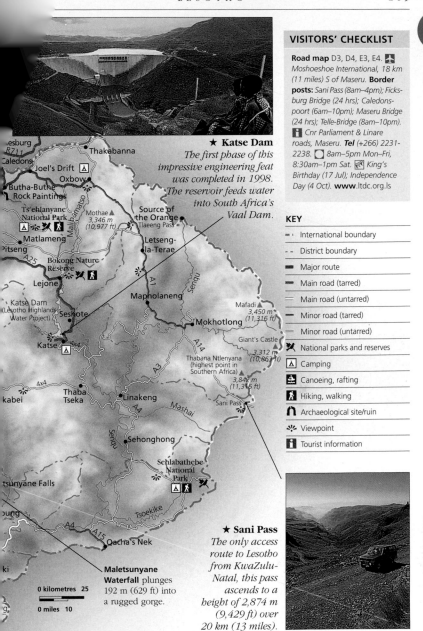

★ Katse Dam

The first phase of this impressive engineering feat was completed in 1998. The reservoir feeds water into South Africa's Vaal Dam.

VISITORS' CHECKLIST

Road map D3, D4, E3, E4. ✈
Moshoeshoe International, 18 km (11 miles) S of Maseru. **Border posts:** *Sani Pass (8am–4pm); Ficks-burg Bridge (24 hrs); Caledons-poort (6am–10pm); Maseru Bridge (24 hrs); Telle-Bridge (8am–10pm).* ℹ *Cnr Parliament & Linare roads, Maseru.* **Tel** *(+266) 2231-2238.* ⏰ *8am–5pm Mon–Fri, 8:30am–1pm Sat.* 🎉 *King's Birthday (17 Jul); Independence Day (4 Oct).* www.ltdc.org.ls

KEY

- -ı- International boundary
- - - District boundary
- ━ Major route
- ━ Main road (tarred)
- ═ Main road (untarred)
- ─ Minor road (tarred)
- ═ Minor road (untarred)
- 🏃 National parks and reserves
- 🅰 Camping
- 🚣 Canoeing, rafting
- 🚶 Hiking, walking
- ⌂ Archaeological site/ruin
- ☀ Viewpoint
- ℹ Tourist information

Joel's Drift 🅰
Oxbow
Butha-Buthe
Rock Paintings
Thakebanna
R711
esburg
Caledons
Ts'ehlanyane
National Park 🅰
Matlameng
Mothae ▲
3,346 m
(10,977 ft)
Source of
the Orange
Tlaeeng Pass
Pitseng
Bokong Nature
Reserve
Letseng-
la-Terae
Lejone
Katse Dam
(Lesotho Highlands
Water Project)
Seshote
Mapholaneng
Mafadi ▲
3,450 m
(11,316 ft)
Mokhotlong
Katse 🅰
4x4
Giant's Castle
3,312 m
Thabana Ntlenyana
(highest point in
Southern Africa) ▲
3,842 m
(11,315 ft)
4x4
kabei
Thaba
Tseka
Linakeng
Mashai
Sani Pass
Senqu
Sehonghong
tsunyane Falls
Schlabathebe
National
Park 🅰
oung
A4
A15
Tsoekike
Qacha's Nek
ki
Maletsunyane Waterfall plunges 192 m (629 ft) into a rugged gorge.

0 kilometres   25
0 miles   10

★ Sani Pass
The only access route to Lesotho from KwaZulu-Natal, this pass ascends to a height of 2,874 m (9,429 ft) over 20 km (13 miles).

ROCK PAINTINGS AND DINOSAUR TRACKS

Due to its remoteness, Lesotho has remained relatively uncommercialized. The high mountains, where stout Basotho ponies are often the only form of transport, contain some of the finest examples of rock art in southern Africa. Thaba Bosiu near Maseru and the Sekubu Caves at Butha-Buthe in the north are just two of the more than 400 worthwhile sites. Fossilized dinosaur tracks are found at places like Moyeni (Quthing), and the Tsikoane Mission at Hlotse.

Monochrome and polychrome art

Kamberg ❸

Road map E3. Estcourt. ℹ️ *(and reservations) Ezemvelo KZN Wildlife, (033) 263-7312.* ◯ *daily.* 🏷️ 🏃 🍴 🔼 www.kznwildlife.com

Nestling in the foothills of the uKhahlamba-Drakensberg Park, Kamberg is known for its trout-fishing locations. There are several small dams near the trout hatchery, which is open to the public and offers guided tours. Walking trails explore the valley or meander along the river.

Shelter Cave has superb San Bushman rock paintings and can be visited with a guide; the return walk takes about four hours. A small chalet camp overlooks the valley.

The high-lying Giant's Castle is covered with snow in winter

Kamberg offers good trout fishing in a beautiful setting

Giant's Castle ❹

Road map E3. Estcourt. ℹ️ *(036) 353-3718.* ◯ *daily.* 🏷️ 🏃 🍴 www.kznwildlife.com

In 1903 a sanctuary was established in this area to protect some of the last surviving elands in South Africa. They now number around 1,500 – one of the largest populations in the country.

A camouflaged hide allows visitors to view endangered bearded vultures (lammergeier), an estimated 200 pairs of which are found here.

Accommodation is in comfortable bungalows and small cottages. The main camp overlooks the Bushman's River, with Giant's Castle (3,314 m/ 10,770 ft) dominating the skyline. A short walk brings visitors to the Main Caves, where 500 San Bushman rock paintings, some of which are 800 years old, can be seen.

Champagne Castle ❺

Road map E3. Winterton.

Champagne Castle, at 3,377 m (10,975 ft), is the second-highest peak in South Africa. It juts out from the surrounding escarpment and dominates the horizon in a delightful valley. A 31-km (19-mile) connecting road from the N3 provides convenient access to a cluster of luxury hotels and timeshare resorts, such as the The Nest and the luxurious Drakensberg Sun. Famous institutions like the internationally acclaimed Drakensberg Boys' Choir School, as well as the Dragon Peaks and Monk's Cowl caravan parks, are found in this region.

uKhahlamba-Drakensberg Park ❻

Road map E3. Winterton. ℹ️ *(and reservations) Ezemvelo KZN Wildlife, (033) 845-1000.* 🏷️ 🏃 🍴 🔼 www.kznwildlife.com

The Drakensberg's dramatic and rugged escarpment provides an awesome backdrop to much of the pastoral KwaZulu-Natal Midlands.

The uKhahlamba-Drakensberg Park covers an area of 2,350 sq km (907 sq miles) and preserves some of South Africa's finest wilderness and conservation area, as well as its highest mountain

THE DRAKENSBERG RANGE

The Drakensberg, "dragon mountains", is South Africa's greatest mountain wilderness. It follows the border of Lesotho for 250 km (155 miles) – an escarpment that separates the high, interior plateau from the subtropical coast of KwaZulu-Natal. The Drakensberg is divided into the rocky High Berg and the pastoral Little Berg. Both are superb hiking venues.

Hodgson's Peaks

Giant's Castle

Giant's Castle Pass

Die Hoek

...ks. Secluded valleys and ...se, mist-shrouded forests ... home to an abundance ... wildlife, while many rock ...verhangs shelter some of ...he finest remaining examples of San Bushman rock art in South Africa today. Since these ancient paintings and etches represent a priceless cultural heritage, they must never be touched, or, even worse, splashed with water to enhance their colours.

Ezemvelo KZN Wildlife has established several rest camps in uKhahlamba-Drakensberg, and there are many pleasant campsites, mountain huts and caves that cater for hikers and mountaineers. On the park's boundaries, hotels and resorts offer comfortable accom-modation and outdoor sports.

Cathedral Peak ❼

Road map E3. Winterton.

Some of the Drakensberg's finest scenery is found in this region, and the area around Cathedral Peak offers some of the best hiking in the entire range.

The road from Winterton winds for 42 km (26 miles) through Zulu villages that are scattered across the gentle folds of the Mlambonja Valley. The Drakensberg's towering peaks form a dramatic back-drop. From the conservation office near the Cathedral Peak hotel, Mike's Pass gains 500 m (1,625 ft) in 5 km (3 miles). Ndedema Gorge, where many San Bushman paintings adorn rocky overhangs, protects the largest forest in the range.

Royal Natal National Park ❽

Road map E3. Winterton.
🛈 (033) 845-1000, (036) 438-6411.
⬤ daily. 🏞 🏃 🎣 🅰
www.kznwildlife.com

The Royal Natal National Park has some of Africa's most spectacular scenery. The awe-inspiring Amphitheatre, a crescent-shaped basalt wall 6 km (4 miles) wide, soars to a height of 1,500 m (4,875 ft). Here, the Tugela River plunges 948 m (3,080 ft) into the valley below on its journey to the Indian Ocean, making it the second-highest waterfall in the world.

Tendele rest camp, above the Tugela River, provides unrivalled views of the countryside below.

In the valleys, the Mahai campsite provides easy access to an extensive network of trails that explore the 88-sq-km (34-sq-mile) reserve.

Bearded vulture

Golden Gate Highlands National Park ❾

Road map E3. Clarens. *Tel* (058) 255-0000. ⬤ daily. 🏞 🏃 🎣 🅰
🏠 www.sanparks.co.za

Situated in the foothills of the Maluti Mountains in the eastern Free State, this national park encompasses 48 sq km (18 sq miles) of grassland and sandstone formations. The park was proclaimed in 1963 to protect the sand-stone cliffs above the Little Caledon valley. Black wildebeests, grey rheboks, blesboks, moun-tain reedbucks, elands and oribis can be seen, as well as the endangered bearded vultures, black eagles, steppe buzzards and bald ibises.

Accommodation in Glen Reenen Camp consists of cha-lets and a campsite; a more upscale option is provided by the Golden Gate Hotel (formerly the Brandwag).

The Royal Natal National Park, an unspoilt wilderness

Woman Grinding Corn | Cathedral Peak | Mnweni Needles | Eastern Buttress | Mont-aux-Sources

Cathkin Peak | Champagne Castle | Pyramid | South Peak | Amphitheatre

Gatberg

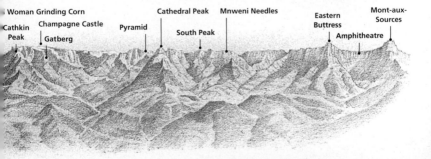

Cattle grazing at the foot of the mighty Drakensberg Mountains ▷

Battlefields Tour ⑩

The peaceful, rolling grasslands and treed hills of northwestern KwaZulu-Natal retain few reminders of the bloody battles that were waged in this corner of South Africa during the 19th century. In the 1820s, Zulu king Shaka's campaign to seize control over the scattered tribes plunged the entire region into turmoil. Over

Monument at Rorke's Drift

the following 80 years many wars were fought, pitting Zulu against Ndwandwe, Afrikaner against Zulu and English against Afrikaner and Zulu. A detailed guide to the battlefields lists over 50 sites of interest and is available from the local publicity associations and the Talana Museum, where expert guides can be hired as well.

Elandslaagte ②
The Boer and British forces clashed here on 22 October 1899, during a severe storm. The British were forced to retreat to nearby Ladysmith.

Talana Museum ③
This museum commemorates the first battle of the South African War (20 October 1899) when 4,500 British soldiers arrived in Dundee to defend the town and its coal mines.

Rorke's Drift ⑤
This museum depicts the battle during which some 100 British soldiers repelled 4,000 Zulus for 12 hours, earning them a total of 11 Victoria crosses.

Ladysmith ①
On 2 November 1899, Boer general Piet Joubert laid siege to Ladysmith and its 12,000 British troops for 118 days.

KEY

▬	Motorway
▬	Tour route
═	Other roads
☀	Viewpoint
⚔	Battle site

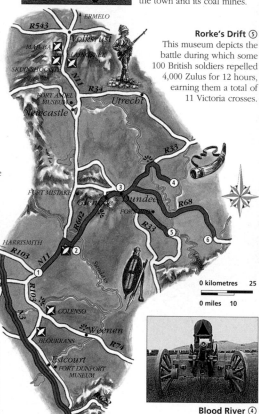

0 kilometres 25

0 miles 10

TIPS FOR DRIVERS

Length: 380 km (236 miles).
Stopping-off points: The towns of Ladysmith and Dundee have restaurants and accommodation. Audio tapes can be bought from the Talana Museum in Dundee and at Fugitives Drift, which also offers guided tours and accommodation.

Isandhlwana ⑥
Zulu *impis*, angered by an invasion of their territory, attacked a British force on 22 January 1879.

Blood River ④
For years seen as a symbol of the Afrikaners' victory over the Zulus, this battle gave rise to a public holiday – 16 December, now called Day of Reconciliation.

Midmar Dam is surrounded by a tranquil nature reserve

Spioenkop Game Reserve ⓫

Road map E3. 35 km (22 miles) SW of Ladysmith on Winterton Rd. **Tel** (036) 488-1578. ⬜ 6am–6pm daily (Oct–Mar: to 7pm daily). 🅿 ⛺ 🛈 ⬆ **www**.kznwildlife.com

The picturesque dam nestles at the foot of the 1,466-m- (4,810-ft-) high Spioenkop, which in 1900 was the scene of a decisive battle between British and Boer forces in the South African War *(see p53)*. The battlefield site is accessible from the road, and countless graves and memorials are scattered across the mountain's summit as a grim reminder of one of the worst defeats suffered by British forces during that conflict.

Today, Spioenkop is very popular with outdoor enthusiasts. The dam offers fishing and boating, while elands, hartebeests, zebras, giraffes, kudu and white rhinos can be seen in the surrounding nature reserve, together with a wide variety of bird species. There is also a pleasant camp-site here, as well as a small shop. Picnic sites are situated along the southern shoreline, and two short trails, in an area free of dangerous animals, encourage visitors to view game on foot.

Situated at the foot of Spioenkop on the northern shore of the dam, Iphika Bush Camp offers rustic tented self-catering accommodation and is reached by a private track. As other vehicles are not permitted in this sector, visitors are offered a unique wilderness experience.

Midlands Meander ⓬

Road map E3 Mooi River. 🛈 (033) 330-8195. **www**.midlandsmeander.co.za

The undulating hills of the Natal Midlands, with their green patches of forest and their dairy farms, have long been a retreat favoured by artists and crafts-people. In 1985, six studios established an arts and crafts route: the Midlands Meander. The route quickly gained popularity and now consists of around 400 participating members and studios.

Tapestry detail, Rorke's Drift

There are four routes that meander between the small towns of Hilton, Nottingham Road, Howick and Mooi River. Goods on offer include herbs, cheese, wine, pottery, woven cloth, leather items, furniture, stained glass and antiques.

On the R103, just past Midmar Dam, a monument marks the spot where Nelson Mandela *(see p57)* was arrested by security police on 5 August 1962.

Accommodation along the way ranges from idyllic country hotels, tranquil guest farms and picturesque lodges to comfortable bed and breakfast establishments. There are also many quaint country pubs and eateries and a health spa.

The monument to the Battle of Spioenkop overlooks the dam

For hotels and restaurants in this region see pp394–6 and pp421–2

Street-by-Street: Pietermaritzburg ⑬

From its humble beginnings as an irrigation settlement established by Afrikaner farmers in 1836, Pietermaritzburg (in the municipality of Msunduzi) has developed into the commercial, industrial and administrative centre of the KwaZulu-Natal Midlands. An intriguing blend of Victorian, Indian, African and modern architecture and culture combine to produce a distinctly South African city. Many historic buildings and monuments, as well as galleries and museums, are located around the city centre and in the western suburbs, which nestle at the foot of a range of densely wooded hills. Visitors can ramble through the surrounding forests and botanic gardens, and visit several nature reserves and recreation resorts located within the city or a few minutes' drive away.

Gandhi Statue
In Pietermaritzburg, in 1893, Gandhi had to leave a first-class train, because he wasn't white.

Church Street Mall
is shaded by stinkwood trees and lined with well-preserved historic buildings.

★ Tatham Art Gallery
Housed in the old Supreme Court, displays at this gallery include works by South African artists, as well as European masters like Edgar Degas, Henri Matisse and Pablo Picasso.

Presbyterian Church

Parliament Building
The seat of the colonial government prior to 1910, it now houses Kwa-Zulu-Natal's provincial legislature.

CHURCH

KEY

– – – Suggested route

STAR SIGHTS

★ Tatham Art Gallery

★ City Hall

★ Natal Museum

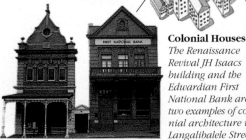

Colonial Houses
The Renaissance Revival JH Isaacs building and the Edwardian First National Bank are two examples of colonial architecture in Langalibalele Street.

FIRST NATIONAL BANK

VISITORS' CHECKLIST

Road map E3. 🏘 928,000.
✈ Durban, 80 km (49 miles) SE.
✈ Pietermaritzburg Airport, S
of the city. 🚌 Top of Church
Street. 🚌 Publicity House, cnr
Langalibalele and Chief Albert
Luthuli streets. ℹ Publicity
House, (033) 345-1348. 🕐
8am–5pm Mon–Fri, 8am–1pm
Sat. 🎪 Royal Agricultural Show
(May). www.pmbtourism.co.za

★ **City Hall**
*This edifice, the largest brick
building in the southern
hemisphere, was completed
in 1893. The clock tower, a
later addition, rises 47 m
(153 ft) above the street.*

```
0 metres      50
0 yards       50
```

**Publicity
House**

**Msunduzi Voortrekker
Museum Complex**
*The Church of the Vow, built by
the Voortrekkers after the Battle
of Blood River (see p51), is the
focus of this complex on the
corner of Langalibalele
and Boshoff streets.*

★ **Natal Museum**
*Gigantic insects cling
to the outside walls of
this museum, whose
superb displays include
African mammals,
birds and dinosaurs.*

Exploring Pietermaritzburg
The town is a treasure trove
of architecture and lends itself
well to walking excursions.
One of the oldest quarters, the
Lanes – a labyrinth of narrow
alleys between Church and
Langalibalele streets – gives an
idea of what Pietermaritzburg
was like in days gone by.

Environs: Midmar Dam, a
weekend and holiday venue
for watersports enthusiasts
and fishermen, lies 27 km
(17 miles) north of Pietermaritzburg in the **Midmar
Dam Nature Reserve**,
which is home to several
antelope species, among
them black wildebeests,
elands, hartebeests, springboks, blesboks and zebras.
    The origins of Howick, some
18 km (11 miles) north of
Pietermaritzburg, date back to
1850. In the town, a viewing
platform and restaurant overlook the beautiful Howick
Falls, equal in height to the
Victoria Falls in Zimbabwe.
    On the Karkloof Road, just
outside Howick, the **Umgeni
Valley Nature Reserve** offers
hiking trails through the
steep-sided, boulder-strewn
valley carved by the Umgeni
River. The track leading from
the entrance gate provides
scenic views of the gorge.

🏞 **Midmar Dam Nature
Reserve**
Howick. **Tel** (033) 330-2067. 🕐
24 hours daily. 🌐 🚻 🅿 🚻 🚤 ⚠

🏞 **Umgeni Valley Nature
Reserve**
Howick. **Tel** (033) 330-3931.
🕐 8am–4:30pm daily.
● 25 Dec. 🌐 🚶

The Howick Falls

DURBAN AND ZULULAND

*C*aressed by the warm currents of the Indian Ocean, this
picturesque region is one of the country's leading tourist
destinations. Abundant rainfall and year-round sunshine
sustain a prosperous sugar industry and a profusion of coastal
holiday resorts. North of the Tugela River, an untamed tapestry of
wildlife, wilderness and wetland evokes the essence of Africa.

Near the end of the 15th century, a sailing ship captained
by the Portuguese mariner
Vasco Da Gama passed
the east coast of Africa on
Christmas Day. The intrepid
seafarer sighted a large
bay, flanked by forested
dunes, and named it "Rio de Natal",
the Christmas River. Subsequently,
on sailors' maps, the name "Natal"
was given to the uncharted land that
lay beyond the wide beaches and
forested dunes along the coast.

In the 1820s, rumours of the Zulu
chief and military genius Shaka *(see
p49)* began to reach the Cape Colony.
Shaka forged the scattered clans of the
Natal region into a near-irrepressible
force, and 60 years would pass before
the British Empire succeeded in sub-
duing the mighty Zulu army. The
passage of time has brought many
changes. "Rio de Natal" has
developed into Durban,
today the largest port in
Africa and third-largest city
in the country. Where the
coastal grasslands and forests
once tumbled down to the sea,
a wide band of sugar cane plantations now separates luxury hotels
overlooking sandy beaches and the
warm currents of the Indian Ocean
from the rolling hills of the interior.
Many major rivers meander through
the undulating hills of the interior, and
the coastline is enhanced by tranquil
estuaries and lagoons rich in birdlife.

In the northern corner of the region,
some of the country's finest game
reserves, with melodious Zulu names
like Hluhluwe-Imfolozi, Mkhuze,
Ndumo and Tembe, preserve a timeless landscape that has remained
unchanged since the reign of Shaka.

Traditional reed fishtrap, Kosi Bay

◁ The marvellous interior of the Hindu Temple of Understanding near Durban

Exploring Durban and Zululand

This region is renowned for its subtropical climate, sandy beaches, tepid ocean currents and unspoilt game reserves. Durban, with its superb hotels, beach-front and shopping centres, is perfectly situated for exploring a scenic and varied coastline, and the N2 coastal motorway allows holiday-makers easy access to many attractions. Apart from tourism, this coastal belt also sustains the vast plantations that produce most of South Africa's sugar. North of Richards Bay, three hours from Durban on excellent roads, beckons a wilderness of swamps, forests and savannah. The iSimangaliso Wetland Park is a paradise for bird-watchers and nature lovers. The wooded hills of the nearby Hluhluwe-Imfolozi Game Reserve are home to rhinos, zebras, elephants, buffaloes and lions.

Grazing Burchell's zebras in the Hluhluwe-Imfolozi Game Reserve

SIGHTS AT A GLANCE

Durban ①
Hluhluwe-Imfolozi
  Game Reserve ⑥
iSimangaliso Wetland Park ⑧
Ithala Game Reserve ⑦
Kosi Bay Nature Reserve ⑩
North Coast ③
Phinda Private Game
  Reserve ⑨
Shakaland ⑤
Simunye Zulu Lodge ④
South Coast ②
Tembe Elephant
  Park ⑪

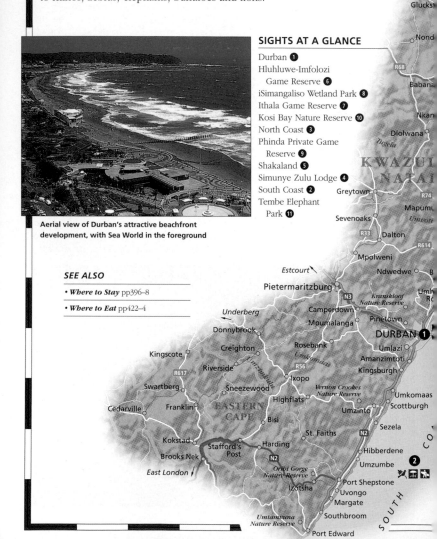

Aerial view of Durban's attractive beachfront development, with Sea World in the foreground

SEE ALSO

- *Where to Stay* pp396–8
- *Where to Eat* pp422–4

Ndumo Game Reserve

TEMBE ELEPHANT PARK **11**

10 KOSI BAY NATURE RESERVE

Ingwavuma

Emangusi

rmelo

Pongola

7 ITHALA GAME RESERVE

Louwsburg Magudu

Golela

Jozini

Ubombo

Phongola

R22

Lake Sibaya

Mbazwana

Sodwana Bay National Park

eilrand

R66

Mkuze

Mkhuze Game Reserve

Nongoma

R618

lack Umfolozi

Hlabisa

Hluhluwe Dam

R66

Ulundi

6 HLUHLUWE-IMFOLOZI GAME RESERVE

N2

9 PHINDA PRIVATE GAME RESERVE

Hluhluwe

8 ISIMANGALISO WETLAND PARK

Cape Vidal

Lake St. Lucia

Somkele

Mtjobanembi Mtubatuba

St. Lucia

Mtonjaneni

Melmoth

4 SIMUNYE

walini R34

Teza

N2

Kwambonambi

Empangeni

5 SHAKALAND

Eshowe

Richards Bay

gindlovu

Mtunzini

Mandini

N2 Tugela Mouth

anger **3**

INDIAN OCEAN

NORTH **COAST**

0 kilometres   50

0 miles   25

The unspoilt beach at Cape Vidal, near St Lucia, on the North Coast

GETTING AROUND

The N2 national route that leads from the Eastern Cape Province and Wild Coast runs parallel to the coast from Port Shepstone onwards. It provides quick and safe access to the region's attractions. Durban has an international airport, and there is a domestic airport at Richards Bay. Several Durban-based touring companies offer package tours to the splendid northern game reserves.

Sugar cane is a major crop in subtropical Zululand

KEY

▬▬	Motorway
▬	Major road
▭▭	Minor road
▭▭	Untarred road
▬	Scenic route
▬▬	Main railway
▬	Minor railway
▬▬	International border
▬	Provincial border

Durban 1

Life ring

Vasco Da Gama's Port Natal was renamed Durban in honour of Cape Governor Benjamin D'Urban after Zulu chief Shaka gave the land to the British in 1824. Today the former trading post is the holiday capital of KwaZulu-Natal. Sunny days and the warm Indian Ocean draw visitors to a beachfront flanked by high-rise hotels and holiday apartments. Attractions such as Waterworld and the Umgeni River Bird Park lie north of South Africa's principal harbour.

An aerial view of the Paddling Pools on Durban's Golden Mile

Exploring Durban

Most of the city's attractions are located along the beach-front, close together and within walking distance from the hotels. But Durban is not only about seaside fun; the city centre has many historic buildings, as well as museums, theatres and exciting markets. For safety reasons, visitors are advised not to explore the city on their own but to join one of the many organized tours.

The Golden Mile
OR Tambo Parade.

The land side of this 6-km (4-mile) long holiday precinct is lined with a continuous row of hotels, while the seaward edge consists of amusement parks, an aerial cableway, craft sellers, pubs, restaurants, ice-cream parlours, piers, sandy beaches and a promenade.

Along the Golden Mile is where visitors will find many brightly decorated rickshaws. Their colourful drivers, festooned in beads and tall, elaborate headdresses, are a curious amalgamation of traditional African practices and Indian influences.

uShaka Marine World offers an excellent aquarium and dolphinarium. The aquarium's main tank is home to many species of tropical fish, turtles and sting rays. Scuba divers enter the tank twice a day to feed the fish. Shows at the dolphinarium feature dolphins, seals and penguins. A short drive from central Durban, the **Umgeni River Bird Park** exhibits more than 4,500 birds of some 400 species in walk-through aviaries. There are daily free-flight bird shows.

uShaka Marine World
1 King Shaka Ave, Point.
Tel (031) 328-8000. 9am–5pm daily. www.ushaka marineworld.co.za

Umgeni River Bird Park
490 Riverside Rd, 16 km (10 miles) north of Durban off M4. **Tel** (031) 579-4600. 9am–5pm daily (bird shows at 11am, 2pm).

Durban Waterfront
Margaret Mncadi Avenue.

The bright murals and pink staircase that lead to the **BAT Centre** (Bartel Arts Trust) are an appropriate introduction to Durban's innovative dock-side art and music scene. The centre has a 300-seat theatre and music venue, a dance studio, art galleries and shops.

Photographs and memora-bilia of Durban's seafaring past are displayed in the **Port Natal Maritime Museum**. The tug-boats *Ulundi* and *JR More* and the minesweeper SAS *Durban* form part of the exhibits.

Just to the west of the museum is the Dick King statue, commemorating a British trader who embarked on an epic horseride to Grahamstown to request reinforcements during the Boer siege of Port Natal in 1842.

BAT Centre
Margaret Mncadi Avenue.
Tel (031) 332-0451. 8:30am–4:30pm Mon–Fri, 9am–2pm Sat. public hols. www.batcentre. co.za

Port Natal Maritime Museum
Margaret Mncadi Avenue. **Tel** (031) 311-2230. 8:30am–4pm Mon–Sat, 11am–3:30pm Sun.

Modern art exhibit at the BAT Centre

The mock-Tudor façade of The Playhouse

Central Durban

Beautifully restored buildings and interesting museums can be found in the city centre, all within walking distance. The cafés and restaurants that line the streets offer respite from the heat and humidity.

Completed in 1910, Durban's **City Hall** was modelled after that of Belfast, in Northern Ireland. The central dome is 48 m (156 ft) high while statues symbolizing art, literature, music and commerce flank the four smaller domes.

The **Natural Science Museum** is situated on the ground floor of the City Hall. Exhibits vary from a display of South African wildlife to a mammal gallery, a bird hall, a dinosaur exhibit and an Egyptian mummy. Fascinating, if disturbing, are the oversized insects featured in the *Kwa-Nunu* section of the museum.

Upstairs, the **Durban Art Gallery** began collecting black South African art in the 1970s, the first in the country to do so.

What was once Durban's Court now houses the **Old Court House Museum**. It contains relics of early colonial life in what was then Natal.

The Playhouse offers top-class entertainment, from opera to experimental theatre.

🏛 **Natural Science Museum**
City Hall, Anton Lembede St.
Tel (031) 311-2256. ⬜ 8:30am–4pm daily (from 11am Sun). ⬤ Good Fri, 25 Dec.

🏛 **Durban Art Gallery**
City Hall, Anton Lembede St.
Tel (031) 311-2265. ⬜ 8:30am–4pm daily (from 11am Sun). ⬤ Good Fri, 25 Dec.

VISITORS' CHECKLIST

Road map F3. KwaZulu-Natal Province. 👥 3,200,000. ✈ 35 km (22 miles) NE of city centre. 🚉 New Durban Station, Umgeni Rd. 🚌 New Durban Station. ℹ Old Station Bldg, 160 Monty Naicker Street. (031) 366-7500. 🎭 Comrades Marathon (Jun); Vodacom July Handicap (Jul). **www**.zulu.kzn.org.za

🏛 **Old Court House Museum**
77 Samora Machel St. *Tel (031) 311-2229.* ⬜ 8:30am–4pm Mon–Sat. ⬤ Good Fri, 25 Dec.

🎭 **The Playhouse**
231 Anton Lembede St.
Tel (031) 369-9555.

In the Natural Science Museum

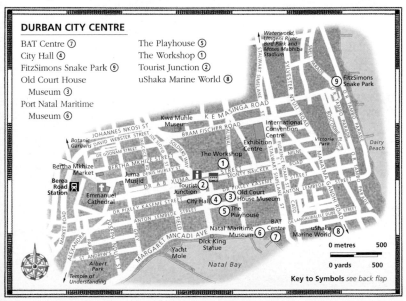

DURBAN CITY CENTRE

BAT Centre ⑦
City Hall ④
FitzSimons Snake Park ⑨
Old Court House Museum ③
Port Natal Maritime Museum ⑥

The Playhouse ⑤
The Workshop ①
Tourist Junction ②
uShaka Marine World ⑧

Waterworld, Umgeni River Bird Park and Moses Mabhida Stadium

SHELL PARADE

STALWART SIMELANE

SYLVESTER NTULI ROAD

FitzSimons Snake Park ⑨

O R TAMBO PARADE

Botanic Gardens

JOHANNES NKOSI ST
DAVID WEBSTER STREET

DR GOODNAM STREET

BERTHA MKHIZE STREET

Bertha Mkhize Market

Berea Road Station

Emmanuel Cathedral

Juma Musjid

Kwa Muhle Museum

K E MASINGA ROAD

BRAM FISCHER ROAD

SOLDIERS' WAY

DENIS HURLEY ST

DR A.B. XUMA

The Workshop ①

Tourist Junction ②

International Convention Centre

Exhibition Centre

MONTY NAICKER ST

DR PIXLEY KASEME

Old Court House Museum ③

City Hall ④

The Playhouse ⑤

Victoria Park

MILNE
ROAD

FLORENCE NZAMA ST

STALWART SIMELANE ST

ANTON LEMBEDE ST

CATO

MAHATMA GANDHI ROAD

Dairy Beach

O R TAMBO PARADE

Natal Maritime Museum ⑥

BAT Centre ⑦

uShaka Marine World ⑧

DR LANGALIBALELE DUBE ROAD

MARKET ROAD

JOSEPH NDULI

DR PIXLEY KASEME STREET

ANTON LEMBEDE STREET

FIELD

GREY

ALEXANDRA PARK

ST ANDREW'S ST

Albert Park

Temple of Understanding

MARGARET MNCADI AVE

Dick King Statue

Yacht Mole

Natal Bay

0 metres 500
0 yards 500

Key to Symbols see back flap

Exploring Durban

Away from the city centre, beautiful mosques, richly decorated temples and vibrant street markets await the visitor. Nature reserves and sanctuaries are situated on the outskirts of Durban, among them the Umgeni River Bird Park, north of the city, which houses exotic birds in walk-through aviaries. Waterworld is a perfect destination on a hot day, while the Hindu Temple of Understanding, in the suburb of Chatsworth, never fails to impress with its grandiose opulence. Tour operators offer tailor-made coach trips to all of these sights.

Exotic curry and masala spice

ℹ️ Tourist Junction

Station Building, 160 Pine St. *Tel (031) 366-7500.* ⏰ *8am–5pm Mon–Fri, 9am–2pm Sat, 9am–1pm Sun.* ♿

Tucked between Commercial and Pine streets stands the former railway station. The four-storey, red-brick building was completed in 1894 and now houses the tourist centre. In the entrance of the building stands a statue in memory of Mahatma Gandhi, who bought a train ticket to Johannesburg here in June 1893.

The building's most curious feature is the roof, designed to carry the weight of 5 m (16 ft) of snow. The London firm of architects accidentally switched plans – and the roof of Toronto station caved in during the first heavy snowfalls.

The Tourist Junction has a comprehensive range of maps and brochures, and the staff can advise on several walking tours of the city centre. There is also a useful booking office for accommodation at the national parks (the only other offices are in Cape Town and Pretoria) and a booking office for long-distance bus tours.

🛍️ The Workshop

99 Aliwal St. *Tel (031) 304-9894.* ⏰ *8:30am–5pm Mon–Fri, 10am–4pm Sat & Sun.* ♿ 🍴 📷
www.theworkshopcentre.co.za

The Workshop offers over 100 shops, boutiques, jewellers, a supermarket and several cinemas, as well as a large fast food and restaurant area. It is housed in a vast, steel-girded Victorian building that was once the railway workshop.

Extensive renovations have transformed it into a postmodern complex, with "old-world" touches like fanlights and brass- and wrought-iron trimmings.

Facing The Workshop, on the opposite side of Aliwal Street, in the direction of the beach, are the big grounds of the International Convention Centre (ICC) Durban. As well as trade conventions, numerous public events are held here throughout the year, including lifestyle and food and wine expositions.

Bananas

🕌 Bertha Mkhize Street Market

Cnr Bertha Mkhize & Denis Hurley sts. ⏰ *6am–6pm Mon–Sat, 10am–4pm Sun.*

At the end of the N3 flyover, where the highway meets the streets of central Durban, is the Bertha Mkhize Street Market (formerly the Victoria Street Market). The building is striking – each of its 11 domes was modelled on a notable building in India.

In this crowded bazaar, visitors can sample the tastes and aromas of the Orient as they browse through more than 120 stalls offering spices and incense, fabrics, leather goods, brassware and ceramics.

☪️ Juma Masjid Mosque

Cnr Denis Hurley & Grey sts. *Tel (031) 306-0026.* ⏰ *9am–4pm Mon–Sat.* 📷 *book in advance.*

The impressive Juma Masjid Mosque, also known as Grey Street Mosque, lies across the road from the Bertha Mkhize Street Market. Completed in 1927, it is the largest mosque on the African continent.

Visitors are allowed inside at certain times. A strict dress code is enforced, and shoes must be removed before entering the building.

🌿 Durban Botanic Gardens

John Zikhale Rd. *Tel (031) 322-4021.* ⏰ *7:30am–5:15pm Apr–Sep; 7:30am–5:45pm Sep–Apr.* ♿ 📷

Heading north on Grey Street, the Durban Botanic Gardens are located near the Greyville

The Workshop houses a wide variety of shops

racecourse. It was established in 1849 as an experimental station for tropical crops.

The Ernest Thorp Orchid House, named after an early curator, gained renown as the first naturalistic botanical display in South Africa.

The spectacular cycad and palm collection on the 15-ha (38-acre) property is one of the largest of its kind in the world. It includes several rare species, like a male *Encephalartos woodii* from the Ngoye forest, which was successfully transplanted in 1916.

Among the garden's 480 tree species are the oldest jacarandas in South Africa, originally imported from Argentina.

Other attractions include a sensory garden, a Victorian sunken garden and an ornamental lake with pelicans.

The Temple of Understanding in Chatsworth

Durban's Botanic Gardens are the perfect setting for a picnic

🔆 Waterworld

Battery Beach Rd. *Tel* (031) 903-3034. ⬤ 10am–5pm daily. 🈳

This theme park is based on having fun in the water and is easily accessible from the northern beaches, which are situated along the Golden Mile.

Given Durban's hot, at times even sultry, climate throughout most of the year, Waterworld is an extremely popular destination. It offers thrilling water slides, cool wave pools and water chutes in a tropical setting framed by palm trees.

🦜 Umgeni River Bird Park

490 Riverside Rd, Northway. *Tel* (031) 579-4600. ⬤ 9am–5pm daily. ⬤ 25 Dec. 🈳 🗖 🛆

Bordered on three sides by steep cliffs, and overlooking the north bank of the Umgeni River, 1.5 km (1 mile) from its mouth, the Umgeni River Bird Park enjoys a superb location. Four waterfalls cascade down the cliffs into ponds fringed by palms and lush vegetation. The four large walk-through aviaries allow visitors a face-to-face encounter with some of the 3,000 birds. Among the 400 resident species are rare exotic parrots, toucans, cranes, macaws, and hornbills.

Entertaining bird shows are held daily at 11am and 2pm.

Temple of Understanding

Bhaktiveedante Swami Rd, Chatsworth. *Tel* (031) 403-3328. ⬤ 4:30am–8pm daily. 🈳 🚻

This large, ornate temple of the International Society for Krishna Consciousness was designed by the Austrian architect Hannes Raudner. It is encircled by a moat and a beautiful garden laid out in the shape of a lotus flower.

The daily guided tours take in the awe-inspiring marble temple room and the inner sanctuary, as well as an interesting audio-visual show.

THE HINDU POPULATION OF DURBAN

When the first sugar was produced from sugar cane in 1851, the Natal Colony experienced a major economic boom. Cheap labour was required to work in the plantations, and the colony entered into negotiations with the colonial government in India. Between 1860 and 1911, a total of 152,000 indentured labourers were shipped to Durban from Madras and Calcutta. Tamil and Hindi were the main languages spoken. At the end of their five-year contracts, the workers were offered a free passage back to India. Over half of them opted to remain in South Africa, and became active as retailers and vegetable farmers; in later years many entered commerce, industry and politics. Of the current population of 1.2 million (the largest Indian community outside Asia), an estimated 50 per cent are Hindu. Deepavali is their most important festival, and begins with the lighting of a lamp for the Goddess of Light, symbolizing the conquest of good over evil.

Statue of Bhaktivedanta Swami, a respected religious teacher

Durban's North and South Coasts

Traditional
Zulu basket

Durban is the central focus of South Africa's most popular holiday coastline. Blessed with a subtropical climate, this picturesque area is a delightful blend of sun, sand, surf and nature reserves. Extending 162 km (100 miles) south of Durban is a string of coastal towns and holiday resorts, like Scottburgh and Port Edward. Uncrowded beaches at holiday villages such as Ballito are hallmarks of the 154-km (96-mile) stretch of coast that lies north of Durban.

Oribi Gorge

The Oribi Gorge, 21 km (13 miles) inland from Port Shepstone, is a scenic, thickly forested area where cliffs rise from the deep chasms and open out to reveal the spectacular Samango Falls.

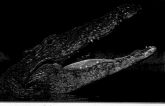

Croc World

In a 60-ha (148-acre) indigenous botanic garden near Scottburgh, Croc World has 12,000 Nile crocodiles and the largest eagle cage on the African continent.

Port Edward

This village near the Umtamvuna Nature Reserve is the location of Caribbean Estates, a popular timeshare resort.

San Lameer

Two good golf courses, a private beach and a nature reserve make San Lameer a sought-after holiday resort.

For hotels and restaurants in this region see pp396–8 and pp422–4

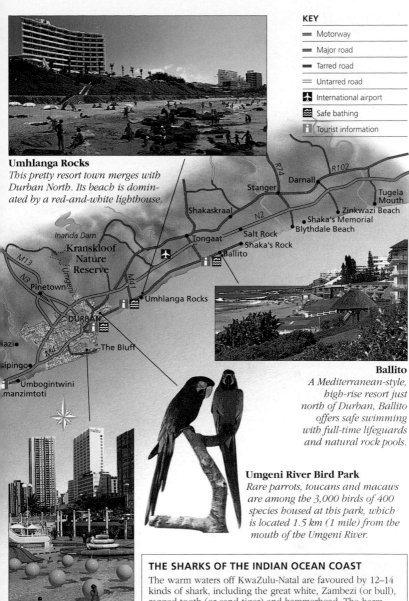

KEY

▬	Motorway
▬	Major road
▬	Tarred road
═	Untarred road
✈	International airport
≋	Safe bathing
ℹ	Tourist information

Umhlanga Rocks
This pretty resort town merges with Durban North. Its beach is domin-ated by a red-and-white lighthouse.

Ballito
A Mediterranean-style, high-rise resort just north of Durban, Ballito offers safe swimming with full-time lifeguards and natural rock pools.

Umgeni River Bird Park
Rare parrots, toucans and macaws are among the 3,000 birds of 400 species housed at this park, which is located 1.5 km (1 mile) from the mouth of the Umgeni River.

THE SHARKS OF THE INDIAN OCEAN COAST

The warm waters off KwaZulu-Natal are favoured by 12–14 kinds of shark, including the great white, Zambezi (or bull), ragged tooth (or sand tiger) and hammerhead. The harm-less whale shark also visits this coast in summer. Major beaches from Port Edward to Richards Bay are pro-tected by shark nets beyond the surf, 500 m (545 yds) from the shore. These are maintained by the KwaZulu-Natal Sharks Board, which finds about 1,200 sharks caught in the nets each year.

A "great white" encounter

Durban
This large city has the most developed beachfront in the country, with amusement parks, paddling pools, fun rides, a water park and a salt water pool.

The South Coast

A year-round combination of sunshine, sand, sea and surf has created an irresistible drawcard for visitors coming from the cooler inland climates or the Northern Hemisphere. Some 30 inviting resort towns form a coastal playground that stretches for 162 km (100 miles) from the Eastern Cape border to Durban. The attractions entail much more than the obvious seaside fun. From nature reserves and bird sanctuaries to glittering casinos – this coast has it all.

Furry-ridged triton

Port Edward
Road map E4. N2, 20 km (12 miles) S of Margate. 🚉 *Margate.* ℹ️ *Panorama Parade, Margate, (039) 312-2322.* **www**.southcoasttourism.co.za

The village of Port Edward on the Umtamvuna River is the southernmost beachside resort in KwaZulu-Natal. Port Edward is popular for swimming, fishing and boating, and the estuary is navigable far upstream, making it ideal for ski-boats.

The lush Caribbean Estates on the north bank is rated as one of the country's top timeshare resorts.

Between 1976 and 1994 the land south of the Umtamvuna River bridge fell within the homeland known as Transkei. At that time, gambling was illegal under South African law and a casino resort, the Wild Coast Sun, was built here to lure visitors from Durban and the South Coast. Today, it overlooks an unspoilt coast-line covered in dense forest and grassland. A challenging 18-hole golf course stretches from the banks of the river to the shores of the lagoon.

The Mzamba Village Market opposite the resort's main entrance offers a range of locally crafted curios, such as woven grass baskets, stone and wood carvings and beadwork. The **Umtamvuna Nature Reserve**, some 8 km (5 miles) north of Port Edward, protects a 30-km (19-mile) section of the Umtamvuna River gorge. The trails that explore the dense, subtropical forest are excellent for bird-watching.

🌿 **Umtamvuna Nature Reserve**
Port Edward. Road to Izingolweni. **Tel** (039) 313-2383. ⭕ sunrise–sunset daily. 📷 **www**.kznwildlife.com

Margate
Road map E4. N2. 🏠 45,000. ✈️ 4 km (2.5 miles) inland. 🚉 Beachfront. ℹ️ Panorama Parade, (039) 312-2322. **www**.southcoasttourism.co.za

Margate is the tourist capital of the South Coast. Its focal point is a broad expanse of golden sand lined by the tall, white towers of dozens of hotels and apartments. Marine Drive, which runs parallel to the coast one block inland, is the town's main business centre, and banks, restaurants, pubs, fast-food outlets, shops, estate agencies and cinemas all compete for the available street frontage.

The approach to the sandy beach leads across well-tended palm-shaded lawns that attract many sunbathers. Along the main beachfront there is a variety of attractions for holiday-makers to enjoy. Among these are the paddling pools, a fresh-water swimming pool, water slides, a mini-golf (putt-putt) course, paddle boats and many ice-cream parlours.

Margate's fishing area is one of the drawcards of the town

Uvongo
Road map E4. N2, 12 km (7 miles) N of Margate. ℹ️ Panorama Parade, Margate, (039) 312-2322.

Just before it empties into the sea, the Vungu River plunges down a 23-m (75-ft) waterfall into a lagoon. High cliffs, overgrown with wild bananas, protect the sheltered lagoon. With its spit of sandy beach separating the river from the ocean, Uvongo is one of the most attractive features along the South Coast.

Boating is popular in the lagoon and the beach, a safe playground for children, is also the site of a daily craft, fruit and basketry market. A restaurant, timeshare resort, tidal pool and paddling pool are a short walk inland.

On the main road, less than 2 km (1 mile) south of the beach, the small Uvongo Bird Park is home to many species of exotic birds.

The swimming pool of the Wild Coast Sun resort

For hotels and restaurants in this region see pp396–8 and pp422–4

THE HIBISCUS COAST

Lying approximately 120 km (75 miles) south of Durban, the Hibiscus Coast extends from Hibberdene in the north to Port Edward in the south. As well as beaches and golf courses, this stretch of coastline is home to the famous "Sardine Run". Every June or July, millions of the tiny silver fish head north from their spawning grounds off the Eastern Cape to reach the waters of Port Edward. They are followed by predators such as dolphins, sharks and seals, while numerous sea birds rain down from above to take their fill. The Sardine Run lasts for several weeks, then lessens as the shoal continues its northbound migration.

Birds diving into a shoal of fish during the Sardine Run

Oribi Gorge Nature Reserve

Road map E4. 21 km (13 miles) inland of Port Shepstone. **Tel** (039) 679-1644. ○ 6:30am–7:30pm daily. www.kznwildlife.com

In a region where population densities are high and where sugar cane plantations and coastal resort developments have replaced most of the natural vegetation, the ravine carved by the Umzimkulwana River is a delight for nature lovers. The impressive gorge is 24 km (15 miles) long, up to 5 km (3 miles) wide and 300 m (975 ft) deep.

The reserve has a small rest camp with seven huts perched on the southern rim of the chasm. There is a scenic circular drive, as well as three walking trails and many beautiful picnic spots along the river.

Small, forest-dwelling animals like bushbucks, duikers, samango monkeys and leopards occur in the dense forest, which comprises some 500 different tree species.

Oribi Gorge was formed by the Umzimkulwana River

Scottburgh's beaches and lawns are popular with sunbathers

Scottburgh

Road map E4. N2, roughly 30 km (19 miles) S of Amanzimtoti. ■ **i** Blue Marlin Hotel, Scott St, (039) 978-3361.

An almost continuous carpet of sugar cane plantations lines this stretch of South Coast, and the town of Scottburgh was once used as a harbour for exporting the crop. Today, the neat and compact little town has a distinct holiday atmosphere, and is a popular beach resort. It occupies the prominent headland overlooking the mouth of the Mpambanyoni River, and most of the hotels and holiday apartments offer superb sea views.

Frangipani

In the previous century, a spring used to cascade from the bank above the river, but today a large water slide occupies the site. A restaurant, small shops, a miniature railway and tidal pool are added attractions. Further south, a caravan park adjoins the beach and the town's popular golf course has a prime site overlooking the Indian Ocean surf.

Amanzimtoti

Road map F4. N2, 27 km (17 miles) S of Durban. ✈ Durban. ■ **i** 95 Beach Rd, (031) 903-7498.

It is claimed that Amanzimtoti derives its name from a remark made by Shaka Zulu *(see p49)*. In the 1820s, returning home from a campaign further down the South Coast, Shaka drank from a refreshing stream and is said to have exclaimed, *"amanzi umtoti"* (the water is sweet). Today, Amanzimtoti is a lively coastal resort. Its beaches are lined with hotels, holiday apartments, take-away outlets, restaurants and beachwear shops.

The most popular beach extends for 3 km (2 miles) north of the Manzimtoti River and offers safe bathing, picnic sites and a fine salt-water pool.

The N2 passes within 400 m (400 yrds) of the coast, providing easy access to the town's attractions, such as the small bird sanctuary, a nature reserve and two fine golf courses in the vicinity of the beach.

North Coast

This subtropical region is renowned for its attractive towns, sheltered bays and estuaries, uncrowded beaches and forested dunes that give way to a green carpet of sugar cane and timber plantations. Northern KwaZulu-Natal has escaped the rampant development that characterizes the South Coast and offers unspoilt nature at its best.

One of the guest rooms at the cross-cultural bush lodge of Simunye

Umhlanga Rocks

Road map F3. 20 km (12 miles) NE of Durban. 🏃 22,000. 🚌 Umhlanga Express. 🛈 Chartwell Drive, (031) 561-4257. ◯ Mon–Sat.

The premier holiday resort on the North Coast, Umhlanga Rocks has excellent beaches, timeshare resorts, hotels and restaurants. This is a fast-growing, upper-income town, but the stylish outdoor cafés and bistros make it seem more like a peaceful coastal centre than a fast-paced resort. The promenade, which extends along the coastline for 3 km (2 miles), provides stunning views of the golden sands that have made Umhlanga famous.

Hibiscus flower

Further north, at the mouth of the Ohlanga River, forested dunes fringing the beach form part of a nature reserve. Here a boardwalk crosses the river and the forest teems with blue duikers, birds and monkeys.

Ballito

Road map F3. N2, 30 km (19 miles) N of Umhlanga Rocks. 🏃 14,000. 🚌 Baz Bus. 🛈 Dolphin Coast Publicity, cnr Ballito Dr/Link Rd, (032) 946-1997. ◯ Mon–Sat. 🎾 Mr Price Pro (Jul).

Ballito and the neighbouring Salt Rock extend for 6 km (4 miles) along a coast known for its beaches, rocky headlands and sheltered tidal pools. Lining the main coastal road are many good restaurants. Accommodation ranges from luxury holiday apartments and timeshare resorts to family hotels and attractive caravan parks.

Mtunzini

Road map F3. N2, 29 km (19 miles) SW of Richards Bay.

The pretty village, whose name means "in the shade", is set on a hillside overlooking the sea. Its streets are lined with coral trees and in winter their red flowers add splashes of colour to the townscape. A golf course adjoins the main shopping street, and near the railway station there is a grove of raffia palms. The nearest known group of these plants is on the Mozambique border, 260 km (163 miles) north. The rare palm-nut vulture is a fruit-eating raptor that may be spotted here, and the swamp forest and raffia palms can be seen from a raised boardwalk.

Mtunzini lies in a belt of unspoiled coastal forest that falls within the Umlalazi Nature Reserve. Comfortable log cabins, tucked into the forest, border a broad marsh, and along the banks of the Mlalazi River there is a circular walk through a mangrove swamp that is alive with crabs and mud-skimmers.

From the picnic site on the bank of the Mlalazi River, a boat trip to the river mouth will reveal glimpses of fish eagles and kingfishers, and walking trails lead through the forest to a wide, sandy beach. Along the many trails, shy forest animals such as vervet monkeys, red duikers and bushbucks are often seen.

Simunye Zulu Lodge ❹

Road map F3. Melmoth. D256. **Tel** (035) 450-0101. ◯ 7am–5pm daily. 🍴 🏠 www.simunyelodge.co.za

A unique lodge tucked into the Mfule Valley 6 km (4 miles) from Melmoth allows visitors to experience both traditional and contemporary Zulu culture. The creation of linguist Barry Leitch, Simunye overlooks the Mfule River in a

Holiday apartments and hotels line the beach at Ballito

◁ Shaka's Rock, near Ballito, is a subtropical holiday resort, typical of the North Coast

typical Zululand scenery of thorn trees and grassy hills. Visitors can reach the lodge on horseback, by ox-wagon, donkey cart, 4x4 or on foot, on a one-hour guided trail.

Overnight guests have the option of staying in a stone lodge or traditional Zulu *kraal* (see pp258–9). Guides tell the fascinating history of the Zulu nation, and there are demonstrations of traditional dances, sparring and spear-throwing. Guests also visit working Zulu homesteads for a first-hand experience of rural Zulu life.

The entrance to the cultural village of Shakaland

Shakaland ❺

Road map F3. Eshowe. R68, Norman Hurst Farm, Nkwalini. *Tel* (035) 460-0912. ⬜ *6am–9pm daily.* 🔲 *Daytime visitors: 11am & noon daily (3-hour tours); overnight guests: 4pm culture tour, Zulu dancing after dinner & 9am morning tour.* 🍴 📷 **www**.shakaland.com

For the 1984 TV series *Shaka Zulu*, several authentic 19th-century Zulu *kraals* were constructed. For the series' grand finale, the villages were set alight; only that of Shaka's father was spared and opened to the public as Shakaland.

The unique Zulu village is open for day visits, while those wishing to stay overnight are accommodated in one of the Protea Hotel chain's most unusual destinations. A video explaining the origin of the

Zulu "love-letter" pouch, Shakaland

Zulu people is shown, and guests sleep in beehive huts and enjoy traditional Zulu fare, followed by a dancing display.

On a tour of the 40-hut village, visitors are introduced to a variety of traditional skills such as hut-building, spear-making, beer-brewing, artistic beadwork and pottery.

Framed by thorn trees and aloes, Goedertrou Dam in the valley below is an attractive body of water. The sunset river boat cruises are an added attraction. In the hills east of Shakaland, and commanding a superb view over the wide Mhlatuze Valley, is the site of Shaka's famed military stronghold, KwaBulawayo. Construction of this historic facility began in 1823, but today almost nothing remains of the citadel that once held so much of southern Africa in its grasp.

TRADITIONAL HEALING

In traditional Zulu society, the *inyanga* (herbalist) was male and concentrated on medicinal cures, while the *isangoma* (diviner) was a woman who possessed psychic powers and the ability to communicate with the ancestral spirits. Today, this strict division is no longer accurate. *Muthi* is an assortment of medicine and remedies made from indigenous bulbs, shrubs, leaves, tree bark and roots. Animal products like fat, claws, teeth and skin are also often used. Despite the advances of Western culture, the faith in traditional healing methods is still wide-spread in rural and urban settlements. In order to meet the demand for the plants and to ensure a regular supply, special "*muthi* gardens" have been established in a number of nature reserves.

Zulu *inyanga* (herbalist)

Shakaland offers unusual hotel accommodation

For hotels and restaurants in this region see pp396–8 and pp422–4

Hluhluwe-Imfolozi Game Reserve ⑥

Road map F3. *30 km (18 miles) W of Ulundi, or from N2.* 🏠 *(and reservations) Ezemvelo KZN Wildlife, (033) 845-1000.* ⭕ *Apr–Sep: 6am–6pm daily; Nov–Feb: 5am–7pm; Oct & Mar: 8am–7pm.* 🚯 🚻 📷 www.kznwildlife.com

An unspoilt wilderness of rolling hills, subtropical forest, acacia woodland and palm-fringed rivers, the 964-sq-km (372-sq-miles) park is world-renowned for its rhino conservation programme.

In 1895 two wildlife reserves, Hluhluwe and Imfolozi, were established to protect the last rhinos in South Africa. In the early 1950s a corridor of land between the two was added. The park was consolidated in 1989, and is now the fourth-largest in the country. One of Africa's leading wildlife sanctuaries, it is home to an astonishing diversity of wildlife. The varied vegetation supports large herds of nyalas, impalas, wildebeests, kudu, zebras and buffaloes, as well as elephants, rhinos, giraffes, lions, leopards, hyenas and cheetahs.

Over the years, animals that had become extinct in this region were re-introduced.

In 1958 a single male lion suddenly appeared – possibly from the Kruger National Park some 350 km (220 miles) to the north. Two lionesses were relocated from Kruger some time later, and their offspring have re-established prides throughout the park.

Southern bald ibis roosting site in Hluhluwe-Imfolozi Game Reserve

Elephants, first transported from Kruger in 1981, have adapted extremely well to their new environment and now number around 200.

Nyalazi Gate, the park's main entrance, is reached from the N2 at Mtubatuba. It is a perfect starting point for exploring the park's 220-km (138-mile) road network. Heading south, the route traverses open woodland before fording the Black Imfolozi River. Then it ascends to Mpila Camp, which has magnificent views over the reserve.

A trio of exclusive reed-and-thatch rest camps on the banks of the Black Imfolozi, Sontuli, Gqoyeni and Nselweni rivers allow visitors to savour the most secluded corners of this wilderness. Game rangers conduct game-viewing walks.

From Nyalazi Gate north, the route follows a tarred road that curves across rolling hills teeming with wildlife. The journey to Hluhluwe climbs a range of hills, 400 m (1,300 ft) above the Hluhluwe River.

These hills trap moisture-laden clouds, resulting in an average rainfall of 985 mm (38 inches) per year. In the dense woodland and forests live red duikers, bushbucks, nyalas and samango monkeys. Buffaloes, zebras, white rhinos and elephants can be seen roaming the northeastern grasslands near Memorial Gate.

Hilltop Camp, at an altitude of 450 m (1,460 ft), offers panoramic views over the surrounding countryside and can accommodate up to 210 guests in its chalets. Facilities at the central complex include a restaurant, bar, shop, petrol station and swimming pool.

A short trail through the adjoining forest is excellent for bird-watching.

A female waterbuck at Hluhluwe-Imfolozi Game Reserve

Ithala Game Reserve ⑦

Road map F3. *Vryheid. R69 via Louwsburg, 50 km (31 miles) NE of Vryheid.* 🏠 *(and reservations) Ezemvelo KZN Wildlife, (033) 845-1000.* ⭕ *Oct–Mar: 5am–7pm daily; Apr–Sep: 6am–6pm daily.* 🚯 🚻 www.kznwildlife.com

From the unhurried village of Louwsburg on the R69, a tarred road descends a steep escarpment to the wilderness of Ithala, a 296-sq-km (114-sq-mile) tract of grassland with dramatic mountain scenery and densely wooded valleys.

The reserve was established in 1972, and over the years 13 farms have become one of South Africa's top sanctuaries.

Hilltop Camp at Hluhluwe-Imfolozi Game Reserve

For hotels and restaurants in this region see pp396–8 and pp422–4

Mhlangeni Bush Camp, Ithala Game Reserve

The Phongolo River flows along the northern boundary for some 37 km (23 miles). Seven tributaries have carved the deep valleys that dissect this park and enhance its scenic splendour. The Ngoje escarpment rises dramatically to 1,446 m (4,700 ft), providing a striking backdrop to Ithala's game-viewing roads.

A 7-km (4-mile) tarred road leads from the entrance to the prestigious Ntshondwe Camp, which nestles at the foot of an imposing escarpment. Its 67 chalets (some self-catering) have been carefully tucked away between boulders and wild fig trees. The central complex contains a reception area, restaurant, store and coffee shop, and offers panoramic views over the entire reserve. In front of the building, an extensive wooden platform overlooks a reed-fringed water hole and is perfect for bird-watching.

As no fences surround the camp, animals such as warthogs often wander between the chalets. A path leads to a swimming pool tucked into a clearing at the base of the mountain.

Ntshondwe Lodge is a lavish, three-bedroomed cabin perched on a hill top. The far-reaching vista from its wooden deck and sunken swimming pool is arguably Ithala's finest.

Game-viewing at Ithala is excellent. Visitors will see white rhinos, giraffes, harte-beests, kudu, elands, impalas, wildebeests, warthogs and zebras, as well as the only population in KwaZulu-Natal of the rare tsessebe antelopes. Elephants, buffaloes, leopards and black rhinos are also present, but are generally more difficult to locate.

Ngubhu Loop, a 31-km (19-mile) circuit, which crosses a broad basin backed by the escarpment and then hugs the cliff face on the return journey, is the best drive in the park. Another route winds down the thickly wooded Dakaneni Valley to the Phongolo River. Although game is not as plentiful here as on the higher grasslands, the scenery is spectacular.

Game-viewing in the Ithala Game Reserve

A white (square-lipped) rhino

THE WHITE AND THE BLACK RHINO

At first glance, it may seem impossible to classify the grey hulks, yet there are a number of clear distinguishing factors between the white *(Ceratotherium simum)* and black *(Diceros bicornis)* rhino. The term "white" does not describe colour, but is a bastardization of the Dutch *wijd* (wide), referring to the lips of the animal. The white rhino is a grazer that carries its large, heavy head close to the ground as it rips off grass with its wide, square lips. The black rhino, on the other hand, is a browser and holds its small head up to feed off leaves with its elongated, prehensile upper lip. Black rhinos are smaller and occur singly or in very small groups, while white rhinos may weigh up to 2,300 kg (5,000 lb) and gather in larger social groups. Today the Hluhluwe-Imfolozi Game Reserve protects a total of 2,200 white and 220 black rhino.

ISIMANGALISO WETLAND PARK

African fish eagle

iSimangaliso Wetland Park ⑧

Road map F3. St Lucia. Approx. 53 km (33 miles) NE of Empangeni. ◯ *daily, some areas are restricted.* ⬛ ⬛ 🍴 ⬛ ⬛ ⬛ **www**.isimangaliso. com; **www**.kznwildlife.com

Lake St Lucia, 368 sq km (142 sq miles) in size, is the focal point of the third-largest wildlife sanctuary in South Africa. Stretching from the game-filled Mkhuze plains in the north to the St Lucia Estuary in the south, the 1,700-sq-km (656-sq-mile) iSimangaliso Wetland Park encompasses a diversity of habitats: mountain, bushveld, palm groves, sand forest, grassland, wetland, coastal forest, coral reef and ocean.

The coastal village of St Lucia is a popular holiday destination, with a range of facilities and accommodation. Regular cruises offer close-up views of hippos, crocodiles, pelicans, fish eagles and rare waterbirds. The Crocodile Centre, north of the village, is the finest in the country.

Cape Vidal, 32 km (20 miles) north of St Lucia Estuary,

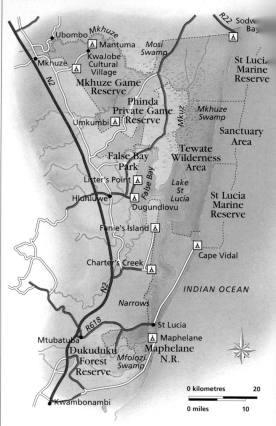

KEY

▬	Major route
▬	Road (tarred)
═	Road (untarred)
Ⓐ	Camping

boasts a reef-shielded beach, tropical waters, deep-sea fishing and a freshwater lake.

The coastline from Cape Vidal to Ponta Do Ouro is a protected marine reserve; the sandy beaches provide vital nesting sites for loggerhead and leatherback turtles. Fishing is allowed in certain areas.

Located 65 km (41 miles) north of St Lucia Estuary, along an unspoilt and unin-habited coastline, **Sodwana Bay** is a popular destination for deep-sea fishing and scuba diving expeditions.

The road from Sodwana to the N2 passes the southern boundary of the **Mkhuze Game Reserve**; its four game-viewing hides are renowned for their close-ups. **KwaJobe Cultural Village** near Mantuma camp gives visitors an insight into traditional Zulu culture.

St Lucia Estuary offers excellent shore-based fishing

For hotels and restaurants in this region see pp396–8 and pp422–4

One of the beaches at Kosi Bay, the northernmost part of KwaZulu-Natal

Environs: About 50 km (31 miles) west of Kosi Bay is the **Ndumo Game Reserve**, famous for the richness of its riverine life, particularly its water birds – an amazing 420 species have been recorded. Hides on the Nyamithi and Banzi pans offer excellent views. The pans also sustain large hippo and crocodile populations, as well as animals such as nyalas, red duikers, and white and black rhinos. To appreciate the pans, book a guided Land Rover tour. A small rest camp overlooks Banzi Pan.

Ndumo Game Reserve
Tel (035) 591-0098. 6am–6pm daily (Oct–Mar: 5am–7pm).

Sodwana Bay
Tel (035) 571-0051.

Mkhuze Game Reserve
Tel (035) 573-9004/1.

KwaJobe Cultural Village
Tel (035) 562-0255.

Phinda Private Game Reserve ❾

Road map F3. 80 km (50 miles) NE of Empangeni. **Tel** (011) 809-4300. restricted access. www.phinda.com

Extending over 170 sq km (65 sq miles) of bushveld, wetland, savannah and sand forest, luxurious privately owned Phinda adjoins the iSimangaliso Wetland Park. Activities on offer include sunset cruises on the Mzinene River, outdoor meals under an acacia tree, game-viewing drives led by experienced rangers as well as bush walks and fishing or diving expeditions to the nearby coast. Wildlife includes nyalas, kudu, wildebeests, giraffes, zebras, elephants, lions, white rhinos and cheetahs. Visitors can stay in one of six lodges, including Mountain Lodge, which offers panoramic views over the surrounding bushveld, or the exclusive, glass-walled Forest Lodge, which is so much a part of the sand forest that its rooms are framed by trees and enclosed by dense foliage. The reserve has its own air strip and arranges air transfers from Johannesburg, or road transfers from Richards Bay.

Kosi Bay Nature Reserve ❿

Road map F2. Approx. 155 km (96 miles) NE of Mkhuze. **Tel** (035) 592-0236. 6am–6pm daily. www.kznwildlife.com

Kosi Bay Nature Reserve is an 80-sq-km (31-sq-mile) aquatic system that incorporates an estuary, mangrove swamps and four interconnecting lakes. It can be reached from Mkhuze, just south of Pongolapoort Dam. The system hosts many fresh- and salt-water fish species, and angling and boating are popular. Tonga fish traps (fences built from sticks and reeds) have been a feature of the Kosi system for over 500 years. There is a campsite and a few thatched chalets, and guided walks and boat trips can be arranged. A four-day circular trail allows hikers to explore the lakes on foot.

Tembe Elephant Park ⓫

Road map F3. Approx. 110 km (68 miles) N of Mkhuze. **Tel** (031) 267-0144. 6am–6pm daily (Oct–Mar: 5am–7pm). www.tembe.co.za

This 290-sq-km (112-sq-mile) wilderness reserve bordering South Africa and Mozambique protects the flood plain of the Phongolo River along the northern boundary of KwaZulu-Natal. The park was established in 1983 to protect the KwaZulu-Natal elephants. Access is limited to 4WD vehicles, and only ten groups of visitors are allowed in per day. There is a tented camp near the entrance, and two hides overlook areas where elephants come to drink. The park has South Africa's largest population of suni antelopes and 430 species of birds.

Loggerhead turtles lay their eggs on sandy beaches

GAUTENG AND MPUMALANGA

INTRODUCING GAUTENG
AND MPUMALANGA 300–305

GAUTENG AND SUN CITY 306–325

BLYDE RIVER CANYON AND KRUGER 326–343

Introducing Gauteng and Mpumalanga

From natural wonders and wildlife to the "City of Gold", this region offers something for everyone. Johannesburg is the throbbing life of the streets and the sophistication of exclusive suburbs, while Soweto, Johannesburg's "other half", provides an insight into the daily lives of the country's urban black people. To the east, the land drops over 1,000 m (3,281 ft) to the hot Lowveld plains and the Kruger National Park. West lies the arid heartland of the subcontinent, and beyond, the Magaliesberg range seems to rise from the waters of the Hartbeespoort Dam. The most fascinating destinations of all, perhaps, are glittering Sun City and the near-mythical grandeur of the Lost City.

The Palace of the Lost City, *a part of the opulent Sun City resort and casino complex, is a spectacular architectural indulgence of age-stressed concrete, beautifully crafted pillars and ornate domes set in a man-made tropical garden and surrounded by a variety of water features such as Roaring Lagoon.*

Sun City

GAUTENG AND SUN CITY
(See pp306–25)

Johannesburg

Johannesburg *is the largest city in South Africa and the one in which extremes are most evident. Poverty and wealth, historic buildings and modern office blocks create stark contrasts.*

◁ Seen here in the Kruger National Park, the lion is one of the "Big Five" African animals

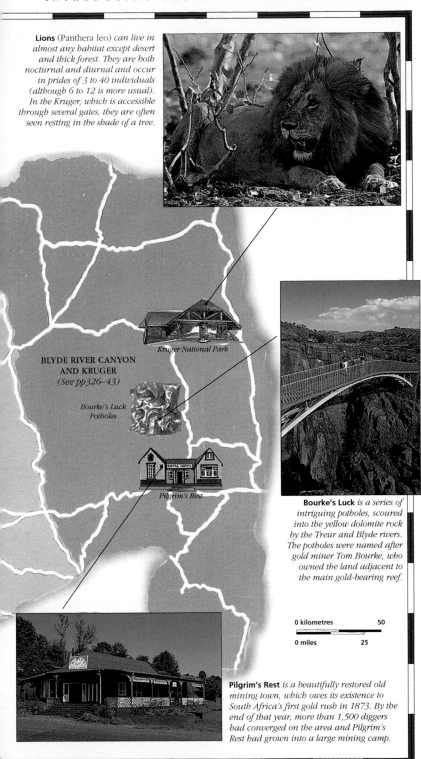

Lions (Panthera leo) *can live in almost any habitat except desert and thick forest. They are both nocturnal and diurnal and occur in prides of 3 to 40 individuals (although 6 to 12 is more usual). In the Kruger, which is accessible through several gates, they are often seen resting in the shade of a tree.*

Kruger National Park

BLYDE RIVER CANYON AND KRUGER
(See pp326–43)

Bourke's Luck Potholes

Pilgrim's Rest

Bourke's Luck *is a series of intriguing potholes, scoured into the yellow dolomite rock by the Treur and Blyde rivers. The potholes were named after gold miner Tom Bourke, who owned the land adjacent to the main gold-bearing reef.*

| 0 kilometres | 50 |
| 0 miles | 25 |

Pilgrim's Rest *is a beautifully restored old mining town, which owes its existence to South Africa's first gold rush in 1873. By the end of that year, more than 1,500 diggers had converged on the area and Pilgrim's Rest had grown into a large mining camp.*

Conservation in the Kruger National Park

National Parks Board logo

The Kruger National Park stretches for 352 km (220 miles) along South Africa's northeastern border. The 19,633-sq-km (7,580-sq-mile) conservation area supports an astounding array of fauna and flora. Although the park sustains the animals in their natural habitat, a fence along much of its boundary does restrict their free movement. Wildlife is concentrated in the lusher southern parts, which calls for careful management. Periodically, rangers have to limit the numbers this contained ecosystem can safely support by translocating young and healthy animals to other reserves.

EXTENT OF THE KRUGER NATIONAL PARK

■ *Park boundaries*

Dry hills provide a habitat for kudu and eland, animals that do not need to drink water regularly.

Zebras flourish when artificial water points are provided. Large zebra herds have a negative impact on animals like roans, sables and reedbucks, which require tall grass.

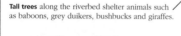

Zebras

Giraffes

The Olifants River *is the largest of the park's seven major watercourses. Since water is scarce, artificial water points have allowed elephants to move into areas that were previously only accessible in wet summer months.*

Tall trees along the riverbed shelter animals such as baboons, grey duikers, bushbucks and giraffes.

MANAGING FOR DIVERSITY

Scientists are only now beginning to understand the complicated African savannah. In an effort to manage the ecosystem in a way that maintains its diversity, artificial water points, which caused habitat-modifiers like elephants to flourish (to the detriment of other species), are now being closed.

Giraffes *are the tallest of the browsers and favour areas where acacias are abundant.*

Kudu *are large antelopes that do not need to drink frequently, and occur in dense woodland.*

Sable antelopes *require tall grass of a high quality that grows on well-drained soils.*

Radio tracking *enables scientists to monitor the endangered predators. Only 120 cheetahs and 120 wild dogs inhabit the park's vast expanse. Research has shown that competition from the more aggressive lion is a major limiting factor.*

DROUGHT STATISTICS

Although park managers endeavour to limit the impact of drought, animal populations in the park are never static. Some species like wildebeests and giraffes are hardly affected, while sables and roan antelopes exhibit sharp declines.

SPECIES	1995	2005	2011
Elephant	8,371	11,672	13,750
Rhino	2,800	4,509	9,000
Wildebeest	12,723	9,612	9,750
Giraffe	4,902	5,114	10,300
Impala	97,297	85,869	176,400
Buffalo	19,477	27,000	37,130
Sable	880	550	290
Roan	44	70	90

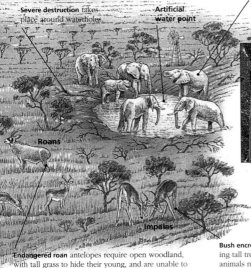

Severe destruction takes place around waterholes

Artificial water point

Roans

Impalas

Elephants are termed habitat-modifiers, because they destroy trees, which brings about significant changes in vegetation.

Destructive feeders, *elephants strip bark off umbrella thorn acacias and fever trees. Kruger's 8,700 elephants each consume up to 250 kg (550 lb) of vegetation daily and comprise one-quarter of the park's total biomass.*

Endangered roan antelopes require open woodland, with tall grass to hide their young, and are unable to adapt to the short-grass conditions caused by an increase in zebra herds around artificial water points.

Bush encroachment, resulting from elephants damaging tall trees and from concentrations of grazing animals near water, benefits browsers like impalas, kudu and giraffes.

TOURIST GUIDELINES

To ensure the safety of visitors and maintain the park's essential attributes, a few regulations are necessary. It is important to observe speed limits, as the animals, too, use the roads as thoroughfares. Since camp closing times are strictly enforced, a good rule of thumb is to calculate an average travelling speed, including stops, of 20 kph (12 mph). Visitors are not permitted to leave their cars except at the 22 designated picnic sites and facilities at 13 of the larger camps – all of the animals are wild and unpredictable, and the predators are superbly camouflaged. Although baboons and vervet monkeys may beg for food, particularly on the road between Skukuza and Lower Sabie, feeding is a punishable offence. It disrupts natural behaviour, and often produces aggression, particularly in male baboons.

Baboons can be aggressive

Visitors blatantly ignoring the rules

Gold Mining

Kruger rands

Vast natural resources make South Africa one of the richest countries on earth. Ancient sediments in this geological treasure chest yield silver, platinum, chromite, uranium, diamonds – and gold. Over the years, small-scale miners have left behind evidence of their labour all around the country. The most poignant of these historic sites is Pilgrim's Rest (see p332), a well-preserved mining town in Mpumalanga. Today, controlled by giant corporations, South Africa produces about one-quarter of the world's gold.

EXTENT OF GOLD FIELDS

▨ Main mining operations

The processing plant produces gold bars of 90 per cent purity, ready for transport to the refinery.

Johannesburg in 1889 *was a sprawling tent settlement. Three years earlier, a prospector named George Harrison had discovered the greatest gold reef in history on a farm named Langlaagte, just west of today's Johannesburg.*

Office blocks house the administration and human resources staff, as well as engineers, geologists, surveyors, mechanics and planners.

SHAFT 9 – VAAL REEFS
This vast gold mine near Klerksdorp straddles the North West and Free State provinces. It is the world's largest gold-mining complex, and is now in the process of selling some of its 11 shafts to black empowerment groups such as Rainbow Mining.

The main shaft, *sunk to a depth of 60 m (197 ft), is encased in a concrete "collar" to support the headgear. South African gold-mine shafts are the deepest in the world, because the reefs are located several miles underground.*

Miners *work underground on 8-hour shifts. Rock temperatures in the confined working place (stope) may reach up to 55°C (131°F).*

Canteen staff *have to cater for the different traditional diets of miners, as well as their exceptionally high calorie intake.*

The ore *is crushed and pumped into a leach tank where cyanide is added to dissolve it. The product is then heated to remove impurities and smelted into gold bars of about 90 per cent purity. A yield of one troy ounce (31.1 grams) of gold from a ton of ore is considered very rich indeed.*

e headgear, set up after the initial
aft has been sunk, carries the ropes,
eels and other mining equipment.

Mine dumps, *yellow heaps, on the outskirts of Johannesburg contain the waste solids of the extraction process. "Greening" the dumps has seen the return of smaller animals and birds.*

Miners' accommodation also
includes sporting facilities,
libraries and parks.

The gold price *is determined twice daily (except on weekends and British bank holidays) by a group of London bullion dealers. It is quoted in US dollars per troy ounce.*

A carat *denotes the purity of gold (measured per part of gold in 24 parts other metal).*

THE KRUGER MILLIONS

Legend has it that when Paul Kruger, last president of the
Zuid-Afrikaansche Republiek (1883–1900), left to go into exile
in Europe in 1900, all the gold in the State Mint at Pretoria
travelled with him to keep it out of the hands of the advancing
British army. At the town of Nelspruit (Mpumalanga), the
presidential train was delayed while mysterious wooden crates
were unloaded and carried away into the bush. Kruger had little
money (or any assets at all) in Europe, and it is surmised that
the missing gold – in Kruger pounds, coin blanks and bars –
still awaits discovery somewhere between Nelspruit and
Barberton. The search continues to this day.

President Paul Kruger

GAUTENG AND SUN CITY

*S*oweto and Johannesburg are part of the urban conglomerate that developed around the rich gold mines of the Witwatersrand in Gauteng. To the north of these cities lies sedate and elegant Pretoria/Tshwane, founded before the discovery of gold and today South Africa's administrative capital. In the northwest, the glittering Sun City resort and casino complex offers fast-paced entertainment.

After the discovery of the main reef in 1886, gold fast became the basis of the national economy and dictated the development of the then mostly rural Transvaal Boer republic. Gold prospectors uncovered many other minerals, such as the coal fields of the eastern Highveld, which now provide the power for further development.

Those who wish to escape the cities do not have far to go. Northwest of Johannesburg and Pretoria/Tshwane is the Hartbeespoort Dam, where watersports enthusiasts flock at weekends, and the shores are lined with resorts and holiday homes. The Magaliesberg mountain range is a nearby nature retreat, whose lower slopes are all but immersed in the water. To the south, the Vaal Dam is another source of water, and recreation, for the province.

The ambitious Sun City development turned the most unpromising terrain in the former homeland of Bophuthatswana, now part of the North West Province, into an opulent leisure resort. Subsequent expansion on a tide of success produced the exotic fantasy called The Palace of the Lost City, where the visitor wants for nothing. Tropical jungle now covers what once was overgrazed farmland in the crater of an extinct volcano, and computer-generated waves wash onto pristine, man-made beaches. Even those who do not find the complex to their taste have to admire the effort and planning that went into its creation.

Visitors in search of an authentic Africa experience should head for the tranquil beauty of the Pilanesberg Game Reserve, a little further north.

In October, the streets of Pretoria/Tshwane are ablaze with lilac jacaranda blossoms

◁ **The impressive Elephant Walk leads to the Palace of the Lost City at Sun City**

Exploring Gauteng and Sun City

The rocky Witwatersrand "ridge of white waters" lies about 1,600 m (5,250 ft) above sea level and stretches for 80 km (50 miles) from west to east. Johannesburg and its satellites have grown, literally, on gold. Here live almost half of South Africa's urban people. Although summers are hot and lush, languid afternoons are frequently torn apart by short, violent thunderstorms. The Highveld grasslands do experience frost and occasional snow in winter. To the northwest, Sun City and The Palace of the Lost City are part of a glittering complex offering superb accommodation, casinos and fast-paced entertainment.

History comes alive in Gold Reef City

SIGHTS AT A GLANCE

KEY

▬▬ Motorway	⋯ Main railway
▬ Main road	— Minor railway
⋯ Minor road	▬ International border
▬ Untarred road	▬ Provincial border
▬ Scenic route	△ Summit

Map place names: Matlabas, Spanwerk, Rooibost, Sentrum, Maricosdraai, Thabazim, Derdepoort, Ramotswa, Madikwe Game Reserve, Ganskuil, Wiljoenteinrant, Middelw, Nietverdiend, Silkaatskop, Bier, Northam, PILANESBERG GAME RESERVE ❾, △ 1687 m, Blairbeth, Mabaalstad, ❽ SUN C, Kromellenboog Dam, Zeerust, R565, R51, Millvale, Bospoort Dam, Groot-Marico, N4, Rustenburg, Mmabatho, Wondermere, Magalie, Mafikeng, Elandsputte, Koster, Derby, Lichtenburg, Swartplaas, R53, R30, NORTH WEST, Klerkskraal, Deelpan, Biesiesvlei, Coligny, Madibogo, N14, Carletonville, Sannieshof, Gerdau, Ventersdorp, Harts, Kuruman, Delareyville, Brakspruit, Fochvi, N12, Hartbeesfontein, Potchefstroom, Ottosdal, Renosterspruit, Klerksdorp, Parys, Orkney, Wolmaransstad, Vierfontein, Vaal, FRE, Leeudoringstad, Kimberley, Viljoenskroon, Rooiw, Makwassie, Bothaville, Bloemfontein

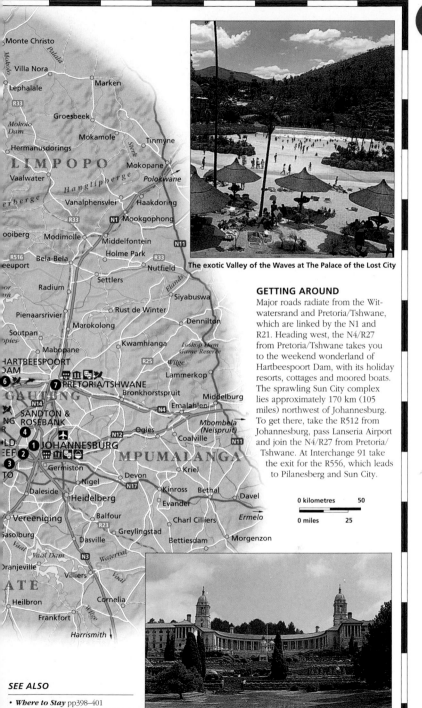

The exotic Valley of the Waves at The Palace of the Lost City

GETTING AROUND

Major roads radiate from the Witwatersrand and Pretoria/Tshwane, which are linked by the N1 and R21. Heading west, the N4/R27 from Pretoria/Tshwane takes you to the weekend wonderland of Hartbeespoort Dam, with its holiday resorts, cottages and moored boats. The sprawling Sun City complex lies approximately 170 km (105 miles) northwest of Johannesburg. To get there, take the R512 from Johannesburg, pass Lanseria Airport and join the N4/R27 from Pretoria/Tshwane. At Interchange 91 take the exit for the R556, which leads to Pilanesberg and Sun City.

| 0 kilometres | 50 |
| 0 miles | 25 |

The Union Buildings, the seat of parliament in Pretoria/Tshwane

SEE ALSO

Johannesburg

A taste of Africa

The densely populated city of Johannesburg is the country's financial and commercial heartland. The city has many names, and most of them, like Egoli and Gauteng, mean "place of gold". Indeed, gold and, of course, glamour are close companions in this place, which has grown from primitive mine camp to metropolis in little over a century. The city pulsates with entrepreneurial energy while, at the same time, it retains the spirit of a frontier town. It lies at an altitude of 1,763 m (5,784 ft) above sea level but at the Western Deep gold mine, the shafts reach an astonishing 3,777 m (12,388 ft) below ground.

Traditional arts and crafts are sold at many markets

Exploring Johannesburg
Johannesburg is undergoing considerable change. The once quiet neighbourhoods of Sandton and Rosebank, north of the city, have become fashionable places to live, and the city centre has a host of interesting sights.

Johannesburg is not a safe city to explore on foot; visitors should join an organized tour.

City Centre
⊞ University of the Witwatersrand
1 Jan Smuts Ave, Braamfontein. **Tel** (011) 717-1000. ☐ 9am–5pm Mon–Fri, 9am–1pm Sat. ● public hols. 📷 **www**.wits.ac.za
Splendid African carvings and ceremonial and ritual objects can be seen at the Wits Art Museum on the campus.

The Origins Centre traces the origins of man from the Stone Age to the present day and is home to the country's most important examples of Khoi and San rock art.

▣ Market Theatre Complex
56 Margaret Mcingana Street. **Tel** (011) 832-1641. ☐ 9am–5pm daily. 🍴 🖥 ♿ **www**.markettheatre.co.za
The Market Theatre Complex is the centre of the Newtown Cultural Precinct that includes the SAB World of Beer, the Workers' Museum and Library, and MuseuMAfricA. A great effort has been made to make Newtown a safe place to visit.

Originally an Indian fruit market, it now houses three theatres, two art galleries, restaurants, cafés and shops. Each Saturday morning, flea-market traders gather on the square outside to sell all kinds of curios.

Opposite the Market Theatre, but part of the complex, the Africana Museum (1935) was relaunched in 1994 as **MuseuMAfricA**. The theme is Johannesburg and its people at various stages of socio-political transformation.

Situated west of the Market Theatre and along Jeppe Street, the **Oriental Plaza** bazaar is permeated by the aroma of Eastern spices. Here, some 360 shops and stalls sell every-thing from carpets to clothing. Many of the traders are the descendants of Indians who came to the Witwatersrand in the 19th century after their contracts on the sugar plantations had expired.

⊞ MuseuMAfricA
Newtown. **Tel** (011) 833-5624. ☐ 9am–5pm Tue–Sun. 📷 ♿ 🄳
⬚ Oriental Plaza
Main & Bree sts. **Tel** (011) 838-6752. ☐ 8:30am–5pm Mon–Sat. ● 12:30–1pm Fri. 🍴 🄳 🖫 **www**.orientalplaza.co.za

⊞ Johannesburg Stock Exchange Building
17 Diagonal Street, Newtown. ● to the public.
This rather impressive glass-walled building is set somewhat incongruously in a downtown area that is busy with street vendors and tiny shops selling everything from plastic buckets to blankets and traditional herbal medicines. The building once housed the Johannesburg

MuseuMAfricA, part of the Market Theatre Complex in Newtown

Stock Exchange (JSE) on one of its floors, but the exchange is now located in other premises in Sandton.

SAB World of Beer, a museum tour with refreshments

🏛 SAB World of Beer

15 President St (entrance in Gerard Sekoto St), Newtown. **Tel** (011) 836-4900. ◯ 10am–6pm Tue–Sat. 🅿 🕅 🛗 www.worldofbeer.co.za

South African Breweries (SAB), which was established in 1895, is the largest brewer by volume in the world, boasting 150 brands and a production of 120 million barrels annually. In this modern museum there is an entertaining display of the company's long history. Other exhibits focus on the development of brewing in ancient Mesopotamia and illustrate how beer-brewing came to Africa and Europe, with excellent reconstructions of a "gold rush" pub, a traditional Soweto *shebeen*, and a full-scale brewhouse where you can see how the brewing process works.

At the end of the tour, adult visitors are rewarded with two ice-cold "frosties". Those under 18 are given a choice of several non-alcoholic cocktails.

🏛 KwaZulu Muti

14 Diagonal St. **Tel** (011) 836-4470. ◯ 8am–5pm Mon–Fri, 8am–1pm Sat. ● Sun, public hols.

This working herbalist shop represents a traditional side of Africa that is very much a part of daily life for many South Africans. It sells a variety of herbs and plants, both dried and fresh. Not all the potions, remedies and medicines are herbal, however. Its fascinating stock includes animal skins, bones, horns and claws, as well as dried bats, frogs and insects. Visitors can get advice from a *sangoma*, a traditional African healer.

VISITORS' CHECKLIST

Road map E2. Gauteng Province. 🏘 3.2 million. ✈ 20 km (12 miles) E of the city. 🚌 Park City, cnr Rissik and Wolmarans sts, Braamfontein. 🚃 Park City. ℹ 195 Jan Smuts Ave, Grosvenor Corner, Parktown North 2193, (011) 214-0700. ◯ 8am–5pm Mon–Fri, 9am–1pm Sat. 🎭 FNB Dance Umbrella (Feb); Standard Bank Joy of Jazz (Aug); Arts Alive (Sep). www.joburgtourism.com

Traditional African herbal remedies

JOHANNESBURG

0 metres   750
0 yards   750

Key to Symbols *see back flap*

The impressive Carlton Centre, a landmark on the downtown Johannesburg skyline

🏛 Johannesburg Central Police Station

Commissioner St. *Tel (011) 375-5911.* 🚫 *to the public.*
Formerly known as the infamous John Vorster Square, this police station was the nerve centre of apartheid repression, a place that in its own way was as sinister as the KGB or the Gestapo headquarters. The nondescript blue and white building was the home of the dreaded Security Branch, where many people, including a large number of political activists, were held, tortured and died while in custody. Among them was Steve Biko *(see p266)*. Renamed, the building still functions as a police station.

🏛 Standard Bank Art Gallery

Cnr Simmonds and Fredericks sts. *Tel (011) 631-4467.* 🕐 *8am–4:30pm Mon–Fri, 9am–1pm Sat.* 🚫 *public hols.* ♿ **www.** standardbankarts.co.za
The unusual setting of a working bank conceals a sophisticated gallery that provides a remarkable showcase for talented local and international artists. As well as changing exhibitions, the display features part of the Standard Bank's own extensive collection. This started as an informal project and was augmented by approved art purchases of each successive chairman of the bank. The gallery has easy-to-follow explanations of both the collection and the African fine art form. The building also hosts recitals and concerts.
Across the road in the Standard Bank's headquarters is Ferreira's Stope – an interesting old mine shaft with a small museum attached.

🏛 Gandhi Square

Built in 1893 as Government Square, this central business district plaza has undergone many transformations. In 1949, it was remodelled and renamed Van der Byl Square after a prominent local politician. The area then became a bustling and anarchic bus station before being thoroughly refurbished in 2002, as part of a wider redevelopment of the surrounding district. The square was also given a new name, after the prominent Indian politician Mahatma Gandhi, who came to Johannesburg in 1903 and worked as a lawyer and civil rights activist. Gandhi's profession often brought him to the Transvaal Law Courts (now demolished), which were located in the square.
In 2003, a life-size statue of Gandhi, by sculptor Trinka Christopher, was unveiled here. Buses still pass through the area, albeit in a more orderly fashion, and there is also a row of trendy shops, restaurants and cafés lining the southern side of the square. A pleasant arcade has been added to provide a link with Marshall Street, and the retail space created was sold out in days.

🏛 Carlton Centre

150 Commissioner Street. *Tel (011) 368-1331.* 🕐 *9am–6pm daily (to 5pm Sat, to 2pm Sun).* 📷 🖥 🎧
A key downtown landmark, the Carlton Centre is 50 storeys or 223 m (730 ft) tall, making it the African continent's highest building. For a small fee visitors can take the lift up to the Top of Africa observation deck on the 50th floor, where amazing panoramic views of the city can be enjoyed. The building was completed in 1973 as part of a five-star hotel complex, although the hotel no longer operates. Today there is a shopping mall on the lower levels.

Gandhi Square, with a statue of the Indian pacifist

🏛 Johannesburg Art Gallery and Sculpture Park

Klein St, Joubert Park.
Tel (011) 725-3130. ⏲ *10am–5pm Tue–Sun.* ⚫ *Good Fri, 25 Dec.*
📷 📷

This gallery offers displays of traditional, historical and modern South African art, as well as several works from European schools, including 17th-century Dutch and Flemish paintings and a collection of Pre-Raphaelite artwork. There are also interesting collections of ceramics, sculpture, furniture and textiles on view.

Unfortunately, the small park here has now become a haven for hustlers, so visitors must be on their guard.

🏛 Constitution Hill

San Hancock St. *Tel (011) 381-3100.* ⏲ *9am–5pm Mon–Fri, 10am–2pm Sat.* ⚫ *Good Fri, 25 Dec.* 📷 ♿ 📷 *www.constitutionhill.org.za*

This remarkable development is a living museum documenting South Africa's turbulent past and its transition to democracy. The site incorporates the Old Fort Prison Complex, a notorious jail for more than a century where many, including Nelson Mandela, were imprisoned. South Africa's Constitutional Court, established in 1994 after the country's first democratic elections, now occupies the eastern side of the complex.

Blackburn Buccaneer in the South African National Museum of Military History

🏟 Ellis Park Stadium

Cnr Cerrey and Staib sts. *Tel (011) 402-8644.* 🚌 *from Park City.* 🚆 *Ellis Park station.* **www.ellispark.co.za**

Home ground of the Gauteng Lions rugby team, this 60,000-seat stadium was built in 1982. It also features an Olympic-sized swimming pool.

🏛 South African National Museum of Military History

20 Erlswold Way, Saxonwold 2132. *Tel (011) 646 5513* ⏲ *9am–4:30pm daily.* ⚫ *Good Fri, 25 Dec.* 📷

Initially opened by the then prime minister Field Marshall Jan Smuts in 1947 to commemorate South Africa's role in the two world wars, this outstanding museum also covers the Anglo-Zulu War, the Anglo-Boer War and the South African resistance movements. It displays more than 44,000 items, divided into 37 separate categories, including the nation's official war art and war photography collections. It also has a vast library of books, journals and archive material, along with some of the world's rarest military aircraft, including the only extant night fighter version of the feared German Me 262 pioneer aircraft.

🏛 Apartheid Museum

Northern Parkway and Gold Reef Road, Ormonde. *Tel (011) 309 4700.* ⏲ *10am–5pm Tue–Sun.* ⚫ *Good Fri, 25 Dec.* 📷 📷 📷 *www.apartheidmuseum.org*

The darkest days of South Africa's turbulent past are chillingly evoked at this fascinating museum. To set the mood, there are separate entrances for whites and non-whites. Documenting the triumph of the human spirit over adversity, the displays recall the National Party's apartheid policy after their election to power in 1948, which turned 20 million non-whites into legally defined second-class citizens. Particularly powerful exhibits include a room with 131 nooses representing the number of political prisoners hanged during apartheid, BBC footage taken in 1961 of Nelson Mandela when he was in hiding from the authorities and a series of evocative photographs taken by Ernest Cole before he was sent into exile during the late 1960s.

Allow at least two hours to visit the museum, but note that it is not suitable for children under 11 because of the harrowing nature of the material on display.

The entry to the Apartheid Museum, with its separate doorways

Gold Reef City ❷

This imaginative reconstruction of Johannesburg of the 1890s is situated some 8 km (5 miles) south of the city. The Gold Reef City theme and fun park was built around Shaft 14, a gold mine that was in use from 1887 to 1971, and aims to recapture that transient time during which Johannesburg slipped from mining camp to city. There is an informative underground tour of the now-disused mine, as well as daily displays of tribal, gumboot and cancan dancing, a daily bird show and rides, including the biggest Ferris wheel in Africa.

Cancan dancer

Golden Loop
The daring loop is one of 33 rides that can be enjoyed free of charge.

Main Gate
People short enough to pass under the miner's hands without touching (1.2 m/4 ft) pay a children's fee.

Gemstone World

Gold Reef City Train
For visitors wishing to gain an overview of the theme park, the Gold Reef City Train offers a leisurely mode of transport and stops at three different stations.

★ **Traditional Dancing**
One of several traditional dances performed here, the gumboot dance is said to be based on a folk dance taught by missionaries who were scandalized by "pagan" African dances. The deliberately heavy-footed response is a gentle rebuke to those who saw merit only in their own customs.

STAR FEATURES

★ Traditional Dancing

★ Main Street

★ Jozi Story of Gold

★ Main Street
Restaurants, pubs, shops, banking facilities, and the Gold Reef City Hotel line this wide street, which also acts as a stage for impromptu dance displays.

VISITORS' CHECKLIST

Road map E2. Shaft 14, Northern Parkway, Ormonde, Johannesburg. **Tel** (011) 248-6800. ⬭ 9:30am–5pm Wed–Sun (daily during school hols). ⬤ 25 Dec. 🎫 incl. all rides & shows. 🎭 9am, 10am, 11am, 2pm & 3pm; multilingual. ♿ 🍴 ⬛ 📷 www.goldreefcity.co.za

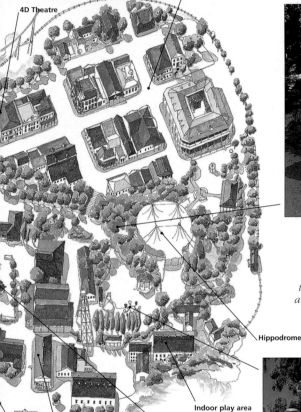

4D Theatre

Hippodrome

Indoor play area

Tower of Terror

Town square

0 metres 50
0 yards 50

★ Jozi Story of Gold
This interactive tour brings the old mining town of Johannesburg to life. It includes a visit to the underground mine and the chance to see gold panning and pouring.

Kiddies' Corner
This delightful funfair is specifically designed for younger children. Here kids can enjoy gentle, old-fashioned rides such as bumper cars and merry-go-rounds.

Gold Pouring
The country's only public gold-pouring demonstration takes place here as part of the Jozi Story of Gold tour.

The Spirit of Sophiatown

Sophiatown – 10 km (6 miles) from Johannesburg's city centre in the 1950s – was a rather seedy shanty town, yet it was also the cradle of urban black culture and became part of South Africa's mythology. Much of the creative black African talent of Johannesburg lived in this overcrowded slum. Artists, journalists from *Drum* (the first "black" magazine in **Township shuffle** the country) and musicians would meet in the vibrant dance halls and debate politics in the shebeens (illegal bars). In the 1950s the government ordered the forcible removal of the community to Meadowlands, a characterless settlement on the far edge of the city – and the white suburb of Triomf replaced Sophiatown. The name Sophiatown was reinstated in 1997.

Shebeens
The Casbah Gang Den was the most notorious shebeen. At these illegal drinking spots, workers and teachers, both white and black, would meet.

Tap water was unavailable in most homes.

Sophiatown Gangs
Gangsters looked to the USA for role models. The most admired gang in Sophiatown was a snappily dressed, limousine-driving group known as "The Americans".

ESSENCE OF SOPHIATOWN
Despite the poverty, squalor, petty crime and violence, Sophiatown's stimulating vibe differed from that of other townships in the country. People of all races could (and did) buy and own properties here.

Skokiaan was a potent, back-yard-brewed cocktail.

Building materials were bits of wood, cardboard boxes, tin and old sacks.

The Sounds of Music
The sounds of the penny whistle, saxophone, harmonica, piano, trumpet and clarinet filled the streets and halls.

Leaving Sophiatown
It took four years to remove all of the inhabitants to Meadowlands (now Soweto). By 1959 Sophiatown had been demolished.

Graffiti on a wall in Soweto

Soweto ❸

Road map E2. 👥 *1 million.*
ℹ️ *Walter Sisulu Square (cnr Union Rd & Klipspruit Valley Rd), (011) 342-4316.* 🕐 *8am–5pm Mon–Fri.*

Few white South Africans have visited Soweto or any of the other townships built beyond the limits of the once "whites-only" suburbs. Although Soweto has few parks or reserves, museums or malls, it is home to at least one million people.

It was in Soweto, in 1976, that the final phase of resistance to apartheid began. The anniversary of this student-led uprising, 16 June, is commemorated as Youth Day. There is a modest monument in the suburb dedicated to the victims of that day's violence.

Numerous reliable tour companies organize day trips to Soweto, usually including a visit to a traditional shebeen, as well as a back-yard, or spaza, shop. It is not advisable for visitors to enter Soweto alone.

Sandton and Rosebank ❹

Road map E2. 👥 *600,000.*
✈️ *OR Tambo International Airport.*

North of Johannesburg, the metropolitan sprawl blends into expensively laid-out residential areas with high walls, spacious gardens, swimming pools and tennis courts.

Affluent Sandton is a fashionable shoppers' paradise, with **Sandton City** reputedly the most sophisticated retail centre in the southern hemisphere. It is especially noted for its speciality shops, trendy boutiques, jewellers and dealers in African art, curios and leatherwork. The centre also has 11 cinemas and 14 superb restaurants and bistros. A number of five-star graded hotels adjoin the Sandton City complex and Nelson Mandela Square, where an Italianate fountain is the focal point in a little piazza lined with coffee shops and restaurants.

The residential suburb of Rivonia, north of Sandton, is home to **Liliesleaf Farm**, once a rural farmhouse and now a museum dedicated to the apartheid era. It was on this farm that, on 11 July 1963, the South African security forces carried out a raid that ended with the arrest of most of the leaders of the African National Congress. The ANC representatives, including Walter Sisulu and Govan Mbeki, were imprisoned after the Rivonia Trials later that year. Although Nelson Mandela had been arrested six months earlier, he was also part of the Rivonia Trials, which marked the beginning of his 27 years' incarceration.

Nelson Mandela's statue, Sandton

South of Sandton is Rosebank, where **The Mall of Rosebank** offers chain stores, upmarket boutiques, restaurants and entertainment, including a ten-pin bowling alley and cinemas. The African Craft Market is an indoor facility with more than 140 stalls. Every Sunday a lively market is held on the rooftop of the mall.

🏢 **Sandton City**
Cnr Sandton Dr & Rivonia Rd. *Tel (011) 883-2011.* 🕐 *9am–6pm Mon–Fri, 9am–5pm Sat, 10am–4pm Sun.*
♿ 🍴 www.sandton-city.co.za

🏛️ **Liliesleaf Farm**
George Ave, Rivonia. *Tel (011) 803-7882.* 🕐 *9am–5pm Mon–Fri, 9am–4pm Sat & Sun.* 📷 ♿ 🛍️ 🍴
www.liliesleaf.co.za

🏢 **The Mall of Rosebank**
Cradock St, Rosebank. *Tel (011) 788-5530.* 🕐 *9am–6pm Mon–Sat, 10am–4pm Sun.* ♿ 🍴
www.themallofrosebank.co.za

The indoor African Craft Market, part of The Mall of Rosebank

Touring Gauteng ❺

Mask, Heia Safari Ranch

Much of Gauteng consists of the industrial areas that have helped to shape the national wealth, but the vibrant metropolitan centres of Johannesburg and Pretoria/Tshwane are surrounded by a green belt that offers various facilities for outdoor recreation. Popular destinations like the Ann van Dyk Cheetah Centre, Hartbeespoort Dam and the hiking trails of the Magaliesberg mountain range are accessible via an excellent network of highways.

Ann van Dyk Cheetah Centre ⑦
This sanctuary near Brits initiated a breeding programme for captive king cheetahs in 1971. The project is a great success. Booking is essential.

The Magaliesberg Range ⑥
This chain of low hills between Pretoria/Tshwane and Rustenburg is popular with hikers. The area has many hotels, guest farms, caravan parks and camp sites.

KEY

- Motorway
- Tour route
- Other roads
- Viewpoint

Lesedi Cultural Village ⑤
This mock-up of four typical African villages – Xhosa, Zulu, Pedi and Sotho – illustrates all aspects of tribal life, including traditional singing and dancing. The three-hour tour includes a meal.

TIPS FOR DRIVERS

Length: *200 km (124 miles). Hartbeespoort Dam is an hour's drive from Pretoria/Tshwane and Johannesburg.*
Stopping-off points: *There are good restaurants at Heia Safari, the Aloe Ridge Game Reserve and around the Hartbeespoort Dam area.*

Sterkfontein Caves ④
This extensive cavern network – a World Heritage site – is one of the world's most important archaeological locations. Guided tours leave every 30 minutes.

Aloe Ridge Game Reserve ②
At this reserve near Muldersdrift, visitors can see giraffes, buffaloes, hippos and many antelope and bird species. There is also a Zulu craft centre.

Hartbeespoort Dam ⑧

A 17-sq-km (7-sq-mile) water surface makes this a prime week-end destination for Johannesburg and Pretoria/Tshwane citizens.

Crocodile Ramble ⑨

Visitors driving along this arts and crafts route can stop off at a variety of workshops to watch the craftspeople in action and buy fine art, furniture and metalware.

Lion Park ⑩

A one-way road passes through a 200-ha (493-acre) lion enclosure and a separate park stocked with blesboks, black wildebeests, impalas, gemsboks and zebras, to reach a picnic site. There is also a restaurant.

R566
R513
⑦
R514
TSHWANE/ PRETORIA
N4
R511
R511
R512
N1
Johannesburg

Walter Sisulu National Botanical Garden ①

The Witpoortjie Falls form the focus of the gardens, where indigenous highveld flora like aloes and proteas attract many bird species.

Heia Safari Ranch ③

Impalas, blesboks and zebras wander freely through the grounds, which also incorporate a conference centre, restaurant, and bungalows on the banks of the Crocodile River.

Power-boating is popular on Hartbeespoort Dam

Hartbeespoort Dam ❻

Road map E2. On R514 take cableway turnoff.

This dam forms part of the **Hartbeespoort Nature Reserve**. Boating is permitted, and the dam is popular with waterskiers, boardsailors and yachtsmen, while anglers cast for *kurper* (a species of bream), carp and yellowfish.

The circular drive includes a short tunnel leading to the dam wall, which offers views over the captive waters of the Crocodile and Magalies rivers.

Other attractions include a snake and animal park housing most species of South African reptiles, plus penguins and seals. There is also a zoo with a cheetah trust and predator park.

The **Elephant Sanctuary** is also nearby. Visitors can feed, ride and walk hand-in-trunk with the pachyderms, or observe them from a tree-house deck.

Environs: In the Ysterhout Kloof is the **Magalies Canopy Tour**. Enjoy the magnificent greenery of the ancient Magaliesberg range from 11 platforms connected by cables. Tours start from the Sparkling Waters Hotel & Spa.

🗡 Magalies Canopy Tour
Ysterhout Kloof. **Tel** *(014) 535-0150.* ☐ *Summer: 7am–4:30pm daily; winter: 8am–3:30pm daily.* 🖼
www.magaliescanopytour.co.za

Pretoria/Tshwane ❼

The monuments and grandiose official buildings, some dating back to the 1800s, are softened by Pretoria/Tshwane's many parks and gardens. Each spring, the flowers of the jacaranda trees add splashes of lilac to the streets of South Africa's administrative capital, which is also one of the country's foremost academic centres. The South African government is currently going through the process of changing the name of the city to Tshwane, which means "we are the same".

Voortrekker Monument

Paul Kruger Monument, Church Square, Pretoria/Tshwane

Exploring Pretoria/Tshwane

Historical buildings, gracious parks, theatres, and restaurants can be found throughout this elegant, compact city, which centers on the attractive, pedestrianized Church Square.

🐾 National Zoological Gardens

232 Boom St. *Tel (012) 339-2700.*
◯ 8:30am–5:30pm daily. 🎫 ♿ 🍴
www.nzg.ac.za
Better known as Pretoria Zoo, this parkland lies in the heart of the city on the bank of the Apies River. One of the top ten zoos in the world, it is very conservation conscious. Much time and effort is spent on breeding programmes of rare or endangered species like the Cape mountain zebra and the stately Arabian oryx.

⛪ Church Square

Cnr WF Nkomo and Paul Kruger sts.
Among the buildings on the square are the **Raadsaal** (1890), one-time parliament of the former Boer Republic, and the **Palace of Justice** (1899), used as a military hospital until 1902 by the British.

Anton van Wouw's statue of Paul Kruger was cast in Italy in 1899, the year the Transvaal Republic went to war against the British Empire.

🎭 South African State Theatre

Cnr Sisulu & WF Nkomo sts.
Tel (012) 392-4000. ◯ daily.
This Japanese-style complex houses five theatres where ballets, dramas, operas, musicals and classical concerts are performed regularly.

⛪ City Hall

Paul Kruger St.
This imposing building is a mixture of Neo-Greek and Roman architecture. Two statues depict Marthinus Pretorius, founder of the city, and his father, Andries. A statue of the mythical chief Tshwane stands nearby.

🏛 National Museum of Natural History

Paul Kruger St. *Tel (012) 322-7632.*
◯ 8am–4pm daily. ● Good Fri, 25 Dec. 🎫 ♿
This natural history museum has a remarkable collection of stuffed animals, as well as permanent archaeological and geological exhibitions.
Many of South Africa's indigenous birds are displayed in the Austin Roberts Bird Hall.

⛪ Melrose House

275 Jeff Masemola St. *Tel (012) 322-2805.* ◯ 10am–5pm Tue–Sun.
● public hols. 🎫
In the 1880s, British architect William Vale designed this house for transport contractor George Heys. The house features nearly all forms of precast embellishment available, and the style was inspired by Cape Dutch architecture, English country houses and Indian pavilions. Today, the museum still has many of its original contents.
During the South African War, Melrose House was the residence of Lord Kitchener, British commander-in-chief. It was here that the Treaty of Vereeniging was signed on 31 May 1902, ending the war.

NDEBELE ARTS AND CRAFTS

The Ndebele are noted for their colourful dress and their art, which includes sculpted figurines, pottery, beadwork, woven mats, and their celebrated wall painting *(see p429)*. An outstanding example is the beaded *nguba*, a "marriage blanket" which the bride-to-be, inspired by her ancestors, makes under the supervision and instruction of the older women in her tribe. Traditionally, the women work the land and are the principal decorators and artists, while the men fashion metal ornaments such as the heavy bracelets, anklets and neck rings that are worn by women.

Typical Ndebele art

⚜ Union Buildings

Government Ave, Meintjies Kop.
◯ *daily (grounds only).*
Designed by the renowned
architect Sir Herbert Baker,
the Union Buildings were
built to house the administrative offices of the Union of
South Africa in 1910. Baker
himself chose the imposing
hill site from where the two
large office wings overlook
landscaped gardens and an
impressive amphitheatre.

Although the building is not
open to the public for reasons
of security, the impressive
Renaissance building with
its Cape Dutch and Italian
influences may be admired
from the peaceful gardens.

Environs: Visible on the left
as one approaches Pretoria/
Tshwane on the N1 from
Johannesburg, the **Voortrekker
Monument** and museum
commemorate the Afrikaner
pioneers who trekked from
the Cape in the 1830s to
escape British domination.

Begun in 1938, the centenary
of the Battle of Blood River
(see p51), it became a focus of
Afrikaner unity. The structure
features a cenotaph in the Hall
of Heroes which is lit by a
beam of sunlight at noon on
16 December, the day of the
Battle of Blood River.

The Voortrekker Monument

East of Pretoria/Tshwane on
the R104 lies **Sammy Marks
Museum**, once the elegant
residence of industrial pioneer
Sammy Marks (1843–1920),
the founder of the South
African Breweries. The house
has been beautifully furnished
in a Victorian style.

VISITORS' CHECKLIST

Road map E2. Gauteng Prov-
ince. ⚜ *1,400,000.* ✈
*Johannesburg, 50 km (31 miles)
SW of Pretoria/Tshwane.* 🚌 *Cnr
Scheiding & Paul Kruger sts.*
🚌 *Tourist Information Centre.*
ℹ️ *Church Square, (012) 358-
1430.* ◯ *7:30am–4pm Mon–
Fri.* 🎪 *Spring Show (Sep).*
www.tshwane.gov.za

⚜ Sammy Marks Museum
Route 104, Bronkhorstspruit Rd.
Tel *(012) 755-9541.* ◯ *10am–4pm
Tue–Sun (tours obligatory).*
● *Good Fri, 25 Dec.* 🎫 ♿

⚜ Voortrekker Monument
Eeufees Rd. ***Tel*** *(012) 326-6770.*
◯ *8am–5pm daily.* ● *25 Dec.* 🎫
Museum ***Tel*** *(012) 323-0682.* 🎫

Historic Melrose House is set in a splendid garden

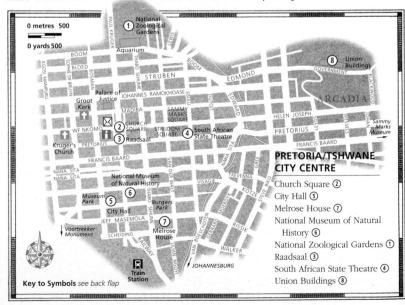

0 metres 500

0 yards 500

PRETORIA/TSHWANE CITY CENTRE

Church Square ②
City Hall ⑤
Melrose House ⑦
National Museum of Natural
History ⑥
National Zoological Gardens ①
Raadsaal ③
South African State Theatre ④
Union Buildings ⑧

Key to Symbols *see back flap*

The Cascades Hotel at Sun City

Sun City ❽

Road map D2. Rustenburg. N4, take R565 turnoff. **Tel** *(014) 557-1000.* ✈ *Pilanesberg, (014) 522-1115.* 🚌 *Johannesburg (011) 780-7800.* 🏷 ♿ 🍴 🛏 🔒 🛍

Set in a fairly bleak part of southern Africa, two hours by road from the metropolitan centres of the Witwatersrand, "the city that never sleeps" is a glittering pleasure resort. Sun International *(see p379)* and Computicket *(see p431)* offer regular coach tours from Gauteng and there are charter flights from Johannesburg's OR Tambo International Airport.

Sun City was the inspiration of hotelier Sol Kerzner. In the 1970s, when the complex was built, the land formed part of the quasi-independent "republic" Bophuthatswana, where gambling, officially banned in South Africa at the time, was legal. The casino was a key element in the resort's initial success, which then included only one luxury hotel, a man-made lake and a challenging 18-hole golf course designed by the former South African golfing champion Gary Player.

It soon became apparent that the complex could not cope with the influx of visitors, and a further two hotels were added in 1980 and 1984 respectively, the Cabanas and the attractive

Casino entrance

Cascades. Accommodation at the 284-room Cabanas caters mainly for families and day visitors with outdoor interests, and costs slightly less than elsewhere in the resort.

Although changes in gambling legislation, introduced in 1996, mean that casinos have sprung up around the country, Sun City continues to attract visitors due to its many other features, particularly the entertainment centre. Not only does it offer a chance of winning a fortune at the spin of a wheel, there are also elaborate stage shows featuring sequined dancers, music concerts, beauty pageants and a variety of sports events.

The complex also houses restaurants and coffee shops, curio shops, boutiques, a cinema and entertainment areas for kids. **The Palace of the Lost City at Sun City** *(see pp324–5)* is the latest addition to the complex; a fourth hotel has been built here, along with a second golf course.

In the vicinity of Sun City are several worthwhile natural attractions that should not be missed. At the entrance to the

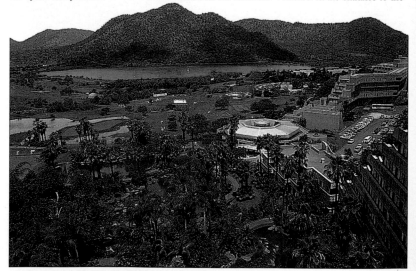

Sun City is a spectacular man-made oasis in the North West Province

For hotels and restaurants in this region see pp398–401 and pp424–7

The jungle gardens of the Lost City at Sun City

resort is the fascinating **Kwena Gardens**, where Nile crocodiles can be viewed in their natural habitat, with special walkways leading to observation areas.

🐊 Kwena Gardens
Sun City. **Tel** (014) 552-1262.
⬜ 10am–6pm daily. Feeding: 4:30pm daily. 🎫 🖥 🎁

Pilanesberg Game Reserve ➒

Road map D2. Take Mogwase turnoff from R510. **Tel** (014) 555-1600.
⬜ 6am–6pm daily (times may vary).
🎫 🍴 🚙 www.pilanesberg-game-reserve.co.za

The circular layout of the park can be traced to prehistoric times, when this area was the crater of a volcano. Around the central Mankwe Dam lie three rings of little hills – mounds of cooled lava – and the whole area is raised above the plain.

The decision to establish a reserve here was economic: to benefit the local people, and to complement the nearby resort of Sun City.

Re-stocking the overgrazed farmland turned into one of the most ambitious game relocation ventures ever attempted in South Africa. Appropriately called Operation Genesis, it involved the release of 6,000 mammals of 19 species into the new reserve. To ensure the success of the ambitious venture, alien plants were removed and replaced with indigenous ones, telephone lines were diverted, farming structures demolished and the ravages of erosion repaired.

Elephants, black rhinos and leopards head an impressive list of wildlife that can be seen at Pilanesberg today. Qualified rangers take guests on safaris in open vehicles. For visitors staying overnight, there is the excitement of night drives.

The Pilanesberg is also home to a number of birds, notably a variety of raptors. Cape vultures nest on the steep cliffs of the Magaliesberg mountains and a number of feeding stations have been established to encourage the survival of this endangered bird.

Pilanesberg Game Reserve offers a choice of accommodation, from the luxurious Kwa Maritane Resort, Tshukudu Bush Lodge and Bakubung Lodge, which overlooks a hippo pool, to tented camps and thatched huts. In the vicinity is a private camp with bungalows and a pleasant caravan park.

Young elephants in the Pilanesberg Game Reserve

The Palace of the Lost City at Sun City

In an ancient volcanic crater, some 180 km (112 miles) northwest of Johannesburg, lies the mythical "lost city" of a vanished people, where time seems to have stood still. Here, innovative design and fanciful architecture in a lush, man-made jungle have created a complex that promises an unforgettable holiday: luxurious hotels, world-class golf courses, the glamorous Superbowl entertainment centre, glittering casinos and blue waves lapping palm-fringed beaches.

Palace light

The Desert Suite
Oak panelling, a private library, bar and panoramic views make this one of the hotel's most opulent suites.

King's Tower

Buffalo Wing

Lost City Golf Course
This 18-hole championship course offers a choice of tees. A crocodile pool at the 13th hole is a unique water hazard.

Cheetah Fountain
This superb bronze sculpture shows impalas, frozen in flight from the feared predator.

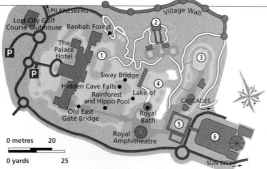

LOST CITY COMPLEX

1. Grand Pool
2. Temple of Courage
3. Adventure Mountain
4. Roaring Lagoon
5. Bridge of Time
6. Entertainment Centre

KEY

— Road (tarred)

▇ Building

P Parking

PILANESBERG
Village Wall
Lost City Golf Course Clubhouse
Baobab Forest
The Palace Hotel
Sway Bridge
Hidden Cave Falls
Rainforest and Hippo Pool
Lake of
Old East Gate Bridge
Royal Bath
CASCADES
Royal Amphitheatre
SUN CITY

0 metres   20
0 yards   25

★ **Elephant Atrium and Shawu Statue**
This sculpture honours an elephant bull that roamed the Kruger National Park, until his death in 1982, aged 80. It graces a large chamber at the end of the vaulted Elephant Atrium.

VISITORS' CHECKLIST

Road map D2. N4 from Pretoria/Tshwane, then R565; or R556. North West Province. ✈ Pilanesberg (014) 522-1115. 🚌 from Johannesburg (014) 557-1000. ℹ Sun International Central Reservations (011) 780-7800. **Tel** The Palace of the Lost City at Sun City (014) 557-1000. ◯ daily. ♿ 🅿 🛒 🍴 🛍 💻 📷 📀 ⛽ 🎿

www.suninternational.co.za

Desert Suite and Presidential Suites

Queen's Tower

Elephant Atrium

Some **1,600,000** trees, shrubs, plants and groundcovers were planted at the Lost City.

★ **Central Fresco**
The fresco that adorns the dome of the reception area measures 16 m (52 ft) in diameter and took 5,000 hours to complete.

The porte-cochère leads to the domed lobby.

Roaring Lagoon
Every 90 seconds a 1.8-m (6-ft) wave rolls onto the white sand beach.

STAR FEATURES

★ Elephant Atrium and Shawu Statue

★ Central Fresco

BLYDE RIVER CANYON AND KRUGER

The attractions in the northeastern part of the country include a deeply carved canyon and the nature reserves that surround it, panoramic views, trout-fishing dams, and the charming gold-mining town of Pilgrim's Rest, preserved as a living museum.

South Africa's topography is at its most dramatic where the Drakensberg's northern reaches drop sheer to the hot bushveld plains below. From here, visitors can look out over the Eastern Escarpment to where the savannah merges with the distant coastal plains of Mozambique, and hike through the ravines of the Blyde River Canyon.

High rainfall on the steep mountain slopes contributes to the growth of dense forests, as well as the country's greatest concentration of waterfalls. More timber is produced here than anywhere else in South Africa, and there are vast pine and eucalyptus tree plantations. Scenic drives include the Panorama Route, with its unobstructed view sites, which is accessible from the busy little town of Graskop.

Much of the Lowveld plains is occupied by the Kruger National Park, one of the world's oldest and largest wildlife reserves. The southern part, south of the Letaba River and closer to the metropolitan area of Gauteng, is very popular and more frequently visited. Tourist numbers are considerably lower in the east and remote north, renowned for its long-tusked elephants. Strict management policies preserve the park from becoming a victim of its own success, while some of the tourist pressure is relieved by the privately run luxury reserves along the Kruger National Park's western border.

Lowveld farming produces a variety of citrus fruit from a number of large estates. Tobacco, nuts, mangoes and avocados are also sucessfully grown.

The graceful impala, a common sight in the Kruger National Park

◁ At the confluence of the Blyde and Treur rivers, pebbles have scoured gigantic potholes into the rock

Exploring the Blyde River Canyon and Kruger

Early prospectors flocked to the eastern part of the country in search of gold, and found it in the rivers and streams. Today, visitors are attracted by the natural beauty and the superb nature reserves. Here, the Blyde River has cut a mighty canyon, and close by, the edge of the Drakensberg range rises from the grassy plains a kilometre below. This is wildlife conservation country, home of the renowned Kruger National Park and a cluster of exclusive private reserves. There are airstrips and excellent accommodation – just a few hours' drive away from the Witwatersrand.

SIGHTS AT A GLANCE

Blyde River Canyon **5**
Dullstroom **1**
Kruger National Park **6**
Lydenburg **2**
Pilgrim's Rest
  Alanglade pp334–5 **4**
Private Reserves **8**
Swaziland pp342–3 **9**

Tour

Southern Kruger Tour p340 **7**
Waterfalls Tour p331 **3**

SEE ALSO

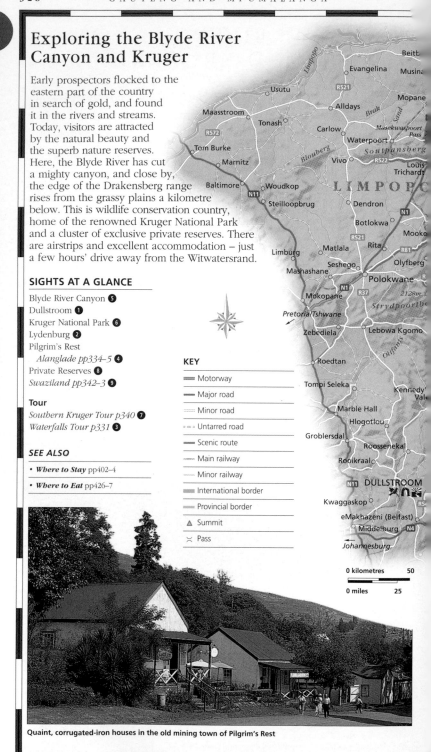

KEY

▬▬	Motorway
━━	Major road
┅┅	Minor road
= = =	Untarred road
━━	Scenic route
⎯⎯	Main railway
⎯⎯	Minor railway
▬▬	International border
▬▬	Provincial border
▲	Summit
⤬	Pass

0 kilometres   50

0 miles   25

Quaint, corrugated-iron houses in the old mining town of Pilgrim's Rest

For additional map symbols *see back flap*

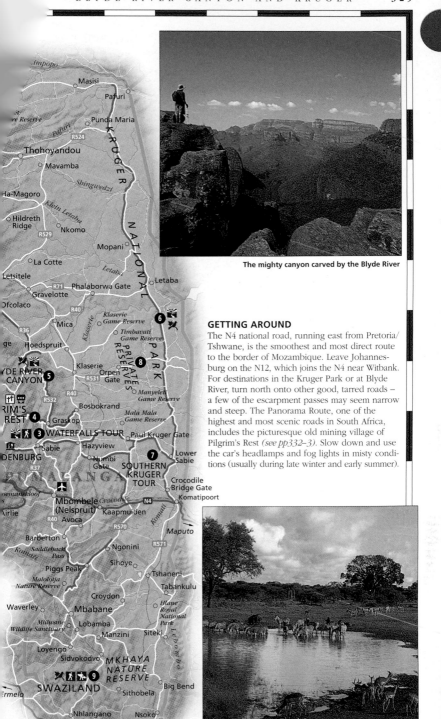

The mighty canyon carved by the Blyde River

GETTING AROUND

The N4 national road, running east from Pretoria/Tshwane, is the smoothest and most direct route to the border of Mozambique. Leave Johannesburg on the N12, which joins the N4 near Witbank. For destinations in the Kruger Park or at Blyde River, turn north onto other good, tarred roads – a few of the escarpment passes may seem narrow and steep. The Panorama Route, one of the highest and most scenic roads in South Africa, includes the picturesque old mining village of Pilgrim's Rest *(see pp332–3)*. Slow down and use the car's headlamps and fog lights in misty conditions (usually during late winter and early summer).

Wildlife gathers at a waterhole in the Kruger National Park

The serpentine curves of Long Tom Pass near Lydenburg

Dullstroom ❶

Road map E2. Middelburg. 🏠 500.
ℹ️ *Naledi Drive, (013) 254-0254.*
⭕ daily. **www**.dullstroom.biz

Named in 1893 after a Dutch official called "Dull" and the *stroom* (stream) of the Crocodile River, Dullstroom is South Africa's fly-fishing centre. It has the highest railway station in South Africa, at 2,076 m (6,811 ft) above sea level. In winter, temperatures can drop to -13°C (9°F).

Environs: The **Dullstroom Dam Nature Reserve**, on the eastern outskirts of the town, is an area of attractive wooded gorges surrounding a tranquil dam known for its trout-fishing. Sheltered camping and caravan sites lie close to the shores amid the unusual and luxuriant sub-alpine vegetation. Bird life is rich, and the countryside is traversed by scenic hiking trails like Misty Valley, Ratelspruit and Salpeterkrans.
Verloren Vlei Nature Reserve lies 14 km (9 miles)

by road north of Dullstroom, at the heart of a wetlands conservation area boasting a wealth of floral species. The endangered wattled crane is the subject of a conservation project, which aims to release the bird back into the wild.

Along the road to Nelspruit, the **Sudwala Caves** are filled with bizarre dripstone formations. There are regular guided tours. The network of caverns is named after a Swazi leader who took refuge here during the mid-1800s.

A short walk from the caves is an interesting timeline of the development of man, as well as a park with life-sized models that portray prehistoric wildlife in a convincing setting of palms, shrubs and cycads.

🏞️ **Dullstroom Dam Nature Reserve**
Tel (078) 168-8741. ⭕ daily. 🏞️
🏞️ **Verloren Vlei Nature Reserve**
Tel (013) 254-0799. ⭕ by appt. 🏞️
🕳️ **Sudwala Caves**
Tel (013) 733-4152. ⭕ 8:30am–4:30pm daily. ⭕ 25 Dec. 🏞️

Lydenburg ❷

Road map F2. 58 km (36 miles) N of Dullstroom. 🏠 6,000.

Lydenburg means "town of suffering" and refers to the failed attempt to establish a town in the malaria-infested area to the north. Survivors headed south in 1850 to found a new settlement. Interesting historic buildings from that early period are the old church and the Voortrekker school.

The most interesting exhibits in the **Lydenburg Museum** are replicas of the Lydenburg Heads *(see p45)*, seven large, unique terracotta masks dating back to about AD 500 and believed to have been used in ceremonial rituals.

🏛️ **Lydenburg Museum**
Long Tom Pass Rd. *Tel (013) 235-2213.* ⭕ 8am–4pm Mon–Fri, 8am–5pm Sat, Sun. ⭕ 25 Dec.
www.lydenburgmuseum.org.za

Environs: Sabie, some 53 km (33 miles) east of Lydenburg, is surrounded by vast forestry plantations and is reached via the scenic **Long Tom Pass**, originally part of a wagon road. In places the rocks still bear the marks of metal-rimmed wheel ruts. In the 19th century exotic, fast-growing trees were planted around Sabie to provide timber for use in the many local gold mines. Timber is still the area's mainstay. The **Forest Industry Museum** is dedicated to wood and its many uses.

🏛️ **Forest Industry Museum**
10th Ave, Sabie. *Tel (013) 764-1058.* ⭕ 8am–4pm Mon–Sat (to noon Sat). 🏞️ **www**.komatiecotourism.co.za

---

TROUT-FISHING IN DULLSTROOM

In 1890, brown trout were successfully introduced to the inland waters of KwaZulu-Natal for the first time and were later distributed in cold streams throughout the country. The rainbow trout, with its sparkling reddish-mauve side stripe, was introduced in 1897. The trout-rich waters around Dullstroom allow for dam and river angling, mostly from private ground. Temporary membership of the Dullstroom Fly-Fishers' Club allows temporary access to sites, as well as sound advice from experienced local anglers. Details may be obtained on admission to Dullstroom Dam, or from the town clerk. Accommodation in the district ranges from wooden cabins to luxurious guesthouses.

Tranquil dam near Dullstroom

The Waterfalls Tour ❸

High-lying ground, generous rainfall and heavy run-off have created spectacular waterfalls in this old gold-mining area along the Drakensberg escarpment. There are, in fact, more waterfalls here than anywhere else in southern Africa. Several of them can be seen on an easy round trip of under 100 km (60 miles) between the towns of Sabie and Graskop. Most are well signposted and easy to reach by car. Enchanting as they are, waterfalls can be slippery and dangerous and visitors are urged to heed the warning notices.

Lisbon Falls ⑥
The Lisbon Falls crash 90 m (295 ft) down a rocky cliff. The old miners named many local places after towns in their home countries.

Maria Shires Falls ⑤
These falls in the forest are noted for their thundering sound, especially after heavy rainfall.

Bridal Veil Falls ③
Delicate wisps of spray that billow like a veil have given this waterfall its name.

Berlin Falls ⑦
The water flows through a natural sluice before falling 80 m (263 ft) to the deep, dark-green pool below.

MacMac Falls ④
The 70-m (230-ft) fall was named for the Scottish miners who panned for gold in this area. There is a picnic site at the nearby MacMac pools.

KEY

- ▬ Tour route
- ═ Other roads
- ⸗ Trail
- ✲ Viewpoint

Lone Creek Falls ②
From almost 70 m (230 ft), the spray of the falls drifts down onto dense pockets of fern and mountain forest.

TIPS FOR DRIVERS

Starting point: *Sabie.*
Length: *100 km (60 miles).*
Getting there: *From Sabie, turn left on to the R532 for the Horseshoe, Lone Creek and Bridal Veil falls. For the MacMac, Maria Shires, Lisbon, Berlin and Forest falls, take the R532 from Sabie towards Graskop.*

Horseshoe Falls ①
Cascading in an almost perfect horseshoe, these falls are on private land and reached after a short walk through a campsite.

0 kilometres   5

0 miles   3

Pilgrim's Rest ●

Gravestone

Prospectors struck it rich in 1873, ending their search for gold in a picturesque valley of the Eastern Escarpment. Their original village, today restored to its modest glory, is unique: the diggers built in "tin and timber" thinking that, once the gold was exhausted, they would move on. But the gold lasted almost 100 years, and Pilgrim's Rest, 15 km (10 miles) west of the Drakensberg escarpment, is a living part of history.

VISITORS' CHECKLIST

Road map F2. 35 km (21 miles) N of Sabie. ▮ (013) 768-1060. ◯ 9am–4pm daily. ▨ multi-entry. ⚠ (013) 764-1177.

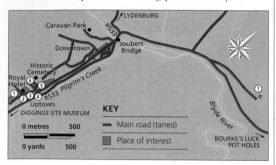

KEY

■ Main road (tarred)
▪ Place of interest

0 metres 500
0 yards 500

Dredzen's shop, with its colourful bargains from a bygone era

KEY TO TOWN PLAN

Pilgrim's & Sabie News Museum ①
Information Centre ②
Victorian House Museum ③
Central Garage ④
Dredzen Shop & House Museum ⑤
Thelwell's Transformation Museum ⑥
Alanglade ⑦

Exploring Pilgrim's Rest

The entire village is a National Heritage Site. A stroll from St Mary's Church to the Post Office passes the old "uptown area", where one can visit the cemetery. Most interesting of all the tombstones is the enigmatic Robber's Grave.

At the Diggings Site Museum, on the bank of Pilgrim's Creek, visitors may try their luck at panning for alluvial gold.

The Pilgrim's & Sabie News Museum displays hand-printing equipment from the 1900s.

The Victorian House Museum, a typical building of corrugated iron sheets on a timber frame, shows that, despite being surrounded by gold, prospectors led a simple life.

The Central Garage houses a transport museum, while the Dredzen Shop & House is a typical general store from the 1930s–50s, with the owner's house at the back. Thelwell's Transformation Museum has displays on the Sekhukhumne Wars and the history of local black miners.

Stately Alanglade, the mine manager's residence, is located in a wooded glen, well away from the dust and noise of the village (*see pp334–5*).

Environs: Timber and tourism are the mainstays of this area on the dramatic escarpment of the Drakensberg mountains.

From the village, the tarred R533 winds across Bonnet Pass to Graskop, a convenient centre for exploring both the escarpment and the Kruger National Park, whose main camp, Skukuza, is just 70 km (44 miles) away.

View from God's Window

The R534, also known as the Panorama Route, starts 3 km (2 miles) north of Graskop and passes cliff-top sites and lovely waterfalls (*see p331*). The escarpment drops almost 1,000 m (3,281 ft) to the Lowveld plains below. In places, the view extends 100 km (60 miles) towards Mozambique. The scenery in this area has been called the most beautiful in South Africa, and the vistas are spectacular.

The bar of the Royal Hotel was once a chapel

The Three Rondavels in the Blyde River Canyon

Blyde River Canyon 5

Road map F2. On R534. 🎣 🄰

The fast-flowing Blyde River has, over the centuries, carved its way through 700 m (2,300 ft) of shale and quartzite to create a scenic jumble of cliffs, islands, plateaus and bush-covered slopes that form a 20-km (12-mile) canyon. At the heart of this canyon lies the Blydepoort Dam.

The forested slopes of the ravine are home to several large antelope species, as well as smaller mammals, birds, hippos and crocodiles. Only in the Blyde River Canyon are all the southern African primates found: chacma baboons, vervet and samango monkeys, and both species of bushbaby. The abundant flora ranges from lichens and mosses to montane forest, orchids and other flowering plants.

Exploring the Blyde River Canyon Nature Reserve

A 300-km (186-mile) circular drive from Graskop via Bosbokrand, Klaserie, Swadini and Bourke's Luck affords panoramic vistas of the escarpment rising above the plains, the Blydepoort Dam and the breathtaking view deep into the canyon itself. There are several overnight trails and short walks, and accommodation is available at the resorts of Swadini and Blyde Canyon.

Kowyn's Pass

The tarred R533 between Graskop and the Lowveld provides views of the escarpment and its soaring cliffs. It also passes the scenic Panorama Gorge, with its feathery waterfall.

Forever Resorts Swadini

On R531. **Tel** (015) 795-5141. ⬜ daily. **www**.foreverswadini.co.za

This resort, set deep in the canyon on the shores of Blydepoort, offers accommodation, a restaurant and a base for boating trips on the dam. The visitors centre and low-level view site have information on the dam and the Kadishi Falls, the world's largest active tufa (calcium carbonate) formation.

Three Rondavels

Resembling the traditional cylindrical huts of the Xhosa or Zulu, these three hills were shaped by the erosion of soft rock beneath a harder rock "cap" that eroded more slowly. The capping of Black Reef quartzite supports a

Bourke's Luck potholes

growth of evergreen bush. The Three Rondavels is one of three sites that can be viewed from the road which overlooks the canyon – the other two are World's End and Lowveld View.

Bourke's Luck

⬜ 7am–5pm daily. 🏞 🄱

Grit and stones carried by the swirling waters at the confluence of the Blyde ("joyful") and Treur ("sad") rivers have carved potholes, from which early prospectors extracted large quantities of gold. Off the R532, Bourke's Luck is the reserve's headquarters, with an information centre.

The Pinnacle, Panorama Route

Panorama Route

The 18-km (11-mile) stretch of the R534 that loops along the top of the cliff, right at the very edge of the escarpment, is a scenic marvel. Wonderview and God's Window may sound like purely fanciful names until one explores the sites and stands in silent awe at the breathtaking scenery.

The Pinnacle

This impressive column of rock, also on the Panorama Route, appears to rise sheer from a base of evergreen foliage. Optical illusions seem to place it almost within reach. Exposed layers of sandstone show the rock's sedimentary origins. It becomes clear that, even at this lofty height above present sea level, the top of the escarpment was once covered by a primordial sea.

Pilgrim's Rest: Alanglade

Palatial by Pilgrim's Rest standards, Alanglade was
occupied by a succession of Transvaal Gold Mining
Estate managers. It is, however, most strongly
associated with its first occupants. Alan and Gladys
Barry moved into the newly built house with their
young family in 1916. Today, the mansion is a
period museum furnished in the Edwardian style,
and seems to await the return of its first owners.

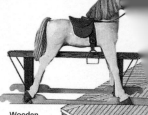

**Wooden
rocking horse**

★ The Kitchen
*The kitchen staff
had to cook for many
people, so the kitchen
includes two pantries,
a larder, scullery and
milk room.*

Electric Bell
*An ingenious bell
system connected to
a numbered, glazed
box informed the
staff in which
room service
was required.*

**Blocks of
local stone** line the
base of the house.

Glazed double doors
separate the rooms and let in light.

Arched windows offset
the entrances from the
rest of the house.

Enclosed Verandahs
*Airy verandahs doubled as sleeping space for the Barry house-
hold, which included seven children and many servants.*

STAR FEATURES

★ The Kitchen

★ Erica's Bedroom

For hotels and restaurants in this region see pp402–4 and pp426–7

Alanglade, built in 1915

VISITORS' CHECKLIST

Pilgrim's Rest. 3 km (2 miles) NE at R533 fork. ☎ (013) 768-1060.
🕐 11am, 2pm daily. Book ahead at Pilgrim's Rest info centre. ♿

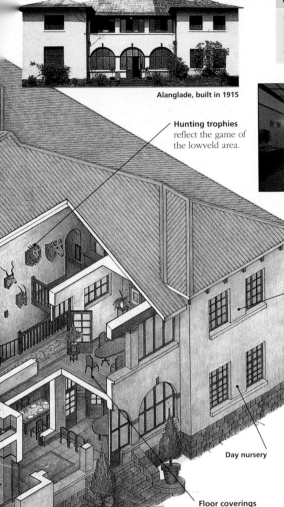

Hunting trophies reflect the game of the lowveld area.

★ Erica's Bedroom
The eldest daughter, Erica, was the only child to have her own bedroom, even though she only visited during school holidays.

Antique Furniture
Museum Services furnished Alanglade with a number of exquisite antiques, such as this rosewood armoire.

Day nursery

Floor coverings consist of woven mats made of coir, grass or sisal fibre.

ALAN BARRY'S LEGACY

On 15 August 1930, Richard Alan Barry, the General Manager of Transvaal Gold Mining Estates Ltd, wrote this diary entry: "Leave Pilgrim's Rest. A very sad parting from work and friends and associates." This, the third Alanglade (the other two were in Johannesburg), had been the family's home for 14 years and had seen a new generation of Barrys grow up. So strong was the association with these first owners that the house is called Alanglade to this day.

Three of the Barry children

The Rose Garden
Only the small rose garden still displays the strict, original period layout of bold lines, geometric patterns and herbaceous borders.

The Kruger National Park ❻

Kruger is South Africa's largest national park, and unquestionably one of the best wildlife sanctuaries in the world. From the Limpopo River in the north to the Crocodile in the south, the park extends for 352 km (220 miles), and averages 60 km (38 miles) from east to west. This vast wilderness covers an area of 19,633 sq km (7,580 sq miles), equivalent in size to Israel. The park has 16 distinct sections, based on the type of vegetation found there.

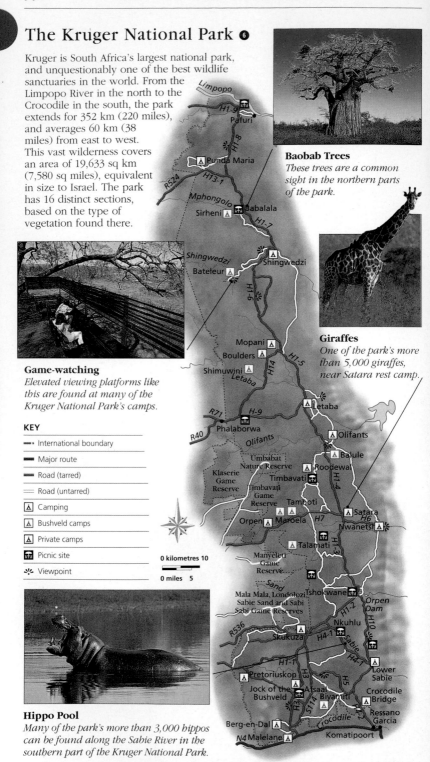

Baobab Trees
These trees are a common sight in the northern parts of the park.

Giraffes
One of the park's more than 5,000 giraffes, near Satara rest camp.

Game-watching
Elevated viewing platforms like this are found at many of the Kruger National Park's camps.

KEY

- **—·** International boundary
- **—** Major route
- **—** Road (tarred)
- **=** Road (untarred)
- **Ⓐ** Camping
- **Ⓐ** Bushveld camps
- **Ⓐ** Private camps
- **⌂** Picnic site
- **✳** Viewpoint

0 kilometres 10

0 miles 5

Hippo Pool
Many of the park's more than 3,000 hippos can be found along the Sabie River in the southern part of the Kruger National Park.

◁ **Zebras and impalas share a drink at one of the Kruger National Park's many waterholes**

Mopane trees and red sand near Punda Maria in northern Kruger

NORTHERN KRUGER

Kruger's semi-arid northern region is an immense, barren wilderness of mopane trees. Several rivers, often little more than sandy courses, sustain some of the park's most intriguing habitats. The north provides sanctuary for large herds of elephants and buffaloes and also hosts antelope species such as sables, roans, elands, Lichtenstein's hartebeests, tsessebes and grysboks.

Punda Maria

The remote northernmost corner of Kruger will appeal to visitors seeking solitude. Punda Maria's huts date back to 1933. The Pafuri picnic spot, at the northern extremity of the park, attracts bird-watchers in pursuit of the exquisite crimson-and-green Narina trogon. Longtailed starlings, crested guinea fowl and white-fronted bee-eaters are also found in this tranquil haven within the park. Wild fig, fever, mahogany, jackalberry and baobab trees border the Luvuvhu River, where nyalas feed quietly in the shade.

Shingwedzi and Mopani

Shingwedzi, 47 km (29 miles) south, offers stunning views over the Shingwedzi River and flood plains, home to some of the biggest elephants in Kruger. In this hot, dry region, the camp's pool gives year-round relief to the elephants. Mopani, 63 km (39 miles) further, is an ideal base from which to explore the area. A network of roads follows both banks of the river, which sustains elephants, nyalas, buffaloes, waterbucks, lions and leopards.

Letaba

Enjoying a commanding position on the south bank of the Letaba River is one of Kruger's finest camps. Chalets are arranged in semi-circles overlooking the river. In the Elephant Hall is a display of tusks from the "Magnificent Seven", believed to be the largest tusks ever found in southern Africa.

CENTRAL KRUGER

Although no major rivers flow across the flat plains of Kruger's central region, the open grassland supports large herds of antelopes and other game. As prey animals are plentiful, half of the park's lions inhabit this region and are regularly sighted. During winter, large herds of impalas, zebras, wildebeests, buffaloes and giraffes gather to drink at the artificial waterholes and dams that have been constructed across sandy riverbeds.

Crested guinea fowl

There are some superb vantage points on the road north from Lower Sabie that overlook the Kruger's dams. Mlondozi Dam has good picnic facilities and a shady terrace overlooking the valley. The very popular Nkumbe lookout point offers unparalleled views over the plains below. The water of Orpen Dam, at the foot of the N'wamuriwa hills, attracts kudu, elephants and giraffes.

Olifants

This attractive camp overlooks the broad floodplain of the Olifants River. This area supports large herds of elephants. Lions antelopes and buffaloes can often be found along the roads that follow the river.

Satara and Orpen

Satara, the second-largest camp, is located in an area where lions are common. Gravel roads along the Sweni, Nw'anetsi and Timbavati rivers offer superb game-viewing. To the west of Satara, Orpen camp is close to the private Timbavati Game Reserve.

Near Satara, zebras and giraffes enjoy fresh grazing after the summer rains

For hotels and restaurants in this region see pp402–4 and pp426–7

Southern Kruger Tour ❼

Although the Southern region covers only about one-fifth of the Kruger National Park's total area, it attracts the most visitors, as it is easily accessible from Gauteng. Three of the five largest camps are found here, and the traffic volume can be high, but it is considered to be the best game-viewing area. It is also a very scenic region, where granite *koppies* (outcrops) punctuate the woodland, and the Sabie River carves a verdant corridor across the plains.

Skukuza ①
The largest camp, able to accommodate around 1,000 visitors, is at the centre of the Kruger's best wildlife-viewing area. Camp facilities include an airport, car-hire service, bank, post office, museum, library, restaurant, shop and bakery.

Nkuhlu Picnic Site ⑤
On the shady banks of the Sabie River, the picnic spot is often visited by monkeys who descend from the trees to snatch food off plates. Fish eagles may be seen, and crocodiles float in the river.

Lower Sabie Road (H4-1) ④
Connecting Skukuza to Lower Sabie, the road closely follows the Sabie River for 43 km (27 miles). It is the most popular road in the park, as there is much wildlife in the area.

Tshokwane Picnic Site ②
A pleasant place for breakfast, lunch or a cup of tea. Tshokwane is located on the old transport wagon trail, cut through the bush in the 1880s. Refreshments can be bought from the kiosk.

0 kilometres 25

0 miles 25

KEY

━ Tour route

═ Other roads

🌼 Viewpoint

Lower Sabie ③
At the modest-sized Lower Sabie camp, many of the chalets survey an expanse of the Sabie River where elephants, buffaloes, hippos, ducks and herons are often seen.

TIPS FOR DRIVERS

Starting point: *From Paul Kruger Gate to Skukuza, Tshokwane and Lower Sabie, and onto the H4-1.*
Length: *100 km (62 miles).*
Getting there: *Take the N4 from Nelspruit, the R538 to Hazyview and R536 to Paul Kruger Gate.*

'rivate Reserves ❽

Along the western boundary of the national park, and bordered by the Sabie and Olifants rivers, a mosaic of private reserves provides a vital buffer between the densely populated areas of Lebowa and Gazankulu and the Kruger. A fence, erected along the park's boundary in the 1960s to prevent the spread of diseased animals, also blocked migration routes. An agreement between all parties made possible its removal, and by 1994 herds were free once again to trek along their ancient paths.

Hippos in the natural pool at Sabi Sand Game Reserve

Exploring the Private Reserves
Luxury lodges, often recipients of international awards for service excellence, offer exclusive "bush experiences" to small groups of visitors. Emphasis is placed on personal attention, and experienced rangers guide visitors on night drives and interesting bush walks.

Sabi Sand Game Reserve
Mpumalanga. *Bookings: Londolozi (011) 280-6640,* **www**.*londolozi. co.za; Mala Mala (011) 442-2267,* **www**.*malamala.com; Sabi Sabi (011) 447-7172,* **www**.*sabisabi.com* ⬤ *restricted access.* 🎨 🍴 *fully incl.* **www**.*sabisand.co.za*
This famous reserve includes the Mala Mala, Londolozi and Sabi Sabi private game reserves and shares a 50-km (31-mile) boundary with Kruger National Park. There are no fences within this area, and animals are free to roam. Thanks to the Sand and Sabie rivers, the area has a rich water supply, which translates into a lush environment that animals enjoy all year round. Sightings of the Big Five are virtually guaranteed, and hyenas, cheetahs and wild dogs may also be seen.

Manyeleti Game Reserve
Mpumalanga. **Tel** *(011) 341-0282.* ⬤ *restricted access.* 🎨 *fully incl.* **www**.*manyeleti.co.za*
This reserve adjoins the Orpen area of the Kruger National Park, known for its varied wildlife. Visitors can stay in the comfortable tented Honeyguide Camp, the luxurious Khoka Moya chalets and other lodges.

Tourists on a game drive

Timbavati Game Reserve
Mpumalanga. **Tel** *bookings for the different lodges: (015) 793-2436.* ⬤ *restricted access.* 🎨 🍴 *fully incl.* **www**.*timbavati.co.za*
This 550-sq-km (210-sq-mile) reserve, adjoining Kruger's central region, has some of the best game-viewing in South Africa. Several lodges, each with access to a different part of the reserve, offer drives and guided walks.
Umlani Bush Camp is situated in the north, while the luxurious Ngala and Tanda Tula lodges lie in the central region. Also renowned is the Gomo Gomo Game Lodge.

Klaserie
Mpumalanga. **Tel** *bookings: Thornybush (011) 253-6500; Maduma Boma Game Conservancy (015) 793-2813,* **www**.*madumaboma.co.za; Gwalagwala Safari Lodge (015) 793-3491.* ⬤ *restricted access.* 🎨 🍴 *fully incl.* **www**.*thornybush.co.za*
Klaserie encompasses many private reserves and is the country's second-largest private sanctuary. It extends over 620 sq km (235 sq miles) and borders on the Kruger National Park, as well as on the Olifants River.
The Klaserie River meanders across the semi-arid bushveld as the reserve's central focus as countless animals and birds gather on its banks to drink. Klaserie's bushcamps and lodges are firm favourites with visitors.

A luxurious lounge at Mala Mala Lodge, within Sabi Sand Game Reserve

Swaziland ❾

Traditional Swazi hut at Mlilwane

The kingdom of Swaziland achieved its independence from Britain on 6 September 1968. King Mswati III has ruled the almost one million Swazis since 1986. In the west of the country, the highlands offer many opportunities for hikers. The middleveld has the perfect growing conditions for tropical fruit and is known for its arts and crafts. In the east, lush sugar cane plantations contrast with the dense brown bushveld of game reserves and ranches.

★ Mbabane

Swaziland's capital city developed around the site where Michael Wells opened a pub and trading post at a river crossing in 1888. Today, trade is brisk at the Swazi Market.

★ Mlilwane Wildlife Sanctuary

Mlilwane, which supports white rhinos, giraffes, zebras and antelopes, covers 45 sq km (17 sq miles). The rest camp's Hippo Haunt restaurant overlooks a hippo pool.

STAR SIGHTS

- ★ Mlilwane Wildlife Sanctuary
- ★ Mbabane
- ★ Peak Craft Center, Piggs Peak
- ★ Hlane Royal National Park

Manzini
Swaziland's biggest town is situated close to the airport. An industrial centre, it also has colourful markets that sell fresh produce, crafts and fabric.

For hotels and restaurants in this region see pp402–4 and pp426–7

★ **Peak Craft Center, Piggs Peak**
Local artists display their craft on the road leading to a casino hotel further north.

Phopanyane Lodge and Nature Reserve is privately owned. The sub-tropical vegetation attracts many birds.

Malolotja Nature Reserve
Ngwenya, in the reserve, is the oldest mine in the world. Specularite and haematite, used for cosmetics, were excavated here 43,000 years ago. From here there are spectacular views over the countryside.

At Big Bend, near the Lubombo Mountains, sugar cane thrives along the Lusutfu River.

0 kilometres 20
0 miles 10

★ **Hlane Royal National Park**
Hlane and the adjacent Mlawula Reserve protect 370 sq km (143 sq miles) of dense woodland and the Lubombo Mountains. Elephants, white rhinos, antelopes, hippos and giraffes can be seen. Lions and cheetahs are kept in separate camps. Guided walking safaris can be arranged on request.

KEY

‑ ‑ International boundary
- - Provincial boundary
▬ Major route
▬ Road (tarred)
═ Road (untarred)

▲ Camping
🛶 Canoeing, rafting
🚶 Hiking, walking
🔆 Viewpoint
ℹ Tourist information

THE ARID
INTERIOR

Introducing the Arid Interior

The semi-arid, sparsely populated Karoo extends across the Northern Cape and parts of the Free State, Eastern and Western Cape provinces. Sleepy country towns and villages, often treasure chests of Cape Dutch and Victorian architecture, serve as supply centres for surrounding farms. North of the Orange River lie the red dunes of the Kalahari Desert, one of South Africa's finest wilderness areas. A rich assortment of wildlife inhabits this remote territory. In the Northern Cape, the most famous diamond mines in the world extract shining riches from the earth.

The Ai-Ais Richtersveld Transfrontier Park *is a bleak moonscape with curious flora such as the* kokerboom *(quiver tree), from which Khoi hunters made arrows.*

Ai-Ais Richtersveld Transfrontier Park

Upington

SOUTH OF THE ORANGE
(See pp352–63)

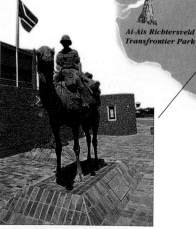

The Camel Rider Statue *in Upington honours the memory of the policemen and their tireless mounts who patrolled the Kalahari in the early 20th century.*

◁ A *kokerboom* (quiver tree) in the barren semi-desert of the Augrabies Falls National Park

Kimberley's diamond mines, *once owned by De Beers Mining Company, are nowadays controlled by the Anglo-American Corporation. Impressive headgear dominates the skyline on the outskirts, while in the town itself lie many beautiful historic buildings, like the City Hall.*

Bloemfontein's Civic Centre, *a tall modern structure of glass and concrete, represents a bold departure from the traditional, stately sandstone buildings in the town.*

NORTH OF
THE ORANGE
(See pp364–73)

Kimberley

Bloemfontein

The Gariep Dam *is the largest water project on the Orange River and has become a popular weekend resort.*

Gariep Dam

Nieu-Bethesda

Nieu-Bethesda's *quaint Dutch Reformed Church was completed in 1905. The main drawcard of this little Karoo town, however, is the bizarre Owl House.*

```
0 kilometres        100

0 miles        50
```

Life in the Desert

Velvet mite

The Kalahari Desert forms part of a vast inland steppe that stretches from the Orange River to the equator. It extends across portions of the Northern Cape and Namibia, and also covers much of Botswana. Rainfall in this region varies from 150–400 mm (6–16 in) per year and is soon soaked up or simply evaporates. There is little surface water and the flora consists mainly of grass, shrubs and the hardy camelthorn acacias that line the dry beds of ancient rivers. Although the landscape may appear to be lifeless, it supports an astonishing variety of wildlife that is superbly adapted to survive in this harsh environment.

Seasonal river beds, *such as that of the Auob, carry water only every few years, usually after exceptionally heavy downpours.*

The quiver contains arrows poisoned with the juice of beetle larvae.

The *Gemsbok* (oryx) *feeds on grass, leaves and roots, and can do without water. The animal's temperature fluctuates in response to climatic changes: during the day it may soar to above 45°C (113°F).*

Kalahari lions *are unique to the Kgalagadi Transfrontier Park, and have learned to depend on smaller prey, taking porcupines and bat-eared foxes when antelopes migrate.*

Bat-eared foxes' *large ears allow them to detect underground prey, such as harvester termites and beetle larvae, in the barren areas.*

The brown hyena *is primarily a scavenger, but also eats wild fruit, beetles, termites, birds' eggs and small animals. Restricted to the drier desert regions of southern Africa, it can survive without fresh water for extended periods of time.*

The Tsama melon's *bitter-tasting flesh is eaten by Bushmen and animals, as it is a vital source of vitamin C and moisture.*

Steppe buzzards *are one of the many raptor species that can be seen in the Kalahari. Migrant visitors, they arrive in southern Africa during October and depart in March.*

Namaqua sandgrouse *males fly distances of up to 60 km (37 miles) every three to five days to drink and to soak their specially adapted chest feathers. The water retained in these feathers sustains the chicks.*

Digging sticks are used to unearth a variety of edible and water-bearing roots and tubers.

Ostrich eggs are a source of moisture and protein.

The puff adder *is highly poisonous and bites readily when threatened. The snake propels itself forward leaving deep, straight tracks which can sometimes be seen on the Kalahari sand dunes.*

THE BUSHMEN

These nomads have all but vanished from the subcontinent. A small band lives on land south of the Kgalagadi Transfrontier Park allocated to them in 1997. The modern age has severely affected their culture. Even in the remote reaches of Botswana, clans now live in settlements around waterholes – the nomadic lifestyle replaced by a sedentary existence. Before these camps were established, water and food were obtained from the bush: the Bushmen knew of 20 edible insects and 180 plants, roots and tubers.

Barking geckos *herald sunset in the desert by emitting a series of sharp clicking sounds. When threatened, they tend to freeze, camouflaged against the red sand.*

The *Sparrmannia flava* *scarab has a furry coat which enables it to remain active at night when temperatures can drop drastically.*

Windmills *pump precious water from below the surface into metal reservoirs. Farming activities in the Kalahari region include Karakul sheep, goat and wildlife rearing, while hardy Afrikander cattle only survive where a water supply is assured.*

The Orange River

South Africa is predominantly a dry country, with precipitation decreasing from east to west and only 8 per cent of rainfall reaching the few major rivers. The mighty Orange and its tributaries drain 47 per cent of the country. For much of the 2,450-km (1,530-mile) long journey from its source in northeast Lesotho to the Atlantic Ocean, the Orange meanders across the arid plains of the Northern Cape. Here, wooden wheels draw the precious water from canals to sustain a narrow, fertile corridor of vineyards, date palms, lucerne and cotton fields, tightly wedged between the river and the unrelenting desert.

Quiver tree

The Ai-Ais Richtersveld Transfrontier Park *is located in a jagged, mountainous landscape where water is scarce. The hardy vegetation relies on the early morning fog that rolls in from the Atlantic.*

Alexander Bay *is the site of large-scale diamond dredging operations. The nearby Orange River estuary is a wetland renowned for its splendid birdlife.*

The Fish River Canyon lies across the Namibian border.

Rosh Pinah
Ai-Ais Richtersveld Transfrontier Park
Restricted Access
Ai-Ais Richtersveld Transfrontier Park
Khubus
Oranjemund
Alexander Bay
Noordoewer
Vioolsdrif
Goodhouse
Haib
B1
N7
Brak
Hom
Wa
R382

0 kilometres   50
0 miles   25

Orange River canoe trips (see p434) *have become increasingly popular since the 1990s. Several Cape Town-based adventure companies offer exciting canoeing and rafting tours that include camping along the river banks.*

Augrabies Falls, *christened Aukoerebis ("place of great noise") by the early Khoi inhabitants of this region, is where the Orange River plunges 56 m (182 ft) into a constricted granite gorge. The falls and surrounding area were declared a national park in 1966.*

Onseepkans, a small settlement and border post, serves as a departure point for canoe trips down the Orange River.

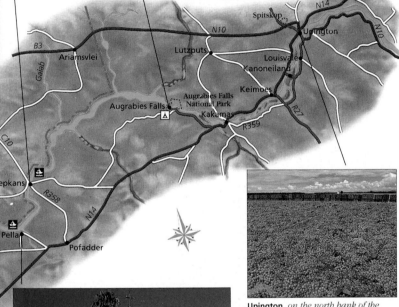

Upington, *on the north bank of the Orange River, is the largest town along its course. As it is an important centre for the dried fruit industry, sultanas drying in the sun are a common sight along the road. The municipal resort, on an island in the river, is a popular stop-over.*

Pella Mission, *with its rows of date palms and the tall spire of its Catholic church, exudes a distinctly Mexican ambience. The church was built by two missionaries whose only building manual was an encyclopaedia.*

KEY

—·—	International boundary
▬	Major route
▬	Road (tarred)
═	Road (untarred)
▲	Camping
⚑	Canoeing / rafting

SOUTH OF THE ORANGE

Vast and unrelenting, the great Karoo is a uniquely South African landscape of dolerite outcrops, buttes and endless plains. In restful towns and villages the harshness of the terrain is softened by the large, low, sandstone homesteads, typical of Karoo architecture. Since the 1970s, several nature reserves have been established to conserve the territory's fascinating wildlife.

The indigenous Khoi called the region *Karoo* ("land of great thirst") and the Dutch colonists of the 17th century were hesitant to venture into this forbidding terrain. Ensign Schrijver was the first European to explore the eastern reaches of the Karoo in 1689, and by 1795 the Cape Colony had expanded to include the southern and eastern Karoo regions. The vast plains were partitioned into sheep ranches, and large migrating herds of springbucks, hartebeests, black wildebeests, elands and quaggas were decimated through uncontrolled hunting. Some 80 years later, the quagga was extinct, and the large herds of Cape mountain zebras and black wildebeests had been reduced to tiny remnant populations.

With the expanding frontier, several new towns were established. Graaff-Reinet, founded in 1786, prospered quickly as it became an important centre for the surround-ing community of sheep farmers. Today, it has the highest number of national monuments in South Africa and is renowned for its Cape Dutch architecture. Elsewhere, the typical Karoo vernacular includes steep-roofed sandstone farm houses surrounded by broad verandahs and delicate latticework.

The Camdeboo National Park surrounds Graaff-Reinet on three sides, while the Karoo National Park lies just north of Beaufort West. The Mountain Zebra National Park, near Cradock, is credited with saving the Cape mountain zebra from extinction. In the eastern Karoo, where South Africa's largest water project, the Gariep Dam on the Orange River, provides water to the drought-prone Eastern Cape, many water-based resorts have sprung up.

A fiery show of low-growing *vygies,* drought-resistant plants that flower only after it has rained

◁ The windpump silhouetted against a glowing sky is the unofficial emblem of this arid region

Exploring South of the Orange

The Karoo is a region of endless vistas and clear blue skies, where the road runs straight as an arrow to the distant horizon. Large sheep farms produce much of South Africa's mutton and wool. Steel windmills, standing in the blazing sun, supply the area's life-blood: water. Only 70 small towns and villages, of which Beaufort West is the largest, cling tenaciously to the drought-prone land. Many of them, for example Graaff-Reinet, are architectural treasure chests. At Beaufort West, Graaff-Reinet and Cradock, nature parks conserve the characteristic landscape, fauna and flora of the region.

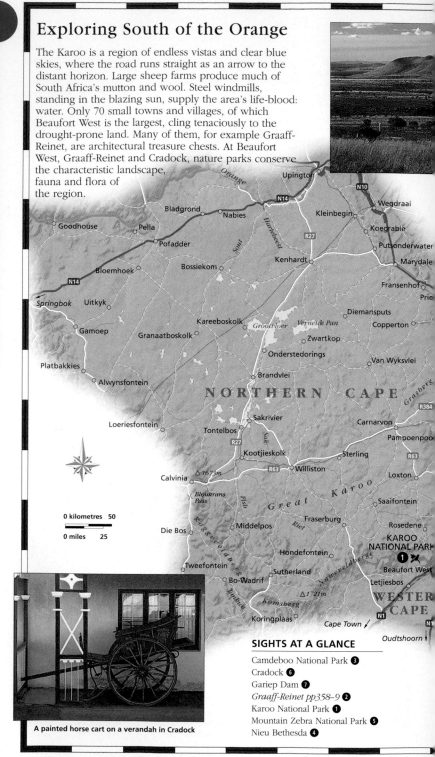

A painted horse cart on a verandah in Cradock

SIGHTS AT A GLANCE

GETTING AROUND

The N1 national route that links Cape Town and Johannesburg passes right through Beaufort West. The N9, which connects Graaff-Reinet to the Southern Cape coast, branches off the N1 at Colesberg. Cradock and the nearby Mountain Zebra National Park to the west of the town are located on the N10. Tarred provincial roads connect most of the smaller villages, allowing visitors to explore the more remote parts of the region. Although distances are great, traffic volumes are moderate and many of the Karoo towns have comfortable bed-and-breakfast establishments and restaurants. The long-distance bus companies stop in Beaufort West, Graaff-Reinet and Cradock.

Ostrich in the Mountain Zebra National Park

The Drostdy in Graaff-Reinet, a typical example of a Cape Dutch-style magistrate's office

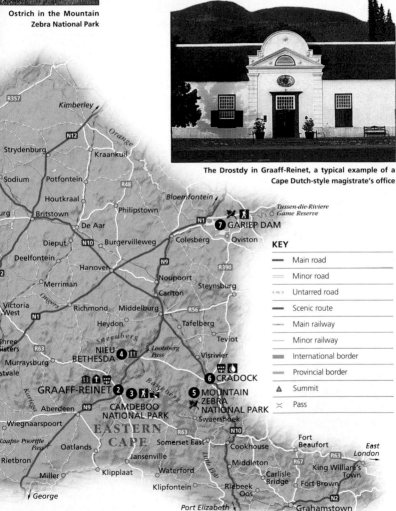

KEY

———	Main road
=====	Minor road
= = =	Untarred road
———	Scenic route
—+—	Main railway
———	Minor railway
▬▬▬	International border
▬▬▬	Provincial border
▲	Summit
✕	Pass

SEE ALSO

Karoo National Park ❶

Road map C4. N1, 7 km (4 miles)
S of Beaufort West. ⓘ (023) 415-
2828. **Tel** Reservations: (012) 428-
9111. ◯ 5am–10pm daily. 🅿 ♿
🍴 🚶 www.sanparks.org

The Karoo National Park was
established on the outskirts
of Beaufort West in 1979, to
conserve a representative
sample of the region's unique
heritage. It has been enlarged
over the years and now encompasses vast, flat plains as
well as the rugged Nuweveld
Mountains. Animals such as
mountain reedbucks, grey rheboks, kudu, steenboks, jackals
and aardwolves occur naturally,
while reintroduced species
include springboks, hartebeests, gemsboks (oryxes),
black wildebeests (gnus), Cape
mountain zebras and the
endangered black rhinos and
riverine rabbits. Some 196 bird
species have been recorded,
and the park also sustains
more than 20 black eagle pairs.
   A comfortable rest camp is
set at the base of the Nuweveld Mountains. Its spacious
Cape Dutch chalets provide
a convenient overnight stop
that is easily accessible from
the N1. The camp has a shop,
swimming pool, restaurant and
caravan park. Nearby, the
historic Ou Skuur Farmhouse
contains the park's information

Springbok once roamed the Karoo plains in their thousands

centre. A 4WD trail has been
laid out in the rugged western
region of the park, and night
drives provide the very best
chances of seeing many of
the region's shy nocturnal
animals, such as the aardwolf.
   The short Fossil and Bossie
trails are accessible from the
rest camp and allow visitors
to learn about the Karoo's
fascinating 250-million-year-
old geological history and its
unique vegetation. The Fossil
Trail accommodates wheel-
chairs and incorporates Braille
boards. An easy circular day
hike of 11 km (7 miles) is also
accessible from the rest camp.

Graaff-Reinet ❷

See pp358–9.

Camdeboo National Park ❸

Road map C4. R63, 8 km (5 miles)
NW of Graaff-Reinet. ⓘ (049) 892-
3453. **Tel** Reservations: (012) 428-
9111. ◯ 6am–6pm (Oct–Mar: to
7pm). www.sanparks.org

In a bid to conserve typical
Karoo landforms and wild-
life, an area of 145 sq km
(56 sq miles) around Graaff-
Reinet (see pp358–9) was set
aside. West of the town is the
Valley of Desolation, where
spectacular columns of weathered dolerite tower 120 m
(390 ft) over the valley floor.
   A 14-km (9-mile) road leads
to a view site and a short walk,
while the circular day hike is
reached from the Berg-en-dal
gate on the western edge of
town. A two- to three-day hike
explores the scenic mountainous terrain in the southeast.
   The eastern region of the
nature reserve includes the
Driekoppe peaks, which rise
600 m (1,950 ft) above the
plains. This section sustains
more than 220 species of bird.
The population of Cape mountain zebras, buffaloes, hartebeests, springboks, kudus and
blesboks is expanding, and
many of them may be seen.
   There are game-viewing
roads and picnic sites around
the Van Ryneveld's Pass Dam
in the centre of the reserve,
and both boating and fishing
are permitted.

The Valley of Desolation in the Camdeboo National Park

The back yard of the Owl House is populated with many strange figures

Nieu Bethesda ④

Road map C4. 50 km (31 miles) N of Graaff-Reinet. 🏘 950. 🍴 Karoo Lamb Restaurant, New St, (049) 841-1642. www.nieubethesda.co.za

The turn-off to this village lies on the N9, 27 km (17 miles) north of Graaff-Reinet. From there, a good dirt road traverses the Voor Sneeuberg ("in front of snow mountain") and leads to Nieu Bethesda.

The Kompasberg (Compass Peak), at 2,502 m (8,131 ft), is the highest point in the Sneeuberg range. It received its name in 1778 when Cape Governor Baron van Plettenberg, accompanied by Colonel Jacob Gordon, visited the mountain and noted that the surrounding countryside could be surveyed from its summit.

Nieu Bethesda was founded by Reverend Charles Murray, minister of the Dutch Reformed Church in Graaff-Reinet. The fertile valley in the arid terrain reminded him of the Pool of Bethesda (John 5:2), and so he named the town after it.

In 1875 he acquired a farm in the valley and by 1905 the church (now in Parsonage Street) was completed. It cost £5,600 to build, but at the time of its consecration two-thirds of the amount was still outstanding. To raise funds, arable church land was divided into plots and sold at a public auction. The debt was finally settled in 1929.

Today, Martin Street, the quaint main road, is lined with pear trees, and many of the bordering properties are framed by quince hedges. Irrigated fields and golden poplar trees complement and soften the rugged Karoo mountains, which create a bold contrast.

Pienaar Street crosses over the Gat River to its western bank, and passes an old water mill that was built in 1860 by the owner of the original farm, Uitkyk. The first water wheel was made of wood, but was later replaced with the existing steel wheel.

The peaceful village has attracted much artistic talent, including one of South Africa's leading playwrights, Athol Fugard, who achieved world acclaim for his thought-provoking plays such as Master Harold and the Boys (see p248).

🏛 The Owl House

River St. ◯ 9am–5pm daily. Tel (049) 841-1603. 🖳 www.owlhouse.co.za

The Owl House is considered one of South Africa's top 50 heritage sites. Its garden is cluttered with an intriguing assembly of concrete statues: owls, sheep, camels, people,

Owl statue

sphinxes and religious symbols, created over more than 30 years by Helen Martins and her assistant, Koos Malgas. The walls, doors and ceilings of the house are decorated with finely ground coloured glass. Mirrors reflect the light from candles and lamps. Her work, unusual in its quantity and range of subject, has been classified as "Outsider Art" (art that falls outside the artistic mainstream as a result of isolation or insanity) and "Naïve" (an expression of innocence and fantasy).

HELEN MARTINS (1897–1976)

Born in Nieu Bethesda on 23 December 1897, Helen left home to study at a teachers' training college in Graaff-Reinet, and later married a young diplomat. The relationship did not last. Neither did a second marriage, and Helen returned home to nurse her irascible, elderly father. After his death, the naturally retiring woman retreated increasingly into her own fantasy world, and began to populate her garden with bizarre figures, an expression of her personal, mythical universe. In later years her eyesight began to fail due to having worked with ground glass over a long period of time. In August 1976, aged 78, she committed suicide by drinking a lethal dose of caustic soda. As an artist she remains an enigma.

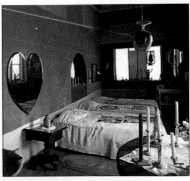

The bedroom with its "wallpaper" of ground glass

Street-by-Street: Graaff-Reinet ❷

Display in Urquhart House

In 1786 a *landdrost* (magistrate) was appointed by the Dutch East India Company to enforce Dutch law and administration along the remote eastern Karoo frontier. The settlement that grew up around the magistrate's court was named after Governor Cornelis Jacob van de Graaff and his wife, Hester Cornelia Reinet. Nine years later, the citizens of Graaff-Reinet expelled the *landdrost* and declared the first Boer Republic in South Africa. Within a matter of a few months, however, colonial control was re-established.

The War Memorial
The memorial honours the fallen of both World Wars.

Huguenot Monument

PARK STREET

Town Hall

Valley of Desolation

Spandau Kop

NORTH STREET

CALEDON STREET

CHURCH STREET

SOMERSET STREET

PARLIAMENT STREET

STRETCH'S COURT

Dutch Reformed Church
The beautiful Groot Kerk *(great church), completed in 1887, was constructed using two different types of local stone.*

The South African War Memorial
This monument, unveiled in 1908, commemorates the efforts of Boer soldiers against the British troops.

0 metres 100
0 yards 100

KEY
- - - Suggested route

★ Stretch's Court
These cottages were built in the 1850s to house labourers and freed slaves.

STAR SIGHTS
★ Stretch's Court
★ Reinet House
★ The Old Residency

Spandau Kop looms over the town

VISITORS' CHECKLIST

Road map C4. 63,000.
Port Elizabeth, 236 km (147 miles)
SE. Kudu Motors, Church St.
Graaff-Reinet Tourism Office
(049) 892-4248. 8am–5pm
Mon–Fri, 9am–noon Sat. **Reinet
House Tel** (049) 892-3801.
8am–4:30pm Mon–Fri,
9am–1pm Sat & Sun.
www.graaffreinet.co.za

Exploring Graaff-Reinet

Graaff-Reinet lies in a valley eroded by the Sundays River. The gardens and tree-lined avenues form a striking contrast to the bleak expanse of the surrounding Karoo. Many of the town's historic buildings have been painstakingly restored, and over 200 of them have been declared national monuments. The main architectural attractions lie between Bourke and Murray streets.

Dutch Reformed Church

This beautiful church is considered to be the finest example of Gothic architecture in the country. Completed in 1887, it was modelled on Salisbury Cathedral.

Stretch's Court

In 1855 Captain Charles Stretch bought land near the Drostdy for his labourers. Restored in 1977, the cottages are now an annexe of the Drostdy Hotel.

Old Library Museum

Church St. **Tel** (049) 892-3801.
8am–1pm, 1:45–4:30pm Mon–
Fri, 9am–1pm Sat & Sun.
Completed in 1847, this building displays Karoo fossils, historic photographs and reproductions of rock art.

Hester Rupert Gallery

Church St. **Tel** (049) 892-2121.
9am–12:30pm, 2–5pm Mon–Fri,
9am–noon Sat & Sun.
This former Dutch Reformed Mission Church displays works by contemporary South African artists, among them Irma Stern and Cecil Skotnes *(see p372)*.

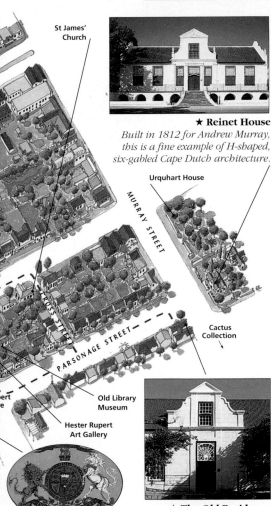

St James'
Church

MURRAY STREET

Urquhart House

CROSS STREET

PARSONAGE STREET

Cactus
Collection

pert
re

Old Library
Museum

Hester Rupert
Art Gallery

★ Reinet House
*Built in 1812 for Andrew Murray,
this is a fine example of H-shaped,
six-gabled Cape Dutch architecture.*

The Drostdy
*Heraldic detail on a plaque
at the Drostdy (magistrate's
court), a building designed
by French architect Louis
Michel Thibault in 1804.*

★ The Old Residency
*This imposing, gabled Cape
Dutch manor was completed
in the 1820s, and the
original fanlight can still
be seen above the front
door. Today the manor is
an annexe of Reinet House.*

The Dutch Reformed Church

A Cape mountain zebra in the Mountain Zebra National Park

Mountain Zebra National Park ❺

Road map D4. 26 km (16 miles) W of Cradock. **Tel** Park: (048) 881-2427; reservations: (012) 428-9111. ⬜ 7am–6pm May–Sep; 7am–7pm Oct–Apr. ♿ ⚒ 🚶 🅿 🍴 🚻
www.sanparks.org

While the national park west of Cradock is the second-smallest in the country, its modest acreage in no way detracts from the visitor's enjoyment. It was originally conceived as a sanctuary that was intended to rescue the Cape mountain zebra from imminent extinction. When the park was proclaimed in 1937, there were six zebras; by 1949 only two remained. Conservation efforts were successful, however, and the park now protects about 300 zebras. Several breeding herds have been relocated to other parks, but the Cape mountain zebra still remains rare. Also to be seen are springboks, hartebeests, elands, mountain reedbucks and black wildebeests. Black rhinos have also been re-introduced.

The rest camp, which overlooks a valley, consists of chalets, a caravan park, a restaurant, shop and information centre. A short walk leads past the chalets to the swimming pool set at the base of a granite ridge.

For convenience, the park can be divided into two sections. From the camp, a circular drive of 28 km (18 miles) explores the wooded Wilgeboom Valley, noted for its rugged granite land forms. The road passes the Doornhoek Cottage where *The Story of an African Farm* was filmed, and leads to a shady picnic site at the base of the mountains. The northern loop, which starts just before Wilgeboom, climbs steeply to the Rooiplaat Plateau, and offers splendid views across the vast Karoo where most of the park's wildlife congregates. The early mornings and late afternoons are the best times to visit the area. Alternatively, a three-day circular hike explores the southern part of the park, where the granite Bankberg mountains are at their most spectacular.

Cradock ❻

Road map D4. 🏘 20,000. 🚉 Church St. 🚌 Struwig Motors, Voortrekker St. 🛈 JA Calata St, (048) 801-5000. ⬜ Mon–Fri. **www.**cradocktourism.co.za

In 1812, towards the end of the Fourth Frontier War, Sir John Cradock established two military outposts to secure the eastern border. One was at Grahamstown, the other at Cradock. Merino sheep flourished in this region, and Cradock soon developed into a sheep-farming centre. The Dutch Reformed Church was inspired by London's St Martin's-in-the-Fields. Completed in 1867, it dominates the town's central square. The **Great Fish River Museum** behind the town hall preserves the history of the early pioneers. In Market Street, **Die Tuishuise** (*see p405*) is the result of an innovative project to restore a series of 14 mid-19th-century houses and create comfortable bed-and-breakfast establishments. Each portrays the architectural style of a particular era.

The Dutch Reformed Church in Cradock

About 5 km (3 miles) north of town, the **Cradock Spa** is renowned for its indoor and outdoor swimming pools that are fed by hot sulphur springs.

🏛 **Great Fish River Museum**
87 High St. **Tel** (048) 881-4509. ⬜ 8am–4pm Mon–Fri, 8am–noon Sat. ♿

OLIVE EMILIE SCHREINER (1855–1920)

The Story of an African Farm is widely regarded as the first South African novel of note. Olive Schreiner began writing while she worked as a governess on farms in the Cradock district. The manuscript was released in 1883 under the male pseudonym Ralph Iron, and was an immediate success. Schreiner, an active campaigner for women's equality and a supporter of "Native" rights, wrote extensively on politics. She died in Wynberg (Cape Town) in 1920. Her husband, Samuel Cronwright-Schreiner, buried her on Buffelskop, 24 km (15 miles) south of Cradock, beside their daughter who had died 25 years earlier just 18 hours after her birth, and Olive's dog.

Olive Schreiner

Cottages with striped awnings and painted *stoeps* (verandahs) line the streets of Cradock

🔥 Cradock Spa
Marlow Rd. *Tel* (048) 881-2709.
🔲 6:45am–7:30pm daily. 📷

Gariep Dam ❼

Road map D4. NE of Colesberg
on R701. 🏨 *De Stijl Gariep Hotel,*
(051) 754-0060. 📷 🚶 ♿ 🅿️

The Orange River is South
Africa's largest and longest
river. Together with its tributaries (excluding the Vaal
River), it drains a total of
one-third of the country.

In 1779, when Colonel
Robert Gordon reached the
banks of a watercourse that
was known to the Khoina as
Gariep, he renamed it the
Orange River, in honour of
the Dutch Prince of Orange.
Little did he know that a dam
would be constructed at this
point nearly 200 years later.

In 1928 Dr AD Lewis
advanced the idea of building
a tunnel linking the Orange
River to the Eastern Cape.
Although a report was presented to the government in
1948, it was only in 1962 that
then prime minister Hendrik
Verwoerd gave the ambitious
project the go-ahead. Work
began in 1966 and in September 1970 the last gap in the
wall was closed. The Gariep
is South Africa's largest body
of water. The dam wall rises
90 m (297 ft) above its foundations and has a crest length
of 948 m (3,110 ft). At full
supply level it covers an area
of 374 sq km (144 sq miles).

At Oviston, midway along
the shoreline, the Orange-
Fish Tunnel diverts water
along a stretch of 83 km
(52 miles) to the headwaters
of the Great Fish River near
Steynsburg. This tunnel,
completed in 1975, is the
second-longest water conduit
in the world. With a diameter
of 5 m (17 ft), it can divert
one-quarter of the Orange
River's water flow.

A corridor of bushveld
surrounds the Gariep Dam,
and the land that lies between
the Caledon and the Orange
rivers has been developed
into three beautiful nature
reserves with a combined
area of 452 sq km (174 sq
miles). Springboks, blesboks
and the rare Cape mountain
zebra and black wildebeest
have been successfully
re-introduced here.

The **Forever Resorts Gariep**,
at the dam wall, offers
comfortable chalets, a campsite and a range of activities
such as trampolining, golf
(with own equipment), fishing
and swimming. There are also
tours of the dam wall. At the
headwaters of the dam, a
game reserve, **Tussen-die-
Riviere** ("between the rivers"),
supports herds of springboks,
black wildebeests, hartebeests,
elands, gemsboks, zebras and
white rhinos. Chalets overlook
the confluence of the rivers,
and hiking trails explore the
eastern half of the reserve.

🏕️ Forever Resorts Gariep
Gariep Dam. *Tel* (051) 754-0045.
🔲 daily (day visitors must call
ahead). 📷 🍴 🚶 ♿ 🚣 🅿️

🦌 Tussen-die-Riviere
Gariep Dam. *Tel* (051) 763-1000.
🔲 daily. 📷 📷 🚶 🅿️

Chalets built on the water's edge at the Gariep Dam

Ancient mountains provide a dramatic backdrop to the guest cottages in the Karoo National Park ▷

NORTH OF THE ORANGE

T*he red dunes of the Kalahari Desert stretch north of the Orange River like the waves of an inland sea. Three mountain ranges break the monotony until the dunes give way, at last, to the grasslands of the Highveld plateau. In this remote wilderness, oasis-like towns such as Upington welcome the traveller, and in a narrow band along the river, vineyards produce sultana grapes and fine wines.*

At the beginning of the 19th century, the uncharted Northern Cape was home to the last nomadic hunter-gatherers, the San Bushmen. In 1820, Robert and Mary Moffat built a mission and school in Kuruman, 263 km (163 miles) northeast of Upington, and devoted 50 years to translating and printing the Bible in the Setswana language. The journeys of exploration undertaken by their son-in-law, David Livingstone, focused European attention on Africa.

In the Cape Colony Afrikaner farmers became increasingly discontented with the British administration; many trekked north in search of new land. In 1836, a group of Voortrekkers *(see pp50–51)* crossed the Orange River and settled near Thaba Nchu, east of the present-day Bloemfontein, where they established an independent republic, the Orange Free State, in 1854.

The discovery of diamonds in 1866 transformed South Africa's economy. At the town of Kimberley, countless fortune-seekers carved out the Big Hole, an enormous crater that had yielded a total of 2,722 kg (5,988 lb) of diamonds by the time work stopped in 1914.

Further west along the Orange River, a local Griqua leader invited early missionary Reverend Christiaan Schröder to establish a mission station on the banks of the river, and the town of Upington was founded. Irrigation canals soon transformed the desert into a fertile crescent of vineyards, orchards, wheat and lucerne fields.

Although mining is still the main contributor to the region's economy, today visitors are enticed by the area's history, desert scenery and diverse wildlife, such as various raptor species and the unique Kalahari lion.

Suricates, or slender-tailed meerkats, live in closely knit family groups

◁ A *halfmens (Pachypodium namaquanum)*, or half-human, stands out over misty Richtersveld plains

Exploring North of the Orange

Upington is the perfect base for exploring South Africa's last frontier: the red-dune wilderness bordering the Kalahari Desert. Although no permanent rivers have flowed across this ancient landscape for thousands of years and grass-covered dunes seem to stretch to infinity, wildlife is abundant. Kimberley was once the scene of the world's greatest diamond rush and retains many reminders of its frenetic heyday. Driving eastward, annual rainfall increases. The grasslands of the Free State support cattle and sheep, as well as fields of sunflowers and maize. Historic Bloemfontein, once the capital of a Boer republic named Orange Free State, has many superb old buildings.

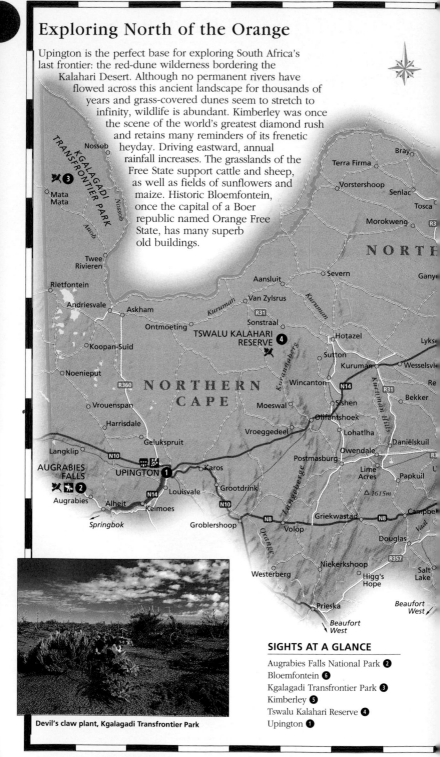

Devil's claw plant, Kgalagadi Transfrontier Park

SIGHTS AT A GLANCE

Augrabies Falls National Park **2**
Bloemfontein **6**
Kgalagadi Transfrontier Park **3**
Kimberley **5**
Tswalu Kalahari Reserve **4**
Upington **1**

KEY

━━ Major road

═══ Minor road

═‑‑ Untarred road

━━ Scenic route

━━ Main railway

── Minor railway

━━ International border

━━ Provincial border

▲ Summit

Gemsbokvlakte

0 kilometres 50

iet Plessis

0 miles 25

VEST

Stella Kameel

Tshwane/Pretoria

R49

Broederput

Vyburg

Migdol

N14

Schweizer-Reneke

Johannesburg

Amalia

Pudimoe Avondster

Kingswood

Bloemhof

N12

Haans

Hartswater

Bloemhof
Dam

R49

Vaal

Jan
Kempdorp

Christiana

Hoopstad

Mount
Rupert

Warrenton

Hertzogville

R700

R59

Bultfontein

FREE STATE

Barkly West Boshof

R700

Kroonstad

5 KIMBERLEY

Dealesville

Brandfort

Wolwespruit

R64

Florisbad

N1

Modder

Soetdoring Nature Reserve

Modderrivier

Petrusburg

2

Jacobsdal

N8

De Brug

6 BLOEMFONTEIN

Riet

aspan

Koffiefontein

Ferreira

N8

Riet

Maseru

Rooipan

Kalkfontein Dam
Nature Reserve

N6

Dewetsdorp

Luckhof

Reddersburg

nia

Fauresmith

Edenburg

Aliwal North

Vanderkloof

Vanderkloof
Dam

Trompsburg

N1

Philippolis

Orange

Donkerpoort

Graaff-Reinet

The Big Hole in Kimberley, begun in the 1870s

GETTING AROUND

Most of the towns north of the Orange River lie more than
200 km (125 miles) apart, and there are few petrol stations or
refreshment stops along the way. But as traffic volumes are low
and all the main roads are tarred, travel in this region need
not be arduous. The R360 runs north from Upington to the
Kgalagadi Transfrontier Park. Although the roads in the park are
sandy, 4WD vehicles are not required. National roads link the
major regional centres to Johannesburg and to the Western
and Eastern capes. The east-west N8 connects Upington,
Kimberley and Bloemfontein. There are regional airports
in all three centres, and long-distance coaches provide
links to other towns.

SEE ALSO

• *Where to Stay* p405

• *Where to Eat* p427

Sunflowers constitute one of the Free
State's major crops

The Reverend Christiaan Schröder's cottage in Upington

Upington ❶

Road map B3. 🏚 76,000.
✈ 7 km (4 miles) NE of town.
🚉 🚌 Upington station. 🛈 Schröder
St, (054) 332-6064. ☐ Mon–Sat.
www.greenkalahari.co.za

Upington lies in a vast plain dotted with low shrubs. Only where the road reaches the Orange River does the landscape change abruptly, as the river paints a green stripe across the barren territory.

The Northern Cape's second-largest town after Kimberley, Upington serves a district of lucerne, cotton, fruit and wine farms lining a fertile corridor on the river.

In the late 19th century the Northern Cape was a wild frontier. The nomadic bands of Khoina hunter-gatherers resented the intrusion of the white settlers into this region and frequently stole livestock from them. In 1871, however, at the request of Korana chief Klaas Lukas, the Reverend Christiaan Schröder established a mission station in the wilderness and the first irrigation canals were dug. His original church is part of the **Kalahari-Oranje Museum** in Schröder Street. Here too, is the statue of a camel and rider,

The "stone" plant

which honours the policemen and their tireless mounts who once patrolled this desert region.

Occupying an island in the Orange River, just outside town, Die Eiland is one of the most attractive municipal resorts in South Africa.

The five wine cellars in this arid region all belong to the **Orange River Cellars**, which offers tastings. On the southern bank of the river, the South African Dried Fruit Co-op on Louisvale Road is capable of processing up to 250 tonnes of dried fruit daily.

🏛 **Kalahari–Oranje Museum**
Schröder St. **Tel** (054) 332-6064.
☐ 8am–12:30pm, 2–5pm Mon–
Fri; 9am–noon Sat. 🚻

🍇 **Orange River Cellars**
Industria St. **Tel** (054) 337-8800. ☐
Mon–Fri & Sat am. ● pub hols. 🚗

Augrabies Falls National Park ❷

Road map B3. 100 km (62 miles)
W of Upington. **Tel** (054) 452-9200;
reservations: (012) 428-9111.
☐ 7am–6:30pm daily. 🚗 🚶 🏃
🏕 🅰 🍴 **www**.sanparks.org

The Augrabies Falls National Park was established in 1966 to protect the Augrabies Falls, which rush through the largest granite gorge in the world. During periods of normal flow, the main waterfall plunges 56 m (182 ft) into the gorge. The lesser Bridal Veil Waterfall, located along the northern wall of the gorge, cascades 75 m (244 ft) into the river below.

At the main complex near the entrance to the park are a shop, restaurant and bar. Paths lead from here down to the falls. Despite safety fences to prevent visitors from falling into the chasm, you should take care near the waterfall, as the rocks are very slippery.

Apart from the waterfall itself and the attractive rest camp, which consists of 59 chalets, three swimming pools and an extensive camp-site, Augrabies has much to offer. The 39-km (24-mile) long Klipspringer Trail explores the southern section of the park and affords superb views of the gorge and surrounding desert. Wildlife to look out for includes klipspringer, kudu, gemsbok and spring-bok, often seen standing in the shade of camel thorn and olive trees to escape the heat.

The Augrabies Falls in the national park of the same name

Kgalagadi Transfrontier Park ❸

Road map B2. 280 km (174 miles) N of Upington. ☎ *(054) 561-2000.* **Tel** *Reservations: (012) 428-9111.* ⭘ *daily; hours vary.* 🎫 🐾 🚶 🏕️ ℹ️ www.sanparks.org

An immense wilderness of grass-covered dunes traversed by two dry, ancient riverbeds, this national park is Africa's largest and extends over 34,390 sq km (13,278 sq miles) across territory almost twice the size of the Kruger National Park. Jointly managed by South Africa and Botswana, the border within the park is unfenced and the wildlife is free to migrate.

From Upington the tarred R360 cuts a course across a landscape that seems devoid of human habitation. The tar roads ends near Andriesvale and a sandy track hugs the border fence for 58 km (36 miles) before reaching the southern entrance. A dusty campsite is situated near the gate, while the nearby camp of Twee Rivieren offers chalets, a restaurant and a swimming pool. From Twee Rivieren, two roads follow the dry courses of the Auob and Nossob rivers on their way to the camps of Mata Mata and Nossob. There are four lovely picnic spots along the Nossob. To cross over to Namibia at Mata Mata, visitors must stay in the park for at least two nights.

Buffalo bull

Although Twee Rivieren is situated in the most arid region of the park, wildlife is surprisingly plentiful, with an astonishing 19 species of carnivore present, including the black-maned Kalahari lion, cheetah, brown hyena, wild cat and honey badger. Several species of raptors – including martial, tawny and bateleur eagles, as well as the pale chanting goshawk – are also commonly sighted.

A total of 40 windmills have been erected in the riverbeds, providing water for wildlife.

Springboks *(Antidorcas marsupialis)*, Kgalagadi Transfrontier Park

Tswalu Kalahari Reserve ❹

Road map C2. 115 km (71 miles) NW of Kuruman. ☎ *(053) 781-9234.* 🎫 www.tswalu.com

An ambitious project without equal, Tswalu is South Africa's largest private reserve. It protects 750 sq km (285 sq miles) of red Kalahari dunes and the picturesque Korannaberg mountains. The reserve came into existence through the tireless efforts of British businessman Stephen Boler. First, he bought and amalgamated 26 cattle farms. Work teams then removed some 800 km (500 miles) of fencing, as well as 2,300 km (1,440 miles) of electric lines, 38 concrete dams and the farmsteads. Approximately 7,000 cattle were sold off and the reserve was fenced.

Boler invested over R54 million to develop the reserve. A total of 4,700 animals, representing 22 species, have been reintroduced, including elephants, leopards, cheetahs, lions, white rhinos, buffaloes, zebras, giraffes, sables, elands and gemsboks. But the jewels in Tswalu's crown are, without doubt, the 20 black desert rhinos (subspecies *Diceros bicornis bicornis*) relocated with the permission of the Namibian government. The reserve is now owned by the Oppenheimer family (of gold and diamond mining fame).

Tswalu's two luxury lodges have their own airstrip, and most visitors arrive by charter plane. Guests are accommodated in nine thatched units and there is an attractive swimming pool.

SIR LAURENS VAN DER POST (1906–96)

Soldier, writer, philosopher, dreamer and explorer, Laurens van der Post was the son of an Afrikaner mother and a Dutch father. During World War II he obtained the rank of colonel and was a prisoner of the Japanese in Java until 1945. Upon his return to South Africa, he began his journeys into the wilderness. A fascinating account of his expedition in search of the San Bushmen of the Kalahari was published in 1958. *The Lost World of the Kalahari* was one of the first books to detail this intriguing and highly spiritual culture. A personal friend of the British Royal Family, the late Van der Post is remembered for his insightful, philosophical writings, most of which deal with the moral and social issues of his time.

Sir Laurens van der Post

Kimberley ⑤

The first Diamond Rush in the Kimberley district took place in 1869 when diamonds were found in the walls of a house on the Bultfontein farm. In July 1871 prospectors camped at the base of a small hill, 4.5 km (3 miles) to the northwest. The party's cook was sent to the summit as punishment for a minor offence and returned with a diamond. Within two years, New Rush tent town, renamed Kimberley in 1873, had become home to 50,000 miners. By the time Cecil John Rhodes *(see p52)* arrived, 3,600 claims were being worked.

A re-created street scene at the Kimberley Mine Big Hole

Exploring Kimberley

The angular street pattern of Kimberley is in contrast to the neat, parallel, grid pattern characteristic of other South African cities, a legacy from its formative, tent-town years. Although reminders of the past are not always apparent, Kimberley has several interesting historic landmarks that are well worth visiting.

🏛 Kimberley Mine Big Hole

Tucker St. *Tel (053) 830-4417.*
🖼 ♿ 📷 🎫 🏪 🛍
www.thebighole.co.za
Centred around the Big Hole, this museum tells South Africa's diamond-mining history through a number of elements. The Old Mining Village consists of cobbled streets lined with historic buildings dating to the

late 19th century, including shops like a watchmaker and a pawnbroker, and an old bar with original fittings. The 90-m (295-ft) viewing platform over the Big Hole allows visitors to look into the murky lake below, and there is a mock-up of a mine shaft too. The Real Diamond Display holds replicas of uncut stones.

🏛 Kimberley Club

70–72 Du Toitspan Rd. *Tel (053) 832-4224.* 🖺 daily. ♿ 📷
www.kimberleyclub.co.za
Completed in 1896, this luxurious club was the meeting place of the mining magnates and saw much wheeling and dealing. The club also has a boutique hotel and conference facilities.

For hotels and restaurants in this region see p405 and p427

VISITORS' CHECKLIST

Road map D3. 🏙 *1 million.* ✈ *7 km (4 miles) S of town.* 🚉 *Old de Beers Rd.* 🚌 *Shell Ultra City.* ℹ *121 Bultfontein Rd, (053) 832-7298.* www.kimberley.co.za

🌿 Oppenheimer Memorial Gardens

Jan Smuts Blvd.
In the gardens, five bronze miners surround the Digger's Fountain. A marble colonnade contains a bust of Sir Ernest Oppenheimer, the German-born diamond buyer who in 1917 founded the giant Anglo American Corporation.

🏛 William Humphreys Art Gallery

Jan Smuts Blvd. *Tel (053) 831-1724.*
🖺 8am–4:45pm Mon–Fri, 10am–4:45pm Sat; 2–4:45pm Sun.
🖼 ♿ www.whag.co.za
This gallery houses a superb collection of paintings by European masters and South African artists.

🏛 McGregor Museum

S Atlas St, Belgravia. *Tel (053) 839-2700.* 🖺 9am–5pm Mon–Sat, 2–5pm Sun. 🖼 ♿ 📷 🎫 🏪
Cecil John Rhodes stayed in this building during the South African War. It now houses a museum of natural and cultural history, with ethnological and archaeological displays, as well as rock paintings.

🏛 Duggan-Cronin Gallery

Egerton Rd. *Tel (053) 839-2700.*
🖺 9am–5pm Mon–Sat, 2–5pm Sun.
The gallery contains 8,000 photographs of anthropological interest taken over a 20-year period by Alfred Duggan-Cronin, who, having arrived in Kimberley in 1897, became deeply interested in the indigenous people of the Northern Cape.

The McGregor Museum, Kimberley

The Kimberley Diamond Rush

Kimberley Mine, or the Big Hole, as it is known, is the only one of four diamond mines in the Kimberley area that is still open. Within two years of the discovery of diamond-bearing kimberlite pipes in 1871, the claims were being worked by up to 30,000 miners at a time. Early photographs reveal a spider's web of cables radiating upward from the edge of the excavation. With little more than picks and shovels to aid them, the miners dug

Barney Barnato

deep into the earth, and by 1889 the hole had reached an astounding depth of 150 m (488 ft). The deeper the miners delved, the more difficult it became to extract the diamond-bearing soil, and the chaotic arrangement of cables, precipitous paths and claims lying at varying heights encouraged the diggers to form syndicates. These groupings were absorbed into various companies that were later acquired by Cecil John Rhodes.

The Cullinan Diamond *is the largest diamond ever found. A replica is displayed at the Kimberley Mine Museum.*

Cecil John Rhodes, *depicted as victorious empire builder in this 19th-century* Punch *cartoon, was one of the most influential people in Kimberley.*

Diamond miners' lives were exhausting during the 1870s: they worked six days a week, surrounded by heat, dust and flies.

THE BIG HOLE

Covering an area of 17 ha (43 acres), the hole has a perimeter of 1.6 km (1 mile). It eventually reached a depth of 800 m (2,600 ft), the first 240 m (780 ft) of which was laboriously dug by hand. An underground shaft increased the depth to 1,098 m (3,569 ft). By 1914, some 22.6 million tonnes of rock had been excavated, yielding a total of 14.5 million carats of diamonds.

Cocopans (wheelbarrows on narrowgauge tracks) were used to transport diamond-bearing rock out of the hole.

De Beers Consolidated Mines, *owned by Cecil John Rhodes, bought Barney Barnato's diamond mines for the sum of £5,338,650 in 1889.*

The Big Hole *was closed as a working mine in 1914. It is the largest man-made hole in the world, and the central focus of the Kimberley Mine Big Hole Museum.*

Bloemfontein ❻

Situated in the heartland of South Africa, Bloemfontein, capital of the Free State and seat of the province's parliament, is also the country's judicial capital. Part of the municipality of Mangaung, it lies at the hub of five major national road routes. An altitude of 1,400 m (4,593 ft) means that summers are moderate and winters mild to cool. The city was named after a fountain where early travellers used to stop on their treks through the interior. The city's history – and that of many of its stately old sandstone buildings – is firmly connected with the Afrikaners' struggle for independence. In 1854, when Major Henry Warden, the region's official British representative, was recalled to the Cape, the Afrikaners established a republic, with Bloemfontein as their capital.

The Appeal Court building, Bloemfontein

Exploring Bloemfontein

Although Major Warden's fort has long disappeared, a portion of Queen's Fort, dating back to 1848, can still be seen south of the city centre.

President Brand Street is lined with many fine old sandstone buildings, such as the **Appeal Court**, built in 1929, opposite the **Fourth Raadsaal**, which now houses the Free State's provincial legislature. This brick-and-sandstone building was constructed around 1893, during the presidency of Frederick Reitz.

🏛 The National Museum

36 Aliwal St. *Tel (051) 447-9609.* ◯ 8am–5pm Mon–Fri, 10am–5pm Sat, noon–5:30pm Sun & pub hols. ♿ 🖼 ▢
📷 www.nasmus.co.za
This museum contains a good collection of dinosaur fossils, and a reconstruction of a typical 19th-century Bloemfontein street, complete with a cluttered general dealer's store.

Detail of the National Women's Memorial

🏛 National Museum for Afrikaans Literature

Cnr President Brand & Maitland sts. *Tel (051) 405-4711.* ◯ 8am–4pm Mon–Fri, 9am–noon Sat.
Near the Appeal Court, this museum is devoted to leading Afrikaans writers, even those who, like André Brink *(see p29)*, opposed apartheid.

🏛 Old Presidency

President Brand St. *Tel (051) 448-0949.* ◯ 10am–noon, 1–4pm Tue–Fri, 1–4pm Sat & Sun. ▢
Three blocks south from the Literature Museum, on the site once occupied by the homestead of Major Warden's farm, stands the Old Presidency, an attractive building completed in 1861. It was the home of the republic's Afrikaner presidents before the British invasion in 1900 and now houses a small museum depicting this time. There is a pleasant café in the stables.

🏛 First Raadsaal

St George's St. *Tel (051) 447-9609.* ◯ 10am–1pm Mon–Fri, 2–5pm Sat & Sun. 🖼 ♿
This, the oldest building in the city, is a white, unpretentious structure near the National Museum. Built by Warden in 1849, it was used as a school. After Warden was withdrawn in 1854, it became the meeting place of the republic's *Volksraad* (people's council).

⛪ Tweetoringkerk

Charles St. *Tel (051) 430-4274.*
Dedicated in 1881, the Dutch Reformed Tweetoringkerk (twin-spired church) is unique in the country. It was inspired by Europe's Gothic cathedrals and designed by Richard Wocke. The interior, too, is Gothic. Especially noteworthy is the woodwork around the pulpit and organ.

🏛 National Women's Memorial and Anglo-Boer War Museum

Monument Rd. *Tel (051) 447-3447.* ◯ 8am–4:30pm Mon–Fri, 10am–5pm Sat, 11am–5pm Sun. 🖼 ♿ www.anglo-boer.co.za
South of the city, this site commemorates the countless Boer and black African women and children who died in British concentration camps during the South African War.

Emily Hobhouse, a British woman who campaigned for better treatment of the prisoners, is buried at the foot of the monument.

Environs: North of the city centre, the **Franklin Nature Reserve** occupies Naval Hill. The name originated during the South African War when a cannon was mounted here by the British Naval Brigade.

Abstract painting by Cecil Skotnes, Oliewenhuis Art Museum

Exterior of the Oliewenhuis Art Museum, Bloemfontein

In 1928, the University of Michigan (USA) built an observatory on the summit. Over 7,000 star systems were discovered before it closed in 1972. It now houses a theatre.

Further north of the city, the **Oliewenhuis Art Museum** is set in a spacious garden. This gallery is renowned for its superb collection of South African art.

Several excellent wildlife reserves can be found north of Bloemfontein. The **Soetdoring Dam Nature Reserve** borders on the expansive Krugerdrif Dam whose wall, at 5 km (3 miles), is one of the longest in South Africa.

The river and shoreline of this reserve provide excellent picnic spots and attract many birds. Antelope species like black wildebeests and gemsboks roam free, while predators like lions and

wild dogs are kept in a large separate camp.

The turn-off to the **Willem Pretorius Game Reserve** lies some 150 km (93 miles) north of Bloemfontein on the N1. The grassland around the Allemanskraal Dam supports large herds of gazelles. The hills on the northern shore are home to kudu, elands, buffaloes, giraffes and white rhinos. Birds such as korhaans and double-banded coursers are also commonly seen.

✕ Franklin Nature Reserve
Union Ave, Naval Hill. ◯ daily.

血 Oliewenhuis Art Museum
Harry Smith St. *Tel* (051) 447-9609.
◯ 8am–5pm Mon–Fri, 10am–5pm
Sat, 1–5pm Sun. ● Good Fri, 25
Dec. ♿ 🅿

✕ Soetdoring Dam Nature Reserve
R64 (Kimberley Rd). *Tel* (051) 433-9002. ◯ 7am–6pm daily. 🎫 🍴 🚶

VISITORS' CHECKLIST

Road map D3. 🏘 500,000. ✈
N8, 10 km (6 miles) E of the city.
🚌 Harvey Rd. 🚌 Tourist Centre.
ℹ Bloemfontein Tourist Centre,
60 Park Rd. (051) 405-8489.
◯ 8am–4:15pm Mon–Fri, 8am–
noon Sat. 🎭 Bloem Show (Apr–
May); Rose Festival (Oct). **www.**
bloemfonteintourism.co.za

✕ Willem Pretorius Game Reserve
N1 to Kroonstad. *Tel* (057) 651-4003. ◯ 7am–6:30pm daily. 🎫
www.sa-venues.com/game-reserves/fs_willempretorius.htm

Giraffe, Franklin Nature Reserve on Naval Hill, Bloemfontein

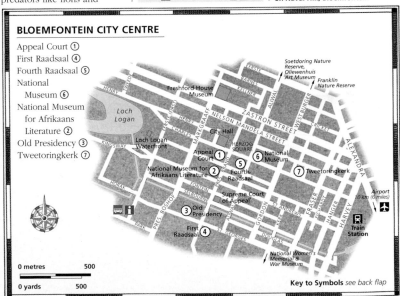

BLOEMFONTEIN CITY CENTRE

Appeal Court ①
First Raadsaal ④
Fourth Raadsaal ⑤
National
  Museum ⑥
National Museum
  for Afrikaans
  Literature ②
Old Presidency ③
Tweetoringkerk ⑦

Soetdoring Nature
Reserve,
Oliewenhuis
Art Museum
Franklin
Nature Reserve

Freshford House
Museum

Loch
Logan

Loch Logan
Waterfront

City Hall

HERZOG
SQUARE

Appeal
Court ①

National Museum for ②
Afrikaans Literature

Fourth
Raadsaal ⑤

⑥ National
Museum

⑦ Tweetoringkerk

Supreme Court
of Appeal

③ Old
Presidency

First ④
Raadsaal

National Women's
Memorial &
War Museum

Airport
10 km (6 miles) ✈

Train
Station

0 metres   500
0 yards   500

Key to Symbols see back flap

TRAVELLERS' NEEDS

WHERE TO STAY

The slow journeys of earlier centuries, when the vast distances between settlements had to be covered on horseback or by ox wagon, led to a proud local tradition. In South Africa "hospitality" is more than a catchword, and establishments, from the largest hotel chain to the smallest bed and breakfast, do their utmost to make the modern traveller feel welcome. The wide range of accommodation available is a reflection of the diversity of the country itself. A fantasy resort hotel like the Palace of the Lost City at Sun City *(see pp324–5)* and Cape Town elegant colonial hotel, the Moun Nelson *(see p381)*, offer every conceivable luxury and bear comparison with the best in the world. Charming alternatives are the guest cottages found in most *dorp* (country villages), where tranquillity and hearty, home-cooked fare are valued far more than modern convenience. Farmsteads and safari lodges provide a lavish and expensive Africa experience, while camp sites and backpacker's hostels offer basic amenities and cater for younger visitors on limited budgets.

Doorman at the Mount Nelson Hotel

WHERE TO LOOK

Visitors touring South Africa by car may be worried by the distances that separate cities and towns. Fortunately, hotels, bed and breakfasts, motels and self-catering cottages are found in even the remotest villages. Farm accommodation is also plentiful.

South Africa's cities offer a great variety of places to stay, whether you want family, luxury or business accommodation. In well-visited country and resort areas, there is also accommodation to suit every taste and pocket: many game parks, for example, offer luxurious lodges as well as basic camp sites, while most coastal resorts offer hotels, camp sites, B&Bs and guesthouses. Enquire at the local tourist information office (usually well signposted) or contact one of the many umbrella associations such as **AA Travel Accommodation**, the **Tourism Grading Council of South Africa**, **Hostelling International** or the **Guest House Association of Southern Africa** *(see p379)*. If you are travelling through the smaller towns without having made prior arrangements, ask at the post office, one of the local stores or police stations for accommodation advice.

If you are seeking quiet surroundings, try the smaller and more simple hostelries, inland or away from obvious attractions on the coast. Most private game reserves offer superb safari lodges.

HOTEL PRICES

Prices quoted tend to be per person rather than per room. Taxes (and sometimes gratuities) are usually included in the rates, but tips are appreciated. Ten

The Sabi Sabi Game Lodge (see p403)

to 15 per cent of the cost or value of goods or service received is the norm.

Where rates are stated as "dinner, bed and breakfast" or "bed and breakfast", you are likely to be charged for these meals whether or not you take them. If you advise the host in time, it may be possible to avoid payment for advertised meals that are not taken. Also notify the hosts in advance if you are vegetarian, for example. "Special offers" are seldom further negotiable.

Rooms with a shower are usually cheaper than those with a bath, and those with views are more expensive.

Prices vary slightly outside of high season (Nov–Feb, Easter weekend and the mid-year school holidays). But do ask your travel agent about possible special offers made by hotel groups, or contact them directly. Hotels do not close during winter (May–Aug).

Thatched rondavels at Olifants camp, Kruger National Park (see p339)

◁ **A herd of elephants makes its way across the Addo Elephant Park near Port Elizabeth**

The pool at the Singita Private Game Reserve *(see p403)*

HOTEL GRADING

South African hotels are classified by a number of organizations, such as Satour, the national tourism authority, and the Tourism Grading Council of South Africa. Satour divides hotels into five categories, indicated by a plaque carrying from one to five stars. A typical five-star hotel is luxurious, offering suites as well as rooms and a wide range of services, such as hairdressing, dry cleaning and room service. In a country town, a one-star hotel may prove to be comfortable and entirely satisfactory, while in a city it may be little more than a noisy local rendezvous spot.

Many charming hotels have lower ratings, and some hotels with higher ratings – although they boast more than the required minimum of facilities and service – turn out to be impersonal business warrens.

Self-catering cottages and guesthouses are generally also graded.

FACILITIES

Facilities vary according to location and grading. Parking is usually available, but is not always under cover or supervised by a guard. Some hotels offer a daily car-wash, and may also have courtesy vehicles for hire, either with or without a driver.

Most hotels provide a telephone in the bedroom, but it is usually cheaper to use a public telephone. Television sets in rooms (with satellite channels) are fairly common, and there is almost always a set in the guests' lounge.

Central heating in winter is not the norm, although most places of accommodation do provide portable heaters. Many self-catering cottages, particularly those on farms, have indoor fireplaces.

Some more up-market small guesthouses and B&Bs offer an "honesty bar" with cold beers, wine, soft drinks and mineral water.

In country towns, the hotel frontage may be on the main street. If there is no bypass road, the noise level may be uncomfortable, especially at night. Before asking to be moved to a room at the back, however, check that there are no large cooling units tucked away, as those are likely to be even more disturbing.

Hotels usually have a locked and secure safe where guests can deposit valuables.

HOTEL GROUPS

Many of the better-class hotels are controlled by one of the national hotel chains *(see p379)*, offering incentives or package deals that include lower family rates or out-of-season tariffs. Some, however, are graded lower than others, so have a different rates' structure.

CHILDREN

Don't presume that your venue of choice will cater for children. Many up-market hotels, guesthouses and safari lodges do not accept children under the age of 10.

Where children are accepted, families may be able to share a room at little extra cost, if tariffs are per room rather than per person.

BOOKING

If possible, confirm a telephone booking in writing, by fax or by email. It is likely that a deposit will be required, which you will forfeit if you cancel your booking at short notice.

The hotel is legally obliged to inform you if there has been a tariff increase since you made your booking.

Even if you have reserved a specific room, ask to see it before you sign the register. And if you require special arrangements, first ensure that these are satisfactory.

Unless otherwise stated, the occupation period generally extends from 2pm to 10am.

Reception area in the Palace of the Lost City at Sun City *(see pp324–5)*

SELF-CATERING

Choice in style and price of self-catering accommodation in South Africa is vast, with cottages sometimes also referred to as chalets, bungalows or *rondavels* (if they are round and grass-thatched).

Many of the game parks have luxurious, East African-style safari tents with private outdoor kitchens, while farm-style cottages in the vast Karoo *(see pp356–7)* feature large, indoor hearths to fend off the bitter cold on winter nights. Municipal chalets in caravan parks may offer only the mere basics, while cottages on the wine estates of the Cape *(see pp190–203)*, for example, may even be equipped with microwaves and satellite television.

Club Mykonos, Langebaan (see p213)

The larger resorts and game reserves will usually have a selection of cottages. These may be self-contained units or have shared kitchen, laundry and bathroom facilities. Self-catering cottages usually have well-equipped kitchens, are comfortably furnished and

Guest cottage at the Blyde River Canyon resort (see p333)

may even include towels and bedding, although it is always advisable to ask beforehand.

Upon arrival, a member of staff may check to ensure that all the items on the inventory are supplied and intact. You could also be asked to pay a small deposit (refundable at the end of your stay) to cover potential loss or breakage.

It is advisable to approach individual tourist information offices of towns or regions for the addresses and contact numbers of self-catering cottages. Agencies like **Roger & Kay's Travel Selection** may also be able to assist.

COUNTRY COTTAGES

Cottages on farms and in peaceful villages are to be found in Mpumalanga (**Jacana Collection**), the KwaZulu-Natal Midlands (**The Underberg Hideaway**),

and in the wine- and fruit-farming areas around Cape Town. A memorable aspect of a stay in the country is the hospitality and catering in true local style.

BED AND BREAKFAST

Accommodation in private homes has become very popular, especially along the Garden Route and in bigger cities like Cape Town, Port Elizabeth and Johannesburg. The hosts, who concentrate on a small number of guests staying only a night or two, take pride in being able to provide personal attention.

GUEST FARMS

Relatively inexpensive outdoor family holidays are provided by guest- or holiday-farms all around the country. Visitors stay in the farmhouse or in a nearby cottage. Sometimes meals are eaten with the resident family, otherwise there are equipped kitchens. Guests can also take part in daily activities, such as collecting the eggs and milking the cows.

GAME LODGES

Game lodges in most private reserves *(see pp62–7)* cater for affluent visitors. They typically offer excellent cuisine, luxurious pseudo-rustic accommodation, highly skilled staff and game rangers who ensure that guests see as much of the African wildlife as possible. National parks are much more basic, yet very comfortable.

Entrance of the Table Bay Hotel, on Cape Town's V&A Waterfront (see p381)

...MMODATION

...ling International ...ides accommodation ...several hostels. There are ...so many private back-packers' hostels, especially in the cities and along the coast. For more details, try to acquire a copy of the accommodation guidebook published by **Coast to Coast**; it is available for free from hostels. No age limit is imposed on guests, although preference is usually given to the younger travellers.

Backpackers' lodges are more suited to young people, as facilities and meals are few and privacy is non-existent. Staying in a youth hostel may be fairly accurately described as "roughing it".

CARAVAN PARKS

You don't have to tow a caravan to qualify for residence, since many caravan parks have caravans to let, along with prefabricated or rustic cottages. Allocated sites are usually connected to water mains and electricity supplies.

Larger caravan parks have a shop, restaurant and swimming pool, and sometimes even tennis courts or a bowling green.

Camping in the uKhahlamba-Drakensberg Park *(see p270)*

Most campers do their own cooking– the method of choice is the South African *braaivleis* or barbecue. Cooking-places or "braai sites" are provided – one per site – and firewood is usually available from the park office.

Camping sites can be noisy at night, so choose a spot well away from the entrance gate, which usually also serves as the exit point. AA Travel Accommodation will be able to supply contact details of caravan parks and camping sites.

REST CAMPS

Rest camps are the "standard" version of the luxurious game lodge and are found in national parks and provincial game reserves *(see pp62–7)*. Most of them offer a variety of facilities such as swimming pools, shops and communal dining areas, with accommodation options ranging from bungalows to bigger chalets.

UNDER CANVAS

Numerous camping grounds are situated along South Africa's major rivers or by the sea. Sites are separated from each other by calico screens or hedges. Communal ablution blocks are provided. Many of the camp sites are run as part of a local caravan park.

DIRECTORY

HOTEL GROUPS BOOKING OFFICES

City Lodge
Tel (011) 557-2600 or (0861) 563-437.
www.citylodge.co.za

Forever Resorts
Tel (012) 423-5660.
www.foreversa.co.za

Portfolio Collection
Tel (021) 701-9632.
www.portfolio collection.com

Protea Hotels
Tel (021) 430-5000.
www.proteahotels.com

Sun International
Tel (011) 780-7878.
www.suninternational. com

Tsogo Sun Hotels
Tel (011) 461-9744.
www.tsogosunhotels. com

COUNTRY HOMES

Jacana Collection
Tel (041) 378-1439, or (0861) 522-262. www. jacanacollection.co.za

The Underberg Hideaway
Tel (033) 343-1564.
www.hideaways.co.za

CAMPING

Ezemvelo KZN Wildlife
Tel (033) 845-1000.
www.kznwildlife.com

SAN Parks
Tel (012) 428-9111.
www.sanparks.org

GUESTHOUSES AND B&BS

Bed and Breakfast Association South Africa
Tel (012) 420-4012.
www.babasa.co.za

Guest House Association of Southern Africa
Tel (021) 762-0880.
www.ghasa.co.za

Roger & Kay's Travel Selection
Tel (021) 715-7130.
www.travelselection. co.za

GENERAL

AA Travel Accommodation
Tel (011) 713-2000.
www.aatravel.co.za

Coast to Coast
Tel (021) 783-4003.
www.coastingafrica. com

Hostelling International
www.hihostels.com

South African Tourism
Tel (011) 895-3000.
www.southafrica.co.za

Tourism Grading Council of SA
Tel (027) 895-3000.
www.tourismgrading. co.za

Choosing a Hotel

The hotels in this guide have been selected from a wide price range for their good value or exceptional location, comfort and style. The chart highlights some of the factors that may influence your choice and gives a brief description of each hotel. Entries are listed by price categories within the towns.

PRICE CATEGORIES
The following price ranges are for a standard double room per night, including tax and service charges, not including breakfast.

Ⓡ Under R400
ⓇⓇ R400–R800
ⓇⓇⓇ R800–R1,200
ⓇⓇⓇⓇ R1,200–R2,000
ⓇⓇⓇⓇⓇ Over R2,000

CAPE TOWN

CITY BOWL Acorn House   ⓇⓇⓇ

1 Montrose Avenue, Oranjezicht, 8001 **Tel** *(021) 461-1782* **Fax** *(021) 461-1768* **Rooms** *9*   **Map** 5 A4

Acorn House was originally built for the editor of a local newspaper and has a 1904 Herbert Baker-designed edifice. Today the house is the home of Bernd and Beate, who have made a name for this hotel in Cape Town's German quarter through their meticulous hospitality, beautiful decor and passionately compiled wine list. **www.acornhouse.co.za**

CITY BOWL Daddy Long Legs Art Hotel   ⓇⓇⓇ

134 Long Street, 8000 **Tel** *(021) 422-3074* **Fax** *(021) 422-3446* **Rooms** *13*   **Map** 5 A2

Each room in this hostel has been put together by a different local artist, and the results are individual, irreverent and representative of Cape Town's lively cultural landscape. There are also five self-catering apartments. Daddy Long Legs is located on a bustling strip that hosts much of Cape Town's thriving nightlife. **www.daddylonglegs.co.za**

CITY BOWL Leeuwenvoet House   ⓇⓇⓇ

8 Kloof Nek Road, Tamboerskloof, 8001 **Tel** *(021) 424-1133* **Rooms** *15*   **Map** 4 F2

An excellent guesthouse in a lovingly restored Victorian building, Leeuwenvoet is situated around the corner from trendy Kloof Street, with its superb restaurants and boutiques. Start the day with a hearty breakfast and then head over Kloof Nek to the beach. Alternatively, ask your friendly hosts for daytripping tips. **www.leeuwenvoet.co.za**

CITY BOWL Table Mountain Lodge   ⓇⓇⓇ

10a Tamboerskloof Road, Tamboerskloof, 8001 **Tel** *(021) 423-0042* **Fax** *(021) 423-4983* **Rooms** *8*   **Map** 4 F2

This large, colourfully restored Cape Dutch farmhouse on the slopes of Signal Hill has received a four-star grading from the Tourism Grading Council of South Africa. Freshly cut flowers adorn the halls of the house, and there are eight en-suite rooms all furnished in a classically elegant style. **www.tablemountainlodge.co.za**

CITY BOWL Tudor Hotel   ⓇⓇⓇ

153 Longmarket St, 8001 **Tel** *(021) 424-1335* **Fax** *(021) 423-1198* **Rooms** *26*   **Map** 5 B1

Overlooking Greenmarket Square, famous for its arts and crafts market and varied choice of restaurants, this stylish three-star hotel has a historical façade. The interiors, however, are ultra-modern. Parking is not available, but it can be arranged with a nearby garage. Breakfast is included in the price. **www.tudorhotel.co.za**

CITY BOWL Urban Chic Boutique Hotel   ⓇⓇⓇ

172 Long Street, 8001 **Tel** *(021) 426-6119* **Fax** *(021) 423-2086* **Rooms** *20*   **Map** 5 A2

The ultimate in cosmopolitan and contemporary boutique hotels. Sip cocktails in the cigar lounge, while you make use of the wireless Internet connection, or step outside into the throbbing heart of Cape Town's nightlife. Each room has a large corner window affording great views of Table Mountain and Signal Hill. **www.urbanchic.co.za**

CITY BOWL Cape Diamond Hotel   ⓇⓇⓇ

Cnr Longmarket & Parliament sts, 8001 **Tel** *(021) 461-2519* **Fax** *(021) 462-2741* **Rooms** *60*   **Map** 5 B2

Centrally located near City Hall and the Castle of Good Hope, this hotel is housed in a converted Art Deco building that in the 1930s was a diamond dealership. The ground-floor restaurant and bar is popular with the after-work crowd. Rates include breakfast. **www.capediamondhotel.co.za**

CITY BOWL Cape Town Hollow Boutique Hotel   ⓇⓇⓇ

88 Queen Victoria Street, 8000 **Tel** *(021) 423-1260* **Rooms** *56*   **Map** 5 B2

Situated in Cape Town's old centre, overlooking the Dutch East India Company's Garden, this four-star boutique hotel offers tasteful modern furnishings and a relaxing wellness centre. For excellent views of Table Mountain, request a room on the fifth floor or above, facing the gardens. **www.capetownhollow.co.za**

CITY BOWL Townhouse Hotel   ⓇⓇⓇ

60 Corporation Street, 8000 **Tel** *(021) 465-7050* **Fax** *(021) 465-3891* **Rooms** *106*   **Map** 5 B2

Set in a tranquil corner of the city centre, close to the South African Parliament buildings, this four-star hotel has well-appointed rooms with hi-tech features, including satellite television, electronic safes and free high-speed Internet access. **www.townhouse.co.za**

BOWL Underberg Guesthouse 🏠 🅿 ®®®®

...boerskloof Road, Tamboerskloof, 8001 **Tel** *(021) 426-2262* **Fax** *(021) 424-4059* **Rooms** *9*   **Map** *4 F2*

...eautifully renovated Victorian house at the bottom of Kloof Nek, with ten en-suite rooms available. Wireless ...net and a self-service honesty bar are available to guests. Your hosts are on hand to help with travel tips, ...ort transfers and any theatre or restaurant reservations. **www.underbergguesthouse.co.za**

ITY BOWL Villa Lutzi 🛏 🏠 🅿 ®®®®

6 Rosmead Avenue, Oranjezicht, 8001 **Tel** *(021) 423-4614* **Fax** *(021) 426-1472* **Rooms** *17*   **Map** *4 F4*

Located on the slopes of the mountain in Oranjezicht, a ten-minute walk from the city, Villa Lutzi offers a luxurious home from home, with an exotic garden and a large pool deck overlooking the Lions Head. Hosts Dagmar and Eric are clued up on local restaurants and nightlife and keen to point guests in the right direction. **www.villalutzi.com**

CITY BOWL Cape Heritage Hotel 📋 ®®®®®

Heritage Square, 90 Bree Street, 8001 **Tel** *(021) 424-4646* **Rooms** *17*   **Map** *5 B1*

Contemporary design meets colonial charm at this four-star luxury boutique hotel in a historic 18th-century building. Cape Heritage borders a shady courtyard around which six independent restaurants compete for business. All 17 rooms are individually decorated and full of Old World character. **www.capeheritage.co.za**

CITY BOWL Derwent House Boutique Hotel 🛏 📋 🅿 ®®®®

14 Derwent Road, Tamboerskloof, 8001 **Tel** *(021) 422-2763* **Rooms** *11*   **Map** *4 F3*

This owner-managed hotel is conveniently located in trendy Tamboerskloof, within walking distance of a wide selection of fashionable restaurants and shops and just a few minutes' drive from Table Mountain. It offers excellent service and top-notch facilities in an elegant and stylish setting. **www.derwenthouse.co.za**

CITY BOWL Kensington Place 🍴 🛏 🍽 📋 🅿 ®®®®

38 Kensington Crescent, Higgovale, 8001 **Tel** *(021) 424-4744* **Fax** *(021) 424-1810* **Rooms** *8*   **Map** *4 F4*

An award-winning and unique place to stay in exclusive Higgovale, on the slopes of Table Mountain. Setting a high benchmark for intimate boutique hotels, Kensington focuses on sexy contemporary stylings with unobtrusive yet attentive service. There are fabulous mountain and city views from the pool deck. **www.kensingtonplace.co.za**

CITY BOWL Mount Nelson Hotel 📺 🍴 🛏 🏠 🍽 📋 ♿ ®®®®®

76 Orange Street, Gardens, 8001 **Tel** *(021) 483-1000* **Fax** *(021) 483-1001* **Rooms** *209*   **Map** *5 A3*

A colonial masterpiece and Cape Town's most famous hotel, the "Pink Lady" is at the foot of Table Mountain. It is spread over a large plot of lovely gardens, and has been voted the Best Hotel in South Africa in the *World Travel Awards* for several years running. Nelson Mandela celebrated his 79th birthday here in 1997. **www.mountnelson.co.za**

CITY BOWL The Westin Cape Town 📺 🍴 🛏 🏠 🍽 📋 ♿ ®®®®®

Convention Square, Lower Long Street, 8001 **Tel** *(021) 412-9999* **Fax** *(021) 412-9001* **Rooms** *483*   **Map** *5 B1*

State-of-the-art technology and uncompromising luxury permeate the guest's experience at this architectural landmark, from the slick, contemporary furnishings and African art on the walls to the oversized beds and e-butler facility, which passes your requests to the relevant member of staff. **www.westincapetown.com**

V&A WATERFRONT Breakwater Lodge 🍴 🏠 🍽 📋 ♿ 🅿 ®®®

Portswood Road, V&A Waterfront, 8001 **Tel** *(021) 406-1911* **Fax** *(021) 406-1070* **Rooms** *191*   **Map** *1 A1*

A budget hotel built in a converted 19th-century prison, Breakwater Lodge is comfortable, inexpensive and full of character. Rooms overlook Table Bay on one side of the hotel, and Table Mountain on the other. The hotel is linked with the UCT Graduate School of Business, and its conference facilities are impressive. **www.bwl.co.za**

V&A WATERFRONT Victoria Junction 📺 🍴 🛏 🍽 ♿ 🅿 ®®®

Cnr Somerset & Ebenezer Rds, Green Point, 8001 **Tel** *(021) 418-1234* **Fax** *(021) 418-5678* **Rooms** *172*   **Map** *2 D5*

Half in Green Point and half inside the V&A, the Victoria Junction offers the full designer hotel experience. The industrial interior is offset by chic furnishings, and the rooms have the feel of contemporary loft-style apartments. The excellent in-house restaurant is constructed around a working film set. **www.proteahotels.com**

V&A WATERFRONT Cape Grace 📺 🍴 🛏 🏠 🍽 📋 🅿 ®®®®®

West Quay Road, V&A Waterfront, 8001 **Tel** *(021) 410-7100* **Fax** *(021) 418-0495* **Rooms** *120*   **Map** *1 B2*

A member of the Leading Hotels of the World group, the Cape Grace is the stately jewel in the crown of the Waterfront's crop of hotels. It has scooped numerous international awards since the Brand family first opened the doors in 1996. The atmosphere is intimate, with exquisite decor and personalized service. **www.capegrace.co.za**

V&A WATERFRONT Radisson Blu Hotel 📺 🍴 🛏 🏠 🅿 ®®®®

Beach Road, Granger Bay, V&A Waterfront, 8002 **Tel** *(021) 441-3000* **Fax** *(021) 441-3520* **Rooms** *177*   **Map** *1 C3*

The Radisson is a well-established hotel located on a Granger Bay promontory that overlooks a private marina. The plentiful modern facilities include an in-house spa and multiple restaurants. The service is always impeccable, but never intrusive. All rooms offer either mountain or sea views. **www.radissonblu.com**

V&A WATERFRONT The Table Bay 📺 🍴 🛏 🏠 🍽 📋 ♿ 🅿 ®®®®®

Quay 6, V&A Waterfront, 8001 **Tel** *(021) 406-5000* **Fax** *(021) 406-5686* **Rooms** *329*   **Map** *1 C1*

Exuding the nautical charm of a cruise liner, the Table Bay has a heated salt-water pool, perhaps the only tropical sea water you'll find during your stay in the Western Cape. Other features include an in-house spa, a small gym, an elegant ballroom, an executive boardroom and dramatic sea views. **www.hoteltablebay.co.za**

V&A WATERFRONT Victoria & Alfred Hotel

Pier Head, V&A Waterfront, 8001 **Tel** *(021) 419-6677* **Fax** *(021) 419-8955* **Rooms** *94*   **Map**

The Victoria & Alfred is the original waterfront hotel, offering spacious rooms with expansive panoramas of the mountain or the basin. Service is prompt and includes a chauffeur facility if required. For the less demanding commuter, a shuttle bus takes guests to and from the centre of town on a regular basis. **www.vahotel.co.za**

ATLANTIC SEABOARD Bateleurs Guesthouses

81 Theresa Avenue & 12 Rontree Street, Camps Bay, 8001 **Tel** *(021) 438-1697* **Fax** *(021) 438-9588* **Rooms** *9*

At the top of Camps Bay's network of mountainside avenues, Jasper and Zonia offer stylish accommodation, including two spacious suites with king-size beds and a selection of slightly smaller options, all with luxury en-suite facilities. All rooms have lovely views across Camps Bay and the Atlantic Ocean beyond. **www.bateleurshouse.co.za**

ATLANTIC SEABOARD Primi Royal

23 Camps Bay Drive, Camps Bay, 8040 **Tel** *(021) 438-2741* **Fax** *(021) 438-1718* **Rooms** *10*

The theme at this boutique hotel belonging to the Primi Group is the fusion of African and Asian styles. Suites afford spectacular views that take in Lions Head, Bakoven and the vast expanse of Atlantic inbetween. Popular Camps Bay Beach is just across the road, with plenty of restaurants on the main thoroughfare. **www.primi-royal.com**

ATLANTIC SEABOARD Villa Rosa Guesthouse

277 High Level Road, Sea Point, 8005 **Tel** *(021) 434-2768* **Fax** *(021) 434-3526* **Rooms** *8*

Villa Rosa is a Victorian family home located at the foot of Lions Head, in upper Sea Point. Breakfasts are a hearty affair, with muesli, breads, eggs and home-made jam to order. This is an established and safe bet for a warm welcome and a comfortable stay. **www.villa-rosa.com**

ATLANTIC SEABOARD Villa Sunshine

1 Rochester Road, Bantry Bay, 8001 **Tel** *(021) 439-8224* **Fax** *(021) 439-8219* **Rooms** *7*

The four-star Villa Sunshine offers B&B accommodation in seven individually decorated en-suite rooms. All modern home comforts are provided, as well as high-speed Internet, a beautiful salt-water pool and a secluded location on spectacular Bantry Bay. **www.villasunshine.co.za**

ATLANTIC SEABOARD Albatross B&B

24 Queens Road, Bantry Bay, 8050 **Tel** *(021) 434-7624* **Fax** *(021) 434-7666* **Rooms** *10*

This comfortable bed and breakfast in Bantry Bay offers non-smoking en-suite and triple rooms. The house itself is spacious, with two large palm trees presiding over the beautiful garden, where guests can have breakfast. Cape Town tours, airport transfers and car rental can all be arranged. **www.albatrossct.co.za**

ATLANTIC SEABOARD Ambassador Hotel

34 Victoria Road, Bantry Bay, 8005 **Tel** *(021) 439-6170* **Fax** *(021) 439-6336* **Rooms** *68*

This large, established four-star hotel is located along Bantry Bay's jagged coastline, wedged between the main road and the surf-weathered rocks below. The rooms and suites feature luxury finishes, wireless Internet and flat-screen TVs. All have dramatic views of the surrounding granite cliffs. **www.newmarkhotels.com**

ATLANTIC SEABOARD Blackheath Lodge

6 Blackheath Road, Sea Point, 8005 **Tel** *(021) 439-2541* **Fax** *(021) 439-9776* **Rooms** *10*

Located under Signal Hill, close to the V&A Waterfront and Clifton and Camps Bay beaches, Blackheath Lodge is housed in an 1880s Victorian building. The spacious interior features high ceilings, wooden floors and eclectic African decor. The delicious breakfast includes freshly baked quiches and muffins. **www.blackheathlodge.co.za**

ATLANTIC SEABOARD The Bay Hotel

69 Victoria Road, Camps Bay, 8040 **Tel** *(021) 437-9701* **Fax** *(021) 438-4433* **Rooms** *78*

This large hotel has a prime position on Camps Bay's main drag. The grounds are large, with plenty of activities to keep restless guests happy. The Bay Hotel boasts four swimming pools, a tennis court and a luxury wellness centre for those in need of pampering. The city is five minutes' drive away, over Kloof Nek. **www.thebay.co.za**

ATLANTIC SEABOARD Ellerman House

180 Kloof Road, Bantry Bay, 8005 **Tel** *(021) 430-3200* **Fax** *(021) 430-3215* **Rooms** *11*

A historical landmark on the granite outcrops of Bantry Bay, this classic turn-of-the-century mansion is recognized as one of the top boutique hotels in the world. The emphasis is on immaculate service and perfection at every level. Ellerman Villa next door is available as a serviced home for a hefty nightly fee. **www.ellerman.co.za**

ATLANTIC SEABOARD Hout Bay Manor

Baviaanskloof, off Main Road, Hout Bay, 7872 **Tel** *(021) 790-0116* **Fax** *(021) 790-0118* **Rooms** *19*

The Manor dates back to 1871 and offers the ultimate in rest and relaxation for visitors to the self-proclaimed "Republic of Hout Bay". The beach is a short walk away, and there are shops, restaurants and an excellent weekend craft market nearby. All rooms are child-friendly and furnished with sleeper couches. **www.houtbaymanor.com**

ATLANTIC SEABOARD O on Kloof

92 Kloof Road, Bantry Bay, 8005 **Tel** *(021) 439-2081* **Fax** *(021) 439-8832* **Rooms** *8*

This impeccably decorated villa on the slopes of Lions Head is all about attention to detail. The wooden deck of the honeymoon suite on the top floor is the ideal location to enjoy panoramas of both mountains and ocean. It boasts a gym and an attractive heated indoor pool; in-room spa treatments can also be arranged. **www.oonkloof.co.za**

Key to Price Guide *see p380* **Key to Symbols** *see back cover flap*

NTIC SEABOARD Peninsula All-Suite Hotel

each Road, Sea Point, 8060 **Tel** *(021) 430-7777* **Fax** *(021) 430-7776* **Rooms** *110*

seafront tower block has a varied range of luxury self-catering studios, suites and apartments. Facilities include ate-of-the art gym and swimming pool, as well as a frequent shuttle service to the V&A Waterfront. Close to autiful beaches and gardens. The surrounding area also boasts a good range of shops. **www.peninsula.co.za**

TLANTIC SEABOARD The Twelve Apostles Hotel & Spa

Victoria Road, Oudekraal, Camps Bay. 8005 **Tel** *(021) 437-9000* **Fax** *(021) 437-9001* **Rooms** *70*

Sandwiched between the mountains and the Atlantic Ocean, this secluded five-star retreat has uninterrupted views of the pristine coastline. Rooms are beautifully appointed, though guests may wish to trade their king-size four-poster bed for a little extra elbow room in one of the smaller standard suites. **www.12apostleshotel.com**

ATLANTIC SEABOARD Villa Clifton

7 Leckhampton Court, 234 Kloof Road, Clifton, 8005 **Tel** *(021) 919-1752* **Fax** *(021) 919-1758* **Rooms** *2*

Positioned high on Kloof Road, this self-catering house (with butler and chef if required) has a large deck overlooking some of the world's most beautiful beaches. The Atlantic Seaboard's spectacular sunsets are best enjoyed with a well-stirred cocktail in hand and the sound of the crashing waves below. **www.newmarkhotels.com**

ATLANTIC SEABOARD Winchester Mansions

221 Beach Road, Sea Point, 8005 **Tel** *(021) 434-2351* **Fax** *(021) 434-0215* **Rooms** *76*

A renowned, privately owned four-star hotel on Sea Point's coastal boulevard. Tailor-made tours to the Winelands or to Cape Point can be arranged through consultation with the management. The hotel restaurant, Harveys, is run by an award-winning local chef. **www.winchester.co.za**

GREEN POINT AND MOUILLE POINT Jambo Guest House

1 Grove Road, Green Point, 8005 **Tel** *(021) 439-4219* **Fax** *(021) 434-0672* **Rooms** *5*   **Map** *1 B4*

Relax in a hot Jacuzzi surrounded by tropical foliage at this B&B. Hosts Barry and Mina Thomas are on hand to advise on local places of interest. Decor varies in theme from African animal skins to the ornately colonial. Jambo has won several AA Accommodation Awards in recent years and offers good value for money. **www.jambo.co.za**

GREEN POINT AND MOUILLE POINT Brenwin Guest House

1 Thornhill Road, Green Point, 8001 **Tel** *(021) 434-0220* **Fax** *(021) 439-3465* **Rooms** *16*   **Map** *1 C4*

Built in 1830 to accommodate Cape Town's port captain, Brenwin can be found in cosmopolitan Green Point, just off High Level Road, overlooking the Waterfront. Rooms range from spacious doubles with extra sleeper couch to self-contained apartments that can be booked as either B&B or self-catering. **www.brenwin.co.za**

GREEN POINT AND MOUILLE POINT La Splendida Luxury Suites

121 Beach Road, Mouille Point, 8005 **Tel** *(021) 439-5119* **Fax** *(021) 439-5112* **Rooms** *24*   **Map** *1 B3*

Situated on Mouille Point's coastal boulevard, La Splendida offers clean, modern accommodation at a good price, although it should be noted that the emphasis here is not on round-the-clock or overly attentive service. A two-storey penthouse is also available. The V&A Waterfront is a ten-minute walk away. **www.newmarkhotels.com**

GREEN POINT AND MOUILLE POINT Cape Royal Luxury Hotel

47 Main Road, Green Point, 8051 **Tel** *(021) 430-0500* **Fax** *(021) 430-0797* **Rooms** *95*   **Map** *1 B3*

The attractive mock Victorian façade hides an ultra-modern hotel. The Cape Royal features one- and two-bedroom apartments and penthouses. Guest facilities include the 1800° Restaurant, rooftop swimming pool and luxury spa. There are also fabulous views across the V&A Waterfront. Breakfast is included. **www.caperoyal.co.za**

GREEN POINT AND MOUILLE POINT Romney Park All-Suite Hotel

Cnr Hill & Romney Roads, Green Point, 8005 **Tel** *(021) 439-4555* **Fax** *(021) 439-4747* **Rooms** *18*   **Map** *1 B4*

Afro-colonial decor has been carefully selected for the well-appointed, spacious suites at Romney Park. Facilities are extensive, with a lap pool outside and a wellness spa offering all kinds of invigorating treatments. Suites have creamy carpets and are painted in neutral tones, which offsets the mahogany furniture. **www.romneypark.co.za**

KHAYELITSHA Kopanong Bed & Breakfast

C329 Velani Crescent, Khayelitsha, 7783 **Tel/Fax** *(021) 361-2084* **Rooms** *3*

Run by Thope Lekau and her daughter Mpho, Kopanong B&B is a friendly family home where guests are invited to share in the host's knowledge of the history and culture of the townships. Breakfast is included; with advance notice, guests can also enjoy a hearty, traditional dinner. **www.kopanong-township.co.za**

KHAYELITSHA Malebo's

18 Mississippi Way, Graceland, 7784 **Tel** *(021) 361-2391* **Fax** *(021) 361-7098* **Rooms** *3*

Lydia Masoleng offers visitors a warm welcome at her B&B. If you want to find out how the majority of South Africans live, staying at Malebo's is the way to do it. A traditional African meal is served at dinner time, and guests are also invited to visit the local shebeen to share in the latest township gossip.

KHAYELITSHA Vicky's B&B

C685a Kiyane Street, Site C, Khayelitsha, 7784 **Tel** *(082) 225-2986* **Rooms** *6*

Vicky's B&B is constructed in the typical cut-and-paste style of most township dwellings, forged from a collage of corrugated-iron, tree trunks and hardboard. Inside, however, guests want for nothing, particularly warmth and hospitality. The house is opposite the "original" V&A waterfront shebeen. **www.vickysbedandbreakfast.com**

SOUTH PENINSULA Lord Nelson Inn

58 St George's Street, Simon's Town, 7975 **Tel** *(021) 786-1386* **Fax** *(021) 786-1009* **Rooms** *10*

A traditional inn in this well-preserved former Royal Navy town, the Lord Nelson is located close to Cape Point Nature Reserve and Boulders Beach, with its renowned African penguin colony. Also nearby are tennis courts and a golf course. Rated three stars by the Tourism Grading Council of South Africa. **www.lordnelsoninn.co.za**

SOUTH PENINSULA Toad Hall

9 AB Bull Road, Froggy Farm, Simon's Town, 7975 **Tel** *(021) 786-3878* **Fax** *(021) 786-3878* **Rooms** *2*

Toad Hall is a B&B in a quiet cul-de-sac on the outskirts of Simon's Town. Watch the sun come up over False Bay, and expect to see whales between late August and early November. Your hosts can arrange a boat trip for you to get a closer look. Explore nearby Cape Point, or visit Kalk Bay and its fantastic restaurants. **www.toad-hall.co.za**

SOUTH PENINSULA Boulders Beach Lodge & Restaurant

4 Boulders Place, off Bellvue Road, Simon's Town **Tel** *(021) 786-1758* **Fax** *(021) 786-1825* **Rooms** *12*

Only a few short strides from Boulders Beach and its penguins, this hidden gem offers an east-facing location for spectacular sunrises, great food and no TV to distract you from the glorious environs. Double or twin rooms are available in the lodge, while self-catering units sleep a maximum of six. **www.bouldersbeachlodge.com**

SOUTH PENINSULA Afton Grove Country Retreat

Chapman's Peak Road (M6), Noordhoek, 7979 **Tel** *(021) 785-2992* **Rooms** *11*

Located in rural Noordhoek, at the southern end of Chapman's Peak Road, this classy four-star guesthouse offers B&B or self-catering cottages. All mod cons are available, as well as poolside dinners and picnic baskets on request. Nearby activities include horse riding, surfing, whale-watching and white shark viewing/diving. **www.afton.co.za**

SOUTH PENINSULA Quayside Hotel

Jubilee Square, St George's St, Simon's Town, 7975 **Tel** *(021) 786-3838* **Fax** *(021) 786-2241* **Rooms** *26*

Superbly located overlooking Simon's Town's busy marina and False Bay, this modern hotel offers sunny rooms with balconies and a jaunty blue-and-white marine-style decor. Museums, shops and restaurants are just a short walk away. Breakfast is included in the rates. **www.quayside.ahagroup.co.za**

SOUTH PENINSULA Villa St James

36 Main Road, St James, 7945 **Tel** *(021) 782-9356* **Rooms** *8 (sleeps up to 20)*

A landmark building on the False Bay coast, with 360-degree views of the ocean and the mountains. The villa, which can be hired for exclusive use, has a fascinating history, and has played host to many VIPs, including royalty and South African premier Jan Smuts. Close by is Kalk Bay, with its quirky shops and cafés. **www.villastjames.co.za**

SOUTH PENINSULA Whale View Manor Guest House

402 Main Road, Murdock Valley, Simon's Town, 7995 **Tel** *(021) 786-3291* **Fax** *(021) 786-1290* **Rooms** *10*

This stately manor house is perched upon a strip of lawn that runs down to Fisherman's Beach. The interior is impressively furnished, with high ceilings that convey an airy colonial ambience. The penguin colony at Boulders Beach is a short walk along the coast. A four-star haven in this secluded corner of the deep south. **www.whaleviewmanor.co.za**

SOUTH PENINSULA The Last Word, Long Beach

1 Kirsten Avenue, Kommetjie, 7976 **Tel** *(021) 783-4183* **Fax** *(021) 783-4735* **Rooms** *6*

In the fishing village and surfing spot of Kommetjie is The Last Word, Long Beach, the least metropolitan of Cape Town's boutique hotels, and one of The Last Word Group's luxury small hotels. Each room faces the sea, and the tranquil ambience fills this unexplored corner of the Cape Peninsula. No children under five. **www.thelastword.co.za**

SOUTH PENINSULA Stillness Manor & Spa

16 Debaren Close, Tokai, 7945 **Tel** *(021) 713-8800* **Fax** *(021) 713-8829* **Rooms** *7*

Set among the vineyards in the Constantia Valley, this hotel in a Cape Dutch manor house offers seven elegant suites, a peaceful garden, outdoor and indoor swimming pools and a relaxing spa with steam room and sauna. From here, it is only a short drive to Constantia's wine estates. Breakfast included. **www.stillnessmanor.com**

SOUTHERN SUBURBS Allandale Holiday Cottages

72 Swaanswyk Road, Tokai, 7945 **Tel** *(021) 715-3320* **Fax** *(021) 712-9744* **Rooms** *15*

Allandale is located at the end of a cul-de-sac on the slopes of Constantiaberg, adjacent to the Tokai Forest Reserve. Cottages are self-catering, with metered telephones. Towels and bedding are also provided. A pool and all-weather tennis court are available and mountain-bike hire is arranged on request. **www.allandale.co.za**

SOUTHERN SUBURBS Constantia Lodge

5 Duntaw Close, off Rhodes Drive, Constantia, 7806 **Tel** *(021) 794-2410* **Fax** *(021) 794-2418* **Rooms** *7*

On the southern slopes of Table Mountain, in serene and densely wooded Upper Constantia, lies this lodge. Suites are decorated with simple elegance, and they are reasonably priced for the location. There are wonderful views across False Bay from the front garden and pool area. Meals by arrangement. **www.constantialodge.com**

SOUTHERN SUBURBS Dongola House

30 Airlie Place, Constantia, 7806 **Tel/Fax** *(021) 794-8283* **Rooms** *7*

Wake up to the sound of the guinea fowl's call in this B&B. The interior is chic-contemporary-meets-traditional-African. The Constantia Wine Route starts nearby, and the beaches and restaurants of the Southern Peninsula are a short drive away. Host Peter Eckstein is on hand to provide travel tips and advice. **www.dongolahouse.co.za**

SOUTHERN SUBURBS Hampshire House
10 Willow Road, Constantia, 7806 **Tel** *(021) 794-6288* **Fax** *(021) 794-2934* **Rooms** *7*

The English and continental breakfast buffet is renowned at this sedate Constantia home with a large secluded garden. Ricky and Carole Chapman are charming and obliging hosts with a wicked sense of humour. Four-star graded and just a short drive to many excellent restaurants. **www.hampshirehouse.co.za**

SOUTHERN SUBURBS The Wild Olive Guest House
4 Keurboom Road, Newlands, 7708 **Tel** *(021) 683-0880* **Fax** *(021) 671-5776* **Rooms** *8*

The Wild Olive is nestled amid leafy suburban Newlands, close to Newlands Cricket Ground and the shopping mecca of Cavendish Square. The property has spacious grounds that feature a pool, a gym and a sauna. The atmosphere is serene and welcoming, with rooms that offer luxurious decor in warm earthy tones. **www.wildolive.co.za**

SOUTHERN SUBURBS Andros
Cnr Newlands & Phyllis Rds, Claremont, 7708 **Tel** *(021) 797-9777* **Fax** *(021) 797-0300* **Rooms** *13*

A Sir Herbert Baker-designed Cape Dutch homestead in leafy Claremont, Andros is a B&B-cum-boutique hotel with an in-house chef and wonderfully elegant rooms. The shopping at Cavendish Square, just around the corner, is on a par with what's on offer at the Waterfront and is an altogether less brash retail experience. **www.andros.co.za**

SOUTHERN SUBURBS Harfield Guest Villa
26 First Avenue, Harfield Village, Claremont, 7704 **Tel** *(021) 683-7376* **Fax** *(086) 604-0236* **Rooms** *9*

Within walking distance of Cavendish Square shopping mall and with beautiful views of the eastern side of Table Mountain, this elegant, small guesthouse offers nine rooms with garden entrances. Three of them also have a kitchen. Breakfast is included, dinner is by prior arrangement, and there is a wine bar on site. **www.harfield.co.za**

SOUTHERN SUBURBS Houtkappersspoort
Constantia Nek Estate, Hout Bay Main Rd, 7806 **Tel** *(021) 794-5216* **Fax** *(021) 794-2907* **Rooms** *26*

Houtkappersspoort is spread out across an ample piece of Constantia Nek, the pass that takes you to Hout Bay on the other side of the mountain. Despite four- and five-star gradings for the cottages, prices are remarkably affordable. Tennis, a heated pool and high-speed Internet access are all available. **www.houtkappersspoortresort.co.za**

SOUTHERN SUBURBS Southern Light Country House
24 Hohenort Avenue, Constantia, 7806 **Tel** *(021) 794-4500* **Fax** *(021) 794-4300* **Rooms** *11*

Set in two acres of gardens, with a large pool area and a tennis court, this family-friendly guesthouse features stylish decor in bold primary colours and marble bathrooms. It is located within easy reach of Constantia's wine estates, several golf courses and many restaurants. The rates include breakfast. **www.southern-light.com**

SOUTHERN SUBURBS Alphen Hotel
Alphen Drive, Constantia, 7806 **Tel** *(021) 795-6300* **Fax** *(021) 794-5710* **Rooms** *21*

This converted manor house and national monument dates back to 1753. Situated in Cape Town's most exclusive and leafy suburb, at the heart of a now-defunct wine estate, the Alphen includes a hair studio and a health and beauty salon. Personalized tours and transfers to the airport are available on request. **www.alphen.co.za**

SOUTHERN SUBURBS Cellars Hohenort
93 Brommersvlei Road, Constantia, 7800 **Tel** *(021) 794-2137* **Fax** *(021) 794-2149* **Rooms** *53*

Home to the famous restaurant of the same name, this five-star hotel is a luxury country-living experience in close proximity to everything that Cape Town has to offer. As well as luxury doubles, standard doubles, suites and single rooms, there is a private cottage and another detached villa within the grounds. **www.cellars-hohenort.com**

SOUTHERN SUBURBS Constantia Uitsig Country Hotel
Spaanschemat Road, Constantia, 7800 **Tel** *(021) 794-6500* **Fax** *(021) 794-7605* **Rooms** *16*

A working vineyard since the 17th century, the Uitsig offers superior accommodation and unparalleled gastronomic treats as two of South Africa's top restaurants – Constantia Uitsig and La Colombe – are within the hotel grounds. Sixteen garden rooms offer stunning panoramas of the Constantia Valley. **www.constantia-uitsig.com**

SOUTHERN SUBURBS Greenways Hotel
1 Torquay Avenue, Upper Claremont, 7708 **Tel** *(021) 761-1792* **Fax** *(021) 761-0878* **Rooms** *16*

Commanding six acres of rolling manicured gardens, the five-star Greenways offers boutique-hotel attentiveness and individual charm in a Cape Dutch manor house from the 1920s. There are five golf courses nearby, and the hotel is also close to Kirstenbosch National Botanical Garden and the Cavendish Square shopping mall. **www.greenways.co.za**

SOUTHERN SUBURBS Steenberg Hotel and Winery
10802 Steenberg Estate, Tokai Road, Constantia, 7945 **Tel** *(021) 713-2222* **Fax** *(021) 713-2251* **Rooms** *24*

Set on a working wine farm up against the Constantiaberg Mountains, this hotel is housed entirely within the original listed Cape Dutch buildings and offers a tranquil setting and great views across the vineyards. Other amenities include a superb 18-hole golf course, three restaurants and a luxury spa. **www.steenberghotel.com**

SOUTHERN SUBURBS Vineyard Hotel & Spa
Colinton Road, Newlands, 7700 **Tel** *(021) 657-4500* **Fax** *(021) 657-4501* **Rooms** *207*

The Vineyard is a four-star hotel with three excellent restaurants on its premises and the beautiful Angsana Spa. There is a conference centre in a separate building. The Cavendish Square shopping mall is nearby, and the city centre and the V&A Waterfront are only 15 minutes away by car. **www.vineyard.co.za**

CAPE WINELANDS

FRANSCHHOEK Auberge Bligny   ®®®

28 van Wijk Street, Franschhoek, 7690 **Tel** *(021) 876-3767* **Fax** *(021) 876-3483* **Rooms** *8*

An 1860 homestead in the historic centre of Franschhoek, this Huguenot home is furnished with period antiques that add to the period atmpophere. Some of South Africa's greatest restaurants are within easy walking distance. In the summer months, breakfast is served on the terrace, with a view of the pool and the mountains beyond. **www.bligny.co.za**

FRANSCHHOEK La Fontaine Guest House   ®®®

21 Dirkie Uys Street, Franschhoek, 7690 **Tel** *(021) 876-2112* **Rooms** *14*

This beautiful guest house is centrally located in the village, and it offers great value for money. Rooms in the main house afford beautiful mountain views. Among the activities on offer at La Fontaine are fly fishing, horse riding and hiking, and children of all ages are welcome. **www.lafontainefranschhoek.co.za**

FRANSCHHOEK Plumwood Inn Country Guest House   ®®®

11 Cabriere Street, Franschhoek, 7690 **Tel** *(021) 876-3883* **Fax** *(086) 672-6030* **Rooms** *11*

Eleven rooms all sumptuously and uniquely decorated in a contemporary style are available here. The Plumwood experience offers unrivalled pampering, superb views and a daily soundtrack of garrulous birdlife. Franschhoek's cosmopolitan centre is a mere 2 minutes away on foot. **www.plumwoodinn.com**

FRANSCHHOEK Rusthof Country House   ®®®

12 Huguenot Street, Franschhoek, 7690 **Tel** *(021) 876-3762* **Fax** *(086) 614-2799* **Rooms** *8*

This small and exclusive country house hosts a maximum of 16 guests at a time. The Rusthof is on the main street of Franschhoek, within a minute's walk of the town's restaurants and delis. A wide range of activities can be arranged, including wine tours, horseback wine tastings, hot-air ballooning and scenic drives to Route 62. **www.rusthof.com**

FRANSCHHOEK Akademie Street Boutique Hotel & Guest House   ®®®®®

5 Akademie Street, Franschhoek, 7690 **Tel** *(021) 876-3027* **Fax** *(021) 876-3293* **Rooms** *6*

Located in a quiet area of the village, this property comprises three separate guesthouses that are effectively individual cottages, each with its own private pool and garden attended by cooing doves and chirping crickets. Rooms have been nominated as the Winelands' best for honeymoons. **www.aka.co.za**

FRANSCHHOEK Franschhoek Country House & Villas   ®®®®

Main Road, Franschhoek, 7690 **Tel** *(021) 876-3386* **Fax** *(021) 876-2744* **Rooms** *25*

At this restored manor house and perfumery, the emphasis is on classic luxury, attention to detail and utter indulgence. It has spectacularly furnished villa suites and a wine cellar. The venue's Monneaux restaurant, headed up by chef Adrian Buchanan, has been winning accolades since the mid-1990s. **www.fch.co.za**

FRANSCHHOEK Le Quartier Français   ®®®®®

Cnr Berg & Wilhelmina sts, Franschhoek, 7690 **Tel** *(021) 876-2151* **Fax** *(021) 876-3105* **Rooms** *15*

Focusing on "ultimate luxury and romantic charm", Le Quartier Français is located in the centre of Franschhoek. The innovative restaurant regularly appears on international top-50 lists. Beauty therapy is available, with some rooms featuring private pools and iPod docking stations. **www.lqf.co.za**

HERMON Bartholomeus Klip Farmhouse   ®®®®®

Hermon, 7308 **Tel** *(022) 448-1087* **Fax** *(086) 604-4321* **Rooms** *5*

Endless vistas, herds of roaming antelope, mountains turning pink as the sun dips below the horizon: the Bartholomeus Klip enjoys a magical setting. Explore the farm and nature reserve on a mountain bike, chill by the lake, or visit the quagga-rebreeding and buffalo-breeding projects. The rate is all inclusive. **www.bartholomeusklip.com**

KUILSRIVER Zevenwacht Country Inn   ®®®

Langverwacht Road, Kuils River, 7580 **Tel** *(021) 903-5123* **Fax** *(021) 903-3373* **Rooms** *24*

All modern comforts are installed in these air-conditioned luxury suites with private terraces and views across False Bay. The Zevenwacht's working wine farm is also an integral part of the Stellenbosch Wine Route. Cellar tours, cheese and wine tastings, horse riding and quad biking are all available on the premises. **www.zevenwacht.co.za**

MONTAGU Airlies Guest House   ®®

36 Bath Street, Montagu, 7560 **Tel** *(023) 614-2943* **Fax** *(086) 617-8360* **Rooms** *7*

This charming Edwardian house, on the scenic Route 62, offers elegant, spacious bedrooms with high ceilings and polished wooden floors. Amenities include a large garden with fruit trees and a pool, and log fires in winter. A varied selection of good restaurants lies within easy walking distance. **www.airlies.co.za**

MONTAGU Mimosa Lodge   ®®®

Church Street, Montagu, 6720 **Tel** *(023) 614-2351* **Fax** *(086) 535-0722* **Rooms** *23*

Sleek modern decor adorns the spacious rooms in this intimate Edwardian hotel renowned for its hospitality. The food is also well-regarded, presided over by owner-chef Bernhard Hess. Montagu is central to Route 62 and affords easy exploration of this increasingly popular alternative to the Garden Route. **www.mimosa.co.za**

Key to Price Guide *see p380* **Key to Symbols** *see back cover flap*

MONTAGU Montagu Country Hotel
27 Bath Street, Montagu, 6720 **Tel** *(023) 614-3125* **Fax** *(023) 614-1905* **Rooms** *33*

⚇❋☒目 ⓇⓇⓇ

Simple country charm and relaxation are the key themes at this airy hotel with Art Deco accents. Staff are on hand to pamper with massages, facials and all manner of organic beauty treatments. Fruit trees line the streets in this Winelands oasis and infuse the dry air with their aromas in the spring and summer. **www.montagucountryhotel.co.za**

PAARL Goedemoed Country Inn
Cecilia Street, Paarl, 7646 **Tel** *(021) 863-1102* **Fax** *(021) 863-1104* **Rooms** *9*

❋目 ⓇⓇⓇ

A Cape Dutch manor house on a working wine farm, this B&B also offers dinner by prior arrangement. Surrounded by Shiraz and Chardonnay vineyards, Goedemoed is in close proximity to both the Berg River and a superb 18-hole golf course. Nine double rooms are available, all with free high-speed wireless Internet. **www.goedemoed.com**

PAARL Lemoenkloof Guest House
396a Main Street, Paarl, 7646 **Tel** *(021) 872-3782* **Fax** *(021) 872-7532* **Rooms** *26*

❋目 ⓇⓇⓇⓇ

A 19th-century listed Victorian homestead with a manicured garden. There is a secluded pool area and a sun terrace where you can sunbathe after enjoying a generous cooked breakfast. The ambience is one of great tranquillity. Horse riding on neighbouring farms is available by arrangement. **www.lemoenkloof.co.za**

PAARL Pontac Manor Hotel & Restaurant
16 Zion Street, Paarl, 7646 **Tel** *(021) 872-0445* **Fax** *(021) 872-0460* **Rooms** *22*

⚇❋☒目 ⓇⓇⓇ

A historic piece of 18th-century architecture tucked below Paarl Rock, the Pontac Manor is surrounded by oak trees and imbued with the generous spirit and hospitality of the Boland region. An award-winning and gastronomically accomplished restaurant is housed in a restored barn on the estate, which also produces its own wine. **www.pontac.com**

PAARL Grande Roche Hotel
1 Plantasie Street, Paarl, 7646 **Tel** *(021) 863-5100* **Fax** *(021) 863-2220* **Rooms** *35*

⚇❋☒⛭目 ⓇⓇⓇⓇⓇ

This 18th-century Paarl manor house has a sophisticated contemporary flavour to its decor. The hotel facilities include floodlit tennis courts, two swimming pools, gym, massage parlour, hair salon, sauna and steam bath. Bosman's is an award-winning restaurant and Allegro is an informal bistro. **www.granderoche.co.za**

PAARL Palmiet Valley Estate
Sonstraal Road, Paarl, 7628 **Tel** *(021) 862-7741* **Fax** *(021) 862-6891* **Rooms** *11*

⚇❋目P ⓇⓇⓇⓇ

Located on a farmstead that dates back to 1642, this establishment features luxury suites that have been lovingly decorated with antiques and Persian rugs. Most have French doors leading to the leafy garden. On sunny days, breakfast (included in the rates) is served on a long table under an oak tree. **www.palmietvalleyestate.co.za**

ROBERTSON Rosendal Winery & Wellness Retreat
Klaas Voogds West, Robertson, 6705 **Tel** *(023) 626-1570* **Fax** *(023) 626-1571* **Rooms** *10*

⚇❋目P ⓇⓇⓇⓇ

Breathtaking Breede River Valley views, game drives embarking from the doorstep, an intimate wine cellar, one of the area's most accomplished restaurants and, of course, the beautifully appointed wellness centre combine to create an outstanding hotel. A stay at Rosendal is always a special experience. **www.rosendalwinery.co.za**

SOMERSET WEST Penny Lane Lodge
5 North Avenue, Westridge, Somerset West, 7130 **Tel** *(021) 852-9976* **Fax** *(021) 851-2520* **Rooms** *6*

❋☒目 ⓇⓇⓇ

Located in the beautiful town of Somerset West, Penny Lane Lodge offers its guests the choice of B&B-style accommodation or self-catering units sleeping two to four people. It is located close to six major golf courses. Staff can arrange day trips and activities such as whale-watching or fishing. **www.pennylanelodge.co.za**

SOMERSET WEST Ivory Heights Boutique Hotel
17 L Botha Ave, Monte Sereno, Somerset West, 7130 **Tel** *(021) 852-8333* **Fax** *(021) 852-8886* **Rooms** *10*

❋☒⛭目 ⓇⓇⓇ

An award-winning boutique hotel offering splendid views of False Bay from the infinity pool, as well as free wireless Internet, pool, satellite TV and home cinema, gym, tennis and squash courts. Contemporary architecture and sleek decor set the mood in this airy and elegant five-star establishment. **www.ivoryheights.co.za**

SOMERSET WEST The Lord Charles Hotel
Cnr Main Rd & Broadway Blvd, Somerset West, 7130 **Tel** *(021) 855-1040* **Fax** *(021) 855-1107* **Rooms** *156*

⚇❋☒⛭目♿P ⓇⓇⓇⓇ

A large four-star hotel with panoramic views of the Helderberg Mountain, the Lord Charles has a good range of amenities, including two swimming pools, tennis courts, a country-style restaurant and a pub. It is located close to several golf courses and wine estates. **www.nh-hotels.co.za**

STELLENBOSCH Knorhoek Country Guest House
Knorhoek Road, off R44, off N1 between Stellenbosch and Klapmuts, 7600 **Tel** *(021) 865-2114* **Rooms** *7*

❋☒目P ⓇⓇⓇⓇ

The wine farm here dates back to 1710. Enjoy a traditional Cape breakfast as the farmyard hubbub fizzes around you. During harvest time, you will be invited to sample the first fermentations of the year and enjoy the award-winning wines on offer. In addition to the seven en-suite rooms, there is also one self-catering suite. **www.knorhoek.co.za**

STELLENBOSCH Protea Hotel Dorpshuis
22 Dorp Street, Stellenbosch, 7600 **Tel** *(021) 883-9881* **Fax** *(021) 883-9884* **Rooms** *27*

⚇❋目P ⓇⓇⓇ

Elegant country-style accommodation close to the University of Stellenbosch is on offer here. The comfortable rooms, furnished with antiques, have all modern conveniences. Light meals are available throughout the day, and the Oak Leaf restaurant serves South African fare. Spa and sauna are available. **www.proteahotels.com**

STELLENBOSCH Ryneveld Country Lodge   ℝℝℝ

67 Ryneveld Street, Stellenbosch, 7600 **Tel** *(021) 887-4469* **Fax** *(021) 883-9549* **Rooms** *10*

Luxurious antiques adorn the halls of this national monument. Self-catering cottages, as well as individually furnished en-suite rooms, are available. Children are welcome, and golf and wine tours can be arranged on request. The management have been collecting accolades and awards since 1999. **www.ryneveldlodge.co.za**

STELLENBOSCH Batavia Boutique Hotel   ℝℝℝℝ

12 Louw Street, Stellenbosch, 7600 **Tel** *(021) 887-2914* **Fax** *(021) 887-2915* **Rooms** *9*

With its blend of 19th-century antiques and hi-tech amenities, Batavia offers something exclusive and unique. Renovated from a derelict house by the inspired hand of Matilda de Bod, it stands just off Dorp Street in the historic heart of Stellenbosch and is within walking distance of museums and restaurants. **www.batavia-stellenbosch.co.za**

STELLENBOSCH D'Ouwe Werf Hotel   ℝℝℝℝ

30 Church Street, Stellenbosch, 7600 **Tel** *(021) 887-4608* **Fax** *(021) 887-4626* **Rooms** *50*

In business since 1802, this four-star inn lends new meaning to the word "established". It offers a heated outdoor pool, free valet parking and 45 individually decorated en-suite rooms and five apartments. The staff pride themselves on their attentive service. D'Ouwe Werf is also renowned as a fine dining destination. **www.ouwewerfhotel.co.za**

STELLENBOSCH Eendracht Boutique Hotel   ℝℝℝℝ

161 Dorp Street, Stellenbosch, 7600 **Tel** *(021) 883-8843* **Fax** *(021) 883-8842* **Rooms** *12*

Located in the heart of old Stellenbosch, the Eendracht is close to many shops, restaurants and the major museums. The emphasis is firmly placed on luxury and traditional Afrikaans hospitality. Next door to the hotel is the fascinating village-museum complex, which consists of the four oldest houses in town. **www.eendracht-hotel.com**

STELLENBOSCH Sante Hotel, Resort & Spa   ℝℝℝℝ

Simonsvlei Road, Paarl-Franschhoek Valley, 7625 **Tel** *(021) 875-8100* **Fax** *(021) 875-8111* **Rooms** *49*

Focusing entirely on health and lifestyle, Sante offers manor house suites and spa village rooms, all arranged around a piazza. The sumptuous spa has vineyard views, and their signature "vinotherapy", or grape cure, is said to relax, rejuvenate and de-stress. **www.santesa.co.za**

STELLENBOSCH Summerwood Guest House   ℝℝℝℝ

28 Jonkershoek Road, Mostertsdrift, Stellenbosch, 7600 **Tel** *(021) 887-4112* **Fax** *(021) 887-4239* **Rooms** *9*

This turn-of-the-century mansion has been lovingly restored by an Italian architect to appeal to contemporary tastes. The grounds are extensive and there are only nine rooms, so guests never feel overcrowded. Staff are always on standby to help with tips on Stellenbosch, guided wine tours or golfing outings. **www.summerwood.co.za**

STELLENBOSCH The Village at Spier   ℝℝℝℝ

R310 Lynedoch Road, Lynedoch, Stellenbosch, 7600 **Tel** *(021) 809-1100* **Fax** *(021) 809-1973* **Rooms** *155*

At this luxury wine-estate village, the grounds are immense and dotted with pretty, self-contained cottages. The estate dates back to 1692 and is now a throbbing cultural hub in the area. The complex also plays host to three excellent restaurants, including the unique Moyo, as well as art collections and the Camelot Spa. **www.spier.co.za**

STELLENBOSCH Lanzerac Hotel & Spa   ℝℝℝℝℝ

Lanzerac Road, Stellenbosch, 7599 **Tel** *(021) 887-1132* **Fax** *(021) 887-2310* **Rooms** *48*

The Lanzerac is one of South Africa's finest examples of Cape Dutch architecture. It is located amid landscaped gardens and surrounded by ancient oak trees that add to the historic atmosphere. The rooms include Presidential and Royal Pool suites, the latter with its own private pool, as the name would suggest. **www.lanzerac.co.za**

TULBAGH De Oude Herberg   ℝℝℝ

6 Church Street, Tulbagh, 6820 **Tel** *(023) 230-0260* **Fax** *(086) 666-0260* **Rooms** *4*

Originally established in 1885, this guesthouse has been a national monument since it was rebuilt after the town's devastating 1969 earthquake. Occupying a prime position near the centre of the village, it has four double en-suite rooms decorated in a simple contemporary and elegant style. **www.deoudeherberg.co.za**

TULBAGH Rijk's Country House   ℝℝℝℝ

Rijk's Wine Farm, Winterhoek Road, Tulbagh, 6820 **Tel** *(023)230-1006* **Fax** *(023) 230-1125* **Rooms** *15*

On the outskirts of town and part of a new wine estate, the Rijk's offers secluded and luxurious tranquillity. Each room has its own verandah overlooking the lake and mountains. Other facilities at this resort include a wine-tasting room and the popular Iceberg Terrace, with views over the lake and the vineyards. **www.rijkscountryhouse.co.za**

WELLINGTON Diemersfontein Wine and Country Estate   ℝℝ

Jan van Riebeck Drive (R301), Wellington, 7654 **Tel** *(021) 864-5050* **Rooms** *14*

Diemersfontein has been turning heads in the wine trade since its first selection of reds in 2001. Its heavenly Pinotage is now very hard to find. There is no better way to pick up a case than to go to the source. Rooms are furnished in a comfortable country style, and activities include mountain biking and horse riding. **www.diemersfontein.co.za**

WORCESTER Church Street Lodge   ℝℝ

36 Church Street, Worcester, 6850 **Tel** *(023) 342-5194* **Fax** *(023) 342-8859* **Rooms** *21*

Situated in the historical and most attractive part of town, Church Street Lodge offers a Roman-themed swimming pool, fountains and a serene leafy garden in which to relax. All rooms are air-conditioned, with fridges and TVs with M-Net (subscription channels). Self-catering units are also available. **www.churchst.co.za**

WESTERN COASTAL TERRACE

CEDERBERG Mount Ceder

Grootrivier Farm, Cederberg **Tel** *(023) 317-0848* **Fax** *(023) 317-0543* **Rooms** *7*

A river etches a path through rugged mountain scenery at this Cederberg retreat. There are seven self-catering cottages with three bedrooms each, and a small country shop nearby, allowing guests to stock up on essentials. Hiking, canoeing, bird-watching, swimming and horse riding are all on offer. **www.mountceder.co.za**

CITRUSDAL Kardouw Country Retreat

Take Citrusdal turnoff off N7, Citrusdal, 7340 **Tel** *(022) 921-2474* **Fax** *(072) 286-2044* **Rooms** *6*

Experience tranquil riverside living in the compact farmhouse or one of the cabins on stilts, connected by elevated boardwalks. One cabin features a barbecue area overlooking the Olifants River. Canoes are available for paddling down the river, and a hot spring with swimming pools is a short drive away. **www.citrusdal.info/kardouw**

CLANWILLIAM Saint du Barry's Country Lodge

13 Augsberg Road, Clanwilliam, 8135 **Tel** *(027) 482-1537* **Fax** *(027) 482-2824* **Rooms** *5*

Hosts Wally and Joan foster an atmosphere of light-hearted generosity in this luxurious home from home. Bedrooms are all en suite, with high ceilings and wooden rafters. The Saint du Barry's is highly commended by the AA, and the enchanting hospitality here leaves guests longing to return. **www.saintdubarrys.com**

CLANWILLIAM Bushmanskloof Wilderness Reserve

Over Pakhuis Pass, towards Wuppertal, 8135 **Tel** *(021) 481-1860* **Fax** *(021) 481-1870* **Rooms** *16*

The Bushmanskloof features one of the densest concentrations of rock art in South Africa: paintings are found on 130 separate sites. In spring, the landscape bursts with colour as wild flowers carpet the ground. Guided walks and botanical tours allow you to explore the local eco-system. Rates include all meals and activities. **www.bushmanskloof.co.za**

LANGEBAAN The Farmhouse Hotel

5 Egret Street, Langebaan, 7357 **Tel** *(022) 772-2062* **Fax** *(022) 772-1980* **Rooms** *30*

Built on the hill above the lagoon in 1860, this dignified Cape Dutch building exudes a stately charm, with its reed ceilings, oversized fireplaces and majestic vistas. Stretch your legs on a hike in the adjacent nature reserve, or head out to Langebaan's bars and restaurants to experience the local culture. **www.thefarmhousehotel.com**

MOOREESBURG Sewefontein

Follow Palaisheuwel Road, in Piekenierskloof Pass, off N7 **Tel** *(022) 921-3301* **Fax** *(022) 921-2502* **Rooms** *2*

A working farm at the top of majestic Piekenierskloof with two self-catering houses available for hire. A great option for independent travellers on a budget, Sewefontein is also a good base from which to explore the surrounding areas of Clanwilliam and Lamberts Bay, or the Cederberg and Kouebokkeveld. **www.citrusdal.info/sewefontein/**

PIKETBERG Dunn's Castle Guesthouse

R399 Veldrif Road, Piketberg, 7320 **Tel** *(022) 913-2470* **Fax** *(086) 613-1907* **Rooms** *28*

A Herbert Baker-designed home in the heart of the Swartland, the Dunns Castle has cosy rooms with a Victorian feel, each with its own fireplace. Twenty self-catering cottages have been added to the accommodation options. The hosts are renowned for their caring and helpful hospitality. **www.dunnscastle.co.za**

RIEBEEK KASTEEL The Royal Hotel

33 Main Street, Riebeek Kasteel, 7307 **Tel** *(022) 448-1378* **Fax** *(022) 448-1073* **Rooms** *10*

The Royal boasts four stars, a state-of-the-art kitchen and an outdoor amphitheatre. The fittings are of excellent quality: contemporary, but full of character. The porch has been described as "the most convivial stoep south of the Limpopo", so expect a lively atmosphere with plenty of locals. **www.royalinriebeek.com**

RIEBEEK WEST Riebeek Valley Hotel

4 Dennehof Street, Riebeek West, 7306 **Tel** *(022) 461-2672* **Fax** *(086) 549-7049* **Rooms** *28*

A well-appointed country house that exudes tranquillity, the Riebeek Valley Hotel overlooks a picture-postcard valley of vineyards, with the Cederberg beyond. The en-suite bedrooms and suites are mostly spacious and adorned in a romantic fashion. High-quality fusion cuisine is served at Bishops restaurant. **www.riebeekvalleyhotel.co.za**

ST HELENA BAY The Oystercatcher Lodge

1st Avenue, Shelley Point, St Helena Bay, 7382 **Tel** *(022) 742-1202* **Fax** *(022) 742-1201* **Rooms** *6*

The Oystercatcher, quietly positioned at the water's edge, presents spellbinding views from the private verandahs. In the spring you can watch the whales from your room, or stroll down to the nine-hole golf course. There are also five self-catering apartments. The decor has a Mediterranean beach house feel to it. **www.oystercatcherlodge.co.za**

VELDRIF Doornfontein Guest Farm

R399, Veldrif, 7368 **Tel** *(022) 783-0853* **Rooms** *9*

The Doornfontein is a working farm, and the Melck family go all out to ensure a genuine West Coast experience for their guests. A riverboat is available for bird-watching and sundowner cruises through the wetlands. Choose from rooms in the restored farmstead or the cottage adjacent to the indoor heated pool. **www.doornfonteinfarm.co.za**

VELDDRIF Kersefontein Guest Farm 🔟 🅿 ⓇⓇⓇ

Between Hopefield & Velddrif, 7355 **Tel** *(022) 783-0850* **Fax** *(022) 783-0850* **Rooms** *6*

This family-run farm dates back to 1770, when it was established by settler Martin Melck. Today Julian Melck's large en-suite bedrooms are lovingly furnished with period antiques salvaged from the farm's attics. The *Architectural Digest* described the farm as "...appearing to exist in a glorious and romantic time warp". **www.kersefontein.co.za**

YZERFONTEIN Emmaus on Sea 🔝 ⓇⓇ

30 Versveld Street, Yzerfontein, 7351 **Tel** *(022) 451-2650* **Fax** *(022) 451-2650* **Rooms** *6*

This well-appointed retreat is only one hour's drive from Cape Town and 19 km (12 miles) from the West Coast Nature Reserve. Enjoy picturesque views over the quaint fishing harbour, long walks on unspoilt beaches, and opportunities for whale- and bird-watching. B&B-style accommodation or self-catering.

SOUTHERN CAPE

BETTY'S BAY Buçaco Sud Guesthouse 🖼 ⓇⓇ

2609 Clarence Drive, Betty's Bay, 7141 **Tel** *(028) 272-9750* **Fax** *(028) 272-9750* **Rooms** *6*

Individually decorated rooms with a Provençal feel are found at this beautiful Betty's Bay guesthouse. The Kogelberg Mountains behind are South Africa's first UNESCO Biosphere Nature Reserve, while the bay in front is a popular destination for whale-watchers. Both Cape Town and Hermanus are easy day trips. **www.bucacosud.co.za**

GANSBAAI Crayfish Lodge Sea and Country Guest House 🔟 🖼 🅿 ⓇⓇⓇⓇ

2–4 Killarney Street, De Kelders, 7220 **Tel** *(028) 384-1898* **Fax** *(028) 384-1898* **Rooms** *5*

Great sea and *fynbos* views can be enjoyed from this fine contemporary building. There is a large heated swimming pool and a sandy beach just a short stroll down the hill. The Crayfish Lodge boasts its own wellness clinic. Two luxury suites and three superior garden rooms are available, each with its own private patio. **www.crayfishlodge.co.za**

GREYTON The Greyton Lodge 🔟 🖼 🔝 ⓇⓇⓇ

52 Main Street, Greyton, 7233 **Tel** *(028) 254-9800* **Fax** *(086) 626-4750* **Rooms** *15*

A former police station renovated as a series of cottages, this hotel is evocative of the unique, elegant Greyton character. The GL restaurant offers award-winning cuisine and a superb selection of local and international wines, while the adjacent gallery hosts regular exhibitions by local artists. **www.greytonlodge.com**

HERMANUS Harbour Vue Guesthouse 🖼 🅿 ⓇⓇⓇ

84 Westcliff Road, Hermanus, 7200 **Tel** *(028) 312-4860* **Fax** *(086) 503-2424* **Rooms** *4*

Tastefully decorated en-suite rooms with high-quality finishes in this four-star luxury B&B. Watch the whales from your bedroom, or stroll down to the cliff paths and breathe in the heady *fynbos* aromas. The dining room also features large glass panels that can be opened to enjoy the sounds of the waves crashing below. **www.harbourvue.co.za**

HERMANUS Whale Rock Lodge 🖼 🔝 🅿 ⓇⓇⓇⓇ

26 Springfield Avenue, Westcliff, Hermanus, 7200 **Tel** *(028) 313-0014* **Fax** *(028) 313-2932* **Rooms** *11*

One of the most pristine and lovingly maintained old buildings in Hermanus, Whale Rock Lodge is covered in heavy thatch, which hints at the cosy ambience inside. Breakfast is served in the sun room, with a view over the koi pond and pool below. Water sports such as kayaking, scuba diving and fishing can be arranged. **www.whalerock.co.za**

HERMANUS The Marine 🔝 🔟 🖼 🔝 📋 🅿 ⓇⓇⓇⓇⓇ

Marine Drive, Walker Bay, Hermanus, 7200 **Tel** *(028) 313-1000* **Fax** *(028) 313-0160* **Rooms** *42*

Individually decorated bedrooms and suites, each with its own facilities, can be found here. The Marine boasts a spa and heated salt-water swimming pool in the large central courtyard. A dip in the tidal pool in front of the hotel gives the impression of swimming with the whales, which can often be seen off shore. **www.marine-hermanus.co.za**

MCGREGOR The Old Mill Lodge 🔟 🖼 🔝 ⓇⓇ

McGregor, 6708 **Tel** *(023) 625-1841* **Fax** *(023) 625-1941* **Rooms** *8*

Consisting of four cottages, each with two separate en-suite bedrooms, the Old Mill has been lovingly restored and provides a perfectly secluded spot along the world's longest wine route. A delightfully cosy bar and lounge overlooks the vineyards and the majestic Langeberg Mountains. **www.oldmilllodge.co.za**

OUDTSHOORN De Oude Meul Country Lodge 🔟 🖼 🔝 🅿 ⓇⓇ

R328, near Cango Caves, 6620 **Tel** *(044) 272-7190* **Fax** *(082) 272-7190* **Rooms** *40*

Halfway between the Cango Caves and Oudtshoorn, in the beautiful Schoemanspoort Valley and surrounded by mountains, is the three-star De Oude Meul. Owners Boy and Marianne assure their guests of a supremely comfortable stay and a delicious ostrich steak at dinner time. **www.deoudemeul.co.za**

OUDTSHOORN Feather Nest Guest House 🗐 🖼 📋 ⓇⓇ

12 Tiran Street, West Bank, Oudtshoorn, 6620 **Tel** *(083) 415-5407* **Fax** *(086) 617-7793* **Rooms** *3*

Mia Steyn's home is comfortable, relaxed and affordable. Recline beside the pool and listen to the sound of hundreds of birds chattering in the lush foliage above, or take in the spectacular Karoo sunset with a cocktail in hand on the spacious balcony. **www.feathernest.co.za**

Key to Price Guide *see p380* **Key to Symbols** *see back cover flap*

OUDTSHOORN Queens Hotel

Baron van Reede Street, Oudtshoorn, 6625 **Tel** *(044) 272-2101* **Fax** *(044) 272-2104* **Rooms** *40*

Children are welcome at this popular Oudtshoorn hotel, the third-oldest in South Africa, having been built in colonial style in 1880. It is close to shops and restaurants in the centre of town. All 40 rooms have their own bath and shower, and the Colony restaurant features an award-winning menu. **www.queenshotel.co.za**

OUDTSHOORN La Plume Guest House

Volmoed, Route R62, 6620 **Tel** *(044) 272-7516* **Fax** *(044) 272-3892* **Rooms** *12*

La Plume is a working ostrich and alfalfa farm with wonderful views over the Olifants River all the way to the Swartberg Mountains. Hosts Bartel and Karin offer extraordinarily warm hospitality, great service and high levels of personal attention at this 1902 Victorian homestead. **www.laplume.co.za**

OUDTSHOORN Rosenhof Country Lodge

264 Baron van Reede Street, Oudtshoorn, 6625 **Tel** *(044) 272-2232* **Fax** *(044) 272-3021* **Rooms** *14*

A collection of antiques offsets the original exposed yellowwood beams and ceilings. The two executive suites are separated from the main house for extra privacy, and they have their own swimming pools, too. There are excellent wellness and fitness facilities available to work off the restaurant's cordon bleu meals. **www.rosenhof.co.za**

STANFORD Mosaic Farm

Hermanus Lagoon, Provincial Road, 7210 **Tel** *(028) 313-2814* **Rooms** *9*

Spacious en-suite rooms under thatch and canvas are seamlessly integrated with the surroundings, which feature magnificent *fynbos*, ancient milkwood thickets, Stanford's Kleinrivier Lagoon and the craggy Overberg Mountains. Nature-related activities are on offer. Rate includes breakfast and dinner. **www.mosaicfarm.net**

SWELLENDAM Aan de Oever Guest House

21 Faure Street, Swellendam, 6740 **Tel** *(028) 514-1066* **Fax** *(086) 216-6884* **Rooms** *7*

The Aan de Oever offers spacious, open-plan rooms with simple but elegant furnishings. Casual luxury abounds in this serene location. Relax by the salt-water pool, play a round of golf on the nine-hole course or watch the birdlife through the telescope in the garden. **www.aandeoever.com**

SWELLENDAM Old Mill Guest House & Restaurant

241–243 Voortrekker Street, 6750 **Tel** *(028) 514-2790* **Fax** *(028) 514-1292* **Rooms** *6*

This guesthouse – a collection of converted historical farm cottages located in a beautiful garden with a stream running through – is also renowned for its restaurant, which specializes in local dishes such as *bobotie* and *melktert* (*see p409*). The owners are Belgian, so visitors can expect a number of European languages to be spoken. **www.oldmill.co.za**

SWELLENDAM De Kloof Luxury Estate

8 Weltevrede Street, Swellendam, 6740 **Tel** *(028) 514-1303* **Fax** *(028) 514-1304* **Rooms** *9*

De Kloof offers guests daily complimentary wine tastings, as well as a cigar lounge, a pool and a fully equipped gym. Extra-long beds and oversized duvets add to the ambience of sheer indulgence in the deluxe and honeymoon suites. A candle-lit table for a gourmet dinner can be set up on the estate's rolling lawns. **www.dekloof.co.za**

SWELLENDAM The Hideaway

10 Hermanus Steyn Street, Swellendam, 6740 **Tel** *(028) 514-3316* **Fax** *(086) 645-9735* **Rooms** *4*

Considered by many to be one of South Africa's best guesthouses, this charming Victorian house is among the oldest in Swellendam. Rooms are individually furnished with handcrafted furniture and antiques. The house is set in a lush green garden, from which there are spectacular views of the mountains behind. **www.hideawaybb.co.za**

WITSAND Breede River Resort & Fishing Lodge

Joseph Barry Avenue, Witsand, 6666 **Tel** *(028) 537-1631* **Fax** *(028) 537-1650* **Rooms** *24*

Located at the mouth of the Breede River, this lodge organizes a wide range of activities for its guests, from deep-sea fishing charters to skippered boat hire, spearfishing, horse riding, kayaking and quad biking. The hotel has been graded as three-star accommodation; the self-catering option has four stars. **www.breederiverlodge.co.za**

GARDEN ROUTE TO GRAHAMSTOWN

ADDO Cosmos Cuisine Guesthouse

Sunland, Addo, Sundays River Valley **Tel** *(042) 234-0323* **Fax** *(042) 234-0796* **Rooms** *15*

Ten minutes from Addo Elephant Park, Cosmos draws visitors in with traditional country hospitality in the heart of the Sundays River Valley. The restaurant has been voted one of the best in South Africa, and its sumptuous five-course gastronomical extravaganzas are a welcome respite after a long day's game driving. **www.cosmoscuisine.co.za**

THE CRAGS Hog Hollow Country Lodge

Askop Road, The Crags, Plettenberg Bay, 6600 **Tel** *(044) 534-8879* **Fax** *(044) 534-8879* **Rooms** *16*

A unique eco-venture and a labour of love set on the edge of an indigenous forest and private nature reserve, the Hog Hollow is a little slice of paradise on the Garden Route. Beautifully decorated log cabins offer sweeping vistas of the surrounding woodlands. The superb team of friendly staff comes from the local community. **www.hog-hollow.com**

GEORGE Hilltop Country Lodge ®®®

Victoria Bay, George, 6529 **Tel** *(044) 889-0142* **Fax** *(044) 889-0199* **Rooms** *8*

A country guesthouse in a private reserve overlooking the Indian Ocean. The lodge layout makes full advantage of the incredible panoramas, with big windows and glass doors opening on to lawns that roll down to lush forests and the sea. Hosts Magda and Hennie will provide advice for your daytrips and meals. **www.hilltopcountrylodge.co.za**

GEORGE Protea Hotel King George ®®®

King George Drive, King George Park, George, 6529 **Tel** *(044) 874-7659* **Fax** *(044) 874-7664* **Rooms** *109*

Close to the George Golf Course, this hotel offers attentive service and a wide range of amenities, including two swimming pools, a tennis court and a children's playground. A bowling green, squash courts and hiking trails are all nearby. There's also a terrace overlooking the majestic Outeniqua Mountain Range. **www.proteahotels.com**

GEORGE Fancourt Hotel ®®®®

Montague Street, Blanco, George, 6529 **Tel** *(044) 804-0010* **Fax** *(044) 804-0710* **Rooms** *115*

Cape colonial decor has been tastefully applied at the Fancourt, and a variety of restaurants offer gourmet treats for weary fairway trudgers. Facilities include two Gary Player-designed golf courses and a golf school, four tennis courts, a squash court, lawn bowls and outdoor swimming pools. **www.fancourt.co.za**

GRAHAMSTOWN 137 High Street ®®®

7 Worcester Street, Grahamstown, 6139 **Tel** *(046) 622-2843* **Fax** *(046) 622-2846* **Rooms** *7*

This restored Victorian residence is close to the town centre, where you can enjoy many shopping opportunities, as well as numerous cultural events. Expect boutique hotel-style luxury, a warm welcome from the attentive staff and good, traditional meals in the attached restaurant and tea room. **www.137highstreet.co.za**

GRAHAMSTOWN The Cock House Guest House & Restaurant ®®®

10 Market Street, Grahamstown, 6139 **Tel** *(046) 636-1287* **Fax** *(046) 636-1287* **Rooms** *9*

The Cock House is a G-Town landmark and former winner of the heritage category in the AA Travel Awards. The interior is adorned with yellowwood floors, sublime fabrics and attractive antiques. The library played host to novelist André Brink, of *A Dry, White Season* fame, who wrote four of his novels here. **www.cockhouse.co.za**

KNYSNA Point Lodge ®®®

The Point, Knysna, 6570 **Tel** *(044) 382-1944* **Fax** *(044) 382-3455* **Rooms** *9*

Ryk and Amanda Cloete's guesthouse offers panoramic views across the lagoon to the Knysna Heads. Point Lodge is a good base from which to explore Knysna; bicycle and canoe hire are both available. The ambience is quiet and peaceful, with a wide variety of birds to be found in the garden. **www.pointlodge.com**

KNYSNA Waterfront Lodge ®®®

The Point, Knysna, 6570 **Tel** *(044) 382-1696* **Fax** *(044) 382-1652* **Rooms** *8*

Marion and Gavin's establishment is set on the edge of tranquil Knysna Lagoon. You will be amazed by the birdlife you can admire from the lagoon-view garden. Facilities at the lodge include a sauna and Jacuzzi. A relaxing massage is available on request; the more energetic will enjoy the golf courses nearby. **www.waterfront-lodge.co.za**

KNYSNA Belvidere Manor ®®®

Belvidere Estate, 169 Duthie Drive, Knysna, 6570 **Tel** *(044) 387-1055* **Fax** *(044) 387-1059* **Rooms** *28*

Belvidere Manor is a historic estate dating from 1834. Guests stay in individual cottages, each with its own verandah, living room and double en-suite bedroom, set in colourful gardens with sweeping lagoon views. Dine at Caroline's Bistro or The Bell Tavern, Knysna's smallest pub. Small conference venue available. **www.belvidere.co.za**

KNYSNA The Lofts Boutique Hotel ®®®

Long Street, The Boatshed, Thesen Island, Knysna, 6570 **Tel** *(044) 302-5710* **Fax** *(044) 302-5711* **Rooms** *10*

This small boutique hotel is tucked away in a boatshed on Thesen Island. Amenities include a heated pool and a lounge bar. Selected rooms have balconies with lagoon views, and the harbour and a plethora of fine restaurants and interesting shops are a mere 7-minute walk away. **www.thelofts.co.za**

KNYSNA St James of Knysna ®®®®

The Point, Knysna, 6570 **Tel** *(044) 382-6750* **Fax** *(044) 382-6756* **Rooms** *15*

A five-star country hotel on the shores of the lagoon, the St James is owner-managed and offers an exclusive retreat on the outskirts of Knysna. The emphasis here is firmly on privacy and high standards of service. Guests are afforded lots of individual attention in this hotel, which is set on a beautifully landscaped estate. **www.stjames.co.za**

MATJIESFONTEIN The Lord Milner Hotel ®®®

Matjiesfontein, off the N1 Karoo, 8900 **Tel** *(023) 561-3011* **Fax** *(023) 561-3020* **Rooms** *58*

The Lord Milner is a well-preserved colonial vestige of what was once a glamorous Victorian spa town. In the early 1900s, this building was used as a military hospital during the Anglo-Boer War. The colonial atmosphere extends to the daily raising of the Union Jack on the turret of the hotel. **www.matjiesfontein.com**

MOSSEL BAY Bella Sombra Guesthouse ®®

72 21st Avenue, Mossel Bay, 6500 **Tel** *(044) 690-8150* **Rooms** *5*

This is a beautiful guesthouse with breathtaking views across Mossel Bay. Breakfast can be enjoyed on the patio while watching whales play in the waters below. The Mossel Bay Golf Course is situated just 800 m (9 yards) from your doorstep. **www.bellasombra.co.za**

Key to Price Guide *see p380* **Key to Symbols** *see back cover flap*

MOSSEL BAY Cheetah Lodge

Take R328 Hartenbos/Oudtshoorn, Brandwag **Tel** *(076) 744-9957* **Fax** *(044) 694-0029* **Rooms** *5*

African decor, an outdoor *braaivleis* area and a heated pool are some of the attractions at Cheetah Lodge. A variety of birdlife and buck can be spotted within the grounds. The management will be pleased to arrange activities such as game drives, deep-sea fishing, quad-bike rides and bird-watching. **www.cheetahlodge.com**

MOSSEL BAY Eight Bells Mountain Inn

Robinson Pass, R328, between Mossel Bay & Oudtshoorn **Tel** *(044) 631-0000* **Fax** *(044) 631-0004* **Rooms** *25*

Great bed-and-breakfast hospitality is on offer from the Brown family, who have run Eight Bells for more than 30 years. Accommodation ranges from thatched rondavels to log cabins and rooms in the main house. Horse riding and tennis courts are available on the premises. **www.eightbells.co.za**

MOSSEL BAY The Point Hotel

Point Road, The Point, Mossel Bay, 6500 **Tel** *(044) 691-3512* **Fax** *(044) 691-3513* **Rooms** *52*

A four-star hotel built upon the rocks below the lighthouse, The Point Hotel is a three-minute drive from Mossel Bay town and offers spectacular views of the breakers crashing on to the jagged shoreline. Whales swim by regularly in the spring. The St Blaize hiking trail that hugs the coastline starts nearby. **www.pointhotel.co.za**

PLETTENBERG BAY Crescent Country Hotel

Piesang Valley Road, Plettenberg Bay, 6600 **Tel** *(044) 533-3033* **Fax** *(044) 533-2016* **Rooms** *39*

Budget accommodation in Plettenberg Bay is increasingly rare. However, this established and clean hotel offers great-value B&B lodgings in park-like grounds in Piesang River Valley, 1.5 km (1 mile) from the beach. There are good recreational facilities, including canoeing, pony rides, tennis and volleyball. **www.crescenthotels.com**

PLETTENBERG BAY Anlin Place

33 Roche Bonne Avenue, Plettenberg Bay, 6600 **Tel** *(044) 533-3694* **Fax** *(044) 533-3394* **Rooms** *4*

The Indian Ocean and white sands of Robberg Beach are only a short walk away from this guesthouse, also known as Anlin Beach House. The four apartments are fully equipped with all mod cons for self-catering. Suites are serviced daily and offer satellite TV and wireless Internet connections. Decor is contemporary African. **www.anlinplace.co.za**

PLETTENBERG BAY Emily Moon River Lodge

End of Rietvlei Rd, off N2, after Plettenberg Bay, 6600 **Tel** *(044) 533-2982* **Fax** *(044) 533-0687* **Rooms** *8*

All lodges at the Emily Moon River are individually and stylishly furnished and accommodate one couple each, apart from the family lodge, which sleeps four. All feature wooden decks overlooking the sprawling wildlife-rich Bitou River wetlands. Bathrooms include under-floor heating and open-air showers. **www.emilymoon.co.za**

PLETTENBERG BAY Tsala Treetop Lodge

From Plettenberg Bay, take N2 west for 10 km (6 miles), 6600 **Tel** *(044) 501-1111* **Fax** *(044) 501-1100* **Rooms** *16*

Tsala is a unique and luxurious forest-canopy living experience: glass-and-wood huts are perched high on stilts and connected by wooden boardwalks above the Tsitsikamma forest floor. Each treetop dwelling has its own plunge pool, fireplace and sunken bathtub. In addition, there are six two-bedroom villas. **www.hunterhotels.com**

PORT ALFRED Halyards Hotel & Spa

Albany Road, Port Alfred, 6170 **Tel** *(046) 624-8525* **Fax** *(046) 624-8529* **Rooms** *49*

This three-star Cape Cod-style landmark hotel is located in the Royal Alfred Marina and is popular for family holidays. A range of activities is available, including cruises on the Kowie river, deep-sea fishing and game drives at the Halyards-owned Mansfield Private Reserve. **www.riverhotels.co.za**

PORT ALFRED Fort d'Acre Game Reserve

Box 394, Port Alfred, 6170 **Tel** *(040) 676-1091* **Fax** *(040) 676-1095* **Rooms** *4*

Enjoy sweeping views of both the ocean and the grassland bushveld at this exclusive private game park situated at the mouth of the Great Fish River. The thatched safari lodge is decorated with African art and artifacts. Game drives and horse safaris can be arranged by the management. **www.fortdacre.com**

PORT ELIZABETH Brighton Lodge

21 Brighton Drive, Summerstrand, Port Elizabeth, 6001 **Tel** *(041) 583-4576* **Fax** *(041) 583-4104* **Rooms** *11*

A boutique hotel-styled establishment close to the airport and central shopping areas of the city, Brighton Lodge is positioned to cater for both leisure and business travellers. As well as Internet and fax facilities, a swimming pool and airport shuttle services are available on request. **www.brightonlodge.co.za**

PORT ELIZABETH Forest Hall

84 River Road, Walmer, Port Elizabeth, 6001 **Tel** *(041) 581-3356* **Fax** *(086) 660-4848* **Rooms** *6*

Wake to the sound of abundant birdlife before enjoying a leisurely breakfast in the Tuscan-style dining room at this charming bed and breakfast. All rooms have a private patio overlooking the garden and the Romanesque swimming pool. The Little Walmer Golf Estate is nearby. **www.foresthall.co.za**

PORT ELIZABETH The Beach Hotel

Marine Drive, Summerstrand, Port Elizabeth, 6001 **Tel** *(041) 583-2161* **Rooms** *58*

A standard hotel on Port Elizabeth's beachfront, close to several shopping centres and Bayworld. Nearby are the famous Hobie Beach, the casino and a variety of watersports and recreational activities. Non-smoking rooms, Jacuzzis and separate showers are available on request. **www.thebeachhotel.co.za**

PORT ELIZABETH Hacklewood Hill Country House ⓇⓇⓇⓇ

152 Prospect Road, Walmer, Port Elizabeth, 6070 **Tel** *(041) 581-1300* **Fax** *(041) 581-4155* **Rooms** *8*

A luxurious, serene and private country house full of Victorian character. All rooms have a large bathroom and several also have a balcony; the grounds include a crystal-clear pool and a tennis court. The decor is made up of rich and sumptuous colours, exquisite fabrics and a considerable antiques collection. **www.hacklewood.co.za**

PORT ELIZABETH Shamwari Game Reserve ⓇⓇⓇⓇⓇ

Off N2, between Port Elizabeth and Grahamstown, 6139 **Tel** *(041) 407-1000* **Fax** *(041) 407-1001* **Rooms** *60*

Shamwari, South Africa's leading malaria-free game reserve, has seven luxury lodges, each independent and individually decorated. The reserve and its ecosystem are meticulously maintained by a dedicated team of experts. After a long day game driving, relax at the luxury spa. The rate is all-inclusive. **www.shamwari.com**

SEDGEFIELD Lakeside Lodge ⓇⓇⓇ

Wilderness National Park, Wilderness, 6560 **Tel** *(044) 343-1844* **Fax** *(044) 343-1844* **Rooms** *10*

An eco-tourism retreat on the banks of the Swartvlei Lake inside the Wilderness National Park. There are either lake-facing self-catering rooms or B&B accommodation. The limited number of rooms at Lakeside Lodge – and the fact that it is closed to non-residents – guarantees a private and exclusive stay. **www.lakesidelodge.co.za**

TSITSIKAMMA Tsitsikamma Lodge ⓇⓇⓇ

Storms River, Tsitsikamma, 6308 **Tel** *(046) 624-8525* **Fax** *(046) 624-8529* **Rooms** *32*

This lodge comprises a series of log cabins, each with its own spa bath, situated in a garden setting with splendid mountain or forest views. Other facilities include a pool, spa and games room. Spectacular trails are nearby, including the famous Striptease River Trail. **www.riverhotels.co.za/tsitsikamma**

WILDERNESS Ballots Bay Coastal Lodges ⓇⓇⓇ

Victoria Bay turnoff, George Industria, 6536 **Tel** *(044) 880-2299* **Fax** *(044) 880-1153* **Rooms** *8*

Ballots Bay is a rocky cove nestled amid the steep cliffs of a rugged coastline. Beautiful rustic timber homes are available for hire in this dramatic private reserve, the ideal retreat for nature lovers who appreciate hiking, fishing, and bird- and game-watching. There are magnificent views over the *fynbos*-covered hills. **www.ballotsbay.co.za**

WILDERNESS Moontide ⓇⓇⓇ

Southside Road, Wilderness, 6560 **Tel** *(044) 877-0361* **Fax** *(044) 877-0124* **Rooms** *8*

This cluster of five charming en-suite cottages, each with its own entrance and patio, is set among 400-year-old milkwood trees along the shores of the Wilderness lagoon, a paradise for bird-watchers. The beach is a five-minute walk away, and a spa and several fine restaurants and craft shops are within easy reach. **www.moontide.co.za**

WILD COAST, DRAKENSBERG & MIDLANDS

BALGOWAN Granny Mouse Country House & Spa ⓇⓇⓇⓇⓇ

Box 22, Balgowan, KwaZulu-Natal, 3275 **Tel** *(033) 234-4071* **Fax** *(033) 234-4429* **Rooms** *20*

The deluxe thatched cottages of Granny Mouse are found at the foot of the Drakensberg Mountains, in the heart of the Natal Midlands. Located among golf courses and battlefields, the four-star hotel has an award-winning restaurant and spa. Canopy tours, quad biking and hot-air ballooning can all be arranged. **www.grannymouse.co.za**

BARKLY EAST Reedsdell Guest Farm ⓇⓇ

Box 39, Barkly East, Eastern Cape, 9786 **Tel** *(045) 974-9900* **Fax** *(045) 974-9900* **Rooms** *5*

This working holistic farm is located in mountain country, close to the highest passes of the southern Drakensberg. The scenic surroundings, which include waterfalls, sheer cliffs, pristine grasslands and rock art, are perfect for hikers to explore. The farm organizes arts and crafts courses, as well as skiing tuition in the winter. **www.snowvalley.co.za**

BERGVILLE Orion Mont aux Sources Hotel ⓇⓇⓇⓇ

Mont aux Sources, Bergville, 3350 **Tel** *(036) 438-8000* **Fax** *(036) 438-6201* **Rooms** *107*

The Mont aux Sources Hotel lies in the spectacular setting of the Amphitheatre area of the Drakensberg, where the Tugela River creates the second-highest waterfall in the world, plunging more than 950 m (3,000 ft). Outdoor activities include giant chess, a playground, ball games, hiking and climbing. **www.oriongroup.co.za**

BUTHA BUTHE, LESOTHO Afriski Ski + Mountain Resort ⓇⓇⓇ

Mahlasela Pass, Lesotho **Tel** *(266) 595-44734* **Rooms** *40*

The ideal destination for active holiday-makers: as well as a ski slope and lift, there is an Austrian-operated ski school, an après-ski restaurant and a selection of bars. In the summer, facilities include the highest Gary Player golf course on earth, fishing, mountain and quad biking, rock climbing, rafting and trekking. **www.afriski.net**

BUTHA BUTHE, LESOTHO New Oxbow Lodge ⓇⓇⓇ

Box 60, Ficksburg, Free State, 9730 **Tel** *(051) 933-2247* **Fax** *(051) 933-2247* **Rooms** *35*

This lodge is made up of thatched and tin-roofed rondavels on the banks of the Malibamatsoe River, in the Lesotho Maluti Mountains. This is strictly 4x4 territory, and a haven for bird-watching, hiking and climbing. There is a ski slope with equipment for hire at Mahlasela Hill, 11 km (7 miles) away. Children under 12 stay free. **www.oxbow.co.za**

Key to Price Guide *see p380* **Key to Symbols** *see back cover flap*

CHAMPAGNE VALLEY Inkosana Lodge ⬜⬜ ®

Box 60, Winterton, 3340 **Tel** *(036) 468-1202* **Fax** *(036) 468-1202* **Rooms** *13*

Surrounded by luxuriant gardens, Inkosana offers a variety of accommodation options, including dorms for up to 150 people. Good climbing opportunities await nearby, and the lodge offers guidance for climbers, as well as white-water rafting. Dinner is often a barbecue. Winner of the AA Overnight Backpackers Award. **www.inkosana.co.za**

DUNDEE Royal Country Inn ⬜ ®®

61 Victoria Street, Dundee, 3000 **Tel** *(034) 212-2147* **Fax** *(034) 218-2146* **Rooms** *32*

The Royal Country Inn, located on the Battlefields Route, offers a mix of well-appointed bedrooms and economical backpackers' lodgings. Hiking, bird-watching, mountain biking, abseiling and white-water rafting are all available. There are several nature reserves nearby, as well as the Zulu Cultural Experience. **www.royalcountryinn.com**

EAST LONDON Bunkers Inn ⬜⬜⬜ ®®

23 The Drive, Bunkers Hill, East London, 5241 **Tel** *(043) 735-4642* **Fax** *(043) 735-1227* **Rooms** *10*

Located on a golf course in a quiet suburb, the Art Deco-style Bunkers Inn attracts visitors thanks to its proximity to game reserves and museums. A snake park, an aquarium and the beach are also nearby. There is an Internet connection in every room, and picnics can be arranged by the management. **www.bunkersinn.co.za**

EAST LONDON Kennaway Hotel ⬜⬜⬜⬜ ®®®

Esplanade, Orient Beach, East London, 6280 **Tel** *(043) 722-5531* **Fax** *(043) 743-3433* **Rooms** *107*

This three-star, seven-storey balconied block on the Esplanade offers a vast array of lodgings, including spacious rooms, suites, family rooms and honeymoon suites. Nearby, visitors will find a spa and an aquarium, as well as whale-watching opportunities. Township tours can also be arranged. **www.katleisure.co.za**

GONUBIE The White House ⬜⬜⬜ ®®

10 Witthaus Street, Gonubie, Eastern Cape, 5257 **Tel** *(043) 740-0344* **Fax** *(086) 616-3768* **Rooms** *11*

Fifteen minutes from East London, on a Blue Flag beach and the Gonubie River, is this attractive four-star B&B, which also offers self-catering rooms. Surfing, sailing, waterskiing and boating are all available. A casino and a game park are nearby. **www.thewhitehousebandb.co.za**

HOWICK Mulberry Hill Guest House ⬜⬜⬜ ®®

Curry's Post Road, Howick, 3290 **Tel** *(033) 330-5921* **Fax** *(033) 330-4424* **Rooms** *6*

Located on an estate near the Howick Falls, the four-star Mulberry Hill Guest House is on the Midlands Meander Art & Craft Route. There are two trout dams for fishing enthusiasts, as well as glorious mountain views and forest walks. Riding, bird-watching, croquet, polo and golf are all available nearby. **www.mulberryhill.co.za**

LIDGETTON Pleasant Places ⬜ ®®®

Lidgetton Valley, KwaZulu-Natal, 3270 **Tel** *(033) 234-4396/(082) 456-2717* **Fax** *(086) 615-2988* **Rooms** *6*

Lying in the green Natal Midlands, this thatched country house is surrounded by forests and farming country. Guests can either relax in the rambling garden or opt for more energetic pursuits in the nearby river and rapids. Nature lovers should also keep an eye out for the otters and birds that frequent this area. **www.pleasantplaces.co.za**

MAZEPPA BAY Mazeppa Bay Hotel ⬜⬜⬜⬜ ®®®®

Mazeppa Bay, Eastern Cape **Tel** *(047) 498-0033* **Fax** *(047) 498-0034* **Rooms** *49*

On its own island, reached by a suspension bridge, is the highly recommended Mazeppa Bay Hotel. Thatched single-storey rooms and rondavels cluster around a central building. Among the activities available are fishing, canoeing, hiking, volleyball, tennis, sandboarding and mountain biking. **www.mazeppabay.co.za**

MOOI RIVER Sycamore Avenue Treehouse ⬜⬜ ®®®®

11 Hidcote Road, Mooi River, 3310 **Tel** *(033) 263-2875* **Fax** *(086) 688-5949* **Rooms** *8*

Located in the Giants Castle area of the Drakensberg, one of the most scenic parts of KwaZulu-Natal, Sycamore Avenue offers beautifully appointed wooden pavilions in the trees. All rooms come with balconies and Jacuzzis. Children under 12 stay at half price; those under the age of two for free. **www.sycamore-ave.com**

MOOI RIVER Hartford House ⬜⬜⬜ ®®®®®

Hlatikulu Road, Mooi River, 3300 **Tel** *(033) 263-2713* **Rooms** *16*

The former home of Natal's prime minister, Hartford House is now a luxurious boutique hotel. It is surrounded by beautiful gardens and boasts a wellness centre and a helipad. The management offers guided tours of nature reserves, as well as drives and picnics to Bushman painting sites and battlefields. **www.hartford.co.za**

NEWCASTLE Newcastle Inn ⬜⬜⬜ ®®®

Cnr Hunter & Victoria Roads, Newcastle, 2940 **Tel** *(034) 312-8151* **Fax** *(034) 312-4142* **Rooms** *165*

Situated in the economic heart of KwaZulu-Natal, with views of both downtown Newcastle and luxuriant gardens, the Newcastle Inn is conveniently located for the Zululand Battlefield tour. There is a casino nearby, as well as a golf course. **www.africanskyhotels.com**

NOTTINGHAM ROAD Rawdon's Hotel ⬜⬜ ®®®®

Box 7, Nottingham Road, Midlands, KwaZulu-Natal, 3280 **Tel** *(033) 266-6044* **Fax** *(033) 266-6048* **Rooms** *28*

Officially described as a "hotel and fly-fishing estate", Rawdon's Hotel provides warm, friendly hospitality in a building with a thatched roof, dormer windows and log fires. Restaurants, a coffee shop and a brewery offer welcome refreshment after activities such as tennis, bowls and volleyball. **www.rawdons.co.za**

NOTTINGHAM ROAD Fordoun Hotel & Spa ⓇⓇⓇⓇⓇ
Nottingham Road, Midlands, KwaZulu-Natal, 3280 **Tel** *(033) 266-6217* **Fax** *(086) 603-8778* **Rooms** *22*

Built in the 1880s, this dairy farm amid scenic rolling grasslands has been turned into a boutique hotel and restaurant. Relax in the steam room or hydrotherapy bath. Alternatively, go fishing with the local guru, or try horse riding, hot-air ballooning or mountain biking. There is also a golf course nearby. **www.fordoun.com**

PIETERMARITZBURG Protea Hotel Hilton ⓇⓇⓇ
1 Hilton Avenue, Hilton, 3245 **Tel** *(033) 343-3311* **Fax** *(033) 343-3722* **Rooms** *97*

This hotel has been welcoming guests since 1936. Housed in a Tudor-style building, located amid rolling green grounds, the terrace has a swimming pool, a tennis court and Ellington's Restaurant and Cocktail Bar, which is well known for its Sunday lunch. A good base for the Midlands Meander Art & Craft Route. **www.proteahotels.com**

PORT ST JOHNS Khululeka Retreat ⓇⓇ
Box 128, Port St Johns, 5120 **Tel** *(072) 194-3644* **Fax** *(086) 672-4096* **Rooms** *12*

Off the beaten track, the Khululeka Retreat offers catered or self-catering cottages in indigenous forest on a hill with views of the sea and the estuary of the Ntafufu River. Meet the local tribal people, visit the Magwa tea plantation or the Isinuka sulphur springs. Fishing, whale-watching, hiking and biking are all available. **www.khululeka.co.za**

PORT ST JOHNS Umzimvubu Retreat ⓇⓇⓇ
380 Golf Course Drive, First Beach, Port St Johns, 5120 **Tel** *(047) 564-1741* **Fax** *(047) 564-1310* **Rooms** *12*

This guesthouse is within walking distance of the town centre and a golf course. Overlooking the mouth of the Great Umzimvubu River and the Indian Ocean, the three-star Umzimvubu is ideally located for exploring the Wild Coast. Enjoy local crafts, angling, canoeing, biking and forest trails. **www.umzimvuburetreat.co.za**

PORT ST JOHNS Umngazi River Bungalows & Spa ⓇⓇⓇ
Box 75, Port St Johns, Wild Coast, 5120 **Tel** *(047) 564-1115* **Fax** *(047) 564-1210* **Rooms** *64*

Spacious thatched bungalows, a spa and fresh local food are just some of the reasons for staying here. Add pristine beaches, breathtaking views, indigenous forests and mangrove swamps, and the Umngazi River Bungalows become very appealing. Activities include fishing and tennis; there is also a spa. Rate includes all meals. **www.umngazi.co.za**

QOLORA MOUTH Trennery's ⓇⓇⓇ
Southern Wild Coast, Eastern Cape, 4960 **Tel** *(047) 498-0004I(082) 908-3134* **Fax** *(047) 498-0011* **Rooms** *37*

Thatched rondavels and bungalows provide the accommodation in lush, tropical gardens close to the lagoon and the river. Among the activities on offer are tennis, bowls, golf, sailing, fishing, 4x4 adventures and sea cruises. Saturday nights see Trennery's famous Seafood Extravaganza. A good place for children. **www.trennerys.co.za**

RORKE'S DRIFT Fugitives' Drift Lodge ⓇⓇⓇⓇⓇ
Rorke's Drift, KwaZulu-Natal, 3016 **Tel** *(034) 642-1843* **Fax** *(034) 271-8051* **Rooms** *17*

The Rattray family are pioneers of historical tourism, and their stylish guesthouse houses an impressive collection of Zulu and Anglo-Boer war-related memorabilia. The lodge is located in a vast nature reserve with abundant wildlife, including zebras, giraffes and over 250 species of birds. Rate is all inclusive. **www.fugitivesdrift.com**

WINTERTON Dragon Peaks Mountain Resort Ⓡ
PO Winterton, 3340 **Tel** *(036) 468-1031* **Fax** *(036) 468-1104* **Rooms** *30*

Choose between B&B and self-catering accommodation at this family- and pet-friendly resort. Cottages, chalets and campsites are located in the shadow of Champagne Castle, the second-highest peak in South Africa, and the Cathkin Mountains in the Ukhahlamba World Heritage Site. A game reserve is nearby. **www.dragonpeaks.com**

WINTERTON Cathedral Peak Hotel ⓇⓇⓇⓇ
Winterton, Drakensberg, KwaZulu-Natal, 3340 **Tel** *(036) 488-1888* **Fax** *(036) 488-1889* **Rooms** *94*

A collection of thatched buildings on a hillside in the Drakensberg, this three-star hotel was opened in 1939. Located in a dramatic setting, it has a wedding chapel among its facilities, along with a helicopter pad, children's programmes, biking, fishing, riding and hiking trails. The rate is all inclusive. **www.cathedralpeak.co.za**

DURBAN AND ZULULAND

BALLITO Dolphin Holiday Resort ⓇⓇ
Compensation Road, Dolphin Crescent, Ballito, 4420 **Tel** *(032) 946-2187* **Fax** *(032) 946-3490* **Rooms** *12*

This informal resort with cottages, caravan stands and campsites is situated in a peaceful forest north of Durban. Shopping facilities, beaches, golf and restaurants are all available nearby. Outdoor chess, volleyball, trampolines and a playground make it a great destination for families with young children. **www.dolphinholidayresort.co.za**

BALLITO Izulu Hotel ⓇⓇⓇⓇ
Rey's Place, Ballito, 4420 **Tel** *(032) 946-3444* **Fax** *(032) 946-3494* **Rooms** *19*

The five-star Izulu Hotel is a mere five-minute walk from the sea and offers splendid views of subtropical dunes. Relax in the luxuriously appointed beauty spa, or take part in more active pursuits such as visits to the nearby crocodile farm, animal reserve, and historic and cultural sites, including battlefields. **www.hotelizulu.com**

Key to Price Guide *see p380* **Key to Symbols** *see back cover flap*

DOLPHIN COAST The Lodge at Prince's Grant
Prince's Grant, Dolphin Coast, 4404 **Tel** *(032) 482-0005* **Fax** *(032) 482-0040* **Rooms** *15*

The four-star Lodge at Prince's Grant is situated on the KwaZulu-Natal golf estate, in the vicinity of other golf courses. As well as a private lagoon, guests can enjoy the beautiful unspoilt coastline near Rorke's Drift, not to mention the stunning views of the Indian Ocean. **www.princesgrant.co.za**

DURBAN 164 Guest House
164 St Thomas Road, Musgrave, Berea, Durban, 4001 **Tel** *(031) 201-4493* **Fax** *(031) 201-4496* **Rooms** *7*

In the heart of trendy Musgrave, the 164 benefits from its proximity to boutiques, cafés, shops and bars. Built in 1928 in luxurious colonial style, this five-star guesthouse also offers self-catering cottages. A wealth of activities, such as riding, cycling, fishing, golf, bird-watching and paragliding, is available nearby. **www.164.co.za**

DURBAN Bali on the Ridge
28 Mazisi Kunene Road, Glenwood, Durban, 4001 **Tel** *(031) 261-9574* **Rooms** *10*

A stylish guesthouse decorated with Indonesian furnishings from the owners' shop, Bali on the Ridge boasts sweeping views over the city centre and harbour. Generous breakfasts (included in the price) are served on the verandah, and the restaurants of Musgrave are only a short drive away. **www.baliridge.co.za**

DURBAN City Lodge
Cnr Silvester Ntuli and K.E. Masinga, Durban, 4001 **Tel** *(031) 332-1447* **Fax** *(031) 332-1483* **Rooms** *160*

This reliable chain hotel strikes the right balance between corporate and leisure hospitality. City Lodge is centrally located and is only a couple of minutes from relaxing beaches and the convention and exhibition centres. Although the rooms are basic, luscious gardens and a swimming pool add to the appeal. **www.citylodge.co.za**

DURBAN Elangeni Hotel
63 Snell Parade, Durban, 4001 **Tel** *(031) 362-1300* **Fax** *(031) 332-5527* **Rooms** *449*

Part of the Tsogo Sun group, the fashionable Elangeni is situated on the beach, within walking distance of shops and restaurants, and close to attractions such as Durban's Snake Park, Seaworld and flea market. Tennis, bowling, squash, fishing and windsurfing can be arranged by the management. **www.tsogosunhotels.com**

DURBAN Garden Court South Beach
73 OR Tambo Parade, Durban, 4001 **Tel** *(031) 337-2231* **Fax** *(031) 337-4640* **Rooms** *414*

A modern Art Deco building on the beach, close to the city centre and several attractions, including the Juma Musjid Mosque (the largest in the southern hemisphere), the Indian market, the Botanical Gardens and the BAT Arts Centre. The rooms are standard but well turned out, with coffee- and tea-making facilities. **www.tsogosunhotels.com**

DURBAN North Beach Hotel
83 Snell Parade, Durban, 4001 **Tel** *(031) 332-7361* **Fax** *(031) 337-4058* **Rooms** *295*

North Beach is a world-famous surfers' paradise, but within walking distance of this three-star establishment you will also find museums and art galleries. The hotel is close to the convention centre, Durban's Snake Park and Mini Town. A pool on the 32nd floor offers amazing views of the Indian Ocean. **www.tsogosunhotels.com**

DURBAN Protea Hotel Edward
149 OR Tambo Parade, Durban, 4001 **Tel** *(031) 337-3681* **Fax** *(031) 337-3628* **Rooms** *101*

This elegant four-star hotel on the Golden Mile is located within walking distance of Durban's central business district, the convention centre, the casino and the shops. Built in 1911, the Edward has been constantly updated. It features an internationally recognized restaurant. Children under 12 stay free. **www.proteahotels.com**

DURBAN Royal Hotel
267 Anton Lembede Street, Durban, 4001 **Tel** *(031) 333-6000* **Fax** *(031) 333-6002* **Rooms** *204*

This 150-year-old grand hotel in Durban's city centre is decorated with warm yellowwood and blue tones. The butler service adds a touch of luxurious sophistication, and there are massage and sauna facilities. Six restaurants, three bars and views over the yacht harbour all contribute to the appeal. **www.theroyal.co.za**

DURBAN Audacia Manor
11 Sir Arthur Road, Morningside, 4001 **Tel** *(031) 303-9520* **Fax** *(031) 303-2763* **Rooms** *10*

Built in 1928, this family home in a secluded cul-de-sac is the *grande-dame* of the Durban hotel scene, exuding a genteel charm. Sit in the drawing room or on the Arts and Crafts-style verandah, cooled by the breezes of the Berea. Among the services on offer are a beautician, chauffeur and croquet on the lawn. **www.africanpridehotels.com**

DURBAN Quarters Hotel
101 Florida Road, Morningside, 4001 **Tel** *(031) 303-5246* **Fax** *(031) 303-5269* **Rooms** *23*

Four gracious Victorian houses provide a successful combination of Old World charm and modern sophistication. The rooms are exquisitely appointed, with balconies, air-conditioning and double-glazed windows, and the Brasserie Restaurant offers a wide-ranging menu. Minutes from the sea and the city's dining district. **www.quarters.co.za**

ESHOWE Shakaland
Normanhurst Farm, Nkwalini, Eshowe, 3816 **Tel** *(035) 460-0912* **Fax** *(035) 460-0824* **Rooms** *55*

Experience the disappearing Zulu culture at this resort overlooking Umhlatuze Lake. Shakaland is an authentic re-creation of a historic Zulu village, Shaka's Great Kraal. Guests stay in traditional beehive huts and enjoy Zulu activities such as tribal dancing, spear-making, beadwork and a beer-drinking ceremony. **www.shakaland.com**

HLUHLUWE Zululand Tree Lodge   🍴 ≋ 🏃   ®®®®®

PO Box 116, Hluhluwe, 3960 **Tel** *(035) 562-1020* **Fax** *(035) 562-1032* **Rooms** *24*

Enjoy an unusual accommodation experience in these thatched houses on stilts in a fever-tree forest, part of the Ubizane Wildlife Reserve. Each tree lodge includes a luxury bedroom, en-suite bathroom and private balcony. Guided walks and drives, boat cruises and bird-watching can all be arranged. The rate is all inclusive. **www.ubizane.co.za**

KOSI BAY Rocktail Beach Camp   🍴 ≋ 🏃   ®®®®®

Manguzi, Kosi Bay, KwaZulu-Natal, 3886 **Tel** *(021) 424-1037* **Fax** *(021) 424-1036* **Rooms** *17*

Located in the iSimangaliso Wetland Park, Rocktail Beach Camp has easy access to 29 km (18 miles) of ocean coast. The Maputaland Marine Reserve lies just offshore, providing unique diving and snorkelling opportunities. Accommodation is in thatched tree-house chalets with balcony and en-suite bathrooms. **www.wilderness-safaris.com**

LINKHILLS Zimbali Resort   🍴 ≋ 🏃 🍽 🎬 🅿   ®®®®®

PO Box 17, Zimbali, 3652 **Tel** *(032) 538-5000* **Fax** *(032) 538-5001* **Rooms** *154*

A five-star boutique hotel overlooking the Indian Ocean and set within a conservation area rich in local flora and fauna. The luxurious rooms are located in lodges with viewing decks and furnished with wooden furniture. Bird- and butterfly-watching, golf, horse riding and swimming are just some of the activities on offer. **www.fairmont.com**

NORTH KWAZULU White Elephant Safari Lodge & Bush Camp   🍴 ≋ 🏃   ®®®®®

Pongola Game Reserve, North KwaZulu **Tel** *(034) 413-2489* **Fax** *(034) 413-2499* **Rooms** *15*

Surrounded by the majestic Lebombo Mountains and Lake Jozini are these 15 luxury safari tents, all featuring private verandahs, bathrooms with views and outdoor showers. The Kors family are conservation pioneers and organize elephant-viewing programmes, game drives and bush walks. The rate is all inclusive. **www.whiteelephant.co.za**

PORT EDWARD The Estuary Country Hotel   🍴 ≋ 🏃 🎬 🅿   ®®®

PO Box 71, Port Edward, 4295 **Tel** *(082) 380-9890* **Fax** *(039) 311-2689* **Rooms** *44*

Offering easy access to the nature reserves on the south coast and to the golf courses at the Wild Coast Sun and San Lameer Resort, the Estuary Country Hotel is a friendly option in a restored Cape Dutch manor house. A safe swimming beach is a short walk away, and there is a beauty spa on the estate. **www.estuaryhotel.co.za**

SAN LAMEER Mondazur Resort Estate Hotel   🍴 ≋ 🏃 🎬 🅿   ®®®®

Old Main Road, San Lameer, 4277 **Tel** *(039) 313-0011* **Fax** *(039) 313-0157* **Rooms** *40*

The beneficiary of a multimillion-rand renovation, this resort hotel is located on a lagoon on the Indian Ocean. Mondazur is a great option for a beach holiday, but it also has plenty to keep more active guests happy: abundant wildlife, boat rides, tennis courts, a golf course, volleyball and squash. **www.mondazur.com**

UMHLANGA ROCKS Beverly Hills Hotel   📺 🍴 ≋ 🏃 🍽 🎬 🅿   ®®®®®

Lighthouse Road, Umhlanga Rocks, 4320 **Tel** *(031) 561-2211* **Fax** *(031) 561-3711* **Rooms** *88*

A favourite luxurious modern hotel on the seafront, with superb views of the Indian Ocean and miles of unspoilt beaches within easy access. The recently refurbished rooms are decorated in brown and cream tones; the suites have rich suede and leather furnishings and plasma TV screens. Close to amenities and shops. **www.tsogosunhotels.com**

UMHLANGA ROCKS The Oyster Box   📺 🍴 ≋ 🍽   ®®®®®

2 Lighthouse Road, Umhlanga Rocks, 4319 **Tel** *(031) 514-5000* **Fax** *(031) 561-4072* **Rooms** *86*

This Art Deco building from the 1930s has been renovated and extended, but it maintains its original atmosphere of old-fashioned elegance. Right on the beach, and featuring its own lighthouse, The Oyster Box is also close to the city centre and its amenities. It is famous for high tea and oysters served in many ways. **www.oysterboxhotel.com**

GAUTENG AND SUN CITY

DUNKELD WEST Backpackers Ritz of Johannesburg   🍴 ≋   ®

1a North Road, Dunkeld West, 2196 **Tel** *(011) 325-7125* **Fax** *(011) 325-2521* **Rooms** *15*

Basic accommodation, friendly service and tourist tips are available at the longest-established hostel in Johannesburg. Located in a beautiful mansion, it boasts a swimming pool, a bar and pretty views. It is close to shopping malls, restaurants and flea markets, and staff can organize day tours in and around Johannesburg. **www.backpackers-ritz.co.za**

DUNKELD WEST Ten Bompas   🍴 ≋ 🎬   ®®®®®

10 Bompas Rd, Dunkeld West, 2196 **Tel** *(011) 341-0282* **Fax** *(011) 341-0281* **Rooms** *10*

Ten suites, each individually decorated by a different interior designer with their own interpretation of "Home from Home in Africa". Neutral colours and cherrywood furniture are used throughout. The restaurant serves classic dishes and old home favourites. A magnificent wine cellar overlooks the swimming pool. **www.tenbompas.com**

EASTERN SUBURBS Brown Sugar Backpackers   ≋ 🅿   ®

75 Observatory Avenue, 2198 **Tel** *(011) 648-7397* **Fax** *(0865) 080-0153* **Rooms** *10*

This "castle-like" mansion was built by a Mozambiquan mafioso in the 1970s. Rooms are clean and comfortable, and many offer views of Johannesburg. In-house entertainment includes a bar, a pool table and a swimming pool; the Bruma flea market and OR Tambo International Airport are nearby. **www.brownsugarbackpackers.com**

Key to Price Guide *see p380* **Key to Symbols** *see back cover flap*

FOURWAYS Amaqele Bed & Breakfast ®®

213 Seven Oaks Lane, Chartwell, Fourways, 2021 **Tel** *(011) 875-2105* **Fax** *(011) 507-5060* **Rooms** *6*

Amaqele allows its guests to experience the African countryside while still being close to the city. All rooms are housed in free-standing cottages with kitchenettes and private verandahs overlooking the garden. Amaqele also has much to keep children entertained, including a playground, sand pit and tree house. **www.amaqele.co.za**

FOURWAYS The Palazzo Montecasino ®®®®®

Montecasino Blvd, 2021 **Tel** *(011) 510-3000* **Fax** *(011) 510-4001* **Rooms** *246*

Montecasino is a Tuscan-style village resort in the up-market suburb of Fourways, close to the major highways. It houses a massive gaming, leisure, entertainment and retail complex. The Palazzo is one of three hotels here, and it offers five-star luxury in landscaped gardens. **www.montecasino.co.za**

HARTBEESPOORT Leopard Lodge ®®®

Box 400, Broederstroom, 0240 **Tel** *(083) 267-6406* **Fax** *(086) 651-9998* **Rooms** *15*

Leopard Lodge offers visitors the full bush experience, including game drives, bush walks and a bush *boma*. Two swimming pools are available, as well as a bird-watching deck and an African-style pub. The restaurant overlooks the Hartbeespoort Dam, where you can enjoy a wide range of watersports. **www.leopardlodge.co.za**

ILLOVO Protea Wanderers Hotel ®®®

Cnr Corlett Drive & Rudd Road, Illovo, 2196 **Tel** *(011) 770-5500* **Fax** *(011) 770-5555* **Rooms** *229*

Part of the Protea Hotels group, the Wanderers Hotel offers comfortable rooms within close proximity to all business and entertainment centres. Just around the corner is the hi-tech Planet Fitness Gym, open 24 hours. Little homely touches include a fresh apple placed in each guest room every day. **www.proteahotels.com**

JOHANNESBURG The Westcliff ®®®®®

67 Jan Smuts Avenue, Westcliff, 2193 **Tel** *(011) 481-6000* **Fax** *(011) 481-6010* **Rooms** *117*

Created in the image of a Mediterranean village, with cobbled pathways, fountains and lush greenery cascading down the hillside, The Westcliff offers high luxury and impeccable service, as well as sweeping views of Johannesburg. A club-car service is available to transport guests around the property. **www.westcliff.co.za**

KEMPTON PARK InterContinental Jo'burg OR Tambo Airport ®®®®®

Johannesburg OR Tambo International Airport, 1619 **Tel** *(011) 961-5400* **Fax** *(011) 961-5401* **Rooms** *138*

Conveniently situated within walking distance of the terminals of OR Tambo International Airport outside Johannesburg. Special features for travellers include in-room flight information, a health spa to ease the stress of travel and an indoor heated swimming pool with a panoramic view over Johannesburg. **www.intercontinental.com**

MAGALIESBERG Hunters Rest Mountain Resort ®®®

Box 775, Rustenburg, 0300 **Tel** *(014) 537-8300* **Fax** *(014) 537-8400* **Rooms** *91*

An extensive resort with excellent recreational facilities, including golf, tennis, game drives, quad bikes, hiking, dancing, heated pools and games room. Little ones can be kept entertained at the children's barnyard, and there is even a crèche on site. Weekend highlights include a Saturday lunch *braai* at the pool. **www.huntersresthotel.com**

MAGALIESBERG Lesedi African Lodge & Cultural Village ®®®

Box 699, Lanseria, 1748 **Tel** *(012) 205-1394* **Fax** *(086) 515-0084* **Rooms** *30*

A unique and powerful experience, Lesedi African Lodge consists of five villages, each with a different cultural theme (Zulu, Sotho, Xhosa, Pedi, Ndebele) and decorated accordingly. In the evenings, guests can witness or take part in singing, dancing and storytelling. The rate is inclusive of accommodation, meals and cultural tour. **www.lesedi.com**

MAGALIESBERG Mount Grace Country House & Spa ®®®

Old Rustenburg Road, R24, 2805 **Tel** *(014) 577-5600* **Fax** *(086) 630-5834* **Rooms** *121*

Elegant yet unpretentious country retreat located in 4 hectares (10 acres) of gardens. English country-style decor dominates in the stone-and-thatch bedrooms with private patios. Enjoy swimming, fishing, bird-watching, croquet and walking. A good spa, delightful cuisine and an excellent wine list add to the experience. **www.mountgrace.co.za**

MELROSE Premiere Classe Suite Hotel ®®®

62 Corlett Drive, Melrose, 2196 **Tel** *(011) 788-1967* **Fax** *(011) 788-1971* **Rooms** *30*

Centrally located, this affordable, self-catering apartment hotel is suitable for both short- and long-term stays. Serviced daily, the lodgings consist of fully equipped kitchen, lounge and dining area. Telephone and satellite TV are also available, and you can arrange for breakfast to be served in the apartment. **www.premiereclasse.co.za**

MELROSE Melrose Arch Hotel ®®®®

1 Melrose Square, Melrose Arch, 2196 **Tel** *(011) 214-6666* **Fax** *(011) 214-6600* **Rooms** *118*

Situated in the secure urban Melrose Arch lifestyle development, this hip five-star hotel offers designer decor with warm, natural tones and mood-enhancing lighting. The stylish restaurant provides a fusion of tastes from around the world. Sink into one of the inviting leather couches at the library bar. **www.africanpridehotels.com**

MELVILLE Die Agterplaas B&B ®®

66 Sixth Avenue, 2092 **Tel** *(011) 726-8452* **Fax** *(086) 616-8456* **Rooms** *13*

Homely accommodation at the foot of the historical Melville Koppies, a short walk from the eclectic restaurants and shops of Melville. In addition to the en-suite rooms, a spacious cottage is available for longer stays. Badia's coffee shop offers delicious *bobotie* and *biryani*. **www.agterplaas.co.za**

MELVILLE Pension Idube

11 Walton Avenue, Melville, 2092 **Tel** *(011) 482-9512* **Rooms** *7*

An ideal option for budget travellers to Johannesburg. Accommodation at the Idube has personal touches by the owner, who lives on site. Facilities include a sparkling pool and patio area, fully equipped kitchen for self-catering guests, laundry service and TV lounge. Game drives can be organized on request. **www.idubeguesthouse.co.za**

MIDRAND Protea Hotel Midrand

14th Street, Halfway House, Midrand, 1685 **Tel** *(011) 318-1868* **Fax** *(011) 318-2429* **Rooms** *177*

This Protea hotel is a good-quality corporate and leisure option located halfway between Johannesburg and Pretoria/Tshwane, with easy access to the highways and the airport. Modern contemporary interiors include a striking glass and beamed ceiling in the reception area. **www.proteahotels.com**

MULDERSDRIFT Misty Hills Country Hotel, Conference Centre & Spa

69 Drift Boulevard Road, 1747 **Tel** *(011) 950-6000* **Fax** *(086) 173-2237* **Rooms** *215*

Located between Johannesburg and Pretoria/Tshwane, Misty Hills offers accommodation in stone-built thatched rooms. The Carnivore restaurant is well known for its charcoal-grilled game and other traditional local meats, skewered on swords and cooked over an open fire. **www.recreationafrica.co.za**

MULDERSDRIFT Avianto Village Hotel

Driefontein Road, 1747 **Tel** *(011) 668-3000* **Fax** *(011) 668-3060* **Rooms** *34*

Nestled along the Crocodile River is this stylish yet unpretentious hotel with a distinctive Tuscan character. Romantic touches include a calming sprig of fresh lavender on your pillow at turndown. Golf fans may want to try Qolf, a fun, challenging lawn game that combines golf and croquet. **www.avianto.co.za**

NORWOOD Garden Place

53 Garden Road, Orchards, 2192 **Tel** *(011) 485-3800* **Fax** *(011) 485-3802* **Rooms** *24*

Garden Place provides comfortable self-catering accommodation with fully equipped kitchens. There is a communal breakfast room for those who prefer to mingle. Located near the trendy suburb of Norwood, it is a great place to relax, with a pretty, tree-filled garden. A free shuttle service to surrounding areas is available. **www.gardenplace.co.za**

ORMONDE Southern Sun Gold Reef City

Shaft 14, Northern Parkway, 2159 **Tel** *(011) 248-5000* **Fax** *(011) 248-5100* **Rooms** *38*

Set in a mining theme park, this Victorian-style hotel offers an experience reminiscent of a bygone era with all modern amenities. Each of the en-suite rooms is uniquely decorated and themed. Gold Reef City will keep children happily entertained with rides, clowns and other entertaining diversions. **www.tsogosunhotels.com**

PILANESBERG Bakubung Bush Lodge

Box 294, Sun City, 0136 **Tel** *(014) 552-6000* **Fax** *(014) 552-6300* **Rooms** *76*

En-suite chalets on the edge of the Pilanesberg Game Reserve, which is situated in an ancient volcanic crater. View lions, leopards, cheetahs and antelopes during game drives. There is a regular shuttle bus to Sun City, where you can visit a crocodile farm, a casino and several theatres and cinemas. The rate is all inclusive. **www.legacyhotels.co.za**

PILANESBERG Kwa Maritane Bush Lodge

Pilanesberg National Park, Sun City, 0316 **Tel** *(014) 552-5100* **Fax** *(014) 552-5333* **Rooms** *90*

Luxury suites and self-catering chalets on the doorstep of Pilanesberg National Park. Kwa Maritane is a particularly child-friendly resort, with a playground, trampoline, floodlit bush putt, outdoor chess board and water slide. Grown-ups will enjoy activities such as volleyball, tennis and swimming. The rate is all inclusive. **www.legacyhotels.co.za**

PILANESBERG Tshukudu Bush Lodge

Box 6805, Rustenburg, 0300 **Tel** *(014) 552-6255* **Fax** *(014) 552-6266* **Rooms** *6*

Built high on a hilltop, the six private luxury cottages offer a view of Pilanesberg National Park's bush and a waterhole where wild animals gather to drink. Cool off in the rock plunge pool in the daytime, and gather by the fire for dinner. The hotel offers twice-daily game drives and morning game walks. The rate is all inclusive. **www.legacyhotels.co.za**

PRETORIA/TSHWANE Oxnead Guesthouse

802 Johanita Street, Moreleta Park, 0044 **Tel** *(012) 993-4515* **Fax** *(012) 998-9168* **Rooms** *6*

One of the first guesthouses established in Pretoria/Tshwane, this Cape Georgian-style manor is located in a quiet and safe suburb of the city. Most of the tastefully decorated rooms have kitchen facilities and private entrances. There is easy access to a driving range for golfing enthusiasts. **www.oxnead.co.za**

PRETORIA/TSHWANE La Maison Guesthouse

235 Hilda Street, Hatfield, 0083 **Tel** *(012) 430-4341* **Fax** *(012) 342-1531* **Rooms** *6*

Located close to the Hatfield Shopping Centre, this inviting guesthouse boasts a long tradition of excellence. Enjoy the views from the rooftop patio or sip a cocktail by the pool. Gustav Klimt fans will enjoy the ambience in one of the dining rooms, which features a mural depicting the Austrian artist's famous *Kiss*. **www.lamaison.co.za**

PRETORIA/TSHWANE Kievits Kroon Country Estate

Plot 41, Reier Road, Kameeldrift East, 0035 **Tel** *(012) 808-0150* **Fax** *(012) 808-0148* **Rooms** *142*

This Cape Dutch-inspired estate, situated in the beautiful Kameeldrift Valley, is an ideal romantic getaway. The Kievits Kroon prides itself on its catering options, which range from fine dining at the elegant restaurant to picnic baskets by the poolside. Also on offer is a state-of-the-art spa. **www.kievitskroon.co.za**

PRETORIA/TSHWANE Illyria House

37 Bourke Street, Muckleneuk, 0002 **Tel** *(012) 344-6035* **Fax** *(012) 344-3978* **Rooms** *12*

A magnificent colonial manor boasting fine antiques, 17th-century tapestries and exquisite cuisine. Guests will enjoy the enchanting colonial lifestyle with white-gloved butlers and classical music playing in the background. Take advantage of the pampering beauty treatments in one of the wooden treatment rooms in the garden. **www.illyria.co.za**

ROSEBANK 54 on Bath

54 Bath Avenue, Rosebank, 2196 **Tel** *(011) 344-8500* **Fax** *(011) 344-8501* **Rooms** *75*

This independent five-star hotel is set in a vibrant, cosmopolitan area, with a covered, elevated walkway linking the hotel to The Mall of Rosebank, with its many shopping options. The dining room's unpretentious yet creative menu, the tranquil roof garden and outdoor heated pool make this elegant hotel a favourite. **www.tsogosunhotels.com**

SANDTON Melleney's Exclusive Guest House

149 12th Avenue, Rivonia, 2128 **Tel** *(011) 803-1099* **Fax** *(011) 803-1190* **Rooms** *10*

An exclusive guesthouse close to the shops and restaurants in Rivonia. One of the highlights at Melleney's is the salt-water pool, which enables guests to experience a rare taste of the ocean inland. The recently renovated pub offers a friendly, relaxed atmosphere. **www.melleneys.co.za**

SANDTON City Lodge Morningside

Cnr Rivonia & Hill Roads, Sandton, 2146 **Tel** *(011) 884-9500* **Fax** *(011) 884-9440* **Rooms** *160*

Affordable quality accommodation is on offer at this elegant outpost of the City Lodge chain. The hotel is situated in the heart of one of Johannesburg's most fashionable suburbs, close to major highways, exclusive shops and restaurants. Children sharing a room with their parents stay free. **www.citylodge.co.za**

SANDTON Protea Hotel Balalaika

20 Maude Street, Sandton, 2196 **Tel** *(011) 322-5000* **Fax** *(011) 322-5023* **Rooms** *330*

A tranquil hotel in the heart of Sandton, the Balalaika features two private gardens and two swimming pools. The recently refurbished hotel is located at the heart of a vibrant shopping hub that includes the Sandton shopping complexes, the mall at the waterfront and the Oriental Plaza. **www.proteahotels.com**

SANDTON Zulu Nyala Country Manor

270 Third Road, Chartwell, 2146 **Tel** *(011) 702-9300* **Fax** *(011) 702-9322* **Rooms** *43*

This thatched country manor in beautifully landscaped gardens is a mere ten-minute drive from Johannesburg and offers comfortable, spacious rooms and warm hospitality. The popular Lion Park is so close that, according to the hotel's website, you will probably hear the lions roar at night. **www.zulunyala.com**

SANDTON Fairlawns Boutique Hotel & Spa

Alma Road, off Bowling Avenue, Sandton, 2191 **Tel** *(011) 804-2540* **Fax** *(011) 802-7261* **Rooms** *19*

This elegant boutique hotel was built on one of the original homesteads of the area and is inspired by the romantic architecture of 18th-century Europe. Fairlawns' cellar is renowned for the rare and vintage wines on offer, and the hotel's list appears regularly at the Diners Club's Wine List of the Year Award. **www.fairlawns.co.za**

SANDTON Michelangelo

135 West Street, Sandton, 2128 **Tel** *(011) 282-7000* **Fax** *(011) 282-7172* **Rooms** *242*

A member of The Leading Hotels of the World, this prestigious five-star Renaissance-style hotel is set in a piazza surrounded by up-market shops and restaurants. Expect discreet service and the attention to detail typical of such a top-class hotel. Gourmet African cuisine is on offer in the restaurant. **www.michelangelo.co.za**

SANDTON Saxon Hotel & Spa

36 Saxon Road, Sandhurst, Sandton, 2132 **Tel** *(011) 292-6000* **Fax** *(011) 292-6001* **Rooms** *24*

Set in tranquil, tree-lined Sandhurst, a five-minute drive from Sandton city, this lush boutique hotel and spa sits on 2 hectares (6 acres) of landscaped gardens and epitomizes tasteful African elegance. For total relaxation, try the signature sound therapy at the world-class spa. **www.thesaxon.com**

SUN CITY The Cascades

Box 7, Sun City, 0316 **Tel** *(014) 557-5840* **Fax** *(014) 557-3447* **Rooms** *243*

Accommodation is split between three different venues at this massive five-star complex close to Sun City's casino and entertainment centre. The luxury rooms are decorated in ochre and yellow tones and feature dark-stained furniture, while the cabanas are particularly suitable for families with children. **www.suninternational.com**

SUN CITY The Palace of the Lost City at Sun City

Box 308, Sun City, 0316 **Tel** *(014) 557-4307* **Fax** *(014) 557-3111* **Rooms** *338*

Masterminded by entrepreneur Sol Kerzner, this hotel recreates an ancient African fantasy temple rising out of a subtropical jungle. The grand architecture is complemented by animal statuary and exotic works of art. The Valley of the Waves water park is a fun treat for children. **www.suninternational.com**

VEREENIGING Riviera on Vaal Hotel & Country Club

Mario Milani Drive, Vereeniging, 1930 **Tel** *(016) 420-1300* **Fax** *(086) 606-8856* **Rooms** *89*

This well-appointed boutique hotel is situated on the banks of the Vaal River, in close proximity to Johannesburg, and caters to both corporate and leisure travellers. Each of the rooms boasts expansive panoramic river views. The hotel's well-known floating restaurant offers guests a unique dining experience. **www.rivieraonvaal.co.za**

BLYDE RIVER CANYON AND KRUGER

DULLSTROOM Peebles Country Retreat ®®®®
Cnr Lyon Cachet & Bosman Streets, Dullstroom, 1110 **Tel** *(013) 254-8000* **Fax** *(013) 254-8014* **Rooms** *10*

At this gracious country house set in the trout-fishing village of Dullstroom you can choose from a variety of activities: trout-fishing, bird-watching, horse riding, clay-pigeon shooting, archery and mountain biking. There is a relaxing spa and a fine dining restaurant with a large collection of single malt whiskies.. **www.peebles.co.za**

DULLSTROOM Walkersons Hotel & Spa ®®®®®
Walkersons Private Estate, Dullstroom, 1110 **Tel** *(013) 253-7000* **Fax** *(013) 253-7230* **Rooms** *26*

A luxurious stone-and-thatch lodge set in a vast estate in the heart of fly-fishing country. Bedrooms have lake views, private patios and fireplaces. Indulge in country cuisine and choose your wine from the award-winning cellar. Fish for rainbow trout on private rivers and lakes – all the necessary equipment is provided. **www.walkersons.co.za**

GRASKOP Mac Mac Forest Retreat ®
Box 907, Sabie, 1260 **Tel** *(013) 764-2376* **Fax** *(013) 764-3124* **Rooms** *9*

Close to the thunderous Mac Mac and Forest Falls, this relaxed resort offers activities such as 4x4 trails, archery, canoeing, gold-panning and mountain biking. Accommodation is provided in safari tents and renovated forestry houses, which are self-catering, with all appliances, cutlery, crockery and bedding included. **www.macmac.co.za**

GRASKOP The Graskop Hotel ®®®
3 Main Street, Graskop, 1270 **Tel** *(013) 767-1244* **Fax** *(013) 767-1244* **Rooms** *34*

Located in malaria-free Graskop, within easy reach of Kruger National Park. The superb sights of the area include God's Window, Pilgrim's Rest and Bourke's Luck Potholes. The rooms are artistically decorated, and the food is prepared with home-grown produce and herbs. There is a crafts studio and gallery on site. **www.graskophotel.co.za**

HAZYVIEW The Windmill Wine Shop & Cottages ®®
R536 Box 204, Hazyview, 1242 **Tel** *(013) 737-8175* **Fax** *(013) 737-8966* **Rooms** *7*

The Windmill is located on 22 hectares (54 acres) of malaria-free indigenous bush populated by small game, including vervet monkeys, caracals and bushbucks. The cottages are well spaced to give guests privacy. Enjoy bird-watching from your own private deck or join the wine, beer and cheese tastings at the Wine Shop. **www.thewindmill.co.za**

HAZYVIEW Sabi River Sun Resort ®®
Main Road, Perry's Farm, Hazyview, 1242 **Tel** *(013) 737-7311* **Fax** *(013) 737-7314* **Rooms** *60*

This resort hotel offers comfortable accommodation and unrivalled sporting activities, including an 18-hole golf course, five swimming pools, three floodlit tennis courts, a bowling green, squash court, volleyball and jogging trail. Sabi River Sun caters particularly well for children, with a daily activity programme. **www.tsogosunhotels.com**

HAZYVIEW Perry's Bridge Hollow Boutique Hotel ®®®®
Perry's Bridge Trading Post, cnr Main St & Sabie Rd (R40), 1242 **Tel** *(013) 737-6784* **Fax** *(086) 509-5688* **Rooms** *31*

This modern hotel, part of the popular colonial-themed Perry's Bridge Trading Post, is located a ten-minute drive from Kruger National Park's Phabeni Gate. Rooms are spaciously laid out in motel-style low buildings around a swimming pool; extras include outdoor showers and private patios. **www.perrysbridgehollow.co.za**

HAZYVIEW Rissington Inn ®®®®
R40 Box 650, Hazyview, 1242 **Tel** *(013) 737-7700* **Fax** *(013) 737-7112* **Rooms** *16*

This affordable lodge, just ten minutes from Kruger National Park, offers stylish but relaxed accommodation. Each of the warm rooms has its own entrance and verandah, so you can enjoy the breathtaking views down the valley in privacy and comfort. Golf, riding and a host of other activities are available nearby. **www.rissington.co.za**

HAZYVIEW Thulamela Bed & Breakfast ®®®
R40, White River Road, Hazyview, 1242 **Tel** *(013) 737-7171* **Fax** *(086) 676-6047* **Rooms** *6*

This is a lovely honeymoon destination, as children under the age of 16 are not allowed. Each charming timber cabin at Thulamela has been built and decorated to ensure total privacy for its occupants: they are set in indigenous bush and feature a spa bath on the patio. Guests can expect generous breakfasts. **www.thulamela.co.za**

HAZYVIEW Highgrove House ®®®®®
R40 Box 46, Kiepersol, 1241 **Tel** *(083) 675-1500* **Fax** *(086) 528-5665* **Rooms** *8*

A colonial-style, award-winning lodge with a pastoral setting. The rooms have open fireplaces, overhead fans and secluded verandahs opening on to spectacular views. Expect gourmet dishes, fine wines and personal service at the candlelit restaurant. Easy access to the area's panoramic drives and wildlife reserves. **www.highgrove.co.za**

HOEDSPRUIT Camp Jabulani ®®®®®
Kapama Private Game Reserve, Hoedspruit, 1380 **Tel** *(015) 793-1265* **Fax** *(015) 793-1261* **Rooms** *6*

This exclusive lodge provides every modern luxury and convenience, yet blends in perfectly with the surrounding wilderness. Each suite, set in its own garden, offers total privacy and seclusion, and includes an outdoor plunge pool. Elephant-back safaris are a key attraction. The rate includes all meals, drinks and activities. **www.campjabulani.com**

Key to Price Guide *see p380* **Key to Symbols** *see back cover flap*

KRUGER NATIONAL PARK Satellite Camps

Box 787, Pretoria/Tshwane, 0001 **Tel** *(012) 428-9111* **Fax** *(012) 343-0905* **Rooms** *13*

The ideal camp for people who want to embrace nature and don't mind roughing it. Staying at Maroela, Tamboti, Balule and Malelane camps requires booking in at the main camp. It is important to note that facilities are often basic with self-catering, and there are no staff on site overnight. **www.sanparks.org**

KRUGER NATIONAL PARK Bushveld Camps

Box 787, Pretoria/Tshwane, 0001 **Tel** *(012) 428-9111* **Fax** *(012) 343-0905* **Rooms** *67 units*

This accommodation is great for families who are looking for a real bush experience. Bateleur, Biyamiti, Sirheni, Shimuwini and Talamati camps offer several self-catering cottages. There is no mobile-phone signal, so you are guaranteed a quiet, uninterrupted stay. **www.sanparks.org**

KRUGER NATIONAL PARK Main Camps

Box 787, Pretoria/Tshwane, 0001 **Tel** *(012) 428-9111* **Fax** *(012) 343-0905* **Rooms** *1,636 units*

The wide variety of lodgings is perfect for first-time safari visitors. Camps offer restaurants, shops and other amenities. They all have swimming pools, apart from Olifants. Berg-en-Dal, Skukuza, Satara and Letaba camps offer children's programmes over the holidays. Skukuza is the only camp with an ATM and a post office. **www.sanparks.org**

LYDENBURG De Ark Guesthouse

37 Kantoor Street, Lydenburg, 1120 **Tel** *(013) 235-1125* **Fax** *(013) 235-1125* **Rooms** *9*

Dating back to 1857, this delightful guesthouse is one of the oldest remaining buildings in Lydenburg. Located at the foothills of Long Tom Pass, De Ark has been lovingly restored and decorated with eclectic period furniture. Owners François and Francis Le Roux are always pleased to advise their guests on itineraries. **www.dearkguesthouse.co.za**

MALALANE Serenity Forest Eco Reserve

PO Box 1285, Malalane, 1320 **Tel** *(013) 790-2000* **Fax** *(013) 750-2801* **Rooms** *9*

Honeymooners and bird-watchers will love this spot – the windows and decks of the private suites look directly into the canopy of trees. The place offers spa treatments and scenic walks to nearby mountain streams where you can have a swim. The southern gates of Kruger National Park are only a short drive away. **www.serenitylodge.co.za**

PILGRIM'S REST Crystal Springs Mountain Lodge

Robber's Pass, Pilgrim's Rest, 1290 **Tel** *(013) 768-5000* **Fax** *(013) 768-5024* **Rooms** *192*

Individual self-catering cottages situated within a game reserve high above Pilgrim's Rest. Tennis and squash courts, mini-golf and a gym surround an indoor heated pool and Jacuzzi area. You can relax in the pub, by the fireplace in your room, or on the open wooden deck of your cottage, which includes a *braai*. **www.crystalsprings.co.za**

ROOSSENEKAL Old Joe's Kaia Country Lodge

Schoemanskloof Valley, Roossenekal, 1207 **Tel** *(013) 733-3045* **Fax** *(086) 518-1778* **Rooms** *13*

Old Joe's is a friendly country home decorated with vibrant colours in authentic African colonial style. Choose from log cabins, rondavels or "Kaia" rooms. Meals are prepared using garden-fresh produce and can be eaten in the dining room, garden or by the river. Don't miss out on the home-baked bread. **www.oldjoes.co.za**

SABIE Hillwatering Country House

50 Marula Street, Sabie, 1260 **Tel** *(013) 764-1421* **Fax** *(086) 750-3323* **Rooms** *5*

In a quiet residential area, a few minutes from the centre of Sabie, is this welcoming country home. Four of the rooms have French doors leading on to a private porch where guests can enjoy the view of the Drakensberg Mountains. Owners Hazel and Richard are happy to book day trips and other activities. **www.hillwatering.co.za**

SABIE Bohm's Zeederberg Country House

Box 94, Sabie, 1260 **Tel** *(013) 737-8101* **Fax** *(013) 737-8193* **Rooms** *10*

This farm, with its majestic views, borders the pine and eucalyptus forests of Sabie on one side and the agricultural heartland of subtropical fruit on the other. The garden has a swimming pool, sauna and Jacuzzi, as well as a variety of indigenous trees, all labelled for easy identification. **www.bohms.co.za**

SABIE Lone Creek River Lodge

Old Lydenburg Road, Sabie, 1260 **Tel** *(013) 764-2611* **Fax** *(086) 523-9466* **Rooms** *21*

Accessible from all major routes, this five-star boutique hotel offers elegant accommodation in a variety of lodgings, from self-catering timber cottages to luxury river suites located on the banks of the Sabie. Children are welcome in the timber lodges, and those under seven are accommodated at half price. **www.lonecreek.co.za**

SABI SAND RESERVE Sabi Sabi Game Lodge

Box 52665, Saxonwold, 2132 **Tel** *(011) 447-7172* **Fax** *(011) 442-0728* **Rooms** *25*

This multi-award-winning establishment includes four unique rest camps – Bush, Little Bush, Selati and Earth – each of which offers the ultimate luxury safari experience. Experienced guides accompany visitors on day and night game-viewing drives in open vehicles. Fully inclusive. **www.sabisabi.com**

SABI SAND RESERVE Singita Private Game Reserve

Box 23367, Claremont, 7735 **Tel** *(021) 683-3424* **Fax** *(021) 671-6776* **Rooms** *30*

Singita's lodges offer exceptional standards of luxury. Gourmet cuisine, an extensive wine cellar, day and night game drives and walking safaris are all included. Suites in the Boulders Lodge feature stunning stone bathrooms and bedrooms. **www.singita.com**

SWAZILAND Malolotja Lodge ®

Malolotja Nature Reserve, Nkhaba **Tel** *(268) 416-1151* **Fax** *(268) 416-1480* **Rooms** *13*

Rustic log cabins and campsites are dotted throughout this scenic nature reserve catering for self-sufficient hikers. At the front of each cabin is a *braai* for evening barbecues. The reserve has many interesting walking trails, and the shop at the main gate sells basic provisions. **www.stntc.org.sz**

SWAZILAND Mlilwane Wildlife Sanctuary ®®

Mlilwane Wildlife Sanctuary, lobamba **Tel** *(268) 2528-3943/4* **Fax** *(268) 2528-3924* **Rooms** *54*

At Mlilwane Lodge, you can choose between various accommodation options situated right in the sanctuary, from twin huts in the rest camp, to family huts or cottages, from traditional beehive huts to rondavels and camping sites. There is also an inexpensive youth hostel. **www.biggameparks.org**

SWAZILAND Royal Swazi Spa Hotel ®®®®®

Main Road, Mbabane–Manzini **Tel** *(268) 2416-5000* **Fax** *(268) 2416-8807* **Rooms** *149*

One of two hotels under the Royal Swazi Sun Valley umbrella, the Royal Swazi Spa is nestled in the scenic Ezulwini Valley. It is renowned for its superb golf course, casino and high-quality cuisine. Other facilities include tennis, squash, a games room, Camp Kwena for children, horse riding and a spa. **www.suninternational.com**

TIMBAVATI PRIVATE GAME RESERVE Tanda Tula Safari Camp ®®®®

Box 32, Constantia, 7848 **Tel** *(015) 793-3191* **Fax** *(015) 793-0496* **Rooms** *12*

Luxury tented camp in an exclusive reserve near Kruger Park. The thatched East African-style tents are fitted with roll-top baths, outdoor showers and spacious wooden decks overlooking the dry river bed. All meals and drinks are included, and they can be taken on your private verandah or convivially around the *boma*. **www.tandatula.co.za**

TZANEEN Coach House Hotel & Spa ®®®®®

Box 1034, Tzaneen, 0850 **Tel** *(015) 306-8000* **Fax** *(015) 306-8008* **Rooms** *30*

Built in 1892 to cater to travellers in the days of the Gold Rush, the Coach House is situated on a high plateau. Individual chalets are set in beautiful gardens; each features a private verandah with views of the Drakensberg Mountains. The 8,000-bottle wine cellar and the renowned Coach House nougat are big attractions. **www.coachhouse.co.za**

WHITE RIVER Kirby Country Lodge ®®

Jatinga Road, White River, 1240 **Tel** *(084) 643-4344* **Fax** *(086) 602-8880* **Rooms** *11*

Only 25 minutes by car from Kruger National Park, this tranquil thatched lodge set in woodland gardens is owned by a hospitable Swiss family. They are on hand to help their guests book all sorts of activities, from game drives to gold-panning or hot-air ballooning. Families with children are welcome. **www.kirbylodge.com**

WHITE RIVER Cybele Forest Lodge and Health Spa ®®®®

R40 Box 346, White River, 1240 **Tel** *(013) 764-9500* **Fax** *(013) 764-9510* **Rooms** *12*

Tucked away in forest country is this exquisite old farmhouse. The gardens are filled with the varied vivid colours of indigenous trees, and the rooms are lavish, with log fireplaces and private gardens – some with heated pools. Spa and beauty treatments, bird-watching and horse riding are some of the activities on offer. **www.cybele.co.za**

WHITE RIVER Jatinga Country Lodge ®®®®

Jatinga Road, White River, 1240 **Tel** *(082) 655-4397* **Fax** *(086) 635-9788* **Rooms** *17*

Once a hunting lodge, this luxurious homestead dates back to the 1920s. Although renovated, its African colonial style and ambience have been retained. The hammocks in the garden are a great way to wind down. The restaurant caters well for diabetics and vegetarians. **www.jatinga.co.za**

SOUTH OF THE ORANGE

BEAUFORT WEST Lemoenfontein ®®

Off Jagers Pass, Beaufort West, 6970 **Tel** *(023) 415-2847* **Fax** *(086) 650-9928* **Rooms** *12*

Built in 1850 as a hunting lodge, Lemoenfontein is an oasis in the heart of the arid Great Karoo, under the Nieuweveld Mountains. The extensive game reserve surrounding it teems with buck, giraffes and bird life. Enjoy the views from the wide verandahs, and tuck into the hearty breakfasts and traditional Karoo dinners. **www.lemoenfontein.co.za**

BEAUFORT WEST Treetop Guest House ®®

17 Bird Street, Beaufort West, 6970 **Tel** *(023) 414-3744* **Fax** *(023) 415-1329* **Rooms** *11*

A pleasant residential building surrounded by a garden in a small town full of history. The Treetop offers a great home-away-from-home vibe, with a pool and *braai* facilities for the guests. Start the day with a full English breakfast, and enjoy a traditional Karoo dinner by candlelight in the evening. **www.treetopguesthouse.co.za**

COLESBERG Kuilfontein Stable Cottages ®®

Box 17, Colesberg, 9795 **Tel** *(051) 753-1364* **Fax** *(051) 753-0200* **Rooms** *12*

A farm that produces Karoo lamb, Kuilfontein has been in the same family for more than a century. The rooms are located in former racing stables, and activities include bird-watching and game viewing. Nearby are historical and Stone Age sites, water sports at Gariep Dam and a local museum for Karoo fossils. **www.kuilfontein.co.za**

Key to Price Guide *see p380* **Key to Symbols** *see back cover flap*

CRADOCK Die Tuishuise 🏨 👥 🖥 🅿 ⓇⓇⓇ

36 Market Street, Cradock, 5880 **Tel** *(048) 811-322* **Fax** *(048) 881-5388* **Rooms** *27*

These traditional iron-roofed Karoo cottages have been restored and beautifully converted into tourist accommodation. Each cottage is furnished with antiques and four-poster beds, reflecting the style of English and Dutch settlers in the mid-1800s. Activities include game drives, township tours and rock art. **www.tuishuise.co.za**

GRAAFF REINET Caledonia Guest House 🏨 🚰 ⓇⓇ

59 Somerset Street, Graaff Reinet, 6280 **Tel** *(071) 868-2889* **Fax** *(086) 733-0708* **Rooms** *6*

In the historic quarter of this interesting town – the fourth-oldest in South Africa – is this 150-year-old colonial-style stone house. Shops, banks and museums are all within walking distance, as is the Valley of Desolation, where you can see zebras, wildebeests and springboks. The restaurant serves delicious Karoo-style dishes. **www.caledonia.co.za**

KING WILLIAM'S TOWN Dreamers Guest House 🏨 🚰 👥 ⓇⓇ

29 Gordon Street, Hospital Hill, 5600 **Tel** *(043) 642-3012* **Fax** *(086) 677-6016* **Rooms** *11*

This guesthouse in historic King William's Town is a good stopover on the way from Cape Town to Durban. Meals are served on request, and owners Marieta and André take pride in the challenge of special-request cuisine. Given a little notice, they will also arrange a visit to a Xhosa kraal to observe local culture. **www.dreamersguesthouse.com**

LADY GREY Comfrey Cottage Guest House 🏨 🅿 ⓇⓇⓇ

51–59 Stephenson Street, Lady Grey, 9755 **Tel** *(051) 603-0407* **Fax** *(086) 212-4694* **Rooms** *4*

One of four family-run cottages in a garden in a tranquil village below the Witteberg Mountains, the four-star Comfrey Cottage provides great comfort and good food. It is an ideal base from which to enjoy local attractions such as hiking, biking, fly-fishing, bird-watching and flower tours. Fully licensed. **www.comfreycottage.co.za**

NORTH OF THE ORANGE

BLOEMFONTEIN Dias Guest House 🚰 🖥 🅿 ⓇⓇ

14 Dias Crescent, Dan Pienaar, 9301 **Tel** *(051) 436-6225* **Fax** *(051) 436-7733* **Rooms** *8*

Rhyno and Mariette's award-winning, gay-friendly guesthouse is located near several museums and historic monuments, including the Women's War Memorial, the War Museum and the Rugby Museum. Each room features an Internet connection, fridge and microwave. **www.diasgh.co.za**

BLOEMFONTEIN Florentia Guest House 🖥 ⓇⓇ

2c Louis Botha Street, Waverley, 9301 **Tel** *(082) 853-7472* **Fax** *(086) 530-5177* **Rooms** *3*

On a tree-lined street at the foot of Naval Hill, this four-star guesthouse is renowned for owner Jolena van Rooyen's collection of quilts, which can be admired on the beds as well as hanging on the walls. A game reserve, orchid house and theatre are all located nearby. **www.florentia.co.za**

BLOEMFONTEIN Halevy Heritage Hotel 📺 🏨 🚰 🅿 ⓇⓇⓇⓇ

Markgraaff & Charles Streets, 9301 **Tel** *(051) 403-0600* **Fax** *(051) 403-0699* **Rooms** *21*

Originally built as accommodation for theatre-goers at the end of the 19th century, the renovated Halevy Heritage Hotel has maintained its Edwardian appeal and features spacious rooms, high ceilings, dark furniture and attractive Tiffany bedside lamps. **www.halevyheritage.com**

KIMBERLEY Kimberley Club 🏨 🖥 ♿ ⓇⓇⓇ

35 Currey Street, Kimberley, 8301 **Tel** *(053) 832-4224* **Fax** *(053) 832-4226* **Rooms** *17*

Founded by a cluster of diamond magnates who missed their London clubs, the Kimberley Club has had a recent facelift and an upgrade to four-star boutique hotel in colonial style. Formal but comfortable, it is close to excellent museums, mining buildings, the Big Hole, the Magersfontein battlefield and a casino. **www.kimberleyclub.co.za**

KIMBERLEY Protea Hotel Diamond Lodge 🏨 🚰 📺 🖥 ⓇⓇⓇ

124 Du Toitspan Pan Road, Kimberley, 8301 **Tel** *(053) 831-1281* **Fax** *(053) 831-1284* **Rooms** *34*

This small, comfortable, friendly hotel is conveniently located near Kimberley's central business district. The three-star Diamond Lodge is also within easy walking distance of historical and recreational facilities, including the Big Hole. Most rooms have two double beds. **www.proteahotels.com**

KIMBERLEY Garden Court 📺 🏨 🚰 👥 📺 🖥 ⓇⓇⓇ

120 Du Toitspan Road, Kimberley, 8301 **Tel** *(053) 833-1751* **Fax** *(053) 832-1814* **Rooms** *135*

A standard city hotel that caters to both business and leisure travellers, the Garden Court is close to the main tourist attractions and to a tram stop that takes you to the Big Hole, the world's largest man-made excavation. Tours to local places of interest, including the Ghost Trail and the battlefields, can also be arranged. **www.tsogosunhotels.com**

UPINGTON Le Must River Manor 🚰 🖥 🅿 ⓇⓇ

12 Murray Avenue, Upington, 8800 **Tel** *(054) 332-3971* **Fax** *(054) 332-7830* **Rooms** *5*

This beautiful Georgian-style guesthouse is surrounded by a splendid manicured garden on the banks of the Orange River, in the central business district of Upington. The Kalahari, the Augrabies Falls, the Kgalagadi Transfrontier Park and the Tswalu Reserve are all within a short driving distance. **www.lemustupington.com**

WHERE TO EAT

South Africa has a wide variety of restaurants and eateries, from franchise steakhouses and sizzling street-corner *boerewors* stands to elegant business venues and seafood, Oriental, French and Mediterranean-style restaurants. Whenever the weather is fine, eating is done outside, and coffee shops do a roaring trade. African eateries for the Western palate are found in the cities, while some township tours *(see p436)* include traditional meals. South Africa's multi-cultural heritage is also evident in the proliferation of Indian restaurants and stalls serving spicy eastern and Kwa-Zulu-Natal-style curries. In the Western Cape, fragrant, sweet Malay curries are popular quick lunches and in the winelands, more formal fare.

Outdoor tables in Sandton, with Nelson Mandela's statue in the background

SOUTH AFRICAN EATING PATTERNS

Restaurants are most likely to be open for lunch from Mondays to Fridays and for dinner from Tuesdays to Sundays. It is common to find restaurants closed on Mondays (Italian restaurants often close on Tuesdays). Coffee shops are open during the day, usually from 9am to 5pm, and serve breakfasts, light lunches and teas. For breakfasts, try the traditional cooked dish of eggs, bacon and sausages. Healthy muffins (also available at supermarkets, delis and even petrol-station stores) such as bran, banana and date are popular, too. Salads, open sandwiches and quiches are good choices for lunch, while cakes (carrot, chocolate and cheese) are usual afternoon-tea fare. Dinner is the main meal of the day, served from 6:30pm to 10pm. In the urban areas, bars, popular restaurants and fast-food outlets stay open until midnight or even later.

PLACES TO EAT

You can always eat well in South African cities and in the well-visited outlying areas.

The annual guide *Eat Out* magazine, available at newsagents, recommends restaurants nationwide and has a website with user reviews (www.eatout.co.za). Another good website is www.diningout.co.za.

BOOKING AHEAD

It is best to phone ahead and reserve a table in order to avoid disappointment.

Established or fashionable venues may be booked up for weeks in advance. If you cannot keep a reservation, call the restaurant and cancel.

PRICES AND TIPPING

Eating out in South Africa is usually inexpensive. The average price of a three-course meal for one (excluding wine and a tip) at a good restaurant is about R140–160. But certain items, such as seafood, can increase the total substantially. A freshly made deli sandwich with delicious fillings will seldom cost more than R30, while a large, hearty breakfast costs around R50.

Tipping should always be based on service. If simply average, leave 10 per cent; if excellent, 15 per cent. Tips are sometimes placed in a communal jar near the cashier.

Seafood *braai* at a *skerm* (sheltered barbecue area) on the West Coast

WHAT TO EAT

Try to visit one of the African, Indian (in Kwa-Zulu-Natal) or Malay (in Cape Town) restaurants in the cities. If you're at the coast, don't miss the delicious seafood – calamari, mussels, tuna, crayfish, yellowtail and *kabeljou* (cob). On the West Coast there are scenic open-air seafood *braais* (barbecues). The cities and larger towns offer excellent international cuisine: Portuguese, Thai, Indonesian, Italian, Greek, French and Chinese. There are also typical South African restaurants, where traditional fare and drinks like *witblits*, strong spirit distilled from peaches, are served.

Witblits
(peach brandy)

South Africa is a meat-loving nation; beef steaks are good, and franchise steakhouses offer great value for money; the selection of substantial salads and vegetable dishes will satisfy vegetarians, too. *Boerewors* (spicy-sausage) on a bread-roll can be bought from informal street vendors. At someone's home, you might sample a South African meat *braai*, or barbecue *(see p21)*. Pizza chains are very popular and offer good value.

WINE CHOICES

South African wines offer something for everybody, and most restaurants stock a mainstream selection of local labels – usually with a significant price mark-up. Many serve a great variety: from easy-drinking wines to vintage bottlings. Some venues offer a choice of bottled wines by the glass, although house wines are, more usually, from an inexpensive 5-litre box. Fine-dining venues provide an international winelist, and the better Italian eateries, for example, offer Italian wines. Corkage (from R25) is charged if you bring your own bottle.

DELIVERY SERVICES

In the cities and larger towns, food-delivery services are popular. The company known as "Mr Delivery" is contracted to a variety of eateries and restaurants (not only fast-food outlets) and will deliver hot food, for a reasonable fee, during lunch times and from early to late evening. The local telephone directory will provide details.

SMOKING

Strict anti-tobacco laws are enforced in South Africa. Smoking in the main dining area of restaurants is not allowed. Most restaurants have a smoking section, and patrons should specify their requirements when booking.

CHILDREN

Restaurants and eateries are not always child-friendly in South Africa, especially at dinner times when, for many patrons, dining out is the entertainment for the evening and children are left at home.

Outdoor, informal and day-time venues (and their menus) are more likely to suit little people. High chairs and mini menus are not common; expect to pay three-quarters of the price for a half-size meal.

Franchises like the Spur Steakhouses are a very good bet: they all have an appetizing children's menu, crayons, colouring-in competitions, balloons and resident clowns.

The Spur Steakhouse franchise also caters for younger patrons

DRESS CODE

Many up-market restaurants do require patrons to wear smart, but not formal attire. While you will not be able to wear shorts and sports shoes at such venues, you may comfortably do so just about anywhere else.

WHEELCHAIR ACCESS

A growing awareness for the special needs of the physically disabled visitor has led to the construction of ramps and wider toilet doors at some, mostly up-market, venues. Many restaurants, however, still cannot accommodate visitors in wheelchairs, and it is advisable to check in advance.

Eating alfresco, on the patio of a South African restaurant

The Flavours of South Africa

In 1652, the Dutch East India Company established a refreshment station in the Cape to provide their ships with fresh supplies. These early settlers learned much from the hunter-gatherer skills of the local people and a multi-ethnic cuisine began to emerge. The spice traders brought exotic flavours to the country, and the diversity of ingredients increased with the arrival of British, Indian and German settlers. Finally the French Huguenots contributed culinary finesse. This rainbow of influences is evident today in both traditional and modern dishes.

Rooibos tea

Preparing for a *braai* at a restaurant on the West Coast

CAPE MALAY COOKING

Malay slaves were brought from Java to the Cape Colony in the late 1600s, bringing with them an intimate knowledge of spices that had a profound influence on Cape cooking. Authentic specialities can still be found in Cape Town's historic Bo-Kaap district. Although spiced with traditional curry ingredients such as turmeric, ginger, cinnamon, cardamom, cloves and chilies, Cape Malay cuisine is never fiery. Meat is often cooked with fruit, marrying sweet and savoury flavours, while fish, especially snoek and seafood, is also important. Malay cooks were much sought after by the settlers and soon learned how to prepare traditional Dutch fare such as *melktert* (custard tart), adding cinnamon and grated nutmeg to suit their own tastes. Other baked puddings and tarts show a strong Dutch influence, while the delicious fruit preserves are mainly French Huguenot in origin.

KWAZULU NATAL CUISINE

In the mid-1800s, indentured labour was brought from India to work in Natal's

Oysters   **Sea bass**   **Squid**   **Prawns**   **Orange roughy**   **Mussels**

Selection of fresh South African seafood

SOUTH AFRICAN DISHES AND SPECIALITIES

Biltong

From the Malay kitchen comes *bobotie*, served with *geelrys* (rice with raisins and spices) and *blatjang* (spicy fruit chutney). Durban's most popular dish is *bunny chow* (food of the Indians), a hollowed-out loaf filled with curry and garnished with pickles. The dish dates from apartheid when black South Africans were not allowed in restaurants, so were served this portable meal through the back door. Larded saddle of venison is the signature dish of the Karoo, and venison is also dried, salted and spiced to create a type of jerky called *biltong*. The Cedarberg region has its own speciality, Rooibos tea, which has a light and fruity taste. The warm Benguela and cold Atlantic currents ensure a plentiful supply of fresh fish, and snoek is a traditional favourite.

Smoorsnoek *mixes flaked snoek (a barracuda-like fish) with potato slices and tomato in a tasty braise.*

Vast array of South African fruit laid out at a Cape Town market

sugar cane fields. Many workers stayed on after their contracts expired and Gujarati traders soon began supplying traditional spices to the growing community, who blended them with local foodstuffs to create distinctly South African flavours. Today, spice stores specialize in all manner of blends, some unique to South Africa, which create delicious dishes. The early Indian settlers later gained a strong foothold in the regional fruit and vegetable trade, introducing tropical Asian fruit to KwaZulu Natal. Mangoes, lychees, banana, *paw paw* (papaya) and watermelon are enjoyed fresh, or as ingredients and accompaniments to curries.

Fresh fish is also very popular in this region and the annual sardine runs on the Natal coast are awaited with great anticipation. As soon as the fish are spotted, locals rush to the sea collecting them by the dozen. The sardines are immediately sprinkled with salt, dipped into a South African Red Spice mixture and fried.

South African bream caught by a local Natal fisherman

BRAAIVLEIS

The South African *braai* (barbecue) is much more than a meal cooked over an open fire. It is a social tradition cherished throughout the land. Lamb chops, steak, chicken, *sosaties* (kebabs) and *boerewors* (farmer's sausage) are the most common items. The Western Cape is famous for grilling whole snoek, basted with a mixture of apricot jam, white wine and fruit chutney. Grilled crayfish is another favourite *braai* dish.

ON THE MENU

Erwtensoep Dutch pea soup, slow cooked then liberally laced with diced, salted pork.

Groenmielies Corn on the cob, grilled over an open fire and thoroughly basted with butter. A favourite for a summer *braai*.

Koeksisters "Cake sisters" is a sweet Malay snack, best described as a doughnut infused with sugary syrup.

Perlemoen Tenderized and soaked in milk, abalone is lightly pan fried, which brings out the fresh sea taste.

Sosaties Skewers of meat, onions and dried fruit are marinated in a curry sauce and then grilled over an open fire.

Waterblommetjiebredie A Cape stew made of lamb and *waterblommetjies*, a water plant which resembles an artichoke.

Bobotie *is minced beef, spiced with bay and turmeric, topped with an egg custard and baked.*

Roast springbok *or venison remains succulent when basted continuously with a sour cream marinade.*

Melktert *dates back to early Cape Malay-Dutch cooking. This sweet custard tart is sprinkled with cinnamon.*

What to Drink in South Africa

South African wine may be classified as "New World", but the country actually has a long history in winemaking. The first vines were planted in the Cape of Good Hope by Commander Jan van Riebeeck in 1655. The most important figure in the industry, however, was Simon van der Stel, who founded both the Stellenbosch and Constantia vineyards, the latter's dessert wine gaining an international reputation by the end of the 17th century. In 1885, the vineyards were devastated by an infestation of the phylloxera insect. The subsequent recovery led to over-production and this, along with the establishment of trade sanctions as a result of apartheid, led to a decline in quality. Recent years have seen major changes in the industry, with a move towards smaller, independent vineyards producing some world-class wines. South Africa is now the world's eighth-largest producer.

Grape picker, in the scenic Dieu Donné vineyard

WHITE WINE

With its Mediterranean-style climate, the country's southwestern tip is the best area for wine production. The growing conditions are perfect for the once-ubiquitous Chenin Blanc grape used in high-volume, low-cost wines and for brandy-making. Since the quota system ended in 1992, a greater variety of grapes has been planted. Sauvignon Blanc, Chardonnay and even some German, Spanish and Portuguese vines are now well established, and have taken on their own distinctive style. Stellenbosch, Constantia and the cool-climate Walker Bay all produce some of the finest white wines.

Meerlust Estate wine

Cellars of Avondale, on Klein Drakenstein slopes, near Paarl

RED WINE

The dominant red grape variety is Merlot but it now has strong competition from the homegrown Pinotage cultivar *(see pp182–3).* South Africa still produces plenty of basic red drinking wine but producers such as Hamilton Russell with his Pinot Noir, and Neil Ellis with his Cabernet Sauvignon have dramatically expanded the country's portfolio of excellent reds.

Morgenhof Estate bottled red, near Stellenbosch

SPARKLING AND OTHER WINES

Méthode Cap Classique is the nomenclature devised for the Champagne-style sparkling wines produced in all of the country's major wine districts *(see p188).* The delightfully honeyed Constantia dessert wine was first produced over 350 years ago, but the wine industry has not stood still and a wide range of increasingly popular rosé wines are being produced from grapes such as Gamay and Shiraz. Additionally, South Africa offers a number of port-style fortified wines, with Calitzdorp, in the Klein Karoo region, the main area of production, although Paarl and Stellenbosch also offer some good examples. Axe Hill, J P Bredell and De Krans are among the best on offer.

Graham Beck brut non-vintage

BEER

Incorporated in London in 1895, South African Breweries (SAB) has been swallowing up rival breweries and beer brands across the globe for the past two decades and is now second in size only to Belgium's InBev group. Castle is the company's ubiquitous home-brand label – it has even inspired the popular Beef & Castle pie recipe. The company operates the SAB World of Beer Museum in Johannesburg (see p310), the guided tour, which illustrates the brewing process has guaranteed refreshment at the end in the form of a couple of cool "frosties".

Black Label   Castle   Hansa

BRANDY

Set up in Stellenbosch in 1984, the South African Brandy Foundation represents virtually all of the country's 50 brandy trademarks. In 1997, on the 325th anniversary of South African brandy distilling, the foundation launched the world's first Brandy Route. The trail stretches from Stellenbosch through Paarl and Franschhoek to the Breede River Valley town of Worcester. Attractions include the Van Ryn Brandy Cellar (see p193), 8 km (5 miles) outside Stellenbosch where visitors can learn about brandy production methods; the Oude Molen Brandy Museum in Stellenbosch itself, and the tasting rooms at the Backberg Distillery near Paarl.

A KWV 10-year-old   Boplaas Potstill Brandy

Spectacular vineyard setting in the Franschhoek Mountains

READING THE LABEL

South Africa operates strict wine labelling laws as a guarantee of quality. According to the WO (Wine of Origin) system, information provided on the grape variety and the vintage must apply to at least 85 per cent of what's gone into the bottle. However, 100 per cent of the grapes must have come from the stated place of origin. This can be the region (for example, Olifants River, Breede Valley River or Cape Point), the precise district therein (such as Paarl, Stellenbosch and Swartland) or, narrowing it down even more, the ward (Elgin, Waterberg, Cedarberg). Top-end wines can be labelled as estate wines provided that the product is grown, vinified and bottled on one parcel of land that is farmed as a single unit and registered as such.

VARIETY	REGIONS	PRODUCERS
WHITE		
Chenin Blanc	Breede River Valley, Stellenbosch, Cedarberg, Swartland	De Trafford, Kleine Zalze, Nederburg, Beaumont Hope
Sauvignon Blanc	Darling District, Elim Ward Overberg, Cape Point, Stellenbosch	Groote Post, Paul Cluver, Steenberg Vineyards, Hamilton Russell
Chardonnay	Breede River Valley, Overberg, Paarl, Swartland, Cedarberg	Springfield Estate, Neil Ellis, Glen Carlou, Jordan Wines
RED		
Cabernet Sauvignon	Cedarberg, Paarl, Stellenbosch, Swartland, Tygerberg	Thelema Mountain Cedarberg Cellars, Neil Ellis, Rupert & Rothschild
Shiraz	Franshhoek, Paarl, Stellenbosch	Fairview, Neil Ellis, Boekehnhoutskloof
Pinotage	Overberg, Tulbagh, Breede River Valley, Stellenbosch	Rijk's Private Cellar, Fairview Primo, Graham Beck
Merlot	Constantia, Tygerberg, Paarl	Le Riche, Veenwouden, Glen Carlou
Pinot Noir	Overberg, Elgin, Constantia, Walker Bay, Darling District	Newton Johnson, Bouchard Finlayson, Paul Cluver, Groote Post
SPARKLING		
Cape Classic	Cape Peninsula	JC Le Roux, Villiera Wines, Graham Beck Wines
FORTIFIED		
(Port style)	Klein Karoo	Axe Hill, De Krans, JP Bredell

Choosing a Restaurant

The restaurants in this guide have been selected for their good value, interesting location and exceptional food. This chart lists additional factors that may assist your choice, such as the presence of a vegetarian selection or outside tables. Entries are divided by region and listed alphabetically within price categories.

PRICE CATEGORIES
The following price ranges are for a three-course meal for one, including a half-bottle of house wine, cover charge, tax and service.
® Under R200
®® R200–R250
®®® R250–R300
®®®® R300–R350
®®®®® Over R350

CAPE TOWN

CITY BOWL Biesmiellah
Cnr Wale Street & Pentz Road, Bo-Kaap, 8001 **Tel** *(021) 423-0850*   **Map** *5 B1*

This no-frills café and bakery specializing in Cape Malay cuisine is just up the road from the Iziko Bo-Kaap Museum (*see p128*). Typical fare on the menu includes *denningvleis* (lamb stew cooked in tamarind) and *bobotie* (baked mince with raisins and cloves and topped with a savoury custard). Biesmiellah is open until 11pm daily.

CITY BOWL Chef Pons
12 Mill Street, Gardens, 8001 **Tel** *(021) 465-5846*   **Map** *5 A3*

Popular with young and stylish locals, this Thai and South-East Asian restaurant is always buzzing from around 7pm onwards. If you're after an incendiary culinary experience, try the fiery jungle curry. Alternatively, go for one of the milder stir fries if hot and spicy is not to your taste.

CITY BOWL Deer Park Café
2 Deer Park Avenue, Vredehoek, 8000 **Tel** *(021) 462-6311*   **Map** *5 B5*

This is an excellent venue for families with small children, since the outside tables allow parents to keep an eye on their offspring as they play in the grounds. The Deer Park Café serves breakfasts and light meals like burgers and salads in both adult and child-sized portions.

CITY BOWL Greens on Park
5–9 Park Road, Gardens, 8001 **Tel** *(021) 422-4415*   **Map** *5 A2*

Housed in a listed building that used to serve as an inn, Greens is the sister restaurant of a successful Constantia establishment. There is a large terrace where you can enjoy a gourmet brie-and-cranberry pizza or one of the hearty ground-beef burgers on offer. The interior is carefully put together with a calming palette of earthy colours.

CITY BOWL Lola's
228 Long Street, 8001 **Tel** *(021) 423-0885*   **Map** *5 A2*

The excellent vegetarian food served at Lola's is a compulsory experience for veggies during their Cape Town stay. However, the restaurant also caters for carnivores, and daily chalkboard specials might include dishes such as sticky beef ribs or lamb chops with butternut couscous. Lola's is always busy and has a great vibe.

CITY BOWL Manna Epicure
151 Kloof Street, 8001 **Tel** *(021) 426-2413*   **Map** *4 F3*

A trendsetting restaurant with a sleek, white interior. Wholesome home-baked breads complement the inventive and tasty tapas dishes. The menu is divided into sweet, bitter, sour and savoury, with freshly squeezed juices and highly original cocktails on hand to wash it down. Try the coconut bread with scrambled egg, avocado and salmon.

CITY BOWL Mr Pickwicks
158 Long Street, 8001 **Tel** *(021) 423-3710*   **Map** *5 A2*

A quirky deli-cum-coffee shop that is popular with trendy youngsters and tourists alike. Big open sandwiches are custom-made to order at the counter. Try the Bar One milk shake, the ultimate ice cream and chocolate-bar smoothie. Service can be haphazard, so don't be afraid to make yourself known to the often inattentive waiters.

CITY BOWL Mugged on Roeland
37 Roeland Street, East City, 8001 **Tel** *(084) 589-4665*   **Map** *5 B2*

This thriving Lebanese coffee shop offers free Wi-Fi access along with delicious crescent-shaped pies filled with a variety of fresh Mediterranean ingredients. The coffee is great, and there is also a delicious selection of muffins on offer or a meze platter to share with your fellow diners.

CITY BOWL Oasis
Mount Nelson Hotel, 76 Orange Street, Gardens, 8001 **Tel** *(021) 483-1948*   **Map** *5 A3*

Located within the Mount Nelson Hotel, Oasis overlooks the picturesque hotel gardens and pool. Fresh seafood, the finest cuts of meat cooked to order and oven-baked pizzas are all available. Home-baked *ciabatta*, *kitka* and *focaccia* rolls stuffed with smoked salmon and shrimps are a superb treat for those with less time.

Key to Symbols *see back cover flap*

BOWL Royale Eatery

   ng Street, 8000 **Tel** (021) 422-4536

Map 5 A2

ed amid the bustle of Long Street, Sacha Berolsky's homage to *Pulp Fiction* is a gourmet burger experience
excellence. Lamb, ostrich and a variety of vegetarian burgers are on offer, all served with regular or sweet-
ato fries. There is also a rather trendy bar upstairs, the Waiting Rooms.

CITY BOWL Vida e Caffe Kloof Street

34 Kloof Street, Gardens, 8001 **Tel** (021) 426-0627

Map 5 A2

This happening coffee shop on Kloof Street is particularly popular with stylish locals and international visitors who
come here to see and be seen. Vida e Caffe also serves great coffee, the latte is considered to be the best in town,
and delectable giant savoury or apple-and-cinnamon muffins.

CITY BOWL Arnold's

60 Kloof Street, Gardens, 8001 **Tel** (021) 424-4344

Map 5 A2

Arnold's is a veritable Cape Town institution, a popular eatery that attracts both locals and visitors with its good
food, pleasant location, magnificent views of Table Mountain and friendly, attentive service. On the menu are game
dishes such as crocodile and warthog ribs and ostrich fillet. The signature dish is fillet steak with mushrooms.

CITY BOWL Carlyles

17 Derry Street, Vredehoek, 8000 **Tel** (021) 461-8787

Map 5 C4

This is a fantastic and informal place to grab a filling meal on the slopes of the mountain in Vredehoek. The specials
list is crammed with delicious pizza, pasta and meaty dishes. Reciting them all and their method of preparation – as
the waitresses do – is quite an impressive performance piece.

CITY BOWL Mama Africa Restaurant & Bar

178 Long Street, 8001 **Tel** (021) 426-1017

Map 5 A2

Mama Africa is exactly that: a thoroughly African matriarch among Cape Town eateries, with an irreverent and
joyful vibe that infuses visitors with a lust for life. There is often live music on the go, with humming marimbas to
get you into the cultural vibe. Try the mixed-game grill or mopane worms for a more adventurous meal.

CITY BOWL Savoy Cabbage

101 Hout St, 8001 **Tel** (021) 424-2626

Map 5 B1

Located in a historic building on the Hout Street side of Heritage Square, Savoy Cabbage is an elegant restaurant
with an open-plan kitchen. The menu changes daily, but favourites include carpaccio chicken liver parfait followed
by mains of game meat. Reservations recommended. Closed Sat lunch; Sun.

CITY BOWL Gold Restaurant

96 Strand Street, 8000 **Tel** (021) 421-4653

Map 5 B1

Housed in the Gold of Africa Museum, this stylish restaurant offers a complete African experience, including live
entertainment and an optional drumming workshop before dinner. The menu consists of a selection of set dishes
from all corners of the African continent. Open for dinner only.

CITY BOWL Miller's Thumb

10b Kloofnek Road, Tamboerskloof, 8001 **Tel** (021) 424-3838

Map 4 F3

Solly and Jane Solomon's seafood restaurant has an ever-changing specials board utilising simply prepared ingredients
fresh from the ocean. There is a definite leaning towards Cajun and Creole cuisine, although their interpretation of
the Japanese dish *yaki soba* (prawn, chicken and cashews with noodles) is also a firm favourite with the locals.

CITY BOWL 95 Keerom

95 Keerom Street, 8000 **Tel** (021) 422-0765

Map 5 B2

Somehow a century-old olive tree continues to grow inside this established city-centre restaurant. Chef-owner
Giorgio Nava's northern Italian-inspired cuisine is big on seafood, which he sources himself, going out to sea in
his own boat. The seared tuna with tomato, olives and capers is a popular choice.

CITY BOWL Bukhara

33 Church Street, 8001 **Tel** (021) 424-0000

Map 5 B1

Bukhara is perhaps the most respected Indian restaurant in the city; the high-quality, immaculately prepared dishes
are a delight. The ambience of the restaurant is enhanced by the layout, with the glass-encased open-plan kitchen
and authentic tandoori ovens on one side offset by large windows and a pretty view of Church Street on the other.

CITY BOWL Café Paradiso

110 Kloof Street, Gardens, 8001 **Tel** (021) 423-8653

Map 4 F3

A down-to-earth and well-established restaurant serving hearty Mediterranean meals with an extensive wine list
to match. The steaks are renowned, as is the meze buffet. The outdoor area on Kloof Street, overlooking the City
Bowl, is a great place to soak up Cape Town's attractive landscape.

CITY BOWL Haiku

33 Church Street, 8001 **Tel** (021) 424-7000

Map 5 B1

This über-trendy offshoot of Bukhara (just around the corner) specializes in modern Asian dining tapas-style. Loud
lounge music permeates the venue, but otherwise the ambience is very Zen, with soft overhead lights and black
granite walls. Brighter lighting shines on the open-plan kitchen.

CITY BOWL The Opal Lounge

30 Kloof Street, Gardens, 8001 **Tel** *(021) 422-4747*

Map

Set in a Victorian villa on Kloof Street, this chic eatery offers a fusion of Asian, African and French dishes. The restaurant prides itself on its culinary flair, stylish decor, service and attention to detail. Try the slow-roasted pork belly or rare seared tuna, or sip a delicious cocktail at the bar, which is one of South Africa's best.

V&A WATERFRONT Il Paninaro

Shop 14–15, Alfred Mall, 8001 **Tel** *(021) 421-6052*

Map *1 B1*

The name translates as "the sandwich maker", but at Il Paninaro you will also find salads, pizzas and pasta dishes. As well as offering the finest coffee in Cape Town, this place is renowned for its quality ingredients – all cold meats are imported from Italy. Stop here on your way to Robben Island to pick up one of their famous sandwich boxes.

V&A WATERFRONT Quay Four

Quay 4, 8001 **Tel** *(021) 419-2008*

Map *1 B1*

One of the oldest and most popular restaurants at the Waterfront, Quay Four boasts a broad wooden deck overlooking the harbour. Not surprisingly, seafood dominates the menu, with highlights including linefish and calamari served in giant frying pans. In the evening, dining is accompanied by live music.

V&A WATERFRONT Den Anker Restaurant and Bar

Pierhead, 8001 **Tel** *(021) 419-0249*

Map *1 B2*

The focus at Den Anker is on keeping it Belgian. The building is a glass wrap-around affair presenting views of the marina, City Bowl and the mountain beyond. Mussels with fries and mayo is a signature dish, or try the châteaubriand of springbok for a combination of European preparation and local ingredients.

V&A WATERFRONT Baia Seafood Restaurant

Upper Level, Victoria Wharf, 8001 **Tel** *(021) 421-0935*

Map *1 C1*

The menu at this Mediterranean-styled seafood restaurant with views over the Waterfront and Table Mountain features freshly caught Cape crayfish, Mozambique prawns, West Coast mussels and Knysna oysters. The sweeping terrace is an ideal venue to watch the sunset. Reservations and formal wear are recommended.

V&A WATERFRONT Sevruga

Shop 4, Quay 5, 8001 **Tel** *(021) 421-5134*

Map *1 B1*

The sister restaurant to the ever-popular Beluga in Green Point *(see p415)*, Sevruga is the Waterfront's – and Cape Town's – latest spot to see and be seen. It offers its beautiful patrons an extensive menu of sophisticated fare such as ocean-fresh sushi, grilled meats and carpaccios.

V&A WATERFRONT Belthazar Restaurant and Wine Bar

Shop 153, Victoria Wharf, 8001 **Tel** *(021) 421-3753/6*

Map *1 C1*

Food is prepared to perfection at this restaurant and the menu includes steak and seafood. There is an immensely varied and impeccable wine list to match. Having the world's largest selection of wine by the glass is an aspiration the management is striving to achieve. Book ahead.

ATLANTIC SEABOARD La Cuccina

Victoria Mall, Victoria Road, Hout Bay, 7872 **Tel** *(021) 790-8008*

A spacious deli and restaurant offering freshly baked cakes and buffet lunches. Despite being a little off the beaten path, La Cuccina is well known to most Hout Bay residents. The breakfast menu is also excellent, and the restaurant stays busy throughout the day. Plates are charged by weight at the buffet.

ATLANTIC SEABOARD Café Caprice

37 Victoria Road, Camps Bay, 8001 **Tel** *(021) 438-8315*

A popular haunt with models and fashionable twentysomethings, Café Caprice is always busy, particularly in the summer months. The breakfast menu is popular too, and the eggs Benedict are particularly good. In the evening a resident DJ plays in the bar, and on Sundays it becomes the place to party.

ATLANTIC SEABOARD La Perla

Beach Road, Sea Point, 8005 **Tel** *(021) 439-9538*

Delicious fresh fish and shellfish are on the menu at this grand old dame of seafood restaurants. For each fish on the menu, three dishes are created using different sauces and preparation. The ambience is elegant, but not stuffy, and children are welcome. In good weather you can sit outside and watch the breakers. Service can be hit or miss.

ATLANTIC SEABOARD Blues

The Promenade, Victoria Road, Camps Bay, 8001 **Tel** *(021) 438-2040*

Blues is a product of Cape Town's 80s yuppie restaurant boom. It has performed solidly over the years and was recently refurbished to include a wine cellar complete with a 12-seater table to accommodate tastings and intimate private dinners. Food is contemporary Mediterranean, with lots of seafood and dashes of global influences.

ATLANTIC SEABOARD Codfather

37 The Drive, Camps Bay, 8001 **Tel** *(021) 438-0782/3*

One of Cape Town's first dedicated sushi restaurants (although they serve other seafood as well), Codfather opened its doors to the public in 2001. The restaurant has no menu, instead waiting staff must consult with guests and help them put together tailor-made dishes. Chose a table with a panoramic view of the ocean.

GREEN POINT AND MOUILLE POINT Giovanni's Deliworld

Main Road, Green Point, 8051 **Tel** (021) 434-6593

Map 1 A4

The Italian-owned Giovanni's is Cape Town's most fashionable deli, and the semi-open coffee bar at the front is the place to see and to be seen. Many of the cheeses and cold meats are imported from Italy, and there is a hot buffet counter where meals are charged by the weight.

GREEN POINT AND MOUILLE POINT Sotana

121 Beach Drive, Mouille Point, 8005 **Tel** (021) 439-5119

Map 1 B3

A family affair on Mouille Point's sea-facing boulevard, Sotana is a reliable choice for delicious alfresco pizzas or various bistro dishes. There is a children's playground nearby with a miniature train to keep the little ones occupied while you wait for your main course to arrive.

GREEN POINT AND MOUILLE POINT Andiamo

Cape Quarter, 72 Waterkant Street, Green Point, 8001 **Tel** (021) 421-3687/8

Map 2 D5

A bustling Italian venue full of *joie de vivre* in the fashionable Cape Quarter section of Green Point. The food is blissfully unpretentious, focusing on straightforward recipes done properly. Among the signature dishes are lamb chops and fish, which is baked in the pizza oven. In the deli is a promotions table featuring tastings seven days a week.

GREEN POINT AND MOUILLE POINT Pigalle

57 Somerset Road, Green Point, 8001 **Tel** (021) 421-4848

Map 2 D5

Occupying a converted ice rink, no expense was spared in fitting out this up-market eatery. Pigalle is somewhat of an anomaly in Cape Town's fickle restaurant scene. Most similar ventures have lasted only a few months, but this restaurant has gone from strength to strength. Expect a smattering of celebrities enjoying a classy night out.

GREEN POINT AND MOUILLE POINT Wakame

Cnr Beach Drive & Surrey Road, Mouille Point, 8005 **Tel** (021) 433-2377

Map 1 B3

The dramatic interior will no doubt impress as you enter this first-floor sushi bar on Mouille Point's Beach Road. The restaurant's mascot is a long fish skeleton that hangs above the sushi bar. Take a seat inside or choose a table in the balcony area. You may see whales in the bay during the spring and early summer months.

GREEN POINT AND MOUILLE POINT Anatoli

24 Napier Street, Green Point, 8005 **Tel** (021) 419-2501

Map 2 D5

Serving up Cape Town's best Turkish cuisine since 1984, Anatoli is located in a 100-year-old warehouse. The vibrancy of Turkish culture is reflected in the decor and the cuisine, with an ever-changing list of specials. On arrival, hot flat breads and meze are carried to your table on oversized trays for immediate consumption.

GREEN POINT AND MOUILLE POINT Beluga

The Foundry, Prestwich Street, Green Point, 8001 **Tel** (021) 418-2948

Map 2 D5

Taking advantage of an industrial space, Beluga has made its home inside a century-old metalworks. Serving up a contemporary mix of seafood and grilled meats, the restaurant includes a sushi bar where you can watch Asian chefs at work slicing up the catch of the day. The two-for-one lunchtime sushi offer is very popular.

NORTHERN SUBURBS La Masseria

Cnr Bluegum & Huguenot Streets, Durbanville, 7550 **Tel** (021) 976-0036

The emphasis is on hearty, home-made dishes at this family-run establishment. The menu is dictated by what produce is in season, and nothing is rushed to ensure that the tradition of attention to detail is maintained. Owner Lorenzo Ciman now has a deli alongside the restaurant where he does a roaring trade in cured meats and Italian cheeses.

NORTHERN SUBURBS De Tijgerkombuis

12 Old Oak Road, Bellville, 7530 **Tel** (021) 914-0186

An old-fashioned Dutch pub and restaurant serving Cape Provençal-style meals, this establishment is extremely popular with the locals. A good selection of traditional South African dishes is on offer, along with meatier favourites such as oxtail, *bobotie* and top-notch tripe.

SOUTH PENINSULA Cape to Cuba

165 Main Road, Kalk Bay, 7975 **Tel** (021) 788-1566

Essentially a series of adjacent corrugated-iron shacks beside the railway line, Cape to Cuba is a marvel of South Africa's enterprising spirit. Every last piece of Latin American and African decor masking the rudimentary nature of the restaurant structure is for sale, usually with a significant price tag. Best enjoyed for cocktails and light snacks.

SOUTH PENINSULA Kalky's

Kalk Bay Harbour, Kalk Bay, 7945 **Tel** (021) 788-1726

This is Cape Town's best fish-and-chip shop, so don't be put off by the slightly seedy harbour surrounds. Kalky's offers excellent value for money and the freshest possible ingredients. The best option is the "family meal", which will buy you enough fish, chips, calamari and bread rolls to feed a small army.

SOUTH PENINSULA The Meeting Place

98 St Georges Street, Simon's Town, 7975 **Tel** (021) 786-5678

A deli and coffee shop opposite Simon's Town's yacht basin and Jubilee Square, The Meeting Place has a lo colonial-style balcony overlooking the old main road and plenty of couches to sink into on the inside. Cho a selection of freshly baked cakes and muffins, toasted sandwiches and other light meals.

SOUTH PENINSULA Octopus' Garden
The Old Post Office Building, Main Road, St James, 7945 **Tel** *(021) 788-5646*

An idiosyncratic venue in St James and a delicious lemon meringue pie, which is claimed to bestow amorous skills upon the dinner, are only two of the attractions at this delightful restaurant. Children and dogs are welcome here, and the ambience is laid-back and friendly. The restaurant's hammock is the perfect place to relax after a meal.

SOUTH PENINSULA Olympia Café & Deli
134 Main Road, Kalk Bay, 7975 **Tel** *(021) 788-6396*

An irreverent ambience and strong culinary skills have won this café the Award for Everyday Eating. This accolade has been hung in one of the bathrooms for patrons to appreciate. The breakfasts are justifiably legendary, as is the seared tuna and other regularly rotated specials.

SOUTH PENINSULA Tibetan Teahouse
2 Harrington Road, Seaforth, Simon's Town, 7975 **Tel** *(021) 786-1544*

A holistic café featuring an art gallery, the Tibetan Teahouse specializes in wholesome vegetarian food such as stews, soups and dairy-free cakes and desserts. And, of course, there is tea, home-grown and herb-infused. The shop also sells jewellery and crafts from Nepal. Open until 5pm daily.

SOUTH PENINSULA The Brass Bell
Kalk Bay Station, Main Road, Kalk Bay, 7975 **Tel** *(021) 788-5455*

Before tourism came to the area, this established live-music and drinking venue was reliant on a regular stream of patrons from the neighbouring town of Fish Hoek, which had an alcohol ban. These days it is a much smarter restaurant with good pizzas from the wood-fired oven.

SOUTH PENINSULA Carla's
9 York Road, Muizenberg, 7945 **Tel** *(021) 788-6860*

Named after Carla, a Mozambiquan expat now happily installed in bohemian Muizenberg, the signature dish "LM prawns" is a firm local favourite, served with rice or chips and a home-made peri-peri sauce. The restaurant itself is small and cosy and presided over by Carla herself on a nightly basis. Booking is always a good idea.

SOUTH PENINSULA The Black Marlin
Main Road, Millers Point, Simon's Town, 7995 **Tel** *(021) 786-1621*

To get to Cape Town's oldest seafood restaurant at Millers Point, you have to drive through Simon's Town and past Boulders' penguin colony until the coastline is more or less deserted. The long drive is worth it for the incredible views alone. During whale season you can enjoy freshly caught crayfish while watching the giant mammals swim past.

SOUTH PENINSULA Polana
Kalk Bay Harbour, Kalk Bay, 7945 **Tel** *(021) 788-7162*

A little slice of Café del Mar on the South Peninsula. Polana's setting is a bigger draw than its food, which is arguably overpriced. Have a cocktail in the bar before heading to your table. In summer the large glass frontage is open, and the sea spray is almost tangible as you recline on the generous couches waiting for the next course.

SOUTH PENINSULA Harbour House
Kalk Bay Harbour, Kalk Bay, 7945 **Tel** *(021) 788-4133*

Perhaps the most up-market restaurant in this popular fishing village, Harbour House is located within the harbour and above two other restaurants. The interior is airy, with the bar area almost as big as the restaurant itself. Sipping a cocktail on the deck while watching the seals glide through the water below will make you feel like a millionaire.

SOUTHERN SUBURBS Rhodes Memorial Restaurant
Rhodes Memorial, Groote Schuur Estate, Rondebosch, 7740 **Tel** *(021) 689-9151*

Famous for its home-made desserts, this restaurant behind the granite Rhodes Memorial offers unbeatable views across the City Bowl and Cape Flats. It is also an ideal breakfast venue. Take an early morning hike along the mountain's contour path and end it here with a fry-up and some freshly squeezed orange juice – or even a beer.

SOUTHERN SUBURBS Peddlars on the Bend
Spaanschemat River Road, Constantia, 7800 **Tel** *(021) 794-7747*

A local institution, Peddlars serves up consistent pub fare to a steady stream of loyal patrons. On a fine day, the garden area is full to capacity and alive with the hubbub of local gossip. Try the *ferrari prego* for the Peddlars' twist on the classic steak roll, or the kingklip calabrese with anchovies. Veggies will enjoy the spinach and lentil bake.

SOUTHERN SUBURBS Constantia Uitsig
Constantia Uitsig Estate, Spaanschemat River Road, Constantia, 7800 **Tel** *(021) 794-4480*

A much-lauded establishment that gets it right on all levels: from the service to the food, down to the wine list. Installed in the original manor house of the Constantia Uitsig wine estate, the restaurant is hugely popular and often listed as one of South Africa's top dining venues.

SOUTHERN SUBURBS La Colombe
Constantia Uitsig Estate, Constantia, 7800 **Tel** *(021) 794-2390*

On the Uitsig working wine farm, La Colombe consistently features among the top 50 restaurants in the [wor]ld. [The] flavours are of French origin, but with a distinctive Cape accent. Ideal for special occasions that require [...]nce. The emphasis is on well-crafted meals rather than overblown service.

CAPE WINELANDS

FRANSCHHOEK Essence   🔊 🚫 📋 Ⓥ   ®

7 Huguenot Square, Huguenot Road, Franschhoek, 7690 **Tel** *(021) 876-4135*

A relaxed café with comfortable couches and sunny outdoor tables, Essence offers generous breakfasts, filled paninis and bagels, local favourites such as *bobotie* and lamb curry, and good, old-fashioned scones with cream and strawberry jam. Open 7am–6pm daily.

FRANSCHHOEK Bread & Wine   🔊 🚫 📋 🍴 Ⓥ 🅿   ®®®

Moreson Winery, Happy Valley Road, Franschhoek, 7690 **Tel** *(021) 876-3692*

This characterful restaurant has won numerous accolades for its rustic Mediterranean-inspired food. Set in a winery and surrounded by vineyards, it has a courtyard and a covered terrace for outdoor dining. Grilled meat and seafood are on offer, along with homemade pasta dishes. The speciality of the house is home-cured charcuterie.

FRANSCHHOEK Haute Cabrière   📋 🍴 Ⓥ 🅿   ®®®®

Cabriere Estate, Pass Road, Franschhoek, 7690 **Tel** *(021) 876-3688*

A supremely elegant cellar restaurant high up on the Franschhoek Pass. A great many of the dishes on the menu use ingredients found in the valley below, including fresh salmon and trout bred and caught in the cold-water stream that flows off the mountain. Haute Cabrière routinely features in most South African top ten restaurant lists.

FRANSCHHOEK La Petite Ferme   🚫 📋 🍴 Ⓥ 🅿   ®®®®®

Franschhoek Pass Road, Franschhoek, 7690 **Tel** *(021) 876-3016*

The cellar at La Petite Ferme is impressive, to say the least, and the winery has produced several award-winning vintages over the years. Head chef Olivia Mitchell and sous chef Carina Bouwer are a *tour de force* in the kitchen, crafting contemporary African and Malay masterpieces.

FRANSCHHOEK Reubens Restaurant, Bar & Deli   📋 🍴 Ⓥ 🅿   ®®®®®

Oude Stallen Centre, 19 Huguenot Road, Franschhoek, 7690 **Tel** *(021) 876-3772*

This stylish modern restaurant was set up by chef Reuben Riffel, who is South Africa's top celebrity chef, having appeared on TV's *Masterchef* and numerous commercials. The relaxed ambience, great service, and particularly good seafood all make for a memorable dining experience.

FRANSCHHOEK The Tasting Room (at Le Quartier Français)   🚫 📋 🍴 Ⓥ 🅿   ®®®®®

16 Huguenot Road, Franschhoek, 7690 **Tel** *(021) 876-2151*

Le Quartier Français regularly features in *Restaurant* magazine's top 50. Chef Margot Janse is the star of the show and offers guests a choice of four-, six- or eight-course dining experiences from a menu that uses only seasonal local ingredients. Le Quartier's attached bistro, The Common Room, has a less expensive, but just as excellent, menu.

PAARL Eat@Simonsvlei   🔊 🚫 🍴 Ⓥ 🅿   ®

Simonsvlei Winery, Old Paarl Road (101), Paarl, 7646 **Tel** *(021) 863-3040*

Child-friendly, with extensive indoor and outdoor seating, this restaurant provides all-round value for money and is an antidote to the more gastronomic options that are found all over the Winelands. Large parties are catered for, and buffet or picnic lunches are served around the water feature in the summer months.

PAARL Kikka   🚫 🍴 Ⓥ 🅿   ®

217 Main Street, Paarl, 7646 **Tel** *(021) 872-0685*

Situated just off the village main road, Kikka unusually houses both a florist and a coffee shop. Don't let the interesting trinkets that fill the shop distract you from the excellent buffet or light meals served in a comfortable and casual environment. The speciality cheesecakes are not to be missed.

PAARL Laborie   🚫 🍴 Ⓥ   ®®®

Laborie Estate, Taillefert Street, Paarl, 7646 **Tel** *(021) 807-3095*

Reservations are recommended at this restaurant offering gourmet fare on the Laborie wine estate, at the foot of Paarl Mountain. In winter, diners can enjoy the cosy fireplace, and in summer they can eat alfresco, at the tables set under the large oak trees. Dishes are paired with Laborie's own wines. Open daily for lunch; Wed–Sun for dinner.

PAARL Bosmans   🔊 🚫 📋 🍴 Ⓥ 🅿   ®®®®®

The Grande Roche Hotel, Plantasie, 7646 **Tel** *(021) 863-2727*

Named South Africa's Top Deluxe Restaurant by *Style* magazine for two years running, Bosmans has an international team of chefs who maintain its position as one of the world's great eateries. The food is said to "reflect a sophisticated awareness of what is happening in the international culinary world". A classic fine-dining experience.

SOMERSET WEST The Avontuur Estate Restaurant   🚫 📋 🍴 Ⓥ 🅿   ®®

R44, Somerset West, 7130 **Tel** *(021) 855-4296*

Located on a wine farm between the tasting area and the cellar, Avontuur offers unhurried meals made with fresh country ingredients with a Mediterranean flavour. In fine weather, outdoor seating is available in the patio garden, with sweeping views across the vineyards all the way to Table Mountain.

SOMERSET WEST Wine Women & Sushi   ®®
Urtell Crescent, The Triangle, Somerset Mall, 7130 Tel (021) 851-0271

Sushi is pretty much all Wine Women and Sushi does, and it does it properly, which is why this is one of the best Japanese restaurants in the Cape Winelands. The menu offers several vegetarian options as well as a takeaway service. In summer there are outdoor tables for alfresco dinning.

SOMERSET WEST La Vigna   ®®®
Lord Charles Hotel, cnr Main Rd & Broadway Blvd, Somerset West, 7130 Tel (021) 855-1040

The stylish signature restaurant of the Lord Charles Hotel has modern interiors, a garden terrace and an adjacent wine cellar. The menu features a broad selection of starters, seafood and meat dishes. For a lighter option, choose a gourmet sandwich or an inventive salad. La Vigna also serves a traditional afternoon tea.

SOMERSET WEST Steffanie's Place   ®®®
113 Irene Avenue, Somerset West, 7130 Tel (021) 852-7584

This ever-popular family-run business only gets better. The location is perhaps its biggest coup, as Steffanie's Place is perched right at the crest of Irene Avenue overlooking the mountains and sea beyond. Conan Garrett is a talented head chef, and dishes like grilled kingklip with salsa and queen prawns keep the punters coming back.

SOMERSET WEST 96 Winery Road   ®®®®
Zandberg Farm, Winery Road, Somerset West, 7599 Tel (021) 842-2020

Fresh, organic local ingredients are used to great effect at this well-run Helderberg countryside restaurant. The steaks are aged for 18 days in the restaurant's purpose-built cold room, and they are particularly good. 96 Winery Road received an Award of Excellence for its wine list at the Diners Club Wine List of the Year Awards.

STELLENBOSCH Moyo at Spier   ®®®®®
Spier Estate, Lynedoch Road (R310), 7603 Tel (021) 809-1133

Moyo is about much more than a meal: it's a Cape African culture experience. Food is served as a delicious buffet, while indigenous dancers and musicians entertain with traditional drumming and African storytelling. The garden is filled with bedouin tents and tree houses with water features. A great option for children.

STELLENBOSCH Terroir   ®®®®®
Kleine Zalze, Strand Road (R44), 7600 Tel (021) 880-0740

A Provençal-inspired restaurant with award-winning wines from the host estate of Kleine Zalze. Terroir overlooks a lake, and there is additional seating outside, under the majestic oak trees. Chef Michael Broughton has described his dishes as "deceptively simple", and they are directed by the seasonality of the excellent local ingredients.

WESTERN COASTAL TERRACE

BLOUBERG The Blue Peter   ®
Blue Peter Hotel, 7 Popham Road, Bloubergstrand, 7441 Tel (021) 554-1956

Three restaurants rolled into one, including fine dining in the Upper Deck. The two informal eateries in the Lower Deck are firm child-friendly favourites with the locals, and the pizzas are highly recommended. The famous view across the bay to Table Mountain and the friendly atmosphere are the main draws here.

BLOUBERG On the Rocks   ®®®
45 Stadler Road, Bloubergstrand, 7441 Tel (021) 554-1988

On the Rocks is literally that: enjoy views of the ocean and watch dolphins play in the waves as the sun dips below the Table Mountain skyline. An up-market choice, this restaurant focuses on seafood but also has plenty to satisfy carnivores and vegetarians. Try the catch of the day, or the medallion of kingklip with creamy shrimp sauce.

CLANWILLIAM Khoisan Kitchen   ®
Traveller's Rest, R364, Clanwilliam, 8135 Tel (027) 482-1824

Haffie Strauss serves up hearty traditional Afrikaans and Malay fare on the banks of the Brandewyn River. Mutton stew, *waterblommetjie* stew and *roosterkoek* are long-standing favourites. The Sevilla Rock Art Trail follows the river for 4 km (2½ miles), visiting nine sites of rock paintings left behind by the former Khoi Khoi inhabitants.

DARLING Evita se Perron   ®®®®
Old Darling Railway Station, 8 Arcadia Street, Darling, 7345 Tel (022) 492-2851

The food is pretty good here, but this is more about the show than anything. Evita Bezuidenhout is a national treasure, the alter ego of comedian and international AIDS activist Pieter Dirk Uys. Expect a hilarious and irreverent stand-up routine that ruthlessly satirizes the Rainbow Nation and all of its chequered history.

LAMBERTS BAY Muisbosskerm Open-Air Restaurant   ®®
Elands Bay Road, Lamberts Bay, 8130 Tel (027) 432-1017

The original West Coast seafood *skerm*, Muisbos started as a hobby to entertain family and friends, and grew into something of a phenomenon. The meal is an endless open-air buffet of seafood indulgence. As well as baked, smoked and grilled fish and crayfish, there is also a variety of *potjiekos* on offer.

Key to Price Guide *see p412* **Key to Symbols** *see back cover flap*

LANGEBAAN Die Strandloper

On the beach, Langebaan, 7357 Tel (022) 772-2490

A visit to Die Strandloper necessitates a lengthy and indulgent meal spread out over several hours, starting at noon (or 6pm for dinner). Course after course of freshly caught and expertly prepared seafood is the speciality here. The charge is per head, with children under 12 paying according to their height, and those under five eating for free.

YZERFONTEIN Strandkombuis

16 Mile Beach, Dolphin Way, Yzerfontein, 7351 Tel (022) 451-2360

Located on the immaculate 16 Mile Beach at Yzerfontein, this is an outdoor seafood extravaganza that suits large and informal gatherings. Strandkombuis is great for family occasions: children are welcome, and there is no corkage fee. All food is prepared in a network of *braai* pits and stone ovens, including the freshly baked bread.

SOUTHERN CAPE

GREYTON The Jam Tin

Boschmanskloof, Aster Laan, Greyton, 7233 Tel (028) 254-9075

Traditional cuisine in an authentic Cape home setting is on offer at the quaint Jam Tin. If you call ahead to make a reservation, you might well be asked what your favourite dish is, and they will make it specially for you. Cape Dutch and Malay-style meals are expertly prepared. Open daily for dinner and lunch by arrangement.

HERMANUS Bientang's Cave

Marine Drive, Hermanus, 7200 Tel (028) 312-3454

This restaurant is uniquely located in a cave below Marine Drive. The extended wooden deck right over the waves is the ideal spot from which to enjoy whale-watching in Walker Bay. The menu has a seafood slant, and it is possible to build a platter to share. Open 9am–4pm daily.

OUDTSHOORN Jemima's

94 Baron van Reede Street, Oudtshoorn, 6620 Tel (044) 272-0808

A gourmet feast is assured at Jemima's, voted as one of South Africa's ten best restaurants on several occasions. The gregarious Malherbe family love to share their culinary talents with their guests. They're also keen to recommend the right bottle of wine to accompany the house speciality: leg of Karoo lamb. There are also excellent vegetarian options.

OUDTSHOORN Kalinka

93 Baron van Reede Street, Oudtshoorn, 6620 Tel (044) 279-2596

Set in a beautifully renovated old sandstone house on Oudtshoorn's main street, this elegant restaurant is fast becoming a top destination for Karoo cuisine. Venison, ostrich and lamb are regularly served up by the Russian owner-chef. Specialities include caviar-filled pancakes and Amarula crème brûlée. Open for dinner only.

STANFORD Marianas Home Deli & Bistro

12 Du Toit Street, Stanford, 7210 Tel (028) 341-0272

Open only for breakfast and lunch on Fridays, Saturdays and Sundays, Marianas serves dishes using vegetables grown organically in the field outside. Dishes such as the lamb shanks are heavenly. Booking is advisable at this superb, friendly and unpretentious foodie mecca.

SWELLENDAM The Old Gaol Restaurant

8A Voortrek Street, Swellendam, 6740 Tel (028) 514-3847

Traditional local dishes are served up in this rustic eatery, opposite the beautiful Dutch Reformed Church on Swellendam's historic Church Square. You can see *melktert (see p409)* being baked in copper pans in the outdoor oven in the garden. Sit under the 100-year-old trees along the riverbank, and enjoy a freshly prepared picnic lunch.

SWELLENDAM Herberg Roosje van de Kaap

5 Drostdy Street, Swellendam, 6740 Tel (028) 514-3001

Part of the Roosje van de Kaap hotel, this eatery is regularly rated as a top ten Southern Cape restaurant by *Eat Out*. The menu ranges from Cape Malay to classical French dishes and gourmet pizzas. An Old World ambience is enhanced by traditional décor and soft lighting. Leave room for the wonderful desserts.

GARDEN ROUTE TO GRAHAMSTOWN

GRAHAMSTOWN The Cock House

10 Market Street, Grahamstown, 6139 Tel (046) 636-1287

This established guesthouse and restaurant in a listed building offers home-baked breads, freshly cut herbs from the garden, an innovative menu and a lovingly compiled wine list. Former guests include Nelson Mandela. The restaurant features in Lannice Snyman's book *Reflections of the South African Table*.

KNYSNA Île de païn

Thesen's Island, The Boatshed, Knysna, 6570 **Tel** *(044) 302-5707*

Using a wood-fired oven and only the best ingredients grown on the Garden Route, Liezie Mulder creates the most delicious bread as an integral part of the breakfasts available at Île de païn. Sicilian bruschetta or Cambodian curry are recommended options for lunch. And you can even take goodies for the road.

KNYSNA 34 Degrees South

Quay 19, Knysna Quays, Waterfront Drive, Knysna, 6571 **Tel** *(044) 382-7331*

Named after Knysna's longitudinal position on the globe, 34 Degrees South is a fantastic combination of a deli and a seafood emporium. The focus is definitely on the fruits of the ocean: the hake is freshly caught as opposed to trawled, and there is fresh line fish daily. The ubiquitous Knysna oyster is also available.

KNYSNA East Head Café

The Heads, George Rex Drive, Knysna, 6571 **Tel** *(044) 384-0933*

Situated on the rocks at the famous Knysna Heads, this family-run restaurant serves hearty, uncomplicated fare: grills, pizzas and pasta dishes. These are best enjoyed with a bottle of wine while soaking up the spectacular setting. There is a children's menu and a playground to keep the little ones entertained.

KNYSNA Oyster Catcher

Knysna Quays, Waterfront Drive, Knysna, 6570 **Tel** *(044) 382-9995*

Situated on a working jetty, the Oyster Catcher has been dishing up the finest, freshest seafood since 1998. Enjoy the magnificent waterfront views and watch the boats offloading their day's harvest. Succulent oysters and calamari are highlights of the menu here, but good vegetarian options and great cocktails are also available.

KNYSNA Persellos

41 Main Road, Town Central, Knysna, 6570 **Tel** *(044) 382-2665*

Italian and family-run, this pizzeria is known by the locals simply as "Mamma's". If you are looking for a reasonably priced option away from the tourist hubbub of Thesen's Island, then this is the place to go. Pasta is prepared freshly on the premises, and this really can be tasted in the finished product.

KNYSNA Drydock Food Co

Knysna Quays, Waterfront Drive, Knysna, 6571 **Tel** *(044) 382-7310*

Erected on the site of Knysna's first dry dock, this establishment offers a wide range of fresh seafood, decadent salads and fusion cuisine. Try the line-fish fontana (grilled line fish with vegetables and smoked salmon trout) or the catch of the day. The bar is well stocked with local and imported beers and spirits. The cellar has a decent variety of wine too.

KNYSNA Pembreys

Brenton Road, Belvidere, Knysna, 6571 **Tel** *(044) 386-0005*

Home-made pastas and local dishes infused with Mediterranean flavours rule in Peter and Viv Vadas's kitchen. The simple country setting belies the accomplished menu. Sole is a signature dish, and the desserts, including a mouth-watering *crème brûlée*, are excellent. The couple travel to Europe annually for culinary sabbaticals.

PLETTENBERG BAY Le Fournil de Plett Bakery & Café

Lookout Centre, Main Street, Plettenberg Bay, 6600 **Tel** *(044) 533-1390*

This French bakery and bistro has an attractive tree-covered patio for alfresco dining and an array of delicious aromas emanating from the ovens. Light lunch options include filled baguettes, vol-au-vents and the classic *croque monsieur*. Do not leave without trying a tartlet or a slice of one of their famous gateaux. Open until 5pm daily.

PLETTENBERG BAY The Lookout Deck

Lookout Beach, Plettenberg Bay, 6600 **Tel** *(044) 533-1379*

Lookout Beach is one of the finest beaches in South Africa thanks to its pristine condition. This restaurant is firmly established as one of Plettenberg Bay's best, and it sports an unashamedly seafood-biased menu. Views of the whales, dolphins and sunsets provide the entertainment.

PLETTENBERG BAY Cornuti al Mare

Perestrella Street, Plettenberg Bay, 6600 **Tel** *(044) 533-1277*

Cornuti al Mare (literally, "cuckolds at the seaside") is the coastal counterpart of Piero Carrara's Johannesburg venture. As it is extremely popular with local patrons it is best to book a table. The perfect crisp-based pizzas are a good option, although the coastal location also allows for the addition of seafood meze to the menu.

PORT ELIZABETH Royal Delhi

10 Burgess Street, Richmond Hill, Port Elizabeth, 6001 **Tel** *(041) 373-8216*

Opened 17 years ago, the family-run Royal Delhi offers the best Indian cuisine in the area. The restaurant is centrally located and features a light, richly decorated interior. Krish Pillay offers a wide range of curries, encompassing both North and South Indian dishes, plus seafood and grilled meats. There are some interesting wines on the list.

PORT ELIZABETH Ginger

Marine Drive, Humewood, 6001 **Tel** *(041) 583-1229*

Ginger in Humewood is a popular and chic lounge-cum-restaurant venue with a surprisingly eclectic menu. This "corner café" boasts floor-to-ceiling windows, so you can sip one of their excellent cocktails as you enjoy splendid views over the bay. Resident DJs spin deep-house and lounge music at weekends.

Key to Price Guide *see p412* **Key to Symbols** *see back cover flap*

PORT ELIZABETH De Kelder
🔣 🍴 ♿ Ⓥ 🅿️ ⓇⓇⓇⓇ

Marine Protea Hotel, Marine Drive, Summerstrand, 6001 **Tel** *(041) 583-2750*

Fresh seafood is the speciality at this large and sophisticated restaurant, with line fish and oysters available daily. There are also red-meat and venison platters. Staff are friendly and attentive, and the food is presented with loving panache. Enjoy one of the excellent flambés for dessert.

WILD COAST, DRAKENSBERG & MIDLANDS

BERGVILLE Bingelela Restaurant
♿ 🔣 ♿ Ⓥ 🅿️ ⓇⓇ

Needwood Farm, Box 5, Bergville, 3350 **Tel** *(036) 448-1336*

Nestled at the foot of the Drakensberg Mountains is this old farmhouse, offering food as well as friendly B&B accommodation. Light lunches and dinners are served by owners Paula and Joss in the 68-seat restaurant, which overlooks a beautiful garden with a swimming pool. A non-smoking area is available.

EAST LONDON Ocean Basket
♿ 🔣 🅿️ ⓇⓇ

Vincent Park Centre, Vincent, East London, 5214 **Tel** *(043) 726-8809*

Owned by the largest fish retailer in South Africa and part of a popular national chain, Ocean Basket is a bright, cheerful restaurant offering reasonably priced fare, ranging from seafood to Mediterranean dishes, from Creole and Cajun food to sushi. You can bring your own wine, which will be subject to a corkage fee of R15.

EAST LONDON Michaela's of Chintsa
♿ 🔣 🍴 ♿ Ⓥ 🅿️ ⓇⓇⓇ

Steenbras Drive, Chintsa East, Eastern Cape, 5275 **Tel** *(043) 738-5139*

This two-storey restaurant boasts a spectacular location on top of the dunes, with views that stretch as far as the eye can see. The art and craftwork decorating the venue are all for sale. The menu is contemporary, with the accent on local seafood, but also includes curries, seafood pasta and grilled meats. Good local wines are well priced.

HIMEVILLE Moorcroft Manor
♿ 🔣 ♿ 🅿️ ⓇⓇⓇ

Sani Road, Himeville, 3256 **Tel** *(033) 702-1967*

The restaurant at this award-winning five-star guesthouse in the Drakensberg Mountains offers a selection of light lunches (including a delicious ploughman's platter) and à la carte dinners. In the evening, the stylish menu features the best of local meat, trout, salads, mushrooms and cheeses. There is also an impressive wine list.

HOWICK Corner Post
♿ ⓇⓇ

130 Main Street, Howick, 3290 **Tel** *(033) 330-7636*

This charming pub-cum-restaurant offers a country/fusion menu, which translates on the plate as old favourites with a Mediterranean twist. Try the grilled Karoo lamb chops with aubergine and tzatziki, and be sure to leave room for the fabulous desserts, such as home-made ice creams or *crème brûlée*. Art exhibitions are regularly held at the venue.

HOWICK Yellowwood Café
ⓇⓇ

1 Shafton Road, Howick, 4200 **Tel** *(033) 330-2461*

In the heart of the Natal Midlands, overlooking the Howick Falls, is this country restaurant offering superb views from the verandah tables. The cuisine, based around fresh seasonal delights, matches the vistas. Select your meal from either the à la carte or pub menu, and match it with a suitable wine from the good selection.

LESOTHO Rendez-Vous Restaurant
♿ 🍴 🅿️ ⓇⓇ

Kingsway Street, Maseru **Tel** *(00266) 2231 2114*

Also known as the Lancer's Inn, Rendez-Vous is one of Lesotho King Letsie III's favourite restaurants. You too can eat like royalty here: the dishes available on the à la carte menu are nothing short of excellent. However, be prepared for the service to be on the slow side.

MONT-AUX-SOURCES Tower of Pizza
♿ 🔣 ♿ Ⓥ 🅿️ ⓇⓇ

Mont-aux-Sources, Northern Drakensberg, 3354 **Tel** *(036) 438-6480*

The tower is really a silo on a working farm, but it also indicates this homely Italian eatery. Wood-burning oven pizzas, pasta dishes, *tramezzini*, salads and seasonal specialities all find their way on to the menu here. The desserts are also worth trying. Local art and curios decorate the dining room of this child-friendly, informal eatery.

MOOI RIVER Hartford House
♿ 🔣 ♿ 🅿️ ⓇⓇⓇⓇⓇ

Hlatikulu Road, Mooi River, 3300 **Tel** *(033) 263-7713*

Fine dining is on offer at this international stud farm, which was the former home of the last prime minister of Natal. Young master chef Jacqueline Cameron has devised a sumptuous menu that has earned the restaurant many accolades, such as inclusion in the American Express Fine Dining programme. There is an extensive wine list.

PIETERMARITZBURG Rockafella's Theatre of Food
🍴 ♿ Ⓥ ⓇⓇ

Golden Horse Casino, New England Drive, Pietermaritzburg, 3201 **Tel** *(033) 342-9522*

Come to this 500-seat buffet restaurant overlooking the Scottsville Race Course for a fun night out and a jazzy 1930s–40s atmosphere. The extensive buffet includes spit roasts, curries, pizzas and pasta dishes, as well as create-your-own stir-fries. Reservations are recommended. Closed Mon; Tue–Sat lunch; Sun dinner.

PIETERMARITZBURG Saki Pacific Grill 🖹 🔔 Ⓥ   ⓇⓇⓇ
137 Victoria Road, Pietermaritzburg, 3201 **Tel** *(033) 342-6999*

Featuring a fancy, contemporary interior, this Asian restaurant offers informal communal long tables and a rotating sushi bar. As well as Japanese dishes, there are Thai and Indonesian specialities on the menu. In addition, this family-friendly restaurant has a varied children's list. Open daily.

PORT ST JOHNS Lily Lodge Seafood Restaurant 🖹 🖹 Ⓥ   ⓇⓇ
Box 7, Second Beach, Port St Johns, 5120 **Tel** *(047) 564-1229*

In the dune forests at Second Beach, overlooking the Indian Ocean and its dolphins, Lily Lodge serves a wide-ranging menu of fruits of the sea: crayfish, oysters, prawns, mussels, rock cod and cob are all complemented by a small but perfectly formed selection of Cape wines. A family-run venture staffed by local Pondoland people.

TWEEDIE Snooty Fox 🖹 🖹 🖹 ℗   ⓇⓇ
Fernhill Hotel, Tweedie, 3255 **Tel** *(033) 330-5071*

Hearty breakfasts, filling lunches and romantic, candlelit dinners are all available at the restaurant of this five-star country hotel built in Tudor style. The food is reasonably priced, especially the renowned carvery meal, and you can enjoy it by the fireplace, your dining experience accompanied by the sound of the crackling logs. Excellent service.

UNDERBERG Pile Inn Tea Garden 🖹 🖹 ℗   Ⓡ
27 Old Main Road, Underberg, 3257 **Tel** *(033) 701-2496*

Popular tea garden serving good milk shakes and the best fish 'n' chips and burgers in the area. Located at the foot of Hlogoma Mountain, the Pile Inn is a good stop on the way to or from the Sani Pass. There is a cosy fireplace with logs burning if it's snowing, and a shady patio for alfresco dining in the summer.

WINTERTON The Waffle Hut 🖹 🖹 Ⓥ   ⓇⓇ
At KwaZulu Weavers, R600, Champagne Valley, Winterton, 3340 **Tel** *(036) 488-1500*

KwaZulu Weavers produces quality hand-woven rugs at its shop in the Drakensberg's Champagne Valley. When you are tired of browsing, head over to the attached Waffle Hut, which offers a range of sweet and savoury waffles, but also breakfasts and light lunches. Children will love the milkshakes. Open daily until 4:30pm.

DURBAN AND ZULULAND

BALLITO Al Pescatore   ⓇⓇⓇⓇ
14 Edward Place, Ballito, 4420 **Tel** *(032) 946-3574*

Long established and popular with the local community, this Italian restaurant is renowned for both its great views of the Indian Ocean and its hearty dishes. Try the seafood platter, or the prawn tails wrapped in bacon, and accompany your choice with a good wine from the varied list. Live entertainment on Wednesdays and Thursdays.

DURBAN The Hops Restaurant & Bar 🖹 🖹 Ⓥ ℗   ⓇⓇ
131 Waterkant Road, Durban, 4001 **Tel** *(031) 573-1657*

Part of the Riverside Hotel & Spa complex, and featuring splendid views of the Indian Ocean, The Hops offers an affordable pub-style menu as well as tapas and generous surf-and-turf combos. There is abundant birdlife on the Umgeni River Estuary, just below the hotel.

DURBAN Mo' Noodles 🖹 🖹   ⓇⓇ
Florida Centre, 275 Florida Road, Berea, 4001 **Tel** *(031) 312-4193*

Based within a suburban shopping centre, this restaurant has a great atmosphere. The food is a fusion of Thai, Japanese and Australian styles, with the spotlight firmly on noodles. Specialities include chicken in sesame and chilli peanuts on coconut noodles. There are also healthy chicken, vegetarian and salad options.

DURBAN Vintage India 🖹 Ⓥ   ⓇⓇ
20 Lilian Ngoyi Road, Morningside, 4001 **Tel** *(031) 309-1328*

An up-market dining area decorated with warm colours, wooden furniture and traditional Indian musical instruments on the wall. The food runs the gamut of the Indian sub-continent, from Goan specialities such as the delicately spiced prawns *xacuti* to Hyderabadi dishes. There is also a vast selection of vegetarian dishes.

DURBAN Oyster Bar 🖹 Ⓥ ℗   ⓇⓇⓇ
Wilsons Wharf, Margaret Mncadi Avenue, Durban, 4001 **Tel** *(031) 307-7883*

One of a group of trendy restaurants right on the water. Locally fished (or cultivated) oysters are served with lemon and champagne, or you can try oysters mornay (topped with cheese), oysters wrapped in bacon, or oysters with a Thai sauce of ginger, coriander and soya, grilled. Local and international wines appear on the list.

DURBAN 9th Avenue Bistro & Bar 🖹 🖹 🖹 ℗   ⓇⓇⓇⓇ
2 Avonmore Centre, 9th Avenue, Morningside, 4001 **Tel** *(031) 312-9134*

This unpretentious venue offers a warm welcome, along with innovative cosmopolitan cuisine. The emphasis here is on top-quality seasonal produce. Dishes are exquisitely presented and the matching of flavours is superb. A good choice is the six-course tasting menu. The wine list features rare vintages from some of South Africa's best small vineyards.

Key to Price Guide *see p412* **Key to Symbols** *see back cover flap*

DURBAN Cargo Hold

uShaka Marine World, 1 Bell Street, Point, Durban, 4001 **Tel** *(031) 338-8165*

Nestling in the stern of the Phantom Ship at uShaka Marine World *(see p282)* is this atmospheric upmarket restaurant, with direct views of the ocean and a shark tank. Seafood is the speciality here, although steak, lamb and freshly prepared salads are also highlights. The menu is a creative mix of flavours from all corners of the globe.

DURBAN Jewel of India

Southern Sun Elangeni, 63 Snell Parade, Durban, 4001 **Tel** *(031) 362-1300*

A favourite of Zulu royalty, Jewel of India is a spacious, plush and elegant restaurant with good food and service. The menu offers authentic Cape Malay, South Indian and Gujarat curries. Be warned, though, Durban curries tend to be very hot. End by sampling a dessert from the extensive range. The wines are expertly chosen to complement the food.

DURBAN Le Troquet

Village Market, 123 Hofmeyr Road, Westville, 3630 **Tel** *(031) 266-5388*

Authentically French, this traditional bistro has been in the hands of the same family for more than 20 years. Daily specials of *cuisine regionale* include seafood or mushroom pancakes, rabbit and flamed filet mignon. There are also some rare local wines. The interior features dark walls and furniture, rosy linen and a colonnade across the dining area.

DURBAN Moyo

uShaka Marine World, 1 Bell Street, Point, Durban, 4001 **Tel** *(031) 332-0606*

Part of South Africa's successful chain of African-themed restaurants, and in a great location on the beach (the bar is at the end of a long pier), Moyo offers a varied menu that showcases cuisines from all over the continent. Entertainment includes face painting, live music and a hand-washing ceremony.

DURBAN Gateway to India

Palm Boulevard, Umhlanga Ridge, New Town, 4320 **Tel** *(031) 566-5711*

This sumptuously decorated Indian restaurant is located in an up-market shopping mall. Everything in it comes from India: from the artworks to the chefs. The huge North Indian menu includes tandoori dishes, curries, *roghan josh* and a great and varied vegetarian selection. There is an extensive wine list, including many options by the glass.

DURBAN Roma Revolving Restaurant

32nd Floor, John Ross House, Esplanade, Margaret Mncadi Avenue, Durban, 4001 **Tel** *(031) 368-2275*

Situated 105 m (344 ft) above sea level, Roma gently revolves at the top of John Ross House for 360-degree views of the city. The cuisine is based on Italian and continental fare, with a good mix of seafood and game dishes. Signature dishes include crayfish Portofino, in a creamy white-wine sauce, and the fillet Old Man, flambéed in brandy.

RAMSGATE The Waffle House

Lot 839, Marine Drive, Ramsgate, 4285 **Tel** *(039) 314-9424*

Attentive service, good prices and a play area for children make The Waffle House a great place to relax for families on an active holiday. Enjoy Belgian waffles on the deck overlooking the lagoon. Toppings range from hot apple and ice cream to vegetable curry or smoked salmon with avocado and cream cheese.

RAMSGATE Flavours

2450 Marine Drive, Ramsgate, 4285 **Tel** *(039) 314-4370*

This low-key, award-winning restaurant, a short walk from the beach, serves a varied range of classic dishes from around the world. Try the maple syrup-glazed duck breast or the herbed kinglip with prawns. Seating on the covered terrace overlooks a lush garden. Open only for lunch on Sundays out of season.

UMHLANGA ROCKS Razzmatazz

Cabana Beach Resort, 10 Lagoon Drive, Umhlanga Rocks, 4320 **Tel** *(031) 561-2371*

Choose between formal dining in a terracotta-coloured room with white tablecloths, or a more casual experience alfresco on a terrace overlooking the ocean. Signature dishes include crocodile or ostrich kebabs, and chicken in a pastry basket. Also available are seafood, game and pasta dishes. End your meal with their famous *crème brûlée*.

UMHLANGA ROCKS Grill Room at the Oyster Box

Lighthouse Road, Umhlanga Rocks, 4320 **Tel** *(031) 514-5000*

Located right on the beach, the Grill Room is renowned for its old-fashioned, discreet silver service. The restaurant serves oysters in a variety of ways, but the menu also includes great steaks, chops and curries. Lighter, pub-style meals are on offer on the terrace overlooking the ocean. There is a good list of South African wines.

UMHLANGA ROCKS Lord Prawn

2 Lagoon Drive, Umhlanga Rocks, 4319 **Tel** *(031) 561-1133*

The name pretty much sums it up. Diners here can combine grilled prawns with linefish, oysters, baby chicken or crayfish to create a generous platter. For those who do not wish to go down the prawn route, there are pasta dishes, Durban curries and steaks. The decor is modelled on rustic thatched beach huts, and the atmosphere is informal.

UMHLANGA ROCKS Ile Maurice

9 McCausland Crescent, Umhlanga Rocks, 4320 **Tel** *(031) 561-7609*

Owner Robert Mauvis has installed his brother and mother in the kitchen of his elegant but informal restaurant. On the menu is expertly prepared classic French fare with a twist – Mauritian, Cajun or Creole. There is also an impressive wine list. Expensive, but worth every rand for the excellent food, beautiful view of the ocean and unobtrusive service.

UMHLANGA ROCKS Sugar Club

Lighthouse Road, Umhlanga Rocks, 4320 Tel (031) 561-2211

The luxurious restaurant of the five-star Beverly Hills Hotel is one of the best in the country. In addition to its extensive wine list, the Sugar Club boasts an award-winning chef preparing fusion/contemporary cuisine. Signature dishes include tempura of West Coast oysters and Asian confit of duck, with truffle and stir-fried vegetables.

GAUTENG AND SUN CITY

BRYANSTON Fruits 'n' Roots

Hobart Cnr Shopping Centre, 2191 Tel (011) 463-2928

Those who are health-conscious, vegetarian or vegan will be spoilt for choice with the mouthwatering selection of freshly prepared dishes at Fruits 'n' Roots. Specialities range from a refreshing chilled ginger and butternut soup to sweet chilli "chicken" and green-bean salad, all served in a calm, relaxed outdoor environment.

EASTERN SUBURBS Chinatown

Derrick Avenue, Cyrildene, 2198 Tel (011) 622-0480

A busy, intoxicating strip lined with supermarkets and busy little eateries with plastic chairs and takeaway counters, Johannesburg's Chinatown offers authentic cuisine from a variety of regions, including Mongolia, Korea and Taiwan. One of the most legendary spots is Fisherman Plate, at 18 Derrick Avenue. Arrive early as the kitchens close by 9pm.

EASTERN SUBURBS Primi Piatti

Eastgate Shopping Centre, 43 Bradford Rd, Bedfordview, 2008 Tel (011) 622-1235

This trendy restaurant with giant glass windows and an open industrial feel buzzes with urban energy. Service from staff dressed in bright-orange overalls is excellent, and the tasty Italian food is served in massive portions. Try the signature *minestrone alla genovese*, a hearty vegetable soup with lamb stock and pesto.

EASTERN SUBURBS The Radium Beerhall

282 Louis Botha Avenue, Orange Grove, 2192 Tel (011) 728-3866

The oldest surviving bar and grill in Johannesburg (it was established in 1929), The Radium Beerhall has a great atmosphere and is well known for its resident jazz band and its fascinating collection of old Jo'burg memorabilia. The menu includes such staples as steaks and pizzas, as well as Mozambique prawns and chicken.

FOURWAYS Rodizio

The Leaping Frog Centre, William Nicol Drive, 2055 Tel (011) 493-1910

If you're looking for a festive dancing venue, this bustling Brazilian restaurant is the place. Try the signature Meat Rodizio dish. The meat (chicken, beef, lamb and pork) is marinated in a special sauce, then served off large skewers at your table. You control the flow of this eat-as-much-as-you-like dish with a green or red signal on your table.

GREENSIDE Karma

Cnr Gleneagles Road & Greenfields, 2193 Tel (011) 646-8555

An outstanding and wide selection of Indian fare with a contemporary twist is on offer here. The spices are mellow and well balanced, resulting in dishes that are very easy on the palate, even for non-curry eaters. Karma is also renowned for its extensive gin-cocktail menu. With its warm, earth colours, Karma has a unique energy and vibe.

GREENSIDE Topo Gigio

26 Gleneagles Road, 2193 Tel (011) 646-9573

Named after an Italian cartoon mouse, Topo Gigio is an unpretentious spot on the Greenside strip. Its menu focuses on perennial favourites such as pizzas and pasta dishes, but there are also traditional Mediterranean meat, chicken and fish specialities. The ambience is lively, with a warm, earthy decor and tables spilling out on to the pavement.

HYDE PARK Willoughby & Co

Shop 2, Hyde Park Shopping Centre, 2196 Tel (011) 325-5107

This fish and seafood restaurant is well known for its fresh and delicious fare. The deli selection is large, and the sushi some of the best in town. Try the leek and saffron mussel soup or the delicious seafood linguine. The restaurant doesn't accept advance reservations, so either arrive early or expect a waiting line, which moves fairly quickly.

ILLOVO Parea

Shop 3d, Corlett Drive, 2196 Tel (011) 788-8777

This restaurant offers an authentic Greek dining experience. Things heat up particularly on Friday and Saturday evenings, when the entertainment includes belly-dancing, Greek dancers and much breaking of plates. Their specialities are the lamb shank and flame-grilled line fish, but there is also a good vegetarian platter.

ILLOVO Yamato Japanese Restaurant

198 Oxford Road, Illovo, Sandton, 2196 Tel (011) 268-0511

Only the very best produce finds its way into the authentic dishes served at this traditional Japanese restaurant. A wide variety of superb fish is on offer, as well as homemade tofu, sushi and deep-fried tempura. Fresh ingredients are sourced locally whenever possible, with special dried ingredients and seasonings being imported from Japan.

Key to Price Guide *see p412* **Key to Symbols** *see back cover flap*

LINKSFIELD Afrodisiac ® ® ®

Cnr Civin & Linksfield Drive, 2192 **Tel** *(011) 443-9990*

This African grill house is one of Gauteng's premier tourist destinations. Live entertainment keeps the venue buzzing seven days a week, so you can look forward to the sounds of drums and other traditional instruments, as well as hand-washing and face-painting. Fifteen minutes from OR Tambo International Airport.

MELROSE Moyo ® ®

Shop 5, Melrose Arch Square, 2196 **Tel** *(011) 684-1477*

Set over five levels, Moyo is a spectacular building, with rustic-copper and steel staircases, a water feature, mosaics and sophisticated pieces of African art. The food embraces a variety of African tastes, from Moroccan *tajines* to the curries of the East. All main courses are served with rice, couscous, chips or mashed potatoes.

MIDRAND 33 High Street ® ® ®

33 High Street, Modderfontein, 2065 **Tel** *(011) 606-3574*

High ceilings and Oregon-pine floors set the cosy mood in this family-owned restaurant, with lush gardens that are ideal for weekend lunches alfresco. The menu focuses mainly on Portuguese and other Mediterranean dishes, such as grilled halloumi cheese to start and barbecued meats and fish to follow. Children get a warm welcome.

MULDERSDRIFT The Cradle Restaurant ® ® ® ®

Kromdraai Road, Lanseria, 1748 **Tel** *(011) 659-1622*

Nature takes centre stage at this minimalist stone, steel and glass restaurant set in the Cradle of Humankind, a UNESCO World Heritage site. The fresh Italian-influenced country-style food is served with a twist. Try the venison carpaccio with Parmesan shavings or the veal with sage and Parma ham. There is also a limited children's menu.

NEWTOWN Oriental Plaza ®

Bree, Malherbe, Lilian, Main and Avenue Streets, Fordsburg, 2001 **Tel** *(011) 838-6752/53*

This crowded bazaar offers more than a dozen Indian restaurants and takeaway stands, and it is the best place to visit for the most authentic samosas in Johannesburg. The smells are strong and the experience definitely worth it. Though there is security, be aware of your belongings.

NEWTOWN Gramadoelas ® ® ®

Market Theatre, Bree Street, 2001 **Tel** *(011) 838-6960*

With its timeless charm, fantastic menu and warm interior, Gramadoelas continues to draw locals as well as visiting celebrities. On the menu you will find Nelson Mandela's favourite dish (braised beef, beans and maize), *sosatie*, tomato *bredie* and other traditional fare. This restaurant has a rich history, which the owners are happy to share.

NORWOOD Next Door Pizza ® ®

80 Grant Avenue, 2192 **Tel** *(011) 728-2577*

This informal and friendly place is considered by many to be Johannesburg's top kosher restaurant. It is the ideal venue for family meals, featuring an extensive menu that goes well beyond pizzas to include such fare as sushi, pasta dishes and grilled meats and seafood.

ORMONDE Back o' the Moon ® ® ® ®

Shop 17, Gold Reef City Casino, cnr Northern Parkway & Data Crescent, 2091 **Tel** *(011) 248-5222*

Back o' the Moon was created in the image of the eponymous Sophiatown shebeen, where in the 1950s people would gather to enjoy great jazz music and indulge in fabulous food. Though nothing will compare to the original experience, this restaurant does offer glamorous entertainment, great steak, seafood, stews and curries.

PRETORIA/TSHWANE Café Riche ® ®

2 Church Square, 0002 **Tel** *(012) 328-3173*

This charming Art Nouveau-style building – now a national monument – houses the oldest café in Pretoria/Thswane. Come here for a varied selection of fresh salads and baguettes with a wide range of fillings. Café Riche's pub lunch is great value for money, as is the weekend brunch. Local and imported beers are available at the bar.

PRETORIA/TSHWANE Prue Leith Restaurant ® ® ®

262 Rhino Street, Hennops Park, Centurion, 0157 **Tel** *(012) 654-5203*

Located in the extensive grounds of the Prue Leith College of Food & Wine, this restaurant is effectively a learning ground for aspiring chefs and catering staff. Daily lessons dictate what ends up on the menu, which ranges from classic dishes to contemporary fare, all served with skill and enthusiasm by Leith's students. Closed Sun–Tue.

ROSEBANK Cranks ® ® ®

Shop 169, The Mall of Rosebank, 2193 **Tel** *(011) 880-3442*

A lively and atmospheric restaurant, Cranks is not ideal for anyone looking for a quiet, intimate dining experience. This colourful and festive Thai/Vietnamese restaurant has been going successfully for more than 30 years. All dishes can be adapted for vegetarians. Expect live blues music at the weekend.

ROSEBANK The Grillhouse ® ® ®

Shop 70, The Firs Hyatt Centre, 2193 **Tel** *(011) 880-3945*

This New York-style grillhouse offers choice steaks – basted or pepper-coated – and in different sizes. Though it is primarily a steakhouse, the restaurant also serves seafood, line fish and poultry. The salon area, separated from the restaurant by a corridor, offers a smoking area, a bar for pre-dinner drinks and live music.

SANDTON Browns of Rivonia   🔥 📶 🍽 🍷 V 🅿   ⓇⓇⓇ
*21 Wessels Road, 2128 **Tel** (011) 803-7533*

Once a farmhouse, this restaurant offers a sunny garden for alfresco eating in the summer months and a fireplace in the dining room to warm up the ambience in the colder months. Their exquisite wine and cheese selection, seafood and venison options have won the restaurant several awards.

SANDTON Bukhara   🔥 🍽 🍷 V   ⓇⓇⓇⓇⓇ
*Nelson Mandela Square, Sandton City, cnr Rivonia Rd & 5th St, 2031 **Tel** (011) 883-5555*

The sister establishment to the acclaimed Bukhara in Cape Town *(see p413)*, this top-notch gourmet Indian restaurant is located at the entrance of the luxurious Michelangelo Hotel. On the menu are beautifully presented and aromatic North Indian dishes, and diners can watch their meals being prepared in the glass-fronted kitchen.

SANDTON The Butcher Shop & Grill   🔥 📶 🍽 🍷 V   ⓇⓇⓇⓇ
*Nelson Mandela Square, Sandton City, cnr Rivonia Rd & 5th St, 2031 **Tel** (011) 784-8676*

In an atmospheric setting on Nelson Mandela Square – and overlooked by the giant statue of the formidable former president of South Africa – this is one of the country's top steakhouses and something of an institution. The rump, fillet, ribeye and T-bone steaks are individually cut to diners' preference and come with a range of delicious sauces.

SANDTON Le Canard   🍽 🍷 V 🅿   ⓇⓇⓇⓇⓇ
*163 Rivonia Road, Morningside, Sandton, 2196 **Tel** (011) 884-4597*

Beautifully prepared French-style gourmet food is served in this lovingly restored Georgian homestead, surrounded by majestic oak trees. Classical music, fine wines and flowers, along with produce fresh from the kitchen garden, all contribute to the quality of the experience. A favourite haunt of top politicians and other celebrities.

SANDTON Linger Longer   🔥 📶 🍽 🍷 V 🅿   ⓇⓇⓇⓇ
*58 Wierda Road, 2196 **Tel** (011) 884-0465*

This award-winning restaurant, one of the country's top ten, is set in a gracious colonial home with a large garden. The cuisine is a blend of eastern and western flavours, but the menu also includes classic dishes such as roasted beef fillet with foie gras and crusted lamb rack with pesto mash. A superb selection of wines rounds things off nicely.

SOWETO Wandies Restaurant   🔥 📶 V 🅿   ⓇⓇ
*618 Makhalemele Street, Dube, 1800 **Tel** (011) 982-2796*

A warm, convivial tavern in the middle of Soweto, Wandies is extremely popular among both tour operators and locals. The buffet meals include several vegetarian dishes, including *morogu* (wild spinach cooked with herbs) and *chakalaka* (a local salad made of tomatoes, baked beans, onion and chillies).

STERKFONTEIN Greensleeves   🍽 🍷 V 🅿   ⓇⓇⓇⓇ
*Hekpoort Road (R563), 1739 **Tel** (083) 229-5677/(082) 602-2958*

Take part in a unique medieval experience, indulging in a five-course feast with a goblet of mead. Try *sallamagundy* (salad with fruit, vegetables and fish bites) or pottage (soup) with home-baked bread. There is live entertainment with troubadours and minstrels, and medieval costumes are available for hire for those who want to join in the fun.

SUN CITY Crystal Court   🔥 📶 🍽 🍷 V 🅿   ⓇⓇⓇⓇ
*Palace of the Lost City at Sun City, Sun City, 0316 **Tel** (014) 557-4301*

Surrounded by three terraces and a picturesque lake, this 320-seat restaurant serves international cuisine in a dining room with floor-to-ceiling windows, a beautiful large chandelier and a water fountain in the middle. The high tea served in the afternoon is a delightful treat.

SUN CITY Santorini   🔥 📶 🍽 🍷 V   ⓇⓇⓇⓇ
*Cascades Hotel, Sun City, 0316 **Tel** (014) 557-5850*

Named after the Greek island in the Aegean Sea, this sunny restaurant on the Cascades Hotel's pool deck offers a taste of the Mediterranean with dishes such as *kleftiko* (slow-baked lamb), *dolmades* (stuffed vine leaves) and grilled sardines. Santorini's award-winning wine list is extensive. Reservations are recommended.

BLYDE RIVER CANYON AND KRUGER

GRASKOP Harries Pancakes   🔥 📶 V 🅿   Ⓡ
*Cnr Louis Trichard & Church Streets, Graskop, 1270 **Tel** (013) 767-1273*

Famous for its traditional South African cuisine, Harries real speciality is meal-sized pancakes stuffed with a variety of sweet and savoury fillings – from traditional *bobotie* to chicken livers, and from banana with caramel to chocolate mousse. The restaurant, located next to an African arts and crafts shop, displays local art both inside and out.

MPUMALANGA Kuka   🔥 📶 V 🅿   ⓇⓇⓇ
*Shop 1, Perry's Bridge Trading Post, R40 Hazyview, 1242 **Tel** (013) 737-6957*

Breakfast, lunch and dinner are served in this chic modern restaurant decorated in vibrant colours close to the gateway to the Kruger National Park *(see p338)*. The menu is a sophisticated blend of African and cosmopolitan dishes and includes local venison, crocodile and river trout. Superb cocktails are available at the bar.

NELSPRUIT O'Hagan's Irish Pub & Grill

Sonpark Mall, Barberton Road, Nelspruit, 1200 **Tel** *(013) 741-3580*

Part of a chain of Irish pub-restaurants, O'Hagan's serves up a menu of traditional hearty Irish and South African fare. Great Irish beers, such as Guinness and Kilkenny, are available on tap, along with a selection of fine Irish whiskeys. The relaxed atmosphere and welcoming staff make it an ideal venue for young families and groups.

SWAZILAND Spur Sheba's Rock Steak House

Shop 1, The Gables Shopping Centre, Ezulwini Valley. **Tel** *(268) 416-2888*

This relaxed family restaurant is part of a chain with a slightly overdone Native American theme. The menu consists mainly of grills and burgers, with an extensive buffet offering plenty of different salads. Spur Phoenix caters brilliantly for children, with games and a great kiddies' menu.

WHITE RIVER Magnolia Restaurant & Café

Casterbridge Lifestyle Centre, cnr Hazyview Rd (R40) & Numbi Rd (R538), 2809 **Tel** *(013) 751-1947*

Set in lovely manicured gardens with an attractive balcony, this upmarket bistro has contemporary designer interiors, including murals and hand-made wrought-iron furnishings. Everything on the menu is prepared with ingredients sourced within or near the region – the seafood, for example, comes from nearby Mozambique.

WHITE RIVER Oliver's Restaurant & Lodge

White River Country Estate, Pine Lake Drive, 2809 **Tel** *(013) 750-0479*

The first green of the White River golf course provides the perfect background to a leisurely lunch at Oliver's. The restaurant specializes in Mediterranean cuisine with an Austrian touch. Try the venison platter of kudu, eland and gemsbok, or the prawn and white-wine risotto. The menu has tasty options for kids, too. Closed Mon & Tue lunch.

SOUTH OF THE ORANGE

GRAAFF-REINET The Coldstream Restaurant

3 Church Street, Graaff-Reinet, 6280 **Tel** *(049) 891-1181*

Coldstream is situated in the same building as the second-oldest men's club in the country (founded in 1875) and offers a truly historic experience. Guests here can enjoy breakfast, lunch, dinner or simply a cup of tea and a slice of home-baked cake. The quality of the food on offer is consistently superlative.

GRAAFF-REINET Andries Stockenström Guest House

100 Cradock Street, Graaff-Reinet, 6280 **Tel** *(049) 892-4575*

A gastronomic oasis in Graaff-Reinet. Come here for good, honest South African food prepared with regional ingredients. Dishes include salad of lightly smoked kudu with a sesame wafer, and loin of Karoo lamb served with potato rösti and fine beans. For dessert, try their baked almond cream with berries.

NORTH OF THE ORANGE

BLOEMFONTEIN The Raj

Windmill Casino, cnr Jan Piereweit & Avenue N1, Bloemfontein, 9332 **Tel** *(051) 421-0034*

This top-notch Indian restaurant is housed within the Windmill Casino & Entertainment Centre on the N1 highway, just outside of Bloemfontein. For starters, try the delicious lamb samosas with tamarind chutney; then move on to an expertly cooked spicy masala or vindaloo dish.

BLOEMFONTEIN De Oude Kraal Country Estate

Exit 153 on N1, south of Bloemfontein, 9301 **Tel** *(051) 564-0636*

Extravagant and simple, De Oude Kraal is located on a farmstead 35 km (22 miles) south of Bloemfontein. Both the dinner buffet and the six-course dinner menu are gastronomic adventures, accompanied by a wine list that has received the Diners Club Diamond Award. If dinner stretches too late for the drive back, you can stay the night.

KIMBERLEY Kimberley Club

35 Currey Street, Kimberley, N Cape, 9320 **Tel** *(053) 832-4224*

Fine food is served in the elegant dining room of an updated gentleman's club with warm wooden furniture, white tablecloths and high ceilings. The adventurous chef produces traditional and modern dishes, including T-bone steaks, Karoo lamb chops and *eisbein* (pork knuckle) with apple sauce.

UPINGTON Le Must Country Restaurant

11 Schroeder Street, Upington, 8801 **Tel** *(054) 332-6700*

French-influenced Kalahari cuisine made with locally sourced ingredients is available at this intimate restaurant on the river. Chef Neil Stemmet is an advocate of slow cooking and seasonal produce; try his blue-cheese *crème brûlée*, or the pork with green fig and mustard compote. A great place to stop in the middle of a sightseeing day in this area.

SHOPPING IN SOUTH AFRICA

South Africa's principal shopping attraction is, undoubtedly, its superb range of handcrafted goods, as well as jewellery made from locally mined gold, inlaid with precious or semi-precious stones. Intricate beadwork, woven rugs and carpets, decorative baskets, stone and wood carvings, wood-and-bone spoons and traditional, flowing African garments with geometric motifs are sold at curio shops and

Natural cluster of amethyst crystals

markets countrywide. Crafters from the rest of Africa, attracted by South Africa's thriving tourism industry, frequent markets in the bigger centres, selling, for example, ceremonial wooden masks and malachite bracelets. All manner of other handworks can be found in craft markets, too, from windchimes, wooden beach chairs and painted duvet covers to African chilli sauces and leather goods.

Eye-catching works in malachite

SHOPPING HOURS

City shopping malls have adopted extended hours, staying open until around nine o'clock at night for the convenience of their patrons, while most small-town shops observe the nine-to-five rule. Village shops may even close at noon as siestas are still very much a part of rural South Africa.

Outdoor fleamarkets usually begin trading around 10am and end at sunset.

HOW TO PAY

Credit cards such as Visa and MasterCard are readily accepted in malls and city shops. Small shops and

informal traders prefer cash. In remote areas and rural villages, it is advisable to carry cash in a concealed wallet or pouch. If you need cash after hours, most banks (and many petrol stations and shopping malls) have automatic teller machines (ATMs) that allow you to make withdrawals with your credit card or international ATM card.

BARGAINING

African traders are always prepared to bargain hard, mostly because they would rather make a sale than lose it. Indian salespeople also enjoy haggling over prices and seem to expect a little resistance from their customers.

VAT

Most goods (except basic foodstuffs) are subject to 14 per cent Value Added Tax (VAT), included in the price. Expensive antiques, art and jewellery are best bought from reputable dealers who issue

foreign clients with a VAT refund document, which can be used to claim the VAT amount paid, prior to departure from the international airports.

Vibrant colours at a market stall

A WORD OF WARNING

Hawkers of gold jewellery and watches, theatrically concealed under a jacket or inside a folded piece of cloth, commonly hang around open-air markets and parking lots of shopping malls. Although they approach potential buyers with a very convincing act of secrecy and a lowered voice, the goods are usually cheap brass imitations. They may also be real – and perhaps stolen. In either case, decline briskly and walk away.

REFUNDS

If the merchandise you have bought is defective in any way, you are entitled to a refund. If you decide that you don't like an item, you may have to settle for a credit note or an exchange. In general, the larger the store, the more

The Workshop *(see pp282–5)* in Durban during the festive season

ked you are; if you are
opy with the service,
to the customer services
artment or the manager.

HERE TO SHOP

Many interesting stores
have moved away from
the malls and main centres.
Specialist book, design and
wine stores jostle with delis
and art studios in the city side
streets. There are also always
surprises in the small-town
bric-a-brac shops. Gold and
diamond jewellery, however,
is best sought in the malls;
the variety is more extensive.

SHIPPING PACKAGES

The post office will send
parcels of up to 30 kg (66 lb)
to Great Britain, Australia and
New Zealand and up to 20 kg
(44 lb) to the United States.
They may not be larger than
2.5 sq metres (8 sq feet). A
fixed handling fee is payable,
with additional charges per
100 g. Insurance is an option,
with an upper limit of around
R2,000. Surface mail will take
6–8 weeks; airmail one week.
   Many upmarket stores will
arrange all packaging and
shipping. To organize your
own exports, contact one of
the courier companies, such
as **DHL**, or a shipper such as
Trans Global Cargo Pty Ltd.
They will arrange customs
and packaging, and will
deliver to your home or the
office of their local agent.
There is no maximum or
minimum size or weight,
and prices are competitive.

A bottle of wine to suit any taste

Swaziland is a treasure trove of woven baskets and mats

STRICTLY SOUTH AFRICAN

In Johannesburg and other
large cities, you can buy
almost anything. Johannesburg, in particular, attracts
consumers from all over the
subcontinent. It is the queen
of the mall culture, and the
best place to find indigenous
arts and crafts. But much of
the wood and stone carving
is from West and Central
Africa and Zimbabwe.
   The crafts in Durban (see
pp282–5) and KwaZulu-Natal
(see pp258–9), on the other
hand, are more likely to be
local. Zulu baskets are usually
of outstanding quality, as
are the woven beer strainers,
grass brooms, pots, shields
and drums. Sometimes
brightly coloured baskets are
made from telephone wire.
   These wares, as well as
many charming and often
brightly painted wooden
animal and bird figures, can
be found on the side of the
N2 highway from Durban to
the game parks: Hluhluwe-
Imfolozi and Mkhuze.
   Gazankulu and Venda also
have a reputation for crafts.
Clay pots with distinctive
angular designs in gleaming
silver and ochre are popular,
as are the woodcarvings,
tapestries, fabrics and batiks.
   Ndebele bead blankets,
belts, aprons and dolls are
also worth looking out for
(see p320). They can be
found at Botshabelo Museum
and Nature Reserve near Fort
Merensky, 13 km (8 miles)
north of Middelburg.

Knysna (see pp240–41) is yet
another craftwork "capital".
A major timber centre, this is
the place to buy stinkwood
and yellowwood chairs and
tables, door knobs and other
unusual decor accessories.
Colourful, woven mohair
blankets, shawls, cushion
covers and jackets are also
found in this region.
   The label "Scarab Paper"
represents a truly unique South
African craft: handmade paper,
notelets and cards in nation-
wide craft and curio stores
are produced from (now
fragrance-free) elephant dung!
   Swazi candles are also
sold countrywide: look out
for the distinctive "stained-
glass" effect of these slow-
burning bright candles in
animal, bird and more
traditional candle shapes.
   Throughout the country,
gift stores and jewellers offer
an unusual array of necklaces,
rings, earrings and bracelets
using local diamonds and
semi-precious stones, often
combined with South African
gold and platinum.

ENTERTAINMENT IN SOUTH AFRICA

Johannesburg is said to be the entertainment and nightlife hub of South Africa. In this entrepreneurial city people party as hard as they work, and there is always something happening. This does not mean, however, that other South African cities and towns are dull. Even rural places have their music, restaurant and

CAPAB ballet dancers

clubbing venues. The demar for cinemas and casinos is high and exciting new venues are opened regularly. The dramatic arts are innovative and of a very high standard, with theatre companies committed to the development of a local arts culture. The vibrant music scene spans classical, jazz and the African *genre*.

The Oude Libertas amphitheatre, Stellenbosch *(see p37)*

the local film industry is still in the fledgling stage, and there is relatively little demand for foreign-language films with subtitles.

The cities host regular film festivals: themes range from French, Italian and Dutch to natural health, the environment and gay and lesbian.

INFORMATION

For details of entertainment in the cities, check the local daily press and the weekly papers, such as the *Mail & Guardian*, available nation-wide. They review and list theatre productions, current film festivals, art exhibitions, music performances and other interesting events.

Reviews and listings also appear in a number of magazines that are sold in book stores and at newsagents. The Tonight website (www.tonight.co.za) includes restaurant reviews and details of workshops, gay and lesbian and kids' events in Cape Town, Johannesburg and Durban.

BOOKING TICKETS

Seats for most events can be reserved by calling **Computicket**, which has branches in all the major centres and larger towns countrywide.

To make telephone bookings for Ster-Kinekor cinemas, call the **Ster-Kinekor Ticket-Line**.

Most South African theatres and cinemas do not accept telephone bookings without credit card payment.

CINEMA

Mainstream Hollywood film productions are the main fare in South African cinemas –

THEATRE, OPERA AND DANCE

Comedy, satire, cabaret and musicals are particularly popular in South Africa, as are modernized and "localized" adaptations of Shakespeare.

Theatres are committed to the development of script-writing and directing talent, and talent-scouting festivals are becoming annual events.

Arts Alive, a Johannesburg festival held in September, is a major celebration of the performing arts. The FNB Dance Umbrella, held in Johannesburg in February

Dancers at the Grahamstown Festival *(see p39)*

"Cross Roads", Rupert Museum, Stellenbosch

and March, is an important platform for new choreographers. The National Arts Festival *(see p115)* held in Grahamstown in July is, of course, the best place to go for an overview of innovative, exciting South African theatre, dance, artistic and musical talent.

Opera, too, is well supported, especially in Cape Town, where the Cape Town Opera *(see p168)* performs at the Artscape Theatre Centre from May to September. Artscape is also the main venue for the Cape Town City Ballet *(see p168)*.

Zulu dancer at Heia Safari Ranch

MUSIC

The five symphony seasons throughout the year are well supported in the cities; concerts are held in venues such as the Durban City Hall *(see p283)*, Cape Town's Baxter Theatre *(see p165)* and the Johannesburg College of Music in Parktown.

Outdoor, twilight performances, for example at Durban's Botanic Gardens *(see p285)* and Kirstenbosch National Botanical Garden in Cape Town *(see p158)*, are popular. Look out for the musical fireworks shows in the cities every December.

Nowadays, international bands, pop and opera singers regularly include South Africa on their world tours.

Local bands offer a wide range of sounds: rock, jazz, gospel, reggae, rap and Afro-fusion. The members

of the popular Soweto String Quartet charm audiences with their unique compositions and African-flavoured interpretations of classical pieces.

Local rock bands such as Springbok Nude Girls and Parlotones enjoy a loyal following, and appear at clubs countrywide. Check the listings guides and local radio stations for details of gigs and venues. Music from the rest of Africa is filtering down to South Africa, and clubs are rocking to sounds from Ghana, Mali and Benin.

ART

Johannesburg, Durban, Cape Town, Port Elizabeth and Bloemfontein, as well as some of the larger towns such as Knysna, have excellent art galleries. These showcase local and international works, from the traditional to the somewhat more bizarre, from ceramics

Merry-go-round at the Carousel

and photography to multimedia works and installations. Exhibitions change regularly, and exhibition openings are popular social events, with a high-profile speaker as well as a buffet and drinks.

GAMING

Investors, developers and casino operators have poured billions of rands into this industry. South Africa is said to be the one of the biggest gaming markets in the world.

Spectacular gaming and entertainment centres with names like **Sun City**, **Carousel** and **Sibaya** are now dotted all over the country. Their architectural styles are detailed and lavish, blending fun and fantasy with the latest in technology.

Gaming tables include black-jack, roulette, poker and punto banco. Larger casinos usually have a *salon privé*, in addition to a hall of slot machines.

SPECIAL-INTEREST VACATIONS

South Africa, with its moderate climate, long hours of sunshine, endless coastline and varied landscape, is a country that can provide a wide range of outdoor pursuits almost all year round. South Africans, in general, enjoy the great outdoors: during summer, visitors to Cape Town may well believe that the entire city is in training for forthcoming running and cycling marathons, as locals take to the streets to get fit. Activities go beyond compet-

Bungee jumping

itive sports, however. Whether it is canoeing on the Orange River, taking plant-hunting trips in the coastal forests of KwaZulu-Natal, mountaineering in the Drakensberg, bungee jumping along the Garden Route, board-sailing in the Western Cape or visiting historic battlefields and museums, there is something to interest everyone. Moreover, South Africa's fascinating multicultural past and present can be experienced at regional festivals *(see pp36–7)* and on special tours.

HIKING AND RAMBLING

Hiking is an extremely popular pastime. Even the smallest farms in the most remote regions have laid-out trails, with distance-marked paths and maps provided upon booking and payment. Most overnight hikes are situated on private land or state reserves, with accommodation in rustic huts, with firewood, mattresses and cold-water washing facilities usually included. Favourite trails such as the four-night Otter Trail and four-night Tsitsikamma Trail *(see pp234–5)* need to be booked more than a year in advance. Most outdoor equipment stores are able to advise on day and longer hikes, and they also sell guide books, maps and trail provisions. **Trail Info** has a list of more than 170 accredited hiking trails around the country. The

Kloofing, or madcap jumping, into pools, a new dimension of hiking

list includes a description of the trails, facilities available and reservation details.

Most private reserves and some of the provincial reserves and national parks offer guided game- and bird-watching rambles, as well as overnight bushveld and wilderness trails. The real attraction of these hikes, is the unrivalled experience of walking through the African bush, surrounded by the sounds and smells of its diverse fauna and flora.

The Kruger National Park *(see pp338–41)* offers at least seven such trails: the Bushman Trail includes finding rock paintings in the hill shelters. Due to the popularity of these walks, bookings should be made months in advance. Contact **South Africa National Parks (SANParks)** for details.

KLOOFING AND ROCK CLIMBING

Kloofing is a popular offshoot of hiking: it involves boulder hopping and wading while following the course of a river. It requires you to have a good level of fitness and daring, with long jumps into mountain pools. The **Mountain Club of South Africa** provides information for anyone tempted to try this.

Rock climbing (whether traditional, sport or bouldering) has a large following in South Africa. Climbing equipment stores can provide enthusiasts with gear, information and route ideas. Some of the best traditional climbing is found in KwaZulu-Natal's Drakensberg *(see pp260–61)*, while Cape Town's Table Mountain *(see pp128–9)* offers

Hiking in KwaZulu-Natal

interesting challenges for experienced climbers. Coming back down from the climb can be a fast and thrilling abseil descent, or the Australian SAS-created counterpart, known as a rapp jump. This is even more exciting, as it involves descending at high speed while facing forward with the rope attached to your back and your feet pounding down the rock face.

FISHING

More than a million anglers enjoy the local waters, which are subject to strict regulations – enquire at the nearest police station or through the **South African Deep Sea Angling Association**. Over 250 species of fish can be caught through fly, line, game, surf or reef fishing. The merging of the cool Atlantic and the warm Indian oceans off the Southern Cape coast creates the conditions for a high concentration of game fish, including marlin and tuna. Mpumalanga and KwaZulu-Natal offer excellent trout fishing. Kalk Bay in Cape Town has one of the few line-fishing harbours in the world.

Almost all harbours and marinas offer the opportunity to join commercial or semi-commercial boats on short trips. In addition, many tour groups, including **Big Blue Fishing Charters** in Cape Town and **Lynski Deep Sea Fishing Charters** in Durban offer fishing charters and expeditions.

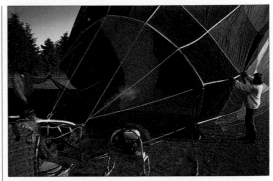

Hot-air ballooning, for a fabulous view of the game

AIR SPORTS

The **Aero Club of South Africa** is the controlling and co-ordinating body for all sport aviation: ballooning, hang-gliding, microlighting and parachuting. With a good head for heights, there is no finer way to see the land than from the basket of a hot-air balloon. Flights are available at many locations, but some of the most popular are the trips over the Winelands or game parks. Early morning or late evening, when the thermals guarantee plenty of lift, are the best times to book. It's important to note that flights are sometimes cancelled due to too much or too little wind. Given the relative silence of the hot-air balloon, it's a wonderful way of getting a close view of shy big game animals. Contact **Airtrackers** for game-viewing trips in Pilanesberg Game Reserve (see p323).

Helicopter rides are widely available and are an exciting way to take in the panorama of Cape Town (see pp114–77) and Table Mountain (see pp132–3). It is even possible to arrange a trial lesson.

Paragliding and parachuting courses (contact the **South African Hang Gliding and Paragliding Association**) and tandem flights are also popular. Bridge jumping and bungee jumping are for real adrenalin junkies and can be found on the Garden Route, including the spectacular 216-m (709-ft) Bloukrans Bungee Jump, which claims to be the highest commercial challenge of its kind in the world. This is operated by **Face Adrenalin**, which also offers a bridge arch walk of Bloukrans Bridge.

Mountain biking in Knysna

CYCLING

In South Africa even the cities offer spectacular cycling routes: at least 35,000 cyclists take to the streets for the annual marathon around the Cape Peninsula (see pp118–19). Cycling organizations such as the **Pedal Power Association** and the **South African Cycling Federation** organize weekend rides, which often include off-road routes on otherwise out-of-bounds farmlands. They can also offer advice about renting bikes. Adventure holiday agencies can book a variety of cycling tours – both off-road and on smooth tar – along the Garden Route, for example, and in the Karoo. Meals, accommodation and luggage transport are provided.

Sport fishing at Cape Vidal, in the Greater St Lucia Wetlands

A close encounter with a great white shark, while cage diving

GAME HUNTING AND CLAY TARGET SHOOTING

Game hunting is a multi-million rand industry today, and in the hunting reserves, such as in the Waterberg region of Northern Province, the area is stocked with game specifically for that purpose. However, by law all foreign hunters must be accompanied by a professional South African hunter. Contact the **Professional Hunters' Association of South Africa (PHASA)** for details of members who can organize your hunting trip and accompany you.

A more humane alternative to hunting is clay pigeon shooting. This has become a very popular sport and is easily arranged through the **Clay Target Shooting Association South Africa**.

White-water rafting on the Orange River (see pp350–51)

WATER SPORTS

South Africa has 2,500 km (1,553 miles) of coastline and many rivers. The country has some of the world's greatest surf, and one of the best spots is Jeffrey's Bay in the Garden Route, where perfect waves abound. Windsurfing and sailing are also popular, and many resorts rent out equipment. The beaches are also ideal for sand boarding, the land-based version of surfing, which takes advantage of the country's abundance of massive sand dunes.

Scuba diving instruction is widely available; instructors should be accredited to the **National Association of Underwater Instructors** (NAUI) or **Professional Association of Diving Instructors** (PADI). The best diving sites are along the St Lucia Estuary Park in KwaZulu-Natal, with coral reefs, tropical fish, turtles, sharks and game fish. In Cape Town, wreck-diving and exploring kelp forests are both popular activities.

River rafting has a growing number of fans. **Felix Unite River Adventures** and **River Rafters** are two Cape Town operators. Qualified guides can take rafters in two- or eight-person inflatable rafts. From white-water running to quiet paddling, there is a trip for everyone, and overnight accommodation and meals are always superb. Popular routes include the Blyde River Canyon and the Breede, Orange and Tugela rivers. One-day or overnight coastal trips from **Kaskazi Kayaks** are available too, usually around the Cape Peninsula, along the Garden Route and in KwaZulu-Natal.

For the ultimate thrill, cage diving takes participants as close to a great white shark as they would ever wish to be. A popular venue is Shark Alley, near the village of Gansbaai (see p224). Several guests at a time are lowered from a catamaran in a steel cage fitted with viewing ports. **White Shark Ecoventures** offer one- to 10-day tours that include accommodation and equipment hire. **Apex Shark Expeditions'** trips depart from Simon's Town, near Cape Town. They offer the smallest groups in the industry (6 to 12 people) and the longest trips.

Pony-trekking in Lesotho (see pp268–9)

HORSE RIDING AND PONY-TREKKING

Sport riding is controlled by the **South African National Equestrian Foundation**. Leisure riding is also very popular; sunset rides along a beach or wine-tasting trails are memorable options.

Malealea Lodge and Horse Treks in Lesotho (see pp268–9) offers a real African experience. Trips are organized with guides to accompany riders through unfenced landscapes to see dinosaur tracks or San Bushman rock art. Accommodation is in Basotho huts, with traditional food and dancing provided by the local people.

Nectar-feeding Malachite sunbird, with emerald plumage

BIRD-WATCHING, FLORA AND FAUNA TRAILS

Blessed with a prodigious variety of indigenous birds, along with vast flocks of migratory birds that pass through during the colder European winters, South Africa is a bird-watchers' paradise. **BirdLife South Africa** is an excellent resource that provides checklists of the more than 800 species recorded in the country. It also recommends the best birding spots.

There is also a wide range of fauna to be seen. Seal or whale watching *(see pp184–5)* are both very popular along the coast, whether you prefer to go on a boat trip or stay on dry land with binoculars. Safaris or wilderness trails both offer an amazing opportunity to view wild animals and flora in their natural habitat, and are an essential part of any trip to South Africa *(see pp62–7)*, but it is essential to book well in advance.

SPECTATOR SPORTS

For visitors who prefer watching to participating, South Africa has much to offer. The country is well known for its love of sports, and world-class rugby and cricket – supported mainly by the white middle classes – can be enjoyed at modern stadiums, such as the New-lands grounds in Cape Town, and the Wanderers cricket grounds in Johannesburg.

The country's favourite sport – supported largely by the black community – is soccer, but the game has only recently started to attract serious financial investment. The legacy of the 2010 World Cup, which was hosted by South Africa, includes 10 major stadiums, but it is doubtful that any South African soccer club could currently generate enough revenue to maintain one.

Stadiums are always open-air, and while some grandstands have canopies, it is advisable to take a hat, sun protection and a good supply of water.

Beautiful view from the green of Leopard Creek golf course

GOLF

The game of golf was introduced to South Africa by British – and notably Scottish – colonialists during the early 19th century and has a long and proud tradition here. The game has produced such great golfers as Gary Player, winner of a record 163 international competitions, and more recently, Ernie Els, who upholds Springbok pride in the world's major tournaments.

Since the 1980s and the start of the global golf boom, South Africa has seen an extensive programme of course upgrades and new builds. These include Jack Nicklaus' signature course at **Pearl Valley Golf Estates** and **Fancourt Golf Club Estate**, which is picturesquely set on the Garden Route and now widely acknowledged as one of the world's best and most scenic challenges.

The most famous course of all is the **Gary Player Country Club** at Sun City, whose immaculate greens host the Million Dollar Nedbank Golf Challenge. Other top courses to have featured on the European PGA Tour, the local Sunshine Tour and the South African Open include Durban's **Erinvale Golf and Country Club, Leopard Creek** and **Glendower Country Club**.

The country's terrain and balmy climate, especially in and around the Winelands *(see pp189–205)* and the Garden Route *(see pp232–41)*, are perfect for the best enjoyment of the game and the facilities are usually just as outstanding. This has led to an increase in the popularity of golf package holidays, and South Africa now claims to be the most successful golfing nation per capita in the world.

Watching cricket at Newlands grounds, with Table Mountain as a backdrop

Robben Island, an important historical and ecological heritage site

TOWNSHIPS AND CULTURAL TOURS

A visit to Soweto is almost always a highlight of a trip to South Africa. In fact, this city receives at least 1,000 foreign visitors a day, and for many it is a destination that is more desirable than Sun City or the game parks. Visitors are accompanied by experienced guides to jazz clubs, clinics, schools, *shebeens* (bars) and cemeteries. Overnight stays and visits to the cultural village of African mystic and writer Credo Mutwa can also be arranged.

Other fascinating tours in and around Johannesburg include a visit to the Lesedi Cultural Village to encounter Zulu, Xhosa and Sotho culture, and to a Ndebele village near Bronkhorstspruit, close to Pretoria/Tshwane. Contact tour operators such as **Vhupo Tours** for more details.

In Cape Town, tours visit the Malay Quarter *(see p129)*, and include traditional meals and hospitality. District Six, craft and education centres, mosques, as well as the rather drab suburbs known as the Cape Flats, are also included on the itinerary. Agencies such as **Legend Tours** will help visitors plan such trips.

For those with an interest in what life was like under the apartheid regime, a trip to the infamous Robben Island *(see pp142–3)* is a must, as are tours of places where protest action occurred. Some of these are led by former *Umkhonto-we-Sizwe* (Spear

of the Nation) activists.

Durban tours offers insights into the Indian community and the nearby townships. They are often the best way to explore the city. A trip to Shakaland *(see p293)* reveals traditional Zulu society, crafts and medicine, and is a popular outing for families.

BATTLEFIELD TOURS

As a frontier land, South Africa's soil has been fought over by succeeding waves of settlers. Battlefield tours *(see p274)* are a major growth area in the tourism industry, and both national and regional governments have invested in landmarking historic sites and plotting trails. Many of the local museums and lodges organize guided tours. The storytelling

skills of many of the guides, such as those of the **Fugitives' Drift Lodge** *(see p396)* and the **Isibindi Lodge**, are remarkable. These trips take in some of the poignant war memorials dedicated to various conflicts, including South Africa's active role in both world wars, that are scattered across the land.

In the 1820s, the ruthless King Shaka created the Zulu nation from nothing – building one of history's most fearsome fighting forces. Rorke's Drift *(see p275)* is the site of the battle in which 150 besieged British soldiers defended a supply station against 4,000 Zulus, earning 11 Victoria Crosses in 12 hours as a result. The battle was immortalized in the 1964 film *Zulu*, starring Michael Caine, which has helped to turn the area into a popular visitor attraction.

Other major stops on the Boer War tour include the siege of Ladysmith *(see p274)*, Mafeking, where Baden Powell later conceived and started the Boy Scout movement, and lofty Spioenkop *(see p275)*, strategically sited on a 1,466-m (4,764-ft) peak, which saw the fiercest of all fighting.

Also on the battlefield trail is Blood River *(see p274)* near Dundee, where Afrikaner forces defeated a huge Zulu army on the 16th December 1838.

Isandhlwana battle site, part of the 1879 Anglo Zulu War in KwaZulu Natal

DIRECTORY

HIKING AND RAMBLING

South Africa National Parks (SANParks)
Tel (012) 428-1111.
www.sanparks.org

Trail Info
www.trailinfo.co.za

KLOOFING AND ROCK CLIMBING

Mountain Club of South Africa
97 Hatfield St,
Cape Town, 8001.
Tel (021) 465-3412.
www.mcsa.org.za

FISHING

Big Blue Fishing Charters
Wharf St, Simon's Town,
Cape Town.
Tel (021) 786-5667.

Lynski Deep Sea Fishing Charters
*Tel (031) 539-3338
or (082) 445-6600.*
www.lynski.com

South African Deep Sea Angling Association
PO Box 4191,
Cape Town, 8000.
Tel (021) 976-4454.
www.sadsaa.com

AIR SPORTS

Aero Club of South Africa
Aeroclub House, Hangar
4, Rand Airport, Gauteng.
Tel (011) 082-1100.
www.aeroclub.org.za

Airtrackers
Tel (014) 552-5020.
www.airtrackers.co.za

Face Adrenalin
Bloukrans Bridge,
Garden Route.
Tel (042) 281-1458.
www.faceadrenalin.com

South African Hang Gliding and Paragliding Association
PO Box 191,
Celtis Ridge, 0130.
Tel (012) 668-3186.
www.sahpa.co.za

CYCLING

Pedal Power Association
PO Box 665,
Rondebosch, 7701.
Tel (021) 689-8420.
www.pedalpower.org.za

South African Cycling Federation
12 Andmar Building,
Ryneveld St,
Stellenbosch, 7600.
Tel (021) 557-1212.
www.cyclingsa.com

HUNTING

Clay Target Shooting Association South Africa
PO Box 812,
Great Brak River, 6525.
Tel (086) 111-4581.
www.ctsasa.co.za

Professional Hunters' Association of South Africa
PO Box 10264, Centurion,
Pretoria/Tshwane, 0046.
Tel (012) 667-2048.
www.phasa.co.za

WATER SPORTS

Apex Shark Expeditions
Quayside Building,
Simon's Town, 7975.
Tel (021) 786-5717.
www.apexpredators.com

Felix Unite River Adventures
14 Stibitz Street, Westlake,
Cape Town 7945.
Tel (021) 702-9400.
www.felixunite.com

Kaskazi Kayaks
179 Beach Rd, Three
Anchor Bay, 8005.
Tel (021) 439-1134.
www.kayak.co.za

National Association of Underwater Instructors (NAUI)
5 Geelhout Close,
Gordon's Bay, 7140.
Tel (021) 856-5184.
www.nauisa.org

Professional Association of Diving Instructors
Tel (+44) 0117-300 7234.
www.padi.com

River Rafters
1 Friesland St, Durbanville,
Cape Town, 7800.
Tel (021) 975-9727.
www.riverrafters.co.za

White Shark Ecoventures
PO Box 50325, V&A
Waterfront, Cape Town,
8002. *Tel (032) 532-0470.*
www.white-shark-diving.com

HORSE RIDING AND PONY-TREKKING

Malealea Lodge and Horse Treks
Malealea, Lesotho.
Tel (082) 552-4215.
www.malealea.com

South African National Equestrian Foundation
Kyalami Equestrian Park,
Dahlia Rd, Kyalami, 1684.
Tel (011) 468-3236.
www.horsesport.org.za

BIRD-WATCHING, FAUNA AND FLORA TRAILS

BirdLife South Africa
239 Barkston Dr,
Blairgowrie, 2194.
Tel (011) 789-1122.
www.birdlife.org.za

GOLF

Erinvale Golf and Country Club
Lourensford Road,
Somerset West,
Western Cape, 7129.
Tel (021) 847-1160.
www.erinvale.co.za

Fancourt Golf Club Estate
Montagu Street,
Blanco, George, 6529.
Tel (044) 804-0000.
www.fancourt.co.za

Gary Player Country Club
Sun City Resort, PO Box 2,
Sun City, 0316.
Tel (014) 557-1245/6.
www.suninternational.com

Glendower Country Club
20 Marias Rd,
Dowerglen, 2008.
Tel (011) 453-1013/4.
www.glendower.co.za

Leopard Creek
Kruger National Park,
Mpumalanga.
Tel (013) 791-2000.
www.leopardcreek.co.za

Pearl Valley Golf Estates
Paarl, 7690.
Tel (021) 867-8000.
www.pearlvalley.co.za

TOWNSHIP AND CULTURAL TOURS

Legend Tours
26 Hayward Rd, Crawford,
Cape Town, 8060.
Tel (021) 704-9140.
www.legendtours.co.za

Vhupo Tours
11749 Mampuru St,
Orlando West, Soweto.
Tel (011) 936-0411.
www.vhupo-tours.com

BATTLEFIELD TOURS

Fugitives' Drift Lodge
PO Rorke's Drift, 3016.
Tel (034) 642-1843.
www.fugitivesdrift.com

Isibindi Lodge
PO Box 1593,
Eshowe, 3815.
Tel (035) 474-1473/1490.
www.isibindiafrica.co.za

Scenic Rail Travel

An increasingly popular holiday choice is taking a land cruise, where travel between each destination is by train. Once perceived as the domain of elderly travellers, scenic train travel now attracts adults of all ages, although it is not aimed at families with young children. This is a year-round activity, but prices will be higher in the busy holiday periods. The advantages of such a tour are many: the "hotel" travels with its guests, it is possible to reach remote destinations while remaining in luxurious surroundings, and then, of course, there is the pleasure of rail travel. The lazy pace of a steam locomotive is perfect for enjoying South Africa's wonderful sights.

A Rovos Rail steam train winding through the Eastern Transvaal

CHOOSING AN ITINERARY

South Africa, with its year-long pleasant climate and beautiful scenery, is the ideal destination for luxury train travel. However, it is not a cheap holiday and it can be sensible to avoid certain times of the year. In general the cheapest fares are available in May and August, while the period from September to December can be markedly more expensive.

South Africa's land cruise itineraries are carefully chosen to reveal some truly stunning views, and reach many destinations that are difficult to access by road. It is a good idea to study the itineraries carefully. The Blue Train, for example, is best taken from south to north as this route passes through the loveliest stretches of scenery by day rather than at night. Other trips include safari expeditions and stops in neighbouring countries. Rovos Rail, in particular,

offers routes to Victoria Falls in Zimbabwe and a magnificent tour to Cairo in Egypt.

CHOOSING WHICH TRAIN

There are several different companies arranging a variety of tours, from short day-trips to more lengthy affairs.

Rovos Rail, which calls itself "the most luxurious train in the world", lives up to its

The Shongololo Express, a great way to enjoy the South African landscape

reputation, with traditional furnishings and exquisite decor. Two beautifully rebuilt trains carry a maximum of 72 passengers each. All suites are of a five-star hotel standard, with air-conditioning and shower or bath facilities. The most expensive suites, occupying half-a-coach each, have a full-size Victorian roll-top bath. The trains provides 24-hour room service and there are two dining cars, which allow the entire complement of passengers to enjoy dinner at a single sitting.

The **Shongololo Express** specializes in adventure and excitement, and is therefore a big hit with the younger crowd. As a result, the style of the trains is more casual, and the cabins are fairly basic but comfortable. There are two en-suite options, but the cheaper twin or single cabins entail a walk to use shower and toilet facilities. All trains carry a fleet of air-conditioned touring cars and include a safari expedition.

Crisp linens, marble-clad bathrooms and faultless service set the tone for the magnificent **Blue Train**, one of the world's most famous scheduled services. Beautiful wood veneers and fine detail add a 1950s ambience to the train. The suites offer a choice of shower or bath and a selection of film and radio channels. The lounge cars are the perfect place to observe the panoramic views as the train winds its way through the Winelands, the Karoo Desert and other impressive scenery.

ROUTES AND SIGHTS

The scheduled route for the Blue Train links Cape Town and Pretoria/Tshwane, and is a 2,600-km (994-mile) journey taking 27 hours through some of South Africa's most spectacular scenery. The Southern Meander tour includes two nights in a top Johannesburg hotel before transferring to the station in Pretoria/Tshwane. There are alternative routes from Pretoria/Tshwane to Durban, which include a two-night stay at the Zimbali Lodge resort, with a spectacular 18-hole course. Alternatively, it is possible to take the train to the Bakubung Game Lodge, in the Pilanesberg Game Reserve, for a two-night stay, with optional game drives.

Rovos Rail has a variety of itineraries. Its three-day Cape Town to Pretoria/Tshwane route, which can be taken in either direction, includes visits to Kimberley's famous Big Hole and diamond museum, as well as the historic town of Matjiesfontein. The three-day route linking Pretoria/Tshwane and Durban skirts Kruger Park and instead visits the Battlefields and Zululand. A game safari in the Nambiti Private Game Reserve, home of the black and white rhino, is also included as part of the fare. Possibly the most intriguing trip is the 14-day African Adventure, which links Cape Town with Dar Es Salaam in Tanzania, passing Zimbabwe, Zambia, Victoria Falls and Selous Game Reserve – the continent's largest – on the way.

The Shongololo Express has itineraries that criss-cross South Africa, dipping into neighbouring countries such as Namibia, Mozambique, Botswana, Zambia and Tanzania. There are two popular "limited edition" trips; one which focuses on wildlife and another which follows in the footsteps of Dr Livingstone.

ON-BOARD CUISINE AND SERVICE

The standard of catering and service on board will be that of a five-star hotel. These trains have a very high ratio of staff to guests, especially in

The Blue Train travels past an impressive Table Mountain view

the restaurant car. The Blue Train, for example, serves a menu that is of a truly gourmet standard, and in 2005 the company won platinum status in the prestigious Diners Club International "Wine List of the Year" awards.

A more unusual way to travel on South Africa's luxury steam trains

WHAT TO TAKE

It pays to pack light because there are limits to the size and number of cases that can be stowed away (check with the train company). However, guests must bring formal wear for evenings as they tend to be rather grand occasions,

with ladies dressing in traditional evening wear and gentlemen either in a smart lounge suit or a tuxedo. The daytime dress code is more relaxed, smart casual clothes.

WHAT IS INCLUDED

Rovos Rail includes food, drink and off-train excursions by luxury coach within the fare. In addition, each suite has an inclusive mini-bar fully stocked to the passengers' choice. This is fairly typical for all the major train companies, although some may charge extra for champagne.

HEALTH AND SAFETY

All trains have a member of staff trained in first aid and will have doctors on call along the route. It is also important to find out if the train is passing through malaria risk areas, as suitable preventative medication will need to be taken. There is little need to worry about personal security, but, as always, keep valuables locked in an on-board safe.

DIRECTORY

Blue Train
Private Bag X637, Pretoria/
Tshwane, 0001. *Tel (012) 334-8459.* **www**.bluetrain.co.za

Rovos Rail
PO Box 2837, Pretoria/Tshwane, 0001. *Tel (012) 315-8242.*
www.rovos.co.za

Shongololo Express
PO Box 1558, Parklands, Gauteng, 2121. *Tel (0861) 777-014.* **www**.shongololo.com

Dining Car 195, Shangani, a Rovos Rail train with original teak pillars

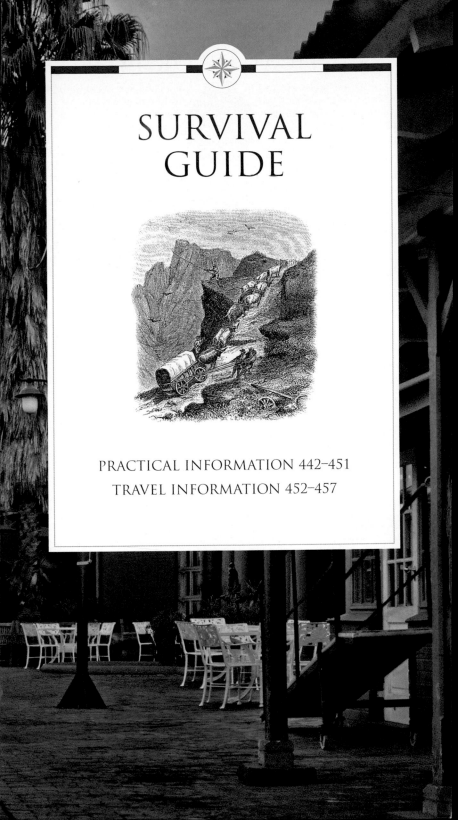

SURVIVAL
GUIDE

PRACTICAL INFORMATION

South Africa hosts around 8 million foreign visitors a year. Throughout the country, the peak seasons coincide with the South African school holidays – the busiest times are from early December to late February, especially along the south and east coasts. The Easter weekend is also busy at both inland and seaside resorts, as are the four-week winter

National Monument logo

school holidays over June and July. Although the number of tourists increases every year, the country nevertheless offers a sense of the "undiscovered". Local people still have wide, sandy beaches largely to themselves, and road travel between cities and the sea is easy. In the interior, the natural splendour of game parks and nature reserves draws crowds of visitors.

WHEN TO GO

Many parts of South Africa are at their best in September and October, when the spring season's growth is fresh and the temperature comfortably warm. Game-watchers may prefer June to August, when many trees are bare and large numbers of animals converge on the diminishing number of drinking places. Winter days are usually sunny and warm, but temperatures drop as the sun sets.

Temperatures from December to February may be close to unbearable in high-lying areas such as the Northern Cape and along the East Coast, but relief is delivered through thunderstorms almost every afternoon. The moderating influence of the sea is welcome at the coast, although some people find the increased humidity difficult to deal with. The southwestern areas have winter rainfall and hot summers. Much of the southern coast receives rain throughout the year. Almost all attractions stay open all through the year.

WHAT TO TAKE

Don't underestimate South African winters, or the wind-chill factor in summer; central heating is an exception so pack warm clothes. Sunblock and specialized provisions can be bought locally, but do carry a supply of medication if you suffer from a chronic condition.

VISA AND PASSPORTS

Citizens of the United States, Canada, Australia, New Zealand and most European Union nationals need only a valid passport to stay in South Africa for 90 days. Citizens of Cyprus, Hungary, Poland, and the Slovak Republic can stay for 30 days.

Visas to enter Swaziland are issued free of charge at the border. Visa requirements for Lesotho depend on your nationality. The South African consulate or embassy in your country will be able to advise.

All visitors must complete a temporary residence permit at the point of entry into South Africa. It shows length and

Summer game-viewing at Addo Elephant Park, Port Elizabeth *(see p250)*

South Africa
Inspiring new ways

Logo and slogan of South Africa

purpose of the visit and a contact address. Visitors may also be asked to prove that they can support themselves financially while in the country and own a return ticket or have the means to buy one. No inoculations are necessary. However, if you arrive from a country where yellow fever is endemic, you will need a vaccination certificate. Malaria is still prevalent in parts of Kwa-Zulu-Natal and Mpumalanga, and caution is advised.

TOURIST INFORMATION

Tourist offices, identified by the letter "i" on a green background, offer invaluable advice about what to see and where to go. They may also carry the name of an umbrella organization or a local publicity association. The offices are usually sited on the main road in the smaller towns, sometimes adjoining (or inside) the offices of the local authority or forming part of the local museum or public library. You should be able to obtain advance information in your own country from **South African Tourism**.

OPENING TIMES AND ADMISSION PRICES

Most businesses (other than retail outlets), museums and galleries open from 8

◁ A beautifully rebuilt classic train, part of the luxurious Rovos Rail fleet, at Capital Park station in Pretoria

The *John Benn* takes sightseers around the Knysna Lagoon *(see p240)*

or 9am until 4 or 5pm. Many, particularly in the smaller towns, close for lunch between 1 and 2pm, except during the peak summer season. Larger museums or galleries usually close for one day each week (usually on a Monday). Entry charges vary. Nature reserves, game parks and botanic gardens all charge entry fees, most of them very reasonable.

ETIQUETTE

Dress code in South African cities is casual, except for a few top restaurants and for events noted as formal. On the beach, however, it is illegal for women to either swim or sunbathe topless. The consumption of alcohol on beaches and in public places is illegal, as is smoking in buses, trains, taxis and most public buildings. It is very important to observe religious customs when visiting mosques, temples and other places of worship.

DISABLED TRAVELLERS

Facilities for the disabled are not as sophisticated as they are in the United States and Europe, but wheelchair users, for example, will nevertheless have a satisfactory holiday. If you're renting a car, ask about a special parking disk, allowing parking concessions. Local airlines provide assistance for disabled passengers, if given prior notice. Many sights – including the Table Mountain Aerial Cableway and Kirstenbosch National Botanical Garden – can be accessed by wheelchairs. South Africa also has a growing number of hotels that cater for the disabled, and most SANParks national parks have specially adapted huts. Contact **Disabled Travel** *(see p445)* for advice on accommodation with facilities.

Disabled parking

VAT AND TAXES

See p428 and p453.

DIRECTORY

EMBASSIES AND CONSULATES

Australian High Commission
Pretoria/Tshwane
Tel (012) 423-6000.

British High Commission
Cape Town *Tel (021) 405-2400.*
Pretoria/Tshwane
Tel (012) 421-7500.

Canadian High Commission
Pretoria/Tshwane
Tel (012) 422-3000.

Embassy of Ireland
Pretoria/Tshwane
Tel (012) 342-5062.

New Zealand High Commission
Pretoria/Tshwane
Tel (012) 435-9000.

US Consulate General
Cape Town *Tel (021) 702-7300.*
Durban *Tel (031) 305-7600.*
Johannesburg *Tel (011) 290-3000.*

US Embassy
Pretoria/Tshwane
Tel (012) 431-4000.

TOURIST OFFICES

Cape Town Tourism
Tel (021) 484-800.
www.tourismcapetown.co.za

Eastern Cape Tourism Board
Tel (043) 701-9600.
www.ectourism.co.za

Free State Tourism
Tel (051) 411-4300.
www.freestatetourism.org

Gauteng Tourism
Tel (011) 085-2500.
www.gauteng.net

KwaZulu Natal Tourism
Tel (031) 366-7500.
www.zulu.org.za

Limpopo Province Tourism
Tel (015) 293-3600.
www.golimpopo.com

Mpumalanga Tourism
Tel (013) 759-5300.
www.mpumalanga.com

Northen Cape Tourism
Tel (053) 833-1434.

South African Tourism
Tel (011) 895-3000.

Visitors must remove their shoes before entering a Hindu temple

Discovery tour at Oudtshoorn's Cango Wildlife Farm *(see p230)*

all over the country, including accommodation options. **MASK** is South Africa's pro-active online forum for the gay and lesbian community.

The drag/theme party held in Cape Town each December by **Mother City Queer Project** draws almost 10,000 party goers – at least 1,000 of them foreign visitors. In September you can join the annual **Johannesburg Gay and Lesbian Pride Parade**, billed as the greatest parade in Africa.

Gay and Lesbian Pride Parade

TRAVELLING WITH CHILDREN

Travelling with children is fairly easy, as the sunny weather allows for a variety of outdoor entertainment. Make sure that they drink plenty of water, though, and that they wear a high-protection sun screen. Consult your doctor about travelling with children in a malaria zone.

Children can be great "ice-breakers" in getting to meet the locals, but do not let them out of your sight.

If you travel during local school holidays, you'll find that even the smaller towns offer children's activities – from aquarium and zoo tours to theatre, baking and craft workshops. The local press, libraries and the **Tonight** website are good sources of ideas. Look out for "Touch and Feed" farms, where children can encounter farm animals.

WOMEN TRAVELLERS

South Africa has an extremely high incidence of rape *(see p446)*, although the careful tourist should be reasonably safe. There are **Rape Crisis** centres in major towns and cities. Travelling alone is not recommended. Women are potential victims of mugging, so keep to well-lit public areas during the day and night and don't exhibit any valuables. Always look as if you know where you are going and don't offer or accept a lift from anyone.

Sexual harassment is not too common, although many South African males do hold rather chauvinistic attitudes, so be careful not to come across as too friendly, as your interest may be perceived as sexual. The incidence of HIV/Aids is high, so don't ever have unprotected sex. Condoms are readily available at pharmacies and supermarkets.

GAY AND LESBIAN TRAVELLERS

Enshrined in the new constitution is a clause protecting the rights of gays and lesbians. But while Cape Town is certainly the "gay capital of Africa", the smaller towns still retain conservative attitudes.

The cities have a host of gay bars and theatre venues; the **Pink South Africa** website is a good resource for gay and lesbian event listings. The **South African Gay Information and Travel Guide** lists gay- and lesbian-friendly venues

STUDENT TRAVEL

Students with a valid **International Student Identity Card (ISIC)** benefit from good airline travel discounts, but reduced admission to venues and events has not taken off in South Africa. **STA Travel**, an agency that specializes in student travel, has branches world-wide. Backpacking is gaining in popularity.

Backpackers' accommodation in the centre of Cape Town

TIME

South African Standard Time (there is only one time zone) is two hours ahead of Greenwich Mean Time (GMT) all year round, seven hours ahead of the United States' Eastern Standard Winter Time and seven hours behind Australian Central Time.

PUBLIC TOILETS

There are public toilets in shopping malls and in many public buildings such as civic centres, libraries or town halls. Most large urban vehicle service stations have toilets, but these are intended for the use of clients. On major tourist routes, most garages that have refreshment centres also usually have well-kept toilets. Public toilets can be found at railway and bus stations, although these are often not very clean. Many have no soap or any means of drying your hands.

An alternative is to use the toilets in a restaurant where you are a customer. Large shopping centres and tourist attractions usually have well-maintained facilities and customized toilets for wheelchair users. Baby-changing facilities are also available.

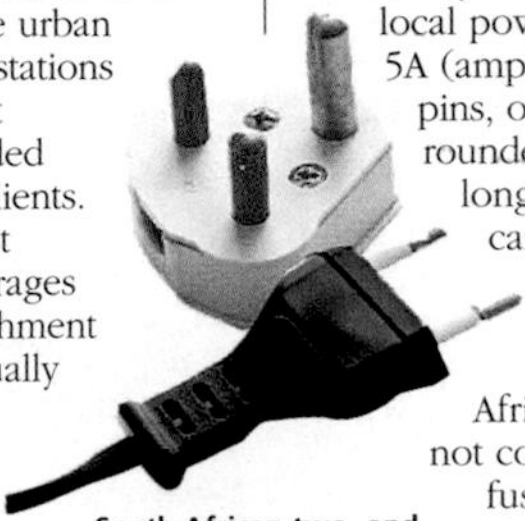

ELECTRICAL SUPPLY

Virtually all electricity (alternating current) is supplied by the state-owned utility company Eskom. Mains voltage is 220/230 volts (220V) at 50 cycles (50Hz). Most local power plugs are 5A (amperes) with twin pins, or 15A with three rounded pins, with the longest of the three carrying the earth connection (brown wire). Standard South African plugs do not contain safety fuses. An open circuit within an appliance should cause a circuit-breaker to trip at the distribution board, cutting off electricity from that board or

South African two- and three-prong plugs

the electricity to the section in which the fault has occurred. Seek advice about adaptors from a local electrical supplier.

WEIGHTS AND MEASURES

South Africa uses the metric system and SI (Système International) units. Normal body temperature of 98.4° F is equal to 37° C. If the weather chart shows 30° C, you're in for a hot day. A pressure of 30 pounds per square inch is equal to two bars.

CONVERSION CHART

Imperial to Metric
1 inch = 2.54 cm
1 foot = 30 cm
1 mile = 1.6 km
1 ounce = 28 g
1 pound = 454 g
1 pint = 0.57 litres
1 gallon = 4.6 litres

Metric to Imperial
1 mm = 0.04 inches
1 cm = 0.4 inches
1 m = 3 feet 3 inches
1 km = 0.6 miles
1 g = 0.04 ounces
1 kg = 2.2 pounds
1 litre = 1.8 pints

DIRECTORY

DISABLED TRAVELLERS

Disabled Travel
82 Mitchell St,
Eastcliff,
Hermanus, 7200.
Tel (028) 312-1889.
www.disabled
travel.co.za

Epic Enabled
Tel (021) 785-7440.
www.epic-enabled.com

Flamingo Tours
Tel (021) 557-4496.
www.flamingotours.
co.za
Tours for the physically disabled or visually impaired.

TRAVELLING WITH CHILDREN

Tonight
www.tonight.co.za

WOMEN TRAVELLERS

AIDS Counselling
Tel (0800) 012-322.
www.aidshelpline.org.za

Rape Crisis
www.rapecrisis.org.za

GAY AND LESBIAN TRAVELLERS

Johannesburg Gay and Lesbian Pride Parade
www.joburgpride.org

MASK
www.mask.org.za

Mother City Queer Project
www.mcqp.co.za

Pink South Africa
14 Cobern Street,
De Waterkant, 8005.
Tel (021) 425-6463.
www.pinksa.co.za

South African Gay Information and Travel Guide
www.gaysouth
africa.net

STUDENT TRAVEL

International Student Identity Card (ISIC)
www.isic.org

STA Travel
14 Main Road,
Rondebosch,
Cape Town, 7700.
Tel (021) 686-6800.

The Mall of Rosebank,
50 Bath Avenue,
Johannesburg, 2196.
Tel (011) 447-5414.

Student Travel
Head Office
Tel (0861) 781-781.
www.statravel.co.za

Personal Security and Health

SA Police logo

South Africa is experiencing a period of profound change. For some, the rate of change is overwhelming; for others it is too slow. Democracy has at last been attained, but a great many problems – such as widespread unemployment and poverty – still need to be solved. In some areas, the incidence of serious crime is alarmingly high, but overall, South Africa is a safe place for visitors who take reasonable precautions. The wildlife should always be taken seriously and treated with respect. Bites and stings from venomous creatures are rare, but malaria and bilharzia need to be considered in certain areas.

PERSONAL SAFETY

Always exercise common sense and extreme caution when out and about. While inner-city areas and townships are probably the most dangerous places in South Africa, villages may also have crime hot spots, so keep your wits about you.

Avoid going out on your own, especially after dark; if you do, stick to busy, well-lit tourist areas. Don't exhibit expensive-looking jewellery and accessories, such as mobile phones. If you are mugged, do not challenge the thief and simply hand over your phone or your money. Carrying a decoy wallet is a good idea.

Don't carry large sums of money, but do keep some change in a side pocket so that you don't have to produce your wallet whenever you need to tip.

Don't put your possessions down when you need your hands (for example, when examining an intended purchase). Leave valuables and purchases in your hotel's safe-deposit box, and carry with you only what you are likely to need. A money belt worn under your clothing is useful for keeping documents and banknotes. Don't go near deserted areas or impoverished neighbourhoods except as part of a tour group.

Avoid any place where unrestricted consumption of liquor takes place.

Avoid suburban trains *(see p454)* at off-peak times, unless you are in a group of at least ten people.

Don't go exploring without a guide. In an emergency, report the incident to the nearest **police** station or police officer. You will need to produce identification. To make an insurance claim you will need to obtain a case reference number from the police station.

ON THE ROAD

When travelling by car, always keep the doors locked and the windows only slightly open. When you do leave the car, lock it, even if you're getting out for just a few moments *(see p456)*. Make sure that nothing of value is visible inside – leave the glove compartment open to show that there's nothing in there either. Use undercover or supervised parking wherever possible. Do not stop for hitch-hikers or to offer any help, even to an accident victim. If a hijacker or other criminal points a firearm at you, obey his or her orders.

Pharmacies offer valuable medical advice and services

MEDICAL FACILITIES

State and provincial hospitals do offer adequate facilities, but they tend to be under-funded and under-staffed. Patients who are members of medical insurance schemes are usually admitted to a private hospital, such as **Medi-Clinic** or **Netcare**; these are found in most South African cities, including Cape Town, Johannesburg and Durban. All visitors should take out travel insurance to cover everything, including emergencies. If you suffer from any pre-existing medical condition or are on any long-term medication, make sure those who try to help you are aware of it.

FOOD AND WATER

Tap water is safe to drink, although chlorinated. There is a wide range of bottled waters available. Be careful of river or mountain water in heavily populated areas. The preparation of food in

Police officers standing guard at Rustenburg Stadium

Ambulance

Police vehicle

Fire engine

most restaurants and hotels meets international standards, but do exercise common sense. In the informal markets, avoid meat or dairy products that may have been lying in the sun, and wash all fruit and vegetables carefully.

Travellers to South Africa do not generally suffer the same stomach upsets as they may in the rest of the continent.

OUTDOOR HAZARDS

In many parts of South Africa, forest and bush fires are a major hazard, especially during the dry winter months. Don't ever discard burning matches and cigarette ends.

Always protect yourself from the harsh sun with a wide-brimmed hat, a high-factor sunblock and sun-glasses. Before you climb or hike at high altitude, ask about the expected weather conditions. Be aware that these can change very

quickly. If you are caught in cloud, keep warm and wait for the weather to lift. Make sure you tell a responsible person at your hotel what route you intend to take and the time you expect to return. Ensure that you are familiar with your route before setting off.

POISONOUS BITES AND STINGS

Few travellers are likely to find themselves in danger of being bitten or stung by any one of the venomous creatures of South Africa. People on safari or on hiking trails should nevertheless watch where they place their hands and feet.

Few snakes in South Africa are deadly, and most are not poisonous at all. They strike only when attacked or threatened. The most dangerous spider is the seldom-encountered button spider (*Latrodectus* species). Most of the species of scorpion are only slightly venomous. In general, those with thick tails and small pincers tend to be more poisonous. Because of their lower body weight, children are more susceptible to the toxins than adults.

MALARIA AND BILHARZIA

Malaria is most likely to be contracted in Mpuma-langa, Northern Province and northern KwaZulu-Natal. The risks of contracting malaria can be minimized by starting a course of anti-malaria tablets a week before

travelling to an affected area and continuing with the treatment for a month after your return.

Bilharzia (*schistosomiasis*) results from contact (whether on the skin or by drinking) with affected water. The areas in which the disease is most likely to be contracted are the Northern Province, Mpumalanga, North-West Province, KwaZulu-Natal and Eastern Cape. Suspect water should not be used for washing or bathing, and should be boiled if intended for consumption.

The charming police station in Pietermaritzburg

Banking and Currency

The Standard Bank

The South African banking system is similar to that in most industrialized Western countries. There are no restrictions on the amount of foreign currency that may be brought into the country. There are, however, limits to the amount of any currency that may be taken out of South Africa. These amounts, like rates of exchange, are subject to fluctuation, so always check with your travel agent. Travellers' cheques may be exchanged at banks, bureaux de change, some hotels and some shops. Banks generally offer the best rate of exchange.

Foreign exchange bureau,
V&A Waterfront, Cape Town

BANKING HOURS

In the larger towns, banking hours are from 9am to 3:30pm on weekdays, and from 9am to 11:30am on Saturdays. Smaller branches and agencies may have shorter hours and be closed on Saturdays. They are all closed on public holidays. A number of sites, such as the V&A Waterfront in Cape Town and the OR Tambo International Airport in Johannesburg, offer a convenient, 24-hour foreign-exchange service. At all the other airports, the reception areas for international arrivals and departures have special banking facilities for international passengers.

ATMS

Automatic teller machines (ATMs) are widely distributed in the cities and towns. Cash withdrawals, up to a set limit per day per card, are made with bank-issued debit cards, but transactions may also be done with local or foreign-issued credit cards encoded with a PIN number. The cards most widely used in South

Africa are Visa and MasterCard. ATMs may run out of notes at the weekend, especially if there is a public holiday on the Monday, so make sure you draw money early. If you find the daily limit inadequate, you can always draw more from a bank (remembering to take your passport along), but it's best to avoid carrying too much cash with you.

Avoid drawing money while on your own, or at deserted ATMs after-hours, and decline all unsolicited offers of "help". ATM fraud is common: a fraudster may, for example, jam the machine slot so you can't retrieve your card. While you alert the bank officials inside, the fraudster un-jams the slot and withdraws money from your account. Rather wait outside at the ATM while a companion goes for help. All ATMs display a 24-hour emergency telephone number to call in the event of any problems with your card.

CREDIT CARDS

Most businesses accept all major credit cards. Keep your card in sight when making a payment, especially in restaurants, to reduce the risk of it being "cloned". Informal traders do not normally accept credit cards. Not all petrol stations take credit cards, but most of the larger ones have ATMs; it is advisable to check before filling up. Find out what charges your bank will levy for use of your credit card in South Africa.

CHANGING MONEY

Most banks offer foreign exchange services. You can also change cash in bureaux like those run by Thomas Cook (represented in South Africa by Rennies Travel) and American Express. Exchange bureaux tend to be clustered together in shopping malls and airports, so it is easy to compare the rates offered.

DIRECTORY

LOST OR STOLEN CARDS

ABSA/Maestro
National free-call (24-hours).
Tel *0800 110 929.*

American Express (Nedbank)
Tel *(011) 710-4710 (24 hours).*

Diners Club International
Tel *0860 346 377.*
www.dinersclub.co.za

First National Bank
National free-call (24-hours).
Tel *0800 110 132.*

MasterCard
National free-call (24-hours).
Tel *0800 990 418.*

Nedbank
National free-call (24-hours).
Tel *0800 110 929.*

Rennies Foreign Exchange Bureaux (Thomas Cook)
National free-call, 24-hours.
Tel *0800 111 177.*

Standard Bank
Tel *0800 020 600.*
www.standardbank.co.za

Visa International
National free-call (24-hours).
Tel *0800 990 475.*

A row of Standard Bank ATMs

TRAVELLERS' CHEQUES

These may be cashed at any bank – provided the currency of issue is acceptable. No commission is charged by a branch of the bank that issued the cheque.

CURRENCY

The South African unit of currency is the rand, indicated by the letter "R" before the amount ("rand" is short for "Witwatersrand", Gauteng's gold-bearing reef).

The rand is divided into 100 cents (c). Older issues of coins and notes are still legal tender. South African currency circulates – usually at face value – in the neighbouring Lesotho, Namibia, Swaziland and Mozambique.

Bank Notes
Bank notes, on which the "Big Five" wildlife animals are represented, are issued in R10, R20, R50, R100 and R200 denominations.

R200 note

R100 note

R50 note

R20 note

R10 note

Coins (actual size)
Copper-coloured, smooth-edged coins are in denominations of 1 cent, 2 cents and 5 cents. The 10-cent, 20-cent and 50-cent coins are a brassy yellow and have milled edges. The R1, R2 and R5 coins are milled in a bright, silver colour.

5-cent piece

10-cent piece

20-cent piece

50-cent piece

R1

R2

R5

Telecommunications

Telkom logo

South African telecommunications systems are among the most advanced in the world. The national telecommunications agency is Telkom SA Limited, and a wide variety of postal options, from insured or signature-on-delivery mail to courier services, are offered by post offices countrywide. Public telephones (payphones) are found in every city and town, and include both coin- and card-operated models. Telephone cards and postage stamps may be bought at many shops and supermarkets. Some shops, especially in the rural areas, have one or more public telephone (rented from Telkom) on their premises.

TELEPHONES

Most telephone exchanges in South Africa are automatic, so you can dial direct as long as you use the correct dialling code. There are public telephone boxes in post offices, train stations and shopping malls; post offices usually keep a complete range of South African telephone directories, but don't rely on finding one in stations or malls. Businesses and restaurants often have a table-model payphone known as a Chatterbox. Even if you are not a patron, ask if you may use the phone. The staff are unlikely to refuse your request. Payphones take a range of South African coins.

Telephone cards can be bought from most post offices, cafés and newsagents. Note that payphones accept either coins or cards, but not both.

Reduced rates are in effect typically from 7pm until 7am on weekdays, and from 1pm Saturday to 7am Monday at the weekend. Calls made from hotels carry a substantial levy.

The AA's roadside emergency number, (083) 84322, is available for all members; non-members may call 10111 for the emergency services.

MOBILE PHONES

Mobile (or cell) phone coverage is very good in most towns and cities and along the main highways. Mobile phones can be obtained in South Africa from private service providers on contract or on a pay-as-you-go tariff with pre-paid airtime. Mobile-phone rental facilities are found at the major airports. Mobiles are often offered as part of a car-hire contract.

To avoid high roaming fees on an international mobile, buy a local SIM card to use in your own phone. Note that you can only do this if your handset is unlocked. SIM cards can be bought inexpensively at any **MTN**, **Cell C** or **Vodacom** shop. MTN and Vodacom also offer Internet packages for use on your mobile phone, as long as you are using a local SIM card; just ask them to set your phone up for Internet access.

RADIO AND TELEVISION

The South African Broadcasting Corporation (SABC) has four television channels and a number of national and regional radio stations. The main TV language is English, but local programming – including news – is produced in several languages including Afrikaans and Zulu; some shows even combine different languages. British and US programmes tend to dominate, but there are some good homegrown productions too. Local radio stations target specific audiences and language-groups. Cable and satellite TV services are provided by the private company MNet.

Stations at an Internet café

INTERNET

Wi-Fi access is becoming increasingly available outside of the big cities, but there are still many areas where broadband is the only option.

There is a growing number of Internet cafés, especially in the main urban centres; to find the nearest one, consult the Yellow Pages. Most of the coffee shops in Cape Town offer Wi-Fi access free of charge; it is not unusual to see people on their laptops in cafés. A lot of restaurants also have this facility during the day, as do the more upmarket hotels and guesthouses and most of the airports and shopping malls. Only at the more remote lodges in the national parks and reserves will the Internet not be available.

Coin- and card-operated public telephones

Post office in Matjiesfontein, Western Cape

POSTAL SERVICE

The South African Post Office (SAPO) provides several ways of sending letters and goods: registered, cash-on-delivery (COD), insured, express delivery, Fastmail and, for guaranteed delivery within 24 hours in South Africa, Speed Services. However, the delivery rate of letters and parcels is somewhat erratic, and coverage, although gradually improving, is still patchy, particularly in remote regions of the country. As a result, private courier services are popular. Post offices also function as banks for the poor, and people collect their social grants here as well. In rural areas, long queues make it impractical to use the post office for postal matters.

Postage stamps are sold at newsagents, some grocery stores and corner cafés. Post offices are open 8am–4:30pm on weekdays and 8am–noon on Saturdays. Smaller centres usually close for lunch hour.

Post office sign in Swellendam, on the Garden Route

COURIER SERVICES

Couriers like **DHL** and **FedEx** have branches in larger South African centres and many small towns as well. They will collect from anywhere in South Africa, and deliver parcels, priced per kilo, country- and worldwide.

Alternatively, try **PostNet**, a private mail and business services company in South Africa that also acts as an agent for DHL. There are more than 230 stores located in the major shopping malls across the country.

NEWSPAPERS AND MAGAZINES

South Africa has 20 daily and 13 weekly newspapers, most of them in English. Of the national papers, the highest-selling is *The Daily Sun*, which is aimed at a predominantly young, black, working class readership. Regional dailies are found in all major cities; most produce both morning and afternoon papers as well as Saturday and Sunday editions. There are also several national weekly and bi-weekly news tabloids.

The main English-language dailies are *The Star* in Gauteng, the *Cape Argus* in the Cape and *The Mercury* in KwaZulu-Natal. Arguably, the best weekly newspaper is the *Mail and Guardian*, known for its hard-hitting reports. Other weeklies are *The Sunday Independent* and the more populist *Sunday Times*.

English-language papers are widespread in the cities, but rural towns may receive fewer copies – often up to a day later. A variety of local and international magazines is widely available. Topics include travel, sport, wildlife and outdoor life.

South Africa receives editions of some overseas newspapers (mainly British), as well as a number of foreign magazines. All of these are distributed through selected newsagents, such as the CNA and Exclusive Books chains, or placed in upmarket hotels.

DIRECTORY

OPERATOR ASSISTANCE

Tel 1023. (Telkom information & local enquiries)

Tel 10900. (International calls)

Tel 10903. (International enquiries)

AREA CODES

Country code (27).
Johannesburg (011).
Pretoria/Tshwane (012).
Cape Town (021).
Durban (031).
Port Elizabeth (041).

MOBILE PHONES

Cell C
www.cellc.co.za

MTN
www.mtn.co.za

Vodacom
www.vodacom.co.za

POSTAL SERVICES

Customer Services
Tel (012) 401-7902.
www.postoffice.co.za

COURIER SERVICES

DHL International
Tel (011) 921-3600.
www.dhl.co.za

FedEx
Tel (087) 742-8000.
www.fedex.com/za

PostNet
Tel (0860) 767-8638.
www.postnet.co.za

TRAVEL INFORMATION

South Africa, historically a welcome stopover for seafarers, is well served by air links with most parts of the globe and by road to the rest of Africa. The national carrier is South African Airways (SAA), but most international airlines operate regular flights to and from here. Domestic destinations are served by SAA and other airlines. The road

Tail of an SAA 747

system in South Africa is fairly comprehensive. Roads are generally in good condition, though the accident rate is high. Intercity bus services operate between major cities. The rail network covers the country and extends beyond the borders to give access to southern and Central Africa. Public transport within cities and towns is seldom satisfactory.

South African Airways and Star Alliance carriers on the runway

ARRIVING BY AIR

Most visitors to the country arrive at and depart from OR Tambo International Airport, which is located outside Johannesburg. Direct international flights also leave from and arrive in Cape Town and Durban.

Internal destinations served by the national carrier SAA and by domestic low-cost, no-frills airlines include Johannesburg, Durban, Cape Town, Port Elizabeth,

Bloemfontein, East London, Kimberley, George and Upington. Smaller centres, as well as the airport at Skukuza in the Kruger National Park, are linked by regular feeder services. Air charter services are available at most of the larger airports.

For flight information, contact the Airports Company of South Africa (Tel: (086) 727-7888; www.acsa.co.za) or send a text message to Tel: 38648 with the relevant flight number.

Public transport to and from the major airports includes airline or privately operated shuttle buses to the nearest city centre (see Directory). In Cape Town, there are also regular MyCiTi buses (see p455) to the city, while visitors travelling from OR Tambo International Airport to Johannesburg also have the option of taking the Gautrain (see p454).

Radio taxi services are also available, while most of the hotels, guesthouses and some backpackers' lodges in the larger cities will be able to provide transport on request.

Facilities at the international airports include banking, currency exchange, car rental, post offices, information centres, duty-free shops (for outbound passengers only), restaurants and bars.

CUSTOMS

Current customs legislation allows visitors to bring duty-free goods to the value of R3,000 into the country.

AIRPORT	INFORMATION	DISTANCE FROM CITY	TAXI FARE TO CITY	BUS TRANSFER TO CITY
✈ Johannesburg	*Tel (086) 727-7888*	24 km (15 miles)	R230	30–35 mins
✈ Cape Town	*Tel (086) 727-7888*	20 km (12 miles)	R200	35–50 mins
✈ Durban	*Tel (086) 727-7888*	20 km (12 miles)	R200	20–30 mins
✈ Port Elizabeth	*Tel (086) 727-7888*	3 km (2 miles)	R50	7–10 mins
✈ Bloemfontein	*Tel (086) 727-7888*	15 km (9 miles)	R160	20–40 mins
✈ East London	*Tel (086) 727-7888*	15 km (9 miles)	R160	10–15 mins
✈ George	*Tel (086) 727-7888*	10 km (6 miles)	R130	10 mins
✈ Kruger Mpumalanga*	*Tel (013) 753-7500*			

* Kruger Mpumalanga International Airport has six British Airways flights a week arriving from Johannesburg.

Visitors may also bring in 50 ml of perfume, 2 litres (3½ pints) of wine, 1 litre (1¾ pints) of spirits, 250 g tobacco, 200 cigarettes and 20 cigars. Children under the age of 18 do not qualify for the alcohol or tobacco allowance. Further items to the value of R12,000 per person are charged at a flat rate of 20 per cent of their value. On amounts above R10,000, normal customs duties apply, plus VAT.

Lesotho, Swaziland and South Africa are members of the Southern African Development Community, a common customs union, so there are no internal customs duties. For more information, visit the South Africa Revenue Services website (www.sars.gov.za).

INTERNATIONAL FLIGHTS

Fares to South Africa tend to be at their highest between September and February, but the cost will depend on the type of ticket. Savings can be made by booking an APEX (Advance Purchase Excursion) ticket in advance, although these are subject to minimum and maximum time limits, thus restricting the visitor's stay.

Specialist agents offer many good deals. Discount agents may also offer attractive student or youth fares.

Make sure that your booking agent is a licensed member of ABTA (the Association of British Travel Agents) or a similar authority; you will then be assured of compensation should something go wrong with your bookings.

DOMESTIC FLIGHTS

Airlines such as **South African Airways**, **Comair**, **Kulula**, **Mango** and **1time** offer regular intercity services.

The current price structures are competitive, with return-fare and other attractive specials regularly on offer. In general, the earlier one books, the cheaper the fare (seven-day advance specials are common). Booking is essential.

PACKAGE HOLIDAYS

Package tours almost always offer reduced airfare and accommodation costs, making them cheaper than independent travel, unless you are travelling on a tight budget and wish to stay in backpackers' lodges, self-catering accommodation or campsites.

Popular package tours and deals include trips to Durban, Cape Town, Johannesburg, Port Elizabeth, the Garden Route, the Wild Coast, Sun City and the Palace of the Lost City, as well as the Kruger National Park.

FLY-DRIVE DEALS

Many travel agents and car-rental firms organize fly-drive packages that enable you to book a flight and have a rental car waiting at your destination. This is usually cheaper and involves fewer formalities than renting a car on arrival. Most major car-rental firms such as Avis, Hertz, Budget and Europcar have offices at the airports (see p457).

AIRPORT TAX

South African Airport tax is paid upon purchase of your ticket. The tax to be paid per international departure is R116. Domestic flights are taxed at R80 per departure. The tax on flights to Botswana, Namibia, Lesotho or Swaziland is R60.

DIRECTORY

AIRPORT SHUTTLES

Cape Town Magic Bus
Domestic Arrivals Hall, Cape Town International Airport.
Tel (021) 505-6300.
www.magicbus.co.za

Durban Magic Bus
Suite 7, Grenada Centre, 16 Chartwell Dr, Umhlanga Rocks.
Tel (031) 263-2647.
www.magicbus.co.za

East London Shuttle
Domestic Arrivals Hall, East London National Airport.
Tel (082) 569-3599.
www.elbusshuttle.com

Johannesburg Magic Bus
Domestic Arrivals, Terminal 3, Johannesburg International.
Tel (011) 394-6902.
www.magicbus.co.za

King Shaka Airport Shuttle Bus
Tel (031) 465-5573.
www.airportbustransport.co.za

King Shaka Airport Shuttle Services
Tel (084) 231-1363.
www.kingshakashuttles.co.za

DOMESTIC AIRLINES

1time
Tel (011) 086-8000.
www.1time.co.za

Comair
Tel (011) 921-0111.
www.comair.co.za

Kulula
Tel (0861) 585-852.
www.kulula.com

Mango
Tel (0861) 001-234.
www.flymango.com

South African Airways
Tel (0861) 359-722.
www.flysaa.com

The interior of Cape Town International Airport

Travelling by Train and Bus

Blue Train logo

Train travel in South Africa is quite comfortable and economical, but seldom very fast. Intercity buses, on the other hand, are fast, far-reaching and affordable, though it's wise to compare long-distance fares to those of the cheaper airlines. City transport is a little more limited. Suburban trains and minibus taxis are largely used by commuters and can be crowded, meaning that personal safety cannot be guaranteed. However, modern buses and high-speed trains with good security are being introduced on many routes, including to and from the major airports. In addition, some forms of transport are specifically designed for visitors, such as luxury trains and sightseeing city buses.

The stately Pretoria/Tshwane Railway Station (see p321)

LONG-DISTANCE TRAINS

Shosholoza Meyl operates trains from Johannesburg to Cape Town (27 hours), Port Elizabeth (21 hours), and Durban (13 hours). The services are affordable but much slower than long-distance buses; in addition, trains run overnight, so they may arrive at or leave some stations at inconvenient times.

There are two types of class: tourist and economy. Tourist class offers sleeping compartments with two or four bunks, a wash basin and a table; bedding can be hired on the train for a fee. Communal toilets and showers are at the end of each coach. Solo travellers share a four-berth compartment with fellow travellers of the same gender. Economy class has reclining seats with headrests and a reasonable amount of legroom; toilets can be found at the end of each coach. Simple meals are available from a

restaurant coach; snacks can also be purchased from a service trolley, and passengers can bring their own food and refreshments.

A tourist-class ticket costs about twice as much as an economy-class ticket. Children under nine travel at half price; note that booking is necessary during the school holidays. Between February and November, holders of valid university student cards receive a discount of 40 per cent and pensioners of 25 per cent.

LUXURY TRAINS

Enormously popular, especially with foreign visitors, are the luxurious train safaris offered by the Blue Train and Rovos Rail (see pp438–9).

Premier Classe is Shosholoza Meyl's upmarket service between Johannesburg and Cape Town and Johannesburg and Durban; cars can be transported on these trains. More comfortable than regular trains, but not as

luxurious as the Blue Train and Rovos Rail services, Premier Classe trains have single, two- and four-berth coupés with air-conditioning, toiletries and room service. There are shared bathrooms and a dining car and bar; fares include breakfast, lunch, high tea and dinner.

SUBURBAN TRAINS

Suburban train services run in most South African cities and are operated by **Metrorail**. These trains are used mainly by commuters and can be overcrowded; theft may also be an issue. Timetables and tickets are available at the stations. A first-class ticket costs about twice as much as a third-class ticket but offers better seating and security. Children under 11 years of age travel at half price.

It is advisable to use suburban trains only in daylight hours, and preferably at peak times (early in the morning and mid- to late afternoon). It is not recommended to travel alone on suburban trains at any time. The exception is in Cape Town, where services are provided by **Cape Metrorail**. Among the Cape Town trains that are popular with visitors is the Southern Line Tourism Route, which runs from the city centre through the Southern Suburbs and along the False Bay coast to Simon's Town. One- or two-day tickets offer unlimited travel on a hop-on/hop-off basis; many of the attractions in this part of the Cape Peninsula are within walking distance of the stations.

The **Gautrain** is a rapid-rail network linking Johannesburg and Pretoria/Tshwane (a journey of about 40 minutes); there is also a branch line between Sandton and OR Tambo International Airport, a journey of around 15 minutes. At peak hours, trains run every 12 minutes, and off-peak about every 20–30 minutes. Fares are paid for by a Gautrain Gold Card, which can be purchased and topped up at ticket offices and vending machines. Children under the age of three travel free.

LONG-DISTANCE BUSES

Citiliner, **Greyhound**, **Intercape**, **SA Roadlink** and **Translux** coaches travel to most towns, and the journeys are safe, comfortable and affordable. Greyhound, Intercape and Translux also run services to the capital cities in neighbouring countries: Maputo (Mozambique), Windhoek (Namibia), Livingstone (Zambia), Harare (Zimbabwe) and Gaborone (Botswana). The coaches are modern and air-conditioned, with on-board toilets and reclining seats, and they stop for refreshments. There are, however, long distances to cover, and some coaches depart or arrive at inconvenient times. Trips can be booked via Computicket *(see p431)*, either online or at any branch in the country.

The **Baz Bus** hop-on/hop-off system, aimed at budget travellers, runs between Cape Town and Durban, and Durban and Johannesburg, picking up and dropping off passengers at backpackers' hostels. Tickets are priced in segments – Cape Town to Port Elizabeth, for example – and allow unlimited hop-on/hop-offs within that segment but no backtracking. This makes the Baz Bus convenient for shorter journeys, especially since buses travel only during the day; however, for longer journeys, conventional bus services offer better value.

Travelling by train, a lovely way to view South Africa's landscapes

Minibus taxis transport workers on some long-distance routes. Services have a poor safety record and vehicles are overcrowded, so they are not recommended.

CITY BUSES

All South African cities have a system of public buses. These are usually inexpensive and easy to use; they can accommodate wheelchairs and prams and are monitored by security cameras. In Cape Town, bus services are run by **MyCiTi**, which also operates a service to and from the airport. In Durban, the **People Mover** runs up and down the beachfront, while in Johannesburg **Metrobus** and **Rea Vaya** cover all the metropolitan areas.

Minibus taxis follow the same routes as regular buses but are driven erratically and are not recommended.

DIRECTORY

TRAINS

Cape Metrorail
Tel (0800) 656-463.

Gautrain
Tel (0800) 428-87246.
www.gautrain.co.za

Metrorail
Tel (0800) 127-070.
www.metrorail.co.za

Premier Classe
www.premierclasse.co.za

Shosholoza Meyl
Tel (0860) 008-888.
www.shosholozameyl.co.za

BUSES

Baz Bus
Tel (0861) 229-287.

Citiliner
Tel (083) 915-9000.

Greyhound
Tel (083) 915-9000.

Intercape
Tel (0861) 287-287.

Metrobus
Tel (0860) 562-874.

MyCiTi
Tel (0800) 656-463.

People Mover
Tel (0861) 000-834.

Rea Vaya
Tel (0860) 562-874.

SA Roadlink
Tel (011) 333-2223.

Translux
Tel (0861) 589-282.

The hop-on/hop-off Baz Bus, a favourite among budget travellers

Travelling by Car

AA logo

Although bus services in South Africa are fast, affordable and comprehensive, a car is the only way to visit the more remote areas. Overall, South Africa's road network is good, although individual roads, even those that are part of the N-prefixed national road system, range from very poor to excellent. In rural areas, only main arteries may be tarred, but dirt roads are usually levelled and in good condition. Unfortunately, long distances and other road users constitute the major hazards. Most sightseeing can be done along tarred roads. Busy routes have many service and petrol stations.

Electronic tolls on the motorway from Pretoria/Tshwane to Johannesburg

When passing semi-urban townships and in rural areas, be alert for pedestrians and straying livestock.

Due to the vast distances between towns, especially in the arid interior, it is advisable to refuel in good time and plan regular rest stops.

STREET & PLACE NAMES

You should be aware that South African street and place names are in a state of flux. For more details, see p23.

FUEL

Motor vehicles run on 97 Octane petrol, unleaded petrol or diesel fuel, and the unit of liquid measurement is the litre (0.22 UK gallons or 0.264 US gallons). Service station attendants see to refuelling and other checks like tyre pressure, oil, water, and cleaning the front and rear windows.

PARKING

Most South African towns and cities have street parking, with numbered bays painted on the tarmac or at the kerb; check for signs posted on a nearby pole. A fee may be paid to a parking marshal with a handheld meter. In unofficial parking areas such as side streets or shopping mall car parks, informal parking attendants expect a tip when you leave, for guarding your car and helping with groceries.

BREAKDOWN SERVICES

In the event of a vehicle breakdown, pull over onto the extreme left and activate your hazard lights. It is a good idea to carry a mobile phone when driving. The **AA** provides a breakdown service for all its members; alternatively, the emergency services can be reached on 10111.

In the event of an accident, you may move your vehicle if there are no injuries, but you have to notify the nearest police station within 24 hours and inform your car rental company immediately. If

WHAT YOU NEED

Persons over 18, who are in possession of a locally issued driver's licence that is printed in English and includes a recent photograph of the owner, will not require an international licence to drive in South Africa. However, if you need an international licence, you must obtain one before you arrive in the country.

Your licence must be carried in the vehicle at all times.

Animal and rock falling warning signs

RULES OF THE ROAD

Traffic in South Africa drives on the left side of the road. Except where granted right of way by a sign or by an official on duty, yield to traffic approaching from your right. It is common courtesy to pull over onto the hard shoulder to let faster traffic pass on the right. Seat belts are

compulsory in the front and in the back. Children must be properly restrained. The speed limit in urban areas, whether there are regulatory signs or not, is 60 km per hour (37 mph). On freeways and roads not regulated to a lower speed, the limit is 120 km per hour (75 mph).

South Africa has strict drink-driving laws. The legal blood alcohol level is 0.05 per cent maximum, which is the equivalent of one glass of beer or wine. Anyone caught driving above this limit is liable for a hefty fine or up to six years' imprisonment.

SAFETY

Police advise travellers not to pick up strangers. Keep car doors locked and windows up. When parking, leave nothing of value in plain sight (see p446). At night, park only in well-lit areas.

there are any injuries, notify
the police immediately and
do not move the vehicles
until they have arrived.

CAR RENTAL

Car rental is inexpensive
in South Africa and is best
arranged through fly-drive
packages *(see p453)* or pre-
booked with international
agents at home. All the
international airports have car-
rental offices on site. To rent a
car you must be over 23 and
have held a valid driver's
licence for at least five years.
Check the small print for
insurance cover. There are
usually specials on offer.

TAXIS

Taxis in South Africa cannot
be hailed in the street, but
there are taxi ranks outside
all airports and bus and railway
stations, shopping malls
and at the major sightseeing
attractions. Additionally, any
hotel or restaurant can call for
a cab. All taxis are metered;
by law they must display a
sticker on the side of the
vehicle showing the price
per kilometre.

GREAT DRIVES

South Africa's natural beauty,
spectacular coastline and
game parks make it an ideal
destination for leisurely self-
driving. Cape Town offers
numerous day trips by road.
The most popular is around
the Cape Peninsula *(see
p150)*, a round trip of about
180 km (112 miles) from the

Car hire facilities at Cape Town International Airport

city centre, with plenty of
distractions along the way,
including seal and penguin
colonies and the stunning
ocean scenery at Cape Point.
The 137-km (85-mile) coast
road to Hermanus is a great
vantage point for whale-
watching (Jul–Nov), while
the roads skirting the West
Coast are lined with wild
flowers between August and
September *(see pp216–17)*.
With its verdant forests,
ocean-facing mountains and
great swathes of beaches, the
Garden Route offers one of
the most scenic drives from
Cape Town. Officially it runs
for 200 km (124 miles), from
Heidelberg in the west to the
Tstsikamma forests in the
east, but the full drive from
Cape Town to Port Elizabeth,
in the Eastern Cape, where
there are more parks and
reserves to explore, is 748 km
(465 miles). Route 62, which
runs on inland roads via
dramatic mountain passes and
quaint farming settlements,
provides an alternative route
back to Cape Town.

The Panorama Route follows
the escarpments adjoining
Kruger, and a day's drive
takes in waterfalls, historic
towns and views of the Blyde
River Canyon. Kruger itself is
very car-friendly thanks to the
numerous entrance gates
along the entire length of the
park, excellent tarred roads
and efficient rest camps.
In the southeast, history
buffs can tour the evocative
battlefield sites of KwaZulu
Natal *(see p274)*, or the
pretty country resorts in
the foothills of the mighty
Drakensberg Mountains.

DIRECTORY

BREAKDOWN SERVICES

AA
Tel (083) 84322.
www.aa.co.za

CAR RENTAL

Avis
Tel (0861) 021-111.
www.avis.co.za

Budget
Tel (011) 398-0123.
www.budget.co.za

Europcar
Tel (0861) 131-000.
www.europcar.co.za

First Car Rental
Tel (0861) 178-227.
www.firstcarrental.co.za

Hertz
Tel (0861) 600-136.
www.hertz.co.za

Tempest Car Hire
Tel (011) 552-3900.
www.tempestcarhire.co.za

Driving a jeep through South Africa's countryside

General Index

Acknowledgments

Dorling Kindersley would like to thank the following people whose contributions and assistance have made the preparation of this book possible.

Main Contributors

Michael Brett has visited many African countries, including Kenya, Malawi, Zimbabwe, Namibia and Mozambique, and has an extensive knowledge of South Africa. His first book, a detailed guide to the Pilanesberg National Park in North West Province, South Africa, was published in 1989. In 1996, he co-authored the *Touring Atlas of South Africa*. He has written *Great Game Parks of Africa: Masai Mara* and *Kenya the Beautiful*. Articles by Michael Brett have been published in several travel magazines, as well as in *Reader's Digest*.

Philip Briggs is a travel writer specializing in Africa. In 1991, his *Bradt Guide to South Africa* was the first such guidebook to be published internationally after the release of Nelson Mandela. Over the rest of the 1990s, he wrote a series of pioneering Bradt Guides including the first dedicated guidebooks to Tanzania, Uganda, Ethiopia, Malawi, Mozambique, Ghana and Rwanda. He also contributes to specialist travel and wildlife magazines including *Africa Birds & Birding*, *Africa Geographic*, *BBC Wildlife*, *Travel Africa* and *Wanderlust*.

Brian Johnson-Barker was born and educated in Cape Town, South Africa. After graduating from the University of Cape Town and running a clinical pathology laboratory for some 15 years, he turned to writing. His considerable involvement in this field has also extended to television scripts and magazine articles. Among his nearly 50 book titles are *Off the Beaten Track* (1996) and *Illustrated Guide to Game Parks and Nature Reserves of Southern Africa* (1997), both published by Reader's Digest.

Mariëlle Renssen wrote for South African general-interest magazine *Fair Lady* before spending two years in New York with *Young & Modern*, a teenage publication owned by the Bertelsmann publishing group. After returning to South Africa, several of her articles were published in magazines such as *Food and Home SA* and *Woman's Value*. Since 1995 she has been the publishing manager of Struik Publishers' International Division, during which time she also contributed to *Traveller's Guide to Tanzania*.

Additional Contributors

Duncan Cruickshank, Claudia Dos Santos, Luke Hardiman, Peter Joyce, Gail Jennings, Loren Minsky, Roger St Pierre, Anne Taylor.

Additional Photography

Greg & Yvonne Dean, Louise Dean, Charley van Dugteren, Hanne and Jens Erikesen, Christopher & Sally Gable, Nigel Hicks, Josef Hlasek, Anthony Johnson, Mathew Kurien, Cyril Laubscher, Ian O'Leary, Gary Ombler, John Reeks, Tony Souter, Linda Whitwam, Jerry Young.

Additional Illustrations

Anton Krugel.

Additional Cartography

Genené Hart, Eloïse Moss.

Research Assistance

Susan Alexander, Sandy Vahl.

Additional Picture Research

Rachel Barber, Ellen Root.

Factchecker

Ariadne Van Zandbergen.

Proof Reader

Michael Fullalove.

Indexer

Helen Peters.

Design and Editorial Assistance

Beverley Ager, Claire Baranowski, Chris Barstow/ Coppermill Books, Uma Bhattacharya, Hilary Bird, Arwen Burnett, Caroline Elliker, Emer Fitzgerald, Sean Fraser, Anna Freiberger, Camilla Gersh, Thea Grobbelaar, Freddy Hamilton, Vinod Harish, Mohammad Hassan, Lesley Hay-Whitton, Victoria Heyworth-Dunne, Jacky Jackson, Vasneet Kaur, Juliet Kenny, Vincent Kurien, Maite Lantaron, Alfred Lemaitre, Carly Madden, Alison McGill, Glynne Newlands, Catherine Palmi, Marianne Petrou, Rada Radojicic, John Reeks, Marisa Renzullo, Gerhardt van Rooyen, Sands Publishing Solutions, Mitzi Scheepers, Azeem Siddiqui, Susana Smith, Conrad Van Dyk, Lizzie Williams.

Special Assistance

Joan Armstrong, The Howick Publicity Bureau; Coen Bessinger, Die Kaapse Tafel; Tim Bowdell, Port Elizabeth City Council; Dr Joyce Brain, Durban; Katherine Brooks, MuseuMAfrikA (Johannesburg); Michael Coke, Durban; Coleen de Villiers and Gail Linnow, South African Weather Bureau; Dr Trevor Dearlove, South African Parks Board; Louis Eksteen, Voortrekker Museum (Pietermaritzburg); Lindsay Hooper, South African Museum (Cape Town); Brian Jackson, The National Monuments Commission; Linda Labuschagne, Bartolomeu Dias Museum Complex (Mossel Bay); Darden Lotz, Cape Town; Tim Maggs, Cape Town; Hector Mbau, The Cape Café; Annette Miller, Bredasdorp Tourism; Gayla Naicker and Gerhart Richter, Perima's; Professor John Parkington, University of Cape Town; Anton Pauw, Cape Town; David Philips Publisher (Pty) Ltd, Cape Town; Bev Prinsloo, Palace of the Lost City; Professor Bruce Rubidge, University of the Witwatersrand; Jeremy Saville, ZigZag Magazine; Mark Shaw, Barrister's; Dr Dan Sleigh, Cape Town; Anthony Sterne, Simply Salmon; David Swanepoel, Voortrekker Museum; Johan Taljaard, West Coast National Park; Pietermaritzburg Publicity Association; Beyers Truter, Beyerskloof wine farm, Stellenbosch; Dr Lita Webley, Albany Museum, Grahamstown; Lloyd Wingate and Stephanie Pienaar, Kaffrarian Museum (King William's Town); and all provincial tourist authorities and national and provincial park services.

Photographic and Artwork Reference

Vida Allen and Bridget Carlstein, McGregor Museum (Kimberley); Marlain Botha, Anglo American Library; The Cape Archives; Captain Emilio de Souza; Petrus Dhlamini, Anglo American Corporation (Johannesburg);

Gawie Fagan and Tertius Kruger, Revel Fox Architects (Cape Town); Jeremy Fourie, Cape Land Data; Graham Goddard, Mayibuye Centre, The University of the Western Cape; Margaret Harradene, Public Library (Port Elizabeth); Maryke Jooste, Library of Parliament (Cape Town); Llewellyn Kriel, Chamber of Mines; Professor André Meyer, Pretoria University; Julia Moore, Boschendal Manor House; Marguerite Robinson, Standard Bank National Arts Festival; Christine Roe and Judith Swanepoel, Pilgrim's Rest Museum; Dr F Thackeray, Transvaal Museum (Pretoria); Marena van Hemert, Drostdy Museum (Swellendam); Kees van Ryksdyk, South African Astronomical Observatory; Cobri Vermeulen, The Knysna Forestry Department; Nasmi Wally, The Argus (Cape Town); Pam Warner, Old Slave Lodge (Cape Town).

Photography Permissions

Dorling Kindersley would like to thank the following for their assistance and kind permission to photograph at their establishments:

African Herbalist's Shop, Johannesburg; Alanglade, Pilgrim's Rest; Albany Museum Complex, Grahamstown; Bartolomeu Dias Museum Complex, Mossel Bay; BAT (Bartel Arts Trust) Centre, Durban; Bertram House, Cape Town; BMW Pavilion, Victoria & Alfred Waterfront; Bo-Kaap Museum, Cape Town; Cango Caves, Oudsthoorn; The Castle of Good Hope; Department of Public Works, Cape Town; Drum Magazine/Bailey's Archives; Dutch Reformed Church, Nieu Bethesda; The Edward Hotel, Port Elizabeth; Gold Reef City, Johannesburg; Groot Constantia; Heia Safari Ranch; Highgate Ostrich Farm, Oudtshoorn; Hindu (Hare Krishna) Temple of Understanding; Huguenot Museum, Franschhoek; Johannesburg International Airport; Kimberley Open-Air Mine Museum; Kirstenbosch National Botanical Garden; Kleinplasie Open-Air Museum; Koopmans-De Wet House, Cape Town; Mal a Mala Private Reserve; MuseuMAfricA, Johannesburg; Natural Science Museum, Durban; Old Slave Lodge, Cape Town; Oliewenhuis Art Gallery, Bloemfontein; Oom Samie se Winkel, Stellenbosch; Owl House, Nieu Bethesda; Paarl Museum; Pilgrim's Rest; Rhebokskloof Wine Estate; Robben Island Museum Service; Sandton Village Walk; Shakaland; Shipwreck Museum, Bredasdorp; Simunye; South African Library; South African Museum, Cape Town; Tatham Art Gallery, Pietermaritzburg; Two Oceans Aquarium, V&A Waterfront; Victoria & Alfred Waterfront; The Village Museum Stellenbosch; Sue Williamson, Cape Town; The Workshop, Durban.

Picture Credits

a = above; b = below/bottom; c = centre; f = far; l = left; r = right; t = top.

Works of art have been reproduced with the permission of the following copyright holders: *6-metre statue Nelson Mandela*, Sandeton Square, © Mr. Kobus Hattingh, Proferro cc, website www. kobushattingh.co.za 317cs; *Lead Ox*, 1995–6, © Cecil Skotnes, Incised, painted wood panel 372br; *Portrait of a Lady*, Frans Hals (1580–1666), Oil on canvas, Old Town House (Cape Town) © Michaelis Collection 124bl; *Rocco Catoggio and Rocco Cartozia de Villiers*,

artist unknown, c.1842, Oil on canvas, © Huguenot Museum (Franschhoek) 199bc; Untitled work, 1998, Hannelie de Clerq, Tempera, © Stellenbosch Art Gallery 193tr.

The publisher would like to thank the following individuals, companies and picture libraries for permission to reproduce their photographs:

ACSA (Airports Company of South Africa): 452t, 453b; Shaen Adey: 1t, 72cl, 30t, 129bl, 138t, 138b, 161cr, 342tl, 342cla, 342cl, 342b, 343t, 343cr; Africa Image Library: 68br, 68cla, 77br; Ariadne Van Zandbergen 79br, 83br, 84bl, 85tl, 87cr, 92tl, 93cr, 95clb, 97tl, 98cl, 98cr, 99br, 99clb, 102bc, 104-5t, 111br; African Pictures: Guy Stubbs 439c; Alamy Images: Ace Stock Limited 76bc; Africa Image Library 69bl; AfriPics. com 77bl, 91clb, 99cra, 101bc; Arco Images / Nienhaus, H. 80br; Arco Images GmbH/ H. Nienhaus 83cla; Arterra Picture Library/Clément Philippe 97br; Peter Barritt 79clb, 113tr; blickwinkel 80clb; blickwinkel/Layer 83ca, 112tl; blickwinkel/ McPHOTO/HPU 107br; blickwinkel/McPHOTO/ PUM 102br; blickwinkel/Poelking 89bl; blickwinkel/ Tuengler 75tl; James de Bounevialle 89br; Penny Boyd 86cla; Bruce Coleman Inc./Michael P. Fogden 11c; Cephas Picture Library/Emma Borg 10br; Cephas Picture Library/Juan Espi 411cr; Cephas Picture Library/ Alain Proust 410clb; Cephas Picture Library/Mick Rock 410cla; Dennis Cox 436br; Danita Delimont/Amos Nachoum 224tl; Tim Davies 100tr; Reinhard Dirscherl 90cla; EcoPic 106cr; Mark Eveleigh 87br; Alissa Everett 81tl; F1online digitale Bildagentur GmbH/Harald Trinkner 95tl; FLPA 107clb; Jason Gallier 111tr; Simon de Glanville 102bl; Dacorum Gold 106br; Greatstock Photographic Library/ SATourism 68clb; Friedrich von Hörsten 69crb, 101bl, 110tr; Andre van Huizen 111tc; Images & Stories 103cla; Images of Africa Photobank/David Keith Jones 82br, 86clb, 87bl, 94clb, 100tc; Images of Africa Photobank/Ivor Migdoll 113bc; Images of Africa Photobank/Lanz von Horsten 77cra; ImageState/Jonathan & Angie Scott 106clb; Mike Lane 112br; Frans Lemmens 69br; LMR Media 110br; Paul Thompson Images/Chris Ballentine 91cr, 234bc; Photodisc/Anup Shah 79bl; Pictorial Press Ltd 81cr; Vic Pigula 102cla; Peter Pinnock 105bl; Stu Porter 105cr; Arco Images / WHJ Sator 112tc; Willie Sator 93tl; Malcolm Schuyl 83tr, 106cla, 108br, 110tc; Steve Bloom Images 89bc; Stockbyte /Tom Brakefield 101tr; Sylvia Cordaiy Photo Library Ltd/Kjell Sandved 98tl; tbkmedia.de 99tl; Peter Titmuss 94cla, 213cra, 408cla, 409c, 410tr, 450bl, 451bl, 457tr; Ann and Steve Toon 81br; Ross Warner 80cr; Sandy Watt 112bc; Terry Whittaker 81clb; Wildviews/Charles Tomalin 78bc, 79bc; WorldFoto 103bc; Ariadne Van Zandbergen 113tl; Danita Delimont 224tl; Reinhard Dirscherl 11br; Greatstock Photographic Library/Michael Meyersfeld 312tc; ImageState/Pictor International 13bl; Jon Arnold Images 12bl; Geof Kirby 436tl; Shaun Levick 65t; Suretha Rous 164tc; Suzanne Long 160tc, 66tr; Eric Nathan 10cl, 12tr; PCL 12c; Stu Porter 238c; Ben Queenborough 66c; Malcolm Schuyl 289tl; Travelstock 410cr; Liam Weer 62tc; World Pictures 129br; Anita Akal: 39cl; Anglo American Corporation of South Africa